OPERAS

and

MUSICAL

COMEDIES

Enlarged Edition

J. WALKER McSPADDEN

THOMAS Y. CROWELL COMPANY
NEW YORK

The author's previous books, *Opera Synopses* and *Light Opera and Musical Comedy*, are incorporated in this book.

PRINTED IN THE UNITED STATES OF AMERICA
BY THE VAIL-BALLOU PRESS, INC., BINGHAMTON, N. Y.

To

The memory of my beloved wife whose
devotion to my work lasted for
half a century and whose
name, as formerly, is
merely inscribed as
"M A C"

INTRODUCTION

That "great oaks from little acorns grow" is exemplified in a work for which I am again privileged to write the introduction. A third of a century ago, a modest, pocket-size volume appeared with J. Walker McSpadden as author, and with the title, *Opera Synopses*. Since then it has been continually reprinted, each time larger as it has kept pace with stage productions old and new. It was for the fifth edition of the book (representing the fifteenth printing) that I wrote an introduction, and I began by remarking that when a book has survived for so many years and repeated editions have been required to supply the public demand for it, we may be sure that it continues to fill a real need. I can only repeat this, adding that it sometimes happens that the name of an author and title of his book become synonymous. Certainly McSpadden and *Opera Synopses* are coupled in the minds of many thousands of music lovers and opera devotees. During its long period of usefulness the frequently revised and enlarged editions of the book have kept it abreast of the changing repertoire of the leading opera companies. With the coming of the radio in the 1920's it acquired many more readers, who have kept it beside their receiving sets and have consulted it before, and often during, the weekly opera broadcasts.

And now a new edition brings the contents up to the middle of the year 1946. My one regret is that the old title has not been retained, and because of some entirely new features, a new name was deemed advisable. However, it is still our old friend, *Opera Synopses—plus*.

In my introduction to the fifth edition, I called attention to a most attractive new feature—the inclusion in a separate section of light operas and operettas. "Obviously," I wrote, "it was possible for Mr. McSpadden merely to skim the surface of the field of light opera, and I hope that his friends or his publishers will urge him to issue, some day, a separate volume devoted to such a tempting subject."

Well, Mr. McSpadden did do so. His *Light Opera and Musical Comedy,* which appeared in 1937, was a pioneer in its field, and has remained the one work on the subject. And now he and his publishers have gotten together on a magnum opus covering Grand Opera, Light Opera, and its modern, related field of Musical Comedy. It is the first such all-inclusive work ever attempted, and to my mind marks a distinct advance in the whole realm of musical study and appreciation.

In many instances, it was probably not easy for Mr. McSpadden to distinguish between "Grand" and "Light" opera. Some music-lovers would consider those works which are traditionally performed in opera

vii

houses as "Grand" operas, and those generally produced in theaters as "Light." The inconsistencies that have resulted from such traditions are so puzzling that the author is no doubt wise in making his own distinctions, based on the nature of each individual work.

The usefulness of Mr. McSpadden's book and the real need for it are not to be questioned. It is true that various types of music lovers enjoy different features of an opera performance, and in varying degrees. To some the music is the principal attraction. They would as soon hear operatic music in the concert hall. Others enjoy the visual aspects, the scenic and lighting effects, the costumes and the ballet. Still others, perhaps the majority, regard opera as drama. They like to know what the singing actors are saying and doing. To these people listening to an opera in a strange language is an incomplete experience, and many of them are advocates of translating the texts into English. But even a familiar tongue is inadequate unless the singers have excellent diction, and the words they sing are easily understood.

It is, of course, to the latter group that a book like Mr. McSpadden's is most useful, but it is safe to say that anyone who listens to any opera, or to any operatic selection, will gain more from hearing it if he has at least a general idea of what it is all about, of the emotions the music expresses, and the action it portrays. Thus, the person who consults this new volume will inform himself briefly and clearly of the outlines of the drama act by act, and scene by scene. When he sits in the opera house he will not have to strain his eyes in a darkened auditorium trying to follow a badly translated libretto while his favorite tenor is singing *Celeste Aida.* He will know already that Rhadames, the warrior, is singing of Aïda, the slave, and he will realize that the music is describing a beautiful maiden and expressing the hero's admiration of her.

This latest edition has still another newly added feature which increases its value and usefulness. In the accounts of many of the more familiar operas, frequent phrases of music are inserted to illustrate the principal arias and to show where they occur. These thematics, as they are called, give musical outlines of the operas to supplement the dramatic outlines of the texts.

As for the contents, the new volume contains all the old favorites that were included in previous editions—the standard operas of the Italian repertoire, the German and Austrian masterpieces from the time of Gluck and Mozart, representative works of the French School, and the outstanding operas of other nations. And once again the works that have been added keep the volume fully up-to-date. The modern "Wozzeck" of Alban Berg and Krenek's "Johnny Plays On" were included in the previous edition, but now are added Hindemith's "Mathis der Mahler," "Goyescas" by Granados, Hageman's "Caponsacchi," Ravel's "L'Heure Espagnole," as well as numerous other operas, grand and light, which are widely discussed and performed either in opera houses or on the radio.

In the new edition the author continues the arrangement he devised for a former edition, of grouping the operas according to the nationalities of their composers in chronological order. Each national group is preceded by a brief account of the development of the opera in that country. Thus the book is actually a condensed history of opera throughout the world, and by reading it the student may trace its development from the ancient Greeks through the era of Italian *bel canto,* of the Wagnerian *leit-motif,* right down to the realism of the ultra-modernists. And if he's interested in the dates of first performances, he'll find them too, together with the names of singers who appeared in the premieres.

The result of these combined features is a book which is written not only for the boxholders at the Metropolitan, but also for the men and woman who stand in line to buy seats for "Oklahoma" and "Up in Central Park." Mr. McSpadden knows that they are very often the same people, for the two types of entertainment represent genuine phases of American life, both of them vital and sincere. The 1946 revival of "Show Boat" has shown us that this nineteen-year-old musical comedy is one of the most genuinely American works of art that has ever been produced on the stage of any theater. Its music, call it light or whatever you wish, is at all times utterly sincere, the words of its songs are in perfect taste, and its plot and dialogue are excellent theater which do not date with the years. The same goes for "Oklahoma!," written by the librettist who produced the book and lyrics of "Show Boat," Oscar Hammerstein, 2nd. And who can dispute the permanent value of the operettas of Offenbach, Lehar, and Strauss, of Gilbert and Sullivan, or of our own Victor Herbert? So let no proponent of this book offer an apology for the inclusion of lighter entertainments. Rather would an apology have been in order if they had been omitted.

As a personal friend and neighbor of J. Walker McSpadden, I know at first hand of the intense thought and planning that has been put into this newly issued book of his. The selection of operas and musical comedies to be included was no slap-dash affair. Months of research and consultation were spent in determining what are the operas that people want to know about, and should know about. Various criteria were set up to show which of them qualified for inclusion, and why. Consequently the reader will find here the latest Broadway hit, because people are going to see it now, and Willard Spenser's "The Little Tycoon" of a generation or two ago, because it was an outstanding product of a significant era in our past. He'll find Gershwin's "Of Thee I Sing," because he's liable to witness a revival of it, almost any season.

And since the book contains so many different kinds of operas, and is the only one now in print that does do so, those who buy it will probably do with it just what I do—put it right in the middle of the nearest bookshelf, where we keep the works we consult most often.

JOHN TASKER HOWARD

AUTHOR'S PREFACE

A word of explanation may be due the reader—certainly to the loyal ones who in the past few months have asked for copies of my *Opera Synopses,* only to be informed that it was out of print. It was a war casualty due to lack of paper. However, in this enforced idleness, the publishers and the author have planned a bigger and better volume, which should include the above work that made its first, modest appearance in 1911 and survived one World War, only to be hit by another, and also combine with it my *Light Opera and Musical Comedy,* a pioneer work in its field.

This has accordingly been done; the two texts have been completely revised; much additional material has been added; many musical notations have been inserted; and the new volume, *Operas and Musical Comedies,* is the result. It is the first work on Opera that offers a comprehensive view of the entire range of such composition both Grand and Light. And recent examples of Musical Comedy are included without apology, to fill in needed details in the canvas.

In the field of operetta the task has been more difficult, and therefore my thanks must be extended to various persons and private sources of material, without which aid the work could not have been completed. I wish to repeat my thanks given in the earlier work to the assistant librarians in the New York Public Library, the Newark Public Library, the Montclair Public Library; Mrs. Robert Bartlett, daughter of Victor Herbert; George Gershwin, now deceased, and his brother, Ira Gershwin; the late Harry B. Smith who was most helpful; the private collections of programs of the late Alvin L. Powell, of Glen Ridge, and of A. Ray Wilkerson, of Richmond, Virginia; John Tasker Howard, author of *Our American Music* and in charge of that division of the New York Public Library; George W. Watson, of that library, whose forte is grand opera programs and librettos; George Freedley, curator of the Theatre Division; Albert Ellis, of New York, for constructive criticism; and others for friendly advice and suggestions.

J. W. McS.

Montclair, New Jersey

AUTHOR'S PREFACE

To the Enlarged Edition

Five years ago, the preface on the preceding page was written, marking the first appearance of my combined works on opera in new dress. This new date and new work are of special significance to me, as it was just forty years ago when my pioneer book, *Opera Synopses,* appeared.

Now a second edition of the combined *Operas and Musical Comedies* is going to press. It necessarily adds new material from the productions on the Metropolitan stage and from busy Broadway humming all about it.

An important new feature is a comprehensive index of characters in grand opera. For example, Rhadames can be instantly identified as a tenor singer in "Aida." Opera-goers and radio listeners as well will doubtless appreciate this added aid.

As formerly I wish to express my grateful thanks to officials in the libraries and others for assistance, not forgetting the unseen friends who get in touch with me, some letters bearing foreign postmarks. These are among any writer's best recompenses.

J. W. McS.

Montclair, New Jersey

CONTENTS

I. GRAND OPERA

GERMANY AND AUSTRIA

ITALY

RUSSIA

OTHER NATIONS

(For English composers, see Light Opera)

THE UNITED STATES

II. LIGHT OPERA AND MUSICAL COMEDY

GERMANY AND AUSTRIA

ITALY

CONTENTS

FRANCE

OTHER NATIONS

THE UNITED STATES

RECENT MUSICAL COMEDIES

RECENT AND REVISED GRAND OPERAS

CONTENTS

PART ONE

GRAND OPERA

GERMANY AND AUSTRIA

HISTORICAL PREFACE

Because they are linguistically allied and the works of these neighboring composers were often performed in Vienna as in Berlin, the composers of Germany and Austria are here grouped together. The roots of Grand Opera, however, were not originally in Teutonic soil. They may be traced through Italy as far back as ancient Greece. For many centuries in Greece the classic drama had flourished. Music with it was incidental, but it had its Prologue and Chorus which, though spoken, were based upon the same stage mechanics. Musical accompaniments gradually crept in. And the dance was a time-honored partner.

The Renaissance brought to Europe a renewed regard for the fine arts, and its first expression was found in Italy. Here in the sixteenth century a group of Florentine noblemen introduced what is regarded as the first of the operas. For further notice of this and other Italian works the reader is referred to that section.

Teutonic opera, however, is given precedence in this book for the reason that the works of at least four major composers from this country, beginning with Gluck, head the list in the beginnings of modern opera. But numerous composers antedated Gluck. We are told of a certain Reinhard Keiser (1679–1739) who wrote over one hundred operas; and of another, Johann Adolph Hasse, who also had a hundred to his credit. Nevertheless, Gluck's "Orpheus and Eurydice," produced in 1762, remains the earliest of such works still holding its place in modern repertory. Those other giants, Mozart (an Austrian), Beethoven, and Weber, were all born before the end of the eighteenth century. Spontini, born in 1774, was of Italian parentage, but his achievements in opera made no lasting impression upon his native soil. His chief work, "The Vestal Virgin," was brought out in Paris and later in Berlin, where for twenty years he was a musical director.

Both Gluck and Mozart were genuine pioneers. While the former studied in Italy and his first operas were produced there, they were experimental and he soon lost patience with the so-called Greek methods and struck out boldly for himself. His efforts to found a new school met with the same violent opposition which greeted Wagner of a later day. Mozart, on his part, was an antithesis of Gluck and was the first

3

to inject pure singing melody in its simplest form into dramatic production.

It would require a volume in itself to trace all the sources of modern opera. Literally hundreds of attempts were made by Italian, French and German composers dating as far back as the thirteenth century. Some of these works won fair success in their day. But the operas of Gluck and Mozart are the only ones of this formative time to linger on. Beethoven's single opera, "Fidelio," was not produced until nearly a quarter of a century after Mozart's death.

With the dawn of the nineteenth century German opera was definitely launched on a national basis. Louis Spohr (1784–1859) aided to bridge the gap from the early masters, and was closely followed in point of time by Weber, whose delightful works revealed the springtime blossoming of the new school. A score of imitators arose, one of the most important being Heinrich Marschner (1795–1861), some of whose works are still produced in Germany. Then came Lortzing, Cornelius, Nicolai, and other noteworthy names. Our list could be prolonged to considerable length. It even includes such great names as Mendelssohn, Schubert, Schumann, and Liszt, but their forte was not that of opera. Liszt in a sense passed on the torch to a blazing genius who was to dominate German opera—Wagner.

Wagner's art was diametrically opposed to that of the prevailing school. He did not view opera as a vehicle merely for some singer, nor yet for some melody. He regarded it as a dramatic work into which all elements should be co-ordinated—the story, the melody, the singer, working together to express the motif of the drama. As a part of his plan he developed a system of *leit-motives,* or leading themes, which should serve to label the characters and even their emotions and thoughts. It was a sort of musical cue. He also chose folk and native German themes, writing his own librettos. Naturally his revolutionary methods and no less radical orchestrations aroused the most determined opposition, but eventually prevailed. So profound has been his influence that German opera now falls into two divisions—before Wagner and since Wagner.

Since Wagner the outstanding composer in Germany has been Richard Strauss. His "Der Rosenkavalier" had the distinction of being performed twice in the first week of the Metropolitan opera season, November, 1945. Some half-dozen other operas in addition to many orchestral suites have given him assured position. D'Albert of "Tiefland" did not realize his first promise. Leo Blech, Alban Berg, Eric Korngold, and Ernst Krenek, are other latter-day figures.

However, the impact of two world wars has snuffed out the divine flame in that unhappy country, perhaps for years to come. The nation under its Nazi leaders turned materialistic, and all the arts suffered, wellnigh to extinction. It will doubtless require an entirely new generation to retake the torch in arts and letters; and meanwhile in the field of opera we shall have to continue to enjoy the fruits of the past.

CHRISTOPHER W. GLUCK

Gluck may be regarded as the great-grandfather of modern opera. He is the earliest composer whose works are still found in the present-day repertory. Born in Weidenwang, Palatine, July 2, 1714, he was from the outset of his career a musical reformer who aroused as intense opposition as did Wagner later. He studied in Milan and thus came under the Italian influence, but his first operas presented in Italy met with scant success. His first successful work was "Helena and Paris." In 1774 he went to Paris, where he presented his masterpieces, among them "Orpheus and Eurydice," "Armide," "Iphigenia in Aulis," "Iphigenia in Tauris," and "Alcestes." The composer, Nicola Piccini, was a bitter rival of his, and adherents of the two frequently came to blows. Gluck died in Vienna, November 15, 1787.

ORPHEUS AND EURYDICE
(Orf'-use and Yoo-rid'-i-see)

(Orfeo.) Legendary Opera in Four Acts. Music by Christopher Gluck. Book by Raniero di Calzabigi. Vienna, October 5, 1762. At New York, the Metropolitan, 1891.

SCENE: Greece and the Lower World.
TIME: Antiquity.

CAST ORPHEUS, *a sweet singer* (Contralto).
EURYDICE, *his bride* (Soprano).
AMOR, *god of love* (Soprano).
Furies, Shades, Friends of Orpheus, etc.

ARGUMENT "Orpheus and Eurydice" is based upon the ancient Greek legend of the musician who went into the depths of Hades to rescue his dead wife.

Act I *The Tomb of Eurydice.* Eurydice, the bride of Orpheus, who charms all things by his music, has perished from the bite of a serpent. After a brief, dirgelike prelude the curtain rises as Orpheus and his friends lament her loss in a touching aria and chorus, "Thou whom I loved." He prays to the gods to restore her to him. He is ready to make any sacrifice, even descend into Hades itself in order to rescue her. Touched by his grief, the god Amor is sent to tell him he may make the journey, trusting only to his powers of song; but that he must on no account turn to look upon the face of his wife, else Death will again seize upon her. "The will of the gods fulfill with joy," sings Amor as Orpheus departs.

Act II *Hades, the Abode of the Departed.* The shades and furies swarm around the entrance to Hades reviling Orpheus for having attempted to enter; but he sings so sweetly of his grief and present quest that they stand aside and allow him to enter. His aria, "A thousand griefs," and recitative, "What pure light," finally win over the furies, who respond with, "Welcome, sweet singer."

Act III *Valley of the Blest.* In the midst of Hades is the Valley of the Blest, where dwell the pure in heart. Here Orpheus on his journey finally finds his wife. The others cannot understand why she wishes to return, but touched by his song lead her to him. He does not turn to look at her, but with averted face takes her hand and leads her from the valley. She, of course, is puzzled and his efforts to re-assure her lead to the lovely duet, "On my faith rely."

Act IV *A Forest before a Cave.* After a long upward journey, Orpheus leads his wife through a cave, finally emerging into a dense forest. Still he does not look at her, but calling back urges that she follow him quickly. She complains that he is indifferent to her; that he has not given her so much as a single glance. Without his love she would prefer death. She continues this plaint until he can resist no longer and turns to reassure her. Immediately she sinks to the ground lifeless. Then it is that Orpheus bitterly reproaches himself in the lament which is best remembered: "I have lost my Eurydice!"

The god Amor is touched, he again appears to Orpheus and says that since he has suffered and toiled greatly he will be forgiven. With a touch he restores Eurydice to life and to her husband's arms.

ARMIDE

(Ar-meed)

Romantic Opera in Five Acts.   Music by Gluck.   Book by Quinault, founded upon Tasso's "Jerusalem Delivered." Académie Royale de Musique, Paris, September 23, 1777.   Metropolitan, New York, November 14, 1910, with Caruso, Fremstad, Gluck, Rappold, Homer.

SCENE: Damascus and Environs.
TIME: The First Crusade, 1098 A.D.

CAST   ARMIDE, *a sorceress* (Soprano).
PHENICE, *her friend* (Soprano).
SIDONIE, *her friend* (Soprano).
HIDROAT, *King of Damascus* (Baritone).
ARONT, *his chief of staff* (Basso).
RINALDO, *Commander of Crusaders* (Tenor).
ARTEMIDOR, *a Crusader* (Tenor).
UBALDO, *a Knight* (Baritone).
A DANISH KNIGHT (Tenor).
   Demons, Naiads, Knights, Courtiers, Servants, etc.

ARGUMENT   "Armide" is a legendary episode connected with the Crusade under Godfrey of Bouillon.   His chief officer falls under the power of a beautiful sorceress.

Act I   *The Palace of Armide.*   The Princess Armide is famed both for her beauty and her powers of magic.   She has remained unmarried, although Hidroat, the King, wishes her to choose a husband. But she cannot free her mind from the thought of Rinaldo, the victorious Crusader.   At every new word of his conquests her heart is torn by hatred of him as an enemy of her country, and love for him as a hero. Tidings are received that the Saracen host is at last victor in a battle, but this is disproved by a later messenger and the arrival of Aront's army which has again suffered defeat.   All swear vengence against the Christian army.

Act II   *An Enchanted Garden.*   Rinaldo, the Crusader, while wandering in the desert, suddenly finds himself in an enchanted garden, conjured up by the wiles of Armide.   Naiads rise up before him and sing him to sleep.   While reclining under a bower of roses, insensible, the sorceress advances toward him with drawn dagger.   At last she has her country's enemy within her power.   But the sight of the man of her dreams once more kindles love in her heart; the sorceress is lost in the woman, and she clasps him in her arms.

Act III   *The Palace of Armide.*   Again in her palace, Armide is torn among the mingled feelings of love, hate, pride, and remorse. Instead of striking her enemy she has yielded to him.   She summons before her the Demon of Hate, who warns her that for this indecision Rinaldo will yet escape her.   Instead of nerving her fury, this only redoubles her love, and the Demon in anger disappears.

Act IV   *The Enchanted Garden.*   Rinaldo has continued under the power of the sorceress.   The Crusaders, alarmed by his absence, send Ubaldo and a Danish knight in search of him.   At their approach Armide bars their path, but is compelled to fall back powerless before a consecrated scepter borne by Ubaldo.   Other visions appear at Armide's command, but are dissipated by the scepter.

Act V   *The Palace (sometimes combined with the Garden scene).* Armide conveys her lover to the palace and seeks to entertain him by ballets and tableaux.   He forgets his past life while subject to her wiles.   She leaves the room for an interval, and Ubaldo and the Danish knight enter, carrying the scepter and a highly polished shield which when held up before Rinaldo reveals to him the warrior he formerly was.   Roused to action by this vision, he grasps his sword just as Armide returns.   She implores him to remain with her.   When he refuses and departs with the Crusaders she sets fire to her palace and perishes in the flames.

Two memorable arias in "Armide" are: "Ah! si la liberté!" and "Plus j'observe ces lieux."

IPHIGENIA IN AULIS
(If-ee-zhee-ny'-a in Ah'-lis)

Legendary Opera in Three Acts.   Music by Gluck.   Book by du Roullot.   Paris, April 19, 1774.

SCENE: Aulis.
TIME: After the Trojan War.

CAST   AGAMEMNON, *King of the Greeks* (Basso).
CLYTEMNESTRA, *wife of Agamemnon* (Contralto).
IPHIGENIA, *daughter of Agamemnon* (Soprano).
CALCHAS, *the High Priest* (Baritone).
ACHILLES, *a warrior* (Tenor).
Soldiers, Courtiers, Priests, etc.

ARGUMENT Although this opera does not rank with "Iphigenia in Tauris," it is yet worthy of preservation
on its own account. And its plot may be regarded as the first part of the
tragedy. Its overture is still frequently played.

Act I *Camp of Agamemnon.* After the Greek victory at Troy, the
victorious soldiers seek to return home, but an unfavorable
wind detains them. The High Priest states that the gods can be appeased only by an innocent offering. Agamemnon is urged to sacrifice
his daughter, Iphigenia. The king is torn between his mistaken sense
of duty and his love for his child. Iphigenia is betrothed to Achilles,
and the two prepare for their wedding, unmindful of the secret danger.

Act II *Portico of the Temple.* Iphigenia is adorned for her wedding, and Achilles comes to lead her to the altar, when Agamemnon's messenger informs them that death awaits Iphigenia.

Clytemnestra, in despair, appeals to Achilles, and the bridegroom
swears to protect Iphigenia. She alone is resigned in the belief that it
is her father's will that she should face this dreadful duty. Achilles
reproaches Agamemnon and leaves the unhappy father a prey to mental
anguish. At last he decides to send mother and daughter to Mycene,
and to hide them there until the wrath of the goddess is appeased.

Act III *Before the Tent of Agamemnon.* The soldiers crowd before
the king and demand the sacrifice. While Achilles implores
Iphigenia to flee with him, she stands ready to offer herself on the bloody
altar. Her mother in turn offers to take her place, but the girl will not
consent. Just as the priest is ready to plunge his knife in the victim,
the goddess Diana appears and saves her; declaring that she does not
want her blood, but her life and service as priestess in a foreign land.

Two arias most often heard are: "Diana impitoyable!" and "O toi,
l'objet le plus amiable."

IPHIGENIA IN TAURIS
(If-ee-zhee-ny'-a in Taw'-ris)

Legendary Opera in Four Acts by Gluck. Book by François Guil-
lard. Académie de Musique, Paris, May 18, 1779. At New York in
the Metropolitan, November 25, 1916, with Kurt, Rappold, and Sun-
delius.

SCENE: Tauris.
TIME: After the Trojan War.

CAST IPHIGENIA, *priestess of Diana* (Soprano).
ORESTES, *her brother* (Baritone).
PYLADES, *his friend* (Tenor).
THOAS, *King of Scythia* (Basso).
DIANA (Soprano).
Scythians, Priestesses of Diana.

ARGUMENT An opera which takes very high rank among early compositions. Both book and music are classic and so harmonious that Herder called the opera "sacred." The plot follows "Iphigenia in Aulis," in point of time.

Act I *Before the Temple of Diana.* Iphigenia, King Agamemnon's daughter, who has been saved by the goddess Diana from death at the altar of Aulis, has been carried in a cloud to Tauris, where she serves as high-priestess in the Scythian temple. Here we find her, after having performed her cruel service for fifteen years. Human sacrifices are required, but more than once she has saved her victims.

She is troubled by a dream in which her father is fatally wounded by her mother, and she herself is compelled to kill her brother Orestes. Thoas, King of the Scythians, orders her to sacrifice two strangers who have been thrown on his shores. They are Orestes and his friend Pylades.

Act II *Temple of Diana.* Orestes bewails his fate. Pylades sings of his undying friendship for him. Pylades is separated from Orestes, who temporarily loses his mind. Iphigenia questions him. Orestes refrains from disclosing his identity. He tells her that he is from Mycene, that Agamemnon has been slain by his wife, and that her son, Orestes, has slain her in revenge, and is himself dead. Of the once great family only a daughter, Electra, remains.

Act III *Temple of Diana.* Iphigenia is struck with the resemblance of the stranger to her brother and, in order to save him from the sacrifice demanded by Thoas, charges him to deliver a letter to Electra. He declines to leave Pylades. The latter agrees to take the letter only because he hopes to bring aid to Orestes.

Act IV *Altar of the Temple.* Orestes is led to the sacrifice. Iphigenia vainly tries to lift her dagger against this stranger but an inner voice forbids. At last when on the point of striking, Orestes reveals himself to her. A touching scene ensues, and Iphigenia declares to the King that she will die with her brother. At this moment Pylades at the head of a rescue party enters the temple. A combat ensues in which Thoas is killed. Diana appears, pardons Orestes, and returns to the Greeks her likeness which the Scythians had stolen when they built their infamous temple.

Two arias still sung: "Unis dès la plus tendre enfonce" and "O malheureuse Iphegénie."

WOLFGANG AMADEUS MOZART

If ever there was "a born musician," Mozart was that one. Stories are still current of his precocity. Born in Salzburg, Austria, January 27, 1756, his extraordinary musical genius early came to public attention. At the age of four he played the clavichord and composed minuets which are still extant. At six we find him and his gifted sister, also a child, playing before the courts at Munich and Vienna. At seven, Mozart took his place in a stringed orchestra and played a difficult score at sight. At the mature age of thirteen he was appointed director of concerts at Salzburg, and made a concert tour with his father to Italy, whither his fame had preceded him. But despite this early popularity Mozart was destined to a life of deprivation and want, due to the pittances which he received for his musical works. His first opera, "Mithridates," was composed at fourteen (1770) and produced in Milan the same year. Ten years later came "Idomeneus" (1780); followed by "The Marriage of Figaro" (1786); "Don Giovanni" (1787); "Cosi Fan Tutte," a comic opera (1788); "The Seraglio," a light opera (1789); "Titus" (1791); and "The Magic Flute" (1791). This does not take into account his quartets, masses, and other compositions, possibly the most noteworthy being his celebrated "Requiem Mass" left unfinished at the time of his decease. That Mozart was "a genius by the grace of God" is revealed by the fact that his career ended at the age of thirty-five. He died in Vienna, December 5, 1791.

THE MARRIAGE OF FIGARO
(The Mar-riage of Fee'-gah-roh')

(Le Nozze di Figaro.) Comic Opera in Four Acts. Music by Mozart. Book by Lorenzo Da Ponte, founded upon the comedy of Beaumarchais.

National Theatre, Vienna, May 1, 1786.   At New York, the Metropolitan, 1895, with Eames, Nordica, De Tusson, Maurel, Carbone.

SCENE: Seville.

TIME: The Seventeenth Century.

CAST   COUNT ALMAVIVA, *a nobleman of Seville* (Baritone).
COUNTESS ROSINA, *his wife* (Soprano).
FIGARO, *valet to the Count* (Basso).
SUSANNA, *his betrothed* (Soprano).
DOCTOR BARTOLO, *a physician* (Basso).
BASILIO, *a music-master* (Tenor).
CHERUBINO, *a page* (Soprano).
MARCELLINA, *the housekeeper* (Contralto).
ANTONIO, *a gardener* (Basso).
BARBARINA, *his daughter* (Soprano).
DON GUZMAN, *a judge* (Tenor).
Members of the Count's household, Friends, Citizens, etc.

ARGUMENT   "The Marriage of Figaro" is a direct continuation of "The Barber of Seville," Rossini's tuneful opera, both being founded upon the uproarious comedy by Beaumarchais.

The sparkling overture represents Mozart at his happiest.   It does not depend upon later arias for its appeal, but blazes a path of its own of riotous, rollicksome melody.   As for the story, the curtain rises to disclose Count Almaviva at last the husband of the fair Rosina, whom he courted under such difficulties with the aid of the "Barber."   But having obtained the lady he proves fickle and susceptible to other beauties who may chance to come his way.   His latest flame is Barbarina, the pretty daughter of his gardener, but he has a rival in the persistent page, Cherubino, whom he seeks to get rid of by placing him in the army.   Figaro, the barber, has entered the Count's service and is looking forward to marriage with Susanna, a ward of the Countess. Susanna also has been pursued by the Count, unsuccessfully.

Act I   *A Room in the Count's Castle.*   Preparations are forward for the marriage of Figaro and Susanna.   He is discovered busily arranging the furniture, while she is trying on a bridal wreath before the mirror.   They plan for the future and she says she will be glad thus to escape the Count's attentions.   Dr. Bartolo, the physician, arrives and is told by Marcellina, the old housekeeper, that Figaro was formerly engaged to marry her. The doctor agrees to help her win justice, and is also glad to have this chance to even up some old scores. Marcellina and Susanna now engage in a war of words: "Go first, I entreat you, Miss, model of beauty!" The page, Cherubino, now appears upon the scene—a fickle youth who finds every petticoat desirable. (This role is taken by a soprano.) He thinks he is once more enmeshed in the grand passion: "Ah, what feelings now possess me!"

His outpourings are halted by the entrance of the Count himself. The page jumps behind a chair. Susanna seats herself before him. The Count makes advances, but is disturbed by the entrance of Basilio, and in turn goes behind the chair. The page slips like an eel into the chair and is covered by a dress which Susanna throws over it. After some further confusion, both the Count and Cherubino are discovered and the page is ordered to depart forthwith.

Act II *Apartments of the Countess.* Cherubino still lingers around the premises, and the Countess decides to use him as a tool to unmask her husband's perfidy. She and Susanna plan to dress him in woman's attire, and he is nothing loath, as this will enable him to remain for the wedding and be near Barbarina.

One of the famous arias of the opera emerges as Cherubino sings the exquisite: "What is this feeling which makes me so sad?"

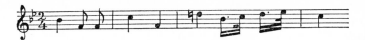

The Count comes to the door and demands admittance. Cherubino jumps out of the window and the Count is baffled. But when the gardener comes in to complain that his flower-pots beneath the window are broken, the Count's suspicions are again aroused. The gardener also produces Cherubino's commission in the army, which has been dropped in the leap. But Figaro, who has entered meanwhile, shoulders all the blame, saying that he had come to see Susanna and also had the letter. Marcellina, the housekeeper, now appears to enforce her claim against Figaro.

Act III *Apartments in the Castle.* Susanna is persuaded by the Countess to meet the Count in the hope of untangling the marital difficulty. The Count is obdurate, until it is found that Figaro is actually the son of Marcellina and so could not possibly marry her. This apparently removes the last obstacle to his happiness. But the Countess and Susanna had agreed to change clothes for the evening in order to confuse the Count still further. The ruse is so successful that Figaro also is fooled and becomes furiously jealous.

In this Act during the concoction of a letter between the Countess and Susanna comes one of the loveliest numbers: "The Song to the Zephyr," a duet which "brought down the house" when the opera was first presented:

Act IV *The Garden.* The last act becomes a farce of confused identities. The Countess and her maid have changed clothes, fooling both the Count and his servant. Barbarina is also in the general mix-up, but it is Figaro who comes in for cuffing whenever he or his master makes a mistake—which is frequently. Finally, lights are brought on, the Count realizes that he has been well punished, and the marriage of Figaro is approved.

DON GIOVANNI
(Don Jo-vahn'-nee)

(Or, The Marble Guest.) Opera Bouffe in Two Acts. Music by Mozart. Book by Da Ponte, after a Spanish tale by Tirso de Molina. Prague, October 29, 1787. Special performance in honor of Mozart's birth, at the Metropolitan, New York, January 27, 1906, with Nordica, Sembrich, and Scotti.

SCENE: Seville.
TIME: The Seventeenth Century.

CAST   DON GIOVANNI (JUAN), *a Castilian dandy* (Baritone).
DON PEDRO, *the Commandant* (Baritone).

ANNA, *his daughter* (Soprano).
ELVIRA, *a former sweetheart of Juan* (Soprano).
DON OCTAVIO, *the fiancé of Anna* (Tenor).
LEPORELLO, *servant of Juan* (Basso).
MASETTO, *a peasant* (Basso).
ZERLINA, *his betrothed* (Soprano).
Spanish Nobles, Ladies, Guests, Guards, Servants.

ARGUMENT Among the many operas on the subject of Don Juan and his amours, none has the merit or the continuing popularity of this of Mozart.

Act I *Scene 1. The Garden of the Commandant's Palace.* Don Juan, a notorious libertine of Seville, goes by night to enter the apartments of Don Pedro's daughter, Anna, who is betrothed to Octavio. As soon as she discovers the intruder's presence she cries for help, and her father hastens to her aid. He is mortally wounded by Don Juan, who escapes in the darkness unrecognized.

Scene 2. Public Square in Front of Don Juan's Palace. Returning from this bloody adventure, Don Juan and his servant Leporello calmly discuss new conquests. While they consult, a former discarded sweetheart, Elvira, appears and upbraids Don Juan for his cruelty. He retreats, leaving the girl with his servant, who reveals to her the amazing list of his master's villainies.

Leporello's recital to Elvira contains the lofty arias, "Madamina" (Gentle Lady) and "Nella Bionda" (Fair One). The former begins thus:

Don Juan's next piece of rascality is an attempt to seduce Zerlina, a peasant girl, on the very eve of her wedding with Masetto, a villager. He is foiled, however, by the entrance of Elvira, who shows the girl her danger. Meanwhile, Octavio and Anna have been searching for the murderer of Anna's father, and come to ask Don Juan to aid them in their search, but they soon begin to suspect the libertine of the deed. Preparations proceed for the peasant wedding, and Don Juan's servant aids him to hoodwink Masetto and Zerlina. The jealous bridegroom is pacified by his bride, while the libertine conducts both to a gaily decorated apartment prepared for them. Masked guests arrive.

Scene 3. The Ball Room. While all the guests engage in a dance, Leporello devotes himself to Masetto, and Don Juan conducts Zerlina to a private room. She resists his advances and her cries attract the masked guests who prove to be Anna, Elvira, and Octavio. Don Juan draws his sword, fights his way through the crowd and escapes. This scene introduces the stately, graceful minuet:

Act II *Scene 1. Before Elvira's House.* Don Juan still pursues Zerlina, who is in the service of Elvira. He exchanges cloaks with his servant, who goes to call upon the mistress while the master devotes himself to the maid. Masetto comes upon the latter, in the midst of a serenade, but is beaten by Don Juan, who again gets away.

Scene 2. Elvira's Apartments. The pretended Don Juan is unmasked by Elvira, Anna and Octavio, and found to be Leporello. Their suspicions are further confirmed as to Don Juan's guilt. Octavio sings the classic aria for tenors, "To my beloved":

Scene 3. A Graveyard, in which stands a statue of the slain Don Pedro. Leporello, who has escaped, comes to tell his master of what has occurred, but the latter's spirits are still gay and he plans further deeds of violence. At this juncture a hollow voice warns him to repent before it is too late. It is the statue of the murdered nobleman speaking to him. The libertine, unabashed, jeers even at this, and invites the statue to attend a banquet which he is to give.

Scene 4. The Apartments of Donna Anna. Love scene between Anna and Octavio (sometimes omitted).

Scene 5. Don Juan's Dining Hall. True to his word, Don Juan has spread a sumptuous meal, and in the midst of it a heavy tread is heard. The marble statue of the Commandant enters and bids the libertine accompany him. The floor opens and both descend into the infernal regions.

THE MAGIC FLUTE

(Il Flauto Magico. Die Zauberflöte.) Fantastic Opera in Two, or Four Acts. Music by Mozart. Book by Emanuel Schickaneder and Gieseke. Vienna, September 30, 1791. New York, the Park Theatre, in English, April 17, 1833. At the Metropolitan, in German, January 11, 1904, with strong cast headed by Sembrich, Gadski, and Ternina.

SCENE: Egypt.

TIME: Antiquity.

CAST   SARASTRO, *Priest of Isis* (Basso).

THE QUEEN OF NIGHT, *a sorceress* (Soprano).

PAMINA, *her daughter* (Soprano).

TAMINO, *a Prince* (Tenor).

PAPAGENO, *his attendant* (Basso).

PAPAGENA, *the latter's sweetheart* (Soprano).

MONASTATOS, *a Moor* (Tenor).

Priests, Ladies, Pages, Fairies, and Wild Creatures.

ARGUMENT   "The Magic Flute" is an allegorical fantasy showing the reward of constancy. It relates the adventures of a Prince and an imprisoned maiden. The bewildering array of scenes is wedded to sensuous music and the effect of the whole is heightened by strange scenic effects. The two acts into which the opera was originally divided have become three or four acts in modern presentations. The overture beginning with a series of stately chords, continuing with a lordly adagio, then a vivacious fugue, again illustrates Mozart's versatility as a composer.

Act I *A Forest.* Prince Tamino has lost his way in a dense forest and is moreover pursued by a gigantic serpent. His outcries bring three fairies to his aid, who slay the serpent with their spears. Tamino now sees a strange being who walks like a man but is clad in birds' feathers. It is the fantastic Papageno, who claims that this is the proper way to catch birds. Papageno is a great braggart and at once claims the honor for having slain the serpent. The fairies fasten a padlock on his lips in punishment for the lie. They show the Prince the portrait of a lovely maiden, Pamina, who is in the power of Sarastro, at the Temple of Isis. Her mother, the Queen of the Night, now appears and invokes his aid to rescue the maiden. The Prince gladly consents to enter upon the adventure, and is given a magic flute which will ward off danger.   Papageno is to accompany him; the padlock is removed and he is given a chime of bells.

Act II   *Scene 1.   The Palace of Sarastro.*   The Moor, Monastatos, has persecuted Pamina with his attentions.   Angered by her disdain he drags her into an apartment, but is frightened away by Papageno, who has been transported thither by her mother to announce the coming of the Prince.   Pamina plans to flee with them.

Scene 2.   Entrance to the Temple.   Tamino approaches the Temple of Isis, conducted by three pages.   At two of its doors he is denied admittance, but at the third a priest appears and tells him he is mistaken in his opinion of Sarastro.   The maiden is really being protected in the Temple to keep her out of the power of her mother's sorceries.   Pamina and Papageno now appear, but the Moor prevents their escape.   Sarastro enters and having heard all the story orders that the Moor be punished.   The two lovers he greets kindly, telling the Prince he must show himself worthy by passing through an ordeal of the Temple.

Act III   *Scene 1.   A Palm Grove.*   The priests meet to consider the case of the two lovers, and agree that they shall be united if the Prince can successfully undergo the ordeals.   This will also prevent Pamina from falling under the evil influence of her mother.   The chorus of priests with its deep harmony from the orchestra is unforgettable:

Scene 2.   A Courtyard.   The first ordeal is that of silence.   Tamino and Papageno must not utter a word.   The three attendants of the Queen of the Night now appear and tempt them, but they remain firm, though at great cost to Papageno.

Scene 3.   A Garden.   While Pamina is asleep the Moor approaches her, then conceals himself when her mother appears with a dagger, which the girl is commanded to employ against Sarastro.   When the Queen is gone, the Moor returns and threatens Pamina, but is again foiled by Sarastro.

Scene 4.   A Corridor in the Temple.   Papageno and his master still continue under the ordeal of silence, which finally becomes too great a strain for the former.   The Prince remains silent even when Pamina meets him and addresses endearing remarks.   She is deeply wounded that he does not reply.

Act IV   *Scene 1.   The Pyramids.*   The Prince is commanded to wander out into the desert.   He parts sadly from Pamina.   Seeing the delights as well as the sorrows of love Papageno wishes for a "little wife" of his own.   An old hag appears before him.   As he is about to run away she changes into the young and pretty Papagena. But he, too, must first prove his worth.

Scene 2.   The Desert.   Pamina believes the Prince to be faithless and is about to kill herself with the dagger, when she is prevented by the three pages.   Papageno likewise is in the depths of despair over the loss of Papagena, but when he finds he can summon her by ringing his chime of bells his sorrow is turned into joy.

Scene 3.   A Fiery Cavern.   Tamino is seen undergoing the last of his ordeals.   He is menaced by great waterfalls and tongues of flame.   Beyond these he beholds Pamina and calls to her, his lips now being unsealed.   The lovers are reunited and a few strains from the magic flute cause the remaining dangers to vanish.

This opera, which is full of difficult vocal passages, has none more exacting than that of Pamina: "All is vanquished"—

Scene 4.   The Temple of Isis.   Despite the interference of the Queen of the Night, the lovers have overcome their trials.   The High Priest solemnly blesses them.   While the clownish Papageno also finds happiness in winning Papagena, the bird woman.   The opera ends amid a blaze of joyous melody.

LUDWIG VAN BEETHOVEN

Although Beethoven is recognized as one of the greatest, if not the greatest, musical composers of modern times, he produced only one opera.   He was born at Bonn, Germany, December 16, 1770.   He died

at Vienna, March 26, 1827.   His works are numerous and in every variety of style—oratorios, chamber music, orchestral suites, vocal music,
and compositions for the pianoforte.   It was Schikaneder, the librettist
of Mozart's "Magic Flute," who first suggested to Beethoven that he
compose an opera.   The completed work, however, was produced under
the patronage of Baron Von Braun, who was then manager of the
Theatre An Der Wien, Vienna, where the opera, "Fidelio," was first
sung.

FIDELIO
(Fee-day'-lee-o)

Dramatic Opera in Two Acts.   Music by Ludwig Van Beethoven.
Book by Joseph Sonnleithner, after Bouilly's "Leonore."   Theatre
An Der Wien, Vienna, November 20, 1805.   In revised form, in Vienna,
May 23, 1814.   In New York at the Park Theatre, September 9, 1839.
At the Metropolitan, January 11, 1891.

> SCENE: A Prison near Seville.
> TIME: The Eighteenth Century.

> CAST   DON FERNANDO, *minister of state* (Baritone).
> DON PIZARRO, *governor of prison* (Baritone).
> DON FLORESTAN, *a noble prisoner* (Tenor).
> LEONORA, *his wife, known as "Fidelio"* (Soprano).
> ROCCO, *jailer* (Basso).
> MARCELLINA, *his daughter* (Soprano).
> JACQUINO, *turnkey* (Tenor).
> CAPTAIN OF THE GUARD (Basso).
> Prisoners, Guards, Citizens, etc.

ARGUMENT   "Fidelio" is of great interest not merely for its
score during the action, but also for its overtures.
Beethoven constantly experimented with these, writing four in all.
Three were entitled "Leonore," his original choice of name for the
opera.   All four are still in the active repertory of orchestras, and if the
opera had been forgotten, they alone would show his mastery in this
field.   The theme itself is a touching story of conjugal love and fidelity.

Act I   *Courtyard of the Prison.*   Don Florestan, a Spanish nobleman,
incurs the hatred of Don Pizarro, governor of the prison, and
soon disappears from the world.   Florestan's wife, Leonora, suspects
that his enemy has hidden him away in one of the prison dungeons, and
disguises herself as a young man known as "Fidelio," and undertakes a
dangerous mission to rescue him.   In an aria of sublime courage she

commits herself to this quest: "Sweet hope, forsake not this abiding heart!"

She enters service with Rocco, the jailer, and soon finds her husband, as she had feared. Meanwhile, she is in danger of discovery, as she wins the approval of the jailer and his daughter, Marcellina, and the latter falls in love with the handsome "young man," much to the sorrow of the turnkey Jacquino, who loves Marcellina. Fidelio cannot refuse the proffered match as she desires to keep on good terms with the jailer. Word is received that the minister, Don Fernando, is coming to inspect the prison. This fills Pizarro with alarm and he resolves to put Florestan out of the way before that time. Rocco refuses to kill the prisoner, but finally consents to dig the grave. Fidelio overhears the plans and is in despair. She obtains the jailer's permission for the prisoners to file out into the courtyard to get the fresh air. She hopes thus to get some message to her husband, but he does not appear with the rest, so she accompanies Rocco to dig the grave.

Act II *Scene 1. Florestan's Dungeon.* In one of the lowest cells of the prison, Fidelio finds her husband weak from exhaustion. He does not recognize her. She gives him food and drink, and with simulated cheerfulness helps to dig the grave. Before the task is ended Pizarro comes down eager to get his dangerous prisoner out of sight. The minister is coming. Pizarro is about to stab the prisoner, when Fidelio, or Leonora, throws herself in front of him crying: "First slay his wife!" She threatens him with a pistol and the cowardly governor flees. Trumpets from without announce the arrival of Don Fernando, while Florestan clasps his wife in his arms and Rocco scratches his head in bewilderment. The trumpet call, the climax to this scene, is lofty and dramatic.

Scene 2. The Courtyard. Fernando quickly frees Florestan, and the chains are ordered upon Pizarro instead. The minister felicitates with the rescued man in having a "Fidelio" for his wife. Marcellina decides that Jacquino will make her a better husband, after all, greatly to the turnkey's delight.

CARL MARIA VON WEBER

A German composer, born in Eutin, Germany, December 18, 1786. His father was a musician and the boy inherited not only this talent, but also painting and engraving. However, music was his grand passion, and he began composing as early as twelve years of age. He went on tour with his father, and about 1803 paid his first visit to Vienna, where he met Haydn. He became successively director of the opera at Prague and Dresden. In 1821 he produced "Der Freischütz" at Berlin, with great success. Five years later he superintended the première of "Oberon," at London. But his career was cut short, this same year, by death, June 5, 1826. His other operas include "The Forest Maiden," and "Euryanthe."

DER FREISCHÜTZ

(Dair Fry'-sheets)

(The Sharpshooter.) Romantic Opera in Three Acts. Music by Weber. Book by Friedrich Kind, after an old legend in "Popular Tales of the 'Northern Nations.'" Berlin, June 18, 1821. At New York in the Park Theatre, in English, March 2, 1825. At the Metropolitan, March 11, 1910, with Gadski, Alten, Jadlowker, Muhlmann, and Witherspoon.

SCENE: Bohemia.
TIME: Seventeenth Century.

CAST   OTTAKAR, *Duke of Bohemia* (Baritone).
KUNO, *his head game-keeper* (Basso).
AGNES, *his daughter* (Soprano).

ANNA, *her friend* (Mezzo-Soprano).
MAX, *a ranger* (Tenor).
CASPAR, *a ranger* (Basso).
KILIAN, *a wealthy peasant* (Basso).
A HERMIT (Basso).
ZAMIEL, *the evil one* (Speaking part).
Foresters, Villagers, Followers of the Duke, Servants.

ARGUMENT   The story of "Der Freischütz," or "The Sharpshooter," is based upon a Teutonic legend that magical bullets may be cast which never miss their mark.

The overture, an abiding concert favorite, is more widely known than the opera itself. It is full of singing melodies.

Act I   *Estates of the Prince of Bohemia.*   The advancing years of Kuno, head ranger of the Duke of Bohemia, make the choice of a new head ranger necessary. Max, who is in love with Agnes, Kuno's daughter, is a candidate for the place, but in order to obtain it he must win in a sharpshooting contest. At a preliminary trial, Max is unsuccessful, the peasant, Kilian, being the better marksman. Max is much cast down and therefore disposed to listen to the evil counsels of Caspar, who has already sold himself to the devil and who hopes to obtain respite by furnishing this new victim. Max is invited to try Caspar's gun, and is astonished to find that he can bring down an eagle from a great height. Caspar then tells him that he can obtain seven magical bullets which will hit any mark, but he must sell his soul for them. Max, undaunted, agrees to meet him at the Wolf's Glen at midnight.

Act II   *Scene 1.* *Agnes' Room.*   Agnes is filled with forebodings over the coming contest. She has met a hermit in the forest, who has warned her of impending danger. Then, while she and Anna are in her room, at the very moment when Max tries the magic bullet, an ancestral portrait falls to the floor. Anna tries to calm her fears. She is reassured by the appearance of her lover and sings the exulting melody first heard in the overture: "Ah, how my pulse is beating!"

However, the joy of their meeting is brief. Max confesses that he is under an obligation and must hurry away to an appointment at the Wolf's Glen.

Scene 2. The Wolf's Glen. Caspar awaits the arrival of his victim, and meanwhile tells Zamiel, the evil one, of his success. When Max arrives, the incantations are under way, and amid scenes of terror the magical bullets are cast.

Act III *Scene 1. Agatha's Room.* Agatha is being prepared for her wedding with Max. She is still filled with foreboding, which is not lessened by finding that a box of flowers contains a funeral wreath. She is comforted, however, by a bridal wreath which the holy hermit has blessed.

Scene 2. Duke Ottakar's Camp. The marksman's tourney is in progress, and is introduced by a rousing chorus in praise of hunting: "What so fine as a huntsman's life?"

Max amazes all the others by his skill. Only one remains of his store of magical bullets, and this one the fiend has in personal charge. The Duke orders Max to shoot at a dove flying through the forest. He obeys and a woman's shriek is heard. Agnes, in her wedding finery, has been struck; but she revives and it is found that the wreath blessed by the hermit has turned the bullet aside. The fiend, cheated of his prey, seizes upon the cursing Caspar, whose day of grace has expired. The horrified Max tells the story of the bullets and confesses his fault, whereupon the Duke imposes a year of penance before he can receive the post of head ranger or the hand of his bride.

EURYANTHE

(Yoo-ree-ahn'-thee)

Romantic Opera in Three Acts. Music by Weber. Book by Helmine von Chezy. Vienna, October 25, 1823. At New York, the Metropolitan, December 23, 1888, with Lehmann, Brandt, and Alvary.

SCENE: Castle Premery and Burg of Nevers, France.
TIME: 1110 A.D.

CAST LOUIS VI, *King of France* (Basso).
ADOLAR, *Count of Nevers* (Tenor).
EURYANTHE OF SAVOY, *his betrothed* (Soprano).
LYSIART, *Count of Forest* (Baritone).
EGLANTINE VON PUISET, *the captive daughter of a mutineer* (Mezzo-Soprano).

ARGUMENT The story of Euryanthe is adapted from an old French romance, entitled "The Story of Gerard of Nevers and the beautiful and virtuous Euryanthe." It is reminiscent of Shakespeare's "Cymbeline." The overture, which is divided into two parts, remains in active repertory and is better known than the opera; the theme of the latter being inane, the music "spotty."

Act I *Scene 1. A Hall in the King's Palace.* In the court of King Louis of France, Count Adolar pays a glowing tribute to the beauty and virtue of Euryanthe, his betrothed. All present applaud except Count Lysiart, who sneers at the chastity of women, and boasts that he could win Euryanthe. Adolar dares him to make the test, staking his fortune on the outcome. The King attempts to dissuade him from the foolish wager, but in vain.

Scene 2. The Palace Garden of Nevers. Euryanthe is discovered alone, but is soon joined by Eglantine, a captive maiden who is secretly in love with Adolar. In a moment of confidence, Euryanthe tells her the secret of a neighboring tomb, in which rests the body of Emma, her sister, who had poisoned herself, and whose ghost can find no peace until tears of innocent distress have been shed upon her ring. Eglantine decides forthwith to make use of this secret against Euryanthe, and takes Lysiart into her confidence when he presently arrives.

Act II *Scene 1. The Same Garden.* Lysiart has tried vainly to win the favor of Euryanthe, and now deplores his failure. When hope of winning his evil wager seems lost, Eglantine brings him Emma's ring from the tomb, to use as evidence of Euryanthe's infidelity.

Scene 2. The King's Palace. Euryanthe and Adolar appear at court. They are confronted by Lysiart, who claims to be the victor. He displays Emma's ring, and Euryanthe is visibly confused at this evidence that she could not keep the secret of her sister's death. Her confusion is taken by Adolar to be evidence of her guilt with Lysiart. He forfeits his lands and leaves the court in humiliation, taking Euryanthe with him.

Act III *Scene 1. A Forest.* Adolar has taken Euryanthe to the wilderness to slay her, but on the way is attacked by a huge serpent. The maiden tries to shield him with her own body. He kills the snake, and renounces his intention of harming her. However, he deserts her in the forest. The King and a band of hunters arrive and rescue her. To him she tells the whole story of Eglantine's treachery. The King takes her back to the palace.

Scene 2. Garden of the Castle of Nevers. Adolar repents his hasty belief in the guilt of Euryanthe, and returns to Nevers to challenge Lysiart. He meets the wedding procession of Eglantine and Lysiart, and in the encounter Eglantine confesses her duplicity and passion for Adolar. In a rage, Lysiart turns and stabs her. The King appears upon the scene, vindicates Euryanthe, orders Lysiart to the scaffold, and restores Adolar to his possessions. The two lovers are reunited, and the soul of Emma is at peace, as tears of innocent distress have been shed upon her ring.

OBERON

(*Oh'-ber-on*)

(Or, the Elf-King's Oath.) Fairy Opera in Three Acts. Music by Weber. Book by James R. Planché. Covent Garden, London, April 12, 1826. At New York, the Metropolitan, in English, December 28, 1918, with Althouse, Rosa Ponselle, Martinelli.

SCENE: Fairyland, France, Tunis, and Arabia.
TIME: Eighth Century.

CAST OBERON, *the Elfin King* (Tenor).
TITANIA, *his Queen* (Mute Character).
PUCK, *his messenger* (Contralto).
DROLL (Contralto).
HUON DE BORDEAUX (Tenor).
SCHERASMIN, *his esquire* (Baritone).
HAROUN EL RASCHID (Baritone).
REZIA, *his daughter* (Soprano).
FATIMA, *her slave* (Soprano).
PRINCE BABEKAN (Tenor).
EMIR ALMANSOR (Baritone).
ROSCHANA, *his wife* (Contralto).
ABDALLAH, *a pirate* (Basso).
CHARLEMAGNE (Basso).
Fairies, Soldiers, Pirates, Courtiers, Ladies of the Harem, etc.

ARGUMENT   Weber's success with "Der Freischütz" had been
so immediate, that he was asked to write "Oberon"
for Covent Garden.   The elfin theme with its graceful music gives no
hint of the physical handicap under which he labored.   His health had
been steadily failing under the ravages of tuberculosis, and by the time
of "Oberon's" first performance he was too ill to wield the baton as he
and his countless admirers had hoped.   The opera was a great success,
the audience being captivated from the start with the fairylike overture,
which is still a favorite with orchestras.   But Weber survived its opening by less than two months.   The story deals with elves and fairies.

Its melodious overture is still a prime favorite with orchestras:
"Ocean, thou mighty monster!" has been sung most recently by Kirsten
Flagstad.

FRIEDRICH VON FLOTOW

A German composer, born in Mecklenburg-Schwerin, April 26, 1812.
He studied music in Paris but did not meet with success there in his
early operas.   At the age of twenty-seven he finally achieved recognition with "Medusa's Shipwreck."   This was followed by "Camoen's
Slave" (1843), and "The Soul in Pain" (1846).   "Alexander Stradella,"
one of the few operas by which he is still remembered, had its première
at Hamburg in 1844, and his most successful work, "Martha," at Vienna
in 1847.   He wrote several other operas, and was director of the court
theatre in his native duchy from 1855 to 1863.   He died in Darmstadt,
January 23, 1883.

STRADELLA
(Strah-del'-la)

Romantic Opera in Three Acts. Music by Flotow. Book by
W. Friedrich. Palais Royale Theatre, Paris, 1837; in revised form as
"Alessandro Stradella," in Hamburg, December 30, 1844. At New
York, the Metropolitan, also in the New Theatre, February, 1910.

SCENE: Venice and Rome.
TIME: Circa 1675.

CAST   ALESSANDRO STRADELLA, *a musician* (Tenor).
LEONORA, *his bride* (Soprano).
BASSI, *a wealthy nobleman, her guardian* (Baritone).
MALVOLIO ⎱ *two desperadoes*
BARBARINO ⎰ (Baritones).
Priest, Friends, Servants.

ARGUMENT   This opera preceded "Martha" in time, but was greatly overshadowed by the latter.   It is remembered chiefly today as being by the composer of the more popular work.

Act I   Stradella, a musician with a lovely voice, wins the hand of Leonora, ward of a wealthy nobleman, Bassi, who has planned to marry her himself.   Aided by friends, Stradella captures the girl during a carnival and flees with her to Rome, where they are married. The infuriated grandee hires two desperadoes to find the singer and kill him.   They secrete themselves in his home and later are admitted, posing as pilgrims.

Act II   A tuneful quartet opens this Act, by Leonora, Stradella, and the two ruffians, in praise of Italy.   So moved are the two villains by Stradella's wonderful voice, that they haven't the heart to murder him.

Act III   Bassi, however, follows them up and tries to bribe them still further to carry out their evil project.   Again they conceal themselves in his house.   When he returns he rehearses a "Hymn to the Virgin," which he is to sing publicly, the next day.   His melting tones again are too much for them.   They implore forgiveness, and Bassi himself relents.   The amazed Leonora, who now enters, unites with the group in a chorus of rejoicing.

MARTHA

Romantic Opera in Four or Five Acts.   Music by F. von Flotow. Book by St. Georges and Friedrich.   Imperial Opera House, Vienna, November 25, 1847.   In Italian and in English, London, 1858.   At New York in Niblo's Garden, November 1, 1852, in English.   At New York, the Metropolitan, April, 1887, with Patti.

SCENE: Richmond, England.
TIME: Reign of Queen Anne.

CAST   LIONEL, *a farmer* (Tenor).
        PLUNKETT, *his foster brother* (Basso).
        LORD TRISTAN, *a courtier* (Basso).
        LADY HENRIETTA DURHAM, *a maid-of-honor* (Soprano). *Also called* HARRIET.
        NANCY, *her attendant* (Contralto).
        SHERIFF OF RICHMOND (Basso).
        Lords, Ladies, Farmers, Servants, Citizens.

ARGUMENT   "Martha" at the end of a century of service is still one of the best loved operas.   It is a "hardy perennial," delighting millions in the past and probably will continue to delight millions yet unborn.   From the tuneful overture with its rounded horn solo as a dominant theme through to the last curtain the opera is a sure escape from the cares of the day.   "Martha" is more Light than Grand, but the greatest singers have not disdained it.   The plot is an old one—love opposed to pride, and pride finally vanquished.

Act I   *The Queen's Court at Hampton.*   Lady Henrietta, a maid-of-honor to Queen Anne, has become weary of humdrum court life and seeks a new diversion.   She talks it over with her saucy maid, who tells her "of the knights so true and charming," but does not fall in with any of the latter's fancies.   "That is really too distressing!" is the theme of a lively duet.   Lord Tristan, an old admirer, meets with as little success when he proposes entertainments for the day.   At this moment a group of villagers and servants pass singing gaily on their way to a county fair.

"Come away, maidens gay, to the fair let's repair!" they sing and their gay abandon strikes a responsive chord in the bored lady's heart. That's the very thing, she decides.   She and her maid shall go also dressed as servants.   What a lark!   The shocked Tristan tries to dissuade her, but the willful lady persists; and he finds himself pressed into service as their unwilling escort.

Act II   *The Richmond Market.*   A chorus of villagers greets the girls seeking service: "Maidens bright and fair, draw near."

While they sing, two well-to-do farmers, Lionel and Plunkett, enter, in quest of servants. A mystery clouds Lionel's birth, as he indicates in his song, "Lost, proscribed."

The sheriff arrives and proclaims that all contracts for domestic servants shall be binding upon both parties for a full year, if money is advanced. Just after this announcement is made, Tristan arrives with the two girls dressed as servants, who immediately capture the fancy of the two farmers. In spite of Tristan's efforts to draw them away, they allow the farmers to haggle with them over terms and finally accept an advance payment for salaries. A pleasing quartet ensues: "Now indeed our love we may be taking."

Without knowing it, they have bound themselves to service for a year. When the farmers now insist upon an immediate departure, objections are raised by the other three. But the crowd prevents Tristan from rescuing the girls, and the sheriff declares that they must go with their new masters.

Act III   *The Farm House.*   Henrietta has taken the name of Martha; and Nancy that of Julia. Lionel and Plunkett try to introduce them to their duties as farm servants. Both are so ignorant, however, of the simplest tasks, that Lionel and Plunkett are in despair. The men try to teach them spinning, but are forced to seat themselves at the wheel, while Harriet admiringly sings, "What a charming occupation!" The Spinning Wheel quartet at this point is one of the gems of the opera. "Presto, presto!" whirls the melody.

But when the men ask, "Do you understand?" Nancy says, "Yes, we do," overturns the wheel and runs out, pursued by Plunkett. When "Martha" makes as if to follow, Lionel restrains her with, "Art afraid?" Then ensues a duet, "To his eye mine kindly meeting." She sees that despite her clumsiness in household matters he is falling in love with her. At first amused, she softens a little, and then sings the crowning aria of the opera, " 'Tis the last rose of summer."

The touching melody has a temporary effect, and the four bid one another a demure good night, in a quartet of rich harmony. The young women, however, by this time realize the predicament they are in. They must get away, and now. The faithful Tristan appears, with a waiting carriage. Out the window they go, to safety and their former station. The farmers find their servants gone and are overcome with grief and fury.

Act IV *A Country Tavern.* While Plunkett is drinking with some of his friends, a party of hunters from the court enter, and he recognizes among them his lost servant girl, "Julia," as she sings "Huntress fair." He demands that she go home with him and complete her contract, but her calls for help bring her friends about her and they chase Plunkett out into the forest. Next Lionel enters, greatly dejected over the loss of "Martha," when whom should he see among the hunters but the girl herself as a court lady. His song, "M'appari" (Like a dream) remains one of the most popular tenor arias.

Lionel stubbornly continues to claim "Martha," and she reproaches him for being an impertinent bumpkin. The others think him a madman, and she is glad to escape in this fashion. He sings in despair, "May Heaven grant you pardon."

Act V *Scene 1. The Farm House.* Lionel's long-standing claim to the earldom of Derby is decided in his favor, but he takes no interest in the matter. He is almost insane with grief. Henrietta is persuaded to visit him, but he does not recognize the "Martha" of his dreams. Nancy and Plunkett come to an understanding and arrange a little scene to restore Lionel's reason.

Scene 2. The Fair at Richmond. Another fair is being held, and Plunkett brings his friend to the square where they had first met the girls. Lo! there they are again, dressed in their servant's attire. Memory and reason return to Lionel, and when "Martha" sings again to him the ballad of the rose his cup of happiness is full. She is willing to become his wife.

RICHARD WAGNER

This foremost German composer, who created a school all his own, was born at Leipsic, May 22, 1813. When eight years of age he had acquired a passable knowledge of the pianoforte; and as a schoolboy he was fond of versifying—Shakespeare being his grand passion. At the age of twenty Wagner began his career as a professional musician, becoming chorus-master at the Wurzburg Theatre. Here he wrote his first opera, "The Fairies," which, however, was not produced until after his death. His next engagements were Königsberg and Riga, and in the latter city he began work on his first great success, "Rienzi," which was produced in Dresden (1842). Not long thereafter the composer was appointed one of the conductors of the Dresden Royal Opera. "Rienzi" was followed by "The Flying Dutchman" (1843); "Tannhäuser" (1845); "Lohengrin" (1850); the "Nibelung" dramas; "Tristan and Isolde," and "Die Meistersinger." Political and other troubles prevented Wagner from producing some of the later operas at the time when written. In fact, so different was his music from the accepted types, that his life was a crusade. His work is remarkable also from the fact that he wrote his own librettos, which reveal a dramatic skill and imagination of high order. His final opera was "Parsifal" (1882). Wagner died in Venice, February 13, 1883.

RIENZI

(Ree-en'-zee)

Grand Opera, in Five Acts. Words and Music by Wagner, after the historical novel, "Rienzi, the Last of the Tribunes," by Bulwer-Lytton. Dresden Opera House, October 20, 1842. At New York in the Academy of Music, 1878; the Metropolitan, February 5, 1886.

SCENE: Rome.

TIME: The Fourteenth Century.

CAST COLA RIENZI, *Roman Tribune and Papal Notary* (Tenor).

IRENE, *his sister* (Soprano).

STEFFANO COLONNA (Basso).

ADRIANO, *his son* (Mezzo-Soprano).

PAOLO ORSINO (Basso).

RAIMONDO, *Papal Legate* (Basso).

BARONCELLO } *Roman citizens* { Tenor.
CECCO DEL VECCHIO } { Basso.

MESSENGER OF PEACE (Soprano).

Ambassadors, Nobles, Priests, Monks, Soldiers, Messengers, and Citizens.

ARGUMENT This first opera of Wagner's, and one which he himself later turned his back upon, is yet a work of great force and beauty. Its theme is semi-historical.

The overture, which remains in repertory, sounds in a long trumpet tone the theme of popular uprising. This is followed by a quieter melody denoting the prayer of Rienzi; then the thunder of revolt; their interplay outlines the turbulent plot.

Act I   *A Street in Rome.* Rienzi, a notary of lofty ideals, cherishes the hope of one day freeing his beloved city from the power of the insolent nobles. His anger against them is heightened by an attempted abduction of his sister Irene by Orsino, a patrician. Orsino is balked by Adriano, son of Colonna, another patrician, and of a family which has already wronged Rienzi's house. Adriano, however, is in love with Irene. During the tumult, Rienzi appears upon the scene, and urges the people to take up arms against the nobility. His cause is espoused by the Church, and is successful. The nobles are driven into flight.

Act II   *The Capitol.* Rienzi is created Tribune, and the nobles are forced to pledge their allegiance. They secretly despise him, and Orsino, one of their party, tries to stab Rienzi. The latter's coat of mail thwarts the blow. The nobles who have taken part in this plot are condemned to death, but Adriano, who belongs to the Tribune's party, pleads for them, and Irene joins in his petition. They are pardoned.

Act III   *A Public Square.* The nobles, far from experiencing a change of heart, are stirred on to fresh excesses. Although Rienzi is again victorious over them, it is at heavy loss of his own men. Adriano feels compelled to turn against the Tribune and side with his own family.

Act IV   *A Public Square.* Adriano denounces Rienzi as a traitor. The credulous people begin to fall away from him. Irene alone clings to her brother, and scornfully repulses her lover when he tries to draw her from Rienzi's side. When the Tribune presents himself at the doors of the cathedral, he is met with a ban of excommunication, instead of a blessing.

Act V   *The Capitol.* The Tribune is now in danger of his life. Adriano, seeing this, once more visits Irene to urge her and her brother to seek refuge in flight. But they will not do so. Rienzi appears on a portico to make one last appeal to the populace. The mob fires the building with torches, and hurls stones at Rienzi and his sister. When Adriano sees that they are doomed to death, he rushes into the blazing building, to perish with them.

THE FLYING DUTCHMAN

(Der Fliegender Hollander.) Romantic Opera in Three Acts. Music by Wagner. Book by the Composer, after Heine's version of the legend. Dresden, January 2, 1843. At New York in the Academy of Music, January 26, 1877. The Metropolitan, December 31, 1890.

SCENE: A Norwegian Fishing Village.
TIME: The Eighteenth Century.

CAST A DUTCH SEA CAPTAIN (Baritone).
DALAND, *A Norse Sea Captain* (Basso).
SENTA, *his daughter* (Soprano).
MARY, *her servant* (Contralto).
ERIC, *a huntsman* (Tenor).
DALAND'S STEERSMAN (Tenor).
Chorus of Maidens, Seamen, Villagers, etc.

ARGUMENT The legend of "The Flying Dutchman," condemned to sail the high seas for many centuries, finds a worthy musical and dramatic setting in this work of Wagner. According to this legend, a Dutch captain, foiled by contrary winds when rounding the Cape of Good Hope, takes a sacrilegious oath that he will succeed if he has to take eternity for it. Thereafter, for long centuries his ship is in charge of demons, who make it the sport of wind and wave. The opera deals with the lifting of the curse.

Like all of Wagner's operas, the overture is one of the dominant parts of the work. Here the composer gives a musical foreword to the piece: the stormy seas, the stubborn Dutchman laboring under a curse, the hint of redemption in Senta's voice, the final victory—all are foreshadowed.

Act I *A Bay in Norway.* Daland, a Norwegian sea captain, is driven by a violent storm to the shelter of a port. During the storm a strange-looking vessel also arrives, riding high upon the waves, and casts anchor alongside. The captain, a man of wild aspect dressed in black, steps ashore. He is the famous Flying Dutchman, whom all mariners fear and dread. By the terms of his oath, he is allowed to go ashore once in seven years, and if perchance he find a wife who will leave all for love of him, the spell will be released. He speaks with Daland, and finding that the latter has a daughter, asks permission to court her, at the same time offering Daland gold. The father's cupidity overcomes his scruples and, the storm having abated, the two vessels set sail in company.

Act II *The Home of Daland.* The curtain discloses a scene in sharp contrast to the preceding. Senta and her friends are busily spinning, the hum of the wheels blending with their voices in the most pleasing chorus of the opera.

Senta is a dreamy, romantic girl, who is already familiar with the strange story of the Flying Dutchman, and feels in her heart that she, at any rate, would be willing to give up all to save him. She tells the others of her wild resolve in a descriptive ballad:

Eric the huntsman, who loves her, enters at this moment and warns her against her dangerous whim. He also tells her that a mysterious stranger is approaching with her father, but Senta is delighted and Eric leaves in dejection. Daland enters with the Dutchman, who gazes fixedly at the maiden and she at him. She readily accepts her father's plan for an early marriage, as she believes herself to be divinely appointed the savior of this sea rover. The two exchange vows of eternal fidelity, and the Dutchman believes his hour of liberation is at hand.

Act III *The Harbor.* The sailors on board Daland's ship give themselves over to merry-making. Girls bring them hampers of refreshments. The Dutchman's ship lies hard by, dark and silent, although his crew has been invited to share in the festivities. Finally they sing a mocking song of their captain's adventures, while the others listen in superstitious fear. Senta comes down to the shore followed by Eric, who makes one last plea for her to relinquish her folly and love him as she had formerly done. The stranger overhears this, and believing himself betrayed, bids her farewell and hastens on board his ship, ordering the anchor raised and all sails set. He admits publicly that he is the Flying Dutchman, upon whom a curse rests, and while Daland and the rest shrink back in horror the ship heads toward the open sea. But Senta tears herself away from Eric and her father, who would restrain her, and rushing to a cliff under which the vessel is passing, throws herself into the sea. Over the roar of the waves her last words ring out:

> *"Praise thou thine angel, for what he saith:*
> *Here stand I faithful, even unto death!"*

Instantly the curse is lifted, the phantom ship sinks beneath the waves, and from its shadow a tableau discloses the Dutchman and Senta ascending heavenward.

TANNHÄUSER
(*Tahn'-hoy-zer*)

Dramatic Opera in Three Acts. Music by Wagner. Book by the Composer. Royal Opera, Dresden, October 20, 1845. At New York in the Stadt Theatre, April 4, 1859; Metropolitan, November 17, 1884.

SCENE: Thuringia and the Wartburg.
TIME: The Thirteenth Century.

CAST HERRMANN, *Landgrave of Thuringia* (Basso).
TANNHÄUSER, *a knight* (Tenor).
WOLFRAM VON ESCHENBACH, *his friend* (Baritone).
WALTER VON DER VOGELWEIDE, *a knight* (Tenor).
BITEROLF, *a knight* (Basso).
REIMAR VON ZWETER, *a knight* (Basso).
HEINRICH, *a scribe* (Tenor).
ELIZABETH, *niece of the Landgrave* (Soprano).
VENUS, *goddess of love* (Soprano).
Retainers, Lords, Ladies, Bacchantes, Shepherd, etc.

ARGUMENT "Tannhäuser" deals with a legend of the Venusberg, a magic grotto in the mountains of Germany. Here the beautiful goddess of love holds court and beguiles any mortals who come her way. Tannhäuser, a Knight of Song, has fallen under her evil spell and dwelt several months with her in luxury and dissipation. But the remembrance of his former high station and the ties of earth still hold him, and when the scene opens he wishes to return to the light of day.

The overture, one of the loftiest, most descriptive, of the Wagnerian suite, interprets the theme: the solemn chant of the pilgrims; the voluptuous strains from Venusberg; the vision of the goddess herself; the minstrel's song of love; the far-off strains of the pilgrim's song, as of warning; the hint of repentance from the flesh—all prepare the auditor for the opening scene.

Act I *Scene 1. The Grotto of Venus.* Tannhäuser is growing weary of the blandishments of Venus and of the elaborate pageants which she prepares to entertain him. Amid the enchanting strains of the Bacchanale, the minstrel nevertheless strives to break away, to return to the world of men and women, but his request only makes her the more jealous of her waning power. She shows him new spectacles of beauty and luxury, but he only insists the more. Seeing that she cannot hold him an unwilling prisoner, she exacts from him a promise that he will sing her praises only, as against the merits of any earthly love. He gives this pledge as a means of escape, and the grotto and its occupants vanish from sight.

Scene 2. The Valley of Wartburg. Tannhäuser finds himself alone in the mountains of the Wartburg. In the distance a shepherd lad plays upon his pipe. By a mountain path stands a rude wayside cross, and presently a throng of pilgrims are heard singing as they go on their mission. After they have passed by, the Landgrave of the country and some of his nobles, among them Tannhäuser's loyal friend, Wolfram von Eschenbach, enter upon a hunting expedition. They recognize Tannhäuser and ask him many questions regarding his long disappearance. He evades their questions. Wolfram urges him to return to court, saying that Elizabeth, the Landgrave's niece, has long held his memory dear. The erring knight is filled with shame at the thought of this pure love which he has cast aside, and promises to return with his friends.

Act II *Hall of Wartburg Castle.* Elizabeth's joyful song of greeting opens this Act, "Dich teure Halle!" All is in readiness for the festival.

Wolfram enters bringing the errant knight, and Tannhäuser is delighted to find her still faithful to his memory. They pledge their love anew in a duet. Then comes one of the musical high spots, the Procession of Guests:

The minstrel knights are the last to enter, and the contest begins. Wolfram sings of love ennobling and spiritual, the highest type of bliss. But Tannhäuser, bound by his unholy promise to Venus, answers scornfully that such love is paltry compared with other delights which he might perchance reveal.   Being pressed for an explanation by other angered knights, he launches into a wild song in praise of Venus.   The court is horrified.   The ladies leave in haste, and the knights press around the daring minstrel with drawn swords ready to kill him.   Elizabeth throws herself before him and pleads for the unhappy man's life. They finally allow him to go unscathed on condition that he join the pilgrims, who now pass by on their journey to Rome, and there obtain the forgiveness of the Pope.   The repentant Tannhäuser sets forth, amid the recurring strains of the Pilgrims' Chorus:

Act III   *The Valley of Wartburg.*   Several months have passed by without news of Tannhäuser.   Both Elizabeth and Wolfram await him.   Wolfram's friendship is unselfish, as he himself has long loved the maiden who pines over the wanderer's departure.   The pilgrims return from Rome, and she comes to the wayside cross to look for him among them.   But he does not appear, and, brokenhearted, she returns to the castle and soon dies.   Wolfram enters, comparing her pure bright spirit to the evening star which shines upon him.

A haggard stranger now appears, who proves to be Tannhäuser returning without the Pope's forgiveness.   The latter refuses to pardon him until his pilgrim's staff blossoms with leaves.   Tannhäuser is ready to return to the haunts of Venus, and she now appears and beckons him. But Wolfram pleads with him and prevails upon him to deny her.   He does so, and the vision vanishes.   Mourners bring forward the bier upon which rests the body of the maiden, and while the troubled Tannhäuser kneels beside it, he dies.   At this moment messengers come from the Pope, bearing the pilgrim's staff.   A miracle has happened.   The staff has put forth green leaves.

LOHENGRIN
(Lo'-hen-grin)

Romantic Opera in Three Acts.   Music by Wagner.   Book by the Composer.   Weimar, Germany, August 28, 1850.   At New York, Stadt Theatre, April 3, 1871; Metropolitan, November 23, 1885.

SCENE: The Scheldt, Flanders.
TIME: The Tenth Century.

CAST   HENRY I, *King of Germany* (Basso).
FREDERICK OF TELRAMUND, *a nobleman* (Baritone).
ORTRUD, *his wife* (Contralto).
ELSA OF BRABANT (Soprano).
LOHENGRIN, *the Knight of the Swan* (Tenor).
HERALD (Baritone).
Courtiers, Soldiers, Citizens, Servants.

ARGUMENT   The basis of "Lohengrin" is a legend connected with one of the Knights of the Holy Grail.   These knights are pledged to aid the oppressed at any time, and it is in an adventure of this sort that the Knight of the Swan appears.

The music of this inspiring opera fits it "like a glove."   The auditor is at once placed in rapport with the story from its opening theme in the Prelude or Vorspiel, which is repeated with many orchestral variations:

Working gradually up to a magnificent crescendo, the final chords crash as the curtain rises.

Act I   *The Banks of the Scheldt.*   According to ancient custom, the King of Germany holds a public outdoor court in which he hears complaints and tries all cases which may be brought before him. Frederick of Telramund, an unscrupulous nobleman, appears before

this court and claims the Duchy of Brabant.   He has been acting as
regent during the minority of Godfrey and his sister Elsa, and now
claims that the maiden has made away with her brother in order to
seize the dukedom.   Elsa is summoned to defend herself and declares
her innocence.   She is willing to leave the merits of her cause to a trial
by combat, stating that she has seen in her dreams a resplendent knight
who promised to come to her assistance.   The arrogant Frederick says
that he is ready to meet any champion and shakes his head scornfully
while the Herald stations his trumpeters and Elsa sinks on her knees in
prayer.   Here occurs again the lovely, flowing melody known as the
Elsa Motif:

The trumpets blare and the Herald announces: "He who by right of
Heaven will come to fight for Elsa of Brabant, let him stand forth!"
Silence.   All watch in awe for any outcome.   Elsa calls out implor-
ingly: "My champion bides afar."   Then a shout goes up.   A swan is
discerned in the distance, drawing a boat on which a figure stands erect.
Nearer and nearer it comes until it stops near the throng, and a knight,
clad in glittering armor, steps forth and announces himself as Elsa's
champion.   He speedily overcomes Frederick, but grants him his life,
and asks Elsa's hand in marriage.   Only one condition is interposed.
She is not to ask the knight's name and whence he came.   She consents
and all rejoice at the happy outcome of events.

Act II   *The Courtyard and Cathedral.*   On the night before the wed-
          ding of Elsa and her champion, Frederick and Ortrud, his wife,
wander into the deserted courtyard.   They have been banished from

the country, but Ortrud revives her husband's drooping spirits by her plans to deceive Elsa, whom she is to persuade to ask the forbidden questions. Elsa receives Ortrud out of pity and grants her shelter. Morning dawns and the people assemble. When all is ready for the ceremony and Elsa and her attendants are about to enter the church, Ortrud steps forward and accuses the knight of being a magician. Frederick also mounts the church steps and proclaims his wrongs. But the knight is undaunted, and, Elsa once more declaring her confidence in him, the procession continues.

Act III *Scene 1. The Bridal Chamber.* This brilliant Act is preceded by the widely known "Introduction," a favorite piece with orchestras. It leads naturally to the famed, "Bridal Chorus," the procession of maidens seen as the curtain rises singing, "Brightest and best, we lead thee on!" Countless thousands of brides have gone to the altar with this lovely melody in their ears. The maidens are followed by Elsa and her knight. But the happy scene is marred. Elsa has been troubled by Ortrud's scoffing accusation, and she now begins to chide her husband for concealing his identity from her. He tries to prevent her from asking the fatal questions, but she persists. At this moment a band of conspirators, headed by Telramund, rush into the room, but the knight easily defeats them all and strikes Telramund dead. He then directs the attendants to carry the body to the king, and promises to follow and tell all.

Scene 2. The Banks of the Scheldt. The court of the king is again assembled as the monarch prepares to set forth for war. The body of Frederick is borne in, and the knight follows it. He defends his act and then in an aria of haunting loveliness at last reveals his identity. He is Lohengrin, a Knight of the Holy Grail and the son of Parsifal. Now he must return to the brotherhood, despite the tears of the penitent Elsa. The swan boat reappears, and as the knight kneels in prayer the swan disappears in the stream, and in its place steps forth Godfrey, Elsa's lost brother. Ortrud confesses that it was her magical arts which caused him to assume this shape. A fluttering dove takes the place of the swan and conveys the boat and Lohengrin on their return journey, while Elsa clasps her brother in her arms, but weeps for the loss of her husband.

THE NIBELUNGEN RING

(*Der Ring des Nibelungen—"Nee'-bel-oong-en"*)

The "Ring" comprises four music-dramas: "Das Rheingold," "Die Walküre," "Siegfried," and "Götterdämmerung." Wagner, who wrote his own books, was familiar with the "Eddas" of Icelandic writers, but probably got his basic idea from another cycle, known as the Saga of Thedrek. The Nibelungen myth based on Teutonic mythology first began to take shape in his mind and on paper, in 1848. However, it was over twenty years until the first opera was produced, and with such revolutionary handling of orchestration and theme that it set a new and an advanced standard.

The entire cycle was first produced at Baireuth, August 13 to 17, 1876. In America it had its first complete presentation at the Metropolitan Opera House, during the week beginning March 4, 1889.

I

DAS RHEINGOLD

(Dahs Rine'-gold)

(The Rhine-Gold.) A Music-Drama in Four Acts. Music by Wagner. Book by the Composer. Munich, August 25, 1869, and authoritatively at Baireuth, August 3, 1876. American premiere at the Metropolitan, January 4, 1889, with Fischer, Alvary, and Moran-Olden.

SCENE: Germany and Upper and Nether worlds.
TIME: Antiquity.

CAST WOTAN, *the mighty* (Basso).
FRICKA, *his spouse* (Mezzo-Soprano).
DONNER, *god of thunder* (Basso).
FRÖH, *god of rain* (Baritone).
LOKI, *god of fire* (Tenor).
FREYA, *goddess of love* (Soprano).
ALBERICH, *a dwarf* (Baritone).
MIME, *a dwarf* (Tenor).

WOGLINDE ⎰ ⎱ Soprano.
WELLGUNDE ⎱ *Rhine-maidens* ⎰ Soprano.
FLOSSHILDE ⎱ ⎱ Contralto.

FAFNER ⎰ *giants* ⎰ Basso.
FASOLT ⎱ ⎱ Basso.

ERDA, *spirit of the Earth* (Contralto).
Gods and Goddesses, Dwarfs, and Spirits.

ARGUMENT "Rheingold," the first of the four operas forming the "Ring" series, tells the story of how the magic ring came to be made, and how its curse rested upon all who came in contact with it, whether gods or men.

A Prelude of masterly musical description opens the work, its central notes the Motif of the Rhine. The horns and 'cellos give their mellowness to this strain, as the curtain rises to an underwater scene.

Act I *The Bottom of the River Rhine.* Down in the bed of the River Rhine a mass of pure gold has been hidden. It is magic treasure, conferring upon its owner boundless power, but whoever possesses it must forswear love. The three Rhine-maidens have been entrusted with the duty of guarding the gold, and they turn the task into a sport, singing and dancing among the grottoes beneath the water, but never venturing far from their charge. Their joyous cry, "Rheingold!" rings out through the waves:

But their careless boasts are short lived. Their song and the glitter of gold attract Alberich, lustful of wealth and power. He knows that once a Ring is fashioned from this precious metal, its owner would be master of the world. The music interpolates this in the Ring Motif. The foolish maidens coquet with him, but he pretends to be indifferent to their charms and to the treasure. Then come the sharp notes of the Nibelung Motif; the dwarf suddenly springs down, lays hands upon the gold, and scales the cliff. "Hark, ye fools!" he cries. "Love I renounce forever!" Amid screams of anguish from the Maidens, rock and waters vanish, leaving the dwarf triumphant.

Act II *The Gardens of Walhalla, Abode of the Gods.* The giants Fasolt and Fafner have built the beautiful castle Walhalla for the abode of the gods. Loki, the god of fire, who is the embodiment of deceit, has persuaded Wotan the mighty to accept the giants' terms for their labors. The Loki Motif which recurs is characteristic:

However, Wotan is dismayed to learn that the giants demand Freya, goddess of love, as their reward, and they now proceed to carry her off despite the entreaties of all the other immortals. Without the presence of Freya the flowers wither and die, the trees refuse to bear fruit, and the gods begin to grow old. The only way in which the giants can be induced to restore the goddess is by a bribe of the magic gold. Wotan and Loki go in search of this treasure, which is now jealously guarded by the dwarfs in the earth caverns.

Act III   *The Dwarfs' Caverns.* Alberich gloats over his treasure, and to watch over it more carefully he has commanded Mime, the smith, to fashion for him a tarnhelm or invisible cap which enables him to assume any shape he pleases. He has also fashioned from the gold a Ring which confers upon its wearer power over gods and men. Wotan and Loki enter to confer with Alberich and he boastingly displays his powers by changing himself first into a dragon and then into a toad—the last at a sly suggestion from Loki. Wotan then quickly places his foot upon the toad, and will not release his squirming victim until he has given up all his treasures, including the cap and the Ring. Alberich, however, puts a curse upon all who shall hereafter wear the Ring.

Act IV   *The Gardens of Walhalla.* The gods carry the gold in triumph to Walhalla, and the giants are summoned to the parley. They return with Freya, and the treasure is heaped before her to excite their cupidity. Wotan secretly hopes to retain the cap and the Ring, but they insist upon these also and threaten otherwise to carry off the goddess again. Wotan is compelled to yield, although he foresees in the terms the ultimate destruction of the gods. The curse of the Ring is shown in an immediate quarrel between the giants, in which Fafner kills Fasolt. While the gods pass over a rainbow bridge to their new mansion of Walhalla, the voices of the Rhine-maidens are heard below lamenting their loss.

II

DIE WALKÜRE
(Dee Vahl-kee'-reh)

(The Valkyrie.) Music-Drama in Three Acts. Music by Wagner. Book by the Composer. Munich, June 24, 1870, and authoritatively at Baireuth, August 14, 1876. At New York, the Metropolitan, January 30, 1885.

SCENE: The Forests of Germany.
TIME: Antiquity.

CAST WOTAN, *the mighty* (Basso).
FRICKA, *his spouse* (Mezzo-Soprano).
HUNDING, *a warrior* (Basso).
SIEGLINDE, *his wife* (Soprano).
SIEGMUND, *her brother* (Tenor).
BRUNHILDE, *a Valkyr* (Soprano).
OTHER VALKYRIE (Sopranos and Contraltos).

ARGUMENT In order to understand the plot of "Die Walküre" as related to the "Ring," a certain amount of narrative is necessary which is not represented upon the stage.

Wotan, foreseeing the doom of the gods because they are pledged to respect the power of the magic Ring, endeavors to protect Walhalla by creating a band of Valkyrie or warrior-maidens whose duty it is to carry on their winged steeds the bodies of the noblest warriors, slain upon the field of battle, to the abode of the gods, where these warriors will live again, a mighty race to defend Walhalla. Upon the earth, also, Wotan has begotten two children of his own, Siegmund and Sieglinde, who grow up in ignorance of each other.

The tumultuous nature of the scenes about to unfold is evidenced by the musical Introduction, which depicts the fury of the elements. Lightning flashes, thunder roars, and a wild wind sweeps around the hut in the forest, upon which the curtain rises.

Act I *The Forest Hut of Hunding.* The abode of the warrior, Hunding, is built around the great trunk of a tree, which pierces the center of the roof. Here Hunding dwells with his wife, Sieglinde, whom he has carried away from her home in childhood, against her will. She has been promised a protector, however, by a mysterious stranger who drives his sword up to the hilt in the ash; and the protector will be known by his ability to withdraw the weapon.

On the night when the scene opens, Hunding is away, and Sieglinde opens the door to an exhausted stranger who begs for food and drink. It is Siegmund, a mortal enemy of Hunding, who has taken refuge here against his foes. Hunding, returning, finds him here and allows him to stay for the night, but challenges him to combat the next morning. Meanwhile Siegmund and Sieglinde feel irresistibly drawn to each other. The Love Motif which recurs throughout the scene is its dominant theme:

They hide their affection, but as soon as Hunding retires, Sieglinde gives him a drug which induces deep sleep. The two, who have discovered that they are really children of Wotan, plan flight; but Siegmund is weaponless. "My father did promise me a sword," he cries. As the Sword Motif rings out, a gleam of light from the dying fire falls upon the tree trunk within the hut—and there gleaming is the hilt of a sword! The Sword Motif gives way to a Song of Victory, as the warrior with a triumphant shout easily draws the weapon from the oak (where it had been placed by Wotan). Again comes the Love Motif as a rush of wind sweeps wide the door, and the lovers flee into the night.

Act II *A Mountain Pass.* The Prelude to this Act is a fusing of the themes in the preceding, then musical passages denoting the flight of the pair, and finally the ride and hail of the Valkyrs.

It has been the will of Wotan that his two earth children shall meet and mate, but he finds unexpected opposition to his plan from Fricka, his wife. She is scandalized by this infraction of marital laws, and demands that he punish the guilty pair. He is finally prevailed upon to summon Brunhilde, his favorite among the Valkyr maidens, and he charges her to deliver over Siegmund to his enemy. The joyous shout of the Valkyrs: "Hoyo to ho! Hyah aha!" echoes through the pass, and the wild ride of the war maidens is heard, while clever stage setting depicts their unearthly parade.

The courageous Brunhilde pleads with her father for the warrior, but in vain; she must on no account disobey this mandate even though she knows it is against the wishes of Wotan himself. She encounters the lovers in a mountain pass, whither they are being pursued by Hunding, and warns Siegmund of his fate; but resolves to shield him at any cost. Hunding now engages him in battle. The Valkyr protects Siegmund. Wotan appears and shivers Siegmund's sword, and the latter is slain by Hunding, who is struck down by Wotan. Brunhilde flees from the wrath of Wotan, carrying with her Sieglinde, whom she conceals.

Act III *Haunt of the Valkyrie.* Wotan goes forth to seek and punish his disobedient Valkyr. Brunhilde implores her sisters to help her, but they are fearful of Wotan's anger. They promise, however, to watch over Sieglinde. The latter is comforted by Brunhilde and told that she shall have a son who will prove the greatest of heroes; meanwhile she is to hide from gods and men, and preserve the broken bits of the sword of Siegmund. Wotan approaches and orders Brunhilde to stand before him. A stormy and pathetic scene ensues, in which he at first consigns her harshly to a fate worse than death. Her pleadings and his harsh answers afford some of the most dramatic musical passages of the opera. Then he mitigates her sentence. Touching her with his staff she falls into a deep slumber. High on a cliff he places her body and summons Loki, the tricky god of fire. "Loki! Loki!" he shouts, "hear me and heed!"—and strikes the rock with his sword. Instantly little tongues of flame appear and circle upward until at last the sleeping war maiden is completely encircled by the fire. "Only a hero will dare this fiery height," is Wotan's last decree. The curtain falls

amid the strains of the lovely Fire Music—in the opinion of many, one
of the supreme melodies of the great composer.

III

SIEGFRIED

(Seeg'-freed)

Music-Drama in Three Acts.   Music by Wagner.   Book by the Composer.   Baireuth, August 15, 1876.   American premiere, at the Metropolitan, November 9, 1887, with Brandt, Alvary, Ferenczy, and Fischer.

SCENE: The German Forests.
TIME: Antiquity.

CAST   WOTAN, *the Wanderer* (Basso).
SIEGFRIED, *the hero* (Tenor).
MIME, *the smith* (Tenor).
ALBERICH, *the dwarf* (Basso).
FAFNER, *the dragon* (Basso).
BRUNHILDE, *a Valkyr* (Soprano).
THE WOOD BIRD (Soprano).

ARGUMENT   "Siegfried" continues the story of the Ring at a
period some twenty years later than the events of
"Die Walküre."

As Brunhilde has foretold, Sieglinde bears a son to the slain Siegmund, and she also dies at the child's birth.   He is sheltered by Mime
the dwarf, who teaches him the smith's trade.   But Siegfried, as he is
called, has the blood of warriors and hunters in his veins, and soon
domineers over the craven fellow.

The quieter music which precedes this third part of the Ring is in
welcome contrast to the stormier music of "Die Walküre."   Now we
listen to the voices of nature; and intermingled with them, the familiar
motives of the Ring, the Sword, the Curse, the dawning Love.

Act I   *The Forest Forge of Mime.*   On Siegfried's reaching manhood,
one of the first tasks which he imposes upon Mime, the dwarf,
is to forge for him an unbreakable sword.   This the coward tries vainly
to do; every one he offers his young master is shivered.   As the scene
opens, the horn of Siegfried is heard in the distance:

In dashes the hunter with the carcass of a bear, to the dismay of the dwarf, who sees more trouble. The musical theme changes to the Joy of Life Motif. "How have you done?" demands Siegfried; and when the smith timidly brings out another sword, his master shatters it also upon the anvil. Meanwhile, the fragments of Siegmund's sword have been preserved, and the next time the young hunter is absent, Wotan appears and informs Mime that Siegfried himself must forge the new weapon. The dwarf, more frightened than ever, decides that he cannot withstand the hand of fate. He gives over the smithy to the hunter, tells him the secret of his birth, and yields the sword fragments. Now at last the hero knows the task before him. Joyously he fashions his sword from the pieces of the old, singing lustily as he labors the Sword Song: "Nothung! Nothung!—Helpneed! Helpneed!"

Act II *The Forest before the Dragon's Cave.* During all these years Fafner has guarded the magic gold jealously. To do so better, he has assumed the form of a dragon, who dwells within a cavern in the depths of the forest. On the outside loiters Alberich, the greedy dwarf, still trying to regain the treasure. Wotan finds him here and warns him that a hero is coming who is stronger than them all. Meanwhile Siegfried has been told of the dragon by Mime, who endeavors thus to frighten him, but the news only fires the young man's spirit, and he resolves to christen the new sword in a combat with Fafner. On his way thither the Wood Bird sings to him warningly, but Siegfried does not understand and goes on his way. The orchestra meanwhile plays a pleasant interlude of "Forest Murmurs." He summons Fafner from his lair and in the fight kills him. A drop of the dragon's blood touches his tongue, and instantly he understands the wood voices. The Bird has told him that Mime is trying to poison him. He is also told of the magical properties of the Ring, which he puts on. He kills Mime, and follows the Bird, who tells of other adventures in store. "Ho, Siegfried, hero, listen!" the Bird chants. "A glorious maid lies sleeping on a mountain top! Only a hero may break through the fire that encircles her." "Oh, Bird, lead on!" challenges Siegfried. And together they make their way up the mountain.

Act III   *A Mountain Pass.*   Erda, the earth spirit, has warned Wotan of the impending doom of the gods.   He therefore resolves to stop Siegfried in his journey up the mountain.   But the latter, undaunted, shivers the great Wotan's spear with his sword, Helpneed, and Wotan stands aside, knowing that the progress of events cannot be stayed.   Neither is Siegfried deterred by the wall of flame which encircles the peak.   He pushes through it and it dies away, leaving him unscathed.   He finds Brunhilde in her warrior's garb, and awakens her. The music of this climactic scene culminating in Brunhilde's awakening rises to sublime heights:

It is followed by Motives of Greeting, Passion, and Peace, denoting the mutual rapture of meeting.   The awakened Brunhilde, delighted with the identity of her rescuer, willingly foregoes her immortal qualities to become his wife.

IV

GÖTTERDÄMMERUNG
(*Gur-ter-dem'-mer-oong*)

(The Dusk of the Gods.)   Music-Drama in a Prelude and Three Acts. Music by Wagner.   Book by the Composer.   Baireuth, August 16, 1876.   In America with the "Ring" at the Metropolitan, 1889.

SCENE: The German Forests.
TIME: Antiquity.

CAST   SIEGFRIED, *the hero* (Tenor).
BRUNHILDE, *the Valkyr* (Soprano).
GUNTHER, *a king* (Baritone).
GUTRUNE, *his sister* (Soprano).
ALBERICH, *the dwarf* (Basso).
HAGEN, *his son* (Basso).
VALTRAUTE, *a Valkyr* (Mezzo-Soprano).

THE NORNS, *spinners of fate* (Mezzo-Sopranos).
THE RHINE-MAIDENS (Sopranos).

ARGUMENT The last of the Ring, "Götterdämmerung,"
brings to a close the adventures and fates of the
chief characters. The downfall of the gods, long foretold, is at hand,
and the Ring of the Curse completes its fatal mission.

Prelude The Norns, who control the fates of both men and gods,
weave their thread of life, and it breaks. They know by this
token that the destruction of all things is near. Siegfried departs from
Brunhilde in order to go upon new adventures, but meanwhile gives
her the Ring to wear while he is gone. He takes with him the Tarnhelm, or invisible cap, and Helpneed, the sword, and Brunhilde lends
him her horse to ride.

The interwoven music is reminiscent of much that has gone before.
We hear the Siegfried Motif, and that of Brunhilde. The leave-taking
between the two is long and tender, and as he rides on his further mission, the notes of his horn are heard.

Act I *Scene 1. Gunther's Court.* Siegfried proceeds to the court of
Gunther, a powerful king, who welcomes him cordially. Hagen, the cunning son of Alberich, is one of the court, and knowing of
Siegfried's deeds, he brews the hero a drink which causes him to forget
all his past. The Motif of Forgetfulness is sounded by the French
horns. It gives way to the Gutrune Motif. The memory of Brunhilde
fades away, and he asks of Gunther the hand of his fair sister Gutrune
in marriage. The King consents on condition that Brunhilde is secured
for himself, and the forgetful Siegfried agrees to go with Gunther and
compel her to yield.

Scene 2. A Mountain Pass. While Brunhilde awaits the return of
her warrior, Valtraute, another Valkyr maiden, comes to plead with her
to restore the Ring to the Rhine-maidens. Thus only can the gods be
spared from destruction. But Brunhilde answers scornfully that the
gods have not been kind to her, and besides the Ring is not her own.
By means of the Tarnhelm, Siegfried assumes the shape of Gunther, and
comes to claim Brunhilde as his wife. She struggles against him but is
overpowered, and he wrests the Ring from her finger. She is compelled
to follow him back to Gunther's court.

Act II *Gunther's Court.* The King publicly proclaims Brunhilde as
his Queen, and gives Siegfried the hand of Gutrune. Brunhilde cannot understand this arrangement and suspects treachery when
she sees the Ring on Siegfried's hand. She upbraids him for fickleness
and falseness, but he is still under the influence of the drug and pays

little heed to her.   Her former love turns to rage and she listens willingly to Hagen's plots to kill Siegfried.   Hagen believes that he can thus
secure the Ring for himself.   They falsely tell Gunther that Siegfried
has been unfaithful with respect to Brunhilde; and the King finally
agrees to his destruction.

Act III   *Banks of the River Rhine.*   While Siegfried is out upon a
        hunting expedition, the Rhine-maidens beseech him to re-
store the Ring to them, telling him that thus only can he escape death.
But Siegfried is fearless and will not yield it up under a threat.
Gunther, Hagen, and other hunters join him, and while they rest they
ask Siegfried to relate his adventures.   The drug has begun to wear
off and Siegfried tells of his past.   When he comes to the meeting with
Brunhilde, he stops, puzzled, to watch the flight of some ravens.   At
this moment Hagen drives his spear in between Siegfried's shoulders,
and the latter falls dying.   But his memory is clear and he calls for
Brunhilde.   Both Hagen and Gunther try to seize the Ring, and in the
struggle the King is killed.   The retainers are in an uproar.   Gutrune
bewails the loss of her husband and her brother.   But Brunhilde, who
has learned the truth, comes in and bids the tumult cease.   She orders
a funeral pyre to be built, and the body of Siegfried to be placed upon it.
Mounting it, she also is consumed.   The waters of the Rhine rise and
engulf all, including Hagen, who has tried to seize the Ring, and the
cursed emblem is at last restored to its rightful owners.   In the sky a
great blaze is seen.   It is the destruction of Walhalla with all the gods.
    Throughout these closing scenes of tragedy, the music skillfully aids
the description.   Theme after theme interplays, even the lighter notes
of the Rhine-maidens, while distant rumblings of thunder herald the
Twilight of the Gods.   Then as they sit in solemn array awaiting their
doom, the music mounts with the flames.   It is the Downfall of Walhalla.

This in turn gives way to a more peaceful note.   "A new day is at
hand!" announces the arpeggio notes of the orchestra.   ("The Dawn of
Peace.")

TRISTAN UND ISOLDE

(*Tris'-tahn oont Ee-sohl'-deh*)

Tragic Opera in Three Acts. Music by Wagner. Book by the Composer. Munich, June 10, 1865. At New York, the Metropolitan, December 1, 1886.

SCENE: Cornwall, Brittany, and the Sea.
TIME: Antiquity.

CAST MARK, *King of Cornwall* (Basso).
ISOLDE, *his Queen* (Soprano).
TRISTAN, *a knight* (Tenor).
KURVENAL, *his servant* (Baritone).
MELOT, *a knight* (Baritone).
BRANGAENE, *Isolde's servant* (Contralto).
STEERSMAN (Tenor).
SHEPHERD (Tenor).
Courtiers, Knights, Servants.

ARGUMENT The story of "Tristan and Isolde" is adapted from a romance by Gottfried of Strasburg, telling of the conflict between love and duty in the hearts of two lovers of medieval days.

As in the preceding dramas of the Ring, the music is an integral part of the theme. The Prelude prepares the auditor for the plot—a series of highly emotional passages dwelling upon mutual love, confession, desire, renunciation. It shares with the concluding love scene in popular appeal.

Act I *On Shipboard.* Tristan, a valiant knight, has been involved in many adventures. In Ireland he has met the beautiful Princess Isolde, and incurred her enmity by killing Morold, an unworthy knight, who was her betrothed. Tristan also was wounded, and the maiden's heart softened toward him as she nursed him back to life. He afterwards gives so glowing an account of her charms, that his royal master,

King Mark of Cornwall, desires her for his wife; and Tristan is sent to conduct her to Cornwall.   The Princess comes most unwillingly as she secretly prefers Tristan, but his lips are sealed on account of his mission. On shipboard he treats her with the most scrupulous courtesy, but will not allow himself to come under her influence.   She sends her attendant, Brangaene, to summon him, but he makes excuses.   Angered, Isolde orders Brangaene to brew a deadly poison for Tristan, and when he finally appears in answer to her repeated requests, she asks him to drink a toast.   Tristan neither knows nor cares as to the nature of the drink, but takes it without protest.   She purposes to drink also and thus perish with him.   But Brangaene has brewed a love potion instead, and the two, after drinking, look into each other's eyes with their mutual passions increased tenfold.   (Love Theme.)

Act II   *The Castle of King Mark.*   Tristan despairingly completes his mission and conducts Isolde to the King.   But the two lovers plan a last meeting, and Melot, who has pretended to be Tristan's friend, arranges a hunting expedition, in order to draw the King and his retainers from the castle.   It is night, and Tristan is summoned by a torch in Isolde's window.   Brangaene keeps watch from the tower. In the midst of their bliss, the lovers are warned by her that the King is returning; and Kurvenal, Tristan's servant, also rushes in warning him to flee.   But it is too late.   Melot has betrayed his friend, and King Mark confronts the guilty pair in dignified surprise.   Tristan is overwhelmed with shame, but when Melot makes a sneering remark, he draws his sword.   The two fight and Tristan falls wounded.

The high point in this scene is the love duet: "Nacht der Liebe"—

Act III   *Scene 1.   A Castle Ruin in Brittany.*   The wounded knight
          is allowed to depart by the generous King, and is conveyed by
Kurvenal to a deserted castle on the coast of Brittany.   But his anguish
of soul and desire for Isolde prevent his wound from healing.   In
despair, Kurvenal sends to Isolde, who is also skilled in drugs.   She answers that she will come in person, and the sick man is buoyed up by
this hope.   At last her ship is sighted—it nears the shore—and she
lands.   With a final effort Tristan rises to meet her, only to sink down
exhausted and die in her arms.

The Liebestod, or Death Music, of this scene, where Isolde pours out
her grief over the dead Tristan, is now considered the supreme achievement of the composer.   Its recurring theme of a love that can triumph
over death itself is a classic of sublime pathos:

Scene 2.   The Same (usually omitted).   King Mark and Melot follow
Isolde.   Kurvenal opposes their entrance and kills Melot, himself receiving a death wound.   The King learns from Brangaene of the love
potion and hopeless passion of the two lovers whom he has separated,
and feels only remorse for their fate.

DIE MEISTERSINGER

(*Dee My'-ster-singer*)

(The Master-Singers.)   Comic Opera in Three Acts.   Music by Wagner.   Book by the Composer.   Munich, June 21, 1868.   At New York
in the Metropolitan, January 4, 1886.

SCENE: Nuremberg.
TIME: The Sixteenth Century.

CAST   HANS SACHS, *a cobbler* (Baritone).
VEIT POGNER, *a goldsmith* (Basso).
EVA, *his daughter* (Soprano).
BECKMESSER, *the town clerk* (Baritone).
KOTHNER, *a baker* (Basso).
WALTER VON STOLZING, *a Knight* (Tenor).
DAVID, *apprentice to Sachs* (Tenor).
MAGDALENA, *maid to Eva* (Contralto).
WATCHMAN (Baritone).
Master-singers, Villagers, Servants, etc.

ARGUMENT   "Die Meistersinger" is the only comic opera that Wagner wrote. It deals with a historic time in Nuremberg when all the tradespeople wrote verses and indulged in singing contests, and may be regarded as Wagner's protest against artificiality.

The "Prize Song" is undoubtedly the mainmast which holds up the swelling canvas of "Die Meistersinger." The overture contains hints of it; it is rehearsed in the Third Act, as both an aria and a quintet; and its closing notes form the climax of this pleasing opera.

Act I *Interior of St. Catherine's Church.*   The whole town of Nuremberg is music-mad.   The master-singers, or head men in this noble profession, hold public contests governed by rigid rules, and the victors are richly rewarded.   Veit Pogner, the goldsmith, finally announces that at the next contest he will bestow his daughter's hand upon the successful man.   Beckmesser, the town clerk, is overjoyed at this, as he has long courted the fair Eva, and thinks he can easily win the contest.   But Eva has had no eyes for the clerk.   She has noted the respectful attentions of a young nobleman, Walter von Stolzing, who has met her at the Church and elsewhere.   Hearing of the contest, Walter resolves to enter it and is instructed in the rules by David, the apprentice of Hans Sachs.   But when Walter first appears before the master-singers, Beckmesser keeps the score and marks down so many mistakes that the young man is ruled out.   Hans Sachs, the cobbler, is the only one who speaks in his favor.

Act II *A Street in Nuremberg.*   On one side is Sachs' cobbler shop, on the other, Pogner's house.   Eva finds an opportunity to meet Walter and console him for his lack of success.   She says that she will not abide by her father's wishes, if some one else wins, but will elope with him. They hasten to conceal themselves as Beckmesser comes out to sing a serenade under Eva's window. But the serenader is interrupted by the hammering and singing of Sachs in his shop. Then David appears and mistaking the attentions of Beckmesser as being directed to his own lady-love, he pounds the clerk over the head. Their cries draw the whole village upon the scene and a small-sized riot is in progress, which ends as suddenly as it began, when the watchman's voice is heard down the street.

Act III *Scene 1. The Cobbler's Shop.* While Sachs and his apprentice are at work, Walter comes in greatly elated. He says that he has dreamed a song so beautiful that, if he can set it down, it will win the prize. As he voices it, Sachs is enchanted. "Wonderful!" he exclaims, and proceeds to write it down. Beckmesser learns of this famous song and steals the manuscript, planning to sing it as his own. Eva comes in to try on some new shoes, and all plan for the coming contest.

Scene 2. An Open Field. The morning of the songfest has arrived, and the different trade guilds bring forward their noted singers. Sachs alone champions Walter, who is not concerned over the loss of his manuscript. His song is superior to the master-singers' rules anyway. Beckmesser tries to sing the stolen song, but his memory proves treacherous and he makes a laughable jumble of it. Walter is grudgingly allowed to follow and speedily wins all his hearers by his song. He is accorded the prize, and Pogner bestows upon him the hand of the happy Eva. (Prize Song.)

PARSIFAL

(Par'-tsee fal)

Music-Drama in Three Acts. Music by Wagner. Book by the Composer after the epic by Wolfram von Eschenbach. Baireuth, July 22, 1882. At the Metropolitan Opera House, New York, December 24, 1903.

SCENE: Montsalvat, in the Mountains of Spain.
TIME: The Middle Ages.

CAST AMFORTAS, *Keeper of the Grail* (Baritone).
TITUREL, *his father* (Basso).
GURNEMANZ, *Keeper of the gate* (Basso).
PARSIFAL, *the guileless one* (Tenor).
KLINGSOR, *a magician* (Basso).
KUNDRY, *his accomplice* (Mezzo-Soprano).
Knights of the Grail, Flower Maidens, Servants, Villagers.

ARGUMENT This closing work of Wagner's is the most deeply religious of all. For a period of years it was held sacred to the precincts of Baireuth; in fact, save in concert form it was not given elsewhere until its New York presentation, in 1903 (a "Christmas piece")—over twenty years after its initial performance.

The title "Parsifal" is familiar to hearers of "Lohengrin," for that knight finally tells Elsa that he is Parsifal's son. The present story is embedded in the legend of the Holy Grail, the cup which Christ blessed and which caught the blood from his wounded side. Both the cup and the spear which wounded him were found by Titurel and his Knights of the Grail, who founded a temple for their service at Montsalvat, in the mountains of Spain.

In his old age, Titurel appointed his son, Amfortas, as Keeper of the Grail. Klingsor, a magician, angered at not being elected a Knight, created an enchanted castle and garden near by. He compelled Kundry, a woman who had laughed at Christ and was condemned to wander until her sin was expiated, to aid him. Kundry tempted Amfortas, who turned aside and was wounded by Klingsor with the sacred spear.

The overture is based upon three religious motifs which recur in the work: the Sacrament, the Grail, and Faith. Later it becomes agitated, foreshadowing the remorse of Amfortas.

Act I *Scene 1. Montsalvat Forest.* Gurnemanz, keeper of the gate, tells of the grievous condition of Amfortas. The wound made by Klingsor refuses to heal and is doubly painful when Amfortas tries to celebrate holy communion. For this reason the Temple service is being neglected. Amfortas is borne in on a litter in search of healing springs, and Kundry, who has repented her share in his woe, comes in bearing a balsam which she has obtained with great difficulty. But it is written that he can find relief only from the touch of the sacred spear in the hands of the Guileless One, and him they await. Gurnemanz repeats the prophecy of the oracle: "By pity lightened, the guileless fool; wait thou for him, my chosen tool" (The Prophecy):

The song is interrupted by a cry of dismay from the near-by lake; then a wounded swan falls to the ground. A half-grown lad, unmindful of the anger he has caused by this desecration of the sacred grounds, comes in blithely to claim his quarry. The fine Parsifal Motif, lofty and joyous, heralds his entrance:

The boy's triumphant mood changes to one of penitence when Gurnemanz reproves him, telling him that he is little better than a murderer. The old keeper then relents and, struck by the boy's demeanor, takes him into the service of the Temple. Now follows a dramatic scene portrayed by both action and music. The lovely Bell Motif is heard, also that of Amfortas' Contrition. The latter again shrinks from his duty of uncovering the Grail, but when he finally does so, an unearthly light streams down from the dome above. Again in a chant the words of the oracle are heard: "By pity lightened, the guileless fool—" The strange lad, however, stands silent, unmoved through the rites. "Don't you know what it is all about?" demands Gurnemanz. The youth shakes his head. "Oh, you are only a fool!" exclaims the old knight in disgust. "Begone, and instead of hunting swans, join the geese where you belong!"

Act II *The Castle of Klingsor.* Several years have passed. The magician is greatly alarmed over tidings that a fearless young knight is coming, who has put his enemies to flight on every side. It is Parsifal grown to manhood. Klingsor summons Kundry to his aid, who obeys him most unwillingly. The castle sinks from view and in place of it are seen enchanting gardens in which the Flower Maidens dwell. As Parsifal comes by the garden, they sing to him seductively; but he turns a deaf ear to them. The Parsifal Motif, again heard, gives way to a lovely Flower Melody:

Then Kundry appears, a dazzling vision of loveliness, and bids him stay until she tells him of his parents, whom he does not remember. He tarries and she relates that he is the son of King Gamuret, slain in battle, and that his mother brought him up as an ignorant peasant in order to keep him from becoming a warrior. His mother—says Kundry —entrusted her with a last message and kiss. With this the enchantress leans over and presses a burning kiss on the young knight's lips; it was in this way that she had formerly betrayed Amfortas. Realizing his danger, Parsifal springs to his feet. Kundry summons the magician to her aid. Klingsor hurls the sacred spear at the knight, but he seizes it in mid-air and strikes Klingsor dead. The gardens vanish and only Kundry is left, an old woman, crouching upon the ground in terror.

Act III *Scene 1. Montsalvat.* Years pass by. Gurnemanz, though grown old, is still the keeper of the gate, and Amfortas is still a sufferer from his grievous malady which will not heal nor let him die. The penitent Kundry lingers about the Temple as a hewer of wood and drawer of water. A strange knight appears, faint and weary from his journeys. It is Parsifal who has completed his self-imposed mission. He kneels in prayer, the sacred spear thrust before him in the soil. Gurnemanz recognizes in him the Guileless One whom he thrust rudely out of doors as a boy, and now ministers to him; while Kundry kneels and washes his feet. He baptizes her. The Temple bells sound for the noonday service, and they array Parsifal in the white robes of a Knight of the Grail.

Scene 2. The Temple Interior. The aged Titurel, father of Amfortas, wishes to see the Holy Grail unveiled once more before he dies, but the pain-racked King shrinks from the task. He begs his knights to kill him and thus remove the curse. At this moment Parsifal enters bearing the spear. He touches the wound of Amfortas and it heals immediately. Parsifal then announces that he has been sent to take charge of the Grail, and he proceeds with the services. As the Grail is uncovered and held aloft, the aged Titurel expires with a smile upon his lips. The Temple is flooded with light, and a dove descends and alights upon Parsifal. Kundry, who has crept in unnoticed, falls at his feet and also dies—redeemed.

The music of this entire scene, with its floating, exquisite arpeggios, lifts the hearer literally up "on wings of song." The heavenly strains persist and die softly in the heights, as the final curtain slowly descends upon the lofty Motif of Faith:

VICTOR NESSLER

Nessler was widely popular during his lifetime, but has since become almost forgotten, unless in Germany. He was born in Baldenheim, Alsace, January 28, 1841, and died in Strassburg, May 28, 1890. He wrote many songs and choruses, chiefly for male voices. Of his operas, beginning with "Fleurette" (1864), only two are now in occasional repertory: "The Piper of Hamelin" (1879) and "The Trumpeter of Säkkingen" (1884).

THE PIPER OF HAMELIN

An Opera in Five Acts.   Music by Nessler.   Book by Fr. Hofmann, from the legend by Julius Wolff. The story is somewhat similar to Robert Browning's later "Pied Piper of Hamelin," where the piper undertakes to rid the town of a plague of rats. He does so by playing on his pipe, and the rats follow him in droves to the river and are drowned. But when Hunold Singuf, the piper, claims his reward and a kiss from the lips of the Burgomaster's daughter, Regina, they condemn him to death as a sorcerer. Hunold then plays one final aria. The citizens dance in spite of themselves; and the children follow him, just as the rats had done. Piping, he leads them straight into a mountain-side which opens and swallows them up forever.

THE TRUMPETER OF SÄKKINGEN

(Der Trompeter Von Säkkingen.) Opera in Prologue and Three Acts. Music by Nessler; text by Rudolf Bunge, after Victor von Scheffel's poem with the same title. Produced, Leipzig, May 4, 1884. At New York, the Metropolitan, 1888.

> SCENE: Germany.
> TIME: Recent.

ARGUMENT   This plot follows the familiar lines of a mysterious hero, who is found to be a missing nobleman. Werner, an unknown trumpeter, wins the favor of Maria, daughter of the Baron von Schonau. Her aunt, Countess of Wildenstein, is also attracted by the young man, but is also suspicious of him. She watches the two young people zealously, while Werner gives Maria music lessons. Damian, the Count's son, a cowardly fellow, has been destined to be Maria's husband; but after a peasant uprising in which he plays the coward, and Werner, the hero, the latter is found to be the long-lost son of the Countess, and he and Maria are united.

The bright music relieves a somewhat stodgy story. The Prologue and First Act bring in a serenade and trumpet strains; a stirring chorus by students and troopers; festival dances; and a charming lyric by Maria: "How proud and grand his bearing!"

In the Second Act we hear: an aria sung by Werner, "On shore I played me a merry tune"; a duet between him and Maria, "Sun, has thy light not grown in splendor?"; a quintet, "Must so soon the sunshine vanish?"; and Werner's sentimental farewell, "Oh, it is sad!"

The Third Act introduces these numbers: Maria's song, "My Love rode out to the wide, wide world"; the Maytime song, "There comes a youth of sweet renown"; the Maytime pantomime and dance; a duet between Maria and Werner, "True love, I give thee greeting"; and a particularly strong final chorus, "Faithful love and trumpet blowing!"

ENGELBERT HUMPERDINCK

This German composer achieved an instant popularity in Germany on the occasion of the production of his fairy opera, "Hänsel and Gretel." It speedily crossed the channel into England, and was also performed in Holland, Belgium, Italy, and America—all within two years. In a sense it violates operatic traditions in substituting for the somber atmosphere and tragic close a simple naïveté that is delightfully refreshing. The success of this opera was repeated in "Koenigskinder," of a slightly later date. Humperdinck was born in Siegburg on the Ahme, September 1, 1854, was educated in the German school, and devoted his life to orchestral and other musical work. His scores reveal the influence of Wagner. He died, September 27, 1921.

HÄNSEL AND GRETEL
(Hen'-sel and Gray'-tel)

Fairy Opera in Three Acts. Music by Engelbert Humperdinck. Book by Adelheid Wette. Weimar, December 23, and at Munich, December 30, 1893. Two years later, at Daly's Theatre, New York, in English. At the Metropolitan, in German, November 25, 1905, with Alten, Abarbanell, Weed, Homer, and Goritz.

SCENE: A German Forest.
TIME: The Seventeenth Century.

CAST   PETER, *a broom-maker* (Baritone).
GERTRUDE, *his wife* (Contralto).

HÄNSEL, *their son* (Mezzo-Soprano).
GRETEL, *their daughter* (Soprano).
THE CRUNCH WITCH (Mezzo-Soprano).
THE SAND MAN (Soprano).
THE DEW MAN (Soprano).
Fourteen Angels, Children, Elves, etc.

ARGUMENT   "Hänsel and Gretel," adapted from a fairy tale by the brothers Grimm, loses nothing of its verve and freshness in this delightful musical setting. The haunting charm of the opera, which while classed as "children's" has no less appeal to adults, begins with the overture. The French horns sound out the Prayer Theme that recurs in the story, followed by that of the Witch and other themes.

Act I   *The Broom-Maker's Cottage.* The two children of Peter, the broom-maker, are trying to finish their stint of work while awaiting the return of their parents with supper. But they finally grow so hungry that they lay aside their tasks and dance about to forget their appetites. Their mother, a hasty-tempered woman, finds them thus wasting time and by way of punishment packs them off into the woods of Ilsenstein, to pick berries for supper. After they have run away in terror, Peter comes in greatly pleased over having sold all his brooms. He brings food in plenty. But when he learns that the children have gone to Ilsenstein, where the bad Crunch Witch dwells, he and Gertrude hasten in search of them.

The music throughout is charming. The two children in the first scene while away the time by singing. Gretel asks, "Susy, pray what is the news?"; and her brother joins in, "Pray, what's to be done?" Then the girl sings, "Brother, come dance with me!" And they suit the action to the word. After the children are sent out into the forest, their mother repents and becomes alarmed. "An old witch within that wood doth dwell," she sings; and then tells in song the fate of children that fall into the witch's hands.

Act II   *In the Forest.* The children wander about picking berries but are so hungry that they eat them as fast as they are picked. They are therefore afraid to return home, and besides it is growing dark. They sink down weary beneath a large tree and the Sand Man comes and sprinkles his sand of slumber in their eyes. Then, in accordance with their childish prayer, fourteen angels descend a staircase from Heaven and assume guard about them.

Both music and setting form one of those unforgettable unions, which have done so much to keep this opera a perennial favorite with all ages

of opera-goers. The lost children try to comfort each other, but with
poor success. "What's glimmering in the darkness?" they ask. The
Sand Man sings, reassuringly, "I send the children happy dreams." As
they fall asleep, celestial strains herald the angels. The lovely Prayer
Theme, first heard in the Overture, is the dominant one here:

Act III *The Witch's Gingerbread Hut.* The next morning the Dew
Man arouses the children and they are surprised to find themselves in front of the Gingerbread Hut of the Crunch Witch. This is
her trap to lure children whom she wishes to devour, but Hänsel and
Gretel do not know it. They are hungry and break off bits of the delicious house to nibble. "Nibble, nibble, mousekin, who's nibbling
at my housekin?" sings a voice from within. And out pops the witch
and seizes them.

"Come, little mousey, come into my housey!" she cackles. "Hocus,
pocus, witch's charm!" she chants. Hänsel she locks up in a cage to
fatten, but Gretel, who is plump enough, is made to bring water and
fuel to help the witch prepare her feast. The witch is impatient for
Hänsel to fatten and meanwhile stirs up her oven fire. As she looks in
at the oven door, Hänsel escapes from the cage, and he and Gretel give
the witch a sudden push, sending her headlong inside the oven. The
children dance about with glee, eating their fill of sweetmeats. "Hocus,
pocus, elder bush!" chants Hänsel, in imitation of the witch's charm.
Then the oven cracks open, and at the same time a row of gingerbread
children, who stood along the façade of the hut, turn into real live children, who thank their deliverers for their escape from the witch's spell.
The witch herself is burned to a crisp. Peter and Gertrude now enter,
overjoyed to find their children alive, and the opera ends in a general
dance and merrymaking.

KOENIGSKINDER
(Kur'-nigs-kin-der)

(The King's Children.) Fairy Opera in Three Acts. Music by Humperdinck. Book by Ernst Rosmer, after the fairy tale by Elsa Bernstein. World premiere at the Metropolitan, New York, December 28, 1910, with Farrar as the "Goose Girl," and Homer, the "Witch."

SCENE: Hellabrun, in the Mountains of Germany.
TIME: The Middle Ages.

CAST　THE KING'S SON (Tenor).
THE GOOSE GIRL, *also of royal descent* (Soprano).
THE WITCH (Contralto).
THE FIDDLER (Baritone).
THE WOODCUTTER (Basso).
THE BROOM-MAKER (Tenor).
THE INN-KEEPER (Baritone).
THE INN-KEEPER'S DAUGHTER (Soprano).
THE COUNCILLOR (Basso).
A LITTLE CHILD (Soprano).
Villagers and Country People.

ARGUMENT　"Koenigskinder" is something more than a fairy opera; it is an allegory upon love which unlocks the eyes of those who have it in their hearts, causing them to see what is denied to ordinary mortals.

The musical themes have been developed in the Wagnerian school, but without imitation; and the story, based on myth, lends itself to this musical structure. The overture and two or three excerpts were known to orchestras some years before the opera's premiere. That event, interestingly enough, was upon the stage of the Metropolitan Opera House. Geraldine Farrar added to her fame as the "Goose Girl."

Act I *The Witch's Hut and Garden.* In a secluded valley a witch has kept a young girl prisoner. She has grown up in ignorance of her parents, and the witch has cast a spell upon the forest round about so that she may not escape. The girl tends her geese and dreams of the sunny world without; but the witch chides her for idling, telling her that there is more evil in the world than good, and bidding her come in and knead the magic bread which is never to grow stale but will some day carry death to the eater. The girl obeys against her will while the witch departs. When the girl returns to the sunshine she is amazed to see a man—the first who has penetrated the forest. It is the King's son who is now in exile. Both having hearts of love, they recognize each other as "King's Children." He tells her to come with him into the world, and she would willingly go but cannot for the witch's spell. He does not understand and departs in anger. Meanwhile the King has died and the citizens of Hellabrun send a delegation—the fiddler, the woodcutter, and the broom-maker—to the witch to ask her who shall be the next ruler. She replies that it will be the one who shall come to the city gates the next day at the stroke of noon. The fiddler alone understands her and lingers behind to talk to the goose girl in whom he also recognizes one of kingly descent. She departs with him despite the witch's curse.

Act II *Gates of the Town of Hellabrun.* The town councillors decide to put the witch's prophecy literally to the test, and all the people gather near the city gates to await the coming of their new ruler. Among the throng is the King's son, clothed in rags and unnoticed. He has been working in menial tasks, no one recognizing his rank. The innkeeper's daughter loves him selfishly but he disdains her. Then a little child with open heart sees him as he is and becomes his friend. The bell strikes the hour of noon and all await feverishly for the gates to open. As they do so, behold! only the goose girl surrounded by her geese and followed by the faithful fiddler. With a cry the King's son springs forward. "My queen!" he cries. But the others laugh them both to scorn and drive them from the city. They cannot accept rulers who come in rags and tatters. Only the little child sobs in grief and tells the chief councillor that they have turned away their King and Queen.

Act III *The Witch's Hut, in Winter.* The witch has been burned by the people in their rage, and now all is cold and desolate around the hut. The fiddler, old and lame, has taken up his refuge there. To him comes the little child who had known the Prince, with her playmates, and asks him to go with them to find the King's children again. He hobbles out to join them. After they are gone, the two lost ones appear, wearied and faint with hunger. The Prince goes to the hut for shelter, but finds the woodcutter there, who denies them admittance. Finally he sells the Prince a loaf of bread for his crown. It is the poisoned bread which has remained always fresh. They eat and are overcome with stupor, falling in the snow. The fiddler and the children presently return from their search and find them cold in death.

Heartbroken, the fiddler bids the children make a grave for the pair upon the summit of the mountain.   There they can lie and dream of the many other children of the King who go through the world unrecognized save by those whose hearts are touched with love.

WILHELM KIENZL

An Austrian composer, born in Weitzenkirchen, January 17, 1857. Of his operas, "The Evangelist," "Urvasi," "Der Kuhreigen," and "Don Quixote," only the first has been produced in this country.   Kienzl died in Vienna, October 3, 1941.

THE EVANGELIST

(Der Evangelimann.)   Musical Drama in Two Acts.   Book and Music by Wilhelm Kienzl.   After the work by Meiszner.   Berlin, 1895. At New York, the Metropolitan, in 1923, but was not retained in repertory.

SCENE: Benedictine Convent, Vienna.
TIME: Latter part of the Nineteenth Century.

ARGUMENT   The story of this drama of village and convent life in Austria is that of a hidden crime and its long-drawn-out expiation.

Act I   *Courtyard of the Convent of St. Othmar.*   Martha, the pretty niece of Engel, head of the Benedictine brotherhood, is beloved by Matthias, the clerk of the convent.   Engel is informed of this fact by Yohannes, Matthias' brother, who is also in love with the maiden, and takes this method of getting Matthias out of the way.   Yohannes watches the lovers, who are planning to elope, and sets in action a plot for their ruin.   A fire breaks out in the convent buildings.   Matthias is accused of having set them on fire, and is arrested and sentenced to a long prison term.

Act II   *Scene 1.   A Courtyard in Vienna.*   Thirty years pass by. Matthias, having served his prison term, turns evangelist, and goes up and down the country on preaching missions.   Martha mean-

while has drowned herself.   Magdalena tells him that she is taking care
of Yohannes, now on his death-bed, who wishes to see a minister before
he dies.
Scene 2. Yohannes' Bedroom.   Matthias goes unrecognized to his
brother's bedside.   Yohannes, not knowing to whom he is confessing,
makes a last statement in which he acknowledges that he is the real incendiary.   Matthias pardons his brother, who then dies.

LUDWIG THUILLE

A German composer, born November 30, 1861, at Bozen, and died,
February 5, 1907.   He studied in German schools and wrote numerous
shorter pieces.   He is known outside his own country for a single opera,
"Lobetanz."

LOBETANZ
(*Loh'-buh-tahnts*)

Fairy Opera in Three Acts.   Music by Ludwig Thuille.   Book by
Otto Julius Bierbaum.   Mannheim, Germany, February 6, 1898.   At
New York, the Metropolitan, November 18, 1911, but did not remain
in repertory.

SCENE: Germany.
TIME: The Middle Ages.

CAST   LOBETANZ, *a wandering minstrel* (Tenor).
        THE KING (Baritone).
        THE PRINCESS (Soprano).
        FORESTER (Basso).
        HEADSMAN (Baritone).
        JUDGE (Basso).
            Prisoners, a Youth, Maidens, Minstrels, Poets,
            Courtiers, Huntsmen, Peasants.

ARGUMENT   A pleasant, old-fashioned fairy tale of a princess
            dying of an illness, who can be healed only by the

strains of a wandering minstrel's song, is the theme of this melodic opera. After much misadventure, Lobetanz is sentenced to be hanged. A crowd gathers on Hangman's Hill. The Princess is borne in, almost lifeless, and Lobetanz craves permission to play his violin for the last time. The sweet strains sound, and at their first echo the Princess begins to recover. When they have ended, she is sitting upright, stretching out her arms to the minstrel. The King pardons him and accepts him as a son. The lovers join hands and lead the dance, in which all join merrily—even the King and the hangman.

EUGENE D'ALBERT

A pianist and composer of mixed English and German stock. He was born in Glasgow, Scotland, April 10, 1864, but obtained most of his schooling on the Continent. He studied the pianoforte under Liszt, at Weimar, early showing marks of genius. At eighteen he became a concert performer. At twenty-five he first visited the United States, where he met with a flattering reception. In 1895 he was appointed royal pianist at the Court of Saxony. "Tiefland" represents his first successful opera. D'Albert died in Riga, Latvia, March 3, 1932.

TIEFLAND
(*Teef'-land*)

(Martha of the Lowlands.) Dramatic Opera in Prologue and Two Acts. Music by Eugene d'Albert. Book by Rudolph Lothar, after the story by A. Guimera. Prague, 1903. At New York, the Metropolitan, November 23, 1908.

SCENE: The Pyrenees and Valley of Catalonia.
TIME: The Present.

CAST SEBASTIANO, *a wealthy landowner* (Baritone).
TOMMASO, *a village patriarch* (Basso).
Others below are servants of Sebastiano:
MARTHA, *a village girl* (Mezzo-Soprano).
PEPA, *a village girl* (Soprano).

ANTONIA, *a village girl* (Soprano).
ROSALIA, *a village girl* (Contralto).
NURI, *a village girl* (Soprano).
MORUCCIO, *a miller* (Baritone).
PEDRO, *a shepherd* (Tenor).
NANDO, *a shepherd* (Tenor).
Priest, Villagers, etc.

ARGUMENT   The simple but strong story of the displacing of
dishonest love and deception by honesty is here
woven into a musical theme of vigor and beauty.

Prologue   *A Rocky Fastness in the Pyrenees.*   All his life long Pedro
the shepherd has lived among the heights of the Pyrenees.
He sees few faces except that of his fellow-shepherd, Nando, and women
almost not at all; but he dreams of the day when the Blessed Virgin will
send him a wife.   Beyond this dream he lives carefree among his beloved hills.   As if in answer to his prayer, his wealthy employer one
day brings to him a beautiful lowlands girl, Martha, and tells him that
she shall be his wife if he will go to the lowlands and live with her at the
mill.   Unknown to Pedro, Martha has been the mistress of Sebastiano,
who is taking this means to keep her in respectable society.

Act I   *Interior of the Mill.*   All of Sebastiano's servants except Pedro
know of Martha's relations with their employer, and have much
sly fun at the simple shepherd's expense.   Sebastiano himself is about
to contract marriage with an heiress.   Martha views her own approaching marriage bitterly.   She is at heart an honest girl, who has been
forced into her present position, and she dislikes to delude Pedro, whom
she has come to admire.   But she is powerless to hinder the course of
events, and the marriage takes place, while Pedro accepts at full value
the boisterous congratulations of the villagers.   It is Sebastiano's intention to continue his relations with Martha, but she avoids him by not
going to her room.   She also avoids Pedro, who is becoming puzzled by
the turn of events.

Act II   *Same Scene. Early Morning.*   Nuri, a peasant girl, who has
taken quite a fancy to Pedro, enters singing and knitting.   She
finds him alone and disconsolate.   He tells her that he is going away.
Martha comes from her room and finding them talking, becomes suddenly jealous for her husband's regard and orders Nuri out of the house.
Pedro goes with her, and Martha, not knowing what course to pursue,
confides in old Tommaso, who advises her to tell Pedro the truth.   This
she does not want to do; she feels that Pedro really loves her, and her

own regard is awakening. Pedro returns and tells her that he does not belong in the lowlands; his place is away from men, among the hills. "Ah, take me with you, then!" she pleads, but he in a rage advances with a knife to kill her. Love and remorse prevent the deed, and the two are reconciled and determine to fly together. They are prevented by the entrance of Sebastiano and the villagers who wish to make merry over the wedding. Sebastiano mockingly thrums on a guitar and bids Martha dance for them. Pedro springs at him, and the villagers interpose to prevent a fight between the two men.

Act III *Same Scene.* Sebastiano's conduct has reached the ears of his fiancée, and she rejects him. He returns to Martha for consolation, and is amazed when she also turns from him. In scorn he seeks to force his attentions upon her, when she calls aloud for Pedro. He has escaped from the villagers and now bounds into the room wild with just anger. At first he draws a knife, but seeing that Sebastiano is unarmed he throws it away and meets him on equal terms. After a furious struggle, Pedro shakes and throws his rival aside, helpless. The crowd gathers, and Pedro defies them all. "Why don't you laugh now?" he demands. Then picking up Martha in his strong young arms he escapes with her to freedom among the hills.

RICHARD STRAUSS

A modern German composer whose work has revealed more vigor, breadth and originality than any other composer of this school since Wagner. Strauss was born in Munich, June 11, 1864, and studied there first under his father, a member of the Royal Opera Orchestra, and in other German schools, before taking up orchestral work. He began composing at so early an age—seeming to take to it naturally—that on the first performance of a work by him, he came out as a mere lad to receive the plaudits of the audience. Strauss is famed in Germany as the composer of many beautiful short pieces and orchestral numbers. His operas include: "Fire Famine" (1901); "Guntram" (1894); "Salome" (1905); "Elektra" (1909); "Der Rosenkavalier" (1911); "Ariadne auf Naxos"; "The Egyptian Helen" (1928); and "Arabella," which was performed at Berlin, in 1933, but has not yet reached America. Strauss died near Berlin, September 8, 1949.

SALOME
(Sa-lo'-meh)

Tragic Opera in One Act. Music by Richard Strauss. Book adapted from the romance by Oscar Wilde. Court Opera, at Dresden, December 9, 1905. At New York, the Metropolitan, January 22, 1907, with Fremstad as "Salome." Also at Manhattan Opera House, with Mary Garden as "Salome"—one of her famous roles.

SCENE: Tiberias, the Capital of Herod, in Galilee.
TIME: 30 A.D.

CAST   HEROD, *Tetrarch of Galilee* (Tenor).
HERODIAS, *his wife* (Mezzo-Soprano).
SALOME, *her daughter, and the King's step-daughter* (Soprano).
JOHN THE BAPTIST, *a prophet* (Baritone).
NARRABOTH, *a Syrian captain* (Tenor).
A PAGE (Contralto).
Jews, Courtiers, Soldiers, Priests, Servants.

ARGUMENT   One of the most revolutionary of modern composers, Richard Strauss did not hesitate to shock his public, and in "Salome" he administered the greatest shock of all— but, this time, not so much on account of his score as of his theme. It is one of sadism and sensuality that even the amoral courts of the Orient cannot quite explain or excuse. The story is based upon a romance by Oscar Wilde, who took his text from the New Testament tale of the death of John the Baptist.

The Palace of Herod. Salome, the beautiful but unprincipled step-daughter of King Herod, falls passionately in love with John the Baptist, the prophet of the wilderness. Because of his bold speech against Herod and Herodias, John has been cast into a deep dungeon. There the King holds him, not caring to take further action for fear of displeasing the Jews. Salome is filled with an unholy desire to kiss the prophet's lips and fondle his long uncut tresses. She persuades Narraboth, a captain who is in love with her, to bring the prisoner before her. When the captain finds that she loves only John, he kills himself; but Salome gives little heed to this in the joy of having the prophet in her clutches. John, however, rejects all her advances, bidding her repent. Filled with rage she has him cast again into the dungeon and bides her time for revenge.

The music, which meanwhile has added to this growing intensity of passion, here depicts through the orchestra the prophet's descent into the well.

Herod the king is also troubled. His problems with the Jews are mounting; he has squabbles with Herodias; he is filled with lust for Salome; and, now that he finds his young captain dead at her feet, he pleads with the girl to show him some favor. She consents to dance for him at a feast for his guests if he will grant her a boon in return. The distracted monarch agrees and Salome then gives the famous Dance of the Seven Veils. The sensuous music follows her lithe body as she removes one by one the diaphanous coverings. Amid the applause, the dancer now demands her reward: it is the head of John the Baptist. The horrified king objects; he is fearful of an uprising; he offers her, instead, his treasures or half his kingdom; but she is obdurate. In desperation the King gives the fatal signal. A dull blow is heard and a moment later the executioner appears with the gory head. Salome is wild with delight. She fondles the trophy as though it were alive, kissing the lips. In disgust and horror the King orders her to be put to death, and the soldiers crush her beneath their shields.

Other musical numbers include a favorite aria for sopranos: "Thou wouldst not suffer me to kiss thy mouth"; and a descriptive aria, "Thy body was a column of ivory."

ELEKTRA

(E-leck'-trah)

Dramatic Opera in One Act. Music by Strauss. Book by Hugo von Hofmannsthal. Dresden, January 25, 1909. The same year in the Manhattan Opera House, New York, with Mazarin as "Elektra."

> SCENE: Greece.
> TIME: Antiquity.

> CAST   QUEEN KLYTEMNESTRA, *widow of Agamemnon* (Mezzo-Soprano).
> ÆGISTHUS, *her paramour* (Tenor).
> ORESTES, *the Queen's son* (Baritone).
> ELEKTRA, *the Queen's daughter* (Soprano).
> CHRYSOTHEMIS, *the Queen's daughter* (Soprano).
> Messenger, Waiting Women, Soldiers, Courtiers.

ARGUMENT   In "Elektra," a modern continuation of an ancient Greek story, the death of King Agamemnon at the hands of the Queen and her paramour is avenged by the crazed daughter. The story is unpleasant but powerful, and lends itself to the unconventional musical treatment given by the composer. The action is confined to a single act, which takes place in an inner court of the royal palace at Mycene.

As servants tell of the strange behavior of the grief-crazed, revenge-driven Elektra, daughter of the murdered Agamemnon, she appears and tells of her plans of vengeance in which she shall be aided by Orestes, her brother. Chrysothemis, her sister, who is actuated by softer, more womanly feelings, now enters and urges Elektra to abate her hatred, lest harm come to them all, and warns her especially against their mother. The Queen appears at a lighted window, and as she and her wild daughter rail at each other, news is brought that Orestes is dead. Elektra, however, states that she alone will slay "the woman and her husband."

But the report as to Orestes proves false, as he presently returns to the court in disguise. At first Elektra does not know him, but when she recognizes him her joy is almost savage. The tragedy from this point rapidly reaches its consummation. Urged on by the implacable sister, Orestes enters the palace and slays both his mother and Ægisthus, while Elektra waits outside in a perfect frenzy of impatience. When she is assured that the bloody revenge is accomplished, she dances madly until she falls prone upon the ground. Chrysothemis runs to her, only to find her dead.

DER ROSENKAVALIER

(Dair Ro-zen-cav-ah-leer')

(The Rose-Knight.) Comic Opera in Three Acts. Music by Richard Strauss. Book by Hugo von Hofmannsthal. Dresden, January 26, 1911. At New York, the Metropolitan, December 9, 1913.

SCENE: Vienna.

TIME: The early years of the reign of Maria Theresa.

CAST PRINCESS VON WERDENBERG (Soprano).
BARON OCHS OF LERCHENAU (Basso).
OCTAVIAN, *a young gentleman of noble family* (Mezzo-Soprano).
HERR VON FANINAL, *a rich merchant, newly ennobled* (High Baritone).
SOPHIA, *his daughter* (High Soprano).
Attendants, Servants, Orphans of Noble Family, Couriers, Musicians, Watchmen, Children, Various Personages of suspicious appearance.

ARGUMENT   As if to make amends for his two earlier works,
              which shocked both the ears and the morals of
some of his hearers, Strauss now rewarded them with a light opera
abounding in gaiety and charm.   Some critics rank it as the best of its
type since "Figaro."   So tuneful is it that complete recordings have
been made of "Der Rosenkavalier."
    The overture gives a foretaste of the work.   It is by turns capricious,
impassioned, tender, and romantic.   Waltz music abounds, recalling
the school of Johann Strauss, although here perhaps more robust.

Act I   *Boudoir of the Princess.*   During her husband's absence the
              Princess von Werdenberg amuses herself by encouraging the de-
votion of Octavian, a young cavalier, seventeen years of age.   An ardent
love scene is interrupted by the entrance of the impecunious and disreputable old Baron Ochs.   Octavian, having no time to escape, and
thinking it to be the Princess' husband, hurriedly dons the clothes of
her maid.   The Baron is anxious to consult the Princess in regard to a
proposed match with Sophia, the daughter of a recently ennobled merchant, but his story is much interrupted by his amorous attentions to
the supposed maid, "Mariandel," whom he ogles violently.   The Princess is urged to suggest a suitable messenger to bear to Sophia the
Baron's *gage d'amour,* a silver rose.   She names Octavian.
    The introduction to this Act is a delightful medley and is often used
as an orchestral number.   The action itself is so interwoven with elusive
melody, as, for instance, the flute solo which entertains the princess, that
it is hard to particularize.

Act II   *A Room in the House of Faninal.*   Faninal takes leave of
              Sophia and departs, promising to return with her noble bride-
groom.   Meanwhile Octavian enters with the silver rose.   The inevitable happens—Octavian and Sophia fall madly in love with one another, and the beauty and elegance of the young cavalier only make
Sophia the more disgusted with the disreputable old Baron, who is cere-
moniously presented to her by her father.   His coarse manners and
attempted familiarities offend Sophia and enrage Octavian, who challenges the Baron to a duel and succeeds in wounding him slightly.   A
tremendous hubbub ensues.   The Baron thinks himself in a dying condition, various people rush to minister to him, Sophia declares that
nothing will induce her to marry the Baron, while Faninal insists that
she shall do so.   Sophia and Octavian concoct a plot, the object of
which is to place Ochs under compromising circumstances.   A letter is
delivered to him purporting to come from "Mariandel," who has attracted him.
    The "Letter Scene and Waltz" are here heard, while the amorous

Baron thinks he is making headway in his suit.   In this Act is also heard one of the most sparkling numbers, "The Presentation of the Rose" in dance rhythm.

Act III   *A Private Room at an Inn.*   Octavian appears, dressed as "Mariandel," the maid.   Various suspicious-looking persons are disposed about the room in hiding-places.   Finally Baron Ochs appears to keep his appointment.   His enjoyment, however, is marred, first by the resemblance of "Mariandel" to Octavian, the young cavalier who wounded him, then by the appearance of the various spies, of the landlord and waiters, of a woman who claims him as her husband, and four little children who hail him shrilly as "papa," of the Commissary of Police, of the enraged Faninal, and finally of the Princess.   The Baron at last departs in the midst of a clamorous host presenting bills. The Princess gracefully gives Octavian his freedom and the young lovers are made happy.

In the closing Act strains of the "Presentation of the Rose" recur; with other memorable music—"Breakfast Scene," and trio sung by the Princess, Octavian and Sophie.

ARIADNE AUF NAXOS

Legendary Opera in One Act.   Music by Strauss.   Book by Hugo von Hofmannsthal.   Written as an interlude to Molière's comedy, "Le Bourgeois Gentilhomme."   Zurich, December 5, 1912.   Berlin, February 27, 1913.   In English by the Juilliard School, New York, December 5, 1934.

SCENE: Island of Naxos.
TIME: Antiquity.

CAST   ARIADNE (Soprano).
BACCHUS (Tenor).
NAIAD (Soprano).
DRYAD (Contralto).
ECHO (Soprano).
ZERBINETTA (Soprano).
Four Clowns: Harlequin, Scaramouche, Truffaldin, and Brighělla.
Three characters from Molière's "Le Bourgeois Gentilhomme," as spectators.

ARGUMENT   In order to understand this "play within a play," some explanation is necessary.   Strauss first wrote some incidental music to accompany Molière's comedy, in which the action there was stressed. In a second version (1916) references to the Molière play were dropped, and a scenic prelude substituted. In the original story, Jourdain, of the bourgeois, strives to break into the uppercrust of society and for this purpose puts on an elaborate entertainment in his own home, to which he invites among others, Marquise Dorimene and Count Dorantes. Jourdain has engaged a ballet troupe, but decides to give a play instead—and "Ariadne auf Naxos" is this play. However, in his ambition to outshine, he has also engaged a troupe of clowns and insists upon their performance, also; so these comedians give a brief performance on the stage, and then make their exit. Despite all these confusing preliminaries, the story of Ariadne follows.

A Cave on a Desert Island. The lovely Ariadne is asleep, while Naiad, Dryad, and Echo sing a charming ballad to soothe her restless spirit; for Ariadne feels herself forsaken, bereft. On awaking she bewails her unhappy lot and says she is only awaiting the coming of Death. An interruption occurs, but instead of the dread guest, four characters from an ancient comedy come dancing across the stage, headed by Zerbinetta, who sings and dances with them—their theme, let us be gay and enjoy life while we may. The disconsolate Ariadne does not appear to notice them, and they whirl off again. Naiad, Dryad, and Echo now announce another visitor. He is youthful and handsome. His tuneful aria is heard in the distance. Ariadne listens eagerly. If this be Death, he is indeed welcome. But when he comes on stage, he is seen to be the god Bacchus. Not oblivion, he tells her, but renewed joy in life is his mission. Eagerly she questions him, then quite as eagerly sinks into his arms.

THE EGYPTIAN HELEN

Dramatic Opera in Two Acts. Music by Strauss. Words by Hugo von Hofmannsthal. Dresden, June 6, 1928.

SCENE: Egypt and Morocco.
TIME: Homeric Antiquity.

CAST MENELAUS (Tenor).
ALTAIR (Baritone).
DA-UD, *his son* (Tenor).
THE ALL-KNOWING MUSSEL (High Tenor).
HELEN, *wife of Menelaus* (Soprano).
HERMIONE, *their young daughter* (Soprano).

AITHRA, *an Egyptian princess and sorceress* (Soprano).
FIRST HANDMAIDEN (Soprano).
SECOND HANDMAIDEN (Mezzo-Soprano).
FIRST GOBLIN (Soprano).
SECOND GOBLIN (Soprano).
THIRD GOBLIN (High Tenor).
Elves, Slaves, Soldiers, Eunuchs, etc.

ARGUMENT   The plot of this opera was suggested by the passage in the "Odyssey" describing how Telemachus visited Lacedæmon, and found Menelaus and Helen living amicably together, the Queen plying the King with draughts of nepenthe whenever he began to remember the awkward history of the Trojan war.   The music is more direct and simple in its emotional and sensuous appeal, more comprehensible and more melodious than "Elektra."

Act I   *In the House of the Royal Sorceress Aithra.*   Aithra is awaiting her divine lover, Poseidon, in company with a mysterious-talking Mussel, a gift from the gods.   A ship is approaching, with Menelaus and Helen, homeward bound from Troy.   The Mussel announces that Menelaus is about to stab Helen to death in her sleep, and urges Aithra to intervene.   Aithra promptly conjures up a violent storm, which she appeases when Menelaus takes Helen in his arms and swims with her through the fierce waves.   Guided by a torch, the royal travelers make their way to the house of the princess.   Helen is anxious to win back the love of her much-wronged husband, but he is proof against all her wiles.   He thinks of all the valiant men, Greeks and Trojans, whom her beauty has done to death.   He tells her how near he came to killing her on the ship, with the same dagger that slew Paris: that she shall never see again their daughter Hermione.   Just as he raises his dagger to smite her, Aithra, by her magic art, stays his hand.   She calls up a horde of spirits to bemuse and perplex him and lead him away.   She gives the Queen a magic potion.   A similar drink is given Menelaus, and the two are conveyed to an island.

Act II   *A Tent in an Oasis under the Shadow of Mount Atlas.*   In a series of four scenes the tangled fortunes of the pair are unraveled.   While they are still under the spell of the magic draught, the first interruption to their bliss comes in the person of Altair, a desert chief.   He like others falls under the spell of Helen's beauty; his son Da-ud also swears his allegiance; while the bemused Menelaus imagines the young man to be Paris, come to life again.   They ride away on a hunting expedition.   Helen implores Aithra to give her a second potion for Menelaus, but before it can be administered, Da-ud falls a victim to his sword. The body of the slain prince is borne in, followed by the distraught Menelaus. To divert him a feast is spread and Helen at last persuades him to drink of the second cup. As he does so, remembrance comes back to him; he recognizes her as his true wife; a white horse is seen bearing their child, Hermione; and as the three, long parted, meet in happy reunion, the curtain falls.

"Helen's Awakening" and "The Funeral March" are memorable numbers.

FIRE FAMINE

(Feuersnot.) Legendary Opera in One Act. Music by Strauss. Book by Ernest von Wolzogen. Dresden, November 21, 1901.

SCENE: Munich.
TIME: Thirteenth Century.

ARGUMENT Following an old superstition, the citizens of Munich go from door to door collecting wood for the fire in honor of the winter solstice. They proceed to one gloomy, shuttered house, in which lives Kunrad, a student of magic. Kunrad bids them take all his wood, but seeing a beautiful girl in the crowd, Diemut, daughter of the burgomaster, he embraces and kisses her. Although she finds the young man's love interesting, she is angry at the public caress; and when he comes later to her house to plead his love, she traps him in an order basket hanging from the window. In a rage he makes use of his magic art to invoke an icy cold upon the town. Instantly cold and darkness descend and grip them until the townsfolk in dismay beseech Diemut to relent. She has, in fact, decided to do so on her own account; and her love for Kunrad is a signal for the welcome light and warmth to return.

The "Love Scene" is an orchestral number from this opera.

ALBAN BERG

Alban Berg was born in Vienna, February 7, 1885, and spent most of his life there. He showed musical talent early and was self-taught until nineteen, when he became a pupil of Arnold Schoenberg. He wrote many pieces for the piano, voice, and instrumental quartets; and one opera, "Wozzeck," said by some critics to be "the first extended opera freed from the bonds of tonality." It has, indeed, roused partisan discussion by reason of its radical departure from accepted tonal methods. Berg died in Vienna, December 24, 1935.

WOZZECK
(Voht'-zek)

Tragic Opera in Three Acts and Fifteen Scenes. Music by Alban Berg. Book by the composer, after the drama by Georg Büchner. Berlin Staatsoper, December 14, 1925. At New York, the Metropolitan, November 24, 1931, by the Philadelphia Opera Co.

CAST
WOZZECK, *a poor soldier* (Baritone).
MARIE, *his mistress* (Soprano).
THEIR YOUNG SON.
CAPTAIN OF WOZZECK'S COMPANY (Basso).
ANDRES, *a soldier* (Baritone).
A DRUM MAJOR (Baritone).
AN ECCENTRIC DOCTOR.
MARGARET, *neighbor of Marie* (Contralto).
Soldiers, Townspeople, etc.

ARGUMENT A musical drama of military life, this opera has no particular locality or time. It relates to the affairs of a poor soldier, Wozzeck, who is a primitive sort of fellow living from day to day and hand to mouth. He is the father of a child, by a mistress, Marie, and though not legally obligated, he strives to provide for them. The only way he can do this is to yield his own body to a medical crank, who makes all sorts of experiments upon him.

Despite his sacrifices on her behalf, Marie is untrue. She has an affair with a Drum-Major, who boasts of his conquest to Wozzeck, and there is further evidence in some earrings she is wearing. Wozzeck surprises the couple dancing together at an inn, and later takes the girl on a woodland stroll and slashes her throat. He comes back to the inn seeking to forget his crime in drink, but instead in a frenzy of fear and remorse, throws the fatal knife into a pond, then in further dread of its recovery wades in after it and is drowned.

PAUL HINDEMITH

Hindemith, who has been called "the playboy of modern music," was born in Hanau, Germany, November 16, 1895. He came of poor Silesian stock, his father being a craftsman, but at an early age showed pronounced musical talent. His father taught him to play the violin, beginning at four, and by thirteen he had mastered the instrument and, two years later, went on a concert tour with his sister as accompanist. In 1936 he was banned by the Nazis, and was invited to come to the United States as performer and guest conductor. He has resided here since 1939. He wrote symphonies, string quartets, an oratorio, "The Eternal," and various operas: a "tabloid," "Hin und Zuruck" (There and Back), 1927; "Cardillac," 1927; "Neues vom Tage" (News of the Day), 1929—an "ingenious and diverting piece" which won added notice by reason of an aria sung in a bathtub; and "Mathis der Maler" (see below).

MATHIS DER MALER

(Matthias the Painter.) Opera in three movements. Music by Hindemith. Book inspired by life and work of Grünewald. Berlin, March 12, 1934, in concert form; same in New York by Philharmonic, Carnegie Hall, October 6, 1934. As an opera, Zurich, May 28, 1938.

ARGUMENT   This work was first presented as a symphony, or synthesis, of three stylistically related excerpts. Its radical modernism so nettled German officialdom that Hindemith's music was subsequently banned from that country. In its finished form as an opera it was based on the story of Mathis Grünewald, a noted sixteenth-century artist. In a peasant uprising he sympathized with the people. His painting was a forerunner of "classic realism" and for this reason appealed to the composer.

The three movements of the opera were inspired by three panels of the artist's masterpiece, a poliptych painted for the Isenheim Altar at Colimar: I. "Angelic Concert"; II. "Entombment"; and III. "The Temptation of St. Anthony."   The musical development has been spoken of by critics as clear and definite.   From a festive and happy chorus of the angels, the music descends gradually to a more somber tone and an elegy marks the entombment scene.   The ordeal of the saint with spirited and almost tumultuous strains leads up to a finale with a "Hallelujah Hymn" and vision of celestial exultation.

ERIC WOLFGANG KORNGOLD

Korngold was born in Brünn, May 29, 1897, the son of Julius Korngold, well-known music critic.   He early showed his versatility, both composing and conducting, church music, symphonies and operas. He came to America in 1936, residing a few years later in Los Angeles where he composed for films.   His works include: "The Ring of Polycrates," "Die Tote Stadt" ("The Dead City"), and "Violanta."

DIE TOTE STADT
(Dee toh-ta staht)

(The Dead City.)   Opera in Three Acts.   Music by Eric Korngold. Book by Schott, after the story by Rodenbach, "Bruges la Morte."   Both Hamburg and Cologne, December 4, 1920.   At New York, November 19, 1921, when Jeritza made her début in America.

SCENE: Bruges.
TIME: End of Nineteenth Century.

CAST   PAUL, *a young citizen of Bruges.*
MARIETTA, *a dancer.*
COUNT ALBERT, *of Brussels.*
FRANK, *a friend of Paul.*
A boating party, players, dancers.

ARGUMENT   "Die Tote Stadt" has a haunting quality, a commingling of the past with the present, which is reflected in the music.   From the opening notes of the overture, the auditor is prepared for the unusual.   Even the final note of tragedy is softened into a dream.

Act I *A Room in Paul's House.* Paul is living in seclusion, nursing
the memory of his deceased wife, Marie. A company of players
comes to his city, and Marietta, a dancer, looks so much like Marie that
Paul thinks it must be his wife restored to him. He invites her in and
Marietta, to humor him, puts on one of Marie's dresses and sings one of
her songs. Paul in a transport of delight fancies that it is really his lost
wife, who has stepped out of her pictured likeness on the wall.

Act II *A Street.* Paul is walking along a moonlit street near the
dancer's home, when he is hailed by a merry party of boatmen
led by Count Albert. They hold an improvised street carnival; Marietta entering into the gaiety, who acts a ghost visitor, a nun in her winding sheet. Paul, horrified, rushes forward and tears the sheet off her.
The boatmen protest, but Marietta quiets them and persuades Paul to
take her to his home.

Act III *Paul's Room.* Once more the distraught man battles with
the image of Marie and this strange woman who threatens to
take her place in his affections. While he strives to reconcile the two,
Marietta, to tease him, winds a lock of Marie's hair about her throat and
dances madly about the room. In a rage, Paul throttles her—only to
awake to discover he has been the victim of a nightmare. The actual
Marietta now enters, but he repulses her and departs with his friend
Frank to another city, to begin life anew.

ERNST KRENEK

Of Czech parentage, Ernst Krenek was born in Vienna, Austria,
August 23, 1900, but came to America and became a naturalized citizen
in 1945. The opera which made him famous was "Jonny Spielt Auf,"
a work so radical that it was shopped around before being produced in
Leipzig, in 1927, and two years later at the Metropolitan, New York.
He was for a time professor of music at Vassar. He was a composer of
great fertility, with seven operas, four symphonies, and numerous other
works to his credit.

JOHNNY PLAYS ON

(Jonny Spielt Auf.) Jazz Opera in Two Acts. Words and Music
by Ernst Krenek. First produced at the Neuen Theater, Leipzig, February 18, 1927. At New York, the Metropolitan, January 19, 1929, but
not continued in repertory.

SCENE: An Alpine resort, a large town in Central Europe,.
        Paris.
TIME: The present.

CAST MAX, *a composer* (Tenor).
    NIGGER JOHNNY, *a performer in a Jazz Orchestra*
    (Baritone).
    DANIELLO, *a celebrated violinist* (Baritone).
    ANITA'S MANAGER (Basso).
    A HOTEL PROPRIETOR (Tenor).
    A STATION EMPLOYEE (Tenor).
    FIRST POLICEMAN (Tenor).
    SECOND POLICEMAN (Baritone).
    THIRD POLICEMAN (Basso).
    ANITA, *a prima donna* (Soprano).
    YVONNE, *a chambermaid* (Soprano).
    Servants, Guests in Hotel, Travelers, etc.

ARGUMENT This opera enjoys the distinction—if distinction
    it can be called—of being the first composed in the
characteristically modern idiom of jazz. The plot and action are as.
highly colored, violent and grotesque as the music.

Act I The action is complete in four scenes—the first, an Alpine
plateau; the second, Anita's room; the third and fourth, a hotel
in Paris. Max, a melancholic composer, at first seeks distraction in the
Alpine scenery; then in Anita's society. She leaves him for a musical
career in Paris, where she is to sing the chief role in his opera. In Paris,.
however, a rival appears in Daniello, a famous violinist, who is besieged
by admirers clamoring for his autograph. Later Johnny, a saxophone
player, forces Daniello's lock and steals his precious violin. The next
morning there is a lively scene between Anita and the violinist. She
tells him "she is another's." When he tries to placate her by playing on.
his violin, he finds it gone.

Act II Seven involved scenes with a jumble of both characters and music further bewilder all but the most determined hearers. The action shifts from an Alpine hotel, where Max impatiently awaits the return of the erring Anita, to a glacier, where the distracted composer hears her voice singing an aria from his opera over the radio. The melody is suddenly interrupted by a lively jazz band. "That's Johnny's band!" some one exclaims, and a lively dance follows. In the next, a scene in a town, Johnny has the center of the stage, but doesn't fancy it. Detectives are seeking the lost violin and suspect him. They follow him to a railway station; he catches sight of them and hides the instrument on top of Max's luggage and "makes himself scarce." The police think Max the thief. A general mix-up follows, with farce comedy worthy of Hollywood. In the final scene, the railway station, Johnny, who has agàin purloined the violin, is seen on a footbridge fiddling away at his jazz. As a clock points to twelve it blurs, the whole scene changes, a terrestrial globe begins to revolve, and there at the top of the North Pole stands Johnny—still playing jazz.

ITALY

HISTORICAL PREFACE

In point of time, Italian opera ranks among the earliest. Modern opera is said to have had its remote beginnings in Greece and was transplanted thence by way of Italy into Europe. Down in the French court at Naples, about the year 1285, Adam de la Halle brought out a dramatic pastoral entitled "Le Jeu de Robin et de Marion," which was but one of many early attempts to string ballads together into a loose plot. They bore the same relation to opera as did the traveling players of the fifteenth century to modern drama.

It was not until the end of the sixteenth century that any concerted attempt was made toward a union of music and drama. Then a coterie of Florentine music lovers known as La Camerata banded themselves together. They enlisted a poet, Rinuccini, and a musician, Jacopo Peri, who wrote "Dafne"—now usually considered the first opera to have been performed in Europe and indeed the first work of this definite type. "Dafne" was privately performed in the Palazzo Corsi, Florence, in 1597. It met with such an enthusiastic reception on the part of the little group and their friends that the librettist and composer were commissioned to write a second piece, "Euridice," which was publicly performed at the wedding festivities of Henry IV of France and Maria de Medici. This performance at the Pitti Palace, October 6, 1600, is a very definite milestone in opera.

During the next fifty years many composers essayed their wings in the new empyrean. Most of them are only names now, but left their mark. We note such men as Claudio Monteverde (1567–1643) and his pupil, Caletti-Bruni, known as Cavalli; Provenzale, Cesti, and many another as this fruitful century drew to its close. The first opera house, the Teatro di San Cassiano, opened its doors in Venice, in 1637. Within the next thirty years eleven opera houses were opened in Venice alone. In Florence, Milan, Rome, and other cities the new form of entertainment flourished.

One would think that from this productive era would have descended a whole flock of operas to sing to modern ears. But such is not the case. Another century was to elapse before Spontini (born 1774) and the greater Rossini (born 1792) were to usher in the succession of famous composers and compositions now known as Italian opera. Meanwhile in the formative years the Italian school undeniably exerted a profound influence upon both Germany and France.

Rossini is the earliest bright, particular star on the Italian horizon. His was a pen of prodigious fertility. No less than fifty operas are placed to his credit, but only two or three are still produced, "The Barber of Seville," "Semiramide," and "William Tell." Hard on his heels follows a brilliant line—Donizetti, Bellini, Verdi, Ponchielli, Ricci, and Boito belonging by birth to the first half of the nineteenth century.

Verdi stands out head and shoulders above his contemporaries and indeed all other Italian composers. He is the proponent of Italian opera as definitely as is Wagner that of the German. He was both a prolific writer and a progressive one. His earlier works, such as "Rigoletto," "Il Trovatore," and "La Traviata," are in the approved melodious style of their period, when plot was subordinated to singer—the *bel canto* (good song). Florid solos were inserted without reference to theme. But in middle life Verdi began to strive for more consistency and dramatic freedom. "Aida" is the first example, to be followed later by such dramatic works as "Othello" and "Falstaff." Verdi's influence upon later composers has been profound.

Following him came such masters as Puccini, Leoncavallo, and Mascagni. The fame of the two latter rests upon only one or two works; but Puccini has attained a position second only to that of Verdi. Of the work of these and others, such as Franchetti, Leoni, Giordano, Montemezzi, and Wolf-Ferrari, record is found in succeeding pages. Among the most recent composers a tendency has been manifest to emphasize the brutal and gruesome, rather than the romantic and lovely. But Italian opera as a whole proves conclusively that this is a singing nation.

GASPARO LUIGI P. SPONTINI

An outstanding, early composer who, even in his lifetime, was the storm center of opposing schools, Spontini had a humble origin. Born of peasant stock at Majolati, near Jesi, Italy, November 14, 1774, he was destined for the priesthood, but ran away from home. Later reconciled to an uncle who had opposed his musical passion, he went, in 1791, to a conservatory in Naples. His first works were church music, but again rebelling he went to Rome where his first opera was put on—"I Puntigli delle Donne"—now forgotten with others that followed. His remembered ones include "La Vestale," "Olympia," and "Cortez." Spontini conducted orchestras in Paris, Berlin, and other cities. He died in 1851.

LA VESTALE

(The Vestal Virgin.) Romantic Opera in Three Acts. Music by Gasparo Spontini. Book by Etienne Jouy. The work was dedicated to Empress Josephine and produced by Napoleon's order at the Tuileries, December 14, 1807. At New York, the Metropolitan, November 12, 1925, with Rosa Ponselle, Johnson, De Luca, Mardones, and Matzenauer.

SCENE: Rome.
TIME: Ancient days.

CAST
LICINIUS, *a Roman General* (Tenor).
JULIA, *a Vestal Virgin* (Soprano).
CINNA, *Captain of the Legion* (Baritone).
PONTIFEX MAXIMUS (Basso).
HIGH PRIESTESS (Mezzo-Soprano).
A CONSUL (Basso).
Vestals, Priests, Senators, Consuls, Soldiers, Gladiators, Citizens.

ARGUMENT   "La Vestale" is of historic as well as musical interest. It foreshadows some of the glow and romance which later entered so largely into Italian composition. It also reveals elements which represent both the older and the newer schools of that nation's music. It was regarded and is still so regarded as one of the most significant pieces of its day.

Act I   *The Roman Forum.* Licinius has covered himself with glory in his campaign against the Gauls. He had hoped by his prowess to win the hand of Julia, a patrician's daughter, but after five years of absence learns that she has taken the veil of a Vestal Virgin. At his triumph she is chosen to place a laurel wreath on his brow and, seeing in her glance that she still loves him, he manages to whisper to her that he will meet her that night before the altar in the Temple.

Act II   *Interior of the Temple of Vesta.* The High Priestess leaves Julia in charge of the sacred flame, and warns her of the fate of

such as are untrue to the trust.   While the virgin kneels and implores
grace to withstand her new-found passion, Licinius enters.   As he
pleads his love to not unwilling ears, the altar's flame dies out!   The
goddess is wrathful and inevitable discovery follows.   Worshipers
and soldiers rush in, in tumult.   Cinna, a captain, rescues his friend,
Licinius.   The Pontifex Maximus bids the lictors tear off the virgin's
white veil, and place upon her a black veil, the symbol of death.

Act III   *The Field of Infamy.*   Cinna has told Licinius that his friends
would rescue the Vestal; but, despite their efforts, plans for
the execution go forward.   A large pyramidal tomb is seen, and into its
depths Julia must descend to be entombed alive.   She is resigned to her
fate.   Licinius now hastens forward and offers to die with her.   As the
throng closes in about them and prevents a rescue, a storm comes up.
Amid the crash of thunder a bolt of lightning ignites the Vestal's veil,
lying on the altar; then the sky clears.   The people, taking this as an
omen that her sin is forgiven, rejoice in the lovers' happiness.

GIOACCHINO ANTONIO ROSSINI

An Italian composer, called the "Swan of Pesaro," from the town of
his birth (February 29, 1792).   In 1807 he entered the Liceo (conservatory) at Bologna, studying 'cello under Cavedagni and composition with
Padre Mattei.   By 1810 he had written and brought out in Venice, and
with applause, a one act comedy opera, "La Cambiale di Matrimonio."
During 1812 he received commissions for no less than five light operas,
scoring, in 1813, with his "Tancredi" his first success.   There was
scarcely a year now that did not see a work from his pen, sometimes two,
until his "William Tell" was produced in Paris, 1829.   This was an entire change of style from his earlier works, possibly, however, foreshadowed by his "Comte d'Ory."   No less than fifty are credited to him.
During the remaining thirty-nine years of his life, Rossini turned aside
from opera.   He resided in Bologna and Florence until 1855, then in
Paris, dying at Ruelle, November 13, 1868.

THE BARBER OF SEVILLE

(Il Barbiere di Siviglia.) Comic Opera in Two Acts. Music by Rossini. Book by Sterbini, founded on a comedy by Beaumarchais. Argentina Theatre, Rome, February 5, 1816. In London at the King's Theatre, March 10, 1818. In New York, in English, at the Park Theatre, May 3, 1819. At the Metropolitan, December 15, 1883, with Sembrich as "Rosina."

SCENE: Seville.
TIME: The Seventeenth Century.

CAST   COUNT ALMAVIVA (Tenor).
FIGARO, *the barber of Seville* (Baritone).
DOCTOR BARTOLO, *a physician* (Basso).
BASILIO, *a music teacher* (Basso).
ROSINA, *a ward of Bartolo* (Soprano).
BERTHA, *a duenna* (Contralto).
FIORELLO, *the Count's servant* (Baritone).
AMBROSIO, *the doctor's servant.*
Musicians, Citizens, Guards, etc.

ARGUMENT   "The Barber of Seville" is a light opera of more than usual interest. It was written by Rossini at top speed in less than three weeks, but is the only one of his works which has persisted continuously in repertory. While it has not the grandeur of his "William Tell," it is a little masterpiece of its kind. Before the curtain rises the bright and merry overture prepares us for the musical feast that is to follow.

Act I   *Scene 1. A Street in Seville.* Count Almaviva, who has fallen in love with Rosina, the ward of Dr. Bartolo, goes to sing a serenade beneath her balcony. His aria, "Dawn with her rosy mantle," is one of the most beautiful. While there Figaro the town barber, a droll, self-important fellow, comes along to tell all and sundry what a fellow he is. "Figaro here! Figaro there!" he rattles off his patter song at break-neck speed, with the orchestra working valiantly to keep the droll pace (Factotem Song):

The Count observes him and decides he is the man he needs to aid in the nobleman's suit. Figaro tells him that he goes every day to shave the old doctor, who is insanely jealous over his ward and wants her to marry him. She is a virtual prisoner. Rosina drops a letter from the balcony, which her guardian cannot find, but it is picked up by the Count, who is overjoyed to see that his attentions are welcome. He pours out his heart to his beloved in another serenade: "Who 'neath thy window sighing." The wily barber then suggests that the Count impersonate the colonel of a passing regiment and demand a billet in Bartolo's house.

Scene 2. *A Room in Bartolo's House.* As the curtain rises, Rosina is seen at her desk just finishing a letter to her unknown admirer. Her soliloquy is one of the best known coloratura arias for sopranos: "A little voice I hear" (Una voce poco fa):

While Rosina is grumbling at her imprisonment and promising herself to lead her guardian a merry dance, Bartolo enters. He is determined to marry his ward, and invokes the aid of Basilio, the music teacher. While the two men go to draw up a contract, Figaro enters and Rosina entrusts him with a letter to "Lindoro" (which she supposes to be the Count's name). Their duet begins, "Am I his love, or do you mock me?" The doctor returns and accuses her of writing letters. At this point the Count staggers in disguised as a drunken officer. An amusing series of incidents follow among all the principals including the wily barber. An officer enters and arrests the Count for disorderly conduct, but on privately learning his true rank he releases him and arrests the doctor instead. A trio, "Awestruck and motionless" leads up to the rousing final chorus.

Act II *Music Room in Bartolo's House.* Count Almaviva returns to the doctor's home, this time disguised as a music master, sent in place of Basilio who is supposed to be sick. Bartolo views him with suspicion and, to prevent his being alone with Rosina, orders Figaro to shave him (Bartolo) in the same room. Rosina enters and the strange combination proceeds amusingly. At this juncture Basilio appears, but is bribed to pretend that he is really ill. During the music lesson the two lovers arrange to elope at midnight, being aided by the tricks of the barber.

The confusion is heightened in this scene by the fact that Rosina still does not know the identity of her suitor, whom she still calls "Lindoro." When she at last learns that he and the Count are the same person, she joyfully accepts him. Bartolo, meanwhile, has hastened to a notary to draw up a wedding contract in favor of himself; but when Basilio later appears with the notary, the Count and the barber intercept them and have it changed to read in the Count's favor. At the final curtain, the lovers are blissful; the doctor grudgingly yields to the inevitable; while the garrulous Figaro showers all with his good wishes. He has been the one indispensable person (so he thinks) all along!

The Act opens with a musical soliloquy by Bartolo, who voices his suspicions of people and things. Then comes the famous "music lesson," beginning with the false teacher's greeting, "Heaven send you peace and joy!" But his actions are not peace inspiring. The music here is a riot of melody. A dialogue quintet is followed by a lengthy aria by the watchful duenna, Bertha. When the lovers finally take their leave of Basilio, they sing the duet, "Fare you well then, good Signore!" (Zitti, zitti.) A melodious finale brings the curtain down.

SEMIRAMIDE
(Say'-me-rah'-me-day)

Tragic Opera in Two Acts. Music by Rossini. Book by Gaetano Rossi, based on Voltaire's tragedy, "Semiramis." Fenice Theatre, Venice, February 3, 1823. At New York, in 1826, in 1855; and at the Metropolitan, April 13, 1887, with Patti.

> SCENE: Babylon.
> TIME: Antiquity.

> CAST   SEMIRAMIDE, *Queen of Babylon* (Soprano).
> ARSACES, *Commander of the Assyrian Army* (Contralto).

GHOST OF NINUS (Basso).

OROE, *Chief of the Magi* (Basso).

ASSUR, *A Prince* (Baritone).

AZEMA, *a Princess* (Soprano).

MITRANUS ⎱ *of the royal household* ⎰ (Baritone).
IDRENUS ⎰   ⎱ (Tenor).

Magi, Guards, Satraps, Slaves.

ARGUMENT   "Semiramide" is one of those "forgotten" operas
which has enough good music to deserve a better
fate.   In the days of Patti and Scalchi its brilliant arias for the soprano
voice were prime favorites; and for many years after the work had left
the boards its stately overture with its sweeping, hymnlike opening bars
remained a pièce de resistance with orchestras.   The story is oriental
dealing with the machinations of a queen in mixing politics with love.
The First Act introduces an especially difficult and brilliant aria, in
which Queen Semiramide sings "Bright ray of hope" (Bel raggio
lusinghier).

Act I   *Babylon.*   Queen Semiramide has put her consort, Ninus, out
of the way, in order to aid the usurper Assur, who is also her
lover.   Meanwhile, her son Ninia, who has grown to man's estate, enters
her service under the assumed name of Arsaces and speedily wins high
rank.   When he returns a victor from the wars, his mother, ignorant of
his identity, falls in love with him and asks him to marry her.   But
Arsaces refuses because already in love with the Princess Azema.

Act II   *A Temple.*   During a gathering of the Babylonians in the
temple, while Semiramide is announcing to her people her
choice for their future King, the gates of Ninus' tomb suddenly open,
and his ghost appears in their midst, asserting that Arsaces will be his
successor to the throne, and commanding him to avenge his death upon
the enemy who shall visit the tomb that night.   In the meantime the
Priest Oroe has revealed to Arsaces the true circumstances of his birth,
whereupon he discloses his story to his mother.   The repentant Queen
declares that he shall be the successor to the crown, and warns him
against Assur.   At midnight Arsaces descends to the tomb of his father,
and is followed by Assur, who has planned to murder him.   Semiramide, fearful for the life of her son, follows Assur into the tomb, and
Arsaces, who is lying in wait for him, hears the footsteps of his mother
approaching, and thinking her to be Assur stabs her.   She dies in his
arms.   Assur is seized, and Arsaces weds Azema, and is proclaimed
King.

WILLIAM TELL

Romantic Opera in Three Acts.   Music by Rossini.   Book by Hippolyte Bis and Etienne Jouy, after the drama by Schiller.   Académie, Paris, August 3, 1829.   In New York, 1857, and at the Metropolitan, season of 1888–89.

SCENE: Switzerland.
TIME: Fourteenth Century.

CAST   GESSLER, a tyrant (Basso).
RUDOLF DE HARRAS, his lieutenant (Tenor).
WILLIAM TELL, a patriot (Baritone).
WALTER FÜRST, a patriot (Basso).
MELCHTHAL, a patriot (Basso).
ARNOLD, his son (Tenor).
LEUTHOLD, a patriot (Tenor).
MATHILDE, daughter of Gessler (Soprano).
HEDWIG, wife of Tell (Mezzo-Soprano).
JEMMY, son of Tell (Soprano).
RUODI, a fisherman (Tenor).
Peasants, Huntsmen, Soldiers.

ARGUMENT   "William Tell" is still another Rossini opera which is far better known for its overture than for the complete work.   Who even among non-opera-goers is not familiar with the lovely melodies in this introduction, beginning with the quiet bars denoting an Alpine calm?   Then comes a storm, in which we can almost see the lightning as with a roar it crashes down upon the trees. It has hardly died away in the distance when we hear the horns of huntsmen, and then a trumpet call—a call to arms for the Swiss peasantry to uprise against their Austrian oppressors.   This gives the opera's theme, a story well-known to all the Swiss, be it history or legend, of a patriot who successfully stirred up his countrymen in the cause of freedom.

Act I   *The Shores of Lake Lucerne, in front of Tell's House.*   William Tell, his wife, and little son are making merry by the shores of Lucerne when their aged countryman, Melchthal, and his son, Arnold, come to greet them.   Arnold is torn between two desires: He wishes to aid Tell and the patriots against the tyrant Gessler, but he is also in love with the latter's daughter, Mathilde, whose life he has saved.   Tell pleads with him to put his country first.   Presently Leuthold, a villager, rushes in, imploring assistance.   He has killed a soldier who tried to abduct his daughter, and he must flee across the lake to escape his enemies. The fisherman, Ruodi, does not dare venture in the face of an approaching storm, but Tell leaps into the boat with Leuthold and rows him across. The soldiers appear led by Rudolf and, in revenge, set fire to Tell's house and other cottages, and seize Melchthal as a hostage.

The most popular musical number in this Act is Arnold's greeting to his sweetheart, "Oh, Mathilde!"—a tour de force for any ambitious tenor.

Act II *Scene 1. A Forest.* The horns of a party of huntsmen sound through the wood, and are answered by a chorus of shepherds. Arnold meets Mathilde and declares his passion for her and learns that she also loves him. But Tell and Fürst enter at this moment to inform Arnold that the soldiers have slain his father. The young man bids his sweetheart a sorrowful farewell and casts in his lot with his country.

Scene 2. The Open Country. Following the call of Tell, Fürst, Arnold, and other patriots, the villagers and shepherds assemble from the various cantons. All take the oath of allegiance to Switzerland and prepare to battle against the tyrant's forces.

The musical climax of the Second Act is the trio of the three leaders, followed by a rousing chorus of the Swiss taking oath to conquer or die: "May glory our hearts with courage exalt!"

Act III *The Open Square at Altdorf.* Gessler has erected a pole in the market place at Altdorf and commanded that all shall bow before the cap, placed thereon, as a recognition of his authority. Tell refuses to do so and is seized by Rudolf. The tyrant has heard of Tell's skill with the crossbow, and will release him only on condition that he give an exhibition of this skill by shooting an apple off of his son's head. Tell does so, but when questioned as to a second arrow which is in his possession, he states that it was intended for Gessler's heart, had the first arrow harmed the lad. For this bold speech Tell is still held prisoner, although Mathilde intercedes for him.

Scene 2. The Shore of Lake Lucerne. Hedwig, Tell's wife, grieves for her husband and child who are both in the hands of the soldiers. Mathilde enters bringing the boy, whom she has aided to escape. The father also soon appears, having made good his own escape. He lies in wait for Gessler and kills him with an arrow from his bow. The patriot army is victorious over the enemy, and Arnold enters at the head of the joyous patriots. All unite in thanksgiving and a prayer that Switzerland may continue to be free.

The final Act brings in a striking tenor aria by Arnold, where he views the ruins of his own home: "O, silent abode!" (O muto asil). As the curtain descends we hear an inspiring hymn to liberty, and to the peaks of their land which typify it: "I boschi, i monti!"

GAETANO DONIZETTI

The Italian composer, Donizetti, was born in Bergamo, Italy, November 29, 1797. His father was a weaver, and wanted his son to study law. But neither the loom nor the bar attracted the young man, who early showed musical ability. He was at last allowed to enter the conservatory in his native town. His father, however, had no intention of continuing his tuition further than to fit him for teaching music; so Gaetano enlisted in the army. While in the service he composed his first opera, "Enrico di Borgogna," which was produced in Venice, 1818, but is now forgotten. Donizetti first came prominently into notice in 1830, when his opera, "Anna Bolena," was produced in Rome. "Belisarius" was produced in Vienna (1836). One opera followed another during his busy life, his total being about seventy. Of these only some half dozen are in the modern repertory, "Lucia di Lammermoor" being by far the most popular. Donizetti was equally facile in serious and lighter operas. Of the latter he is best known by his "L'Elisir d'Amore" (1832); "La Figlia del Reggimento" (1840); and "Don Pasquale" (1843). (See "Light Opera.") Donizetti suffered a paralytic stroke in 1845, and died in his native town, April 8, 1848.

LUCREZIA BORGIA
(Lu-cree'-tsia Borzh'-ya)

Tragic Opera, in a Prologue and Two Acts. Music by Donizetti; words by Felice Romani, after Victor Hugo. La Scala, Milan, 1834; Théâtre des Italiens, Paris, 1840; London, 1839. At New York, the Metropolitan, December 5, 1904, with Caruso, Maria de Macchi, Walker, and Scotti.

SCENE: Venice and Ferrara.
TIME: Early Sixteenth Century.

CAST ALFONSO D'ESTE, *Duke of Ferrara* (Baritone).
LUCREZIA BORGIA (Soprano).
MAFFIO ORSINI (Contralto).

GENNARO — *Young noblemen in* — Tenor.
LIVEROTTO — *the service of the* — Tenor.
VITELLOZZO — *Venetian Republic* — Basso.

GAZELLO (Bass).
RUSTIGHELLO, *in the service of Don Alfonso* (Tenor).

GUBETTA — *in the service of Lucrezia* — Basso.
ASTOLFO — Tenor.

Gentlemen-at-arms, Officers, and Nobles, Ladies-in-waiting, Capuchin Monks, etc.

ARGUMENT Based upon Hugo's story of the celebrated poisoner of history, "Lucretia Borgia," is one of the earliest of the tragic operas which has had a permanent place.

Prologue *Terrace of the Grimani Palace, Venice.* During a night festival, Gennaro, a young nobleman, becomes weary and falls asleep on a bench. Lucrezia Borgia, passing by, masked, is struck with the comeliness of the youth and while wondering if this can be her own son by an early marriage, he awakens. He in turn is interested in this fascinating woman, and when other friends arrive and she is unmasked, he is still more attracted by her beauty. But his friends lose no time in revealing her true character as a murderess. He turns from her in hatred, and she swoons away.

Act I *A Public Square, Ferrara.* Don Alfonso, Duke of Ferrara, and the present husband of the notorious Lucrezia, is jealous of her interest in Gennaro. Like the young man himself, the Duke is ignorant of the fact that Gennaro is really Lucrezia's son. Gennaro now comes to Ferrara with a party of his friends, and in order to show his loathing for her crimes, he hacks her name off the shield on the gates of the palace. The Duke orders his arrest, glad of this excuse to get a possible rival under surveillance.

Lucrezia, ignorant of the offender's identity, demands that he be put to death for this insult. Alfonso cynically consents. Gennaro is brought in, and the now horror-stricken woman pleads for his life; but her husband is adamant. With exquisite cruelty he commands that she herself shall prepare the poisoned cup—a draught in which she is an adept. She does so, but also secretly administers an antidote which saves Gennaro's life. She implores him to flee the city.

Act II *Banquet Hall of the Negroni Palace.* Lucrezia has not forgotten the other young men who were with Gennaro in his
attack upon the palace, and determines to revenge herself by poisoning
them. She invites them to a banquet and drugs their wine. She then
appears before them and announces this fact. What is her horror,
however, to find Gennaro again among them. He threatens to kill her.
She reveals to him the secret of his birth, but he turns from his mother
and dies. The Duke enters to find the hall filled with dead or dying,
and Lucrezia herself expiring from remorse.

Recorded arias from this opera: "Il segreto per essere felice," "Come
e bello quale incento," "M'odi, ah, m'odi!" and "Vieni la mia vendetta."

LUCIA DI LAMMERMOOR
(Lu-chee'-ah dee Lam'-mer-moor)

Tragic Opera in Three Acts. Music by Donizetti. Book by Cammerano, after Scott's "Bride of Lammermoor." Produced at San Carlo
Theatre, Naples, September 26, 1835; in London three years later; and
in English at the Park Theatre, New York, November 17, 1845. The
most celebrated sopranos of the past century have sung "Lucia." Sembrich made her American debut in it, at the Metropolitan, October 24,
1883.

SCENE: Scotland.
TIME: 1700.

CAST HENRY ASHTON, *of Lammermoor* (Basso).
LUCY ASHTON, *his sister* (Soprano).
EDGAR, *of Ravenswood* (Tenor).
LORD ARTHUR BUCKLAW, *friend of Ashton* (Tenor).
NORMAN, *a follower of Ashton* (Tenor).
RAYMOND, *chaplain to Ashton* (Basso).
ALICE, *attendant to Lucy* (Soprano).
Friends and retainers of the Ashtons, Villagers,
etc.

ARGUMENT The story of "Lucia di Lammermoor" follows
closely the well-known novel of Scott dealing with
the tragic fate of two lovers separated by family strife. Although generally regarded as Donizetti's masterpiece, some modern critics have
scoffed at it, saying that it was merely the vehicle for some prima donna.
Nevertheless, the opera remains a favorite for its freshness of melody,
the skillful interplay of the music with its tragic theme, the rich colora-

tura passages, and the fine ensembles including the famed **Sextet**, which is still unchallenged as near the topmost flights of all Italian opera.

Act I   *Scene 1.   A Grove outside Ashton's Castle.*   Lucy Ashton is being urged by her brother to accept the hand of Bucklaw, who will restore their family fortunes, but she persists in refusing him. Henry Ashton is further enraged by learning that she is in love with Edgar of Ravenswood, his worst enemy, and that she has been meeting him secretly.   Henry's confidant Norman, has sent his huntsmen to discover the truth of the matter.   They return and tell in a brisk chorus, that, "Long they wandered o'er the mountain"—and that the suspicion is correct.   Then comes Henry's defiant aria: "From my breast I mercy banish."

Scene 2.   A Fountain in the Grove.   It is evening and a moon shines on a peaceful scene.   A harp breathes the quietude in lovely melody. Lucy enters with her companion, Alice, and sings the "Legend of the Fountain."   Edgar appears and the two again pledge their troth.   He is seeking safety in France, but says he will return for her.   A second aria by Lucy, one of the best-known numbers, "Then swift as thought," is followed by their no less well-known duet, "My sighs shall on the balmy breeze" (Verranno la sull' aure)

Act II   *Scene 1.   Lucy's Apartments.*   Ashton makes preparations for the marriage of his sister with Bucklaw, never doubting that he will obtain her consent at the final moment.   The girl is in deep dejection.   Letters between her and Edgar have been intercepted and she is told that he is faithless.   A forged letter from Edgar is shown in proof of this.   Finally she yields to her brother's entreaties and the arguments of Raymond, her spiritual adviser, and agrees to sign the wedding contract.

Scene 2.   Hall of the Castle.   A brisk chorus of guests assembled to witness the signing of the wedding contract opens this climactic scene. Bucklaw is being congratulated by his friends.   Lucy is a sad and passive figure.   Just as she takes the pen to sign the fatal document, Edgar rushes wildly into the hall.   Then with an orchestral prelude ensues that finest of Italian ensembles, the Sextet.   Edgar sings: "What restrains me at this moment?   Why my sword I do not draw?"   Because

Henry sees his sister "as a rose 'mid tempest bending," he is moved to exclaim: "To my own blood I'm a traitor!" One after another take up the melody until it is a glorious volume of sound with Lucy's despairing voice rising above the rest:

Ashton triumphantly shows Edgar the contract signed by his sister. Edgar loads her with reproaches and leaves the room before Ashton's retainers can interpose.

Act III *Scene 1. Hall of the Castle.* The wedding has been celebrated despite Edgar's interposition, and he has made an appointment to fight a duel with Ashton. The bride and groom have been shown their apartments, and while the guests still make merry the news is circulated that Lucy has gone mad and stabbed Bucklaw. She appears among the horrified guests raving insane. The "mad scene," another pivotal one in the opera, is favored by great prima donni as it challenges their best both in vocalization and in acting. Lucy by turns is reminiscent of her first happy hours with Edgar; then her mood turns ("Shed thou a tear of sorrow"); then comes a brilliant bit of coloratura work, "Yet shall we meet at the altar, dear Edgar"; then grief-stricken ravings with the orchestra in rapid tempo.

Scene 2. A Churchyard. (Sometimes omitted.) Edgar awaits his enemy and dreams of his lost love. A bell tolls and he hears that Lucy is dead, and to the last was faithful as she had promised. "Why lament ye?" he demands of the mourners. When told that she is no more he voices a final plaint: "Thou hast spread thy wings." A 'cello strain accompanies his final prayer, as he stabs himself.

LA FAVORITA
(Lah Fav-o-ree'-ta)

(The King's Favorite). Romantic Opera in Five Acts. Music by Donizetti. Book by Royer and Waëtz, after the drama, "Le Comte de Commingues." Académie Royale de Musique, Paris, December 2, 1840. At New York, Park Theatre, October 4, 1848; and at the Metropolitan, November 29, 1905, with Caruso, Walker, Scotti, and Plançon.

SCENE: Castile.
TIME: 1340.

CAST ALFONSO XI, *King of Castile* (Baritone).
FERNANDO, *an officer of the guard* (Tenor).
BALTHASAR, *Prior of the Monastery of St. Jacob* (Basso).
GASPARO, *an officer* (Tenor).
LEONORE DE GUZMAN, *the King's favorite* (Mezzo-Soprano).
INEZ, *her companion* (Soprano).
Officers, Soldiers, Courtiers, Ladies, Servants, Monks.

ARGUMENT The theme of "La Favorita" is simple but dramatic, treating of lost illusions and blighted hopes. A young anchorite forsakes his vows for the sake of a pretty face, only to find that the promised happiness is a mirage.

Act I *Hall of a Monastery.* Fernando, a novice in orders, of the Monastery of St. Jacob, has shown such earnestness and insight that he is spoken of as the next prior. But between him and his vows comes the vision of a beautiful woman, an unknown whom he loves and who, he finds, loves him in return. He confesses his attachment to his best friend, Balthasar, the present prior, who endeavors to warn him against the snares and pitfalls of the world. But finding that the young man is determined, he releases him from the monastic orders and bids him go in peace.

The "high note" in this Act is the tenor aria by Fernando in which he describes to the prior his lady love: "A virgin, an angel of God" (Una vergine):

Act II *A Palace Garden.* Fernando decides to seek service in the royal army. He comes blindfolded into the palace garden, where ladies of the court who have heard his story, entertain him graciously. Among them, he finds his unknown love, Leonore; but while she reciprocates his affection, she begs him to go away and forget her. She will not even tell him her name and station. She is the King's "favorite" and is afraid Fernando will despise her if he learns her true station. The scene opens with a pleasing solo and chorus of Leonore and her attendants: "Bright sunbeams, lightly dancing," which is followed by the women's chorus: "Gentle zephyr," as Fernando's boat nears shore. Her strange attitude only adds fuel to the flame. While she tries to send him away, Inez enters to announce the approach of King Alfonso. The mystified young man now thinks that his lady is of too high rank for him to presume to address her. Leonore leaves him, after presenting him with a document which proves to be a royal commission as officer in the King's army. Ferdinand resolves to win the King's favor and the lady's hand in the wars.

The Act closes with the martial strain: "Oh, fame, thy voice inspiring!"

Act III *The King's Court.* King Alfonso is delighted with news of his army's victories over the Moors, and with the brilliant conduct of his young officer, Fernando. The latter dreams of happiness at last with Leonore, but he is still ignorant of the fact that she is the King's favorite, and Alfonso does not intend to give her up. A spirited scene ensues between monarch and mistress in which the former reiterates his devotion and the latter reproaches him for putting happiness out of her reach. Before the court she finally hurls defiance at him, being aided by Balthasar, who comes with a message from the Pope threatening the King with excommunication unless he relinquishes Leonore in favor of Fernando. He is given one day in which to decide. Fernando hears nothing of this, but Leonore is cast into the depths of sorrow at the prospect of deceiving her lover.

The two leading arias in this Act are: Alfonso's own plea of passion, "Come, Leonore"; and the prior's vigorous denunciation of the King, "Call not down the wrath of God."

Act IV *A Palace Apartment.* Alfonso decides to yield to the papal pressure and reward Fernando. He tells the young officer that he will give him Leonore in marriage. (Aria, "Thou flower beloved!") While the officer is overjoyed, the lady is a prey to misgivings; she feels that their happiness will not be assured unless she tells her betrothed the truth about her relations with the King. Her plaint, "O, my Fernando!", is one of the best-known songs for the mezzo voice in Italian opera:

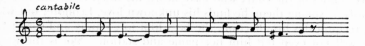

She writes a letter to him and entrusts it to Inez, but is stopped on her way by Gasparo. The King ennobles Fernando and orders an immediate marriage, which ceremony is performed. But during the festivities the bridegroom overhears slurring remarks from Gasparo and the courtiers, and returns to the King demanding an explanation. When he learns the truth, he renounces his bride and honors, breaks his sword, and casts its fragments at the feet of the King. This dramatic scene is the climax of the work. Amid conflicting voices of protest, irony, grief, Fernando departs, while the courtiers salute him with the stirring chorus: "Fernando, the truly brave, we salute and pardon crave!"

Act V   *The Monastery Hall.*   Fernando returns to the monastery and resumes his study for the priesthood. On the day when he is to receive holy orders, Leonore comes to beg his forgiveness. She tells him of the undelivered letter in which she had confessed the truth and which she thought he had received. He forgives her and says that he loves her still, but now the Church calls him. He leaves her swooning and joins the procession of monks.

The closing Act also abounds in melody, beginning with the song of Balthasar and the monks, "Behold the stars in splendor celestial"; and continuing with Fernando's song of renunciation, "Spirit of Light!"— another gem of this school of opera.

LINDA DI CHAMOUNIX
(Linda dee Shah'-moo-nee)

Romantic Opera in Three Acts. Music by Donizetti. Book by Rossi. Vienna, May 19, 1842. At New York, the Metropolitan, 1890, with Patti; and, on February 4, 1919, with Galli-Curci.

SCENE: Chamounix and Paris.
TIME: 1760.

CAST   MARQUIS DE BOISFLEURY (Basso).
        CHARLES, VISCOMTE DE SIRVAL, *his nephew* (Tenor).
        PREFECT (Basso).

PIERROT (Contralto).
LINDA, *a village girl* (Soprano).
ANTONIO, *a farmer, her father* (Baritone).
MADELEINE, *his wife* (Soprano).
INTENDANT (Tenor).
Peasants, Savoyards, Servants, etc.

ARGUMENT   A tuneful opera with a thin and implausible story. In its first act is one of the famed arias for the soprano voice, "Oh, star that guidest!"

Act I   *The Village of Chamounix.*   Linda's parents are poor peasants who are in fear of being dispossessed from their home by the Marquis.   Meanwhile an ardent and pure love affair has sprung up between the Marquis' nephew, Charles, and the girl, who does not know his real rank, but thinks him only a poor artist.   The Marquis and his Intendant arrive, and the old nobleman (who is very much of an old roué) assures Linda's parents that they will be undisturbed.   His kindness however, is only a cloak to get possession of the girl for himself.

Act II   *A Paris Apartment.*   Linda has been set up amid luxurious surroundings in Paris.   It develops that, not the Marquis, but Charles himself, has thus sought to shield her—but without sin!   The old nobleman now enters and tries to win her, but is repulsed.   He laughs sardonically when she tries to explain the true situation. Charles, meanwhile, is being pressed by his mother to make a brilliant match, but still loves his village sweetheart.   Her parents have been turned out of doors by the Marquis, and her father enters her apartment seeking alms.   He does not recognize her at first, but when he does, hurls her money at her feet.   When she realizes her impossible situation, she goes mad.

Act III   *The Village of Chamounix.*   Pierrot alone of her friends has been faithful to Linda.   He has come to Paris for her and brings her back home.   His singing soothes her.   In the meantime, Charles has at last persuaded his mother to allow him to marry Linda; and he has also restored their farm to her parents.   When she learns all this, her reason is restored and there is a joyful reunion.

   The music throughout is sprightly, the few more dramatic passages giving contrast to soft, seductive melodies.   Chief among these are: "Ambo nati ni questa valle," "O luce di quest' anima," and "Romanza di Pierotto."

VINCENZO BELLINI

Bellini was one of those unfortunate examples of a musical genius cut off in his first rich maturity.   Born in Catania, Sicily, November 3, 1802, he died in the village of Puteaux, France, September 23, 1835, at the age of thirty-three.   He was educated at Naples, under Zingarelli, and when only twenty he had composed an opera, "Bianca and Fernando," which was successfully produced.   Several others followed, of which "Il Pirata," "La Sonnambula," "Norma," and "I Puritani" have sufficed to make his fame permanent.

LA SONNAMBULA
(Lah Son-nahm'-boo-lah)

(The Sleepwalker.)   Romantic Opera in Three Acts.   Music by Vincenzo Bellini.   Book by Felice Romani.   Carcano Theatre, Milan, March 6, 1831.   In English at Drury Lane, London, 1833; and at Park Theatre, New York, in 1835.   At the Metropolitan, in 1892; and on December 15, 1906, with Sembrich, Jomelli, and Plançon.

SCENE: A Village in Switzerland.
TIME: Early Nineteenth Century.

CAST   COUNT RODOLPHO, *Lord of the Castle* (Basso).
TERESA, *owner of the Mill* (Soprano).
AMINA, *her foster daughter* (Soprano).
LISA, *owner of the Inn* (Soprano).
ELVINO, *a young farmer* (Tenor).
ALESSIO, *a villager* (Basso).
Notary, villagers, etc.

ARGUMENT   "La Sonnambula" is a simple, human story, written into an opera full of tenderness and color. Its appeal to the sympathies, because of an unmerited punishment falling on the head of a young girl who walks in her sleep, and its dramatic climax, made it widely popular, a century ago.   Its arias were prime favorites with sopranos, among them Jenny Lind and Adelina Patti. Then came the more robust school of German opera culminating in Wagner, and the lighter, more delicate melodies of Bellini went into eclipse. "La Sonnambula" is now seldom heard, yet its melodies retain their old-fashioned charm.

Act I *The Village Green.* The villagers make merry, for they celebrate the betrothal of Amina, the pretty foster daughter of Teresa, who owns the mill, and Elvino, a landowner of the neighborhood. Only one person, however, does not enter into the merry-making —Lisa, the proprietress of the tavern, for she also is in love with the young farmer. Alessio, a villager who is in love with her, is repulsed. Presently the two lovers enter, and a notary brings in the contract, which is duly signed. Just at this moment, a stranger drives up, who is on his way to the castle hard by, but first seeks shelter at the tavern He addresses a polite speech to Amina, much to her lover's annoyance. Teresa, however, warns him against the castle, which is said to be haunted.

Amina has two pleasing songs in this Act: "How for me brightly shining" (Come per me sereno); and "With this heart its joy revealing" (Sovia il sen la man mi posa). There is also a pleasing betrothal duet between her and Elvino, "Take now the ring."

Act II *A Room in the Inn.* The stranger proves to be Rodolpho, who is lord of the castle. He is conducted to his room in the inn by Lisa, who is not averse to flirting with him. They are interrupted by some of the villagers without, and Lisa runs away, dropping her handkerchief in her haste. Shortly afterward, Rodolpho is astonished to behold the figure of Amina, clad in a white nightdress, raise his window and enter his room. He soon sees that she is walking in her sleep, and it is this apparition that has given rise to the village superstition. Rodolpho considerately leaves the room, and the sleeping girl falls upon the bed. Lisa, however, sees in this situation an opportunity to wean away Elvino from his sweetheart. She brings Elvino into the room and points out the sleeping girl. The latter, awakened by the noise, as others have entered, is covered with confusion, and cannot explain her conduct to Elvino, who casts her off in scorn.

The most striking number in this Act is the duet, before the curtain falls, between the two young people—Amina's protestations of innocence, and Elvino's wrath.

Act III *Scene 1. A Valley.* The villagers try to reconcile the lovers, but Elvino, meeting Amina, still scorns her. He snatches his ring from her finger. She is heartbroken, for she still loves him.

Scene 2. Near the Mill. Lisa has lost no time in making Elvino promise to marry her, instead of Amina. Preparations for the wedding are afoot. Rodolpho tries to dissuade Elvino from this step. He tells him about somnambulism, but Elvino is incredulous. Teresa confronts Lisa with her handkerchief, which was found in Rodolpho's room. At this moment the attention of all is directed to Amina, who emerges from a window upon the roof of the mill. She is again walking in her sleep, and she proceeds to cross a rickety foot-bridge near the turning wheel, while the villagers fear for her life. At last she crosses in safety, and as she reaches the ground, she speaks of her lost love. Elvino, convinced and touched, gently replaces his ring on her finger, while her friends crowd around her in congratulation.

The last Act sparkles with melody. Amina's sleepwalking song, "Ah, scarce could I believe how soon my blossoms would wither!", is followed by the joyful greeting of Elvino, "Mingle not an earthly sorrow" —which for many years was a tour de force with tenors.

NORMA

Dramatic Opera in Two Acts. Music by Bellini. Book by Felice Romani. Milan, 1831. In New York, Park Theatre, 1841; and sung at the opening of the Academy of Music, October 2, 1854, with a notable cast. At the Metropolitan, 1890, as a "benefit performance" for Lilli Lehmann.

SCENE: Gaul.
TIME: Circa 50 B.C.

CAST OROVESO, *chief of the Druids* (Basso).
NORMA, *his daughter the High Priestess* (Soprano).
ADALGISA, *a priestess* (Contralto).
POLLIONE, *Roman proconsul* (Tenor).
FLAVIUS, *his friend* (Tenor).
CLOTILDA, *friend of Norma* (Soprano).
Two Children, Priests, Soldiers, Druids.

ARGUMENT "Norma" is an opera of tragic intensity, written around the theme of a woman's scorn. A Druidic priestess, forsaken by her Roman lover, brings down vengeance upon his head, but is yet willing to share his fate. "Norma" appeared the year after "La Sonnambula" and was no less successful. Its technique is that of the earlier Italian school, relying upon directness and simplicity, rather than severe declamation. Nevertheless it is of high emotional quality and its arias tax the ability of the best coloraturas. For this reason it has remained a favorite with the greatest of prima donni for a hundred years and more. The overture gives a foretaste of its changing moods.   The first strains are martial, followed by a tense, minor theme and leading up to a chorus of Druids, which in turn leads logically to the first curtain.

Act I   *Grove of the Druids.*   Norma, the High Priestess of the Druids, is charged with the duties of the Temple, and she alone can declare war or peace.   By cutting the sacred mistletoe she can give the signal for war, and this she is urged to do in order that the Roman invaders may be expelled; but she stays her hand.   Despite her vows to the Temple, she has secretly wedded Pollione, the Roman proconsul, and has had two children by him.   But the Roman is faithless and is even now planning to abduct Adalgisa, another virgin of the Temple. The latter, however, resists his pleas and finally confesses her temptation to the priestess.   Norma is disposed to pardon her, remembering her own weakness, until she learns that the proconsul is the man involved; then she turns upon Pollione, who has entered, and reproaches him.

This Act is filled with fine music of the older tradition: the opening chorus and march of the Druid soldiers, "With thy prophetic oracle" (Dell' aura); then the famous aria by Norma, "Queen of Heaven" (Casta diva)—

This is followed by "Beloved, return unto me" (Ah! bello) in slower tempo.   The Act ends with a melodic trio for Norma, Adalgisa, and Pollione, "O, how his art deceived you!" (Oh, di qual.)

Act II   *Scene 1.   Norma's Apartments.*   While the two children of Norma's secret union with the Roman lie asleep upon a couch, the Priestess enters, resolved to kill them.   But maternal love proves stronger than anger, and she asks Adalgisa, who now enters, to take charge of the children and conduct them to the proconsul.   They may thus escape to Rome, while she herself remains to expiate her sin upon the funeral pyre.   The duet between the two, "Hear me, Norma!" (Mira, O Norma!) is one of the gems of the opera:

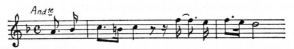

Adalgisa, however, will not aid Norma in her plan; instead she goes to Pollione to urge him to make amends.

Scene 2. (Sometimes presented as a separate Act) While Adalgisa is ministering at the altar, the Roman impiously attempts to seize her by force. Norma enters and strikes upon the sacred shield, summoning all her warriors. She declares that the time has come to make war and drive out the invaders. They seize the proconsul and bring him before her for judgment. Norma condemns him and then tears off the wreath from her brow, saying that she also has been guilty. The proconsul recognizes too late the worth of the woman he has scorned. He begs to die with her. The Druids make ready the funeral pyre and Norma ascends it with her lover, both perishing in the flames.

The impassioned scene between the two lovers, reunited in death, is finely outlined in the music. Another fine passage is the basso aria sung by Oroveso, with chorus of soldiers: "Haughty Roman!" (Oh del Tebro.)

I PURITANI

(*Ee Poo-ree-tahn'-ee*)

(The Puritans.)   Romantic Opera in Three Acts.   Music by Bellini. Book by Count Pepoli.   Théâtre des Italiens, Paris, January 25, 1835. At New York, 1844, and in 1883, at the Metropolitan, with Sembrich as "Elvira."

SCENE: Near Plymouth, England.
TIME: Circa 1635.

CAST   LORD GAUTIER WALTON, *a Puritan* (Basso).
SIR GEORGE WALTON, *his brother* (Basso).
LORD ARTHUR TALBOT, *a Cavalier* (Tenor).
SIR RICHARD FORTH, *a Puritan* (Baritone).
SIR BENNO ROBERTSON, *a Puritan* (Tenor).
HENRIETTA OF FRANCE, *widow of King Charles* (Soprano).
ELVIRA, *daughter of Lord Walton* (Soprano).
Puritans, Soldiers, Guards, Women, Pages, etc.

ARGUMENT   A slight historical background is offered for this opera, in the wars between the soldiers of Cromwell and the followers of the fallen king, Charles I.

Act I   *A Fortress near Plymouth.*   Lord Walton, a loyal adherent of Cromwell the Protector, is in charge of this stronghold, which contains political prisoners, among them Queen Henrietta, widow of

Charles I. Lord Walton's daughter, Elvira, is enamored of Lord Arthur Talbot, a Cavalier, and follower of the Stuarts, but her hand has been promised by her father to Sir Richard Forth, a Puritan. Yielding to her entreaties, however, he allows her to betroth herself to Talbot, and her uncle, Sir George Walton, arranges for the safe conduct of the Cavalier.

Talbot arrives, and then discovers that Queen Henrietta is a prisoner there. As a loyal follower, he plots her escape. He obtains Elvira's bridal veil and drapes it over the form of the Queen. As they pass out they are intercepted by Forth, the disappointed suitor. He halts them, believing the lady to be Elvira, but when her features are partially disclosed, and he sees that it is another woman, he permits them to pass. When the escape is discovered, Elvira is so wrought up over her lover's apparent faithlessness, that she loses her reason.

Three notable musical numbers in this Act are: Sir Richard's cavatina, "Ah, forever I have lost thee!"; Lord Arthur's impassioned, "To thee, Beloved!"; and Elvira's sprightly, "I am a blithesome maiden."

Act II *Another Part of the Fortress.* Elvira seems hopelessly mad. She wanders around like one distraught. Her uncle, Walton, and her Puritan lover, Forth, declare that they will meet Talbot in battle, and avenge her distress.

Here we have the mad scene of Elvira, beginning, "It was here in sweetest accents"; followed by her lovely aria, "Come, dearest love"; and a closing duet between Sir Richard and Sir George, in lusty martial vein.

Act III *A Grove.* Having accomplished the safety of his Queen, Talbot once more becomes the lover. He risks his personal safety to come to a grove near the fortress, in the hope of seeing Elvira. He meets her in the woodland, and is able to lighten her darkened mind no little by his presence and renewed words of love. But she is still in a disturbed state. While he is trying to recall her memory and reason, he hears men approaching. He knows that capture means death, but he will not forsake her. He is arrested and speedily sentenced to death. The execution is about to take place, when word is received that the Cavalier forces have been signally defeated, and Cromwell has proclaimed amnesty for all prisoners. Talbot is accordingly set free, and the sudden joy operates to restore Elvira's full reason. She and Talbot are united.

A charming song by Elvira graces this Act: "Sad and lonely by a fountain." Other good bits are Arthur's plea, "Still to abide"; and her reply, "All words are wanting."

GIUSEPPE VERDI

This supreme master of Italian opera was born at Roncole, near Busseto, Lombardy, October 9, 1813. Verdi early showed a predilection for music, at ten being the village organist, but when at eighteen he applied for admission to the Italian Conservatory, he was refused on the score that he did not reveal sufficient musical talent. Yet this was the composer who a few years later was to astonish the world by his brilliance and sustained excellence of his operas. His first opera, "Oberto," is reminiscent of Bellini. Others appeared until, in 1844, when he was thirty-one, his first really successful opera, "Ernani," was produced. A few years later came "Rigoletto," "Il Trovatore," and "La Traviata," titles which are still household words in every operatic repertory. "The Masked Ball" (1859), "The Force of Destiny" (1862), and "Don Carlos" (1867), which also belong to this middle period, have recently been revived in America. When fifty-eight, he gave evidence of still greater mastery of his art with "Aida." At a still later period came "Othello" (1887), and "Falstaff" (1893), which more nearly resemble music-drama than opera and reveal the influence of Wagner. Verdi passed away at Milan, January 27, 1901.

ERNANI
(Air-nah'-nee)

Dramatic Opera in Four Acts. Music by Giuseppe Verdi. Book by Francesco M. Piavé, after Hugo's "Hernani." Fenice Theatre, Venice, March 9, 1844. New York, Astor Place Theatre, 1846; Academy of Music, forty years later. At the Metropolitan, January 28, 1902, with Sembrich, Bauermeister, De Marchi, Scotti, and Edouard de Reszke.

SCENE: Aragon, Aix-la-Chapelle, and Saragossa.
TIME: 1519.

CAST   DON CARLOS, *King of Spain* (Baritone).
DON RUY GOMEZ DE SILVA, *a Spanish grandee* (Basso).
DONNA ELVIRA, *his niece* (Soprano).
JOHANNA, *her nurse* (Contralto).
ERNANI, *an outlaw* (Tenor).
DON RICCARDO, *royal armor-bearer* (Tenor).

IAGO, *armor-bearer to Gomez* (Basso).
Lords, Ladies, Soldiers, Outlaws, Servants.

ARGUMENT The story of "Ernani" originally followed Hugo's
            tragedy, "Hernani," so closely that the poet ac-
cused the composer of literary piracy and demanded that the libretto be
changed. The title of "Il Proscritto" was therefore given the opera
for a time.

Act I *Scene 1. A Mountain Retreat.* Ernani, the son of a Spanish
          duke, has been outlawed by the King and becomes chief of a
robber band. He has fallen deeply in love with Donna Elvira, a noble
lady, and hearing that she is betrothed to Don Gomez de Silva, a wealthy
grandee, he plans to abduct her.

The opening chorus of the bandits is the drinking song, "Haste, clink
we the glasses," is followed by the tenor aria, "Unhappy one," and one
in faster tempo, "Adoring soul."

Scene 2. Donna Elvira's Apartments. During the preparations for
Elvira's marriage, a cavalier enters her apartments and tries to persuade
her to fly with him. Her cries for assistance bring Ernani upon the
scene, who recognizes the King in her assailant. Carlos, on his part,
recognizes the outlaw whom he has formerly defrauded of his lands
and titles, and a heated dispute arises in which Ernani hurls defiance at
the monarch. Silva now interposes, and the enraged outlaw offers to
fight them both, but is restrained.

Elvira's opening song, a rich, coloratura piece, has long been a
favorite with prima donni. Beginning in a tone of despair, it works up
to a climax of brilliant cadenza: "Ernani, fly with me!" (Ernani, invo-
lami)—

Act II *Hall of Silva's Mansion.* Ernani returns to the grandee's
           home, disguised as a pilgrim, in order to frustrate the wedding
plans of Silva with his niece. He pretends that he is in danger, and
Silva, not discovering his identity, grants him safe harbor so long as he
is under his roof. Later, Silva surprises him in an interview with Elvira
and recognizes him, but the grandee's pledge of safety holds good, and
he postpones his personal vengeance till a later time. Silva will not
even yield up the bandit to the King, who now appears before the castle
walls. The monarch is appeased only by the surrender of Elvira as a
hostage. When the royal troops are withdrawn, Silva releases Ernani

and immediately challenges him to a duel. Both agree, however, to postpone their personal differences until they have rescued Elvira. The outlaw, on his part, pledges himself to appear at any time that Silva shall sound his hunting horn.

An impassioned duet between Ernani and Elvira is a high point in this Act: "Ah, to die would be a blessing!" (Ah, morir!)—

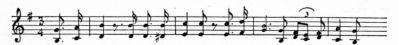

The King's baritone solo, "Come with me," the sounding of the hunting horn, and the spirited chorus, "To horse, to horse!" are other musical features.

Act III   *Charlemagne's Tomb, at Aix-la-Chapelle.*   While Carlos is visiting the tomb of the great emperor, he chances to overhear a conspiracy against him. Among the conspirators are Silva and Ernani. The royal guard appears and the King steps forth and orders the arrest and execution of all present. Ernani then declares that he is Don Juan of Aragon, a proscribed nobleman, who has been urged on to this course by his wrongs. The King's magnanimity is touched, and yielding to Elvira's supplications, he forgives the conspirators and also bestows the lady's hand upon Ernani.

Musical numbers include: Carlos' solemn soliloquy at the tomb; the chorus of the conspirators, "Let the lion roar"; and the stirring finale, "Oh, noble Carlos!"

Act IV   *Don Juan's Castle.*   Ernani has been restored to his rank and ancestral estates. His cup of bliss is filled by his marriage to Elvira. The ceremony has just been completed, when the ominous sound of a bugle is heard. It is Silva come to exact his pledge. The stern old grandee silently enters and hands a dagger to Ernani, who takes it without protest and stabs himself to the heart.

The farewell songs of the lovers: Ernani's plea to Silva, "To linger in misery"; and Elvira's wish to share his fate, "Stay thee, my lord," bring the work to a close.

LUISA MILLER

Tragic Opera in Three Acts. Music by Verdi. Book by S. Cammarano. San Carlo Theatre, Naples, December 8, 1849. New York Academy of Music, October 20, 1886. At the Metropolitan, December 21, 1929, with Ponselle, and De Luca.

SCENE: A Tyrolean Village.
TIME: The Seventeenth Century.

CAST   COUNT WALTER (Basso).
       RODOLFO, *his son* (Tenor).
       FREDERICA, DUCHESS OF OSTHEIM, *the Count's
         niece* (Contralto).
       WURM, *the Count's steward* (Basso).
       MILLER, *a retired soldier* (Basso).
       LUISA, *his daughter* (Soprano).
       LAURA, *a peasant girl* (Contralto).
       Ladies, Pages, Archers, Servants, Villagers.

ARGUMENT   A morbid tale set to melodious music.   The sub-
           titles originally given the opera outline its gloomy
trend.   The plot ends in stark tragedy.   A tenor aria, "Quando le sere
al placido," is well known.

Act I. Love   *Exterior of Miller's house.   Early morn.*   Rodolfo, son
             of the Count, incognito has been courting Luisa Miller,
daughter of an old soldier of humble station, and is loved in return.
Their love affair, however, is beset by difficulties.   Wurm, the Count's
servitor, is a rejected suitor of Luisa, and threatens revenge by telling
all.   Meanwhile, the Count himself has been planning to have his son
wed the widowed Duchess of Ostheim.   When Rodolfo defies him, the
Count in a rage threatens to imprison both Luisa and her father; but is
deterred by his son's threat to reveal a past crime on his father's part.

Act II. Intrigue   *Interior of Miller's house.*   Despite Rodolfo's
                  threat, old Miller is put in prison by the Count's
orders.   Luisa is then told that in order to save her father's life she must
write a letter avowing that she has never really loved Rodolfo, but only
wanted his wealth and station; and that she is ready to flee with Wurm.
Rodolfo is deceived by this note and in both sorrow and anger says he is
ready to marry the Duchess.   He secretly resolves, nevertheless, to kill
both Luisa and himself.

Act III. Poison   *Same as Act II.*   Luisa likewise has determined on
                death, but Rodolfo forestalls her by paying her a
last visit and confronting her with the fatal letter.   Then he pours out
a drink, himself quaffs it, and offers it to her.   He then tells her that
both are facing death.   Feeling the effects of the poison creeping over
her, she tells him that death has released her from her promise; she can
tell all; she had written the letter at Wurm's instigation, to save her
father.   As the now reconciled lovers clasp each other despairingly, to

die together, Miller, the Count, Wurm and the villagers rush in to view the double tragedy with horror.   Luisa sinks in death.   Rodolfo with a last effort runs his sword through the body of Wurm before he dies.

RIGOLETTO
(Ree-go-let'-to)

Tragic Opera in Four Acts.   Music by Verdi.   Book by Francesco M. Piavé, after Hugo's "Le Roi S'amuse."   Fenice Theatre, Venice, March 11, 1851.   Two years later, at Covent Garden; New York, Academy of Music, November 4, 1857.   At the Metropolitan, November 17, 1883, with Sembrich as "Gilda."   A later performance at "the Met," November 23, 1903, is noteworthy as marking the début here of Enrico Caruso, as the Duke.   Sembrich again sang "Gilda," and Scotti, the Jester.

SCENE: Mantua.
TIME: The Sixteenth Century.

CAST   THE DUKE OF MANTUA (Tenor).
RIGOLETTO, *his jester and attendant* (Baritone).
GILDA, *daughter of Rigoletto* (Soprano).
COUNT MONTERONE (Basso).
COUNT CEPRANO (Baritone).
COUNTESS CEPRANO (Soprano).
SPARAFUCILE, *an assassin* (Basso).
MADDALENA, *his sister* (Mezzo-Soprano).
GIOVANNA, *friend of Maddalena* (Contralto).
BORSA, *a Courtier* (Tenor).
Officers, Courtiers, Ladies, Attendants, Servants.

ARGUMENT   "Rigoletto" is an intense tragedy of unbridled desires and retributive vengeance.   Based upon Hugo's powerful drama of medieval court life, "The King Amuses Himself," it is unrelieved by pleasant themes, but has been lastingly successful because of the closely knit plot and the brilliant music with which Verdi has invested it.   "Rigoletto" is remarkable in having been written at top speed, forty days, but is still ranked as one of the four best operas produced by Verdi and, after nearly a century of repertory, one of the Italian works most frequently presented.   Its quartet in the Fourth Act is of almost universal familiarity.   The brief overture sounds a warning note of tragedy in swift contrast to the opening scene.

Act I   *An Open Court in the Duke's Palace.*   The Duke of Mantua, one of the most profligate of rulers, devotes his leisure moments to the pursuit of ladies, and no house high or low is safe from his attentions. The courtiers are embittered, and especially so against Rigoletto, his jester and familiar, who aids him in these adventures. Rigoletto, though deformed, has a keen mind. His own daughter, a beautiful young girl, has been kept carefully hidden away (so he thinks). He can therefore laugh loudly with the Duke when the latter tells of having fallen in love with a fair face he has seen at church, and promises his master another rare adventure. At the same time the Duke is planning an intrigue with the Countess Ceprano. When he is warned by one of the courtiers that her husband might overhear him, he shrugs his shoulders indifferently. Here is heard the first of the tenor arias, as the Duke sings, " 'Mid the fair throng" (Questa o quella). A graceful minuet danced by the courtiers forms a foil for this ironic confession of the Duke's morals. The lively music is broken into by the sudden entrance of Count Monterone. His daughter, also, has fallen a victim to the Duke's lust. As he voices his grief and wrath, Rigoletto treats it as a great jest. Monterone, enraged, turns and hurls a father's curse against both. The Duke treats the matter lightly, but the jester cannot get the curse out of his mind.

Act II *A Secluded Street in Front of Rigoletto's House.* Still thinking of the curse, the jester has an interview with Sparafucile, a hired assassin, who promises to aid him. In a soliloquy cleverly outlined by the music, Rigoletto voices his shifting moods; first the Count's curse—"Yon assassin is my equal. He stabs in darkness—I in daylight" —then a note of scorn for the Duke and his own share in his amours— then an attempt at philosophy, to take things as they are. He is pleasantly interrupted by his daughter, Gilda, the joy of his heart, whom he guards jealously. She answers his questions as to her coming and going, but conceals from him the fact that she has seen a young man at church who has shown her marked attention. It was the Duke, posing as a student. He has found out where she lives, and his men are planning to abduct her this very night. No sooner has the jester gone than the Duke enters, his first greeting a soft melody, "Love in the sun." Meanwhile, Gilda has been singing to herself, "Ah, this is the dear voice!" She desires to know his name. He replies, "Walter." In an emotional duet they pledge their love and part. Alone again, she sings one of the best-known of Italian arias, "Dearest name" (Caro nome)—

Even while she muses tenderly of him, the Duke has put his nefarious plot into action, and his men do not spare his jester.   They think that Gilda is his mistress, and encountering him in the street plan a trick at his expense.   He is informed that they are after the Countess Ceprano, and he is to accompany them blindfolded.   He agrees, and while blinded they place a scaling-ladder against his own house and carry off Gilda.   He discovers the ruse too late to rescue her, and again remembers the curse.

Act III   *An Apartment in the Palace*.   When the curtain rises, the Duke is brooding because he thinks his plot has failed.   He had returned to the jester's home, only to find his bird had flown.   He laments his loss in a very effective song, "Each tear that falls" (Parmi veder le lagrime).   Then his fellow conspirators enter to reassure him. In a lively, amusing chorus they relate the night's adventures, where they have stolen Rigoletto's "mistress"—"On mischief bent" (Scorrendo). The Duke joins in their merriment and goes at once to meet his new sweetheart.   Now ensues one of the most dramatic bits of this or any other opera.   Rigoletto comes to the palace to rescue Gilda, but is prevented from reaching the Duke by the laughing courtiers.   At first he disguises his gnawing anxiety by an airy "Tra-la-la," meanwhile seeking a device to get past them.   When he finds he cannot succeed, he turns upon them in a rage: "Race of courtiers, vile rabble detested!" Then in an agony of despair: "She is my daughter.   Oh, my lords! Will you not have compassion?"   His pleas fall on deaf ears; they have grown hardened to abductions.   At the height of their merriment and his despair, Gilda rushes in.   The others retire, leaving father and daughter alone.   His worst fears have been realized.   She has been dishonored.   Monterone passes by, and Rigoletto tells him his curse has been effective.   "Not so," says Monterone: "the Duke is still happy!" "I join you in vengeance against him!" exclaims Rigoletto.

Act IV   *A Retired Street*.   Rigoletto shudders to learn that Gilda still loves the Duke and would shield him from vengeance.   He therefore hastens to the home of the murderer, Sparafucile, and bargains with him that he shall slay the first person who enters the house, regardless of whom it may be.   The bandit agrees.   The jester then lures the Duke to the house by means of the bandit's sister, Maddalena. The fickle Duke is ready for another adventure.   In his famous aria he charges womankind with his own failing: "All women are fickle" (La donna è mobile)—

Gilda and her father outside the house listen to the flirtation going on between Maddalena and the Duke. Gilda is loath to believe her lover faithless, despite the evidence of her ears. Then comes the wonderful quartet—the voice of the Duke: "Fairest daughter of the graces"; Maddalena's coquettish: "All you say is but to flatter"; Gilda's tearful: "Ah, to speak of love thus lightly"; and Rigoletto's stern reproof: "Silence! Thy tears avail thee naught." (Bella figlia)—

First Theme

Second Theme

The singing over, Sparafucile comes out to get half his fee for killing the Duke. Rigoletto gives it to him, but has meanwhile ordered his daughter to leave the city. Instead, she continues to linger near the house. The Duke has gone upstairs to sleep, while Maddalena pleads with her father to spare him. The rising storm gathers in intensity. The assassin, who has been drinking deeply, stabs Gilda, who in boy's clothes has come to impersonate her recreant lover, and places her body in a sack. Rigoletto comes to claim the remains of his victim, but while gloating over his vengeance he opens the sack only to find the corpse of his beloved Gilda. "Ah, the curse!" he cries.

IL TROVATORE

(Eel Troh'-vah-toh'-ray)

(The Troubadour.) Romantic Opera in Four Acts. Music by Verdi. Book by Salvatore Cammerano after a Spanish drama by Gatteerez. Apollo Theatre, Rome, January 19, 1853. At Covent Garden in 1855, and, a year later in English, as "The Gypsy's Vengeance" at Drury Lane, London.   In Philadelphia, in 1856; and at the Academy of Music, New York, February 25, 1857.   At the Metropolitan, 1888.

SCENE: Biscay and Aragon.
TIME: The Fifteenth Century.

CAST   COUNT DI LUNA (Baritone).
       COUNTESS LEONORA (Soprano).
       AZUCENA, a Gypsy (Contralto).
       MANRICO, the Count's brother, a wandering troubadour (Tenor).
       FERRANDO, servant of the Count (Basso).
       INEZ, friend of Leonora (Soprano).
       RUIZ, a Gypsy (Tenor).
       Gypsies, Gentlemen, Ladies, Servants.

ARGUMENT   "Il Trovatore" is the romantic tragedy of a high-born child kidnapped by Gypsies—to this extent a parallel with "The Bohemian Girl."   Its tragic denouement, which seems forced, does not detract from the brilliant color of its scenes or the pleasing quality of its music. In fact, "Il Trovatore" may be said to have succeeded in spite of its plot, which has been called "jumbled" and "absurd."   A great deal of the action is supposed to have taken place before the first curtain, being narrated by Captain Ferrando in the opening scene; but unless one understands Italian, it would go over the heads of many in the audience.   This is his tale: The former Count di Luna had two sons.   In their childhood the younger one, an infant, was stolen from its cradle by an old Gypsy woman, who was caught and burned at the stake.   Her daughter, Azucena, had seized the child and at first intended to kill it for vengeance, but, instead, slew her own infant and brought the Count's son up as her own.   When the stage action begins, this son grown to manhood is a leader of the Gypsies, known as Manrico the Troubadour.

As for the music it has been so perennially popular that it is as widely known, whistled and sung by non-opera-goers, as by the elect.   Who does not know the "Anvil Chorus" or the "Miserere"?

One further word—each of the Four Acts has been given a title: I, "The Duel"; II, "The Gypsy"; III, "The Gypsy's Son"; and IV, "The Penalty."

Act I   *Scene 1.   Interior of the Count's Castle.*   The present Count di Luna is in ignorance of the fact that his younger brother still

lives.   The story of the kidnapping is related by Ferrando in a ballad,
"The Gypsy Hag sat there."   His melodious story and the chorus of
horrified listeners form a good prelude of what is in store.

Scene 2.   Balcony of the Castle.   The Countess Leonora has become
enamoured of a minstrel, who comes nightly to sing beneath her window.   She describes her sensations in a lovely aria, "Peaceful was the
night."

While awaiting his appearance one evening, Count di Luna, also a
suitor, arrives and she mistakes him for the minstrel.   The surprise is
general a few moments later when Manrico appears.   The two men
quarrel and cross swords.   Manrico is wounded, but escapes before the
Count can summon his attendants.

Act II *Scene 1.   A Gypsy Camp.*   Manrico is being nursed back to
        health by Azucena, his supposed mother.   She confesses to
him that she is not his real mother, but refuses to tell anything more.
Ruiz, Manrico's follower, brings word that Leonora, believing him
dead, is about to take the veil in order to escape from the Count, and
that the latter is pursuing her with his soldiers.   Manrico dons his
armor and despite his weakened condition hurries to the rescue.

The music in this scene strikes the high note of the work.   The opening chorus, a lusty song to the rhythm of beats upon the anvils, tells
of the joys of Gypsy life and especially of their maidens: "Who cheers
the life of the roving Gypsy?" (Anvil Chorus)—

Azucena's wild song, "Upward roll the flames," (Stride la vampa) is almost equally famous:

Scene 2.   A Convent.   It is the day when Leonora is to take the veil. Di Luna is encamped without, to prevent her from doing this.   The nuns march slowly by singing, with Leonora among them.   Di Luna attempts to abduct her, but is in turn surprised by Manrico and his band, who now rush in.   The Count's forces are outnumbered and he is compelled to withdraw.   Leonora is overjoyed to find her lover alive, and renounces the veil in his favor.

Di Luna's song, "The radiant gleaming of her smile," is so engaging that one is tempted to sympathize with him.   The chorus of nuns within is also effective: "Ah, when the shades of night!"

Act III   *Scene 1.*   *The Camp of Di Luna.*   The Count has captured Azucena, and is overjoyed to learn that she is his rival's reputed mother.   Ferrando charges her with having murdered the Count's brother.   She denies it stoutly, but will say nothing more, and the Count orders her to the torture chamber.

Scene 2.   *The Convent.*   Preparations are forward for the marriage of Leonora and Manrico, but before the ceremony occurs, Ruiz enters with the tidings that Azucena is in the Count's power and about to be tortured.   Manrico is loyal to his foster mother, and at once sets forth to rescue her, bidding his tearful bride-to-be a hasty farewell.

Manrico's lyrical address to Leonora, in which he tries to quiet her alarm, "Oh, come, let links eternal," a rich melody, is followed by his still more famous challenge to his enemies: "Tremble, ye tyrants!"

Act IV   *Scene 1.*   *Outside the Prison Tower.*   This time the Count's men are too strong for Manrico, and he is overpowered and made prisoner.   The Count condemns him to death as an outlaw, and he is shut within the fatal tower.   Leonora, on the outside, hears the mournful strains of the Miserere, or death chant, and her voice forms an obligatto:

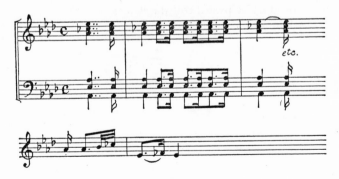

As the solemn strains peal forth, one can also hear the heartbroken cry
of Leonora, while rising above it the farewell of Manrico in the tower:
"Ah, how death still delayeth!" (Ah, che la morte!)—

These climactic passages alone would make the opera famous. Leonora pleads with the Count, who now enters, to spare the life of her
lover, and finally in desperation offers herself to him for this boon.
The Count agrees to sign a reprieve on these terms, and Leonora fur-
tively drinks poison to avoid becoming his victim.

Scene 2. Within the Prison. Azucena, worn and exhausted, lies
upon a pallet in troubled sleep. Manrico watches over her, awaiting
his own summons to the block. This is a final, highly effective musical
scene between the two, when he attempts to comfort her and their voices
join in still another unforgettable duet: "Home to our mountains" (Ai
nostri monti).

The door opens and Leonora, wild-eyed and panting, rushes in to
bid him save himself. He at once suspects that she has sold herself for
him, but sees the whole of her sacrifice as she falls dying. The Count
arrives to find his triumph short-lived, and in a rage orders Manrico at
once to execution. As the blow of the headsman is heard, the dying
Gypsy rises up on an elbow. To the Count's triumphant cry, "It is
ended!" she replies: "Your victim was your own brother!"—then:
"Mother, you are avenged!"—and falls back dead. The Count, horrified at his act, exclaims: "And I still live!"

LA TRAVIATA
(Lah Trah-vee-ah'-tah)

(The Castaway.) Lyric Opera in Three Acts. Music by Verdi.
Book by Francesco M. Piavé, based upon "La Dame Aux Camellias"
(Camille), by Alexandre Dumas, the younger. Fenice Theatre, Venice,
March 6, 1853. New York, 1856, and in 1883 at the Metropolitan, with
Sembrich as "Violetta." Also, in 1883, at the Academy of Music, with
Patti.

    SCENE: Paris.
    TIME: Nineteenth Century.

CAST VIOLETTA VALERY, *a frivolous woman* (Soprano).
FLORA BELOIX, *of her set* (Soprano).
ANNINA, *a servant* (Contralto).
ALFRED GERMONT, *a young Parisian* (Tenor).
GERMONT SENIOR, *his father* (Baritone).
GASTON DE LETORIÈRES, *a Parisian* (Tenor).
BARON DOUPHAL, *a Parisian* (Baritone).
MARQUIS D'ORBIGNY, *a Parisian* (Baritone).
DR. GRENVIL, *a physician* (Basso).
JOSEPH, *a servant* (Baritone).
Members of the gay set, Servants, etc.

ARGUMENT "La Traviata" follows closely the story of "Camille" which tells of the awakening of a pure love in an abandoned woman's heart. Dumas' story is a picture of modern Parisian life; but the Italian libretto harks back to the days of Louis XIV. When first produced the opera was a failure, but on its revival with some changes, a year later, it became a pronounced success and ever since has ranked high in popularity among works of this Italian school. The overture is of soft and tender nature with strings predominating and a theme similar to the prelude which precedes the death of Violetta, in the last Act.

Act I *Banquet Room in Violetta's Paris Mansion.* Violetta Valery, one of the most beautiful and noted of the Parisian demi-monde, gives a supper party to some of her set. Her latest conquest, Alfred Germont, is present, and finds himself taking a strange interest in this talented but dissolute woman. He questions her about her past life, while the guests revel in this and an adjoining ballroom. The woman who has dallied with love all her life finds her better nature awakened by his interest and sympathy, and agrees to leave her folly and devote herself to him alone.

A jovial drinking song by Alfred, in which Violetta and her guests join, is an early feature. Then comes an avowal of love by him, and a response by her, culminating in the duet, "Rapturous Moment" (Un di felice). After her guests have gone, Violetta soliloquizes in two well-known melodies, the first a realization of dawning love: "The one of whom I've dreamed" (Ah, fors' è lui); the other a brilliant coloratura: "What folly! For me there's no returning" (Sempre libera)—

Act II *Scene 1. A Villa near Paris.* True to her word, Violetta retires from Paris and lives quietly but happily with Alfred in a little country place. Their money is spent freely and carelessly, and from time to time Annita, Violetta's maid, goes to Paris, whence she returns with fresh funds. Alfred finally learns from the girl that she has been disposing of all her mistress' property piecemeal in order to run this establishment. For the first time Alfred realizes his true position, and rushes off to the city to raise funds by his own efforts. While he is gone his father, who has just discovered this retreat, arrives to upbraid Violetta for leading on his son in a spendthrift and dissolute life. She smiles scornfully at this charge; but when Germont goes on to say that it is wrecking the young man's chances and also preventing the marriage of his sister, she begins to realize that perhaps she is standing in his way. The music mirrors the intensity of this dramatic scene. Germont's plea, in which he describes his daughter, "Pure as an angel," is followed by Violetta's, "Say to her that one unhappy heart has perished." She finds that the noblest love is unselfish and self-sacrificing, and she proves that this is the quality of her love for Alfred by promising to give him up. Penning a hasty note of farewell, she returns to her old life in the city. When Alfred returns, he pays no heed to the note or to his father's explanations, but hastens back to the city with rage and grief in his heart. His father's attempts to console Alfred and reclaim him to his former life are voiced in the familiar aria, "Thy home in fair Provence."

Scene 2. Flora's Apartments. Another scene of revelry is at its height in the mansion of one of Violetta's friends. A troupe of Gypsy women dance a lively ballet, while they sing, "We're Gypsies gay and youthful." Another group in Spanish costume sing of the matadors. Violetta enters upon the arm of Baron Douphal. Here Alfred finds her. He begins gambling recklessly and soon wins heavy stakes from the Baron. Alfred then upbraids Violetta for leaving him, and implores her to return. She refuses, though giving no explanation of her apparent faithlessness, and Alfred in anger hurls his winnings at her feet, calling them all to witness that he has paid her in full. The Baron interposes, and the two quarrel and challenge each other. Alfred's father now arrives and, chiding his son for his conduct, leads him away. The closing song in this climactic scene is Violetta's despairing, "Alfred, Alfred! Little canst thou fathom the love in my heart!"

Act III *Violetta's Bedchamber.* The pensive quality of the overture is again reflected in the prelude by the orchestra which heralds the rise of the last curtain. It foreshadows the fate which is overtaking the "castaway." Violetta is paying for her former gay life by suffering from tuberculosis and now with hope of a happy love gone, she sinks rapidly. She pines for Alfred, but will not send for him. As she senses the approach of death she sings the aria of haunting loveliness, "Farewell, bright vision!" (Addio del passato) —

Her grief is turned to joy when Annita comes with the tidings that Alfred is on his way to visit her. He has learned of her sacrifice. In the haven of his arms they sing of a new life together: "We shall fly from Paris, beloved" (Parigi, o cara)—

But their happiness comes too late. The doctor arrives with Alfred's father, the latter contrite as he witnesses this tragedy. Sorrowful but helpless, the little group stand about her bedside as the soul of Traviata takes its flight.

SIMON BOCCANEGRA

(See-mon Bo-kan-nay'-grah)

Tragic Opera in Prologue and Three Acts. Music by Verdi. Book by F. M. Piavé and A. Boïto. La Fenice, March 12, 1857. In a revision at Milan, March 24, 1881. At New York, the Metropolitan, January 28, 1932, with Tibbett, as "Simon," and Martinelli, as "Gabriele."

SCENE: Genoa.
TIME: Fourteenth Century.

CAST SIMON BOCCANEGRA, *Corsair, the Doge* (Baritone).
JACOPO FIESCO, *Nobleman* (Basso).
PAOLO ALBIANI, *Goldsmith* (Basso).
PIETRO, *a Follower and Courtier* (Baritone).
GABRIELE ADORNO, *Nobleman* (Tenor).
MARIA BOCCANEGRA, *Daughter of Simon, known as*
    Amelia Grimaldi (Soprano).
MAIDSERVANT (Mezzo-Soprano).

CAPTAIN OF THE GUARD (Tenor).
Soldiers, Seamen, Commoners, Senators, Courtiers, Servants, etc.

ARGUMENT   A tale of personal enmity and intrigue based upon the struggle between the Guelphs and the Ghibellines in northern Italy, in the middle of the Fourteenth Century.

Prologue   *A Public Square in Genoa.*   Paolo and Pietro, two ambitious citizens, are discovered perfecting a plot to elevate Simon Boccanegra to the Doge's throne.   Simon has formerly been a corsair, but has extended the sea power of Genoa and therefore won a wide following.   He has also had a secret union with Maria, daughter of Fiesco, a nobleman, and a daughter is the result.   Simon now consents to the plot as a means of getting possession of Maria and their child. He confronts Fiesco with a plea for this recognition, but the haughty lord spurns him.   Maria dies soon after, and their child disappears. While the populace hail Simon as their new Doge, he is grief-stricken.

Act I   *Scene 1.   The Grimaldi Garden.*   Twenty-five years elapse. Simon's daughter has been living under the assumed name of Amelia Grimaldi, as the ward of Fiesco.   The latter, however, does not know her true name.   The nobleman has never relinquished his enmity for Simon and is secretly plotting to overthrow him.   One of his aides is the young Guelph, Gabriele Adorno, who has fallen in love with, and is loved by, Amelia.   The Doge himself pays her a visit and learns by accident that she is his long-lost daughter.   The two are overjoyed at the reunion; but Paolo, who is also in love with her, plots to abduct her.
Scene 2.   The Council Chamber.   While the Doge is busy with affairs of state, a riot is fomenting in the streets of Genoa.   Amelia has been carried off, and Gabriele is led to believe that the Doge himself is guilty.   With a band of followers he dashes into the Council Chamber and tries to stab Simon, but Amelia enters at this moment and throws herself between them.   The Doge by his dignity awes the crowd, and Paolo, the real culprit, is forced to repeat a curse upon the head of the scoundrel—himself.

Act II   *Doge's Chambers in Ducal Palace.*   Both Adorno and Fiesco are being kept as political prisoners.   Paolo, now plotting against his master, pours poison into his cup; then unlocks the cells in which the two prisoners are confined and seeks to enlist them in his own nefarious projects.   He tells Gabriele that the Doge has evil designs upon Amelia and that the latter loves him.   When Amelia enters,

Gabriele accuses her of this.   She admits it, but says their love is without sin.   As Simon nears the room, she conceals Gabriele and then
pleads for his life.   He grants her prayer on learning of her love for
Gabriele, then dismisses her, wearied by all these conflicting interests.
He drinks of the poisoned cup and falls into a stupor.   Adorno comes
from his hiding place and is about to kill him, when Amelia again saves
her father from his vengeance.   She tells the young man that the Doge
is her father; and Gabriele begs forgiveness and says that henceforth he
will fight at Simon's side.

Act III   *Interior of Palace Court, with view of City.*   The last Guelph
        uprising has been quelled and voices again hail the Doge.
Fiesco is given amnesty, and Paolo is sentenced to death.   On his way to
execution he confesses to Fiesco that it was he who abducted Amelia,
and that even now the poison he gave her father is taking effect.   Fiesco,
a prey to conflicting emotions, watches his lifelong enemy, the Doge,
totter feebly to his chair.   But when the lord learns at last that Amelia
is his own granddaughter he is stricken with remorse.   She now enters
with Gabriele, and with his failing breath the dying Doge gives them
his blessing.

Memorable music: the aria, "Il lacerato spirito," and the quartets,
"Figlia tal nome palpita" and "Piangi su voi."

UN BALLO IN MASCHERA

(The Masked Ball.)   Tragic Opera in Three Acts.   Music by Verdi.
Book by Somma, based on Scribe's libretto for an opera by Auber.
Apollo Theatre, Rome, February 17, 1859.   At New York, the Metro-
politan, in 1889.

SCENE: Naples.
TIME: The Eighteenth Century.

CAST   RICCARDO, *Duke of Olivares and Governor of*
        Naples (Tenor).
        AMELIA (Soprano).
        RENATO, *secretary to the Governor and husband*
        of Amelia (Baritone).
        SAMUEL } *Enemies of the Governor* { (Basso).
        TOMMASO } { (Basso).
        SILVAN, *a sailor* (Soprano).
        EDGARDO, *a page* (Soprano).

ULRICA, *a fortuneteller* (Contralto).
A Judge, a Servant of Amelia, Populace,
Guards, etc., Conspirators, Maskers, and
Dancers.

ARGUMENT   For political reasons, the scene of this opera was
first laid in Boston, but with these reasons re-
moved, the scene shifts more logically back to Italy, as librettist and
composer originally intended.

Act I   *Scene 1.   Reception Hall in the Governor's House.*   Riccardo,
the Governor, is popular with the people, but detested by the
nobility, who plan to get rid of him.   When the action begins, the Governor is giving a public audience.   He is shown a list of guests to be
invited to a masked ball; and notes with satisfaction the name of Amelia,
who is the wife of his secretary.   During the audience, a judge is announced, who brings in for signature a warrant against an aged Negress,
who is said to be a sorceress.

Scene 2.   Ulrica's Hut.   Before signing a decree of banishment
against the Negress, Ulrica, the Governor decides to pay her a secret
visit and test her powers of divination.   He goes in disguise, followed
by two of his enemies, Samuel and Tommaso.   Unknown to him,
Amelia has also come on a visit, and, concealed behind a curtain, he
hears her confess to the fortune-teller her sinful love for himself, and
implore aid to conquer it.   The sybil tells her to pluck a magic herb
which grows beneath the gallows tree.   Amelia shudders but consents.
Riccardo is secretly overjoyed at her confession, and resolves to protect
her on her quest.   After she departs he asks to have his own fortune
told.   Ulrica predicts that he will be slain by a friend—the first one
that shall shake him by the hand.   At this moment his faithful secretary, Renato, enters and greets him with a handshake.   Riccardo laughs
at the prophecy.

Outstanding musical numbers in this Act are: the chorus in praise
of the Governor, "Our welfare is his sole desire"; and the barcarolle by
the disguised sailor, Riccardo, "Declare if the waves will faithfully
bear me."

Act II   *Midnight, beside the Gallows.*   Amelia, deeply veiled, comes
to pluck the magic herb.   The Governor arrives to protect
her.   Amelia is unable to conceal her love for him.   But during their
rendezvous a third person approaches.   It is Renato.   Concern for his
master has called him to the spot.   The conspirators also are lying in
wait near by.   Riccardo exacts from Renato a promise to escort back
to the city the veiled lady, without making an attempt to learn who she

is, while he himself returns by another path. Renato and his companion fall into the hands of the conspirators. The latter do not harm the secretary, but want at least to learn who the Governor's sweetheart is. They lift the veil and Renato sees his own wife. Rage seizes him, and he bids the leaders of the conspiracy meet him at his house the following morning.

It is at the opening of this Act that Amelia sings one of the best known arias, "When at last from its stem I shall sever."

Act III *Scene 1. Room in Renato's House.* Believing his wife guilty, Renato bids her prepare for death. He listens to her pleas and allows her to tell her little son farewell. He finally determines not to slay her, but to wreak vengeance instead upon Riccardo. During her brief absence the conspirators arrive, and they decide that the slayer of Riccardo shall be determined by lot. On Amelia's return she is instructed to draw a name from among others in an urn. Not knowing its purport, she draws her husband's name.

Renato's change of heart is finely shown in his song, "Is it thou?" (Eri tu che macchiavi.)

Scene 2. A Ballroom in the Palace. This festive scene, which gives the opera its name, reveals the revelry of a masked ball. The gay music is itself a mask for the impending tragedy, just as the costumes lend their aid to the conspirators. Riccardo has come to the party despite Amelia's warnings. He has determined to send Renato and his wife abroad on a diplomatic mission, and thus remove temptation from his own path. He informs Amelia of this purpose, but while they talk, Renato again surprises them and plunges his dagger in the Governor's breast. With his dying breath the latter pardons his misguided friend, assures him of his wife's innocence, and tells him of his own intentions now frustrated by death. He begs that no one will seek to avenge him. A crash of music contrasting these conflicting emotions brings the final curtain.

LA FORZA DEL DESTINO
(Lah Fort-zah del Des-tee'-no)

(The Force of Destiny.) Tragic Opera in Four Acts. Music by Verdi. Book by Francesco M. Piavé, based on the play "Don Alvaro," by the Duke of Rivas. St. Petersburg, November 10, 1862. At New York, the Metropolitan, November 15, 1918, marking the début of Rosa Ponselle; also in the cast were Caruso, De Luca, and Mardones.

SCENE: Spain and Italy.
TIME: End of the Eighteenth Century.

CAST The Marquis of Calatrava (Basso).
Donna Leonora, *his daughter* (Soprano.)
Don Carlos di Vargas, *his son* (Baritone).
Don Alvaro, *a gallant* (Tenor).
Preziosilla, *a Gypsy maiden* (Soprano).
Padre Guardiano ⎫*Franciscan Friars*⎧(Baritone).
Fra Melitone ⎭⎩(Baritone).
Curra, *maid to Leonora* (Soprano).
Mastro Trabuco, *a peddler* (Baritone).
A Magistrate, a Surgeon, Muleteers, Peasants, Soldiers, Friars, etc.

ARGUMENT A tragedy of involved plot, in which the motifs of deception, revenge, and magnanimity alternate. They are illustrated by a musical setting of great flexibility.

Act I *Home of the Marquis, Seville.* Leonora, the dearly beloved daughter of the Marquis of Calatrava, has hidden from her father the fact that she has a lover, Don Alvaro. Knowing that her father will not consent to their nuptials, because Alvaro is suspected of being of mixed blood, she agrees to elope with her knight. But just at the moment when the couple are escaping, the Marquis enters. A stormy scene ensues, and he is slain by the accidental discharge of Alvaro's pistol.

Act II *Scene 1. A Village Inn.* Leonora dons male attire and stops at a village inn on her way to the mountains, whither she is fleeing. Her brother, Don Carlos, has sworn to avenge his father's death, and to hunt the wide world over until he finds the guilty pair.
Scene 2. Exterior of a Cloister. Leonora finally reaches a secluded church and, still in male disguise, becomes a recluse. She is protected by Father Guardiano, to whom she tells her story.

Act III *A Wood in Italy, near Velletri.* Don Carlos and Don Alvaro, under assumed names and unknown to each other, are serving in Italy. The former is saved from assassination by the latter, and they vow a lasting friendship. Soon after this Alvaro is wounded in battle, and Carlos discovers, from a portrait of Leonora in his friend's possession, that he is none other than his sister's lover, and the slayer of his father. They fight, but are separated by soldiers. Alvaro announces his intention of entering a monastery.

Act IV *A Monastery.* As Father Raffaello, Alvaro enters a monastery near the cloister where Leonora dwells. Don Carlos, however, follows him and again compels him to draw his sword. Carlos falls, this time mortally wounded.   Leonora enters at this moment, and the three recognize each other.   The dying man asks his sister to embrace him before he dies, and seizes this opportunity to stab her.   Leonora pardons Alvaro with her last breath, and he falls weeping and penitent at her feet.

(In another version of this opera, a final scene is appended, in which Alvaro casts himself from a precipice.)

This opera also has an abundance of good music, too seldom heard: the soprano aria, "Madre, pietosa Vergine"; the duet, "La Vergine degli angeli"; and the tenor arias (sung at various times by Caruso, Martinelli, and Gigli) "O tu che in seno agli angeli," "Solenne in quest ora," and "Sleale! il segreto!"

DON CARLOS

Tragic Opera in Four Acts.   Music by Verdi.   Book by Mery and Du Locle, after the tragedy by Schiller.   Grand Opera, Paris, March 11, 1867.   "Revived" to open the Metropolitan season, as "Don Carlo," November 6, 1950.

SCENE: Spain.
TIME: The Sixteenth Century.

CAST   PHILIP II OF SPAIN (Basso).
DON CARLOS, *his son* (Tenor).
RODRIGO, *Marquis de Posa* (Baritone).
GRAND INQUISITOR (BASSO).
ELIZABETH DE VALOIS, *the Queen; also stepmother of Don Carlos* (Soprano).
PRINCESS EBOLI (Soprano).

ARGUMENT   "Don Carlos" is scarcely remembered today; within five years it was to be completely eclipsed by Verdi's masterpiece, "Aida."   Indeed, it is hard to realize that the two works are by the same composer; yet the "Don" contains some fine passages.   Its scene is laid in Spain in the time of Philip II.

Act I   *Convent of St. Just.*   Don Carlos, the heir apparent to the Spanish throne, has long been enamored of Elizabeth de Valois; but for reasons of state her hand is bestowed upon Don Carlos' father, King Philip.   While the Prince is bewailing his hopeless passion, his friend Rodrigo counsels him to be prudent and seek solace in a foreign country.   He resolves to go on a mission to Flanders, but in an interview with the Queen he again breaks down and declares his love.

Elizabeth reproaches him. The King enters and misunderstands the situation. He charges Rodrigo, his favorite, to keep a watch over the Queen.

Act II *Royal Gardens of Madrid.* In a masked fête, Don Carlos sees a lady whom he mistakes for the Queen, and pours out his tale of love again. The lady, however, proves to be the Princess Eboli, who has been secretly in love with the Prince, and she now turns her thoughts to revenge. She gets possession of a casket from the Queen, containing the Prince's portrait, and shows it to the King. The latter finds a pretext, in the religious wars, to throw his son into prison.

Act III *Scene 1. The Queen's Apartment.* Elizabeth searches for her casket, and is accused of infidelity by the King. She is at a loss to explain matters until the Princess Eboli comes to her rescue and confesses her share in the intrigue. The Queen's innocence is proved, and the Princess is banished from court.

Scene 2. A Prison Cell. While the Prince languishes in prison, he is visited by his friend Rodrigo, who had taken his sword away from him on his arrest. Rodrigo tells Don Carlos that this measure was for the Prince's protection. Meanwhile he himself has taken the blame for the uprising in Flanders, and soon pays the penalty for this pious fraud. He is shot by order of the King. When the latter comes to the prison to return his sword to Don Carlos, the latter turns from him, and tells him he has put an innocent man to death.

Act IV *Convent of St. Just.* Once again the Prince seeks an interview with Elizabeth, and again she meets him, but actuated only by lofty motives. The jealous King again surprises them, and, yielding to the counsel of the Grand Inquisitor, he consigns his son to the tender mercies of the Inquisition.

Best musical numbers: a duet (made famous by Caruso and Scotti) "Dio, che nell' alma infondere"; an aria for contraltos, "O don fatale"; two for bassos, "Ella giammai m'amo" and "Domiro sol nel manto mio regal"; and two for baritones, "Per me giunto" and "O, Carlo, ascolta!"

AIDA

(Ah-ee'-dah)

Romantic Opera in Four Acts. Music by Giuseppe Verdi. Book by Antonio Ghislanzoni, from the French of Camille du Locle. Written for the Khedive of Egypt, and first produced at Cairo, December 24, 1871. In La Scala, Milan, with Verdi conducting, February 8, 1872. At the Academy of Music, New York, November 26, 1873; and, in 1883, with Patti as "Aida."   At the Metropolitan, November 12, 1886, in German.

SCENE: Memphis and Thebes.
TIME: Rule of the Pharaohs.

CAST   THE KING OF EGYPT (Basso).
AMNERIS, *his daughter* (Contralto).
RHADAMES, *a General* (Tenor).
RAMFIS, *the High Priest* (Basso).
AMONASRO, *the King of Ethiopia* (Baritone).
AIDA, *his daughter, a slave* (Soprano).
Soldiers, Courtiers, Citizens, Tire-women, Dancers, etc.

ARGUMENT   "Aida" is considered Verdi's masterpiece, and one of the most brilliant of all operas.   It has remained continuously in favor with the public.   The story, which is full of color, has an ancient Egyptian setting, being a romance woven around a beautiful slave girl, who later proves to be the daughter of a rival king.

Musically the work is of interest as being the first example of Verdi's "mature" style.   It has been likened to the Wagnerian operas in theme and treatment.   This is not exact as it is still of the more florid Italian school, but of more modern pattern.   Verdi was here again exhibiting his great versatility.   After a brief prelude which gives only a hint of the chief motifs, the curtain rises and the reader is transported back to ancient Egypt.

Act I   *Scene 1.   Interior of the Egyptian King's Palace, at Memphis.*
The High Priest, Ramfis, delights the warrior, Rhadames, by informing him that Isis, the goddess, has decreed that he shall lead the army against the warring Ethiopians.   Rhadames is madly in love with Aida, the slave, and sees in this prospective victory an opportunity to obtain her from the King as his bride.   He gives vent to his passion in that magnificent aria beloved of all tenors, "Heavenly Aida" (Celeste Aida).   The first soaring notes:

lead up to the climactic phrase:

His outpourings, however, are interrupted by the entrance of Amneris, the King's daughter, who has long loved the young soldier. As he is cold to her, she begins to suspect the truth, and she jealously watches Rhadames and Aida, when the slave appears. The King and his court enter, and Rhadames is formally invested with the command against the Ethiopians, who have advanced upon Thebes. All rejoice except Aida, who knows secretly that her lover is to meet her father, the rival king, in battle, and that one of them must fall. As the multitude give a great shout of farewell, "Return victorious!"

she expresses her conflicting emotions in the long and difficult aria containing her tender prayer:

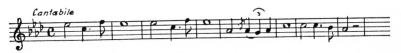

Scene 2. The Temple of Ptah. Ptah is the war god of Egypt, and this short scene is occupied with the consecration of the arms of Rhadames. The music is of solemn character, the prayer of Ramfis, "God, guardian and avenger," being a dominant note.

Act II *Scene 1. The Apartments of Amneris.* By sharp contrast we next look into the luxury of a Princess' rooms. Slave girls sing in praise of their mistress, and a Moorish ballet follows. Some weeks have passed, and Amneris with the rest of the court has heard that Rhadames is returning victorious from war, and, desirous of winning him by her charms, she orders her women to deck her in her finest. Aida enters, and Amneris tricks her into revealing her love for the general by falsely announcing that he has fallen in battle. When Aida's grief betrays her secret, Amneris scorns her.

Scene 2. The Entrance to Thebes. Pharaoh summons his whole glittering court to do honor to his conquering general. The troops enter in formal review, and Rhadames is borne in, in triumph, on the shoulders of slaves. This superb scene where oriental color and display unite with the swelling strains of triumph is the "grand moment" of the opera, and it is a case-hardened auditor indeed who can listen

and watch unmoved.   The triumphal march in which one set of instruments after another takes up the strain: "Glory to Egypt!"

is succeeded by the shouts of the multitude (Chorus of Triumph):

The procession halts at the foot of the throne.   Pharaoh himself comes
down to greet his general and escort him up the steps to a place at his
right hand.   Amneris presents him with a crown signifying her own
desires and as she glances meaningly at her father, he asks Rhadames to
name his own reward.   The captives of war are brought forward, and
the populace demand that they be put to death.   Aida recognizes the
conquered King as her father, but he conceals his true rank.   Rhadames
now asks as his boon, that the lives of the captives may be spared.   The
King grants his request, and in addition bestows his daughter's hand
upon him and proclaims him heir to the throne.

Act III   *A Night Scene on the Nile.*   Amneris, accompanied by the
                High Priest, goes to pay her vows to Isis, on the evening be-
fore her marriage.   Aida follows secretly, to meet Rhadames for the
last time.   While she muses upon her own unhappy fate, another lovely
song emerges: "Oh, native land!" (Oh, patria mia!).   But instead of
seeing Rhadames, Amonasro, her father, suddenly presents himself.   In
a tumultuous scene he alternately reproaches her and urges her to aid
their country by betraying to him the next movements of the Egyptian
army.   This she will not consent to do.   They are interrupted by the
entrance of the young general and the mutual expressions of love are
voiced in an exotic duet: "In ectasy the world forgotten."   However,
in the course of their talk Rhadames tells her his next plans, and Amonasro in hiding overhears them.   The captive King now plays a bold

stroke by presenting himself to Rhadames in his true rank, and urging him to take sides with Ethiopia.   Aida's hand is pledged by way of reward.   Rhadames will not yield to the temptation, and while they parley Amneris comes from the Temple to denounce them.   Rhadames urges the father and daughter to flee, but himself remains to submit to the guards of Ramfis.

Act IV   *Scene 1.   Corridor in the Palace.*   Amneris has repented her
         action against Rhadames, and now seeks to save him.   She tells him that Aida's father was killed in the flight, but that Aida herself still lives.   If Rhadames will renounce her, Amneris says that she will obtain the pardon of Pharaoh.   Rhadames refuses, and the enraged Princess tells him to go to his doom.   But when the tribunal of priests decree that the soldier shall be entombed alive, as the penalty of his supposed treason, Amneris turns upon them in redoubled fury.

Scene 2.   Interior of the Temple, showing the crypt below.   While the priests and priestesses perform the ceremonial temple service above, Rhadames is seen in the shadowy vault, resigning himself to death. Aida now steals to his side.   She has come to die with him.   As he sings the tender aria, "To die, so pure and lovely," she replies with, "Ecstasy of immortal love."   Slowly the light recedes in the vault, in contrast to the lighted room above, where the penitent Princess vainly lifts her voice in prayer.   But below all is peace.   United in death the lovers sing a final duet of haunting loveliness: "Farewell, O earth! Farewell, thou vale of sorrow!   Now opens to us the sky!" (O, terra, addio!)

OTHELLO
(O-thel'-lo)

Music Drama in Four Acts.   Music by Giuseppe Verdi.   Book by Arrigo Boïto, after the play by Shakespeare.   La Scala Theatre, Milan, February 5, 1887.   A year later, at the Academy of Music, New York. At the Metropolitan, March 24, 1891, with Tamagno as "Othello," and Albani, as "Desdemona."

SCENE: Cyprus.
TIME: The Fifteenth Century.

CAST   OTHELLO, *a Moorish general in the service of Venice* (Tenor).

DESDEMONA, *his wife* (Soprano).
IAGO, *lieutenant to Othello* (Baritone).
EMILIA, *his wife* (Contralto).
CASSIUS, *lieutenant to Othello* (Tenor).
RODERIGO ⎱ *Venetian gentlemen* ⎰ (Tenor).
LODOVICO ⎰   ⎱ (Basso).
MONTANO, *former governor of Cyprus* (Basso).
Soldiers, Sailors, Citizens, Servants.

ARGUMENT The story of "Othello" closely follows Shakespeare's play of the same name, except that it
omits the first act of the play dealing with Desdemona's courtship and
marriage. This work followed "Aida" after an interval of nearly sixteen years, and when the composer had reached the age of seventy-four.
It astonished the musical world by the fire and continuity of its composition, no less than by Verdi's versatility. "Othello" is in the style of
the Wagnerian music-dramas.

Act I *Open Square at Cyprus.* Othello, a noble Moor in the service
of the Venetian state, has won the heart of Desdemona, a high-
born Venetian lady, and has brought her with him on his expedition to
Cyprus. The people welcome their arrival. Othello appoints Cassius
as his first lieutenant in command, which act enrages Iago against them
both. Iago is the servant and confidant of the general and had hoped
to win this place for himself. His scheming mind now launches far-
reaching plans of revenge. He succeeds in his first purpose of getting
Cassius drunk and embroiled in a quarrel with Montano, the retiring
governor. Othello enters at this moment—as Iago hoped he would—
and punishes Cassius by depriving him of the command.

Musical numbers in this Act include: Iago's drinking song, "Then
let us quaff the noble wine" (Inaffia l'ugola); and the love duet between
Desdemona and Othello, which she begins by the aria, "When thou
didst speak" (Quando narravi).

Act II *A Room in the Palace.* Iago next endeavors to poison the
mind of Othello against his lovely and virtuous wife. At first
Iago carefully drops hints and innuendoes, some of which, however,
stick. He now makes use of Cassius as a pawn in this game, pretending
friendship for him, and urging him to ask Desdemona to seek his pardon
and reinstatement. Cassius does so, and Iago makes capital of this
with the Moor. Othello finally becomes so suspicious that when his
wife comes to intercede for the lieutenant, he can see in this only evidences of her guilt. He rebuffs her angrily. Her handkerchief has

fallen, and Emilia, Iago's wife, picks it up; but Iago snatches it from her
and keeps it to bolster up his flimsy chain of evidence. When alone
with the Moor, he boldly charges Cassius with having had improper
relations with Desdemona, and states that she has given her lover a
handkerchief which will be found on his person. Othello vows vengeance against the pair.

In the early part of this Act is Iago's remarkable confession of his
cynical creed, known as "Credo," a notable baritone aria; and his great
duet with the indignant Othello, at its close: "Farewell, O sacred memories!" (Addio, sante memorie)—

Act III   *A Room in the Palace.*   Desdemona again intercedes for
             Cassius, but her very innocence leads to her undoing.
Othello sees in it only further confirmation of his suspicions. Cassius
is now led in by Iago. Othello conceals himself, and Iago gives the
harmless conversation such a turn as to make it appear in line with his
accusations. The handkerchief is, of course, found as Iago predicted
and arranged. Othello bursts into a torrent of rage, and as he confronts
his wife with the proofs of her "infidelity" some of the finest dramatic-
musical passages occur. Her tearful plea, "Upon my knees before thee"
(Esterrefatta fisso), only brings a scornful rejoinder from him. He finally hurls her to the floor and is only prevented from doing her further
harm by the arrival of an embassy from Venice. It brings the news
that he is deposed as governor, and Cassius has been appointed in his
place. When they depart, Othello commands Iago to slay Cassius, and
is himself wrought up to such a fury that he falls upon the floor. Their
mingled voices finally merge into an impassioned sextet. The Act
ends ironically with the shouts of the people outside: "Hail, Othello,
thou lion of Venice!"   "A fine lion!" sneers Iago.

Act IV   *Desdemona's Bedchamber.*   Desdemona sits weeping with
             Emilia. All her actions have been misjudged and she is in
terror of her life. Her pathetic narrative to her maid takes the form of
an old Italian folksong, "The Willow" (Salce, Salce)—

After Emilia leaves her, Desdemona intones a lovely "Ave Maria" and then retires. Othello enters and roughly bids her prepare to die. She pleads, but he is obdurate. He suffocates her. Emilia rushes in, but too late to save her mistress' life. She alarms the palace and then reveals to Othello the whole extent of Iago's infamy, stating that he had obtained the handkerchief from her. Othello, too late, sees the truth, and overcome with remorse, stabs himself, falling by the bed of the slain Desdemona. His final outcry shows his grief and remorse: "I kissed thee ere I slew thee!"

FALSTAFF

(Fal'-staff)

Comic Opera in Three Acts. Music by Verdi. Book by Arrigo Boito, after "The Merry Wives of Windsor," by Shakespeare. Teatro Alla Scala, Milan, Feb. 9, 1893. At New York, the Metropolitan, February 4, 1895.

SCENE: Windsor.

TIME: The Fifteenth Century.

CAST SIR JOHN FALSTAFF, *a soldier of fortune* (Baritone).
FORD, *a citizen of Windsor* (Baritone).
MISTRESS ALICE FORD, *his wife* (Soprano).
ANNE FORD, *their daughter* (Soprano).
MISTRESS PAGE (Soprano).
MISTRESS QUICKLY (Contralto).
FENTON, *suitor of Anne* (Tenor).
DR. CAIUS, *a citizen* (Tenor).
BARDOLPH } *followers of Falstaff* { (Tenor).
PISTOL } { (Basso).
ROBIN, *a page*
Innkeeper, Townspeople, Servants, etc.

ARGUMENT "Falstaff" is noteworthy as being Verdi's single incursion into Light Opera. Perhaps tempted by his success with one of Shakespeare's tragic dramas, "Othello," he now turned his hand to this lighter medium. The music while pleasing does not measure up to the high standards which this master composer had set for himself. Shakespeare's comedy is closely followed as to plot in this musical version of the fat knight's misadventures.

Act I *Scene 1. A Room at the Garter Inn.* Falstaff, the doughty knight whose prowess has been tested on the battlefield (if his own word is to be believed), decides to try his skill in the lists of love. He therefore prepares two billets-doux for estimable wives of Windsor, and since his followers, Bardolph and Pistol, balk at taking them, he sends them by a page. He also quarrels with Dr. Caius, who complains of being robbed by Bardolph and Pistol.

In this scene Falstaff sings the praises of Mistress Ford: "O love with starlike eyes!"; and the monologue on "Honor," the words taken from Henry IV.

Scene 2. Ford's Garden. Mistress Ford and Mistress Page, the ladies who have received the epistles, meet and compare them, and with Mistress Quickly plan to revenge themselves upon the sender. Bardolph and Pistol confuse their plans by informing Ford of the affair. The latter is to meet Falstaff in disguise. Meanwhile, a plot of a different sort is afoot. Ford has planned to have his daughter Anne marry Caius, but she is in love with Fenton, who meets her clandestinely.

The reading of the letter by Mistress Ford is delightfully lyrical. This is followed by a quartet of women, unaccompanied, "He'll surely come courting," and a male quartet in sharp contrast, "He's a foul, a ribald thief," with a pleasing aria by Fenton.

Act II *Scene 1. The Garter Inn.* Dame Quickly comes to the inn to give Falstaff a note from Mistress Ford, apparently yielding to his wishes and making an appointment for that afternoon. After she departs, Ford is introduced under the name of Fountain, who pretends that he is a stranger seeking the love of Mistress Ford. Falstaff readily agrees to help him, and states complacently that he has an engagement with that lady for this very day. Ford has heard nothing of the women's plot, and is both astounded and jealous, but hides his feelings. His song is an excellent dramatic outburst, "Do I dream? Or is it real?"

Scene 2. Room in Ford's House. Falstaff arrives at Mistress Ford's and at once begins to make ardent protestations of love. At this moment, Dame Quickly bustles in to say that Ford and his friends are at hand. The fat knight is hastily thrust behind a screen, and a little later, when the search begins in earnest, he is persuaded to hide in a basket of soiled linen. Meanwhile, Fenton and Anne take refuge behind the screen for a little love-making on their own account. Ford returns and thinks he has discovered the villain behind the screen, and is greatly disgusted when the young lovers come to view. While the search proceeds, Falstaff is nearly suffocated in the basket. The women, ostensibly to rescue him, have the basket conveyed to the river brink and its entire contents dumped into the water.

This scene, which has to do with the ludicrous clothes-basket episode, is again utilized to the utmost by the instruments. Vocal numbers include: Mistress Quickly's droll description of her visit: " 'Twas at the Garter Inn"; and Falstaff's song, "Once I was a page."

Act III *Scene 1. The Garter Inn.* Dame Quickly again visits the crestfallen knight to express her sorrow and to make a new appointment. The knight again falls into the trap. As the doughty knight soliloquizes over his misadventures, one instrument after another in the orchestra seems laughing at him. A cacophony of mirth greets his song, "Ungrateful world! Wicked world!" Mistress Ford explains the whole hoax to her husband, and he promises to aid them this time. Dr. Caius is again promised Anne's hand, and Dame Quickly, who learns of it, runs to warn the lovers.

Scene 2. Windsor Park. Fenton is aided by the women, who disguise him as a monk. Falstaff again meets Mistress Ford, but is interrupted by a crowd disguised as witches, elves, and fairies, who belabor the knight soundly. He begs for mercy and, at his promise of good behavior, Ford pardons him. Meanwhile, Dr. Caius finds that he has captured the wrong person, and Anne, for whom he has sought, enters with Fenton. Ford is persuaded to relent and unite the two lovers.

This closing scene brings in Fenton's love song, "From those sweet lips"; and an equally pleasing melody by Anne, "We'll dance in the moonlight"; a dance by elves; and in a spirit of lightheartedness the music blends with the close, "All the world is jesting!"

AMILCARE PONCHIELLI

Ponchielli was born at Paderno Fasolaro, Cremona, August 31, 1834. He studied at the Milan Conservatory. In 1856 he brought out at Cremona an opera, "I Promessi Sposi" (The Betrothed), which, in a

revised version, Milan, 1872, was his first striking success. His second
opera, "I Lituani" (The Lithuanians), brought out in 1874, was revived
ten years later, as "Alguna"; and, while "La Gioconda" (1876) did not
wait so long for success, it, too, was revised and brought out in a new
version before it received popular acclaim. Among his other operas
are, 1880, "Il Figliuol Prodigo" (The Prodigal Son), and, 1885, "Marion
Delorme."   "La Gioconda," however, is the only one of his operas that
has made its way abroad. Ponchielli died at Milan, January 16, 1886.

LA GIOCONDA

(Lah Jo-kon'-dah)

(The Street Singer.)   Dramatic Opera in Four Acts.   Music by Amil-
care Ponchielli.   Book by Tobia Garrio, after Hugo's Tragedy, "Angelo, the Tyrant of Padua."   La Scala Opera House, Milan, April 8,
1876.   At New York, the Metropolitan, December 20, 1883, with
Nilsson, as the street singer, and Scalchi as the blind mother.

> SCENE: Venice.
> TIME: The Seventeenth Century.

> CAST   LA GIOCONDA, *a street singer* (Soprano).
> LA CIECA, *her blind mother* (Contralto).
> ALVISE BADOERO, *an inquisitor* (Basso).
> LAURA, *his wife* (Mezzo-Soprano).
> ENZO GRIMALDO, *a Genoese noble* (Tenor).
> BARNABA, *a spy* (Baritone).
> ZUANE, *a boatman* (Basso).
> ISEPO, *a scribe* (Tenor).
> A PILOT (Basso).
>   Ladies, Senators, Masqueraders, Sailors, Monks,
>   Citizens, Servants.

ARGUMENT   "La Gioconda" is the sole opera upon which Ponchielli's fame rests today, and it had a stormy
career both at home and abroad.   Its first performance at the Metropolitan in New York, in 1883, was unsuccessful and it was withdrawn
from the boards for the next fourteen years.   Today it seems to have
won a permanent and rightful place in repertory, its charming "Dance
of the Hours" alone holding acclaim, even if one forgot its many other
fine musical moments.   As to the plot, it is a swiftly moving Venetian
tale of love, intrigue, jealousy and crime—the sort of dish that many
"Grand" operas seem to demand.   Each Act was given a separate title,
as here shown.

Act I *"The Lion's Mouth." Court of the Ducal Palace.* Called "The Lion's Mouth" because of a receptacle into which letters intended for the Inquisition are dropped. Leading her blind mother, the beautiful La Gioconda, a street singer, enters the ducal square just as a chorus of merrymakers have deserted it. She is in search of Enzo, a nobleman with whom she is in love. But the spy Barnaba bars her way, and when she repulses his advances he takes revenge by stirring up the populace against her mother, La Cieca, charging her with being a sorceress. The latter is rescued by Laura, the Inquisitor's wife, once the sweetheart of Enzo. The latter, who has come upon the scene, also recognizes Laura, and the spy, noting their exchange of glances, plots a new piece of villainy. He arranges a meeting between them on board Enzo's ship, and at the same time sends word to Laura's husband of the adventure. La Gioconda also learns of the meeting.

Chief musical numbers in this Act: the chorus by the populace, "Sports and feasting" (Feste e pane); an expressive aria by La Cieca, "Voice of woman or of angel" (Voce di donna); and the dramatic duet between Barnaba and Enzo, "Prince, thou art pensive" (Principe di Santa Fior).

Act II *"The Rosary." On Board Enzo's Ship.* This act is called "The Rosary" from the fact that La Cieca has given Laura a rosary in token of gratitude and it plays a further part in the action. While Barnaba gloats over the success of his scheme Enzo comes on deck and greets Laura, who arrives in a boat. The two renew their pledges of love. Gioconda who has hidden on board now comes forward with a dagger resolved to stab her rival, but Laura holds up the rosary given by Gioconda's mother, and the street singer, recognizing it, resolves to save rather than slay her. Gioconda advises her that Alvise, the outraged husband, is near at hand and aids her to escape in her (Gioconda's) boat. Seeing his ship surrounded, Enzo sets fire to it.

There is a very effective fisher's ballad sung by Barnaba in this Act: "Ah, fisher, lower now thy net!" (Ah, Pescator!)—

Also a still more famous song, favored of tenors, by Enzo. As he looks upon a scene of great beauty where the moon and stars are reflected upon the waters of the lagoon, he apostrophizes in the delightful melody which matches it: "Heaven and ocean!" (Cielo e mar!)—

Act III *"The House of Gold."* Alvise is determined to avenge himself upon his unfaithful wife and tells her she must die by poison. Deaf to her entreaties he hands her a vial and bids her drain it before his return. Gioconda enters and substitutes a sleeping potion, and Laura is soon stretched upon the couch pale and apparently dead. Alvise's song, "Yes, her doom is to die!" (Si, morir ella de'!) is noteworthy.

After the attempt on Laura's life, the scene changes to a sumptuous ballroom, which stages the magnificent ballet, "Dance of the Hours."

The dancers' costumes, the scenic and lighting effects, and the colorful music depict dawn, noonday, twilight, and night. The combined effect is almost overpowering and the ballet is justly regarded as one of the finest in opera. The furious gaiety of the ball, however, only brings into sharper contrast the calculated villainy of the plot. No sooner has the dance ended than Alvise draws apart the curtains concealing the death couch and reveals the form of Laura. Enzo rushes forward to attack Alvise but is disarmed. Barnaba is placed over him as a guard, and Gioconda now tells the spy that if he will release him, she will agree to his desires. Barnaba does so.

Act IV *"The Orfano Canal."* *A Ruined Palace.* While Gioconda sits alone and dejected, the unconscious form of Laura is borne in. Gioconda fights an inward battle as to whether she shall kill or resuscitate her helpful rival. She finally resolves to kill herself. Enzo comes in and she tells him that Laura has been saved. Overjoyed he hastens to the couch, hearing the voice of Laura. Barnaba enters to claim Gioconda as she has promised, and in reply she stabs herself, falling lifeless at his feet.

The music of the orchestra forms a wonderful foil for the conflicting emotions of this powerful Act. As the voices rise in protest a volume of pure melody pours forth. Laura, regaining her senses, calls out: "Enzo!" A chorus offstage is heard in a serenade, a recurrence of an earlier theme. " 'Tis the rosary!" sings Gioconda. Enzo and Laura join their voices in thanks, "Upon thy hands tears are falling." And as Gioconda stabs herself it is with a defiant cry: "Gioconda is thine!" With a yell of baffled rage the spy tells her deaf ears: "Thy mother, I have strangled her!" But no one heeds him. The curtain falls.

ARRIGO BOÏTO

Arrigo Boïto was known as poet and librettist before turning his hand to composing. He was the author of the books to Ponchielli's opera "La Gioconda," and Verdi's "Othello" and "Falstaff." Boïto was born in Padua, Italy, February 24, 1842. From 1853 to 1862 he studied in the Milan Conservatory, but lived so long thereafter in Germany as to become Teuton in his musical tastes. He was an ardent admirer of Wagner's music. He wrote and composed another opera, "Nerone," but withheld it from production. "Mefistofele" is based on the two parts of Goethe's "Faust." Boïto died in Milan, June 10, 1918.

MEFISTOFELE
(Mef-is-tof'-e-leh)

(Mephistopheles.) Dramatic Opera in Prologue, Four Acts, and Epilogue. Music by Arrigo Boïto. Book by Composer. After Goethe's "Faust." La Scala, Milan, March 5, 1868. At New York, Academy of Music, November 24, 1880. The Metropolitan, January 15, 1896, when "revived" for Emma Calvé. Edouard de Reszke was the Evil One.

SCENE: Germany and Greece.
TIME: Middle Ages.

CAST MEPHISTOPHELES, *the Evil One* (Baritone).
FAUST, *a student* (Tenor).
WAGNER, *a student* (Basso).
NEREUS (Baritone).

PANTALIS (Tenor).
MARGUERITE, *a German girl* (Soprano).
MARTHA, *her mother* (Contralto).
HELEN OF TROY (Soprano).
    Students, Townspeople, Spirits, Witches, Bac-
    chanal Women, Greeks, etc.

ARGUMENT The plot of this opera is not unlike that of Gou-
    nod's "Faust," except that it delves more deeply
into Goethe's theme, and shows the final redemption of Faust.

Prologue *The Court of Heaven.* As the angels prostrate themselves
    before the throne of the Most High, Mephistopheles appears
and wagers that he can seduce the philosopher, Faust. He is bidden to
make the attempt.

Act I *Frankfort.* It is Easter Sunday. Amid the merry throng of
    the streets, Faust and Wagner wander, observing the crowd, but
holding themselves aloof from it. Their attention is finally attracted
by a gray Friar, whom every one seems instinctively to shun. He follows Faust so persistently, that the latter enters his house to avoid him.
However, the Friar also slips in, and presently reveals himself to Faust
as the Evil One. He says that he will open to Faust the riches and happiness of the world, if Faust will serve him in the next world. Faust
accepts the proposition, and Mephistopheles carries him away on his
cloak.

Act II *Scene 1. A Garden.* Mephistopheles first offers Faust love,
    and introduces him to Marguerite, the village girl. The two
walk arm in arm in a garden, while Mephistopheles keeps the coast
clear by making love to Martha, her mother. Faust hands the girl a
phial containing a powerful sleeping potion, which she is to give her
mother.
    Scene 2. The Brocken. The witches' saturnalia is in full progress.
Mephistopheles shows Faust their wild revels. During one incantation, they summon before his eyes the picture of Marguerite, suffering
imprisonment because of crimes instigated by him.

Act III *Interior of a Prison Cell.* Marguerite is shown alone in a
    cell, crazed by grief and remorse. She has been condemned
to death for poisoning her mother and killing her child. She can look
only to Heaven for pardon. Through the power of Mephistopheles,
Faust enters the prison and bids her escape with him, but she will not
do so while he is associated with the Evil One. Until dawn they urge

her to go, but they are forced to leave without her.   She falls back life-less, while an angelic choir chants that she is saved.

Act IV   *A Scene in Ancient Greece.*   In order further to show his power, Mephistopheles transports Faust to ancient Greece, and bestows upon him the hand of the most beautiful of women, Helen of Troy.   She tells Faust her story and the events leading to the fall of Troy.   Faust makes ardent love to her, and she accepts him.

Epilogue   *Faust's Study.*   Faust as an old man is seen reviewing his past life, which he regrets bitterly.   He has not found happi-ness in the gratification of the senses.   Mephistopheles appears, but finds that he has lost his power to tempt him.   Sirens surround Faust and call to him seductively.   He turns away and opens his Bible, read-ing therein that the vilest of sinners can repent and be saved.   He prays for forgiveness, and Mephistopheles sinks into the earth, van-quished.   Faust dies, and a shower of roses falls upon his body from above, in token that Heaven has accepted his soul.

Musical numbers include a soprano aria, "L'Altra notte in fondo al mare," and a quartet, "La notte del Sabba."

ALFREDO CATALANI

An Italian composer who was born in Lucca, July 19, 1854, and died in Milan, August 7, 1893.   He wrote songs and instrumental pieces, but is known in this country for only one opera, "Loreley," which was pre-sented in both Chicago and New York, but has not continued in reper-tory.

LORELEY
(Loh'-ray-lay'-ee)

Romantic Opera in Three Acts.   Music by Catalani.   Book by A. Zanardi and Carlo D'Ormville.   Chicago, and New York, at the Metro-politan, February 13, 1919, by the Chicago Opera Company.

SCENE: The Rhine.
TIME: The Middle Ages.

ARGUMENT   The traditional story of the Loreley is here interwoven into a romantic opera.   While wandering
along the banks of the Rhine, Walter, the governor of Oberwesel, meets
the Rhine-maiden, or Loreley.   Smitten with her charms, he loves her
to her undoing, and his own as well as he forgets that he is already
betrothed to Anna of Rehberg, niece of the Margrave.   He later confides his dark secret to his friend, Herman, who, although himself in
love with Anna, urges him to remain faithful to her.   In the ensuing
action Walter strives vainly to resist the siren.   Anna pines away and
dies.   In the final scene Walter meets a procession of mourners and is
told that Anna has not survived his falseness.   He rushes remorsefully
to the river and is again greeted by Loreley.   She is about to embrace
him, when voices from the deep bid her desist.   She belongs to the river
god.   As she sings her song of enchantment and farewell, Walter throws
himself into the torrent and perishes.

RUGGIERO LEONCAVALLO

A Neapolitan, born March 8, 1858, Leoncavallo is known as a pianist
and man of letters, as well as dramatic composer.   He was his own librettist.   He studied at the Naples Conservatory, but early came under
the influence of Wagner.   His first opera, "Thomas Chatterton," was
unsuccessful at first, but was later produced in Rome (1896).   He then
wrote "I Medici," produced in Milan in 1893; "La Bohème" (Venice,
1897); "Zaza" (Milan, 1900); "Roland in Berlin" (Berlin, 1904); "La
Riginetta delle Rose" (Rome, 1912); and "Zingari" (London, 1912).   It
must be admitted, however, that none of these has had a lasting success,
and Leoncavallo's claim to distinction, a very just one, rests upon his
famous opera, "I Pagliacci."   One other, "Zaza," has recently been revived with considerable success.   Leoncavallo died, August 9, 1919.

I PAGLIACCI
(*Ee Pah-lee-ah'-chee*)

(The Players.)   Dramatic Opera in Two Acts.   Music by Leoncavallo.   Book by Composer.   Milan, May 21, 1892.   At New York,

Grand Opera House, June 15, 1893. At the Metropolitan, December 11, 1893, with Melba, De Luca, and Ancona. The role of "Tonio" has been a favorite with many baritones, because of the famous Prologue.

SCENE: Near Montalto, in Calabria.
TIME: August 15, 1865.

CAST CANIO (Clown), *chief of a troupe of strolling players* (Tenor).
NEDDA (Columbine), *his wife* (Soprano).
TONIO (Taddeo), *a player* (Baritone).
BEPPO (Harlequin), *a player* (Tenor).
SILVIO, *a peasant* (Baritone).
Villagers.

ARGUMENT "Not how much, but how good," might be the motto of this gem of shorter operas. With that other gem, "Cavalleria Rusticana," by a kindred spirit, Mascagni, Leoncavallo reached the heights in a single bound for a completely satisfying evening at the opera. The theme is simple, but strongly developed in both text and music. The keynote is sounded in the Prologue: "We are all players." Before the curtain rises, it parts slightly and Tonio comes forth in his "Taddeo" costume. He warns his audience that a buffoon's heart is human; his tears may be real; and his jests may conceal sadness.

His voice rises in its pleading: "Ah, think then, kind people . . . we are men like you!"—

He concludes with a signal to his company, "Come, then, let us begin!"

Act I *A Village in Calabria.* The curtain rises as villagers sing a joyous chorus, "They're here!" A troupe of players has come, and Canio, their chief, tells the crowd to be sure to be on hand for the night's performance. He then goes down street, leaving his wife, Nedda, alone. Tonio, another player, tries to make love to her, but she strikes him in the face with a whip, and he goes away vowing vengeance. He has suspected a secret love between her and Silvio, a villager. Tonio overhears them making plans, and steals away to summon Canio. Meanwhile as a troupe of bagpipers pass by, the villagers sing a charming "Chorus of the Bells." Nedda soliloquizes over her unhappy lot in an aria, "Ah, ye birds without number!" When Canio hastens back to intercept the lovers, Silvio runs away. Enraged he is about to lay violent hands upon his wife, when other members of the company interpose: the play must go on; they must jest to the end. He echoes their desire in a pathetic song, "On with the play!" (Vesti la giubba)—

Act II *Village Square, with Showman's Stage.* The voice of Beppo (Harlequin) is heard in a lively serenade, "O, Columbine, come to thy window!" Tonio beats a drum to summon the villagers. They bustle in, while Nedda collects the tickets. Silvio reminds her of their assignation, but she cautions him to be silent. The plot of the play, which now begins, deals with a jealous husband who surprises his wife with another man at supper. The unwelcome guest jumps out the window, while the husband loads his unfaithful wife with reproaches; the pair being presented by Canio and Nedda. As he forgets his lines in his own jealous rage, the music rises in ominous intensity: "No, Pagliaccio, no more!" he shouts. "I am a man again!" Nedda, still striving to conceal her emotions and keep the play intact, sings a teasing ditty, "I never knew you were such a tragic fellow." (Suvvia, cosi terrible)—

But her gay song is ended tragically. Canio roughly demands, "His name!"—then plunges his knife into her breast. The terrified Silvio tries to interpose, and Canio kills him also. He regards his victims for a moment, and a final, bitter cry wells from his throat: "The comedy is ended!" (La commedia è finita!)

ZAZA
(*Zah'-zah*)

Lyric Opera in Four Acts. Words and music by Leoncavallo, after the play by P. Berton and Ch. Simon. Milan, 1900. At New York, the Metropolitan, January 16, 1920, with Farrar, Amato, Crimi, and Howard.

SCENE: Paris.
TIME: The Present.

ARGUMENT   "Zaza" avoids the tragic and reaches only the level of melodrama. It is on the familiar theme of a false love which does not bring happiness to either principal. The opera has achieved more success in Italy and Germany than in other lands. The music, while pleasing, lacks the dramatic force of "Pagliacci."

Act I   *Side View of a Stage.*   Zaza, a reigning music-hall favorite, has become smitten with Milio Dufresne, a man about town. The latter does not apparently notice her, and she is much piqued. She finally makes a wager with Bussy, a musical writer, that she will bring the cold Dufresne to her feet. She exerts all her powers of fascination and the latter succumbs.

Act II   *Zaza's Living Room.*   Zaza imperils her singing career because of her attachment for Dufresne. She is reproached by her mother and Cascart, her singing partner, for withdrawing from the music season, then at its height. Dufresne spends most of his time with her, but he finally returns to Paris under the plea of urgent business. In his absence, her mother and Cascart plot to break up this love idyl, and they tell her that her lover has gone to make an appointment with another sweetheart. Zaza, in a huff, departs at once for the city.

Act III   *Dufresne's Home.*   Dufresne has been leading a double life with Zaza, as he is already married and has a child. Zaza and her maid visit the Dufresne home, while monsieur and madame are away. Then it is that Zaza discovers the truth; but after she has seen Toto, the little girl, she departs without making a scene, as she had intended.

Act IV *Zaza's Home.* Zaza goes back home brokenhearted. Cascart tries to console her and win her back to the stage, but without success. The next time her lover comes, she hides her thoughts in order to find out the true state of his affections. When he still tries to keep up the deception she tells him she has seen Toto. She says, his secret is safe, and bids him farewell.

Musical numbers available in records: a duet for soprano and baritone, "Il bacio"; a soprano aria (Geraldine Farrar) "Mama usciva di casa"; tenor songs (Martinelli) "E un riso" and "O mio piccolo"; baritone song, "Buono Zaza" (Titta Ruffo); and another baritone aria, "Zaza piccola zingara" (John Charles Thomas).

GIACOMO PUCCINI

Puccini was born in Lucca, Italy, June 22, 1858, first studied music in his native place as a private pupil of Angeloni. Later at the Royal Conservatory, Milan, he studied under Ponchielli, composer of "La Gioconda." Puccini is generally regarded as the foremost modern composer of the Italian school, and the one man upon whom the mantle of Verdi fell. His work showed more variety and sustained effort than that of either Mascagni or Leoncavallo. He composed at least four operas which promise to become classic: "Manon Lescaut" (1870); "La Bohème" (1896); "La Tosca" (1900); and "Madam Butterfly" (1904). "La Fanciulla del West" (1910) has met with more favor in America than at home, and is better known here as "The Girl of the Golden West." Other works include an early two-act opera, "Le Villi," "Edgar," and "La Rondine." A final work, "Turandot," was incomplete at the time of his death, in Brussels, November 29, 1924.

MANON LESCAUT
(Mah-nohn' Les-co)

Tragic Opera in Four Acts. Music by Puccini. Book by composer, after the novel by Abbé Prévost, and with assistance of group of friends. Produced at Turin, February 1, 1893, and in the same year, in Buenos Aires; in Philadelphia, 1894, in English; and at the Metropolitan in

New York, in Italian, January 18, 1907, under the personal direction of the composer. In the latter cast were Caruso, Cavalieri, Scotti, and Rossi.

SCENE: Amiens, Paris, Havre, Louisiana.
TIME: Second half of Eighteenth Century.

CAST   MANON LESCAUT (Soprano).
LESCAUT, *Sergeant of the King's Guards* (Baritone).
CHEVALIER DES GRIEUX (Tenor).
GERONTE DE RAVOIR, *Treasurer-General* (Basso).
EDMUND, *a student* (Tenor).
Guards, Students, Street Women, etc.

ARGUMENT   A colorful opera, showing how a lifetime of devotion may work reformation in the character of even the most selfish and abandoned.

Act I   *An Inn at Amiens.*   Manon Lescaut, the pretty sister of a sergeant of the Guards, is blessed more with looks than with morals. Her brother, realizing her susceptible nature, determines to place her in a convent.   He brings her to Amiens for this purpose, but on his arrival is inveigled into a gambling game.   Another traveling companion, Geronte, has become infatuated with the girl en route, and now tries to seize this interval to abduct her.   But on this same evening another suitor has appeared in the person of the Chevalier de Grieux, who falls in love with her on sight.   She also likes his appearance and readily consents to meet him later.   So, while her brother is engrossed at the gaming table, she and the Chevalier elope in the carriage which Geronte had placed in readiness for his own use.   Geronte is furious when he discovers that his bird has flown with another, but cannot rouse the cynical brother into action.   "She will soon tire of him and come back to you," the latter says.

The gay singing of the students heralds the curtain rise in this Act. Later when Des Grieux first meets Manon, his song in her praise is a notable one: "Never did I behold a maiden so fair" (Donna non vidi)—

Her clear voice joins him in a charming duet, as she promises to be faithful to this new love: "Behold me!" she sings.

Act II   *Geronte's Mansion.*   Manon, as her brother had predicted, does not linger with her latest lover after his money is gone.

She deserts Des Grieux for the wealthy Geronte, and is now discovered living at ease as the latter's mistress. Yet she is not happy. She finds that she has left her heart with her impecunious lover. Geronte is old and a bore; and although he entertains her with musicians and dancers, she soon tires of them all. During a free moment, the Chevalier enters surreptitiously, and at first reproaches her for her desertion. But soon, overcome by her charms, he renews his ardent vows. Geronte surprises them. He conceals his true feelings under a mask of sarcasm and leaves them. Lescaut enters to warn them to flee from Geronte's anger; he has gone to call the guards. Manon lingers long enough to seize her jewels, but the delay is fatal. The guards enter and seize her. Geronte has preferred charges against her as an abandoned woman, and she is to be deported to America in company with other undesirables. Des Grieux declares his intention to follow her to the end of the world.

The music reflects conflicting emotions. Manon is not happy in her new love nest. She sings of her former happiness with the Chevalier: "O, my little humble dwelling!" Gerone tries to entertain her with a troupe of singers—their madrigal: "Speed o'er the mountain summit, O, my Chloe!" is excellent. A minuet follows, as a dancing master teaches her steps. This gaiety soon gives way to approaching tragedy.

The journey to the port of embarkation is represented by an Intermezzo, a striking bit of orchestration inserted to prepare the auditor for the later action:

Act III *A Public Square near the Waterfront, Havre.* Manon is in prison pending her deportation. Her brother and her lover attempt to rescue her, but are foiled. The utmost that Des Grieux can do is to walk by her side as she makes her way to the waiting ship. The captain is so touched by their story, that he consents to take the Chevalier as one of the crew. Manon is almost reconciled to her lot when she learns that he is to be near her.

The chief musical moments are Des Grieux's plea to the captain, and a dramatic aria by the latter.

Act IV *"A Vast Plain on the Borders of the Territory of New Orleans"* *(then a French possession).* Night is falling. Manon and Des Grieux enter, poorly clothed and weary. Manon is exhausted and leans heavily on Des Grieux. They do not know where to find either food or shelter, or even water to drink. Des Grieux is beside himself with despair. He finds a resting place for her, and goes off to look for water. Manon, thinking he has forsaken her entirely, feels undone. Only the tomb, she cries, can release her. Des Grieux returns in time to be present at her last moments. She dies, declaring to the last her love for him. Des Grieux falls senseless by her side.

The gloom of this scene is again reflected by both voice and instrument. There is a lengthy duet by the two lovers, while she reclines, dying, in his arms.

LA BOHÈME
(*La Bo-ame*)

(The Bohemians.) Romantic Opera in Four Acts. Music by Puccini. Book by Giacosa and Illica, after Henry Murger's "Vie de Bohème." Teatro Regio, Turin, February 1, 1896. Covent Garden, in English, October 2, 1897. Also in English, in America, the next year; and at the Metropolitan, New York, in Italian, December 18, 1901. In the latter cast were Melba, Campanari, Gilibert, and Journet.

> SCENE: Paris.
> TIME: 1830.

CAST   RUDOLPH, *a poet* (Tenor).
SCHAUNARD, *a musician* (Baritone).
MARCEL, *a painter* (Baritone).
COLLINE, *a philosopher* (Basso).
BENOIT, *a landlord* (Basso).
MIMI, *a flower girl* (Soprano).
MUSETTA, *a grisette* (Soprano).
PARPIGNOL, *a toy vender* (Tenor).
ALCINDORO, *a wealthy Parisian* (Basso).
    Sergeant, Guards, Grisettes, Students, Children, Waiters, Citizens.

ARGUMENT   "La Bohème" is a picture of happy-go-lucky artist life in the Latin Quarter of Paris, with its lights and shadows, comedies and tragedies. It is the most popular of the Puccini operas, in America, by reason of its skillful blending of the gay, lighthearted moments of student life with the pathos and tragedy of blighted love.

Act I   *A Garret occupied by Four Bohemians.* Rudolph, a poet, Schaunard, a musician, Marcel, a painter, and Colline, a dreamer, live together in a Parisian attic in a state of chronic poverty,

yet in perfect harmony and good fellowship. The poet and the painter
are discovered, when the curtain rises, sitting in the bare and comfort-
less room, both cold and hungry. They feed one of Rudolph's manu-
scripts to the stove in the effort to extract a little warmth. Enter Colline also to warm up, and he is followed by a boy bringing in fuel and
materials for a feast. While they are overjoyed at this windfall,
Schaunard arrives with a wonderful tale of how he has lined his pockets
and thus can afford to give the spread. All fall to with gusto, but at
this moment Benoit, the landlord, arrives seeking to collect his long-
overdue rent. They ply him with wine until he begins to tell libertine
stories, when they pretend to be greatly shocked and thrust him out of
the door. The rent money is divided for a further carouse in the Latin
Quarter. Rudolph alone remains under a plea that he wants to finish
some writing. Presently a timid knock is heard. He opens the door
to see a girl, who says: "Excuse me, sir, but my candle is gone out." He
aids her to relight it, but a current of the air again extinguishes it.
Through the garret window one can see the snow on the roof. She
shivers and drops her key. As he picks it up, their hands meet. "How
cold your little hand is!" he cries in the first of the tender passages between them. (Tenor aria, "Che gelida mamina!"). He tells her something about himself: "I am a poet" (Sono un poeta); and she replies by
giving him her name: "My name is Mimi" (Mi chiamano Mimi)—one
of the finest flights for the soprano voice:

A no-less lovely duet follows: "O, lovely maiden!" (O, soave fanciulla!).
They decide to cast their lot together and depart to join their friends as
the melody follows them down the stairs.

Act II *A Public Square in the Latin Quarter.* The four friends are
            spending Schaunard's money right and left. Rudolph buys
Mimi a hat, and all seat themselves at a café table and order lavishly.
While they are dining, Musetta, an old flame of Marcel's, enters with a
wealthy admirer, Alcindoro. Musette no sooner sees Marcel than she
tries in every way to attract his attention, and also to get rid of her aged
suitor. She finally sends the latter out to buy her a new pair of shoes,
under a pretext that her old ones hurt her feet, and then rushes over
and embraces Marcel. The Bohemians find that they have spent all
their money and cannot pay the dinner bill, but Musetta tells them not
to worry, that she will add it to her own and leave it for Alcindoro to

pay. All disperse as a party of guards comes by, and Alcindoro upon returning finds a bill of such huge proportions that he falls in a heap on his chair.

The high point in this Act is the waltz song by Musetta, where she dissembles her affections.

Act III *At a Gate of Customs.* It is still winter, and the customs officers examine the passports of all who enter the city. Mimi, who is suffering from consumption, comes to the gate to ask for Marcel who is doing some work hard by. When he appears she tells him that she is miserable as she cannot live with Rudolph and also cannot live without him. They have quarreled. Marcel goes to summon Rudolph, and Mimi hides behind a tree. The poet tells his friend why he has left Mimi. She coughs and reveals her presence, and he takes the sick girl in his arms. Meanwhile Marcel becomes jealous of Musetta, whom he accuses of flirting in the inn.

Another operatic gem is heard when Mimi bids farewell to her lover: "Farewell, then, I wish you well" (Addio, senza rancore)—

Act IV *The Garret as in First Act.* Marcel and Rudolph are at work when the other two Bohemians arrive with materials for a scanty dinner. They make merry, however, over the repast, pretending that it is a banquet. Musetta comes in, saying that Mimi is extremely ill. All bustle to help the invalid. They place her upon a cot and hasten out to pawn their clothing if necessary to buy her food and medicines. Rudolph alone remains, and the two lovers are again reconciled and resolve never to part again.

The closing moments abound in beautiful melody: Rudolph's soliloquy, "Ah, Mimi, false one!" (Ah, Mimi, tu più); the "Song of the Coat" by Colline; and the voices of the reunited lovers, "Have they gone?" (Sono andati), and "Oh God, Mimi!" (Oh Dio, Mimi!) "I only wanted to be with you, Beloved," she whispers. "Do you remember?" And the violins and wood instruments echo the strains in this Death Music of their first meeting. "How cold your hands are!" And, "They call me Mimi."

Their friends now enter bringing food and aid, but it is too late. They can only stand silently by the bed of death. With a last despairing cry, "Mimi, Mimi!" Rudolph sinks across her couch.

LA TOSCA

(*La Tos'-ca*)

Tragic Opera in Three Acts.   Music by Puccini.   Book by Illica and
Giacosa, after the drama by Sardou.   Costanzi Theatre, Rome, January 14, 1900; London the same year; New York, February 4, 1901.   In
the latter cast were Scotti and Ternina.

SCENE: Rome.
TIME: Circa 1800.

CAST   MARIO CAVARADOSSI, *a painter* (Tenor).
BARON SCARPIA, *Chief of Police* (Baritone).
CESARE ANGELOTTI, *an escaped prisoner* (Basso).
FLORIA TOSCA, *a singer* (Soprano).
SPOLETTA, *a police officer* (Tenor).
Churchmen, Police, Jailer, Shepherd Boy,
Servants.

ARGUMENT   "La Tosca," founded upon Sardou's tragedy, is an
intense plot of passion and revenge, unrelieved by
any lighter themes.   Its music, brilliant and somber, closely fits the text.

Act I   *Interior of the Church of Sant' Andrea, Rome.*   The painter,
Mario Cavaradossi, is busily engaged upon mural decorations
within a church when he is appealed to for aid by Cesare Angelotti, an
escaped political prisoner.   The painter promises to assist him to escape and meanwhile hides him in the church.   Tosca, a singer, and
the painter's sweetheart, comes in at this moment and believes that she
has discovered evidences of the painter's fickleness, especially since he
has been using another woman as the model for his "Magdalen."   He
reassures her.   The sacristan and choir-boys enter, and, later, Scarpia,
the Chief of Police, in search of the fugitive.   He finds a fan dropped
by the model and shows it to Tosca in order to excite her jealousy.   He
wishes her to betray her lover, and he is also in love with her on his own
account.

Three crashing chords from the orchestra denoting the sharp sinister
action which is to follow greet the rising of the curtain on Act I.   The
song by the painter, Cavaradossi, "Strange harmony" (Recondita armo-
nia), follows in praise of his lady.

Then comes a fine interlude of choir singing; the impassioned passages between him and Tosca; and the final thrilling outburst of harmony with Scarpia and the choir: "Te Deum"—

Act II *Scarpia's Offices in the Farnese Palace.* Scarpia's men have not been able to catch Angelotti, but still suspecting Cavaradossi they bring him before their chief. Scarpia questions him sharply without being able to obtain any information, and then remands him to the torture chamber. He has sent for Tosca, who now appears. At first she is silent to all his questions, but when he tells her that her lover is being tortured, and proves this by opening the door to the inquisition chamber, she cannot withstand the strain and reveals Angelotti's hiding-place. The painter reproaches her for the betrayal as he is taken away to prison. Scarpia now tells her that her lover will be condemned to death unless she is willing to make a sacrifice to save him—the sacrifice of her honor. He, Scarpia, loves her and under no other condition can the painter be saved. Tosca recoils from this proposition, but when word is brought that Angelotti has poisoned himself to avoid re-capture she fears Cavaradossi will do likewise and says she will consent. The police officer draws up a passport for the prisoner and at the same times gives orders for his execution by a volley of musketry. He carefully explains that it will be a mock-execution, only blank cartridges being used, for the sake of appearances. He advances to Tosca with the passport and endeavors to embrace her. She seizes it and quickly stabs him to the heart. Then piously composing the body, with lights at the head and feet and a crucifix on its breast, she hastens away to the prison.

The supreme number in this Act, and one of the finest in modern Italian opera, is Tosca's exquisite song: "Art and love—these I have lived for" (Vissi d'arte)—

Act III *Battlements of the Prison.* The squad of soldiers prepare to obey the order which they have just received for the execution of Cavaradossi. He is led out to an open court overlooking the battlements, and is there overjoyed to find Tosca, who tells him of the passport which she carries. The execution will only be pretended, she tells him, but he must fall as though slain. The file of soldiers now take their position and fire their volley. The prisoner sinks in a crumpled heap, but when Tosca rushes to his side she finds that he is really dead—pierced by actual bullets. Tosca cannot at first realize the horrible truth, then gives way to despair. The guards now rush in to seize her for the murder of Scarpia, but she evades them.

In the early part of this Act a fine aria for the tenor voice is heard, as Cavadarossi sings a farewell to his beloved: "When the stars are brightly shining" (E lucevan le stelle)—

His final song, "The sting of death I only feared for thee, dear" (Amaro sol per te), comes before he faces the firing squad. Her impassioned, "Now, Mario, all is safe!" is a glad note, all too soon to be followed by her grief when she finds him a corpse. Then amid somber chords from the instruments she leaps from the battlements to her own death—and freedom.

MADAM BUTTERFLY

Dramatic Opera in Two Acts, later Three Acts. Music by Puccini. Italian text by Illica and Giacosa, after the stage play by David Belasco and John Luther Long. Produced unsuccessfully as a two-act opera in La Scala, Milan, February 17, 1904; revised and presented in three acts, at Brescia, May 28, 1904, with success. Covent Garden, London, the next season, in English, Washington, October, 1906; and in Italian at the Metropolitan, February 11, 1907, with Farrar, Caruso, Scotti, and Homer.

SCENE: Nagasaki, Japan.
TIME: The Present.

CAST MADAM BUTTERFLY (Cho-Cho-San), *a Japanese woman* (Soprano).
SUZUKI, *her servant* (Mezzo-Soprano).
PINKERTON, *a lieutenant, U.S. Navy* (Tenor).
KATE PINKERTON, *his wife* (Mezzo-Soprano).
SHARPLESS, *U.S. Consul* (Tenor).
GORO, *a Japanese marriage broker* (Tenor).
YAMADORI, *a Japanese nobleman* (Baritone).
THE BONZE, *uncle to Cho-Cho-San* (Basso).
A baby boy, Relatives of Cho-Cho-San, Villagers, etc.

ARGUMENT "Madam Butterfly" is interesting on several counts. Sung in Italian, its setting is Japan and it also has a strong American flavor, in fact, had its origin on the American stage. The composer has introduced several distinct Japanese melodies, but also artfully contrives to give the work a cosmopolitan touch. For these reasons as well as the dramatic and pathetic story itself, "Butterfly" has remained a favorite on both sides of the Atlantic.

Act I   *A Japanese Villa.*   Lieutenant Pinkerton, U.S.N., finding that he will be stationed in Nagasaki for some months, desires to contract a Japanese marriage. He is assured by the marriage broker who transacts the business for him that this marriage will be binding only so long as he consents to live with his wife, and that afterwards she can marry again. But Cho-Cho-San, the girl who agrees to marry the lieutenant, has fallen deeply in love with him and believes she is entering into a life contract. She goes so far as to renounce her religion, thus severing all connection with her own people. Sharpless, the American consul, tries to prevent the match by telling his friend Pinkerton how seriously the girl considers it. The lieutenant has further proof of this when a fanatical bonze, or priest, an uncle of hers, appears, as the wedding party is seated at the feast, and heaps curses upon her head for renouncing her faith. All her relatives thereupon desert her, but Cho-Cho-San, though sorrowful, clings to her husband, and he soon calms her fears. The scene closes in mutual protestations of love.

The music, quaint and charming throughout, reaches its climax near the close of this Act in the duet between Cho-Cho-San and the lieutenant. Beginning with the quiet, "Evening is falling" (Viene la sera), it gradually rises in passion to "O, night of rapture!" (O quanti occhi fisi)—

Act II   *Scene 1.   The Villa.   Three years later.*   After a short but blissful wedded life, Lieutenant Pinkerton has been recalled to America. He leaves Cho-Cho-San (who is now called "Madam Butterfly") in Japan, promising to return "when the robins nest again." Despite his long absence and silence she still trusts him. Her maid, Suzuki, is not so sure and Butterfly chides her in the famous aria, "Some fine day he'll come!" (Un bel di vedremo)—

with much feeling

As a matter of fact, Pinkerton is returning to Japan, but with no intention of rejoining her. Instead he writes Sharpless, the consul, telling him that he now has an American wife and asking the consul to break this news to Madam Butterfly. The consul brings her the letter, but she is so overjoyed at seeing a missive from him that she pays no heed to its message and the consul has not the heart to disturb her faith. She also turns a deaf ear to Goro, the marriage broker, who comes to arrange a match between her and a Japanese nobleman. When he says that Pinkerton's desertion is equivalent to a divorce she answers proudly: "That may be so in Japan, but I am an American!" Then she brings out her baby boy born of her union with the Lieutenant and asks, "Can this, too, be forgotten?" She bids "Trouble," her boy, not to listen to the bad man. The consul leaves, shaking his head; the sound of a cannon in the harbor is heard, and with a glass Butterfly spells out the name of her lord's ship. In a fever of excitement she and her maid decorate the house. The "Letter Scene" followed by the "Flower Duet" between the two women are particularly charming. But all their preparation is in vain. The night draws slowly by. "Trouble" falls asleep; then the maid; only Butterfly sits erect—watching—waiting—while exquisite music of the night outside brings the fall of the curtain.

Act III (*Also presented as the Second Part of Act II.*) *Setting same as foregoing.* Dawn is breaking as the curtain rises on the little group. Another fine bit of oriental melody greets the rise of the curtain known as the "Vigil Theme":

Butterfly has not closed her eyes. Now Suzuki awakes and persuades her wearied mistress to lie down and rest. She does so, in order that she may look well when "he comes." After she has retired the consul arrives with Pinkerton and his American wife. When Pinkerton hears from Suzuki of Butterfly's devotion and trust he is overcome with remorse and cannot remain to face the deserted bride. Suzuki is commissioned to tell her that Mrs. Pinkerton will care for the child, but Butterfly, entering at this moment, hears it from the American lady's own lips. She retains her composure by a great effort. congratulates Mrs. Pinkerton politely, and says that if they will return in half an hour they may have the child. When the Americans return at the specified time they find that Madam Butterfly has slain herself with her father's sword, on which is inscribed: "Die with honor, when you can no longer live with honor."

The orchestra sounds the final notes, deep, mournful, thunderous— a requiem for a noble love and a sin that never could be expiated.

THE GIRL OF THE GOLDEN WEST

(La Fanciulla del West.) Romantic Opera in Three Acts. Music by Puccini. Book by David Belasco. World premiere at the Metropolitan, New York, December 10, 1910. The cast included Destinn, Caruso, and Amato.

> SCENE: A California Mining-camp.
> TIME: 1848.

> CAST MINNIE, *a Western girl* (Soprano).
> JACK RANCE, *the sheriff, a gambler* (Baritone).
> JOHNSON, *alias Ramarrez, an outlaw* (Tenor).
> DICK, *a servant* (Tenor).
> LARKINS (Baritone).
> HARRY (Baritone).
> Miners, Bandits, Servants, Indians, etc.

ARGUMENT "The Girl of the Golden West" is a romantic and colorful picture of Western pioneer life, which was successful as a drama, before being given a musical setting. The days of the gold fever on the Pacific slope and of the rough-and-ready justice there accorded are here illustrated.

Act I *The Polka Bar.* Minnie, a resourceful "girl of the Golden West," left an orphan, continues to run her father's barroom for the benefit of the miners who flock to the newly discovered gold diggings of California. Minnie herself can gamble and shoot with the best of them if necessary, but she is treated as a sort of ward by the camp whom it would be sudden death to insult. While her friends, the miners, are congregated at her bar, a wandering minstrel halts outside and sings of the "Old Folks at Home," moving some of them to tears. Then Minnie sings a love song which also arouses the sentiments of her hearers. During the singing, Jack Rance, the sheriff, who is also a gambler and who has long loved Minnie, enters. He makes love to her, but she will not listen to him.

The mountains back of the camp have been overrun for some time by a band of outlaws under the leadership of Ramarrez. The miners have offered large rewards for their extermination, but the outlaws are so bold and careless that they plan a robbery in the camp. Their leader comes, under the name of Johnson, to the Polka bar in order to look over the ground and, in the evening, give the signal to his men. But becoming fascinated by the girl, he lingers to make love to her and offers to escort her to her home. She is also interested in him and accepts his attentions.

Act II *Interior of Minnie's Cabin.* The two Indian servants of Minnie crouch in one corner, while she listens, pleased, to Johnson's declarations of love. A noise is heard outside the door and Minnie discovers Rance at the head of a posse. Not caring to have them find a man at her home she conceals Johnson, who is only too willing to go into hiding; then she opens the door. Rance tells her that they are searching for a notorious bandit who, they have reason to believe, is concealed on the premises. Minnie indignantly disclaims knowledge of any such person, but after the posse has gone away she turns upon Johnson and upbraids him for deceiving her. The outlaw tells her that he has been reared to this life, but after seeing her he is ready to reform. She will not listen to him, however, and he leaves the cabin. A few paces from the door a shot is heard. Rance has remained in hiding and now seriously wounds him. Johnson drags himself back to the cabin and Minnie, touched by his plight, conceals him in the loft. Rance returns and demands the fugitive. Minnie again denies knowledge of his whereabouts, but a few drops of blood trickling down from above betray him. In desperation Minnie offers to play a game of poker, the stakes to be the outlaw against her love. The gambling spirit of Rance is aroused and they play. Minnie cheats with the cards and wins. Rance respects his agreement and departs.

Act III *In the Redwood Forest.* Minnie nurses Johnson back to health, and he promises to disperse his gang and go to another state, there to live an honest life. Rance, hearing that he has recovered from his wound and is now on his way to join the outlaws, summons his posse and captures him. The miners promise him short shrift at the end of a rope, and are preparing to lynch him from the first convenient tree, when Minnie rushes forward. She pleads with the miners telling them of Johnson's reformation, and by her influence persuades them to spare his life. Later Rance aids her to effect his escape and she departs with Johnson for an eastern state where they are to be married and begin life anew.

It must be admitted that there has been more interest in the plot than in the music, so far as the American public is concerned. To link up a robust western story with Debussy-like phrases and recitative passages was a task beyond even Puccini's great abilities. There is not enough variety in the orchestration, nor many of the dramatic heights for solo voices. The best of these is perhaps the aria by Johnson, who is facing death: "Let her believe that I have gained my freedom." (Ch'ella mi credo.)

LA RONDINE
(Lah Rone'-dee-neh)

(The Swallow.) Lyric Opera in Three Acts. Music by Puccini. Book by Giuseppe Adami. Monte Carlo, March 27, 1917. At the Metropolitan, New York, March 10, 1928.

SCENE: Paris and Nice.
TIME: The Second French Empire.

CAST   MAGDA, a demi-mondaine (Soprano).
RAMBALDO, a banker (Baritone).
RUGGERO, a student (Tenor).
PRUNIER, a poet (Baritone).
Lisette, Bianca, Yvette, Perichaud, Gobin, Crebillon, and other Guests, Servants, etc.

ARGUMENT   A sentimental work with lilting music and a theme reminiscent of "La Traviata."

Act I   Salon of Magda's Paris House. Magda, who lives a life of ease, under the protection of the rich banker, Rambaldo, holds sway over a Bohemian circle, ranging from poets and artists down to demi-mondaines. During one such levée, the conversation turns on love, and Prunier, a decadent poet, reads an essay which maintains that old-fashioned love is reviving. Derisive laughter. Magda, however, grows pensive; she recalls an idyllic love of her youth. The poet thereupon reads her palm and tells her that she is like the swallow: she will try her wings on romance, only to fly back home again. At this juncture a young stranger is announced—Ruggero, a man from out of town, whose father is an old friend of Rambaldo's. The latter greets him pleasantly, and offers him a guide to the "Bal Bullier," where he can see other night life.

Act II *The Bal Bullier.* Magda has been attracted by the young visitor, and decides to follow him to the Bal. She does so and has a further opportunity to see him, and discovers for him a love which she has long since believed dead. He, unsophisticated, sees in her the beautiful and pure girl of his dreams. They are happy and when the banker appears on the scene and wants to take her back with him, she repulses him.

Act III *A Rustic Cottage at Nice.* Ruggero and Magda have run away to an idyllic existence. She is content at last, while he writes to his mother asking permission to make the girl his wife. She consents, provided that Magda is all that he has depicted. When Magda learns of this, she realizes that it would be unjust to marry Ruggero. She gives him up and—like the swallow—flies back home to her banker.

A soprano solo (sung by Lucrezia Bori) "Ore dolci e divine," is in record form.

GIANNI SCHICCHI
(*Gee'-ah-nee She'-chee*)

Humorous Opera in One Act. Music by Puccini. Book by Gioachino Forzano. Milan, 1918; Metropolitan, New York, December 14, the same year, together with two other shorter works by Puccini, "Il Tabarro" and "Suor Angelica." None of the three has had many performances in recent years, although "Gianni" seems to have more enduring qualities.

SCENE: Florence.
TIME: 1299.

CAST   GIANNI SCHICCHI (Baritone).
     LAURETTA, *his daughter* (Soprano).
      The Relatives of Buoso Donati
     ZITA, *"the Old Woman"* (Contralto).
     RINUCCIO, *Zita's nephew* (Tenor).
     GHERARDO, *Buoso's nephew* (Baritone).
     NELLA, *his wife* (Soprano).
     GHERARDINO, *their son* (Soprano).
     BETTO OF SIGNA, *a cousin to Buoso* (Baritone).
     SIMONE, *a cousin to Buoso* (Basso).
     MARCO, *his son* (Baritone).

La Ciesca, *Marco's wife* (Mezzo-Soprano).
Master Spinellocchio, *physician* (Baritone).
Amanti di Nicolao, *notary* (Baritone).
Pinellino, *shoemaker* (Tenor).
Guccio, *a dyer* (Basso).

ARGUMENT   This little opera is pure sparkling comedy. The
story of the dead man's relatives scheming to ob-
tain for themselves the property he has willed to the Church, and being
outwitted by the clever rogue they have called to their aid, is full of
humor. Puccini's brilliant music is thoroughly attuned to his theme.
Scene: Buoso Donati's Bedroom. The relatives of Buoso are kneel-
ing round the bed upon which his body lies. Their utterances are
choked with feigned sighs and tears. Each hopes that he is his relative's
principle legatee. When Betto suggests that rumor has credited the
Church with the major share, their simulated grief is thrown aside and
a frantic search is made for the will. At last it is found, and their worst
fears are realized. Buoso's wealth is to go to the Church. In their
dilemma Rinuccio suggests asking advice of Gianni Schicchi, with
whose daughter Lauretta he is in love. Schicchi proposes that he shall
impersonate Buoso and dictate a will to a notary and two witnesses,
pretending that his hands are too paralyzed to write. This scheme appeals to the relatives, and they decide to adopt it. The smaller possessions are apportioned between them without difficulty, but there remain the mule, the saw-mills at Signa, and the palace in Florence.
Each in turn privately offers Schicchi a bribe for the legacy of these, and
each is reassured. He is arrayed in nightgown and nightcap and bun-
dled into bed before the notary and witnesses enter. The pretended
Buoso in the quavering voice of an old man dictates his will. To the
Church he leaves five liras, to the relatives the smaller properties as
arranged. Then comes the disposition of the mule, the saw-mills, and
the house in Florence. All hold their breath as he speaks. He leaves
them—to his dear friend, Gianni Schicchi! The relatives fume, but
they are helpless and dare not give themselves away. When the notary
and witnesses are gone they pillage the room and set upon Schicchi, but
he defends himself effectively with Donati's cudgel and pursues them
downstairs. The young lovers, Rinuccio and Lauretta, are seen on the
terrace clasped in each other's arms as Schicchi returns laden with loot.
He glances at the lovers, and appeals to the audience to know if Buoso's
hoards could have been put to better use, and asks for a verdict of "not
guilty."
   Two musical numbers are recorded: the tenor aria, "Firenze e come
un albero fiorito," and the soprano, "O mio babbino caro."

SUOR ANGELICA

(Sister Angelica.) Romantic Opera in One Act, for female voices.
Music by Puccini. Book by G. Forzano. Produced, with "Gianni
Schicchi," in New York, December 14, 1918.

SCENE: Near Florence, Italy.
TIME: Seventeenth Century.

CAST SISTER ANGELICA (Soprano).
THE PRINCESS, *her aunt.*
THE ABBESS.
THE MISTRESS OF NOVICES.
THE SISTER MONITOR.
Other Nuns and Novices.

ARGUMENT Because of a youthful, indiscreet love affair, resulting in a child, Angelica has been forced into a
convent by the wealthy Florentine family to which she belongs. For
seven years she does penance, but meanwhile longs for tidings of her
child. Her aunt, who pays her a visit, tells her coldly that the child is
dead—although, she says, no care was spared. Angelica goes into the
garden, prays the Virgin to forgive her, and ends her life by a drink of
poison. As she is dying, a miracle takes place. The walls of the
cloister shine with unearthly light, and the Virgin herself appears, leading the child, which she places in the mother's arms.

There is a lovely intermezzo in this opera, and a song for the soprano
voice, "Senza mamma."

IL TABARRO
(Eel Tah-bah'-10)

(The Cloak.) Tragic Opera in One Act. Music by Puccini. Book
by Giuseppe Adami, after the story by Didier Gold. Produced, with
"Gianni Schicchi," in New York, at the Metropolitan, December 14,
1918. Revived, January 5, 1946, with Tibbett and Albanese as the
barge owner and his wife; Jagel as "Luigi."

SCENE: Paris.
TIME: The present.

CAST MICHELE, *owner of a barge* (Basso).
GIORGETTA, *his wife* (Soprano).

TALPA, *a longshoreman* (Baritone).
FRUGOLA, *his wife* (Contralto).
LUIGI, *a longshoreman* (Tenor).
TINCA, *a longshoreman* (Baritone).

ARGUMENT The entire action takes place on board a barge, on the River Seine. Michele, owner of a barge, has for some time suspected his wife of infidelity and sets a trap for her and her lover, Luigi. At the end of a day's work all leave the boat except the woman and her lover. Luigi persuades Giorgetta that when all is quiet and it will be safe for him to return to her, she shall strike a match as a signal. When Michele returns he reminds her of their old courtship days and shows her the cloak under which he has sheltered her. She is indifferent and retires. Michele, left alone with his thoughts, strikes a match as if to light his pipe. The lover, mistaking it for Giorgetta's signal, climbs up the side of the barge. He is throttled by the indignant husband, who then covers the body with his cloak. When Giorgetta reappears there is a stormy scene between the two, which reaches its climax when Michele triumphantly lifts his cloak revealing the corpse of Luigi.

The music is a blending of themes only incidental to the action. One of the freshest songs is sung by an outside vendor of ditties, with its refrain, "This is the story of Mimi." An organ-grinder comes by and plays a lively air while tipsy bargemen dance to it. There are few solos by the principals, one being by Luigi in praise of love and wine; and another along the same vein of drinking, by Tinca; a duet between the guilty lovers; and a dramatic bass aria by Michele, before committing the final crime.

TURANDOT

(*Too'-rahn-doh*)

Lyric Drama in Three Acts. Music by Puccini. Book by Giuseppe Adami and Renato Simoni. The score was incomplete at the time of the composer's death, and the last duet and the finale were completed by F. Alfano. La Scala, Milan, April 25, 1926; Metropolitan, New York, November 16, 1926.

SCENE: Peking.
TIME: Legendary.

CAST ALTOUM, *Emperor of China* (Tenor).
TURANDOT, *his daughter* (Soprano).

Timur, *the dethroned Tartar King* (Basso).
Calaf, *the Unknown Prince, his son* (Tenor).
Liu, *the slave girl of Timur* (Soprano).
Ping, *the Grand Chancellor* (Baritone).
Pang, *the General Purveyor* (Tenor).
Pong, *the Chief Cook* (Tenor).
A Mandarin (Baritone).
The Prince of Persia (Baritone).
The Executioner (Baritone).
Guards, Attendants, Wise Men, Priests,
Mandarins, Musicians, Citizens, etc.

ARGUMENT   "Turandot" is a love story employing the familiar
device of the riddle to be solved, under penalty of
death.   The scene is China, but a China of legend and fantasy.   The
music marks a progression along modern lines, especially in intricate
harmony, and while hailed by critics has not won lasting popular appeal.

Act I *The Walls of the Great Violet City—Peking.*   The square in
front of the palace is peopled by a picturesque throng who
listen to a proclamation read by a Mandarin.   It is to the effect that
the Princess Turandot has consented to become the bride of him of
royal blood who shall solve three enigmas; but that if he shall fail, his
head shall be forfeited.   Already several have suffered death and the
latest victim is the young Prince of Persia.   He is to be beheaded at the
rising of the moon.   The crowd grows unruly and in the tumult an old
man falls to the ground.   A slave girl calls for aid in his behalf, and a
young man hastens to their side.   He recognizes the fallen man as his
father, Timur, the former sovereign of Tartar.   The son has chosen to
remain incognito and is styled the Unknown Prince.   He is known only
to his father and to the slave girl, Liu, who secretly loves him.

Meanwhile two assistants to the Executioner appear upon the battlements and whet the huge sword which is to decapitate the luckless
Persian Prince.   The crowd grows more and more ferocious, but when
presently the victim appears, handsome and with a dreamy look in his
eyes, the hatred of the mob turns to pity, and they clamor to the Princess Turandot to show mercy.   In answer to their cry she appears on the
loggia, so divinelike in her beauty that the crowd grow silent and
prostrate themselves upon the ground.   Only the Unknown Prince remains standing.   The funeral procession passes on, leaving him with
Timur and Liu alone in the square.   Then, despite Timur's remon-
strances, the Prince announces his intention of himself trying to solve

the riddles and win the Princess.   As he approaches the gong he encounters three officials, Ping, Pang, and Pong, who also try to dissuade
him.   Liu adds her entreaties, and the ghosts of other princes slain in
the endeavor appear to him.   As a final warning, the Executioner appears with the gory head of the Prince of Persia.   But undeterred, the
Unknown Prince rushes to the gong and strikes it three times, exclaiming, "Turandot! Turandot! Turandot!"

Act II   *Scene 1.   Pavilion in the Imperial Palace.*   This scene is re-
stricted to a colloquy among the three ministers, Ping, Pang,
and Pong, who recount China's ancient glories and bemoan the present
situation.   They mournfully tell of the thirteen unlucky suitors who
have offered the Princess their hearts, and only lost their heads.
Scene 2.   Square in Front of the Imperial Palace.   The curious
throng watches the preparations being made for another test—that of
the Unknown Prince.   Mandarins and Wise Men enter, the latter bearing the scrolls on which the answers to the enigmas are inscribed.   A
flourish of trumpets announces the entrance of the Emperor, who seats
himself on a throne at the top of an outside staircase.   At its foot stands
the Unknown Prince.   A Mandarin reads the proclamation ending
with the sentence of death.   At its conclusion Turandot appears and
tells why she has set this severe test.   It is to avenge the fate of a princess, her ancestress of centuries agone.   Looking menacingly at the
Prince she says: "The enigmas are three; Death is but one!"   "No, Princess," he replies; "The enigmas are three; Life is but one!"   She then
propounds the riddles and he answers each in turn with the words,
"Hope," "Blood," and "Turandot."   The throng acclaims the Prince,
but Turandot appeals to her father to save her from this stranger.   The
Emperor replies: "Sacred is the oath."   While Turandot still rebels,
the Prince in turn gives her a chance to escape.   He says that if she will
tell him his name before the rise of dawn she shall be free and he will lay
down his life.

Act III   *Scene 1.   The Garden of the Palace.*   Heralds announce that
by order of Turandot none shall sleep that night.   The
Prince's name must be disclosed under penalty of death.   The crowd in
terror supplicate the Prince to reveal his name.   The three ministers
try to bribe him.   But he is adamant.   Timur and Liu are seized and
brought before the Princess, as being the only persons who know the
secret.   Timur is on the point of being tortured, but Liu springs in
front of him and exclaims that she alone knows the stranger's name.
Then before they have had time to make good their threat to torture

her, she seizes a dagger and stabs herself. The crowd is moved to tenderness by her self-sacrifice, and even Turandot stands in wonderment at this unseen power. The Unknown Prince seizes this moment to plead to her heart of ice. As she still defies him he takes her in his arms and kisses her. The embrace frees her pent-up emotions and she admits herself vanquished. As dawn breaks he generously whispers to her his name—"Calaf, the son of Timur." On hearing the fatal secret her pride is rekindled, and she haughtily says that she will take him before the people and proclaim his identity—which means death.

Scene 2. Exterior of the Palace. Again are seen the crowd surrounding the Emperor and his dignitaries. Turandot ascends the staircase, saying: "August Father, I know the name of the stranger." Then turning and looking straight at Calaf who awaits his sentence, she murmurs: "His name . . . is Love!" The Prince rushes up the staircase and enfolds her in his arms, while the throng scatter flowers and shout with joy.

ALBERTO FRANCHETTI

A modern Italian composer, born in Turin, September 18, 1860. Franchetti studied at Italian conservatories, and his music is of a somewhat traditional type. He is known in this country for two operas, "Christopher Columbus" and "Germania." He died in Viareggio, August 4, 1942.

CHRISTOPHER COLUMBUS

An historical Opera in Three Acts and an Epilogue; music by Franchetti; text by Luigi Illica. Produced at Genoa (Columbus' birthplace) in 1892—a quadricentennial.

SCENE: Spain and America.
TIME: Circa 1942.

The story and characters of "Christopher Columbus" follow the general lines of history. Columbus obtains aid from Queen Isabella for his voyage of discovery. Incidents of the voyage and with the Indians in America are depicted; and the epilogue shows the aged voyager lying at the tomb of his patron queen.

GERMANIA
(Ger-mah'-nia)

Dramatic Opera in Four Acts.   Music by Franchetti.   Book by Luigi Illica.   Milan, 1902.   At New York, the Metropolitan, January 22, 1910.

SCENE: Various parts of Germany.
TIME: 1806.

ARGUMENT   "Germania" is a picture of the upheaval in Germany caused by the Napoleonic wars.

Act I   *An Old Mill at Nuremberg.*   The revolutionists have converted an old mill at Nuremberg into a printing shop for their literature.   Palm, the author of some of this, is sought by the police, but unsuccessfully.   Meanwhile, books and pamphlets are sent out as bags of flour.   Carl Worms, who is in charge of the press, is visited by Ricke, a Nuremberg girl, who accuses him of betraying her.   She is especially downcast as a letter announces the return of Loewe, her lover.

Act II   *The Black Forest.*   Loewe, Ricke and others seek refuge in a hut, Loewe having been among those proscribed by the victorious Napoleon.   Ricke has consented to marry Loewe.   Worms then summons him to attend a meeting of the secret brotherhood.   Ricke, in terror, flees, leaving a note telling the man she has just wed not to follow her.   The bewildered Loewe finally learns the truth from Ricke's little sister Jane.

Act III   *A Secret Hall at Koenigsberg.*   The patriots meet with the utmost secrecy and lay plans to defeat the invader of their country.   Only one standing apart, masked, jeers at their motives.   He proves to be Loewe, who now challenges Worms to fight.   The latter, however, refuses to defend himself, and others interpose to stop the quarrel.

Act IV   *The Battlefield of Leipzig.*   The plain is covered with prostrate forms after the great battle has been fought.   Ricke seeks among them for the husband she has deserted, and finally finds him not far away from the corpse of Worms.   Loewe is barely alive, and soon expires in Ricke's arms, but she makes no outcry as she lies down beside him.   In life all things conspired to keep them apart; but in death they can be united.

PIETRO MASCAGNI

Mascagni, famous around the world as the composer of one brilliant operatic jewel, was born in Leghorn, Italy, December 7, 1863. He came of humble stock, his father being a baker, and the first years of his life were an unending struggle against hardship. His father wanted him to study law, but the boy had set his heart upon music. An uncle helped him financially; and he studied for two years at the Milan Conservatory, under Ponchielli. After leaving there he made a meager living as a conductor of operas, and finally settled in Cerignola where he conducted an orchestra and taught music. In 1888 while at work on an unfinished opera, he learned of a prize offered for a one-act opera, by Sonzogno, the publisher. On an impulse he wrote "Cavalleria Rusticana" and sent it in. It received the prize, and was performed at the Constanzi Theatre, Rome, in 1890. It aroused the audience to a frenzy of enthusiasm and made the composer famous overnight. His native city, Leghorn, welcomed him home with a torchlight procession. Medals were struck in his honor, and the King conferred upon him the Order of the Crown—all this at the age of twenty-seven. He had "found himself" but never again succeeded in repeating his success, although he lived to eighty-two. His last years were impoverished, due to the ravages of war in his land. He died in Rome, August 2, 1945. Other operas of moderate success include: "Friend Fritz" (1892), "Iris" (1898), "The Maskers" (1901), "Zanetto" (1902), "Isabeau" (1911), and "Lodoletta" (1917).

CAVALLERIA RUSTICANA
(Cah-vah-lee-ree'-ah Rus-tee-cahn'-a)

(Rustic Chivalry.) Dramatic Opera in One Act. Music by Pietro Mascagni. Book by Targioni-Tozzetti and Menasci, after the story by Giovanni Verga. Constanzi Theatre, Rome, May 20, 1890. Chicago, 1891, and the Metropolitan, New York, December 30, 1891. By this time, "Cavalleria" was being performed all over the world.

SCENE: A village of Sicily.
TIME: The Present.

CAST   TURIDDU, *a farmer* (Tenor).
        LUCIA, *his mother* (Contralto).
        ALFIO, *a carter* (Baritone).
        LOLA, *his wife* (Contralto).
        SANTUZZA, *a peasant girl* (Soprano).
        Peasant Neighbors and Villagers.

ARGUMENT   The theme of "Rustic Chivalry" is well described
           by its title and still better by the impassioned
music which follows closely the simple story to its tragic close.   The
music fits the theme so closely and is of such continuing loveliness that
it seems invidious to single out special excerpts.   The Prelude sounds
its keynote in three significant passages: the grief and despair of Santuzza; the dialogue between her and Turiddu where she implores him
to remain true to her; and an aria in Sicilian folk-style sung by him
backstage as a serenade to Lola.   As his voice dies away, the curtain
rises.

A Village Square in Sicily.   The old triangle of love is present.
Turiddu, a young farmer, has had a sweetheart, Lola, but is called to
military duty.   While he is away she marries Alfio, a carter.   Turiddu
turns for consolation to Santuzza, a peasant girl who loves him not
wisely but too well.   Becoming tired of this easy conquest, he turns
again to Lola, despite the fact that she is wedded.   This is the state of
affairs as the curtain rises on a peaceful village scene.   It is Easter, and
the devout peasants are going to church.   While the bells chime, the
peasants sing of their joy in a new springtime.   The swelling tones of
the organ follow them.   They fall upon their knees while Santuzza
leads in the lovely canticle: "Let us sing of our Lord ris'n victorious!"

While the people enter the church, Santuzza lingers outside. She meets Lucia, her lover's mother, and tells her of her trouble in a pathetic melody, "Well, do you know, good mother" (Voi lo sapete). Lucia is sympathetic, but can do nothing beyond going into the church to offer up her own prayers. Santuzza stays behind, feeling unworthy to go in, and next meets the faithless Turiddu. A dramatic dialogue ensues, again interpreted by expressive music. At its height the carefree voice of Lola is heard backstage singing about her "King of Roses." With it still upon her lips she enters and takes in the situation at a glance. A dialogue of bitter irony between the two women ensues. Turiddu again spurns Santuzza and goes with the triumphant Lola into the church. Driven to desperation, Santuzza next confronts Alfio, the carter, and tells him of Lola's conduct. Alfio gives vent to a terrible outburst of rage: "Revenge I'll have upon them this very day!"

The stage is empty, but the curtain does not fall, as the service within the church continues. The storm without suddenly gives way to calm. The first notes of the Intermezzo pray for peace. It is as if the angels on high were adding their voices to this plea.

All too soon the violence of human passion reasserts itself. Church services over, the merry villagers throng the square, meeting and greeting. Cups are passed and Turiddu sings a rollicking drinking song. Alfio returns at this moment and is invited to drink. Instead he refuses and challenges Turiddu to fight, giving this challenge in the Sicilian form of biting his enemy's ear. The two retire, after Turiddu has bidden his mother farewell and asked her to care for the wronged Santuzza, and fight their duel behind the scenes. A short, terrible pause ensues, followed by running messengers, and a cry from the women, "Turiddu has been slain!"

L'AMICO FRITZ

(*Lah'-mee-co Fritz*)

(Friend Fritz.)   Sentimental Opera in Three Acts.   Music by Pietro Mascagni.   Book by Suaratoni, after the story by Erckmann-Chatrian. Rome, 1891, and Dresden, 1892.   At the Metropolitan, New York, January 10, 1894.

SCENE: Alsace.
TIME: The Present.

CAST   FRITZ KOBUS, *a rich bachelor* (Tenor).
DAVID, *a Rabbi* (Baritone).
FREDERICO { *friends of Fritz* { Tenor.
HANEGO   {   { Tenor.
SUSEL, *a farmer's daughter* (Soprano).
BEPPE, *a Gypsy* (Soprano)
CATERINA, *a housekeeper* (Contralto).

ARGUMENT   "Friend Fritz" was the composer's single incursion in the field of Light Opera.   While it has many lilting melodies, it has not won a permanent place in the repertory of either English or Italian singers.   The story deals with the capitulation of a dyed-in-the-wool bachelor.

Act I   *Home of Fritz.*   Fritz Kobus, a wealthy farmer and confirmed bachelor, on his fortieth birthday invites his friends to dine with him.   Among the guests is Susel, his tenant's pretty daughter, who presents him with a nosegay, and sits beside him.   For the first time he realizes a woman's charm.   Rabbi David, a confirmed matchmaker, thereupon wagers with Fritz that he will soon be married, but the latter is obstinate.

After a musical melange of greetings and congratulations on the part of Fritz's friends, Susel sings a lovely flower song, one of the most tuneful bits in the opera.   Others in this Act are: Beppe's song with violin accompaniment; and a stirring march taken from a popular Alsatian melody.

Act II   *A Garden.*   Fritz, however, cannot dismiss Susel from his mind.   He makes a pretext of visiting her father.   The girl mounts a ladder in the garden, picks cherries, and throws them down to Fritz, who is enchanted.   When Rabbi David appears and tells him that he has found a suitable husband for Susel, Fritz cannot help revealing his own chagrin.

Susel's charming ballad, under a cherry tree, "Handsome cavalier!" is followed by a duet between her and Fritz, "Lovely Susel," ending with her own vivacious bird song. Other numbers include: an orchestral scherzo, "The Arrival of Biroccino," a diverting version of the story of Isaac and Rebecca, as interpreted by David and Susel; and a turbulent aria by Fritz.

Act III *Home of Fritz.* Back at his own home again, Fritz finds no peace and doesn't know what is the matter with him. The scheming David tells him Susel's marriage has been decided on. Fritz loses his temper, and says he will forbid the bans. At this moment Susel, pale and sad, comes in with a basket of fruit. When her wedding is mentioned she bursts into tears. Fritz tries to comfort her, and presently the girl is in his arms. David wins his wager, one of Fritz's vineyards, which he promptly bestows upon Susel as a wedding gift.

This Act has for prelude an instrumental number, which has some of the charm of the Intermezzo from "Cavalleria." It was as though the composer were striving again to catch the immortal vision. Two other noteworthy numbers are: an impassioned song by Fritz, "O, love!", and a duet between the two principals, "I love you!"

IRIS
(*Ee'-ris*)

Tragic Opera in Three Acts. Music by Mascagni. Book by Luigi Illica. Theatre Constanzi, Rome, November, 1898, and in revised form the next year, in Milan. At New York, the Metropolitan, December 16, 1907. In the cast were Eames, Caruso, and Scotti.

SCENE: Japan.
TIME: Recent.

CAST   Cieco, *a blind man* (Basso).
Iris, *his daughter* (Soprano).
Osaka, *a wealthy libertine* (Tenor).
Kyoto, *keeper of a dive* (Baritone).
A Geisha (Soprano).
A Peddler (Tenor).
A Rag-Picker (Tenor).
Girls, Villagers, Rag-Pickers, etc.

ARGUMENT   "Iris" is an Oriental opera, telling the tragedy of a lost soul—a Japanese girl who fell into evil ways through no fault of her own, and who passes through the uttermost depths to the light of a happier world beyond.

Act I *A Japanese Garden.* The scene opens with a colorful hymn to the Sun as the Lord of Life. Iris, as an innocent child, is playing with her doll, and her blind father hears her chatter with much contentment. This idyllic scene is disturbed by the entrance of Osaka, an unprincipled man of the town, who has seen the beauty of the young girl and desires her. He arranges with Kyoto, a procurer for an evil resort, to abduct her. The girl goes with other maidens to do their washing at the river brink, and is attracted by a puppet show devised by the crafty Kyoto. She is seized by the men, who leave a purse of gold to make their transaction legal. Geishas dance around her to prevent a rescue, and her father is told that she went willingly. He curses her and their shattered home.

Act II *A Room in the Yoshiwara, or Home of the Geishas.* Iris lies asleep while other girls hum a soft melody. Osaka enters, asking for her, but is informed by Kyoto that her price is high. The libertine agrees, for, as he says, she is a "creature with a soul." When Iris awakens she believes herself in Paradise, her surroundings and gifts are so lovely, and when Osaka approaches she greets him as a "Son of Light." He answers cynically, and at last, wearied by her innocence, he bids Kyoto take her away. The keeper orders the geishas to robe her in transparent garments and expose her to the gaze of the street crowd. Osaka relents and tells Kyoto he shall have his own price for her. During this brutal haggling over the ignorant girl, who still does not know her whereabouts, her father appears in the crowd below and calls to her. She answers joyfully, but he hurls mud upon her and greets her with contempt and curses. Crazed, the girl casts herself into a deep vault, and is given over for dead.

Act III *A Dump Heap on the Outskirts of the City.* Ragpickers are searching over the refuse of the city, in the hope of finding articles of value. They discover the body of Iris, still clothed in its finery. While they try to secure the dress, the body seems to revive. This scatters the ragpickers, who run away in a panic. In a state of semi-consciousness Iris again hears the voices of the world—Osaka telling her that she has perished as a flower that sheds its fragrance in death—her father justifying his brutal act. Still Iris does not understand it all, and murmurs "Why? why?" Why should her simple life at the cottage be destroyed? As if in answer, the sun bursts forth, and she is reminded of her earlier hymn to "My Lord, the Sun!" Flowers spring up around her, enfold her in their expanding petals, and lift her body heavenward.

LODOLETTA

(Lo-do-let'-ta)

Tragic Opera in Three Acts, by Mascagni. Words by Gioacchino
Forzano, after Ouida's novel, "Two Little Wooden Shoes." Rome,
April 30, 1917. At New York, the Metropolitan, January 12, 1918. In
the cast were Caruso and Farrar.

SCENE: A Dutch Village.
TIME: The Second French Empire.

CAST ANTONIO, *a peasant* (Basso).
LODOLETTA, *his foster daughter* (Soprano).
FLAMMEN, *a painter* (Tenor).
FRANZ (Basso).
GIANETTO (Baritone).
A MAD WOMAN (Mezzo-Soprano).
VANNARD (Mezzo-Soprano).
MAUD (Soprano).
A VOICE (Tenor).
A Letter-carrier, an old Violinist, Villagers,
Guests, etc.

Act I *A Village Street.* Lodoletta, foster daughter of old Antonio,
and now grown to be sixteen, desires very much to own a pair
of wooden shoes, but Antonio cannot afford to buy them. Flammen, a
painter from Paris, offers to purchase a picture of the Madonna on the
wall of their cottage. Antonio accepts the gold piece and with it buys
the coveted shoes. Shortly after, he is killed by the fall of a tree.

Act II *The Same.* The painter has conceived a deep affection for
the lovely girl and gets her to pose for his pictures. Their
friendship is innocent, but neighbors regard it with suspicion. To
shield her, the artist returns to Paris, but finds that he cannot forget his
model. Later, when he returns to find her, she has disappeared.

Act III *Flammen's Villa.* Friends of the artist gather at his home
for New Year's festivities. While the celebration is at its
height, Lodoletta enters the garden in rags. She looks through the window at the merry company, then falls exhausted in the snow. Later,
after his guests have departed, Flammen finds two sadly-worn little
shoes on his threshold. Looking further, he discovers his sweetheart
frozen to death.

FRANCO LEONI

A contemporary Italian composer, born in Milan, October 24, 1864. He studied music at the Milan Conservatory, one of his teachers being Ponchielli. Of his four operas, "Rip Van Winkle," "Raggio di Luna," "Ib and Little Christina," and "The Oracle," only the last named is familiar to American music-lovers. Leoni died in Dover, England, November 11, 1938.

L'ORACOLO
(Lo-rock'-o-lo)

(The Oracle.) Tragic Opera in One Act. Music by Franco Leoni. Book by Camillo Zanoni, after the play, "The Cat and the Cherub," by Chester B. Fernald. Covent Garden, London, June 28, 1905. Metropolitan, New York, February 4, 1915.

SCENE: Chinatown, San Francisco.
TIME: The Present.

CAST WIN-SHEE, *a learned doctor* (Baritone).
CHIM-FEN, *keeper of an opium joint* (Baritone).
HOO-TSIN, *a wealthy merchant* (Basso).
WIN-SAN-LUY, *son of Win-Shee* (Tenor).
AH-YOE, *daughter of Hoo-Tsin* (Soprano).
HUA-QUEE, *a nurse* (Contralto).
Chinese Men, Women and Children, Opium Smokers, Policemen, etc.

ARGUMENT An attempt is made in this tragic piece to depict certain phases of Chinese character—the episodical bits in daily life hidden beneath the surface from the passer-by, which, however, are of the most vital importance to the Chinaman himself.

Hatchet Row, in the Chinese Quarter. It is early dawn on the Chinese New Year. Lights gleam from the opium den of Chim-Fen, and the sound of revelry is heard. The keeper ejects one of the most unruly inmates and pauses on his way back to shake his fist at the lighted window of his wealthy neighbor, Hoo-Tsin, the merchant. Why should he work so hard when his neighbor rolls in wealth? The nurse employed in Hoo-Tsin's house approaches, and he demands of her that she obtain a fan given by San-Luy to the merchant's beautiful daughter, Ah-Yoe. Frightened by his threats, she promises. Presently the learned Win-Shee passes. Chim-Fen exchanges New Year's greetings with him, and the Doctor takes opportunity to reprove him for the sort of business he conducts. A policeman passes by, and Win-Shee cautions the other not to notice the "American dog" by word or sign but to pretend to be in earnest conversation. After they have parted company, the Doctor's son, San-Luy, appears beneath the window of Ah-Yoe, where he sings a serenade. The lovers exchange greetings. Now it is broad day and Chinese hail the neighbors everywhere in greeting. Chim-Fen takes this opportunity of general fraternizing to ask of Hoo-Tsin the hand of Ah-Yoe in marriage. The only answer, he receives is the ironical wish, from Hoo-Tsin: "May all the opium in Chinatown pass through your hands!" At this second rebuff that day Chim-Fen is in a rage which is heightened when the crowd reviles him.

As part of the New Year's ceremony, the infant son of Hoo-Tsin is brought in by the nurse, and the oracle is consulted. Part of it is favorable, part unfavorable. Before the child can be taken home, it is kidnapped by Chim-Fen and hidden in a cellar. He then tells the distracted father that he will try to find the child, and makes a bargain with him that it shall be at the price of Ah-Yoe's hand. San-Luy also makes the same bargain. He traces the child to the cellar, but when he attempts to enter he comes to blows with Chim-Fen, and the two fall struggling down the cellar steps. In the outcome San-Luy is killed. When news of the murder is spread abroad there is a great confusion, and the heartbroken Ah-Yoe mourns for her sweetheart. His father, Win-Shee, likewise is disconsolate, but determines to avenge the bloody deed. At nightfall in his wanderings he discovers and rescues the child; then encounters Chim-Fen, whom he reproaches and finally slays. A policeman approaches. Quickly adopting his own advice of the morning, Win-Shee props up the dead body and pretends an animated conversation with it until the officer goes by. Justice has been done according to the Chinese code, so why should the foreign dogs interfere?

The music is not altogether successful in conveying the oriental atmosphere. It relies upon descriptive and dramatic passages familiar to the later Italian school. One of the more delightful numbers is the song of Ah-Yoe on her balcony, in greeting to the new day. Win-Shee also has some good opportunities for the baritone voice.

UMBERTO GIORDANO

Giordano is a contemporary Italian composer of some note. He was born at Foggia, August 26, 1867, and studied at the Naples Conservatory under Serrao. One of his earlier works was the one-act opera, "Marina," which was entered for the Sonzogno prize that Mascagni won with his "Cavalleria Rusticana." This was followed by "Mala Vita," which was produced at Rome, in 1892; "André Chénier" (1896); "Fedora" (1906); "Siberia" (1908); and "Madame Sans Gêne," his most successful work (1915). Giordano died in Milan, November 12, 1948.

ANDRÉ CHÉNIER
(An-dray Shain-yay)

Tragic Opera in Four Acts. Music by Umberto Giordano. Book by Luigi Illica. La Scala, Milan, March 23, 1896. Academy of Music, New York, November 13, 1896. At the Metropolitan, March 7, 1921.

SCENE: Paris.
TIME: The French Revolution.

CAST ANDRÉ CHÉNIER, a poet (Tenor).
CHARLES GERARD, a Revolutionist (Baritone).
COUNTESS DE COIGNY (Soprano).
MADELEINE, her daughter (Soprano).
BERSI, her maid (Mezzo-Soprano).
ROUCHER, friend of Chénier (Basso).
MATHIEU, a Revolutionist (Baritone).
MADELON, an aged woman (Soprano).
FLEVILLE, a writer (Tenor).
THE ABBÉ (Tenor).
SCHMIDT, jailer at St. Lazare (Basso).
A SPY.

Guests, Servants, Pages, Peasants, Soldiers, Judges, Prisoners, Mob, etc.

ARGUMENT This opera in plot follows the familiar lines of the heroine willing to sacrifice honor, then life, for the man she loves. The story is of a poet who gets into the toils of his enemies during the French Revolution. Although based upon a character of history, the librettist has taken many liberties with his actions. The real Chénier was both poet and patriot. The music alternates between tender, lyric passages, and others of high emotion, leading up to "set" numbers of the later Italian school.

Act I *Ballroom in a Château.* Prior to the Revolution, Gerard, a revolutionist, is secretly in love with Madeleine, the Countess' daughter. A ball is given, and among the guests is André Chénier, a poet with revolutionary tendencies. Madeleine asks him to improvise a poem on love, but he sings of the wrongs of the poor. Gerard appears with a crowd of ragged men and women, but the Countess' servants eject the intruders.

The song of the poet, a tirade against Church and State, is the principal number in this Act: "Once o'er azure fields" (Un di all' azzurro spazio).

Act II *Café Hottot in Paris.* Some years later, Chénier has offended the Revolutionists by denouncing Robespierre. A spy is watching Bersi, Madeleine's old nurse, and sees her hand Chénier a letter. It is from Madeleine, who begs him come to her aid, and arranges a rendezvous.

Robespierre enters with citizens. Gerard, now high in favor, wants to possess Madeleine, who has come to meet Chénier. They are about to flee, when Gerard interferes. The rivals fight and Gerard is wounded. The lovers escape.

Act III *Revolutionary Tribunal.* Chénier has been captured, and Gerard brings formal charge against his rival. Madeleine pleads for her lover, finally promising to give herself to Gerard if Chénier is spared. Gerard, moved by the girl's love, agrees to save Chénier if he can. At the trial he declares that the indictment is false. But the mob, thirsting for blood, demands the poet's death.

Gerard's inner conflict between lust and honor is admirably depicted by both voice and instruments. The latter introduce a hint of the "Marseillaise." His song is a favorite one with baritones: "An enemy of his country" (Nemico della patria).

Act IV *Prison of Lazare at Midnight.* Madeleine and Gerard visit Chénier. She has bribed the jailer to allow her to take the place of another prisoner. If she cannot live for her lover, she can, at least, die with him. Together she and Chénier go to the scaffold, to pay the last penalty.

In the opening of this scene the poet is discovered writing his last verses. They are in praise and trust of his sweetheart and give opportunity for a fine lyric for tenor: "As some soft day in May" (Come un bel di Maggio).

MADAME SANS GÊNE
(Ma-dam' Sahn Zhayn)

(Madam Don't Care.) Historic Opera in Four Acts. Music by Giordano. Book by Renato Simoni. After the Comedy by Victorien Sardou and E. Moreau. Metropolitan, New York, January 25, 1915. In the cast were Farrar, Amato, De Segurola, and Martinelli.

SCENE: France.
TIME: Days of Napoleon.

CAST   NAPOLEON (Baritone).
  CATERINA HUBSCHER ("Catherine," "MADAME SANS GÊNE"), *a laundress* (Soprano).
  TONIOTTA, *a laundress* (Soprano).
  GIULIA, *a laundress* (Soprano).
  LA ROSSA, *a laundress* (Soprano).
  LEFEBVRE, *sergeant, then marshal* (Tenor).
  FOUCHÉ, *patriot, then minister of police* (Baritone).
  COUNT OF NEIPPERG, *an Austrian* (Tenor).
  VINAIGRE, *a drummer* (Tenor).
  QUEEN CAROLINE (Soprano).
  PRINCESS ELISA (Soprano).
  GELSOMINO, *valet* (Baritone).
  LEROY, *tailor* (Baritone).
  DE BRIGODE, *court chamberlain* (Baritone).
  MADAME DE BOULOW (Soprano).
  ROUSTAN, *head of the Mamelukes* (Baritone).
   Citizens, Soldiers, Huntsmen, Ladies of the Court, etc.

ARGUMENT   This colorful opera is unique in its attempt to make Napoleon the central figure of a romantic drama—giving him as well as his attendants a singing part. It is full of figures and action, and crosses a considerable period of time.

Act I *Catherine's Laundry, Paris, August 10, 1792.* Catherine Hubscher, a pretty Alsatian, has earned by her saucy manner the popular nickname of "Madam Don't Care." Her laundry is, on this historic morning, a storm center, as the mob is attacking the Tuileries—this is one of the red-letter days of the French Revolution. Fouché, a patriot, enters in great trepidation at the doings of the crowd. He is followed by Catherine, who rallies him for his lack of courage. She herself has great tales to tell of what she has witnessed in the street. Fouché says that it is his ambition to become minister of police. She replies tauntingly that he has about as much chance to become that as she has to become a duchess. A great uproar proclaims that the palace has been taken. So riotous is the street that the laundress prudently barricades her shop. Presently she sees a wounded man, and admits him. It is the Count of Neipperg, an Austrian, who has come to grief in trying to rescue the Queen. Catherine hides him in her room. Her lover, Lefebvre, a police sergeant, enters. He discovers the concealed man and at first is jealous; then believes Catherine and aids her to effect the Count's escape.

The lively action is sustained by both singers and orchestra, without any outstanding single numbers in this Act. A pleasing dance of girls, "La Fricasee," is followed by Catherine's aria on the rudeness of the soldiers. The music then leads up to the curtain in martial strains, the roll of drums, the feet of marching men, and the strains of the "Marseillaise."

Act II *Château of Compeigne.* Nineteen years have passed by. The obscure Napoleon has become a world conqueror, and many of his followers have been ennobled. Lefebvre has been made the Duke of Danzig, and Catherine, his wife, is really a Duchess. But she is still sharp of tongue and bourgeois of action, so much so that the Emperor counsels Lefebvre to divorce her. This the latter laughingly repeats to his wife, and says he doesn't intend to do anything of the sort. Their old acquaintance, Count Neipperg, now enters. He has been dismissed from Court for his too open admiration of the Empress. He is in despair and asks his friends to procure for him a last interview with her. Fouché, now minister of police, enters to announce the royal ladies, for whom the Duke and Duchess are to give a reception. The flunkeys try to tell Madame Sans Gêne how she is to deport herself, but give it up in despair. The reception which follows is conducted without decorum. The hostess flouts her guests to their faces, and it is with open joy they hear that she is summoned to appear before Napoleon, to answer for her conduct.

The music here has more the flavor of Light Opera, as the action alternates between the dramatic and the humorous. The interweaving melody with an unusually vigorous plot keeps the senses quickened.

Act III *The Emperor's Cabinet.* Napoleon receives Madame Sans Gêne, and reproaches her for failing to shed luster on his Court. She should grant her husband a divorce and retire to private life. She retorts that her husband would not exchange her for the proudest princess. Then waxing eloquent she recites the glories of the army life, which she herself has followed. She calls to mind their early days of struggle, and even shows Napoleon his own unpaid laundry bill of nineteen years before. Touched by her naïveté, the Emperor forgives her and stoops to kiss the scar on her arm, received in battle. As she is about to retire, Neipperg enters on his way to the Empress' apartment. There is a sharp encounter between him and the Emperor. As officers rush in, the irate Napoleon orders that he be shot at sunrise.

The musical passages between the former Corporal and laundress are delightful.

Act IV *The Same.* The stage is undisturbed, but a dying fire and gutting candles indicate that the night is far spent and the last hours of the condemned man are running out. There is a brief scene between Catherine and Lefebvre, in which they deplore their own helplessness. Napoleon re-enters in much agitation. Catherine pleads with him to spare the Count, but Napoleon sternly orders her, as a test, to knock at the Empress' door and announce Neipperg's presence. She does so tremblingly. The door opens slightly and a note is handed out. It dismisses the Count and completely vindicates the Empress. The Count's life is spared, and the scene ends amid general felicitations. "As for your divorce," says the Emperor to Lefebvre with mock sternness, "forget it." He tweaks Catherine's ear. "Thank heaven for giving this woman to you!"

A fanfare of hunting horns and a spirited chorus bring the final curtain.

FEDORA

Tragic Opera in Three Acts. Music by Giordano. Book by Colautti, after the play by Sardou. Milan, November 17, 1898. At New

York, the Metropolitan, December 5, 1906, with Cavalieri, Caruso,
Alten, and Scotti.

SCENE: Paris and Switzerland.
TIME: Latter part of Nineteenth Century.

CAST PRINCESS FEDORA (Soprano).
COUNT LORIS (Tenor).
COUNTESS OLGA (Soprano).
DE SIRIEX, *a diplomat* (Baritone).
GRECH, *a police officer* (Basso).
DMITRI, *a groom* (Contralto).
CYRIL, *a coachman* (Baritone).
BOROV, *a doctor* (Baritone).
BARON ROUVEL (Baritone).
Servants, Attendants, etc.

ARGUMENT An opera of love and intrigue, the scene of which
is laid in Russia; based on a drama by Sardou.

Act I *Home of Count Vladimir, in St. Petersburg.* The lovely Princess Fedora impatiently awaits the coming of her accepted
suitor, Count Vladimir. He is brought in, in a dying condition, by
De Siriex, a diplomat, and suspicion points to Count Loris as the murderer. Fedora swears by a jeweled cross she wears that she will be
avenged.

Act II *Fedora's Apartments in Paris.* At a splendid reception given
by the Princess in Paris, she exerts all her wiles upon Loris, in
the hope of obtaining from him a confession. Meanwhile, however,
she finds herself falling in love with him. She fights this emotion unavailingly; and Loris in his turn avows his love. Then he tells her that
the real reason behind his act of vengeance was that fact that Count
Vladimir had betrayed his bride and brought her to the grave. The
Princess embraces him and shields him from Grech, the police officer
whom she had previously stationed outside.

The music in this Act rises to fine lyric heights, as the Count pleads
with the reluctant Princess. His aria is a sustained cantanina: "My
love compels me" (Amor ti vieta non amar).

Act III *A Swiss Villa.* Although Fedora and Loris have escaped to
Switzerland and are now happily married, nemesis pursues
them. The police are on Loris' trail, and he receives word that his
brother has been put in prison, and his mother has died of grief. On
top of this comes word that it is none other than Fedora who has put

the police after him. He is ready to kill her when, in her own despair, she swallows poison. Stricken with remorse, he pleads with her to live for his sake; but she dies in his arms.

The music here reaches its climax when the Count, torn by conflicting emotions at news of his mother's death, sings a pathetic aria, "My dear old mother!"

ITALO MONTEMEZZI

Montemezzi is one of the later group of Italian composers, who established his standing by a single opera, but that a powerful one. He was born in Verona, in 1875, and studied in Italian schools. One of his earliest compositions was a choral, "Cantico dei Cantici," produced at the Conservatory of Music in Milan, in 1900, which attracted attention to his gifts. An opera, "Giovanni Gallurese," was given in Turin, in 1905; and "Hellera" at the same place, in 1909. But it remained for "The Three Kings" to bring him to international fame.

THE LOVE OF THE THREE KINGS

(L'Amore Dei Tre Re.) Tragic Poem in Three Acts. Music by Italo Montemezzi. Book by Sem. Benelli, La Scala, Milan, April 10, 1913. At the Metropolitan, New York, January 2, 1914. In both Paris and London, the same year.

> SCENE: A remote castle of Italy.
> TIME: The Middle Ages.
>
> CAST   ARCHIBALDO, *an aged king* (Basso).
> MANFREDO, *his son* (Baritone).
> AVITO, *Prince of Altura* (Tenor).
> FLAMINIO, *an attendant* (Tenor).
> FIORA, *wife of Manfredo* (Soprano).
> SERVANT GIRL (Soprano).
> YOUNG GIRL (Soprano).
> OLD WOMAN (Contralto).
> Court Attendants, Mourners, Villagers of Altura.

ARGUMENT   Fiora, formerly loved by Avito, Prince of Altura.
has been given as the price of peace to the con
queror of that country.   The story is the struggle of this princess be
tween her old love and her loyalty to her new lord—the tragedy of jeal
ousy and broken faith.   The composer's style is abrupt rather than
flowing—a succession of musical phrases set in eloquent, declamatory
style.

Act I *Spacious Hall in the Castle.*   Archibaldo, the aged King of an
Italian country, has conquered, in earlier years, the neighbor
ing state of Altura.   As the price of peace he receives the maiden, Fiora,
whom he bestows upon his son, Manfredo, for wife.   Manfredo ten
derly loves his young wife, but is often away at the wars.   His father is
suspicious as to her conduct, and having become blind is all the more
distrustful.   In the opening scene, he enters with Flaminio, and ques
tions him as to her whereabouts.   He then retires, after having had a
signal lantern extinguished.   Fiora enters from her apartment and is
met by Avito, her former lover in Altura.   He renews his love-making,
but is warned of danger by the fact that the lantern is extinguished, and
turns to flee as the blind Archibaldo returns.   The latter questions
Fiora sharply as to whom she has been with, and her trembling replies
convince him that she is untrue to his son.   He sends her to her room,
as the sound of trumpets announce the return of Manfredo.   The
Prince is not informed of his father's fears, the latter murmuring, "O
Lord God, let me not see—let me be blind—be blind!"

The music is eloquent in this tense scene.   As the blind King enters,
his groping steps are mirrored by the orchestra.   At his questioning of
Flaminio, the latter replies: "There is no one, my lord.   All is quiet!"
(Tutto è pace!).   Fiora's song to her lover, "Give me thy lips" (Dammi
le labbra) is a central theme:

The extinguishing of the lantern, and the King's suspicious, "I hear
thee breathing!" are other tense moments in the music.

Act II *A Circular Terrace on the Castle Walls.*   Manfredo, recalled
to his troops, bids his wife a kind and affectionate farewell.

He does not demand anything of her—only that she will cheer him and his troops, as they ride away down the valley, by waving a scarf. Touched by his unselfish devotion she promises, and is minded thereafter to be a faithful wife to him. But alas for her good resolutions!—the first person she encounters upon the castle walls is Avito, disguised as a guard. She bids him go, saying that she is "conquered by kindness." He refuses, and makes such ardent love that she is once more overcome and yields to him. When the servants bring a casket containing Manfredo's scarf, she will not let her lover touch it, but waves it wearily to the distant horsemen. Archibaldo again surprises the lovers. Avito is ready to stab him with his dagger, but is prevented by Flaminio in a silent gesture. The King demands to know who is there. Flaminio shields the Prince, and is dismissed by Archibaldo, who rages at his own helplessness. In a fit of frenzy he throttles Fiora, because she withholds the name of her lover, while confessing her guilt. Manfredo returns, alarmed at the cessation of his signal, the waving scarf, and finds the old King crouching beside the dead body of Fiora. Archibaldo tells why he committed the deed, and Manfredo retires, overcome with grief. He is followed by the blind King, carrying the body.

The orchestra gives a vivid tone picture of Manfredo's cavalry riding down the valley. Then comes another frenzied scene between the two guilty lovers. "How art thou trembling, beloved!" sings Fiora in a low voice; to be answered by his triumphant, "Look up! We are in heaven!" (Siamo in cielo.) But the idyllic scene is rudely broken. The aged King again enters with vengeance in his hands. The hoofbeats of the returning Manfredo also spell tragedy. The closing music of the scene pulsates with grief.

Act III *Crypt in the Castle Chapel.* In the center lies the body of Fiora, clad in white, on a bed of flowers. A choir and various single voices sing lamentations. They disperse upon the entrance of Avito, who bows and shields his face as before a shrine. He bemoans his loss and in farewell kisses her upon the lips. A violent pain seizes him and he arises tottering. Manfredo approaches in the shadow. He recognizes the Alturian, and tells him that the girl's lips were poisoned as a trap to catch him, and his moments are numbered. More in sorrow than in anger Manfredo asks: "Did she love thee?" "More than the life they took from her!" replies Avito, and falls dying. Manfredo supports him, crying, "Why cannot I hate!" Overcome with remorse, he casts himself upon the bier and in turn presses the poisoned lips of his dead wife. Archibaldo gropes his way in, to find his son dying. The love of the three kings has brought only death in its wake.

The culminating cry of despair is from the lips of Avito: "Fiora! Fiora! There is naught but silence!" (E silencio!)—

ERMANNO WOLF-FERRARI

A German-Italian composer born in Venice, January 12, 1876. He took his name from both parents, his father being a celebrated German painter, August Wolf. Ermanno took naturally to music and was self-taught until seventeen, when he was placed under Rheinberger's instruction, at Munich. His composition, however, has revealed the Italian rather than the Teutonic influence. His operas include: "Cenerentola" (1900); "Le Donne Curiose" (1903); "I Quattro Rusteghi" (1906); "Il Segreto di Susanna" (1910); "I Giojelli della Madonna" (1911); and "L'Amore Medico" (1913). Three of these, to give them their more familiar English titles, "The Inquisitive Women," "The Secret of Susanne," and "Dr. Cupid," are of lighter texture and will be found in the Light Opera section of this volume. His one serious work, "The Jewels of the Madonna," bids fair to remain longer in repertory. He died in Venice, January 21, 1948.

THE JEWELS OF THE MADONNA

(I Giojelli della Madonna.) Dramatic Opera in Three Acts. Music by Wolf-Ferrari. Book by C. Zangarini and E. Golisciani. Berlin, December 23, 1911, with German title and text. Chicago in the original, January 16, 1912; and the Metropolitan, New York, March 5 following.

SCENE: Naples.
TIME: The Present.

CAST   MALIELLA, *adopted daughter of Carmela*
(Soprano).
CARMELA, *Gennaro's mother* (Mezzo-Soprano).
GENNARO, *a blacksmith* (Tenor).
RAFAELE, *chief of the Camorrists* (Baritone).
Camorrists, Street-sellers, Townsfolk, etc.

ARGUMENT   The scene of action is modern Naples.   The plot
hinges on the rivalry of Gennaro, a blacksmith,
and Rafaele, a Camorrist leader, for the love of Maliella.   The opening curtain is heralded by an orchestral prelude of Neapolitan folk
music, with a hint of the gay dances which enliven a melodramatic plot.

Act I   *A Small Open Square by the Sea.   Afternoon.*   A merry crowd
in a small public square awaits the festival procession in honor
of the Holy Virgin.   Maliella escapes from her house with disheveled
hair and disordered dress, protesting against the restraint of her foster-
mother.   After some banter with Gennaro she sings a challenging
song, inviting the assembled crowd of youths to kiss her.   An im-
promptu dance ensues, she is whirled in and disappears, but soon returns followed by Rafaele.   She repels him, and when he seizes her to
kiss her, stabs him in the hand with a pin drawn from her hair.   He
hesitates, then kisses the wound, swearing she shall be his, and, as she
replaces the pin in her hair, thrusts a flower in her bosom, which she
snatches forth and flings to the ground.   The procession comes in
sight, and he stays by her, pleading.   As the Madonna passes, he offers
to risk his soul for her, by placing the jewels of the Madonna round her
neck.   Terrified at the thought, she shrieks, while Rafaele and his
fellow-Camorrists laugh.   As she is about to enter her home again, Rafaele throws her the flower she has rejected, and this time Maliella
places it between her lips and goes within.

Musical numbers include: the blacksmith's song as he works at his
anvil and offers a prayer to the Virgin: "Madonna, tears and sighing"
(Con sonspiri); Maliella's rebellious story of another girl's love, "Thus
sang poor Cannatella"; a touching duet between Carmela and Gennaro, her son; and the chorus of hymns, with bells and guns in the background, announcing the procession of the Virgin.

Act II   One of the gems of the opera is the lovely intermezzo which
introduces this Act.   Its warmth of melody and sensuous appeal form a haunting picture of a typical Neapolitan night.

Garden of Carmela's House.   Evening of the same day.   Maliella is
with Carmela and Gennaro; the festival is not yet over.   Carmela leaves

them, and Gennaro begins to plead with Maliella, but she complains of the monotony of her life and threatens to leave her home. Gennaro begs for a farewell kiss, and losing control, clasps her in his arms and pours out his passion for her. Maliella escapes from him and proclaims her love for Rafaele, tauntingly repeating the Camorrist's offer to risk his soul for her by robbing the Madonna of her jewels. She returns to the house and Gennaro breaks down. The thought of Rafaele's boast possesses his mind, and his distraught fancy leads him to imagine that only by himself obtaining these jewels can he hope to win Maliella's love. He takes keys and tools with him and locks the garden door after him. Rafaele comes with his fellow-Camorrists to serenade Maliella. She enters the garden and he embraces her through the bars till warned away by the approach of Gennaro, who enters looking like a ghost. In answer to her cry he responds "For you!" and discloses the stolen jewels of the Madonna. She screams, but Gennaro assures her that the Virgin has already forgiven his crime. Fascinated by the jewels glittering in the moonlight, she moves slowly toward them and clasps them about her head, neck and wrists. The sight of the gems calls up the vision of Rafaele to her mind and possesses her utterly; all thought of Gennaro fades and, as if in a trance, she yields herself to him.

The chief music of this Act is the chorus of men's voices in the distance, followed by Rafaele's entrance with his Camorrist friends. He sings an appealing serenade to the accompaniment of mandolins and guitars. The love duet which follows is sustained by the orchestra "with passion," but soon gives way to the more violent scene when the blacksmith claims her.

Act III A second intermezzo is the curtain-raiser for the final Act— and again marks one of the compelling points of an otherwise sordid story. It re-echoes the theme of Rafaele's serenade in the preceding Act, with its graceful waltz rhythm. A scene of wild revelry is shown, with Apache dances and general vulgarity—a fitting prelude to what follows.

Meeting Place of the Camorrists. It is the night of the festival. Some of the Camorrists lie about sleeping, others come in from various expeditions. Rafaele enters and is boisterously greeted. After he has eaten he sings of the charms of Maliella, which piques the Camorrist women, and they begin a wild, bacchic dance, that by degrees degenerates into an orgy. Suddenly there is a loud knocking, and Maliella bursts in, disheveled, pallid and bareheaded. Rafaele forces her terrible secret from her, and at the first mention of Gennaro's name commands his comrades to bring him his rival, alive or dead. Furious at the derision of his fellows following Maliella's confession, Rafaele spurns her brutally, and she falls to the ground, disclosing the jewels. Gennaro rushes in, pursued by the Camorrists, and seeing Maliella cries her name. Filled with consuming hatred, she shrieks that he is accursed, tells how he robbed the Madonna, and, flinging the jewels at his feet, rushes out, crying despairingly, "To the sea!" The wind, whistling through the den, blows out the candles one by one. The company flees, filled with superstitious terror, and Gennaro is left alone. He, not having obtained death from the hands of the Camorrists, crawls to a rude altar beneath a fresco of the Virgin and, craving pardon for his sacrilege, stabs himself. A crowd, armed with various weapons, bursts into the den, seeking vengeance on the sacrilegist. At the sight of Gennaro dead before the Virgin they halt, awe-stricken, on the threshold.

RICCARDO ZANDONAI

Born at Sacco, Trentino, May 28, 1883, Zandonai was a pupil of Gianferrari, at Rovereto; and later of Mascagni. He wrote half a dozen operas, among them, "Conchita" (1911), and "Melenis" (1912). His best known work, however, is "Francesca da Rimini." Zandonai died in Rome, June 19, 1944.

FRANCESCA DA RIMINI
(Frahn-ches'-ca da Rim'-e-nee)

Grand Opera in Four Acts. Music by Riccardo Zandonai. Book by Tito Riccordi, after the drama by Gabriele D'Annunzio. Reggio Theatre, Turin, February 4, 1914. At New York, the Metropolitan, December 22, 1916, with Alda, Martinelli, Amato, and Mason.

SCENE: First act, Ravenna, then Rimini.
TIME: The Thirteenth Century.

CAST GIOVANNI, *the lame* ⎫ sons of ⎧ Baritone.
PAOLO, *the beautiful* ⎬ Malatesta ⎨ Tenor.
MALATESTINO, *the one-* ⎭ da Verruc- ⎩ Tenor.
eyed chio
OSTASIO, *son of Guido Minore da Polenta* (Baritone).

SER TOLDO BERARDENGO, *a notary* (Tenor).
A JESTER (Basso).
A BOWMAN (Tenor).
TOWER WARDEN (Baritone).
FRANCESCA, *daughter of Guido and sister of Ostasio* (Soprano).
SAMARITANA, *sister of Francesca and Ostasio* (Soprano).

BIANCOFIORE	*attendants to*	Soprano.
GARSENDA	*Francesca*	Soprano.
ALTICHIARA		Mezzo-Soprano.

DONELLA (Mezzo-Soprano).
SMARADI, *a slave* (Contralto).
Bowmen, Archers, and Musicians.

ARGUMENT An opera written around one of the world's famous tales of unrequited love—the story of Paolo and Francesca.

Act I *The House of Polentani, Ravenna.* Francesca, the beautiful daughter of Guido da Polenta, is to be given in marriage to Giovanni, a son of Malatesta. There are two other sons, Malatestino, a one-eyed fellow, and Paolo, a handsome young man. Knowing that the maiden would refuse to wed Giovanni, who is a cripple, Paolo is sent to represent him at the betrothal. Francesca falls a victim to this plot which has been hatched for political reasons, and falls in love with Paolo at first sight—a passion which he reciprocates.

The music in this opening Act is of lyric mood. There is a quartet of women's voices which is effective, that of maids attending upon Francesca. This is followed by the aria of a jester, who tells of "Tristan and Isolde," as a sort of prologue to the tale that is to unfold here.

Act II *Tower Room in the Castle of the Malatestas.* Francesca has been tricked into marriage with Giovanni, who is called Gianciotti the Lamester, and nurses in her heart a deep grudge against Paolo for his share in the deception. Paolo seeks her and pleads forgiveness. He does not attempt to conceal his love for her, and now would welcome death. The Malatesta castle is being besieged by the enemy at this moment, and the tower room is the center of warlike activity. Paolo steps out on the parapet to confront his foes, leaving off his helmet and shield. But Francesca, forgetting all save her love for him, rushes out to shield him from danger with her own body. Neither of them is injured; their foes are driven off; and Gianciotti enters the room to tell his brother that he, Paolo, has been appointed to an important post in Florence, for which city Paolo departs.

The music takes on a furious tone as the battle rages around the castle. Gone for the time are the tender moods, even when the lovers again meet. Tragedy is imminent—the instruments uniting with the voices in a tumult of sound.

Act III   *Apartment of Francesca.* In her sumptuous room, Francesca is beguiling her loneliness by reading aloud to her women, from an ancient tome, the story of "Lancelot and Guinevere." During the reading, Paolo is announced, and the attendants retire. He has been unable to remain away at Florence. He and Francesca still make every effort to conceal their mutual passion. They take up the old love story and begin to read it together. But when they come to the passage where Queen Guinevere "takes him by the chin and slowly kisses him on the mouth," they suit the action to the words.

Again the mood of the music is peaceful, tender. Francesca's women sing of the delights of Spring: "March comes and February goes." The greeting between the lovers is restrained. "Welcome, my lord!" she sings. "Paolo, give me peace," she next voices. However, the music takes on a more intimate tone as they read together from another love story.

Act IV   *Scene 1. Hall of the Castle.* Malatestino, the one-eyed brother, has also become infatuated with Francesca, and tells her that he would go to the length of poisoning Gianciotti. She repulses him in horror. They hear a disturbance from a neighboring dungeon, in which a political prisoner is held. Malatestino says he will silence his noise, and goes and kills the prisoner. When his elder brother reproaches him for his act and his attentions to Francesca, Malatestino diverts attention from himself by hinting at improper conduct on the part of Paolo and Francesca.

Scene 2. Francesca's Apartment. It is night, but Francesca cannot sleep soundly. She dreams that harm threatens Paolo. Her women try to soothe her. A gentle knock is heard at the door, and Paolo's voice calls, "Francesca!" She flings open the door and they embrace. As they sit talking together, a violent knock is heard and the deformed husband demands entrance. Paolo hastily hides by going down a trapdoor. The angry husband discovers him, drags him back into the room, and forces him to fight. Francesca rushes between them and receives Gianciotti's sword thrust in her own breast. With another savage thrust Gianciotti pierces his brother's heart; and the two lovers die in each other's arms. Slowly their executioner breaks his bloodstained sword across his knee.

The climax of the music now grown violent again is reached in the final scene. Francesca's wild dream and outcry are followed by the soothing song of the women. It is but a brief calm before the final storm. The last meeting of the lovers is shown in impassioned phrases and a rising tumult of orchestral strings. The rage of the fighting men, as the sword strikes its victims, is mirrored in the orchestra and ends in chords of grief and remorse—a requiem of sorrow.

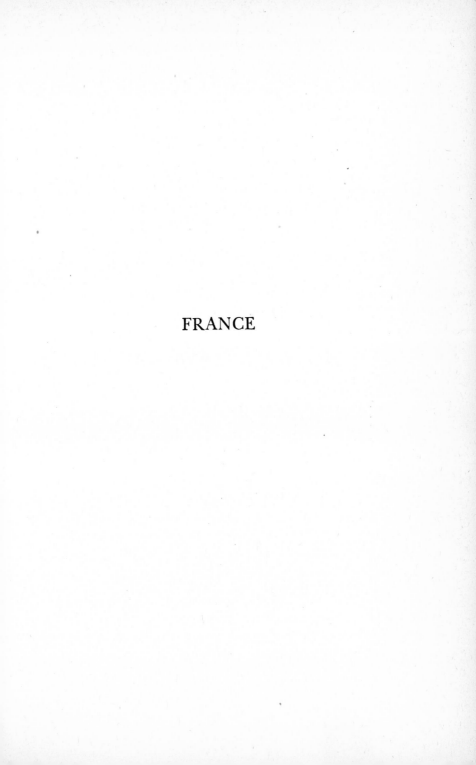

FRANCE

HISTORICAL PREFACE

In tracing the rise of opera in Europe, the student of the French school will encounter many tangled threads. The influence of both the Italian and the German schools is deep and recurring. It was the custom of young French musicians to study in Italy. We have seen how in the French court at Naples, as early as the year 1285, a pastoral with incidental music was performed; and how one of the earliest operas by Peri was given before Henry IV of France, in 1600.

Operas were produced in Paris by foreign composers long before a definite native school was established. The works of Gluck and Mozart vied with those of Rossini and Spontini to such an extent that it was hard for a young Frenchman to get a hearing. Such a one, for example, was Rameau (1683–1764) who had the ill luck to have his "Castor and Pollux" and other works outshone by the German, Gluck. And it was an Italian, Lully, who founded the Grand Opera in Paris, in 1672, and is consequently called the father of French opera.

Early French musicians whose work is still known include: Étienne Nicholas Méhul (1763–1817), whose opera, "Joseph in Egypt," is still studied; François Adrien Boildeau (1775–1834), whose "Caliph of Bagdad" is still remembered for its delightful overture; Daniel F. E. Auber (1782–1871), who achieved immortality with at least one light opera, "Fra Diavolo"; Louis F. J. Herold (1791–1833), of whose opera, "Zampa," only the overture remains in popular esteem; and Jacques Halévy (1799–1862), whose "La Juive" still remains in repertory.

The first commanding figure, however, is Meyerbeer. Though considered the real founder of modern French opera, Meyerbeer was born in Berlin and studied in both Germany and Italy. His earlier work shows the influence of Rossini. But his life work was done in Paris and after the sensational success of his great opera, "Robert le Diable," he became the idol of the French music world. This and succeeding works from his pen made both his own fortune and that of the Grand Opera House in Paris, which was placed soundly on its feet.

Thereafter works by native composers came thick and fast. The reader of this book is referred to later pages for the most notable names and examples. Nevertheless, the few great figures can be numbered with the fingers almost of one hand. When we have called the names of Meyerbeer, Gounod, Offenbach, Saint-Saëns, Bizet, Massenet, and Debussy, we have enumerated the chief ones who represent French opera in other lands. In some instances, also, a composer will be known to fame for a single masterpiece. Witness "Faust," one of the most melodious and popular of all operas; "The Tales of Hoffmann"; "Samson and Delilah"; "Carmen"; "Pelléas and Mélisande"; or the haunting melodies of "Mignon," by Thomas.

French opera, like that of its two great neighbors, Germany and Italy, is characterized by certain elusive yet definite qualities. There is a verve, a brilliance, an elegance, which stamp it with a definite hallmark. Even the more ephemeral elements such as the ballet are yet distinctive.

The work of later composers has run the gamut from light to serious, but always with an unmistakable Gallic quality. In the section devoted to Light Opera we take notice of several typical French composers in this field, beginning with Auber and Lecocq, fifty years later, and continuing often on the border line of grave and gay. "The Tales of Hoffmann," for example, is always classed with Grand Opera, but betrays many traits of the lighter medium.

Among outstanding names of the past century one must mention Massenet, who first won fame by his comic opera, "The Great Aunt," before taking up more serious themes. Later he produced a dozen or more dramatic operas, most of which are familiar to American opera-goers. Charpentier belongs to a more modern school. Witness his "Louise" and its sequels. Debussy is one of the most radical of later composers, but each year sees his fame more secure. Erlanger, Dukas, Rabaud, Fevrier, and Wolff, are among the most promising of contemporary French musicians.

No résumé of French opera would be complete without mention of Opera Comique. (See Light Opera section in this volume.) Here again the Italian influence is seen in Opera Buffa, but the French have made this field peculiarly their own. The true definition of Grand Opera is that in which all conversation is set to music. The more frivolous of the French composers early began to break down this artificial barrier and add other touches such as the ballet. Note, for instance, the technique of Auber or of Offenbach. In still gayer mood, Planquette, in "Chimes of Normandy." This trend we have taken up in detail in the Light Opera section. The field is inviting and will reward the music student, whether he approaches it from the Grand or the Lighter side. It is one of the definite and important trends of the French school.

JACOB MEYERBEER

Meyerbeer is generally considered a French composer and the founder of the so-called school of modern French opera, although he was born in Berlin (September 5, 1791) and studied the piano in Germany. He first came into prominence as a brilliant pianist. Meyerbeer came of a Jewish family. His real name was Jacob Liebmann Beer. He prefixed "Meyer" at the request of a wealthy relative who made him his heir. He was a pupil in pianoforte of Clementi; also studied under Abbé Vogler, being a fellow pupil of Weber. His first operas were German. In 1815 he went to Italy and composed a series of operas in the style of Rossini. Going to Paris in 1826, he became "immersed in the study of French opera, from Lully onward." The first result was "Robert le Diable" (1831). This was followed by "Les Huguenots" (1836); "Le Prophète" (1849); "L'Etoile du Nord" (1854); "Dinorah" (1859). Meyerbeer died May 2, 1864, in Paris. His "L'Africaine" was produced the year following his death.

ROBERT LE DIABLE
(Ro-bair leh Dee-ah-bleh)

(Robert the Devil.) Grand Opera in Five Acts. Music by Meyerbeer. Book by Scribe and Delavigne. Grand Opera, Paris, November 22, 1831, where its tremendous success insured the fortune of the Grand Opera itself. In English, Park Theatre, New York, April 7, 1834; Academy of Music, November 30, 1857.

SCENE: Sicily.
TIME: The Thirteenth Century.

CAST ROBERT, *Duke of Normandy* (Tenor).
ALICE, *foster sister of Robert* (Soprano).
ISABELLA, *Princess of Sicily* (Soprano).
THE ABBESS.
BERTRAM, *the Unknown* (Basso).
RAIMBAUT, *a minstrel* (Tenor).
Knights, Monks, Nuns, etc.

ARGUMENT   A legendary story involving the tempting of human characters by an archfiend, who may be regarded as the prototype of Mephistopheles in "Faust." Although the opera is seldom produced now, it is still of great interest as a forerunner of the romantic school.   Its first enormous success was due to striking scenic effects, to which the plot lends itself, brilliant orchestration, dramatic recitatives, and a running thread of bright melody.

Act I   *A Castle in Palermo.*   Raimbaut, a wandering minstrel, tells the story of Robert the Devil to a group of listening knights.   It seems that Robert is the son of an archfiend by a human woman.   The fiend has roamed the earth under the name of Bertram.   The son is naturally of wild and ungovernable disposition, being still under the secret control of his father.   One of the auditors to whom the minstrel tells this tale is Robert himself.   He is so incensed by this disclosure that he wishes to make away with Raimbaut, but the latter is saved by Robert's foster-sister Alice, who is in love with the minstrel.

Act II   *The Palace of Isabella.*   Robert is enamored of Isabella, the Princess of Sicily, and has come hither to wear her colors in a tournament.   Bertram lures him away, and he fails to meet his opponent, thus losing his honor as a knight and his lady's hand in the bargain.

Act III   *Scene 1.   Rocky Cavern of St. Irene.*   The evil spirits hold high carnival, and to them comes Bertram, who promises a recruit in his son Robert.   They meet Alice, who has had a tryst with Raimbaut, and she seeks to rescue Robert.
Scene 2.   A Ruined Cloister.   In order to strengthen his hold on Robert, Bertram calls to life a group of nuns who in life forgot their vows.   They tempt the knight and finally tell him he can win Isabella, if he steals the mystic cypress from the tomb of St. Rosalie.
In this Third Act some of the more memorable musical numbers are heard: the wild dance of the ghostly nuns; and the two duets between Robert and Bertram, "Our meeting-place" (Du rendezvous), and "Our pleasure lies in constant change" (Le bonheur est dans l'inconstance).

Act IV   *Isabella's Chamber.*   Armed with the magic talisman, Robert enters Isabella's room.   He threatens to abduct her, but yields to her entreaties, spares her, and breaks the cypress branch, destroying the spell.
In this Act we hear the famous aria by Isabella, where her pleadings awake her suitor's better nature: "Robert, whom I love!" (Robert, toi que j'aime).

Act V *A Cathedral Aisle.* Robert comes to the doors of a cathedral seeking divine mercy for his past misdeeds. For the last time his fiendish father seeks to entice him away; but aided by Alice he repulses him. As the fien'd flies, the cathedral door swings open, revealing his bride, Isabella, who is awaiting him.

The final Act brings in a medley of conflict for both voice and instrument, ending in a particularly lovely trio by Alice, Robert, and Bertram.

THE HUGUENOTS

(The Hu-gee-nots)

Dramatic Opera in Five Acts. Music by Meyerbeer. Book by Eugene Scribe. Académie, Paris, February 29, 1836. Astor Place, New York, June 24, 1850; Academy of Music, March 8, 1858; and revived at the Metropolitan, in 1901. On account of its length, the opera is often cut to Three Acts. Patti sang in this opera, at the Academy of Music, in 1883. A "Star" performance was given at the Metropolitan, December 18, 1893, with Jean and Edouard de Reszke, Nordica, and Scalchi.

> SCENE: Paris and Touraine.
> TIME: 1572.

> CAST MARGUERITE DE VALOIS, *the Princess* (Soprano).
> COMTE DE ST. BRIS, *a Catholic nobleman* (Basso).
> VALENTINE, *his daughter* (Soprano).
> RAOUL DE NANGIS, *a Huguenot nobleman* (Tenor).
> MARCEL, *his servant* (Basso).
> DUC DE NEVERS, *a Catholic nobleman* (Baritone).
> URBAIN, *a page* (Mezzo-Soprano).
> BOIS ROSÉ, *a Huguenot soldier* (Tenor).
> Catholic and Protestant Noblemen and Soldiers, Courtiers, Attendants, Citizens.

ARGUMENT The Massacre of St. Bartholomew's Eve forms the historic groundwork of "The Huguenots." The stormy love affair of two young persons belonging to the warring factions is its theme.

Act I *Dining Hall in De Nevers' Château.* In the interests of peace between the warring Catholic and Protestant parties of France, the Duc de Nevers entertains Raoul de Nangis at a banquet of Catholic noblemen. While at table, the diners are asked to toast their ladies, and Raoul tells of a fair unknown, whom he had once rescued from a band of roistering students, and whom he has since searched for in vain.

Raoul's servant Marcel, now enters and warns him of impending danger. Meanwhile, De Nevers has been called from the room, and Raoul, looking out of the window, perceives him in conversation with the very lady whom he has been toasting. He now thinks that he has discovered a liaison between the lady (Valentine) and the noble, when in reality she has come only to ask her release from a promise of marriage. The arrival of a page at this juncture brings in an unexpected element. In a melodious song he informs Raoul that he is to accompany him, blindfolded, to an unknown destination.

The song by Urbain, the Page (taken by a woman with mezzo-soprano voice) is noteworthy: "Noble sirs, I salute you!" (Nobles seigneurs, salut!)—

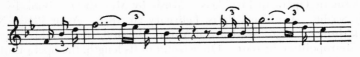

Another song for basso voice, by Marcel, intones Martin Luther's "Ein feste burg," followed by a fierce Huguenot battle song.

Act II   *Garden of Marguerite de Valois.*   Marguerite, like De Nevers, is working for peace, and to this end has invited Raoul to her presence. She is willing to arrange a match between him and Valentine de St. Bris, thus uniting two warring houses. To this end, Valentine has broken her betrothal with De Nevers, but is doubtful as to her father's consent. The princess promises to arrange matters with St. Bris. Raoul is received at court blindfolded, and when unblinded is delighted with his cordial reception. Catholic and Protestant nobles pledge amity, and Valentine's hand is promised to Raoul. But when he discovers in her the same lady that he saw in De Nevers' garden, he thinks that the duke's discarded mistress is being bestowed upon him, and refuses the alliance. St. Bris and De Nevers both wish to avenge this insult, and immediate bloodshed is only averted by the presence of the princess.

In this Act, which is often produced as the second scene of the preceding, Marguerite sings a difficult and beautiful aria for coloraturas, "O, lovely land of Touraine!" with a brilliant passage, "At this word all Nature revives" (A cet mot)—

This is followed by the seductive "Bathers' Chorus" sung on the river bank by women; another song by Urbain in rondeau form: "No, no, no, you never heard it!"; and a charming duet between Raoul and Marguerite, after his bandage has been removed and he sees the glittering court and gracious lady: "Beauty divine!"

Act III   *Banks of the Seine near Paris.*   Valentine has again accepted the faithful De Nevers and preparations are forward for their wedding.   Raoul has sent a challenge to St. Bris, and the latter's friends urge him to involve all the Protestants in the quarrel.   Raoul is warned of treachery through Marcel and Valentine, but keeps his appointment with St. Bris.   Marcel thereupon calls upon all the Huguenots in a neighboring inn, while St. Bris summons all the Catholics.   A general fight is averted only by Marguerite, and as she is in doubt as to whom to believe, Valentine tells her the whole story.   Raoul now learns for the first time of his unjust suspicions, but his knowledge comes too late, as De Nevers appears in a boat to conduct his bride away.

A spirited chorus by the soldiery opens this Act.   As they sing they imitate the beating of drums with their hands and sing the lively "Rataplan."   The vocal protests of the Catholic maidens which follows provides an effective contrast.   Just before the duel, a spirited sextet is sung; "On my good cause relying."   The fall of the curtain is heralded with an exceptional musical and scenic climax, a military band supporting the orchestra.

Act IV   *Room in De Nevers' Mansion.*   It is the Eve of St. Agnes.   Raoul has come to bid farewell to Valentine.   Her grief is voiced in the song, "Amid my tears."   A brief scene between them is interrupted by the entrance of St. Bris and his men.   Raoul hides behind a screen and is the unwilling auditor of a powerful "consecration of the swords," in which the voice of St. Bris leads.   They will wipe out their Huguenot foes.   "With sacred zeal let now your soul be flaming," he sings.   As soon as the soldiers have departed on their bloody quest, a final, affecting parting duet is sung by the two lovers.   It begins with Raoul's impassioned, "Danger presses and time flies!" and reaches to a sublime, "Thou hast said it; thou dost love me!" (Tu l'as dit)—

The close of this touching scene is punctuated by the tolling of bells in the city.   The massacre has already begun.   The girl clings to her lover and begs him not to go; but Valentine gently thrusts her aside. Finding that she has locked the door, he leaps from the balcony to meet his fate.

Act V (Usually Omitted.) *Marguerite's Audience Hall.* Raoul escapes, wounded, to Marguerite's court and begs her protection for the Huguenots. It is too late, however. Murder is afoot and will not cease till the whole party has perished. Valentine now rushes in and begs him to abjure his faith and thus save himself; but Marcel tells him to remember his oath. The two Huguenots go out to meet their enemies, and Valentine declares she will turn Protestant and die with them.

As stated above, the work usually ends with Act IV, and the audience is given the impression that Raoul falls to his death. The opera is further shortened by the compression of the two first Acts into one. The work is not often produced because of its exacting demands upon the singers. The Metropolitan performances of the season of 1901 were called "the nights of the seven stars," as the most famous singers of the day united in the cast.

LE PROPHÈTE
(Luh Prof-ait)

(The Prophet.) Grand Opera in Five Acts. Music by Meyerbeer. Book by Eugene Scribe. Grand Opera, Paris, April 6, 1849. New Orleans, April 2, 1850. New York, Niblo's Garden, November 25, 1853. Sung in German at the Metropolitan, December 17, 1884.

SCENE: Holland and Munster.
TIME: 1534–35.

CAST JOHN OF LEYDEN (Tenor).
FIDES, *his mother* (Mezzo-Soprano).
BERTHA, *his bride* (Soprano).
JONAS, *Anabaptist* (Tenor).
MATTHISEN, *Anabaptist* (Basso).
ZACHARIAS, *Anabaptist* (Basso).
COUNT OBERTHAL (Baritone).
Nobles, Citizens, Anabaptists, Peasants, Soldiers, Prisoners, Children.

ARGUMENT An opera with an historical setting, but the chief motif being the power and beauty of mother love.

Act I *Count Oberthal's Castle.* John of Leyden has won the hand of Bertha, a village lass. His mother, Fides, who keeps an inn at Dordrecht, approves of the match, but permission must also be obtained from the Count, as lord of the domain. The two women now come to seek it. The Count, however, is so pleased with the girl that he refuses his consent and tries to abduct her. Meanwhile a diversion has been caused by the entrance of three Anabaptists, who are zealots urging the people to rise up against their tyrants.

The music in the First Act includes: a lively chorus by the villagers; a cavatina by Bertha in the joy of her courtship, "My heart beats wildly"; a contrasting, gloomy chant in Latin by the Anabaptists; the plea of John's mother to the Count, "One day in the waves of the Meuse"; and his gruff refusal.

Act II *The Inn at Dordrecht.* In his mother's tavern a group of John's friends rejoice with him over his approaching wedding, with a chorus and dance. But the gloomy Anabaptists again appear. They have been struck with his resemblance to David, their guardian saint, and they seek to persuade him to be their new leader. John then tells them of a dream he has had. "Under the great dome of a splendid temple," is the theme of his song. "What does it mean?" he asks. They reply that he is destined to become a king. But he will not give up Bertha, even for a throne. Scarcely have they gone when she rushes in, wildly. The Count had abducted her, but she has escaped. He tries to conceal the weeping girl, as the Count enters in pursuit. He has seized Fides, John's mother, as hostage, and states that she will be slain if he does not relinquish his sweetheart. Torn between the cruel decisions, John at last gives up Bertha. Fides voices her gratitude in one of the sublime arias of all the Meyerbeer operas: "Ah, my son, my son! May you this day be blessed!" (Ah, mon fils!)—

After the triumphant Count has departed, the Anabaptists return and find John a willing instrument to their desires. He now thirsts for revenge against Oberthal. To further their plot, they stain some of his garments with blood and leave them behind in order that his mother and friends may think him dead.

Act III *The Anabaptist Camp.* The Anabaptist soldiers have captured a party of noblemen, who are forced to pay ransom.

All make merry, and the famous ballet on the ice forms part of the amusement. In the background is Münster, still in the hands of Oberthal's father, who refuses to surrender it to the enemy. They resolve to storm it, a resolution which is heard by Oberthal, who has come disguised to the Anabaptists' camp. He is recognized and is about to be killed, when John hears from him that Bertha has escaped. He bids the soldiers spare Oberthal's life, that he may be judged by Bertha herself. John has already endured great pangs of conscience at seeing his army so wild and bloodthirsty. He refuses to go further, but hearing that an army of soldiers has broken out of Münster to destroy the Anabaptists, he rallies. Praying fervently to God for help and victory, inspiration and fresh enthusiasm come over him and are communicated to his soldiers. They resolve to storm Münster.

The well-known ballet of the skaters with its rhythmic, graceful music forms a pleasant interlude to the underlying tragedy. This is followed by a stirring battle song by Zacharias, in which he prays that his foes, "though numerous as the stars," may yet be overthrown. A trio by the three Anabaptists when they recognize the Count follows. The climactic point in action and music here is reached when John and his followers sing the fine "Triumphal Hymn," beginning with the line, "Ruler of Heaven and of Angels!" As it reaches its high point in ecstasy, the sun comes from behind the clouds, as a harbinger of victory.

Act IV *Public Square in Munster before the Cathedral.* Fides thinks her son dead and, reduced to poverty, is on the public square begging for food. Bertha, who also thinks John dead, meets her and in a despairing song they vow vengeance upon the Anabaptists, who, they think, slew him. Meanwhile, the city has been captured by John and his party and he is even now on his way to the cathedral to be crowned king. His "Coronation March" is one of the finest of its type in all opera:

But John's triumph is menaced by the presence of the two women. No sooner than he begins to speak, when Fides recognizes him and cannot restrain an impetuous cry, "My son!" Again he is caught between two currents. With hands upraised he confronts her. He tells his followers that they can run him through his bared breast, if he is an impostor. This woman must be insane. Fides tearfully recants; her old eyes must have deceived her. John absolves her and the crowd exclaim, "A miracle!" thinking it yet another example of their Prophet's divine powers.

Act V *Scene 1.* *The Crypt of the Palace.* A counterplot by the three Anabaptists against John is being hatched. They plan to deliver him over to the German emperor, as the price of their own pardon. Meanwhile, John has had his mother brought to him in secret. As the men lead her through the gloom of a dungeon she exclaims: "O priests of Baal, whither do ye lead me?" (O, Prêtres de Baal!)—

This is the beginning of a cavatina and aria well liked by mezzo-sopranos, by reason of its tumult of emotions, and is known as the "Prison Scene." At first the grief-stricken mother calls down vengeance upon her son, then relenting prays for his forgiveness. When the entrance of the Prophet is announced, her voice rises into an exultant coloratura strain: "He comes!" The meeting between the two is highly dramatic. He pleads her forgiveness, telling her that his bloody deeds have been to avenge Bertha. At this moment they are joined by the girl herself. Her joy at meeting her lover is speedily clouded over, as she learns for the first time that he and the loathed Prophet are one and the same. She is so shocked that she plunges a dagger into her heart.

Scene 2. *A Banquet Hall.* The Prophet's enemies are closing in on him. Bertha had aided them by lighting a fuse leading to a powder magazine. John no longer seeks escape. When the Count comes with the command, "You are my prisoner," he replies, "Nay, ye are all my captives!" He joins a party at the banquet table; smoke and flames rise through the floor. Before the final catastrophe, Fides rushes wildly to his side. "My son!" "My Mother!" they cry in a last reconciliation. "Welcome, sacred flame!" their voices blend as the walls crash down upon them.

DINORAH

Romantic Opera in Three Acts. Music by Meyerbeer. Book by Barbier and Carré. Opéra Comique, Paris, April 4, 1859. Academy of Music, New York, November 24, 1864; revived at the Manhattan Opera House, 1907. At the Metropolitan, February 26, 1908, with Tetrazzini as "Dinorah."

SCENE: Brittany.
TIME: Nineteenth Century.

CAST   DINORAH, *a peasant girl* (Soprano).
HOËL, *a goat-herd* (Baritone).
CORENTINO, *a bagpiper* (Tenor).
Shepherds, Goat-herds, Villagers, etc.

ARGUMENT   The composer's idea here was to write a pastoral opera. The plot, however, has been considered so banal that the occasional bits of fine music have not sufficed to keep it alive. As in his preceding "Star of the North," it is now remembered on account of one famous aria—"The Shadow Song." Dinorah's home has been destroyed by a storm, and her suitor, Hoël, in order to help her father rebuild it, goes to seek a fabled treasure hidden in the mountains. A soothsayer tells him that he must live there for a year. Meanwhile, Dinorah, saddened by her lover's inexplicable disappearance, wanders into the hills seeking a lost goat. She is half demented and her experiences form the chief part of the story. Hoël, Dinorah and Corentino, a bagpiper, occupy the stage in the first act. In the second, Dinorah, again alone, sings her famous "Shadow Song." As a prelude she sings, "The Ancient wizard of the mountains." Then as the bright moon casts shadows upon the glade she imagines them to be living partners and sings and dances with them: "Light, flitting shadow, companion gay, go not away!"

A storm arises. Hoël and Corentino again enter. The former is still seeking the treasure, but the piper is afraid to touch it, lest he die. In a flash of lightning Dinorah sees her pet goat crossing a ravine by means of a fallen tree. She rushes after him and is carried down the gorge by the flood. In the third act, she is shown to have been saved, although at first Hoël thinks her dead. When she revives and her reason also is regained, Hoël thankfully gives up his foolish quest, and the two happily plan for their wedding.

There are other fine musical moments, such as Dinorah's lullaby to her goat (First Act); and a trio at its end; a "Legend of the Treasure," sung by Dinorah; and the villagers' "Pardon Hymn."

L'AFRICAINE
(Laf-ree-cain)

(The African.) Tragic Opera in Five Acts. Music by Meyerbeer. Book by Eugene Scribe. Grand Opera, Paris, April 28, 1865. Academy of Music, New York, December 1, 1865. At the Metropolitan, 1888.

SCENE: Lisbon; a ship at sea; Madagascar.

TIME: The Sixteenth Century.

CAST VASCO DA GAMA, *an officer in the Portuguese Navy* (Tenor).

DON PEDRO, *President of the Royal Council* (Basso).

DON DIEGO, *Member of the Council* (Basso).

DON ALVAR, *Member of the Council* (Tenor).

INEZ, *daughter of Don Diego* (Soprano).

ANNA, *her attendant* (Contralto).

SELIKA, *an African Queen, held as a slave* (Soprano).

NELUSKO, *a slave* (Baritone).

GRAND INQUISITOR (Basso).

Priests, Inquisitors, Councillors, Sailors, Indians, Attendants, Ladies, Soldiers.

ARGUMENT "L'Africaine" was Meyerbeer's last opera, and considered by him his masterpiece. He did not, however, live to see it produced. It is an elaborate work in its scenic setting, and has a quasi-historical background.

Act I *Royal Council Chamber, Lisbon.* The famous voyager, Vasco da Gama, who has been sent to trace a route around the Cape

of Good Hope, has not returned, and is given up for lost.   Admiral
Diego, believing this true, wishes to bestow the hand of his daughter
Inez on another suitor, Don Pedro.   At this juncture Vasco returns,
having been the only one of his ship's party to escape shipwreck.   He
brings with him two strange captives.   He shows the Council maps of
the African coast and endeavors to prove to them the existence of other
lands to the East.   He pleads for ships and funds to start a new voyage
of conquest and discovery.   But his rival for the hand of Inez discredits
him with the Council.   He asserts that Da Gama's contentions are
heretical and contrary to the Holy Word.   Instead of being given cre-
dence and assistance, the Council throws the voyager into prison.

Soon after the first curtain, Inez sings a tender ballad, "Farewell, my
beloved shore," to the birdlike accompaniment of the flute.   It recurs
in the Fourth Act.   In the climax of the First Act, Vasco dramatically
throws down the gauntlet to the powerful Council, culminating in a
stirring chorus.

Act II   *A Prison Cell.*   Vasco languishes in prison.   With him are the
                two captives he has brought from Africa, Selika and Nelusko.
Selika watches over him devotedly.   She was a Queen in her own land,
but is now content to be the slave of this proud foreigner who has saved
her and her companion from a slave ship.   But Vasco is thinking only
of Inez, and Nelusko, who honors in Selika not only his Queen, but the
woman of his love, tries to stab Vasco, the Christian, whom he hates
with a deadly hatred.   Selika prevents him and rouses the sleeping
Vasco, who has been dreaming of another voyage to the unknown country.   Selika now shows him on the map the way to her native isle, and
he vows her eternal fealty.   But presently Inez enters to announce that
Vasco is free.   She has paid dearly for her lover's deliverance, however,
for she has given her hand to Don Pedro, who, having got all Vasco's
plans and maps, is commissioned by the Council to set out on the voyage
of discovery.   On her part, Inez has been told that Vasco has forgotten
her for Selika the slave.   In order to prove his fidelity to Inez, our ungrateful hero immediately presents her with the two slaves, and Don
Pedro resolves to make use of them for his exploration.

Early in this Act we hear the lovely slumber song of the slave queen,
Selika: "On my knees, child of the Sun!"; Nelusko's baritone salutation
to her: "Daughter of kings, my homage!"; and, for finale, a sextet without instruments.

Act III   *On Board Don Pedro's Ship.*   Nelusko has been made pilot,
                 but his actions are open to suspicion.   Two ships of the fleet
have already been lost, but Don Pedro continues to sail on.   At this

moment a Portuguese vessel is seen approaching. It is in command of Vasco da Gama, who has fitted it out at his own expense. Although Don Pedro is his enemy, he comes aboard the admiral's ship to warn him that the vessel is on a wrong course and likely to meet with disaster. Don Pedro, however, accuses him of desiring only to see Inez, who is on the vessel. At his command, Vasco is seized and bound. A few moments later, however, a violent storm breaks over the ship. It is driven upon a reef. Savages, for whom Nelusko has signaled, clamber up the sides of the vessel and massacre all save a few, who are spared by orders of their Queen, Selika.

The musical feature in this Act is Nelusko's impressive invocation: "Adamastor, ruler of the trackless deep!"—a fine baritone aria—

Other numbers are: a pleasing chorus of women: "The swiftly sailing ship"; a sailors' prayer: "O, mighty St. Dominique!" and the orchestration of the storm and battle scene.

Act IV *A Temple and Palace, on Madagascar.* This opera fairly outdoes itself in scenic display, and here in sharp contrast to the violent episodes on shipboard, we are translated to a stage of barbaric splendor. Selika has been restored to her throne. Vasco, with Inez, has been rescued from the ship and now finds himself on the island he has vainly sought. He voices his amazement at the superb scene with a song, "Oh, Paradise!"—

He has just witnessed an Indian march and ballet with its exotic strains, and his aria to woodwind accompaniment, first in exaltation, then in martial spirit, is a favorite with tenors. Vasco is brought in a prisoner and Selika, in order to save him, asserts that he is her husband. She prevails upon the faithful Nelusko to bear witness to this fact, and the marriage is celebrated according to native rites. Vasco is touched by Selika's devotion to him after his past faithlessness, and again vows that he will remain true to her. But alas! he hears the voice of Inez who is being led away to execution, and he cannot conceal his emotion. The duet between the Queen and the explorer, "Oh, transport! Oh, sweet ecstasy!" contains music closely allied to the tender scene.

Act V *Gardens of Selika's Palace.*   Selika divines the cause of Vasco's
emotion, and sends for her rival, resolving to put her to death.
But again her magnanimity conquers her passion.   She sets both her
captives free and provides a ship for them to return to their native land.
As the ship sails away, Selika watches it from a promontory, shaded
by the deadly manzanilla tree.   The odor of its blossoms is poisonous,
but she gladly inhales it, as she has bid an eternal farewell to the king
of her heart.   Her parting soliloquy is filled with poignant grief: "From
here I gaze upon a boundless deep."   For her the deep is eternity.   A
few moments later, Nelusko finds the lifeless body of his beloved Queen
and resolves to join her in the land of the shades.

JACQUES HALÉVY

Halévy was of Jewish extraction, born in Paris, May 27, 1799.   His
musical education was completed in the Paris Conservatory and at
Rome.   In the latter city he devoted himself to church music, as did his
pupil Gounod, and strove to interpolate it into his first operas, "The
Bohemian" and "Pygmalion."   His first success was "Clari" (1828).   A
comic opera, "The Dilettante Avignon," the next year, was also successful, and the two paved the way for "The Jewess" (1835), which made
him famous, and on which his fame still rests.   He wrote eight or ten
other operas which are now forgotten.   Halévy exercised great influence over later musicians, among them Gounod and Bizet, through his
teaching at the Conservatory.   He died in Nice, March 17, 1862.

LA JUIVE
(La Zhoo-eeve)

(The Jewess.)   Tragic Opera in Five Acts.   Music by Halévy.   Text
by Eugene Scribe.   Académie de Musique, Paris, February 23, 1835.
New Orleans, the following February.   At the Metropolitan, New
York, in German, in 1887.   A notable revival here was on November
22, 1919, when Caruso achieved an "historic triumph."   Others were
Ponselle, Orville Harrold, and Rothier.

SCENE: Constance.
TIME: 1414.

CAST   ELEAZAR, *a Jewish jeweler* (Tenor).
       RACHEL, *his foster-daughter* (Soprano).
       CARDINAL DI BROGNI (Baritone).
       PRINCE LEOPOLD (Tenor).
       RUGGIERO, *a judge* (Baritone).
       PRINCESS EUDORA, *the Emperor's niece* (Contralto).
       Courtiers, Soldiers, Citizens, Jews, etc.

ARGUMENT   A tense and dramatic opera involving a conflict of creeds, racial prejudice, and filial love. "La Juive" found great favor with contemporary critics and composers, among them, Wagner, who is said to have been enthusiastic over it. Its plot is dramatic and the role of Eleazar was for long a favorite with tenors. It was sung by Caruso on his last public appearance, in December, 1920. Of recent years it has been seldom performed.

Act I   *A Street.* The Catholic party is celebrating a victory over the Hussites, a heterodox party. They decide to take equally stern measures with the Jews, and all their shops are ordered closed, under pain of death. But Eleazar, a prominent jeweler, keeps his open. He is seized and sentenced to death, when Cardinal di Brogni intercedes for him and protects him from the anger of the crowd. The Cardinal has a secret liking for the Jew and his daughter Rachel, and hopes that the Jew can give him some intelligence of his own long-lost daughter. But despite his favor, Eleazar mistrusts him.

Rachel has a suitor who has won her affections under the name of "Samuel," but who is in reality the powerful Prince Leopold. He also is able to save her and her father from the mob, at a later time, to her own great surprise, as she still does not know his true rank.

The scene opens with a stately "Te Deum" at the Cathedral. Later comes a fine cavatina by the Cardinal, in which he asks the pardon of Heaven upon unbelievers—a baritone song demanding a wide range of voice.

Act II   *Home of Eleazar.* The Jews have gathered around a table in a religious festival. Eleazar leads in the singing of their invocation: "Oh, God of our fathers!" Leopold, posing as a Jew, is present, but quietly thrusts the bread aside. There is a knock at the door and the communion is hastily hidden; but the newcomer is the Princess Eudora, who wishes to purchase a chain for her prospective bridegroom, Prince Leopold—for these nuptials have been commanded by the Emperor. On hearing this, "Samuel" is filled with dismay. After the others have gone he confesses to Rachel that he is a Christian, and persuades her to flee with him. The entrance of Eleazar prevents their

escape. He orders "Samuel" to marry his daughter, but the latter declines. He leaves amid the curses of the old Jew and the grief of the
girl.

Act III *An Imperial Banquet Hall.* The nuptials of Prince Leopold
and Princess Eudora are being celebrated with much festivity.
The bride brings the golden chain which she has purchased. She is
accompanied by Rachel who recognizes in the groom her faithless lover.
She openly denounces him, and the Cardinal pronounces upon him the
curse of the Church, and consigns him to prison, together with the Jew
and his daughter.

The orchestra unites with the voices in this highly dramatic scene.
Rachel's avowal of her faith, and scorn of her faithless lover are swiftly
followed by the Cardinal's stentorian curse: "You who have outraged
Heaven are now by Heaven denounced!"

Act IV *A Dungeon.* Eudora visits Rachel and pleads with her to
pardon Leopold. The Jewess relents and resolves to die
alone in order to save her lover. Meanwhile, in an interview with the
Cardinal, Eleazar tells him that his daughter is still alive, but refuses to
divulge more. Brogni pleads with him for tidings, and also promises
to save Rachel if she will recant, but both refuse.

It is here that the old Jew sings his fine aria, in which he prays God
for guidance in his difficult decision. He can still save his foster-
daughter, whom he loves as his own, but he cannot forswear his faith:
"Rachel, when the grace of the Lord entrusted thee to me" (Rachel,
quand du Seigneur)—

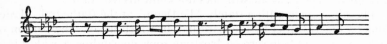

Act V *Court of the Prison.* The Jews have been sentenced to a frightful death by being plunged into a cauldron of boiling oil.
Eleazar and Rachel march to their doom with firm steps. She has forgiven her lover. Now when the old man asks her if she would renounce
the Jewish faith to save her life, she answers with a resolute, "No!"
Just as she is hurled into the cauldron, Eleazar points to her, then to the
Cardinal. "Behold your daughter!" he announces sternly, and plunges
after her. Overcome with horror and grief, the Cardinal tears his
princely robes and falls fainting to the ground.

Again a medley of voice and instruments depict the scene, rising to a
crash as the curtain falls.

HECTOR BERLIOZ

This French composer was educated for the profession of medicine, but turned aside to the more congenial paths of music. He was born in La Cote-Sainte-Andre, near Grenoble, December 11, 1803. At the age of twenty-seven he won first prize in the Paris Conservatory of Music, for his cantata, "Sardanaple." After a few months' study in Italy, he turned seriously to the production of opera, and also to musical criticism in prose. The operas which first brought him fame were "Benvenuto Cellini," "Beatrice and Benedict," and "The Trojans." Strangely enough, he is remembered today for "The Damnation of Faust," which originally was not an opera at all, but a dramatic cantata. Berlioz was also the composer of orchestral symphonies, such as "Episode in the Life of an Artist," in which the various instruments take the part of speaking or singing characters. He may thus be regarded as a pioneer in the school of "chamber music." He died in Paris, March 9, 1869.

BENVENUTO CELLINI

Opera in Three Acts. Music by Berlioz. Book by Du Wailly and Barbier. Grand Opera, Paris, September 3, 1838.

> SCENE: Rome.
> TIME: 1532.

CAST   CARDINAL SALVIATI (Basso).
BALDUCCI, *Papal Treasurer* (Basso).
TERESA, *his daughter* (Soprano).
BENVENUTO CELLINI, *a goldsmith* (Tenor).
ASCANIO, *his apprentice* (Mezzo-Soprano).
FRANCESCO, *artisan in Cellini's workshop* (Tenor).
BERNARDINO, *artisan in Cellini's Workshop* (Basso).
FIERAMOSCA, *sculptor to the Pope* (Baritone).
POMPEO, *a bravo* (Baritone).

ARGUMENT   Cellini is a famous goldsmith of Rome, in the sixteenth century, who is commissioned by the Pope to make a certain statue.   It is carnival time, and his attention is distracted not only by this fact, but also by the love of Teresa, the Papal Treasurer's daughter.   After a tangle of cross purposes, the statue is finished triumphantly.   It proves to be "Perseus," one of the historic art treasures of Florence.

The overture and "Carnaval Romain" have been recorded from this opera.

THE DAMNATION OF FAUST

Dramatic Opera in Four Acts.   Music by Berlioz.   Book by Berlioz, Gerard and Gandonniere.   Paris, 1846, as a dramatic cantata.   In its entirety in Manchester, England, 1880; New York, February 12, 1880; the Metropolitan, December 7, 1906.

<blockquote>
SCENE: A German Village.
TIME: The Eighteenth Century.
</blockquote>

<blockquote>
CAST   FAUST, <i>a philosopher</i> (Tenor).
MEPHISTOPHELES, <i>the tempter</i> (Basso).
BRANDER, <i>a convivial friend</i> (Basso).
MARGUERITE, <i>a peasant girl</i> (Soprano).
Peasants, Troopers, Roysterers, Students,
Sylphs, Fiends, Angels.
</blockquote>

ARGUMENT   This version of the Faust legend is remarkable for its dramatic intensity and the passion of its music. It also forms an interesting parallel with Gounod's popular opera on the same theme.

Act I   *The Open Fields.*   Faust, a learned philosopher, wanders out into the sunrise, tired of books for the nonce and pondering the mysteries of Nature.   He observes a group of peasants who take great delight in a parade of marching soldiers, but he only wonders at their enthusiasm.

The high moment in this scene is the soldiers' march, which is a favorite orchestral number known as the "Rakoczy March"—

Act II *Faust's Study.* The philosopher returns to his books more than ever weary of them and of all the world. Somehow with all his learning his heart is empty and unsatisfied. He resolves to end it all with a dose of poison, but the sound of Easter music stays his hand. Now comes the fiend, Mephistopheles, to tempt him with the pleasures of the world, and Faust yields and goes with him to a tavern. The coarse songs and jests of the roisterers soon disgust him, however, and Mephistopheles takes him to a beautiful garden where he is lulled to sleep by soft music and dreams of a charming peasant girl, Marguerite. Sylphs dance about him as he awakes, filled with desire to find the girl of his dreams. Soldiers and students pass by singing their rollicking songs, and Faust feels the love of the world once more surging through his veins.

The music which the fiend employs in the garden, and the dance of the sylphs, are the occasion for the most exquisite melodies of the work —the "Ballet of the Sylphes"—

Act III *Marguerite's Chamber.* The fiend conducts Faust to the home of his unknown sweetheart, and Faust conceals himself in her room. Marguerite also has dreamed of Faust and enters the room musing upon her vision while she braids her hair. Meanwhile, Mephistopheles sings a mocking song without. Faust reveals himself to the startled girl and pleads his love so ardently that she is finally persuaded to give herself to him. Their love scene is interrupted by the fiend who comes to warn them that Marguerite's mother and friends are near at hand. Faust is dragged away unseen by the exultant demon, while the villagers threaten the defenseless girl.

The song of Marguerite is followed by a mocking invocation by Mephistopheles, and a "Dance of the Will-o'-the-Wisps." There is a love duet, which becomes a trio as the fiend's urgent voice joins in.

Act IV   *Scene 1. Marguerite's Chamber.* Marguerite sits alone and
         grief stricken, sorrowing for her own sin, for her mother's death, and for the absent Faust. Her aria, "Love, devouring flame," is an eloquent confession. It is broken by the martial singing of soldiers outside her window, which grows fainter as "Retreat" is sounded. The unhappy girl falls unconscious.

    Scene 2. A Mountain Gorge. Both music and setting are turbulent. Faust likewise has been yearning for Marguerite and lamenting their interrupted tryst. His soliloquy is titled, "Nature, vast, impenetrable!" The fiend appears and tells him he can save the girl only by surrendering his own soul. The panorama of grinning devils and imminent inferno is depicted musically in the "Ride to Hell"—

Faust's efforts to save Marguerite are thwarted by the demon. She is haled to prison for the murder of her mother, to whom Mephistopheles had given too heavy a sleeping powder and, while Faust descends to Hell, is herself condemned to death.

Epilogue   *The Prison Cell.* The unhappy and penitent Marguerite
         is saved and ascends with angels to Heaven.

BEATRICE AND BENEDICT

Opera in Two Acts. Music by Berlioz. Book by the composer after Shakespeare's comedy, "Much Ado About Nothing." Baden Baden, 1862.

The characters follow those of the Shakesperian play. The plot preserves its spirit, also, except for deleting the intrigue which involves Claudio and Hero. It centers on the spirited interplay between the proud Beatrice and the witty Benedict. The music forms a lively interlude to their quarrels and ends pleasingly as the two decide to "make up."

THE TROJANS

(Les Troyens.) Title given by Berlioz to two lengthy operas, which are now known only to students of music. Text of both by Berlioz.

PART I: "THE CAPTURE OF TROY"

Produced in Karlsruhe, 1890. Characters those of Homer's *Iliad*. Three Acts. I. The Greek camp in front of Troy. The people of that city are rejoicing at the supposed lifting of the siege. Some stand in awe of the gigantic wooden horse left behind by the Greeks. They do not heed the warning voice of Cassandra, the clairvoyant. II. A grove near by. While the Trojans celebrate, Aeneas runs in with the tidings that Laocoon has been throttled by a serpent because he tried to prevent the entrance of the horse into the city. III. Aeneas is sleeping in his tent. Hector's ghost appears to warn him that Troy has fallen. Aeneas must sail away to a far land to found a new kingdom.

PART II: "THE TROJANS IN CARTHAGE"

Produced in Paris, unsuccessfully, in 1863; revived in Karlsruhe, in 1890. This opera in five acts follows closely the later adventures of Aeneas with Dido, in Carthage. The action ends as the unlucky Queen throws herself upon her funeral pyre, while Aeneas and his men sail on for Italy.

Recorded music: overture; "Chasse royale et orage"; and the tenor aria, "Inutiles regrets."

CHARLES AMBROISE THOMAS

A French composer, born in Metz, August 5, 1811. He entered the Paris Conservatory in 1828, winning three prizes there in successive years—for piano playing, harmony, and musical composition, the last being the Grand Prix. Before he had reached the age of twenty-six he had written pieces for the piano, violin, orchestra, and a cantata. His first successful opera was "The Double Ladder" (1837), followed during the course of a long life by many other operas and cantatas, the best known operas being "Mina" (1843); "Betty" (1846); "A Midsummer Night's Dream" (1850); "The Carnival of Venice" (1853); "Mignon" (1866); "Hamlet" (1868); and "Francesca da Rimini" (1882). In 1871 he became Director of the Conservatory. He died in Paris, February 12, 1896.

MIGNON

(Meen-yohn)

Romantic Opera in Three Acts. Music by Charles Ambroise Thomas. Book by Barbier and Carré, after Goethe's "Wilhelm Meister." Opéra Comique, Paris, November 17, 1866. Academy of Music, New York, November 22, 1871; the Metropolitan, October 21, 1883.

        SCENE: Germany and Italy.
        TIME: The Eighteenth Century.

    CAST   WILHELM MEISTER, *a German student* (Tenor).
             BARON FRIEDRICH (Tenor).
             LAERTES, *a strolling actor* (Baritone).
             PHILINA, *an actress* (Soprano).
             LOTHARIO, *an aged minstrel* (Basso).
             GIARNO, *leader of the Gypsies* (Basso).
             MIGNON, *a girl of the Gypsies* (Mezzo-Soprano).
             Gypsies, Peasants, Servants, etc.

ARGUMENT   The story of a girl captured by Gypsies and found to be the long-lost daughter of a nobleman is not new to opera, but the present story, based upon Goethe's "Wilhelm Meister," is one of the most pleasing. Despite the widespread popularity of the song, "Knowest thou the land," and a charming dance, and intermezzo, "Mignon" is not presented frequently. Its plot may be thought too ingenuous, its themes too simple, yet to many opera-goers it is a refreshing change from plots steeped in gloom, or difficult scores. The Overture with its brilliance and charm is a favorite concert piece with orchestras all around the world.

Act I   *Courtyard of an Inn, Germany.* While the strolling actors, Laertes and Philina, are resting in the courtyard of a wayside

tavern, a band of Gypsies also stop there. They are footsore and weary
from a long journey, but despite this fact the leader, Giarno, orders
Mignon, a young girl, to dance for the amusement of other tavern
guests. She refuses from weariness and ill-treatment, and Giarno
rushes forward to beat her. An old harper tries to protect her, and
would himself have been beaten, but is shielded by a young German
student, Wilhelm Meister. Mignon is dressed as a boy, and Wilhelm,
ignorant of her identity, takes her with him as a page. Meanwhile,
Wilhelm has become infatuated with Philina, although Laertes warns
him that she is fickle. His rival is the Baron Friedrich, whose uncle has
invited the players to visit his castle; and much against the Baron's will,
his rival and Mignon go with them.

In this Act while Wilhelm is questioning Mignon about herself and
her past, she sings the nostalgic song which is now recognized as one of
the most beautiful of its type in all opera: "Knowest thou the land
where the orange blooms? . . . 'tis there! 'tis there I'd live!" (Connais-
tu le paye?)—

There is also a pleasing duet between her and the old minstrel, Lothario,
as he bids her farewell: "O, swallows lightly gliding!"

Act II The Second Act is preceded by a dainty Intermezzo, which has
remained deservedly popular; it is in gavotte form:

Scene 1. Boudoir in the Baron's Castle. Philina is making herself
very much at home, "prettying" herself and dreaming of further conquests. The voice of Laertes is heard without, in a madrigal to her:
"Fair one, have pity on me!" He enters with Wilhelm and Mignon,
and the latter jealously looks on from a corner while her beloved pays
ardent court to the actress. When the other two finally leave the room,
Mignon wonders if she might equal her rival's charms, and tries on some
of her dresses and "make-up," meanwhile singing to herself: "I know

a poor fellow." As she thus busies herself in an adjoining apartment, Baron Friedrich enters in search of Philina. He sings the familiar tenor gavotte, "Here am I in her boudoir!" (Me voici dans son boudoir)—

Wilhelm unexpectedly returns and the two men quarrel and are ready to draw swords, when Mignon interposes. The Baron recognizes her borrowed costume and departs laughing. Wilhelm on his part tries to quiet her, in another charming aria, "Farewell, Mignon, take courage, do not weep!"

Scene 2. *Garden of the Castle.* Mignon is so distressed over her false situation that she is on the point of throwing herself into a lake, when the notes of Lothario's harp soothe her. She goes to the old minstrel for counsel, and in her agitation calls down vengeance upon the castle and its occupants. In the meantime the players are giving a performance from "Midsummer Night's Dream" on the terrace. Philina is gorgeous in her costume as Queen Titania. The music of the dance is in polonaise rhythm, again a high point in the work; and with its dashing accompaniment Philina sings the brilliant colorature aria, "I'm fair Titania"—

During the pageant Philina misses the flowers that Wilhelm has sent her and, willing to pique Mignon, sends her into the castle in search of them. Before the girl can return, flames burst from the windows. The aged Lothario has interpreted Mignon's curse too literally and set fire to the castle. Wilhelm rushes into the building and at great peril rescues Mignon, whom he carries forth unconscious in his arms.

Act III *A Castle in Italy.* Lothario takes Mignon, who seems ill in body and mind, to Italy. They are followed by Wilhelm, who has discovered her love for him and reciprocates it, after casting off his passion for the fickle Philina. In Italy the mystery of Mignon's birth is cleared. She is the daughter of Lothario, whose real title is the Marquis of Cipriani. Ever since his daughter had been stolen by the Gypsies he has wandered in search of her, and now proves her identity. He bestows her hand with his blessing upon Wilhelm.

The final Act has its fine musical moments, as when Wilhelm sings to the distressed Mignon: "Soothed is now her sorrow"—a lullaby which soon gives way to a more passionate outburst from him as he at last realizes all she means to him: "Ah, little thought the maid!" Before the final curtain a trio is sung by the two lovers and Lothario, with its recurring refrain, "Knowest thou the land?"

HAMLET

Grand Opera in Five Acts. Music by Thomas. Book by Michel Carré and Jules Barbier, after the play by Shakespeare. Grand Opera, Paris, March 9, 1868. Academy of Music, New York, March 22, 1872. Revived unsuccessfully, twenty years later, by the Chicago Opera Company.

SCENE: Denmark.
TIME: Antiquity.

ARGUMENT While ranking high in France among later operas, "Hamlet" has never won lasting regard in America. The plot takes many liberties with the play by Shakespeare and does not make use of the bard's fine verses. Much of its text is banal. Nevertheless, it has fine dramatical passages and several of its arias are highly esteemed by musicians—notably the spirited Drinking Song, "O, Wine, dispel this gloom!"—a tour-de-force for baritones.

The characters are the same as in the original play, and the action follows its general lines. Hamlet broods over his mother's hasty marriage with Claudius, King of Denmark, and is urged on to revenge by his father's ghost. He then seeks to fasten the guilt of his father's death upon Claudius. The final acts deal with the madness and death of Ophelia, and the vengeance of Hamlet upon the usurping King.

Recorded music: "Doute de la lumiere," sung by Sembrich and Emilio de Gogorza; "Chanson Bachique—O vin dissipe la tristesse" (John Charles Thomas); "Scene de folie," a soprano aria, by Norena, Galli-Curci, and Melba; and "Comme une pale fleur," a song for basso (Tita Ruffo, and Mattia Battistini).

CHARLES FRANÇOIS GOUNOD

Although one of the most popular and voluminous of French composers, Gounod's fame will rest largely upon one opera, "Faust." Gounod was born in Paris, June 17, 1818, and studied at the Paris Conservatory, where he won first prize for composition at the age of twenty-one. He was sent to Rome to complete his musical education, where he specialized on church music, a field in which he was interested all his life. We find traces of this predilection in "Faust." He published many masses, hymns, motets, and sacred songs. In 1851 he produced his first opera, "Sappho," at Paris. This was followed by a comic opera ("The Physician in Spite of Himself," based on Molière's comedy); and "Faust," in 1859. The latter at once brought Gounod to commanding notice, and still remains one of the most popular of all operas. Other operas by him are "Philemon and Baucis" (1860); "The Queen of Sheba" (1862); "Mireille" (1864); "Romeo and Juliet" (1867); "Polyeucte" (1878) ; and "The Tribute of Zamora" (1881). Gounod died in St. Cloud, France, October 18, 1893.

FAUST
(Fowst)

Tragic Opera in Five Acts. Music by Charles Gounod. Book by Barbier and Carré, after Goethe's drama. Lyric Theatre, Paris, March 19, 1859. Academy of Music, New York, in Italian, November 26, 1863; and, in 1883, with Nordica as "Marguerite." At the Metropolitan on its opening night, October 22, 1883, in French, with Nilsson as "Marguerite."

SCENE: A German Village.
TIME: The Eighteenth Century.

CAST   FAUST, *a philosopher* (Tenor).
MEPHISTOPHELES, *the evil one* (Basso).

VALENTINE, *brother of Marguerite* (Baritone).
BRANDER, *a student* (Baritone).
SIEBEL, *a student* (Soprano).
MARGUERITE, *a village girl* (Soprano).
MARTHA, *her servant* (Contralto).
  Students, Soldiers, Citizens, Servants, Fiends,
  Angels.

ARGUMENT This version of the Faust legend so brilliantly in-
          terpreted by a French composer has far outranked
in popularity any other opera, even from the original German source.
Its wealth of melody and sustained exaltation have kept it in continuous repertory. It is probably one of the first ten most frequently heard.

Act I *Faust's Study.* The philosopher Faust has spent his lifetime in
          study, and now feels that he is growing old and that there is
nothing else to live for. He resolves to end it all with a dose of poison,
but his hand is stayed by the sound of Easter carols. Mephistopheles
enters and promises him a new lease of life and many joys which he has
missed, if he will sell his soul. The fiend then shows him a vision of
Marguerite. Faust consents to the compact and is transformed into a
handsome youth.

The music in this opening Act is largely colloquy between the two,
ending with a spirited duet: "For me life's pleasure!" (A moi les
plaisirs!).

Act II *An Open Square.* A festival is in progress, and students, sol-
           diers, and citizens wander about singing and making merry.
Valentine has enlisted as a soldier, but dislikes to go away leaving
his sister, Marguerite, unprotected. Siebel, a boy, promises to be her
champion. Mephistopheles now joins the throng of merry-makers and
arouses popular interest by telling fortunes. He jests with Siebel on
the subject of Marguerite, and Valentine overhears and resents his slurring remark. They draw their swords, but the fiend traces a circle of
fire around himself. Valentine and his friends hold up their swords
like crosses and the evil one slinks away. The dance continues, and
Faust enters and offers his arm to Marguerite, but she repulses him.

This Act opens with a chorus of the villagers, who celebrate "Kermess" or festival day. Its fine harmony is well known. Next comes a
song for baritone voice of breadth and fervency, in which Valentine
asks the favor of Heaven upon his sister while he is away: "Even bravest
heart" (Avant de quitter)—

An ironical bass sung by the fiend, "The Calf of Gold," is succeeded by a dramatic orchestral score, "The Sword Scene," where Valentine confronts the fiend. A chorus of triumph over the latter then gives way to the Kermess dance, known the world around as "the waltz from Faust"—

Marguerite's voice is now heard in a short reply to her new suitor: "No, my lord, I do not need your arm."

Act III *Marguerite's Garden.* Siebel brings a bouquet to Marguerite, but the flowers fade until he dips them in holy water. He then leaves them on the doorstep and departs. Faust and Mephistopheles now enter, the fiend urging Faust to press his suit. Seeing the flowers, Mephistopheles departs to purchase a finer present. He soon returns with a casket of jewels which he places beside the flowers and both retire. Marguerite enters pondering over the handsome young gallant she saw in the market place. She finds the casket and is delighted with the glittering gems, but does not wish to keep them. Martha, her companion, sees them and tells her she would be foolish to reject them. The fiend and Faust return, and the former beguiles Martha into a retired corner of the garden, leaving the coast clear for Faust, who woos Marguerite so ardently that she promises to meet him again on the morrow. But the fiend is persistent. "Wait? Why wait, you dreamer? Hear what she tells the stars!" They pause under her open window, and while the woodwinds hint of rapture, the girl again appears. "Hasten thy return, beloved," she sings. With an answering cry, "Marguerite!" Faust hastens to her. Darkness falls, punctuated by the sardonic laughter of the fiend.

The entire Act is chockful of melody. The first song is that of Siebel (soprano) "Speak to her of love"—the "Flower Song." Faust's fine apostrophe is heard: "All hail, thou dwelling pure and holy!" (Salut demeure)—

Marguerite at her spinning-wheel sings a quaint oldtime melody, "The King of Thule." But when she discovers the casket, her voice rings out in the magnificent "Jewel Song" (Air de Bijoux) —

A ravishing duet between the lovers completes this brilliant Act.

Act IV *Scene 1. A City Street.* The soldiers return victorious from war, among them Valentine. But his joy at seeing his sister again gives way to fury when he learns that she has been betrayed. At dusk, Mephistopheles and Faust approach Marguerite's home and the fiend sings a mocking serenade. Valentine rushes out to avenge his sister's wrongs and crosses swords with Faust, but the latter, aided by the evil one, gives Valentine his death blow. People rush in, and Marguerite bends over her dying brother, only to hear him curse her with his last breath.

Scene 2. Interior of the Church. Marguerite goes to the church and endeavors to pray, but the mocking fiend intrudes even here and tells her she is damned forever. She falls, overcome, upon the floor.

The "Soldiers' Chorus" heard on the curtain rise is yet another of the familiar numbers; the brass and drums accompanying the male voices: "Glory and love to the men of old!"—

By sharp contrast comes Mephistopheles' mocking serenade beneath the girl's window: "Where is thy wedding ring? Ha, ha, ha ha!" A trio between Valentine, Faust and the fiend, "Give double strength, great God!" is the prelude to the fight and the death of Valentine.

Act V   *Scene 1.*   *Walpurgis Revel.* Mephistopheles conducts Faust to the witch revels of Walpurgis night, and for his further tempting conjures up the famous courtesans of antiquity—Lais, Helen of Troy, Cleopatra, and others—who appear in an elaborate ballet. This music is quite familiar, but the scene itself is often omitted. In the midst of this revelry Faust has a vision of Marguerite with a noose around her neck, and at once commands the fiend to transport him back to her rescue.

     Scene 2.   *A Prison Cell.* Marguerite has been condemned to death for the killing of her child. Her mind wanders and snatches of the Kermess music reveal her thoughts of an innocent past. Faust enters and implores her to flee with him. Mephistopheles awaits impatiently without, and the trampling of horses' hoofs is heard. But Marguerite refuses to go, saying that she will submit to the will of Heaven. A superb trio follows, in which the girl's voice rises above the others: "Angels, pure and bright!"

Her voice on a last, triumphant note ends in death. "Condemned!" cries Mephistopheles. "Saved!" proclaim angelic voices, as the rear wall of the prison parts, and in a glory of light and sound Marguerite is carried Heavenward; while the fiend claims Faust as his own.

ROMEO AND JULIET

Tragic Opera in Five Acts. Music by Gounod. Book by Barbier and Carré, after the play by Shakespeare. Théâtre Lyrique, Paris, April 27, 1867. Academy of Music, New York, November 15, 1867. The Metropolitan, December 14, 1891.

        SCENE: Verona.
        TIME: The Fourteenth Century.

        CAST   THE PRINCE OF VERONA (Basso).
               COUNT OF PARIS, *his kinsman* (Baritone).
               CAPULET, *a nobleman* (Basso).

JULIET, *his daughter* (Soprano).
GERTRUDE, *her nurse* (Contralto).
TYBALT, *nephew of Capulet* (Tenor).
ROMEO, *a Montague* (Tenor).
MERCUTIO, *his friend* (Baritone).
STEFANO, *page to Romeo* (Soprano).
BENVOLIO, *friend of Romeo* (Tenor).
GREGORIO, *servant to Capulet* (Baritone).
FRIAR LAURENCE (Basso).
Friends of Capulet and Montague, Retainers of
the Prince, etc.

ARGUMENT Gounod's opera follows closely the accepted version of the story of "Romeo and Juliet," following
the plot, by acts, of Shakespeare's drama. Still earlier versions were the
French tale of Boisteau and the Italian novel of Bandelio.

Between the Veronese houses of Capulet and Montague exists a bitter
enmity. Open warfare of their retainers has continued, until the
Prince threatens the banishment of the next person to engage in the
quarrel.

Act I *Reception Hall in the Mansion of Capulet.* The head of the
house of Capulet gives a fête in honor of his daughter, Juliet.
Romeo, a Montague, comes unbidden to the house and immediately
falls desperately in love with the fair young heiress. She likewise has
eyes for none but him. Tybalt, a kinsman of Capulet, discovers the intruder's identity and wishes to draw upon him, but is prevented by the
host who will not override the laws of hospitality.

Juliet's delight over her party is voiced in the familiar Waltz Song:
"Fair is the dream of youth" (Dans ce reve)—

Romeo's impassioned, "Adorable angel!", and her reply are the occasion
of a charming duet.

Act II *Capulet's Garden.* Romeo lingers beneath the balcony of
Juliet, and is overjoyed to hear her come forth and confess her
love for the young stranger, to the moon and stars. He makes his presence known, and the two pledge their love. Servants of Capulet inter-
rupt them, but only temporarily. They plan a speedy marriage.

With the curtain rise we hear the fine serenade by Romeo: "Ah, fairest dawn, arise!" (Ah, leve toi soleil). With her appearance, a delightful interchange of pledges is reflected by the music.

Act III   *Scene 1. Friar Laurence's Cell.*   The two lovers meet clandestinely in the cell of Friar Laurence, and he consents to unite them, thinking that this will bring about peace between the warring families.   The Friar's prayer, "God, who made man in Thine image," is a notable song for basso.   There is also a quartet by the Friar, Gertrude, and the lovers.

Scene 2. A City Street.   While walking abroad with his friends, Romeo is accosted by Tybalt, who rails at him for having gone to the Capulet home.   Romeo is doubly anxious to keep the peace at this time, and answers him softly.   But soft words will not satisfy either party.   Mercutio, a Montague, draws upon Tybalt and is slain by the latter.   Romeo, in just vengeance, then crosses swords and slays Tybalt.   The Prince orders his immediate banishment from the city.

Act IV   *Juliet's Bedchamber.*   Romeo comes to bid his bride farewell; he cannot tarry on pain of death.   When he is gone, Capulet enters to inform his daughter that a wedding has been arranged between her and the Count of Paris.   She pleads for delay but unavailingly, and she dares not tell her father of her existing marriage.   In despair she consults the Friar, who gives her a sleeping potion which causes the semblance of death.   She is to be entombed, and Romeo is to be informed of the stratagem and rescue her.

The chief numbers in this Act are: a duet between Romeo and Juliet: "Night hymneal"; the lingering parting between them; and a quartet where their voices are joined by those of Gertrude and the Friar.

Act V   *The Tomb of the Capulets.*   Before Romeo can receive word from the friar as to Juliet's feigned death, he hears that she is really no more.   He hastens back to Verona and the tomb where she lies.   At the gate he encounters Paris and strikes him to the ground.   Within he finds his bride apparently lifeless.   He drinks a vial of poison and casts himself upon her bier.   At this moment she awakens from her trance and learns what he has done.   He perishes in her arms, and she seizes his dagger and stabs herself.

There is an effective prelude in the music of the final Act.   Romeo, thinking her dead, voices his sorrow in the lament, "O, my dearly beloved!"   The death music between the two is poignant and gripping.

JACQUES OFFENBACH

The earlier fame of Jacques Offenbach rests upon his operettas in the French opera bouffe school. Born in Cologne in 1819, he went as a lad in his teens to Paris, where he spent his life. From his fertile pen poured a long list of delightful works in this vein; but longing to write an acknowledged masterpiece, Offenbach began his score of "The Tales of Hoffmann" in the spring of 1880. By the time it was completed he became fatally ill and never lived to see it produced. He died on October 5 of that year, leaving this, his greatest musical legacy. Others of his lighter works will be found in the Light Opera section of this volume.

THE TALES OF HOFFMANN

(Les contes d'Hoffmann.) Fantastic Opera in a Prologue, Three Acts and an Epilogue. Music by Jacques Offenbach. Book by Jules Barbier, after three tales by E. T. A. Hoffmann. Opéra Comique, Paris, February, 1881. Fifth Avenue Theatre, New York, October 16, 1882. At the Metropolitan, February 14, 1911, by the Chicago Opera Company, with Renaud, Dalmores, Sylva, Zeppilli and Di Angelo.

SCENE: Various parts of Europe.
TIME: The Nineteenth Century.

CAST HOFFMANN, *a poet* (Tenor).
OLYMPIA ⎫ *his sweethearts.*
GIULIETTA ⎪ Four successive parts usually taken
ANTONIA ⎬ by one person (Soprano).
STELLA ⎭
LINDORF ⎫ *his evil genius.*
COPPELIUS ⎪ Part taken by one person
DAPERTUTTO ⎬ (Baritone).
DR. MIRAKEL ⎭
NICKLAUS, *friend of Hoffmann* (Tenor).
SPALANZANI, *an Italian savant* (Basso).
KRESPEL, *father of Antonia* (Basso).

SCHLEMIL, *admirer of Giulietta* (Baritone).
ANDREAS, *servant of Stella* (Tenor).
LUTHER, *an Inn-keeper* (Baritone).
Several small singing parts, such as Students,
Servants, Messengers, Friends, etc.

ARGUMENT "The Tales of Hoffmann" was derived from the
fantastic and mystical tales written by the Ger-
man author E. T. A. Hoffmann, which attained a wide popularity in
France. The opera is really a musical medley uniting several different
episodes.

Prologue *Luther's Wine Tavern at Nuremberg.* The poet Hoffmann,
who has traveled widely and had many adventures, is now
seeking his latest flame, Stella, who is singing in a theater near by. His
rival, Lindorf (who is really the evil genius of the poet) plans to get
Hoffmann tipsy and unpresentable, and then bring Stella on the scene.
With Hoffmann are a group of his student friends who ask him to relate
his adventures. He at first refuses, but as he begins to drink, his memory is unlocked and he tells the stories of three love affairs. The three
succeeding acts each reveal one of these tales.

Act I *The Home of Spalanzani.* An Italian savant, Spalanzani, is
reputed to have a remarkable daughter, Olympia, who dances
and sings divinely. Hoffmann and his friend, Nicklaus, attend the
large coming-out party. Coppelius, a trickster (the evil genius who
thwarts the poet in each adventure) sells Hoffmann a pair of eyeglasses
for the occasion, and through these the young poet sees a vision of sur-
passing beauty. Olympia sings to the delighted throng, and among
others straight to Hoffmann's heart. He declares his passion to her at
the first opportunity and she responds, although in monosyllables. She
dances, however, better than she talks, and accepts Hoffmann as a partner. They dance faster and faster until he can no longer keep up with
her flying feet and falls exhausted. She flits from the room and a crashing noise is heard. Coppelius returns with a wrecked female figure;
it is Olympia, who was only an automaton! The figure had been constructed by the savant, aided by Coppelius, who now claims that Spalanzani deceived him as to payment. They quarrel while Hoffmann
mourns for his lost love.

The tour de force in this Act is Olympia's "Doll Song," an extremely
clever simulation of whirring mechanism with a birdlike aria. At one
of the loveliest high notes, the doll seems to run down, then the sound
of a winding spring is heard, and up soar the notes again.

Act II *Giulietta's House in Venice.* Hoffmann's next passion is for a beautiful Venetian woman, and he goes to make love to her, although his friend tries to dissuade him, hinting that she is not all she ought to be. But Hoffmann's love blinds him to any defects in her morals. He finds her surrounded by a gay set, her favored admirer being Schlemil, who treats Hoffmann disdainfully. Now both Schlemil and the woman are in the power of Dapertutto (the evil genius under another name). Through Giulietta the evil one has become possessed of Schlemil's shadow (in other words, his soul) and he plans to obtain Hoffmann's in the same manner. The poet falls a victim to her wiles and is promised the key to her room if he will challenge Schlemil who now possesses it. He meets Schlemil and they fight. The latter falls, but when Hoffmann hastens to her balcony he sees her gondola gliding away and the coquette laughing in the embraces of another man.

It is at the beginning of this Act that we hear the famous Barcarolle, as Nicklaus and Giulietta sing to the gentle swaying of a boat on the canal: "Oh, Night of Love!" (Belle Nuit!) —

If this work had been entirely forgotten as a whole, the Barcarolle would still be played and sung as long as there are lovers in the world.

Act III *The Home of Krespel.* The next love of Hoffmann's is a pure one, its object being the lovely but delicate daughter of Krespel. Her mother, who has been a famous singer, has died prematurely from consumption, and the young girl inherits both the talent and the physical weakness. For this reason her father does not wish her to sing; but Dr. Mirakel (again the evil genius) who has treated her mother, secretly plans to hasten the daughter's demise. Hoffmann knows nothing of her disability and urges her to sing. She refuses. Then Dr. Mirakel conjures up a vision of her dead mother, who also seems to join in the request. Antonio yields and sings divinely, but the effort has been too great and she falls from weakness into her lover's arms, where she dies.

Epilogue *The Tavern, as in Prologue.* The tales are ended and Hoffmann's friends have departed one by one leaving him alone with his bottle. His head sinks forward upon his arms as he falls asleep. In his dreams the Muse of Poesy appears saying, "All your earthly loves have forsaken you; henceforth follow me." As he sleeps, the door softly opens and Stella, his last flame, enters upon the arm of Lindorf. The latter, the triumphant evil genius, points to the poet scornfully and leads Stella away.

CAMILLE SAINT-SAËNS

Saint-Saëns was born in Paris, October 9, 1835. He began his musical education at the age of two and a half years. At twelve he studied the organ under Benoist—an instrument on which he later specialized and attained world fame. At sixteen he wrote his first symphony. His first opera, "The Yellow Princess," was given in 1872; followed by "Samson and Delilah," in 1877; "Henry VIII," in 1883; "Ascanius," in 1890; "The Barbarians," in 1901; and "Dejanire," in 1911. Of these, "Samson and Delilah" is far and away his masterpiece. Saint-Saëns' fame as a composer rests upon this opera and his orchestral and church music. He died in Algiers, December 16, 1921.

SAMSON AND DELILAH

Dramatic Opera in Three Acts. Music by Camille Saint-Saëns. Book by Ferdinand Lemaire. Weimar, December 2, 1877. New Orleans, January 4, 1893. The Metropolitan, New York, in 1915.

SCENE: Gaza and Vicinity, in Palestine.
TIME: 1150 B.C.

CAST   SAMSON, *a prophet of Israel* (Tenor).
DELILAH, *a Philistine woman* (Mezzo-Soprano).
ABIMELECH, *a Philistine officer* (Basso).
HIGH PRIEST OF DAGON (Baritone).
A PHILISTINE MESSENGER (Tenor).
Hebrews, Philistines, Priests, Maidens, etc.

ARGUMENT   The Biblical story of Samson and Delilah is faithfully reproduced in this opera, which depicts in
both text and music the dramatic scenes in the life of Israel's warrior-
prophet whose power was wrested from him by a woman's wiles.

Act I   *An open Square in Gaza.*   The people of Israel have been overcome by their enemies the Philistines, and now pray for deliverance.   Samson, their leader and a man of mighty deeds, advises them
to be patient.   During their devotions Abimelech, the satrap of Gaza,
comes out of the temple and ridicules them and their God.   Samson
turns upon him, wrests the sword from his hand, and kills him with one
blow.   Other Philistine soldiers rush to their leader's aid, but Samson
easily withstands them all.   The High Priest urges them forward, but
they answer that they cannot overcome Samson; he is invincible.   Samson bids his people arm and avenge themselves.   They sally forth and
a messenger reports that they are everywhere victorious.   As the strong
man returns, maidens come forth from the temple, led by Delilah, a
Philistine woman.   She praises Samson and says that she can resist him
no longer.   They dance about him, and his eyes follow every motion of
the seductive Delilah.

Before the rise of the first curtain, a chorus of Israelites behind the
scenes is heard bewailing their fate and beseeching Jehovah to intervene.   There are some fine choral and fugue passages here.   Toward
the close of the scene, Delilah exerts her first blandishments on the hero
in her "Spring Song"—"Spring voices are singing" (Printemps qui com-
mence)—

Act II   *House of Delilah in the Valley of Sorak.*   Delilah, gor-
geously attired, awaits the coming of Samson.   He is tardy and

she grows impatient. It was not thus when he was first in her power, but now he is seeking to break the shackles of love. While she waits, the High Priest enters. She must aid them to lay hold upon the warior, he says; and he offers her wealth if she will deliver him into their hands. Delilah refuses the gold, replying that her hatred is enough. The High Priest departs and sets a secret guard about the house. After a time Samson appears but with reluctance and shame. His God commands him to break off this unholy alliance and lead Israel out of bondage. Delilah makes use of all her wiles to bring him again under her power, singing the bewitching song, "My heart at thy dear voice" (Mon coeur s'ouvre a ta voix)—

What man could resist such passion and pleading? Not Samson. As he capitulates, she asks him to tell her the secret of his strength. He refuses, and she leaves him, but he runs after her into the house. While she has been singing, the mutterings of a storm are heard; now it breaks in all its fury, cloaking the advance of Philistine soldiers upon the house. Delilah opens a window and beckons to them in triumph; while Samson is heard in a terrible cry, "Betrayed!"

Act III *Scene 1. The Prison of Gaza.* Samson has been shorn of his long hair, the secret of his strength, his eyes have been put out, and like a blind ox he trudges around a mill wheel. His captors mock him, while from without his people sing in reproach: "For the love of a woman he sold his power—and made us captive!" Presently he is seized and led forth in chains to grace a triumphal procession.

Scene 2. Interior of the Temple of Dagon. Before a great assemblage of Philistines, their High Priest assisted by the triumphant Delilah makes an offering to their god, Dagon. "Dagon, be ever praised!" they sing:

As the flames flash up from the altar, a wild bacchanale is danced by maidens, as the wood instruments wail out an exotic cadenza. It is a riot of voluptuousness. Unnoticed for the moment, the old warrior prays to Jehovah: "Lord, thy servant remember now. For one moment make him strong again!" Delilah turns and taunts him with his help-lessness. She even sings passages from her old love song. All laugh—he is huge sport for them. He is standing between two great pillars which hold up the roof of the temple. His sightless eyes turn toward his tormentors. Then a sudden quickening of his muscles informs him that his prayer has been answered. With one last supreme effort he winds his arms about the columns—they yield—they break—with a rending of timbers the roof crashes down—his enemies are buried be-neath the ruins—and with them Samson—and Delilah!

LEO DELIBES

Delibes was born February 21, 1836, at St. Germain du Val (Sarthe), and died January 16, 1891, at Paris. His chief works are "Coppelia," a ballet in three acts founded upon Hoffmann's story of "The Sand-man"; "The King Has Said It," a comic opera in three acts, and "Lakmé," a romantic opera. Delibes is at his best in ballets and light operas, his music being of singularly graceful, intriguing character.

LAKMÉ
(Lack-may')

Romantic Opera in Three Acts. Music by Leo Delibes. Book by Gondinet and Gille, based upon the story, "The Marriage of Loti."

First produced at the Opéra Comique, Paris, April 14, 1883. At the Academy of Music, New York, March 1, 1886. At the Metropolitan, New York, in the spring of 1890, when "Lakmé" was sung by Patti. Now seldom produced.

SCENE: India.
TIME: Circa 1880.

CAST   NILAKANTHA, *an Indian priest* (Basso).
LAKMÉ, *his daughter* (Soprano).
MALLIKA, *her slave* (Contralto).
GERALD, *a British officer* (Tenor).
FREDERICK, *a British officer* (Baritone).
MRS. BENSON (Contralto).
ROSE (Mezzo-Soprano).
ELLEN (Soprano).
British Officers, Englishwomen, Natives, etc.

ARGUMENT "Lakmé" has been a favorite of divas in the past for its fine opportunities in coloratura, chiefly the "Bell Song." Its oriental plot, a slight, fanciful one, is saturated with exotic, sensuous melody—perhaps an overdose. If this work could be compressed, say within the limits of "Cavalleria" or "Pagliacci," it might rank with them in continuing popularity.

Act I *A Garden in India.* The aged Hindu priest, Nilakantha, has a hearty dislike for all foreigners, the English in particular. Nevertheless, a party of British officers enter his private garden, where they discover some jewels left by Lakmé, the priest's daughter. Gerald, one of the officers, is so delighted with them that he remains behind to sketch them for his fiancée, Ellen, who has come with them but now gone with the others. Gerald's song, punctuated by notes of admiration, "Idle fancies" (Fantaisie aux divins), is a well-known tenor aria.

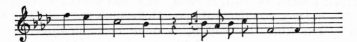

Lakmé comes upon the intruder, and the two are mutually attracted, but the girl warns Gerald of her father's antipathy and possible vengeance.

Act II *Street Scene in India.* The old priest has found a broken fence in his estate and suspects an interloper. He now bends his cunning to find and punish him. Ordering his daughter to follow him, they disguise themselves as penitents and mingle with the crowd at a sacred festival. The priest believes that when his daughter's voice is heard, one of the British officers will betray himself; so she is ordered to sing. Her song, which is recognized as one of the most difficult and exacting of coloratura arias, begins with a legend of a Pariah's daughter: "In the Forest" (Dans le Forêt). "A young girl forward runs; a ring in her grasp she holds tightly, whence tinkles a bell." The singer imitates the notes of a small bell with her voice, in the famous "Bell Song"—

The old man's ruse works. Gerald starts with pleasurable surprise; the priest recognizes him in turn, stabs him, then escapes. The horrified girl rushes to the wounded man as, with a burst of oriental music, still lacking in the dramatic, the curtain falls.

Act III   *A Hut in the Forest.*   Gerald is being nursed back to health by the faithful Lakmé. They confess their love and she goes to procure a sacred potion which will render it deathless. But while she is gone, Frederick, a fellow officer, enters and chides Gerald for his inaction. The soldiers are on the march and his duty is with the colors. Martial music is heard in the distance, as Frederick leaves, and the girl returns with the potion. Gerald, however, refuses to drink it. Lakmé, heartbroken, gathers for herself some deadly datura blossoms. Nilakantha rushes in upon them and again would slay Gerald, but the dying Lakmé warns him that her lover has drunk the sacred draught and cannot be harmed. She dies in the arms of the man she has again saved.

GEORGES BIZET

Georges Bizet was born in Paris, October 25, 1838. He studied music under Halévy, and later at the Paris Conservatory. He composed many pieces of music, long and short, but is chiefly remembered for five operas: "Vasco da Gama" (1863), "The Pearl Fishers" (1863), "The Fair Maid of Perth" (1867), "Djamileh" (1872), and "Carmen" (1875). The last is by far his most famous work, and has remained a prime favorite with opera-goers. Bizet died near Paris, June 3, 1875.

THE PEARL FISHERS

(Les Pecheurs des Perles.) Romantic Opera in Three Acts. Music by Bizet. Book by E. Cormon and M. Carre. Théâtre Lyrique, Paris, September 29, 1863. Thirty years later, in Philadelphia, August 25, 1893. The Metropolitan, New York, January 11, 1896.

SCENE: The Isle of Ceylon.
TIME: Barbaric Period.

CAST LEILA, *a priestess* (Soprano).
NADIR, *a pearl fisher* (Tenor).
ZURGA, *a chief* (Baritone).
NURABAD, *the high priest* (Basso).
Fishermen, Fakirs, Priests and Priestesses, Islanders.

ARGUMENT "The Pearl Fishers" is a rapidly moving opera, woven around a simple theme and involving only four leading characters.

Act I *On the Seashore.* A semi-barbaric tribe meet to elect a chief and to hold an annual festival and vigil to frighten away the evil spirits. They choose Zurga as their chief. While the festival is in progress, Zurga's former friend, Nadir, appears from the forest. The two had become estranged on account of their rivalry for the hand of a beautiful woman who had mysteriously appeared on their shores a year before. Each year she comes to pray for the tribe, and none dares molest her or look upon her face. While the two reunited friends converse, a boat draws near and the fair stranger is again announced, accompanied by Nurabad, the high priest. The people draw near her in awe, asking her to intercede for them. She promises to keep lonely vigil for them, and Zurga promises in his turn that, if she is true to her trust, he will bestow upon her a pearl of great price, but that if she is untrue, death shall be her portion. Nadir is a deeply interested spectator, as he recognizes the voice of the woman he so passionately loved a year before. After all the rest have departed he lingers below the rocks where she is holding her vigil.

In the early part of this Act, a notable duet for tenor and baritone is heard, as Nadir and Zurga reaffirm their friendship: "In the depths of the temple" (Au fond du temple). Near the end, Nadir tells his re-awakened love for Leila in a song of poignant beauty: "I hear as in a dream" (Je crois entendre encore)—

Act II *Ruins of a Temple*. Nurabad, the high priest, installs Leila in her position as priestess of the tribe. He tells her that she must remain in silent watch and prayer throughout the night. She is fearful of the forest sounds, but promises. Nurabad departs. As Leila trembles at the roar of wild beasts, she is suddenly reassured by the sound of a human voice. It is Nadir singing to her in the distance. She answers, and Nadir, overjoyed, tells her of his love. They embrace, but are surprised by the high priest, who has been in hiding. He calls the people together, telling them that their priestess has been false to her vows. The tribesmen are ready to slay her, but Nadir shields her with his body. Zurga, in order to protect his friend, commands the pearl fishers to disperse. Nurabad tears away Leila's veil, and Zurga then recognizes her as the same woman over whom he and Nadir had formerly quarreled. A storm arises and the people pray to the gods while the priests lead Leila away. Nadir is sentenced to death.

Chief musical numbers: Leila's song, "A fugitive one day" (Comme autrefois); and an impassioned duet between her and Nadir, "You have not understood" (Ton coeur n'a pas compris)—the effect of the latter being emphasized by a raging storm outside the temple ruins. Voices, stage setting, instruments, unite in great dramatic effect.

Act III *The Camp of Zurga*. Zurga is torn between conflicting emotions of his love for Leila and his friendship for Nadir. In the midst of his inner struggle, Leila comes, guarded by two pearl fishers, to intercede for her lover. Zurga declares his own love for her, but she disdains him. She is ready to die if Nadir dies. She gives him a chain which she had formerly received as a guerdon. Zurga, much moved, departs, and the tribesmen cluster around their prospective victims, Leila and Nadir, and begin their tribal dance. As they are at last on the point of stabbing the victims with their knives, Zurga re-enters, telling them that their camp is in flames. They hasten away, while Zurga boasts that he is the incendiary and has chosen this method of saving the captives. He strikes off their shackles, while Nurabad, who has overheard, hastens away to the people, to obtain aid in preventing the escape. Nadir and Leila, however, have time to make their way to the cliffs and safety. Zurga remains behind to shield their flight, and is slain by the knives of his followers.

CARMEN

Romantic Opera in Four Acts.   Music by Bizet.   Book by Meilhac and Halévy, after the novel by Prosper Merimée.   Opéra Comique, Paris, March 3, 1875.   Academy of Music, New York, October 23, 1879. The Metropolitan, New York, December 20, 1893, when Calvé made her memorable début.

SCENE: Seville.
TIME: Early part of Nineteenth Century.

CAST   ZUNIGA, *a lieutenant* (Basso).
José, *a sergeant* (Tenor).
MORALES, *a sergeant* (Basso).
ESCAMILLO, *a bull-fighter* (Basso).
DANCAIRO, *a smuggler* (Tenor).
REMENDADO, *a smuggler* (Baritone).
CARMEN, *a Gypsy girl* (Soprano).
FRASQUITA, *A Gypsy* (Soprano).
MERCEDES, *a Gypsy* (Contralto).
MICHAELA, *a peasant girl* (Soprano).
     Gypsies, Peasants, Citizens, Cigarette Girls, Soldiers.

ARGUMENT   "Carmen" is a colorful opera, founded upon Meri-mée's brilliant romance depicting Spanish Gypsy and peasant life.   The central figure is a heartless coquette who lives only for the passion of the passing moment.   Here again is an example of a composer of several operas who is known to fame for a single, striking work.   And yet, so discouraging was its first reception that Bizet died, three months later, disheartened and depressed over the failure of his beloved "Carmen"—now in continuous repertory around the world.

Act I   *A City Square.*   A troop of soldiers under the command of Don José, together with town idlers, throng the open square during the noon hour.   Especially are they interested in the pretty girls who work in a neighboring cigarette factory.   Only the officer, Don José, is indifferent to these coquettes as they jest with the men.   Seeing his indifference, Carmen, the Gypsy girl and the greatest flirt of them all, practices her wiles upon him and flings him a red rose.   Don José's blood is finally fired, but the girls return to their work, and Michaela, a gentle peasant girl from his home village, arrives with a message for him.   The officer is about to throw the Gypsy's rose away when a commotion is heard within the factory and the girls rush out.   Carmen has quarreled with another girl and stabbed her.   The assailant is brought forward and pinioned to prevent further mischief, but she so bewitches the young officer that he connives at her escape.

There is such a wealth of "quotable" music, that it is hard to particularize.   Soon after the curtain rise we hear the ever-popular march of the soldiers as they change the guard:

Carmen's entrance is followed by her captivating song, "Love is a rebellious bird" (L'Amour est une oiseau rebelle)—with its intriguing "Habanera" rhythm—

Near the close, her equally coquettish song, "Near the walls of Seville," making use of another familiar Spanish dance tempo, the "Seguidilla," enables Carmen again to hoodwink the gullible males:

Act II   *A Tavern Room.*   Carmen has returned to her nomadic life and we find her with her companions singing and carousing in a road house.   The famous bullfighter, Escamillo, enters, and Carmen is greatly fascinated by him and also makes him aware of her charms. The inn is closed for the evening, but Carmen and two of the Gypsy men who are smugglers await the arrival of José. The latter is deeply in the girl's toils, and when he appears she urges him to desert the army and join the Gypsy band. At first he refuses, but when a superior officer appears and orders him out, swords are drawn. Carmen summons the Gypsies, who overpower the officer, and all, including José, escape to the mountains.

A brief prelude by the orchestra precedes the rise of the curtain. Then comes the sparkling little Gypsy song, "Ah, when the gay guitars ring out," by Carmen to the accompaniment of these instruments. A lively dance of the Gypsies is supported by full orchestra. When the bullfighter enters, to the shouts of greeting, he struts to the center of the stage, throws out his chest, and sings the unforgettable bravura: "Toreador, on guard! Love is the prize awaits thee, ah, Toreador!"

A fine song for tenor is heard near the end, when José tells Carmen, "You must hear me! This flower you once gave me is dishonored!" It is known as "The Flower Song" (Air de la Fleur).

Act III *Mountain Retreat of the Smugglers.* The smugglers have been busy and successful, aided by José who is still wildly in love with Carmen. She, however, is growing cold to him. He sees this and is deeply dejected by it and at the thought of his perfidy. Carmen's latest conquest, Escamillo, now appears seeking her, and José, wildly jealous, would spring at his throat but for the intervention of the Gypsies. The faithful Michaela again finds José and beseeches him to hasten with her to the bedside of his dying mother. After a struggle between duty and desire, duty prevails and he departs with her.

The Third Act is also given an orchestral prelude marked by delightful, pastoral passages, with harp notes—a calm before the coming dramatic storm. The arrival of the smugglers, after curtain rise, is the occasion of a stirring "Smugglers' March." Carmen's defiant song, "In vain I sort the cards!" is followed by a more pathetic one from the scorned girl, Michaela, who comes seeking the recreant José. "I shall find the guilty one!" she cries. There is a reconciliation between the two, but even as they depart, José calls to Carmen; and the boastful song of the toreador is heard in the distance.

Act IV *Exterior of the Bullfighting Arena.* All Seville is hastening to one of the great fights of the season, where their favorite toreador, Escamillo, is to appear. Carmen has accompanied him, despite the warnings of her friends that the furious José is seeking her. Amid great pomp Escamillo enters the arena, but before she can follow him, her discarded lover appears. At first he pleads with her to return to him. She refuses, and the enraged José stabs her to the heart just as the victorious fighter returns from the arena.

Stirring strains of music herald the final Act. The pace is being quickened to the climax. The street scene is one of a lively ballet. "Viva, Escamillo!" they shout. The music changes. José makes one last plea to the flirt. "Let me pass!" she cries. With a crash of chords, the gates of the arena are thrown open. Escamillo and his friends stop in horror as they see Carmen's lifeless body. José stands by her side. "Yes, I slew her. I am your prisoner." Then with a stricken cry he throws himself beside her. "Carmen, Carmen, how I have loved you!"

JULES MASSENET

One of the most prolific of latter-day composers, Massenet was born in Montaud, France, May 12, 1842. At the age of twenty-one he won the "Prix de Rome" for composition and had already made a name for himself in orchestral work. Three years later began his flood of operas, which were successful almost at once, beginning with two light operas, "The Great Aunt" and "Don Caesar de Bazan." "The Furies," a dramatic work, and an oratorio, "Mary Magdalen" followed. Other operas include: "Herodias" (1881); "Manon" (1884); "Le Cid" (1885); "Werther" (1892); "Thais" (1894); "Cendrillon" (1899); "Griselidis" (1901); "The Juggler of Notre Dame" (1902); and "Don Quixote" (1910). Many of these have been produced in America. Massenet died, August 13, 1912.

HERODIAS

(Herodiade.) Dramatic Opera in Four Acts. Music by Massenet. Book by Paul Milliet and Henri Gremont. Théâtre de la Monnaie,

Brussels, December 19, 1881. The first American production was in New Orleans, February 13, 1892. In New York, Manhattan Opera House, November 8, 1909, with Cavalieri as "Herodias."

SCENE: Palestine.

TIME: 30 A.D.

CAST   HEROD, *the tetrarch* (Basso).
HERODIAS, *his wife* (Mezzo-Soprano).
SALOME, *her daughter* (Soprano).
PHANUEL, *a Chaldean* (Tenor).
JOHN THE BAPTIST, *a Prophet* (Tenor).
VITELLIUS, *a Roman consul* (Baritone).
HIGH PRIEST (Baritone).
Jews, Romans, Soldiers, Priests, Dancers, Servants, etc.

ARGUMENT   "Herodias" presents another version of the character of Salome from that given in the Strauss opera, based upon the Wilde play. Both, of course, go back to the Biblical account for their slender historical setting.

Act I *Courtyard of Herod's Palace.* While servants labor under the direction of Phanuel the Chaldean, Salome enters seeking her mother, whose identity she does not know. Phanuel promises to aid her, but warns her against the intrigues of the palace. They depart. Herod now enters, seeking this maiden whose dancing has already enslaved him. Herodias meets him and complains of a rough-looking prophet who has bitterly denounced her in public. She wishes to be revenged, but Herod counsels caution. John, the prophet, enters at this moment repeating his denunciations. Both Herod and Herodias leave hastily. Salome runs to greet him, her heart won by his former kindness; but he refuses her proffered love.

A lovely aria is heard near the beginning, when Salome tells Phanuel how a man of the desert had befriended her as a child: "He is kind, he is good," she sings (Il est doux, il est bon).

Act II *Scene 1. Herod's Chamber.* The tetrarch reclines at ease watching his dancers; but Salome is not among them and he is unhappy. Phanuel enters to warn him against this life of luxury. But Herod cannot get the vision of the dancing girl from his mind. He drinks a philter brought mysteriously by a slave, and sings of his desire: "Fleeting vision!" (Vision fugitive)—

Scene 2. A Public Square. Urged on by Phanuel, Herod appears before the people haranguing them to throw off the Roman yoke. But they are interrupted by the sound of trumpets announcing the arrival of the Roman consul, Vitellius. The suspicions of the consul are lulled by Herod, who says that the priests desire that their Temple be restored to them. Vitellius says it shall be done. John appears, followed by Salome and others, and the consul is told by Herodias that the prophet is a disturber anxious for power. John retorts that all power is from God.

Act III *Scene 1. An Inner Room.* While Phanuel, the Chaldean, is consulting the stars, Herodias seeks him to know about the future. She is especially desirous to know how to win back Herod's love, and also as to the whereabouts of her lost daughter. For reply, Phanuel shows her Salome who is crossing the court with the dancers. "That my daughter?" exclaims Herodias. "No, my rival!"

Scene 2. The Temple. Salome is in the depths of despair because John has been cast into prison. Herod meets her and offers her his love, but she repulses him. Vitellius enters proclaiming the power of Rome. The priests appear before him urging the condemnation of John. He refers them to Herod. John is brought forward and questioned. Salome throws herself before him begging Herod to pardon him; but this only infuriates Herod, who sentences him to death.

Act IV *Scene 1. A Dungeon.* While John awaits his sentence, Salome enters. Her fortitude and devotion touch him and something like human love enters his heart. But he bids her flee and save herself. The High Priest secretly offers John a pardon if he will use his influence for Herod against Rome, but John refuses.

Scene 2. Audience Hall in the Palace. While Herod, Herodias, and Vitellius hold an audience and are entertained by dancers Salome appears at the special command of Herod. He turns a deaf ear, however, to her requests for John's pardon, and the executioner presently appears with a bloody sword, as a sign that the prophet is dead. Salome turns in fury upon Herodias, saying "This is your deed!" and is about to stab her. Herodias, in fear, cries out: "I am your mother!" "Then take back the life you gave me!" replies Salome, and stabs herself to the heart.

MANON

(Ma'-non)

Dramatic Opera in Five Acts. Music by Massenet. Book by H. Meilhac and P. Gille, after Marcel Prévost's "Manon Lescaut."

Opéra Comique, Paris, January 19, 1884. At the Academy of Music, New York, December 23, 1885. Metropolitan, January 16, 1895, with Jean de Reszke, Plancon, and Ancona in the male roles; and Sybil Sanderson as "Manon."

SCENE: Amiens, Paris, Havre.

TIME: 1721.

CAST   COMTE DES GRIEUX, *a French nobleman* (Basso).
CHEVALIER DES GRIEUX, *his son* (Tenor).
LESCAUT, *a guardsman* (Baritone).
MANON LESCAUT, *his cousin* (Soprano).
GUILLOT MORFONTAIN, *a minister of finance* (Basso).
DE BRÉTIGNY, *a nobleman* (Baritone).
POUSSETTE, *an actress* (Soprano).
ROSETTE, *an actress* (Soprano).
JAVOTTE, *an actress* (Contralto).
    Innkeeper, Citizens, Actresses, Soldiers, Servants, etc.

ARGUMENT   "Manon" is a picture of French life among the gay set, drawn from Prévost's well-known story "Manon Lescaut," which is the same source made use of, some years later, by Puccini in his opera of that name.

Act I   *A Tavern at Amiens.*   Manon Lescaut is a gay and volatile French woman whose spirits her parents very wisely seek to curb by placing her in a convent. On the way thither, escorted by her cousin, she stops at an inn where Morfontain is entertaining some friends. The old roué immediately begins to make advances to her but is repulsed. Not so, young Des Grieux, who has been destined for the priesthood. He finds Manon so attractive, and she him, that they both forsake their prospective vows and run away to Paris.

Manon's opening song is a mixture of the demure and the impish: "I am a simple maiden" (Je suis encore étourdie). Her cousin Lescaut, warns her of pitfalls in his baritone song, "Now give good heed" (Regardez-moi). She speedily forgets the warning, however, as soon as she meets the handsome chevalier. To his question, "If I but knew your name?" and her reply, "I am called Manon"—ensues the usual impassioned duet, "To you, my life and soul!" (A vous ma vie et mon ame). The Act ends with their lively, "We're on our way to Paris!"

Act II   *Des Grieux's Apartments in Paris.*   Manon and the chevalier live quietly in Paris and he writes to his father the Count, asking permission to marry her. Her cousin, Lescaut, comes to demand satisfaction from the chevalier for the abduction. The latter then shows him the letter that he is about to mail to his father, as proof of his honorable intentions. Lescaut seems satisfied, but a new danger threatens. While the two talk, another nobleman has entered, De Bretigny, who takes Manon aside and tells her that the chevalier is on the point of being seized by his father, to prevent this match. She would be wiser to go with him—De Bretigny—who can offer her safety and a life of luxury. She is left alone on the stage to wrestle with this new temptation, and the chevalier on his return from mailing the letter finds her in tears. Seeking to console her, he describes the little dream house he is planning for them: "The Dream" (La reve)—

A sudden knock interrupts their idyl. Manon starts guiltily; she has not warned her lover. Now he goes to the door; she interposes half-heartedly; he is taken by his captors; and she awaits her new lover.

Act III *Scene 1.* *A Parisian Boulevard.* Manon is the center of a laughing crowd of actresses and boulevardiers. True to his word, De Brétigny maintains her in luxury. But she overhears the Count des Grieux telling a friend that the chevalier, disgusted with Manon's conduct, was about to become a monk. She seeks further information, but the Count, guessing her identity, will not say more. She resolves to seek her former lover.

Scene 2. *The seminary of St. Sulpice.* The Count does not wish his son to enter the priesthood and endeavors to dissuade him. Afterwards, Manon enters, but the chevalier only reproaches her with her faithlessness. She says that she still loves him, and after much argument persuades him to come back to her.

In this second scene the chevalier sings a fervent song of renunciation: "Depart, fair vision!" (Ah, fuyez, douce image!), but despite his resolution he cannot drive her image from his mind and as if in answer to his secret desires that fickle vision comes back in the flesh. He upbraids Manon that she has been faithless, and tells her that he is seeking solace in a religious brotherhood. A chanting chorus in the background is heard. But the chameleonlike woman only answers: "Ah, look at me! Am I no longer Manon?" (Ah, regardez moi!) The religious chant and his own fine resolutions are unheeded. "Ah, Manon, I love thee!" he cries; and an impassioned duet of reconciliation marks the fall of the curtain. The clash of contending emotions is faithfully reflected in the tumultuous music.

Act IV   *A Gambling House in Paris.*   In order to maintain Manon in the style to which she is accustomed, the chevalier frequents the gambling houses. He wins large sums, especially from Morfontain. The latter accuses him of cheating and, by way of revenge upon Manon, who jilted him, has both Des Grieux and Manon arrested. The Count also joins forces against her and plots to have her deported where she can do no further mischief.

As the chevalier sweeps in his winnings and the croupier shouts, "Make your plays, gentlemen!" Manon sings a joyous: "Music of Gold" song. However, their joy soon ends with the descent of law. "Oh, despair! Now are our lives parted forever!" she voices her grief.

Act V   *The Open Road near Havre.*   Manon is being escorted out of the country by a guard of soldiers. The chevalier asks Lescaut, her cousin, to aid him in rescuing her. They try bribery. She has a short interview with Des Grieux, begging his pardon for wrecking his life; but even in her last moments a hint of the selfish, fickle woman asserts itself. "What lovely jewels!" she sighs, as she dreams of former luxury. Then she turns repentant to her chevalier. "Forgive me! I love but thee! Take this last kiss—it is all I have left—" As he clasps her in his arms, she dies.

WERTHER

Tragic Opera in Four Acts. Music by Massenet. Book by Blau, Milliet, and Hartmann, after the story, "The Sorrows of Werther," by Goethe. Imperial Opera House, Vienna, with the composer directing, February 16, 1892. At the Auditorium, Chicago, March 29, 1894. In New York, the Metropolitan, April 19, 1894.

> Scene: Wetzlar, Germany.
> Time: 1772.

> CAST   Werther, *a poet* (Tenor).
>   Charlotte, *his cousin* (Soprano).
>   Albert, *her husband* (Baritone).
>   Father of Charlotte (Bass).
>   Friends, servants, etc.

ARGUMENT   This story which closely follows that of Goethe was at first hailed as one of Massenet's greatest works. It contains some of his most persuasive melodies, but as a whole has failed to keep a place in active repertory.

Act I *A Terrace in front of the Bailiff's House.* Werther, a young poet of highly romantic disposition, is in love with Charlotte, his cousin, who reciprocates. Her father, the bailiff, however, has planned to carry out her dead mother's wishes and marry her to Albert, an old friend of the family. Charlotte tells Werther that she feels in honor bound to go through with this marriage, and Werther replies, "If you do so, I shall die."

Act II *Square before the Inn.* The ensuing action takes place three months later. Albert and Charlotte are now man and wife. Albert knows of Werther's love for his wife, but trusts him. The poet, unable to hide his sentiments, finally goes away.

Act III *Albert's Home.* Werther has remained away from his beloved until life becomes unendurable for him. He goes back, in spite of himself, and finding Charlotte at home alone, he begins to read to her a poem by Ossian; but the lines serve only to betray his own passion for her. His song of great intensity, "Do not wake me," is generally called, "Chant d'Ossian"—

Her own agitation reveals her love for Werther, but she entreats him to leave her forever. He departs. Later Albert comes in with a note from him, saying that he is going on a long journey and requesting the loan of his pistol. Charlotte, filled with dread misgivings, hastens to Werther's apartments.

Act IV *Werther's Apartments.* Charlotte finds her worst fears are realized. She finds Werther lying upon the floor, mortally wounded. She reproaches herself for his death, but now at last they can confess all their love for each other. As she holds the dying man in her arms, the voices of children are heard, singing a Christmas carol.

THAIS
(*Tah'-ees*)

Romantic Opera in Three Acts. Music by Jules Massenet. Book by Louis Gallet, after the romance by Anatole France. Grand Opera,

Paris, March 16, 1894.   Manhattan Opera House, New York, November 25, 1908, by the Chicago Opera Company, headed by Mary Garden (her New York début) and Renaud.   At the Metropolitan, February 16, 1917, with Farrar and Rothier.

SCENE: Upper Egypt.
TIME: Early Christian era.

CAST   ATHANAEL, *a monk* (Baritone).
THAIS, *a courtesan* (Soprano).
NICIAS, *a wealthy Alexandrian* (Tenor).
PALEMON, *the head monk* (Basso).
ALBINE, *an abbess* (Mezzo-Soprano).
LA CHARMEUSE, *a dancer.*
CROBYLE, *a slave* (Soprano).
MYRTALE, *a slave* (Soprano).
Monks, Nuns, Citizens, Servants, Dancers, etc.

ARGUMENT   The theme of "Thais" is the struggle between the lower nature and the higher; it personifies the eternal conflict between the beast and the angel, in the human race. Like Mascagni's "Cavalleria," "Thais" has won enduring fame by reason of its Intermezzo, which has become a favorite with violinists.

Act I   *Scene 1.   The Theban Desert.*   Withdrawing from luxury and sin, a small band of Cenobite monks dwell in the desert near Thebes.   Athanael, a young enthusiast of the order, has just returned from a mission to Alexandria, and he gives a gloomy account of the vice rampant in that city.   It is under the control of a beautiful courtesan named Thais, who rules by the power of her charms.   Athanael cannot get the vision of her loveliness out of his head, and he thinks it would be a great victory for the Church if he could convert her.   Palemon, the head of the order, rebukes the idea as foolish, but in his dreams, Athanael witnesses again the lovely woman posing before the populace as Aphrodite, and being acclaimed as a goddess.   He awakes, saying that he must return on this mission, although Palemon and the other monks endeavor to dissuade him.

The music in the opening scene reflects the sober, severe life of the Cenobite monks.   After a quiet but resonant chorus, Athanael enters and recites dramatically his past experiences in the city and vision of Thais.   His song, "Let us have pity in our hearts," is followed by the arguments of the leader and others, to dissuade a further visit to the city of sin.

Scene 2.   The House of Nicias, at Alexandria.   Nicias, a wealthy leader of fashion, is just now the favored admirer of Thais, although he ruefully admits he is paying extravagantly for the distinction. To his house, Athanael directs his steps, and finally gains admittance there. When he unfolds his plan to Nicias, the latter laughs at it, but good-naturedly promises to aid him. Thais is to be present at supper that very evening, and the young monk must make a good appearance. The leader of fashion looks approvingly at Athanael's fine head and athletic figure, and bids his slave array the guest in rich attire. A great acclamation is heard and Thais enters amid a throng of her adorers. The young monk alone stands aloof and she notices his attitude. "Who is he?" she asks. "One who has come for you," Nicias replies jestingly. "Bringing love?" she asks simply; for to her love is all in all. "Yes, love that you know not of," answers Athanael sternly, coming forward; and he tries to tell her of the higher life. She cannot understand him. He reproaches her and the company interfere. Then Thais, piqued, tries to subdue him by her charms. He retreats, but promises to come to her apartments and talk further. It is her challenge which he accepts, confident of his own integrity.

The music here is in striking contrast with the somber first scene. Now all is gaiety, frivolity, sensuality, but with an undertone as the austere monk strives to oppose it.

Act II *Scene 1. Interior of the Palace of Thais.* In a luxuriously appointed room Thais awaits the coming of one whom she thinks will be her next victim. Meanwhile, she prays to Aphrodite for a continuance of youth and beauty, her only weapons. As she contemplates her loveliness in a mirror, she sings the fine aria, "Tell me that I am beautiful" (Dis-moi que je suis belle)—known as the "Mirror Song"—

Athanael pauses at the door, at first spellbound by the vision of loveliness; then advancing, he tells her that the love which he offers is from God and is for her salvation. They argue, she trying upon him all her coquetry, but he is able to resist temptation. This new type of man impresses her even more than his message. The voice of Nicias is heard calling her, and Athanael departs, saying he will wait for her outside the palace. She must follow him if she would find the new and higher love. "On thy threshold till dawn I shall await thy coming," he tells her sternly. The curtain descends and now is heard the hauntingly lovely strains of the "Meditation"—the vigil of the monk, the awakening of a woman's soul.   To a harp accompaniment a solo violin is heard in a strain of pure melody—

Scene 2. Outside the Palace. Moonlight floods the open court, while through the lighted windows come the sounds of revelry and feasting.   Athanael lies upon the stone step.   Presently the door opens and Thais emerges bearing a lighted lamp.   She tells him she has decided to leave all and follow him.   "Then break your image and set fire to your belongings," he replies, "for you cannot take any of these things with you."   She returns within and obeys him, reappearing in a simple garb, bearing a torch.   Meanwhile, Nicias and his friends come forth and order dancers to entertain them.   In the midst of the revelry Thais appears, but they recognize her despite her rough dress, and try to detain her.   Nicias diverts the crowd's attention by scattering handfuls of gold, and the two pilgrims depart while the palace burns.

Act III *Scene 1. An Oasis in the Desert.* Thais is half-dead from the fatigue of this unaccustomed journey, but presses on without murmuring.   She wishes to find the higher love.   Athanael's heart is stirred by her sufferings and fortitude.   He bids her rest beneath the shade of a clump of palms and brings water to bathe her feet, kissing them.   His destination is a convent in the desert, now near at hand. The abbess and her nuns are heard singing as they approach.   Athanael commends the new convert into their keeping and stands silent until they have gone.   Then he utters a cry of anguish.   He has conquered, but now he is alone.

Scene 2. The Cenobite Monastery. Athanael returns to the monastery, where the monks congratulate him upon his success. But he is indifferent to their praise. The vision of Thais still haunts his dreams and he finds that he is miserable since she has gone out of his life.

Scene 3. The Garden of the Convent. Thais is dying, and has sent for Athanael. He comes and the abbess leads him to her cot in the open court. The sisters extol her saintly life, but the monk does not heed. He kneels by her side and begs her to come back to him. It is not the heavenly love which fills his heart, now, but the earthly. She opens her eyes but does not understand him; for visions of heavenly bliss already possess her. Deaf to his entreaties, she calls upon the name of God as she dies, while he grovels upon the ground in despair.

The closing moments between the two are marked by some of the finest passages: his despairing cry to her, and her incoherent answers; the sorrowful chants of the nuns; then again an echo of the celestial strains of the "Meditation," as her soul wings its way upward with the music.

THE JUGGLER OF NOTRE DAME

(Le Jongleur de Notre Dame.) Miracle Play in Three Acts. Music by Massenet. Book by Maurice Lena. Monte Carlo, February 18, 1902; Paris, 1903. Manhattan Opera House, New York, November 27, 1908.

SCENE: Cluny, near Paris.
TIME: Sixteenth Century.

CAST   JEAN, *a juggler* (Tenor).
BONIFACE, *a cook* (Baritone).
PRIOR OF THE MONASTERY (Basso).
POET, *a monk* (Tenor).
PAINTER, *a monk* (Baritone).
MUSICIAN, *a monk* (Baritone).
SCULPTOR, *a monk* (Basso).
Two Angels, apparition of the Virgin, Monks, Cavaliers, Citizens.

ARGUMENT   "The Juggler of Notre Dame" is styled by its librettist a "Miracle" play, but is only such in the sense that it requires a miracle to give value to its denouement. Its theme is medieval and monastic, ignoring love or other affairs of the gentler sex.

Act I *The Cluny Market Place.* During a market day in which all
the villagers gather to barter and make merry, Jean the juggler
wanders about forlorn and hungry. His tricks are time-worn, his songs
weak, and when he presently tries to perform for the crowd, they only
jeer at him. Finally, to arouse them he sings a sacrilegious song, "Alle-
luia to Wine," in which they roar out a chorus. The Prior of a neighboring monastery is shocked and comes out to anathematize the crowd.
All scatter, leaving Jean, who is really a goodhearted fellow, to bear the
blame of the Church. The Prior is finally touched by his penitence,
and pardons him, but urges him to join the band of monks. Jean does
not wish to relinquish his liberty, but the sight of the Cook's donkey
going by with panniers laden with food is too much for his hungry
stomach and he consents.

Act II *The Monastery Study.* The busy monks each labor at their
chosen vocation—poets, musicians, painters, scribes, sculptors,
and what not—but Jean feels himself out of it. He cannot even pray
to the Virgin because he knows no Latin, and he fears that she will not
listen to any other tongue. Meanwhile, the other monks have been
quarreling as to which of their vocations has the most merit. The Cook
alone consoles Jean by relating to him the legend of the humble sage
plant, useful in cooking. The quaint story is that the child Jesus was
once refused shelter by the rosebush, but the lowly sage offered its protection and has since been valued among herbs. The Cook's song,
"The Legend of the Sage" (Légende de la sauge) is a favorite with baritones—

Jean listens to the song open-mouthed and takes new heart. He himself must have something that would be acceptable to the Church and
the Blessed Virgin.

Act III *The Chapel.* Jean lays aside his monastic dress and puts on
his juggler's apparel. He goes before the life-size figure of
the Virgin, in the Chapel, and since he does not know anything else,
he prepares to offer to her his little stock in trade—a juggling performance! Spreading out his shabby outfit, he performs his tricks and sings
his songs, first begging pardon if they do not suit her. In the midst of
his performance, the monks enter to celebrate high mass. They recoil
in horror at this sacrilege and are ready to lay violent hands upon the
poor juggler, when suddenly a miracle happens. The image of the
Virgin becomes animated, the face smiles, and the arms stretch out in

protection and benediction. The monks draw back in awe, and Jean, radiant, exclaims, "Now at last I shall know Latin," and dies. Angels appear and the Prior crossing himself says: "We have had a saint among us!"

DON QUIXOTE
(Don Kee-ho'-teh)

(Don Quichotte.) Romantic Opera in Five Acts. Music by Massenet; text by Henri Cain, after the play by Jacques La Lorrain, based on the romance of Cervantes. Monte Carlo, February 19, 1910. New Orleans, January 27, 1912. At the Metropolitan, New York, February 3, 1914.

SCENE: Spain.
TIME: The Middle Ages.

CAST DULCINEA (Contralto).
DON QUIXOTE (Bass).
SANCHO PANZA (Baritone).
PEDRO, *burlesquer* (Soprano).
GARCIAS, *burlesquer* (Soprano).
RODRIGUEZ (Tenor).
JUAN (Tenor).
TWO VALETS (Baritone).
TENEBRUN, *chief, and other bandits, friends of Dulcinea, and others.*

ARGUMENT "Don Quixote" is based upon the famous novel of Cervantes and depicts phases in the life of the last of the knights-errant.

Act I *Square in Front of the House of Dulcinea.* A throng praises the beauty of Dulcinea. Into the company ride Don Quixote and his comical companion, Sancho. Night and moonlight. Don Quixote serenades Dulcinea, arousing the jealousy of Juan, a lover of the professional beauty, but the latter appears and prevents a duel. She is amused by the avowals of Don Quixote, and promises to become his beloved if he will recover a necklace stolen from her by brigands.

Act II *On the Way to the Camp of the Brigands.* Here occurs the famous tilt with the windmill.

Act III *Camp of the Brigands.* Don Quixote attacks them. Sancho retreats. The Knight is captured. He expects to be put to death. But his courage, his grave courtesy, and his love for his Dulcinea, deeply impress the bandits. They free him and give him the necklace.

Act IV *Fête at the House of Dulcinea.* To the astonishment of all Don Quixote and Sancho put in their appearance. Dulcinea is delighted to have her necklace returned. The Knight pleads with her to marry him. Dulcinea is so touched by his devotion that she confesses her past life to him, and entreats him to forget her.

Act V *A Forest.* Disillusioned and weary, Don Quixote lies down to die. He bequeaths to his faithful squire the most beautiful of all islands, "The Island of Dreams." It is his proudest possession. As his mind wanders, he beholds the beautiful Dulcinea again. He extends his arms to her, and falls back lifeless.

Critics are agreed that if the music of the first four Acts measured up to that of the last, "Don Quixote" would be frequently heard. As the old hero sings of his "Island of Dreams," the orchestra sustains the powerful basso notes with a delicate, wandering melody (first popularized by Chaliapin). Then the voice of Dulcinea is heard, singing of love and joy. He thrills to it, and his last moments are blissful. Only the faithful Sancho is left disconsolate.

ANDRÉ MESSAGER

Messanger was born in Montlucon, December 30, 1853. He belongs strictly to the modern school and has written many shorter musical pieces; but is known in this country for only one opera, "Madame Chrysanthème." Messager died in 1929.

MADAME CHRYSANTHÈME
(Ma-dam Kris-an-thaym)

Lyric Comedy in a Prologue, Four Acts, and Epilogue. Music by Messager. Book by Hartmann and Alexandre, after the story by Pierre Loti. First produced at the Opéra Comique, Paris, January 26, 1893. In New York, the Metropolitan, by the Chicago Opera Company, January 28, 1920.

ARGUMENT This little love story of a temporary romance in Japan is a rather close parallel to "Madame Butterfly."

Pierre, a French naval officer, confides to his attendant, Yves, that while their ship is stationed in Japanese waters he proposes to contract a temporary marriage with some pretty girl of Nagasaki. He meets Madame Chrysanthème. Kangourou, a matrimonial agent, arranges matters, and the bridal veil is handed to her. While Pierre and his temporary bride are enjoying their honeymoon, his comrades arrive with their own feminine charmers and serenade him.

In the Third Act, a festival is in progress, and Chrysanthème is among the gayest of the gay. But Pierre becomes jealous, thinking she is flirting with Yves, and flies into a rage. Peace is later restored between the young couple, but their happiness is short-lived. The boom of guns aboard ship calls the lieutenant back to duty. Chrysanthème does not cry her heart out, but bears up bravely.

The epilogue is again between the lieutenant and Yves, who mourn for Chrysanthème. Pierre tosses the lotus flowers she has given him into the sea, and prays the gods for forgetfulness.

GUSTAVE CHARPENTIER

Gustave Charpentier is chiefly known for his single opera, "Louise." He was born in Dieuze, Lorraine, June 25, 1860, and received his training in the French schools. He describes "Louise" as a musical romance, saying: "Because in a romance there are two entirely distinct sides, the drama and the description, in my 'Louise' I want to treat these different sides."

LOUISE

Dramatic Opera in Four Acts. Music by Gustave Charpentier. Book by the Composer. Opéra Comique, Paris, February 2, 1900. Manhattan Opera House, New York, January 3, 1908. Metropolitan, January 15, 1921.

SCENE: Paris.
TIME: The Present.

CAST LOUISE, *a sewing girl* (Soprano).
HER FATHER (Baritone).
HER MOTHER (Contralto).
JULIEN, *an artist* (Tenor).
IRMA, *a sewing girl* (Contralto).
THE KING OF FOOLS, *a Bohemian* (Baritone).
ERRAND GIRL (Mezzo-Soprano).
FOREWOMAN (Contralto).
Sewing Girls, Bohemians, Peddlers, Rag-pickers, Grisettes, Gamins, etc.

ARGUMENT "Louise" may be regarded as a bit of canvas belonging to the varied panorama of Paris. It depicts home life among the lower working classes as they come in daily contact with the underworld of the great city. Louise herself personifies the struggle between love and duty; between the instincts of virtue and the desire to be free.

In France "Louise" has achieved greater popularity than any opera since "Carmen." Its cross section of Parisian life, no less than its vivacious, dramatic music, have endeared it. It is also of interest in America as providing the first vehicle for the talents of Mary Garden. As an unknown singer she made her début in it, in Paris, April, 1900, and won fame overnight.

Act I *Garret of a Paris Tenement.* Louise, a sewing girl, has fallen in love with Julien, a young artist whose studio balcony adjoins her window. Julien sings charming serenades, but is an improvident bohemian, like the rest of his class. He nevertheless wishes to marry Louise and has written to her father asking permission, but her mother, a hard-working, practical woman, is violently opposed to the match. She overhears the lovers making plans from their adjacent windows and parts them without ceremony. Louise's father returns home wearied from his day's work, but after supper and a pipe he feels in good humor with the world. He reads Julien's letter and the girl pleads her lover's cause, while her mother as strongly berates it. They quarrel, but the father endeavors to act as peacemaker, although he points out to his daughter the improvidence of Julien. Louise is downcast but promises to try to forget him.

A fine song for tenors is heard early in this Act when Louise asks Julien how he happened to fall in love with her. He replies: "A long, long time I have lived in this room" (Depuis longtemps j'habitais cette chambre)—

Act II *Scene 1. The Road to Montmartre.* It is early morning and Paris is waking up. The last of the prowlers—beggars, thieves, bohemians and street-walkers—are still to be seen. Rag-pickers and newsboys are busy. Servants open windows and shake rugs. Presently Julien and some of his bohemian friends appear. He is planning to elope with Louise, since he cannot obtain her father's consent. Meanwhile she comes by on her way to the shop, escorted by her mother. Julien conceals himself until the latter has gone away, then endeavors to persuade the girl to come with him. She refuses and continues on her way to work.

Scene 2. A Dressmaker's Workshop. Louise and many of her companions are seen busily at work sewing and fitting garments over lay figures. They ply their needles and machines and sing carelessly. One or two tell Louise that she does not look well. Presently a serenader's voice is heard; it is Julien, who will not go away. At first the girls applaud, and then his continued singing grows monotonous. Finally Louise complains of being ill and leaves the room, but the others laugh maliciously as they notice that she is going up the street with Julien.

Act III *A Cottage on the Montmartre.* Julien and Louise have set up an establishment for themselves without consent of either parents or the church. But they justify their conduct on the score of love. They are children of the great city and have a right to be free. Louise voices her joy in a lovely aria, "Ever since the day" (Depuis le jour)—

A group of laughing bohemians pause before the doorway. One of them hangs lanterns from its door and windows. The crowd gathers and the lovers are summoned forth. Then the King of Fools makes an address and crowns Louise as the Muse of Montmartre. In the midst of this revelry a woman pushes her way through the throng, which scatters to right and left. It is Louise's mother come to plead with her daughter. She no longer quarrels, but she says that the father is ill and only Louise's presence can help him. Afterwards she will be allowed to return to Julien. The lovers separate upon these terms, and the girl goes with her mother.

Act IV *The Garret Room.* Louise finds, after she returns home, that she is being held a prisoner. She must sew at home. Her father still treats her affectionately, but insists upon her remaining with them. She says she is a grown woman and has the right to be free. He points out that the freedom she claims is the first step to ruin. In a tender scene between father and daughter, he tries to recall to her the carefree days of her childhood, in a Lullaby (Berceuse) of haunting loveliness—

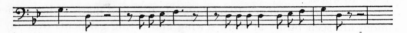

But his pleas are in vain. Louise cannot forget her lover and the little cottage. At last she seizes her shawl and bursts past her parents to the door. Her mother rushes to the window to call her, while her father pursues her as far as the staircase. But she is gone out of their lives. The old workman shakes his fist at the city which has claimed another victim. "Oh, Paris!" he cries out, heartbroken.

CLAUDE DEBUSSY

Claude Achille Debussy was born in Saint-Germain-en-Laye, near Paris, in 1862. He entered the Paris Conservatory at the age of eleven, and won the Grand Prix de Rome, in 1884, with his one-act cantata, "L'Enfant Prodigue." In Italy he produced a symphonic suite, "Printemps," with only moderate success. This was followed with other suites; then his symphonic poem, "L'Apres-midi d'un Faun" (Afternoon of a Faun) came out, in 1902, to establish him firmly as one of the latter-day French composers to be reckoned with. Three years later came his three symphonic sketches, "La Mer." Ballets followed. His one opera, "Pelléas et Mélisande," extended his fame around the musical world. Debussy died March 26, 1918.

PELLEAS AND MÉLISANDE

(Pel-lay-as and May-lis-sand)

Lyric Drama in Five Acts. Music by Debussy. Book by Maurice Maeterlinck. Opéra Comique, Paris, April 30, 1902. At the Manhattan Opera House, New York, February 19, 1908, its première in America, with the role of "Melisande" winning acclaim for Mary Garden. Jean Perier sang that of "Pelleas."

SCENE: Allemonde.
TIME: Antiquity.

CAST   ARKEL, *King of Allemonde* (Basso).
         GENEVIEVE, *his daughter-in-law* (Soprano).
         GOLAUD, *her elder son* (Baritone).
         PELLEAS, *her younger son* (Tenor).
         MELISANDE, *wife of Golaud* (Soprano).
         YNIOLD, *son of Golaud* (Soprano).
         A PHYSICIAN (Baritone).
         Servants, Blind Beggars, etc.

ARGUMENT   "Pelleas and Melisande" is a mystic drama of passion and fate, both text and music being freighted with inner meaning.

Act I *Scene 1. A Fountain in the Forest.* Golaud, a grandson of aged King Arkel, while out hunting discovers a maiden wandering lost and weeping in the forest. She will not tell anything about herself or whence she came, but Golaud, whose wife is dead, persuades her to go with him to the King's court.

Scene 2. Genevieve, daughter of King Arkel, informs him that her son Golaud has taken the strange maiden to wife. He has written his brother, Pelleas, to this effect and asks permission to bring her to court. If it pleases the King a light is to be shown from the tower window; otherwise he will go away. Pelleas is ordered to display the light.

Scene 3. The Castle Gardens. Genevieve shows Melisande (for that is the name given by the strange maiden) the gardens of the castle, but the girl merely shudders and says that it is all old and dark. To divert her mind, Pelleas points out the beacon lights along the shore. She sees a ship sailing away and exclaims that it is her ship. Pelleas, de-

pressed, says that he also is going away.   She answers with the plaintive
cry, "Why must you go?"

The music so subtly interweaves throughout the action that it is almost impossible to differentiate, or to single out special themes.   The
composer's style is distinctively his own.

Act II   *Scene 1.   A Fountain in the Park.*   Pelleas cannot tear himself away from this strange girl.   He walks with her one day
in the park and she seats herself by the edge of a deep pool.   She takes
off her wedding ring, which she plays with carelessly.   It falls into the
depths of the water, and Pelleas says that it cannot be recovered.   The
clock strikes twelve.

Scene 2.   Golaud's Chamber.   By a curious coincidence, Golaud
has met with an accident at the precise moment when the wedding ring
fell into the pool.   His horse stumbled and fell upon him.   Melisande
nurses him back to health.   He notices that the ring is missing from her
finger, and asks her where it is.   She answers that she lost it in a cavern
by the sea while gathering shells for little Yniold (his son).   He commands her to go at once, even though it is nightfall, and search for it.
Pelleas can go with her.

Scene 3.   The Cavern.   Pelleas and Melisande visit the cavern so
that the girl will be able to describe it to Golaud.   They meet three
blind men wandering there and Melisande is frightened.   It portends
ill fortune.

The instruments as well as the voices again give a vivid picture of
setting and action.   In the first scene of this Act, the rippling waters
of the fountain as they fall into the depths of the pool are mirrored by
the orchestra.   In the second scene, Golaud describes his accident in the
song, "Ah, ah! Tout va bien."   Melisande's childish, evasive replies to
his questioning follow.   Before the last scene there is an orchestral interlude, where we hear again the rippling waters of the fountain.   The
terrifying roar of the sea sweeps over it.

Act III   *Scene 1.   Outside Melisande's Balcony.*   Melisande combs
her long tresses while leaning out of the window and the hair
falls in a shimmering mass nearly to the ground.   While she combs it
she sings an old-time legend which gives the names of the saints who
have watched over her.   Pelleas comes up a path and stops to fondle
the wonderful tresses.   He tells her again that he must go away (Il fait
beau cette nuit).   She begs him again not to desert her, but more in the
tones of a child than of a woman.   Golaud surprises them, but chides
them for acting like a pair of children.

Scene 2. The Castle Vaults. The music takes on a tragic tone, as the "Fate" motive rings out from the orchestra; the interlude closing with a note of "Vengeance." By way of covert warning, Golaud takes his brother Pelleas to the vaults of the castle, showing him the deep silent pits from which no victim could escape.

Scene 3. The Gardens. They return to the gardens and Golaud bluntly cautions Pelleas to be less attentive to Melisande. Pelleas, however, still seems unmindful of his danger. As he comes back into the fresh air again, he exclaims, "Ah, I can breathe again!"

Scene 4. Outside the Window of Melisande's Chamber. It is evening, and the still watchful Golaud questions his little son, Yniold, as to the relations of Pelleas and Melisande. The child replies that they are often together, though they have kissed only once. Golaud lifts the boy up on his shoulders so that he can peer in at the lighted window. Yniold says that Pelleas is there but is not near Melisande. They only look at each other with tears in their eyes. Golaud grasps his son so tensely that the child exclaims in pain.

Act IV *Scene 1. A Corridor.* Melisande agrees to meet Pelleas for a farewell interview by the fountain. She is encountered by the aged King, who speaks kindly to her. But after he is gone, her husband enters, greeting her rudely and violently.

During this change of scene a lengthy interlude is played. The "Fate" motive again rings out dramatically; with moments of tenderer passages identified with Melisande. The music becomes gloomy and heavy with despair as the curtain rises.

Scene 2. The Fountain. Pelleas and Melisande meet by the fountain and Pelleas pours forth a torrent of love. Melisande listens half hysterical. Something moves in the shadows behind them. She is sure that it is her husband, but she clings to her lover in despair. Golaud rushes forward and transfixes Pelleas with his sword, and then turns to pursue the fleeing Melisande.

Act V *Melisande's Bedchamber.* Melisande has given birth to a child, but her life hangs upon a thread. Golaud attends upon her, remorseful for what he has done. She does not seem to remember. He questions her about Pelleas, but she returns evasive replies. She has loved him, but she is innocent of wrong-doing. Arkel and the physician bid him cease troubling her. She is shown her child, but is too weak to hold it. The servants enter silently. Golaud bids them begone, but they only fall upon their knees in prayer. The physician looks at his patient and says that they are right. Melisande is dead.

L'ENFANT PRODIGUE

(*Lon-fant Pro-deeg*)

(The Prodigal Son.) A "lyrical episode" by Debussy. Words by
Ernest Guiraud. Sheffield Festival, England, 1908. Covent Garden,
1910. Boston, 1910.

SCENE: Village on Lake Gennasereth.
TIME: First Century.

CAST LIA (Soprano).
SIMEON, *her husband* (Basso).
AZÄEL, *their errant son* (Tenor).

ARGUMENT   This "lyrical episode," with which Debussy won
his first prize, is much more conventional and influenced by tradition than are the later, more typical compositions by
which the composer took his place as the founder of the impressionist
school of music in France.   None the less, there are here traces of that
marked originality of conception and courage in method which were to
set the composer in the very front rank while he was still a comparatively young man.

The hour is early in the morning; the season is the time of harvest.
Far off, joyful chants are heard.   Lia enters alone, inconsolably mourning her son Azäel, who has left home, and whom she hardly dares to
hope that she will ever see again on earth.   Simeon comes, and rebukes
her for this unavailing and untimely sorrow.   A pageant of youths
and maidens appears, followed by servants bearing garlands of flowers,
fruits, and horns of plenty.   They perform a choric dance and then,
headed by Simeon and Lia, depart, their singing dying slowly away in
the distance.   When the stage is clear, Azäel enters, footsore, travel-
stained, and weary.   He has watched the dance from the shelter of the
low-swung boughs, and has recognized his brother and sister among the
dancers.   Overwhelmed with remorse, he thinks of the days of his innocence, when he used to sit by this same lake with his head against his
mother's heart.   He will lie down here and die, within sight of the well-
remembered village which he has neither the courage nor the strength
to enter.

Lia now returns.   She cannot bear the tumult of rejoicing, which
frets her stricken spirit.   Catching sight of Azäel on the ground, she
thinks at first that he is a poor wayfarer, and goes to help him.   Then
she recognizes her long-lost son and folds him in her arms, with passionate words of love, and pity, and pardon.   The servants reappear, and

she tells them that this is the son of their master. Then Simeon himself returns, but, less ready to forgive than his wife, he stands looking down in silence at the prostrate form of his son, uttering only a hurried prayer to Heaven for guidance. Lia throws herself at his feet, imploring forgiveness for their child, and the father relents. He bids the servants make the glad tidings known with sounds of cymbal and tabor, and orders that the wine jars shall be filled and the fatted calf slain. Then Azäel rises, he and his parents are folded in one another's arms, and all three voice an exultant song of thanks to the Lord God of Israel.

CAMILLE ERLANGER

Erlanger was born May 25, 1863, at Paris; and died in the same city, in 1919. He studied under Leo Delibes at the Paris Conservatory, and won the Grand Prix de Rome, in 1888, for his cantata "Velleda." He wrote numerous short pieces, cantatas, and four operas: "Kermaria," (1897); "Aphrodite," (1906); "Noel," (1906); and "L'Aube Rouge," which had its première at Rouen, in 1912.

APHRODITE
(Aph-ro-dy'-te)

A lyric drama in five acts and seven scenes, after the story by Pierre Louys. Adapted by Louis de Gramont. Music by Erlanger. Opéra Comique, Paris, March 23, 1906, with the American singer, Mary Garden, achieving fame both for herself and the opera. She sang the role of "Aphrodite" also at the American première, in the Metropolitan, February 27, 1920. Edward Johnson, in his first season at "the Met," supported her, in "Demetrios."

ARGUMENT   An opera rich in scenic possibilities. Its appeal is directed as much to the eye and the æsthetic sense, as to the ear. The scene is Alexandria; the time, 50 B.C.

The curtain rises to disclose a busy hour of ancient Egypt, upon a crowded wharf at Alexandria. There are citizens of every grade and calling. Some ply their trades, others are there merely for diversion. Rhodis and Myrto play their flutes while Theano dances. All make way for Demetrios, the famous sculptor. A Jewish fortune-teller reads his hand, predicting crime and tragedy because of a woman. At this juncture the beautiful courtesan, Chrysis, enters. Demetrios pays her attention, but she tells him that, to win her favor, he must bring her three precious gifts—the mirror of Bacchis, the ivory comb of Touni, and the pearl necklace of Aphrodite. The sculptor has become so infatuated that he determines to obtain them.

Acts II, III, and IV relate his adventures in quest of these treasures. The people are especially angry at the spoliation of the necklace of Aphrodite. In a fit of compunction Demetrios asks Chrysis if she will wear her trophies in public. She consents. Act V is in two scenes:

Scene 1. The Lighthouse. While the throng gathers to discuss the three crimes that have closely followed each other, and pray the goddess for forgiveness, they suddenly perceive a female figure standing out in relief on the balcony of the lighthouse. She wears the comb in her hair, the necklace around her throat, and holds in her hand the mirror. At first they think it is Aphrodite come to them in person, but soon realize that it is Chrysis. She is seized and thrown into prison.

Scene 2. A Prison. Chrysis is condemned to death, and a poisoned cup is sent her to drink. Demetrios arrives only after she has died. In a vision Demetrios himself sees his fate at the hands of Aphrodite.

PAUL DUKAS

Dukas is a modern French composer, who was born at Paris, October 1, 1865. His only opera that reached the American stage is "Ariane et Barbe-Bleue." Dukas died in Paris, May 17, 1935.

ARIANE ET BARBE-BLEUE
(*Air-ee-an ä Barb-bluh*)

(Ariane and Bluebeard.) Dramatic Opera in Three Acts. Music by Paul Dukas. Book by Maurice Maeterlinck, after the tale of "Blue Beard." Opéra Comique, Paris, May 10, 1907. New York, March 3, 1911.

SCENE: A Medieval Castle.
TIME: Middle Ages.

CAST   BLUEBEARD (Basso).
ARIANE, *his sixth wife* (Mezzo-Soprano).
NURSE (Contralto).
Bluebeard's five earlier wives:
SELYSETTE (Mezzo-Soprano).
YGRAINE (Soprano).
MELISANDE (Soprano).
BELLANGERE (Soprano).
ALLADINE (Silent).
Three Peasants, Crowd of Rustics, etc.

ARGUMENT   The old story of Bluebeard and his wives has been embellished by Maeterlinck with touches of mysticism, which are reflected in the music of the opera. Ariane, the determined wife, may be called a foretype of the New Woman.

Recorded music: "Oh! mes clairs diamants" from Act I; and "Ah! ce n'est ce pas encore la clarte veritable," from Act II.

Act I   *Great Hall in Bluebeard's Castle.* Despite the ugly reputation of Bluebeard, he has found a new wife in Ariane. She has heard that he has done away with five wives, but cannot believe that he has murdered them; it is her mission to discover his secret. As the curtain rises, the angry roar of the crowd outside is heard. They do not want the ogre to have another victim. Unmoved by all this clamor, Ariane enters with her nurse. She has been entrusted with seven keys. Six are of silver, and the last is of gold. It unlocks the one forbidden door. The nurse opens one after another the six silver locks, and in each room finds a delightful surprise—jewels of rare beauty gush out in streams. But Ariane is not satisfied. Her mission is to find what is behind the forbidden door. The nurse begs her to desist, but she turns the golden lock. The door opens and they hear the distant groans of women. Before they can close it, Bluebeard enters, saying coolly, "You, too!" He tells her he will yet forgive her if she will desist, but she defies him. Enraged, he bids her follow him, but the nurse, hearing the renewed tumult of the crowd outside, rushes to the door and admits them. Bluebeard draws his sword and prepares to defend himself from their attack, when Ariane interposes, telling the rioters to disperse, her husband is doing her no harm. They fall back before her and she closes and fastens the door.

Act II   *An Underground Chamber.* Still braving Bluebeard's anger, Ariane and the nurse have been left in the vault leading from the seventh door, but Ariane is undismayed; she is determined to rescue her husband's victims.   By the light of the flickering lamp, carried by the nurse, she discovers the forms of women lying huddled upon the floor.   They prove to be the five missing wives, who are still alive, but leading a wretched existence.   Ariane encourages them, and looks about for some avenue of escape.   The lamp goes out, but they see a faint glow at one end of the chamber.   It proves to be a door leading to the outer world, which they break through, and the whole party pass out to liberty.

Act III   *Great Hall in the Castle.*   The castle and grounds are enchanted, so the wives cannot escape.   They wander back into the great hall and amuse themselves by dressing up in the finery which they find lying about in profusion.   Ariane is showing them how to regain their lost beauty.   Presently the nurse enters in terror to say that Bluebeard, who has been absent, is on his way back to the castle, and that the villagers are lying in wait for him.   It is as she fears, and although he has a bodyguard, they are overcome in the mêlée and Bluebeard is wounded.   The crowd seize him and bind him hand and foot, and are about to throw him into the moat, when Ariane and the other women interpose.   She persuades the villagers to bring him into the hall, stating that she is the one most concerned and should have the decision of his fate.   In the end they leave him and withdraw.   Ariane stoops and cuts his bonds, although the others are fearful.   Then she dresses his wounds, which prove slight.   He rises and looks slowly from one to another of the group, but makes no effort to molest them.   Ariane approaches and bids him farewell; her mission is ended, now she will leave him.   He tries to detain her, pleading his love, but she persists in her decision.   The other women are given an opportunity to go with her, but they decide to cast their lots with Bluebeard.

HENRI FEVRIER

Fevrier was born in Paris, October 2, 1876.   He studied in the Conservatory there under Faure and Massenet.   He wrote shorter pieces for voice and orchestra, and, in 1906, won attention for his opera "Le Roi Aveugle."   "Gismonda" was produced in 1915; "La Damnation de Blanche-Fleur," in 1920; "Aphrodite," in 1920; "La Femme Nue," in 1932; and several operettas.   His chief fame in America, however, rests upon his best work, "Monna Vanna."

MONNA VANNA
(Mo-na Van-na)

Romantic Opera in Four Acts. Music by Fevrier. Book by Maurice Maeterlinck. Paris, 1909. First time in America, at Boston, 1913. New York, 1914, by the Manhattan Opera Company headed by Mary Garden and Lucien Muratore.

SCENE: Pisa.
TIME: The Fifteenth Century.

CAST   PRINZIVALLE, *Commander of the Florentine Army* (Tenor).
GUIDO COLONNA, *Commander of the Pisan forces* (Basso).
BORSO, *Pisan sub-officer* (Baritone).
TORELLO, *Pison sub-officer* (Baritone).
VEDIO, *Secretary to Prinzivalle* (Tenor).
TRIVULZIO, *an envoy* (Baritone).
MARCO VANNA, *a Pisan* (Basso).
MONNA VANNA, *his daughter, wife of Colonna* (Soprano).
Citizens, Soldiers, etc.

ARGUMENT   The plot of "Monna Vanna" is rather thin, but is based upon an historical incident. It is a counter-plot of chivalry and jealousy.

Act I *Office of the Pisan Commander.* Pisa is being besieged by a Florentine army under the command of Prinzivalle. The garrison is in sore straits for food and ammunition. Prinzivalle informs Colonna, the Pisan general, that he will deal leniently with the Pisans if Colonna will send his beautiful wife, Monna Vanna, for an overnight visit to Prinzivalle's tent. She is informed of these terms and professes herself ready to go, to help her city.

Act II *Prinzivalle's Tent.* A plot by Trivulzio, an enemy of Prinzivalle, is thwarted. Monna then enters as agreed. She states that her only purpose is to save her city. The general respects her intentions and treats her as an honored guest.

Act III *A Square in Pisa.* Monna Vanna returns, but her husband distrusts her. His rage is kindled further when he discovers Prinzivalle in the city. The latter has had to flee from treachery in his own camp, but Colonna thinks it is because of an intrigue with Monna. The latter sees that she can save Prinzivalle only by falling in apparently with her husband's evil designs. Prinzivalle is accordingly cast into prison.

Act IV *A Dungeon.* Monna goes to free Prinzivalle from prison. They confess their love for each other, and flee forth into the world together.

GISMONDA

An opera in four acts, which had its first American performance in Chicago, in 1919 with Mary Garden and the Chicago Opera Company. It was brought to New York as the opener for the Lexington Theatre, January 27, 1919. It was only moderately successful. The story follows the play by Sardou.

Gismonda, Duchess of Athens, promises to become the wife of anyone who will rescue her son from the pit of a tiger, into which he has been thrown by a conspirator, who thus plans to help another man, Zacario Franco, seize the Duchy. But after Almerio, a falconer, slays the beast and brings her the boy, she recants from her promise; she will instead spend a night with him, as reward. Zacario spies upon her; she kills him; Almerio to shield her says that he is the slayer; and the repentant lady clears him of guilt and proclaims him as her husband.

ALBERT WOLFF

Albert Wolff, born in 1884, in Paris, is known as both conductor and composer. After studying at the Conservatory he showed such aptitude with the baton that, at the age of twenty-seven, he was appointed second conductor at the Opéra Comique, to which post he returned after the First World War. He was conductor of French repertoire at the Metropolitan Opera House (1919–1923), then resigned to return as first conductor and musical director of the Comique in Paris. His chief operas are: "Le Marchand de Masques" (Nice, 1904); and "L'Oiseau Bleu" (New York, 1919).

THE BLUE BIRD

(L'Oiseau Bleu.) Lyric Opera in Four Acts and Eight Scenes. Music by Wolff. Book by Maurice Maeterlinck. Metropolitan, New York, December 27, 1919. In the cast were Florence Easton, Leon Rothier, Mary Ellis, and Raymonde Delaunois.

SCENE: Fairyland.
TIME: The Present.

CAST MYTYL { *The woodcutter's children* { Tenor.
TYLTYL {   { Soprano.
FATHER TYL, *a woodcutter* (Baritone).
MOTHER TYL, *his wife* (Contralto).
BERYLUNE, *a fairy* (Soprano).
GRANDMOTHER TYL (Contralto).
GRANDFATHER TYL (Basso).
MATERNAL LOVE (Soprano).
JOY OF UNDERSTANDING (Soprano).
LIGHT (Soprano).
FATHER TIME (Basso).
BREAD (Tenor).
MME. BERLINGOT (Mezzo-Soprano).
A Little Girl, Two Lovers, Joy of Being Just, Joy of Seeing the Beautiful, Fairy, Night, Cat, Dog, Happiness, a Child, Sugar, Fire, Other Children, etc.

ARGUMENT Maeterlinck's allegorical story for children and those of larger growth, "The Blue Bird," which was originally brought out as a play, has been utilized in this pleasing opera. The plot follows the book faithfully, only making certain omissions required for a musical setting.

Act I *Scene 1. Room in the Woodcutter's Cottage.* It is Christmas Eve, and the two children of the woodcutter, Tyltyl and Mytyl, awake during the night and sit up in bed to watch the festivities in the great house across the way. Suddenly the door latch is lifted; a little, humpbacked woman enters, who introduces herself as the Fairy, Berylune. She tells the children that her little daughter is ill and unhappy, and asks them if they will go in quest of the Blue Bird of Happiness. They agree, and she gives Tyltyl a green cap with a diamond which, turned one way, enables him to see the future. Tyltyl turns the diamond and immediately everything in the cottage is transformed. The furniture comes to life; the door of the clock opens, and the Hours come out and begin to sing and dance. The loaves of Bread become endowed with souls which, in the forms of little men, are pursued by Fire, a sullen, malicious fellow. The Cat and Dog are changed into persons. The Spinning Wheel hums madly. Water flows from the sink tap and begins to fight with Fire. The Lamp falls from the table with a crash, and its flame turns into a fairy of great beauty; she is Light.

Just then a loud knock is heard. It is the woodcutter returning. Tyltyl quickly reverses the diamond and the enchantment ceases. Berylune asks who will accompany the children on their mission to seek the Blue Bird. All except the Dog and Light refuse; but the time is so short that all have to go. The room grows dark, and when Daddy and Mummy Tyl enter they find the children sound asleep.

Scene 2. The Land of Memory. As the mists lift, the children see a peasant's hut and their dead grandparents sitting on a doorstep. Their little brothers and sisters come out of the house to greet them. Tyltyl catches a Blackbird which at first seems blue, but soon grows dull black. They regretfully go on their way.

Act II *Scene 1. The Palace of Night.* Light shows them the way to the Palace of Night. Tyltyl challenges Night and demands the Blue Bird. Night gives him the keys to gloomy caverns wherein dwell the spirits of evil. Tyltyl opens a forbidden door to Destiny, and sees a beautiful garden. Myriads of blue birds hover about, but when the children catch some of them and show them to Light, the birds are lifeless. As they go into the forest, the Oak tree threatens them with death because they have presumed to catch the Blue Bird—the secret of man's happiness. Light comes to rescue the children.

Scene 2. The Garden of Happiness. In a fabulously sweet garden of peace and serenity they are greeted by a band of little Joys which laugh and dance, but do not aid them. Other greater Joys appear, among them the Joy of Understanding and the Joy of Being Just.

Act III *The Cemetery.* The children enter alone in the darkness. At midnight Tyltyl turns the magic diamond, and the gravestones become changed to a fairly dell—the kingdom of the Future where they meet with the souls of children waiting to be born. Father Time summons them one by one. Light now tells the children that she has secured the Blue Bird and it is safely hidden under her cloak. She bids Tyltyl turn the diamond again so that they can escape.

Act IV *Scene 1. Doorway of the Woodcutter's Home.* The time has come for leave-taking between the children and their comrades, Dog, Cat, Bread, Light, and all the rest. They have come back to the home of Tyltyl and Mytyl, but without the Blue Bird. Light and the other souls bid the children farewell.

Scene 2. Room in the Woodcutter's Cottage. It is morning. Mummy Tyl comes in to awaken the children. They begin to tell her of their strange adventures, and she is alarmed, fearing they are ill. As they talk, a neighbor comes in to ask the children if they will not lend their pet bird to her little girl who is sick. Tyltyl climbs up on a chair to get the dove, and exclaims, "Why it's blue! It's our Blue Bird!" Nevertheless he gives it to her; and later the neighboring child brings it back. She is well and happy. But as they play, the bird escapes and flies away. The children ask the audience, if they find it, to please give it back. "We need it to be happy later on," they say entreatingly.

RUSSIA

HISTORICAL PREFACE

Although the roots of Russian opera reach back as far as the eighteenth century, the western world has become familiar with it only within the past fifty years. Few of the works have come to our stages, the Russian ballet making us familiar with Slavonic music, technique and acting before their operas. The composers were merely names in reference books, and even with foremost composers, only one or two works have been performed abroad. Rachmaninoff is authority for the statement that thirteen works by Rimsky-Korsakoff still await production in America.

The pioneer in the Slavonic school was Glinka (1804–57), who wrote a patriotic opera, "A Life for the Czar," which won such lasting regard at home that it is said to have been performed regularly as a season-opener in Moscow and St. Petersburg so long as there was an imperial house. His "Russlan and Ludmilla" is also marked by national and folk touches. Glinka's influence upon later composers has been profound.

With Dargomijsky (1813–68) we reach the threshold of modern Russian opera. His "Russalska" followed a patriotic theme. His "The Water-Sprite" and "The Stone Guest"—the latter reminiscent of Mozart's "Don Giovanni"—are still heard occasionally in Russia.

Rubinstein (1829–95), more famous abroad as a pianist, was the composer of several operas quite successful in their day. His "Feramors" and "Nero" are still remembered; while others such as two Biblical works, "The Tower of Babel" and "The Maccabees," are forgotten.

Borodin (1834–87) won renown as a chemist as well as musician. His "Prince Igor" was one of the first of Russian operas to win and hold attention in other countries.

César Cui (1835–1918) is still unfortunately little known in America, although he lived to an old age and wrote much for the stage. He was also an authority on engineering, teaching this subject in military schools and writing textbooks on fortifications. He championed the cause of the Young Russians and won the nickname of "Musical Nihilist." His operas include: "William Radcliff" (1869); "Angele" (1876); "The Prisoner of the Caucasus" (1883); "The Saracen" (1899); and others ending with "The Captain's Daughter" (1909).

287

Moussorgsky (1839–81) has become increasingly known to Europe and America. A sketch of his life is given in later pages.

With Rimsky-Korsakoff (1844–1908) we come to the most dominant influence of the modern school. This is due both to the versatility of his talent and the poetry of his themes, which are not overshadowed by the (often gloomy) Slavonic tradition. His "Sadko" stretches its wings as far off as India. He wins agreeable fame, likewise, for the ready aid he gave his contemporaries.

The single figure who challenges his supremacy is Tschaikowsky, a composer of great fecundity and brilliance. His worldwide fame, however, rests upon his symphonies and shorter pieces, rather than his operas. Only one or two of the latter, such as "Eugéne Onégin" and "Pique Dame" have thus far reached an American stage.

More recent composers are still only names to us. We find such men as Napravnik, an organist and director who has guided the production of Imperial Opera, but not make striking contributions of his own; "Harold" being one of his best, followed by "Francesca da Rimini" and a few others. Blaramberg wrote five operas in all, including "The Mummers," a comic opera, and the more ambitious, "The Roussalka-Maiden." Arensky's work is more highly regarded at home. His "A Dream on the Volga" and "Raphael" won the praise of critics and fellow musicians. A more familiar name to us is Rachmaninoff, but as a distinguished pianist and composer for that instrument. He wrote a one-act opera, "Aleko," which had the honor of being produced at the Imperial Opera in Moscow, in 1873.

A more modern figure is that of Igor Stravinsky (b. 1882) who is more famous for his orchestral works in advanced style than for operas. In fact, his works for the stage are more frequently ballet and pantomime. Still another contemporary is Serge Prokofieff (b. 1891). Further notice of these two will be found in later pages.

There are still others in the list, some of whom, we hope, will become more than names to us in succeeding years. The last to challenge attention is Shostakovich, a contemporary writer of symphonies who has achieved sensational success in that field. His opera, "Lady Macbeth," produced in Russia, in 1940, has been hailed as "the most successful written thus far by a Soviet-Russian composer."

The examples of Russian opera included in the present volume are those most likely to appear in our repertory. For convenience they are all included under Grand Opera, and such classification is not wide of the mark, for it is only rarely in the earlier works that one encounters lighter moments on their stage. The roots of Slav music under centuries of oppression were sad, often tragic. Doubtless in the days of troubadours and minstrelsy, the peasantry delighted in their songs and dances—even as they do today. But both Church and State frowned upon any frivolity. In the first centuries of the Christian era, so earnest were the monks in their strife against paganism that songs, dances, and spectacles were anathematized. It is said that as late as the seventeenth century such things were excluded even from the Czars' coronations. Professor Milioukhov, in his "Sketch for a History of Russian Culture," quotes from one of these medieval moralists the following cheerful thought: "Laughter does not edify or save us; on the contrary, it is the ruin of edification. Laughter displeases the Holy Spirit and drives out virtue, because it makes men forget death and eternal punishment. Lord, put mirth way from me; give me rather tears and lamentations." So effective was this dread teaching, that another monk records with sour satisfaction: "There was silence in all the land of Russia!" No wonder there was, when such propaganda was added to the burden of daily life undergone by the serfs and peasantry.

And yet, perhaps because it was officially forbidden, mirth and laughter did not die. It was "bootlegged" into the remoter districts by wandering bands of musicians—the "Guslee" or guzli players; and the "Skomorokhi" or actors. These were welcomed by common folk and nobles alike, to while away the tedium of the long winter nights. Plays, puppet shows, ballets, and other such entertainment followed, some of it crude, some coarse, and some, strange to say, spiritual; but as a whole pointing the way to a lighter form of stage play, interpreted with and without music.

The clergy, however, were still so intolerant that, when Czar Alexis Mikhailovich summoned musicians to his Court and encouraged a national theater, the Patriarch Joseph hurled the curses of the Church at him (1649) and ordered all the musical instruments in Moscow to be seized and burned in the market place. Only those belonging to the Czar were spared. The Czar Alexis, undismayed, continued to encourage the stage, and there is a record of 1664 which says: "Our Musique-master composed a Handsome Comedie in prose, which was acted in our house." Another play ordered by this Czar dealt with the Biblical story of Esther.

It required another hundred years for the Russian stage to take on what may be termed a native form, and for its musical side to receive any consistent development. The operas which gradually took shape were of Biblical, legendary, or historical trend, with music as savage and violent as the text. One of the first Russian composers to attempt a lighter vein was Fomin (1741–1800). He wrote several operas in the folk style, one being called "The Good Maiden," and another, "The

Miller," which had a wide popular success owing to its folk tunes and dance melodies interspersed with more serious strains. A third, which should have some interest for us, was called "The Americans," but dealt with our Indians, as Russia visualized them.

About this time, the end of the eighteenth century, the Russian Court was overrun with foreign composers, chiefly Italian and French; but as this was a foreign graft, we will not try to chronicle it. However, it did have the effect of putting the leaven in the Russian bread.

We find also on record that the first "opera house" was built by the Empress Anne, in St. Petersburg, but was destroyed by fire in 1749. It was not devoted exclusively to musical plays, however. A new building was opened in the year 1759.

A distinctive feature of the Russian school is that of pantomime. Like the ballet, in which the Russian artists also excel, it provides the dual appeal of bodily motion and instrumental music. Using only these means it produces an extraordinary dramatic power.

The distinguishing trait of Russian opera, as indeed of its songs and other musical expressions, is what may be styled the primal element. It is redolent of the life of the people and of the soil.

MICHAEL IVANOVITCH GLINKA

Glinka, who is of the early modern school, was born near Smolensk, in 1804. He studied the piano and the violin under Russian teachers, then spent four years in Italy, partly on account of health. He is credited with writing the first national opera for his country, in "A Life for the Czar" (1836). In his orchestral compositions he was the forerunner of Tschaikowsky and Rimsky-Korsakoff. His second opera, "Russlan and Ludmilla" (1842) is noteworthy in its introduction of oriental music, a practice followed by other Russian composers. He lived in Spain from 1845 to 1847, there writing two Spanish overtures: "Jota Aragonesa" and "Noche en Madrid." Other works are for the piano. Glinka died in 1857.

RUSSLAN AND LUDMILLA

Russian Opera in Five Acts.   Music by Glinka.   Text based upon a poem by Pushkin.   St. Petersburg, 1842.

ARGUMENT   Although this opera has not yet been produced in America, its brilliant and colorful overture has long been esteemed by orchestras.   This and a "Patter Song," popularized by Chaliapin are familiar to listeners of recordings.

The curtain rises upon a scene of festivity.   Prince Svetozar is giving a reception to suitors for the hand of his daughter, Ludmilla.   The visitors include: Russlan, a native nobleman; Ratmir, a Tartar prince; and Farlaf, a Varangian chief, but a coward at heart.   Ludmilla favors Russlan; the god of love, Lel, is invoked; but just then a clap of thunder is heard, and the lights go out.   When they return, the Princess is missing.   Her father promises her hand to the one who will bring her back unharmed.

The Second Act takes place in the cavern of Finn, the wizard.   Russlan learns from him that the maiden is in the clutches of Chernomor, a villainous dwarf.   The evil fairy, Naina, may also interfere with him, says Finn.   In a second scene, Russlan searches for magical weapons on a battlefield, which will aid him to free Ludmilla.

The Third Act is laid in the enchanted palace of Naina.   She has promised her aid to the timorous Farlaf.   To aid her plot, she has imprisoned Ratmir, the Tartar prince.   Three Persian damsels sing to him a siren song.   He is also visited by Gorislava, a former sweetheart whom he has abandoned, and she now pleads with him to return.   Russlan, too, is in danger of listening to the songs of the three sirens, but Finn shields him.

In the Fourth Act, the dwelling of the dwarf Chernomor, Ludmilla is seen a prey to despair.   A ballet is danced to divert her.   It is interrupted by the entrance of Russlan, who employs his magical sword to overcome the dwarf.   But the Princess has been sent into a trance-like slumber, from which Russlan cannot awaken her.   He carries her away, still unconscious.

In the Fifth Act, Russlan makes use of a magic ring.   As he places it upon Ludmilla's finger, she awakens; her father again bestows her hand upon the knight of her choice, and the curtain falls amid melody and rejoicing.

Recorded music: overture; Farlaff's "Rondo," sung by Chaliapin; and an aria by Gorislava, "O, my Ratmir!"

ALEXANDRE BORODIN

Borodin was born in St. Petersburg, Nov. 12, 1834, and died there Feb. 28, 1887. He was equally famed as a scientist and musician, being professor of chemistry, Academy of Medicine, St. Petersburg. As he said: "In winter I can only compose when I am too unwell to give my lectures. At Christmas (1886) I had influenza, so I stayed at home and wrote the Thanksgiving Chorus in the last act of 'Igor.'" He never finished this opera, however. It was completed by Rimsky-Korsakoff and Glazounoff, and presented in 1890, three years after his death. His many other activities prevented Borodin from fully realizing his talents as a composer. He wrote two symphonies, two quartets for strings, some shorter pieces for the piano, and only one opera, "Prince Igor," which, however, has maintained high rank among Russian operas.

PRINCE IGOR
(Prince Ee'-gor)

Dramatic Opera in Prologue and Four Acts. Book and Music by Alexandre Borodin. Imperial Opera House, St. Petersburg, October 23, 1890. New York, the Metropolitan, December 30, 1915.

    SCENE: Russia and Siberia.
    TIME: 1185.

CAST   PRINCE IGOR SVIATOSLAVITCH (Baritone).
       JAROSLAVNA, *his second wife* (Soprano).
       VLADIMIR, *his son by his first wife* (Tenor).
       PRINCE GALITSKY, *brother of Prince Igor* (Basso).
       KONTCHAK, *a Khan of Tartar* (Basso).
       KONTCHAKOVNA, *his daughter* (Contralto).
       OVLOUR, *a Tartar soldier* (Tenor).
       SCOULA, *a minstrel* (Basso).
       EROCHKA, *a minstrel* (Tenor).
       NURSE (Soprano).
       YOUNG TARTAR GIRL (Soprano).
         Russians, Tartars, Soldiers, Courtiers, etc.

ARGUMENT   A tale of early Russian history, which is more concerned with manners and customs than with his-
toric incident.   The opera is full of color and sentiment, and furnishes
the composer with an excellent medium for contrast between native
life and oriental, which are often closely allied.   Folk music, exotic
dances, comedy, tragedy alternate.

The Overture is marked with spirit and fire.   An impressive allegro
movement is followed by a rapid folk dance; then a lovely, more sub-
dued aria, "No sleep, no rest," heard later in the score; all leading up
to a crashing climax as the curtain rises.

Prologue   *Market Place of Poultvle, the seat of Prince Igor.*   Just as
Prince Igor of Seversk is starting out at the head of his army
to crush the Tartars, an eclipse of the sun occurs.   This is regarded as
a bad omen, and the people urge him to postpone his expedition, but he
is determined to proceed.   He takes with him his son, Vladimir, and
commends his wife to the care of his brother, Prince Galitsky, who is
also left at the head of the government.

Act I   *Scene 1.   Courtyard of Prince Galitsky's Mansion.*   No sooner
has Prince Igor departed, than the regent, Galitsky, tries to
overthrow him.   There is feasting and carousing as Galitsky sings a
wild song telling his followers what he would do for them, if he were
Governor: "Song of Prince Galitsky"—

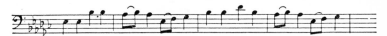

Some timid girls approach to beg him to release one of their number
who has been abducted; but he boasts that he himself is the abductor,
to their further fright.   His scoundrelly rule is aided and abetted by the
minstrels, Scoula and Erochka.

Scene 2.   Apartment in Palace of Prince Igor.   While her husband is
away at the wars, the Princess Jaroslavna contemplates sadly her own
loneliness and the dissoluteness of the court under Igor's brother's reck-
less misrule.   Her mood is reflected in an expressive aria, "Song of Jaroslavna"—

The same group of maidens enter, who had pleaded with Galitsky to release one of their friends; they ask her protection. When her brother-in-law enters the room she upbraids him bitterly for his perfidy and in a stormy scene orders him from her presence. At this moment a messenger enters with the news that Igor's army has been defeated, he and his son are prisoners, and the Tartars are marching against Poultvle. The news of this disaster causes the people to renew their loyalty, and rally to the defense of Jaroslavna.

Act II *Camp of the Tartars.* The beautiful daughter of Kontchak, the Tartar prince, has enslaved the prisoner of war, Vladimir, much more completely than his soldiers could have done. Vladimir, indeed, is becoming reconciled to his captivity, since it brings him near to her. He lingers before her tent, singing a serenade. Igor, however, is anything but pleased with his fate, although his captor has treated him with every consideration. He is offered a means of escape by Ovlour, a Christian soldier, but declines to take advantage of the Khan's chivalry. The Act ends with an elaborate banquet given by the Tartar prince in honor of his royal captive. Here is heard the familiar "Polovetzki Dance"—at first dreamy and sensuous, but mounting by degrees to a savage turbulence:

Act III *Same as Act II.* Victorious soldiers return to camp, bringing trophies from the conquest of Poultvle. At the tidings of the overthrow of his capital, Igor can no longer refuse to escape. While the soldiers are dividing the booty, Ovlour plies them with drink, and in the resulting orgy he and Igor prepare to flee. The Khan's daughter discovers their plans and entreats Vladimir to stay. He hesitates, and is

reprimanded by his father.   However, as the party sets forth, she clings
to the young prince and holds him back.   Igor and Ovlour depart without him.   When the escape is discovered, the soldiers are ready to kill
Vladimir, but the Khan accepts the situation philosophically.   "Since
the old falcon has taken flight, we must chain the young falcon by giving
him a mate," he says, and bestows upon him the hand of his daughter.

Act IV   *Scene 1.   Jaroslavna's Palace.*   Jaroslavna sings a touching
lament for her lost husband and despoiled country.   But as
she gazes out over the ravaged fields, two horsemen are seen approaching.   They are Igor and his faithful attendant, Ovlour.   Husband and
wife are reunited, and in the joy of home-coming much of the interven-
ing sorrow is forgotten.   Igor plans to rehabilitate his country.

Scene 2.   The Kremlin.   As Igor and Jaroslavna enter the Kremlin
to give public thanks, they encounter the two rogues, Scoula and
Erochka, who have been prime movers in the regent's misgovernment.
They know that they will suffer if caught, so forestall discovery by ringing the bells to announce publicly the restoration of Prince Igor.
Their audacity prevents their punishment, and the opera ends pleasantly, amid popular rejoicing.

MODESTE MOUSSORGSKY

Moussorgsky was born at Karevo, March 28, 1839.   His first lessons
on the piano were with his mother.   In 1852 he entered a school for
ensigns, but retained his interest in music.   Later he came in touch
with Borodin and Rimsky-Korsakoff, and with others of a little group
introduced a new school of Russian music.   He wrote chorals, songs,
piano pieces, and an orchestra suite, and three operas—"Boris Godounoff," "Khovantchina" and a folk opera, "The Fair of Sorochintzy."
Some of his work was left unfinished.   Moussorgsky's last years were
spent in poverty, due partly to dissipation.   He died on his birthday,
March 28, 1881.

BORIS GODOUNOFF
(Bo'-ris Go'-do-nof)

Russian National Musical Drama, in Prologue and Four Acts.   Book
and Music by Moussorgsky.   After the historical drama by Pushkin.

St. Petersburg, January 24, 1874. The Metropolitan, New York, November 19, 1913. The early version, which was lengthy, was revised after the composer's death by his friend, Rimsky-Korsakoff. The character of Boris afforded a notable vehicle for the Russian basso, Chaliapin.

SCENE: Russia.
TIME: 1598–1605.

CAST   BORIS GODOUNOFF, *the Czar* (Baritone).
        FEODOR, *his son* (Mezzo-Soprano).
        XENIA, *his daughter* (Soprano).
        NURSE (Contralto).
        MARINA, *a courtesan* (Mezzo-Soprano).
        PRINCE SCHOUISKY (Tenor).
        TCHELLAKOFF, *Secretary of the Duma* (Baritone).
        PIMEN, *a monk* (Basso).
        GREGORY, *the pretended Dimitri* (Tenor).
        WARLAAM, *a vagabond* (Basso).
        MISSAIL, *a vagabond* (Tenor).
        A SIMPLETON (Tenor).
        POLICE OFFICER (Basso).
        COURT OFFICER (Tenor).
        INNKEEPER (Tenor).
        LOVITZKY, *a Jesuit* (Basso).
        TCHERNISKOWSKY, *a Jesuit* (Basso).
        Citizens, Courtiers, Officers, Monks, etc.

ARGUMENT   The theme of this opera is based upon an historical episode, and may be regarded as an epic of Russian life. It involves characters from the highest to the lowest, and the chief figure, the unhappy Czar, is in a sense a lay figure around whom the action revolves.

Prologue *Scene 1. Courtyard of a Monastery.* A mob of people gather about a monastery, in which Boris Godounoff has taken refuge, and clamor for him to become their Czar. Their outcry, however, is instigated by police officers, as it is felt that Boris is a usurper who has been guilty of the murder of Dimitri, the Czarevitch.

A brief prelude by the orchestra brings the first curtain rise. A chorus by the mob outside the walls gives voice to their entreaty: "Why hast thou abandoned us? Have pity, O, Father!"

Scene 2. Square in front of the Kremlin. Boris has yielded to the carefully staged demand on the part of the people, and is publicly crowned amid gorgeous ceremonies. From the portico of the cathedral Prince Schouisky proclaims: "Long live Czar Boris!" And the people answer with a shout: "Glory to Czar Boris!" This is the setting for the lofty Coronation Scene:

Act I *Scene 1. Interior of a Monastery.* The aged monk, Pimen, is engaged in writing the history of the time. He has come to the part dealing with the death of Dimitri and the accession of Boris, when Gregory, a novice, awakens from a sleep, in the corner of the cell, and learns this tragic story. As there seems to be doubt that the prince was actually slain, Gregory inwardly resolves to proclaim himself the lost heir to the throne.

Scene 2. An Inn on the Russian Border. While the hostess of an inn goes singing about her work, a fugitive arrives in haste and demands shelter. It is Gregory, who has escaped from the monastery, and is trying to get over the border, in order to further his plot against the throne. While two monks who have accompanied him are drinking, the police arrive in search of the pretender. They hand a paper to Gregory and ask him to read it for them. He begins it and finds that it is a description of himself, so in the reading he changes it to describe one of the other monks. The latter is seized by the officers, but gets possession of the paper and finds that it applies to Gregory. He, however, jumps through the window and escapes.

Act II *The Czar's Palace.* Xenia, the daughter of Boris, sorrows for the death of her lover, Dimitri. Her nurse sings a song to comfort her, and her little brother, Feodor, also sings a folk song. Boris enters and greets his children. A messenger announces the arrival of Prince Schouisky, who is reported to be in league with the Czar's enemies. When the Prince enters, Boris upbraids him for his duplicity, but the Prince protests that he is loyal. He has seen the pretended Dimitri, in order to learn what manner of man he is. At the mention of Dimitri's name, Boris changes color, and begins to ply him with questions. Finally he dismisses him in order to hide his own terror-stricken condition.

Act III   *Marina's Apartments.*   Marina, an adventuress in the employ of the Jesuits, seeks to entangle Gregory in her net. She knows his true story, but is willing to aid in his plot provided he will grant her party certain rights. Gregory meets her in her garden, and the two exchange vows of love. In this scene a Polish national dance is staged, while the guests sing: "On to Moscow and to victory!" The duet between the lovers is punctuated by the seductive mazurka rhythm of the Polonaise.

Act IV   *Scene 1.   A Street.*   A crowd rushes through the streets, clamoring as loudly for the supposed Dimitri as they had previously shouted for Boris. Gregory arrives and is greeted as the true Czar, while the mob rushes to storm the palace.

Scene 2.   Hall of the Duma.   While the Duma is in session, Prince Schouisky arrives and states that he believes Czar Boris to be demented. He is interrupted by the entrance of Boris, who violently denounces his enemies and asserts his own innocence. The Prince tries to calm him, by asserting that the monk Pimen is at hand, with a written record of the events leading up to his accession. Pimen enters and tells of a supposed miracle which took place at the grave of Dimitri. The latter is undoubtedly dead and has become a saint. Boris again grows violent, giving evidence of insanity. He restrains himself with an effort, and summons his son Feodor, whom he proclaims his heir. In a voice trembling with anguish he sings, "Farewell, my son!"—

Then, "Hark, 'tis the passing bell!" as the solemn tone of the bells is heard without. A choral of great beauty also marks this final scene. Boris, growing weaker, cries, "Lord, grant Thy mercy!" And near the end, as he points to Feodor, he tells the people, "Behold your Czar!" With a final cry of "Mercy!" he falls dead, while the nobles stand with bowed heads; the music dies away into a requiem, and the curtain falls.

KHOVANTCHINA
(Ko-vant-shee'-vah)

Folk Drama in Five Acts. Book and music by Moussorgsky. Marie Theatre, St. Petersburg, November 7, 1911. Philadelphia, April 18, 1928. First performed at the Metropolitan, February 12, 1950.

SCENE: Moscow and environs.
TIME: Seventeenth Century.

CAST   SHAKLOVITOFF, *a Boyard* (Basso).
DOSITHEUS, *leader of "Old Believers"* (Tenor).
IVAN KHOVANSKY, *a patrician plotter* (Basso).
ANDREW KHOVANSKY, *his son* (Baritone).
PRINCE GALITSIN, *a reformer* (Baritone).
MARTHA, *an "Old Believer"* (Soprano).
EMMA, *a German girl* (Mezzo-Soprano).
SUSAN, *an "Old Believer."*
The sect of Streltsy; "Old Believers"; citizens, guards, etc.

ARGUMENT   Like "Boris," the composer here takes an episode from earlier Russian history, in order to show the life of the Russian people in their struggle against the established order of things. The score was unfinished at the time of Moussorgsky's death, and his friend, Rimsky-Korsakoff, again rendered valuable service, not only to him but to the music-loving world, for thus preserving some fine, typical examples of folk music. After a brief Prelude, an engaging tone picture, the curtain rises.

Act I   *The Red Square, Moscow.* A group of the Streltsy, a fierce radical party, is seen near the Kremlin. They boast about a bloody encounter of the previous night. A scribe enters to take up his morning duties; the gang gibes him and then departs. The Boyard Shaklovitoff enters and bribes the scribe to write a letter of denunciation against the house of Khovansky, charging that they are plotting to overturn the throne. Ivan, head of that house, presently comes in, and his proud bearing indicates that the charge has foundation. His son, Andrew, is a libertine. At this moment he is pursuing a German maid, Emma. While she is trying to thrust him off, Martha, a former flame of his enters. Martha is a mystic, and now foretells that he is doomed for his many sins. Ivan re-enters, but instead of reproving his son or shielding Emma, he himself is taken by her charms and quarrels with

Andrew over her; finally ordering her arrest.   The entrance of Dositheus, venerable head of the "Old Believers," restores peace.

Act II   *Apartment of Prince Galitsin.*   Galitsin has been educated in Western Europe and has fine ideas about reform, but is also superstitious.   He summons Martha to read his horoscope, but when she foretells that his riches will be of no avail and that his last days will be in sorrow and poverty, he flies in a rage and orders his servants to take her out and drown her.   Again old Dositheus comes to quell a quarrel.

Act III   *Outside the House of Khovansky.*   Martha has escaped drowning and now, seated near the home of the man who has discarded her, sings of her old passion.   Susan, a fanatical "Old Believer," chides her for her shamelessness and threatens to denounce her as a witch.   Dositheus again pours oil on the troubled waters.   With the fall of night on the deserted street, Shaklovitoff enters.   In a fine musical soliloquy he exclaims: "Yes, they sleep; the Streltsy sleep. Sleep thou, my Russia . . . but thine enemies are even now plotting thy destruction!"   Then he prays for divine guidance to save his beloved country.

He is interrupted by the noisy arrival of the Streltsy, but the latter have antagonists in the persons of their own wives and sweethearts.   Their quarrel is broken up by the scribe, who rushes in to say that the revolt against the Czar has been quelled and their cause is lost.

Act IV   *Scene 1.   Country House of Khovansky.*   Prince Ivan is seeking diversion in the folksongs of his servants and the wild dancing of a group of Persian slaves: "Dance of the Persian Slaves"—

Shaklovitoff enters to announce he is to attend a council of state; but as the Prince is changing his costume, he is assaulted by a group of conspirators and killed by daggers.

Scene 2. A Square in Moscow. During the change of scene, mournful strains are heard from the orchestra, as if bewailing the fate of unhappy Russia; then with the curtain, a stately processional before a church. Through the sorrowing crowd comes a guard with Galitsin in chains. He is being led away into exile—thus proving Martha's prediction. Dositheus in a fine soliloquy mourns over his country. Martha enters to inform him that a trap has been set for the "Old Believers." He charges her to see to it that Andrew is present at the fateful meeting. Then learning that Andrew and Emma are united, he denounces Martha as a witch and orders the Streltsy to kill her. They, however, have given up their cause and bring in headsman's axes for their own execution. At the fateful moment, word comes that the Czar has issued a general pardon.

Act V *A Woodland near Moscow.* A last meeting is held by the "Old Believers," headed by Dositheus, who urges them to remain true to their beliefs. Martha prays for the soul of Andrew, and is ready to mount the great funeral pyre which the Faithful have decided to use as one great, general sacrifice. But Andrew is smitten with remorse at her devotion, and himself climbs the pyre. Others follow fanatically, while Martha applies the torch. As the flames mount up, soldiers enter, but halt appalled at the catastrophe. The dying chant of the Faithful is heard, followed by a blast of trumpets. Old Russia is passing—a new Russia is at hand.

THE FAIR AT SOROCHINTZY

(La Fiera di Sorocinzi.) Comic Opera in Three Acts. Music by Moussorgsky. Book by composer, after the story by N. V. Gogol. French version, by Louis Laloy, produced at the Theatre of Monte Carlo, March, 1923. At the Metropolitan, New York, in Italian, November 29, 1930.

SCENE: A village in Little Russia.
TIME: Uncertain.

CAST   TCHEREVIK, *an old peasant* (Basso).
OKHRIM, *a Cossack, his "Old Crony"* (Baritone).
KHIVRIA, *wife of Tcherevik* (Contralto).
PARASSIA, *his daughter* (Soprano).
GRITZKO, *a young peasant* (Tenor).
IVANITCH, *the Pastor's son* (Tenor).
A GYPSY (Basso).
Youths, Maidens, Gypsies, Vendors, Cossacks.
Jews.

ARGUMENT   A rollicking comedy betraying manners and customs of the peasant folk of Little Russia.   The
music is typically Russian, with folk-songs and native dances.

Act I   *The Fair.   A hot day.*   The market place of Sorochintzy is
filled with jostling crowds and littered with wares on display.
Tcherevik, an old peasant, enters with his pretty daughter, Parassia,
who is at first attracted by all the finery on display, but later by the
ardent glances of a young man, Gritzko.   The latter believes in striking
while the iron is hot; he loses no time in love-making, and soon has his
arms around the fair Parassia.   The old peasant surprises them, and
remarks sarcastically that he seems to know how!   Gritzko then tells
him that he is the son of an old crony, Okhrim, and that he would like
to be his son-in-law.   Tcherevik relents and later he and the Old Crony
celebrate the prospective match by getting drunk.   Fortified by this
potion, Tcherevik reels home to tell the good news to his shrewish
wife, Khivria.   She disapproves so vigorously that the Old Crony beats
a retreat.   Gritzko, disconsolate, meets up with the Gypsy who, for a
consideration, agrees to help him win the girl.   Parassia enters, and the
lovers plight their troth.

Act II   *Tcherevik's Cottage.*   While Khivria cooks the evening meal
her husband is sleeping off his drink.   She bemoans her fate
and thinks how much happier she could be, say, with the Pastor's son.
She arouses Tcherevik with more abuse, but he only laughs tipsily.
She orders him out.   Later, who should come in but the Pastor's son,
with whom she has evidently had an assignation.   They sit down to the
well-filled table.   Just about the time the man is emboldened to pay
compliments to the rather formidable female, her husband and some of
his friends return.   The guest must perforce take refuge in an attic,
which has an indifferent floor.   Among the newcomers is the Gypsy,

whose shrewd glance takes in the situation.   He tells a weird tale, and the others' nerves are further shattered by the dropping of objects down through the rafters.   Eventually the Pastor's son is discovered.

Act III   *The Village Square.*   Due to this disclosure, the sharp tongue
of Khivria is silenced and her husband is boss of the house.
He tells Gritzko and Parassia that they can marry.   When his wife tries
to object she is squelched.   The villagers join in a wild hopak, or
country dance, in honor of the approaching wedding.

PETER ILITCH
TSCHAIKOWSKY

The most widely popular of Russian composers, Tschaikowsky was born at Votinsk in Viatka, April 25, 1840.   His father was a mining engineer, but Peter showed such an early predilection for music, that he was allowed to begin piano study.   In 1862 he entered the Conservatory at St. Petersburg, where he studied under Rubinstein.   He was given a professorship of harmony in the Moscow Conservatory, where he remained until 1878.   After that date he devoted himself to composition, being remarkably prolific as well as outstanding.   In the next quarter-century his name appeared upon eleven operas, three ballets, six symphonies, five orchestral suites, four overtures, besides numerous shorter pieces.   His greater fame in America rests upon such works as his Symphony Pathetique, 1812 Overture, and Marche Slav. His best known operas are: "Valouka" (1876); a prize work, "The Oprichnik" (1877); "Eugéne Onégin" (1879); "Pique Dame"; and "Iolanta."   He left incomplete an opera which he hoped would be his masterpiece, "Romeo and Juliet," from which some fine excerpts are favorite orchestral numbers. In 1891 Tschaikowsky came to New York to take part in the dedication of Carnegie Hall. He died in St. Petersburg (Petrograd), November 13 (25), 1893.

EUGÉNE ONÉGIN

(Yoo-jane' Oh-nay'-gin)

Russian Opera in Three Acts. Music by Tschaikowsky. Text after Pushkin's tale by Modeste Tschaikowsky, the composer's brother; German text by von A. Bernhard. Moscow, March, 1879. New York, in concert form, Carnegie Hall, February 1, 1908. At the Metropolitan, in Italian, March 24, 1920.

SCENE:	Russia.
TIME:	Recent.

CAST LARINA, *owner of an estate* (Mezzo-Soprano).

TATIANA } *her daughters* { (Soprano).
OLGA   (Alto).

FILIPIEVNA, *a waitress* (Mezzo-Soprano).

EUGÉNE ONÉGIN, *a gallant* (Baritone).

LENSKI, *a poet* (Tenor).

PRINCE GREMIN (Baritone).

A CAPTAIN (Basso).

SARETSKY (Basso).

TRIQUET, *a Frenchman* (Tenor).

Guests, Villagers, Servants, etc.

ARGUMENT This opera may be characterized as a series of "lyrical scenes" which follow so closely the epic tale of Pushkin, that the latter should be studied for a thorough enjoyment of the musical work.

Act I *A Country Estate.* Eugéne Onégin, a young society blade, is called from the social diversions of the city by the death of an uncle, who has willed to him a country place. Eugéne comes willingly enough, as he has grown sated with city life, and welcomes a period of retirement. He meets in the country a poet, Lensky, who is somewhat of a fanatic; also Larina, a neighboring landowner, and her two daughters. One of the girls, Olga, is betrothed to the poet. The other, Tatiana, is an over-sentimental girl who proceeds to throw herself at the feet of this worldly-wise city man. Eugéne, however, will not accept her love, and she mopes exceedingly.

Act II   *A Ballroom.*   Tatiana's birthday is the occasion of a ball at her mother's estate.   Thither the two men are invited, but Eugéne is so bored by it all that, as a means of diversion, he begins flirting with Olga, Lenski's sweetheart.   The poet, in a fury, challenges Eugéne, who cannot escape the challenge, though treating it all as a cynical jest.   But in the duel he has the misfortune to shoot his antagonist.   He leaves the country, more cynical and depressed than ever.

In the opening minutes of this Act is heard the brilliant waltz in honor of Tatiana, which has become a prime favorite with orchestras:

Act III   *A Hall in Prince Gremin's Palace.*   Twenty-six years elapse. Eugéne has wandered restlessly from one country to another, but has never found happiness.   Back in St. Petersburg he attends a ball given by Prince Gremin; and in the person of the Princess Gremina recognizes the Tatiana of the country affair.   She has grown to be a well-poised social leader.   He now finds in her all the qualities she formerly lacked, and begins to court her.   She upbraids him for his fickleness, but finally admits that she still cares for him.   She remains true to her marriage vows, notwithstanding, and Onégin sadly bids her farewell.

PIQUE-DAME
(Peek-Dam)

(The Queen of Spades.)   Tragic Opera in Three Acts.   Music by Tschaikowsky.   Book by Modeste Tschaikowsky, after a story by Pushkin. St. Petersburg, 1890. At the Metropolitan, New York, in German, March 5, 1910.

> SCENE: St. Petersburg.
> TIME: Recent.

> CAST HERMAN, *a gambler.*
> "PIQUE-DAME," *a Countess.*
> LISA, *her grand-daughter.*
> PRINCE YELETSKY.
> Gamblers, Society Folk, Servants, etc.

ARGUMENT Herman, an inveterate gambler, is torn between two passions—his love for a girl and his desire to win at cards. The two emotions are exemplified in the persons of Lisa, a young girl, and the Countess, her grandmother—an old dame who is so lucky at cards that she has been nicknamed "The Queen of Spades" (Pique-Dame). She is said to base her phenomenal success on a combination of three cards. Although Herman loves the younger woman, he pays more attention to the older one, in the hope of learning the secret. Lisa also loves Herman, but becomes engaged to Prince Yeletsky. To spy upon the old woman, Herman hides in her bedroom one night. When she sees him the shock kills her, and Herman learns nothing. Half-crazed with remorse Herman is haunted by the old Countess' ghost. The apparition then shows him the three cards that will always win. On the night after her funeral he plays against Prince Yeletsky, and wins twice by the cards shown him by the ghost. Thereupon he stakes everything he possesses on the third card, but he turns up, not the expected card, but the queen of spades. At the same instant he sees a vision of the Countess, smiling derisively. In despair, Herman kills himself.

NICOLAI A. RIMSKY-KORSAKOFF

A Russian composer, born at Tikhvin, Novgorod, March 6, 1844. Both of his parents were passable musicians, and the boy showed early signs of musical aptitude. They planned for him a naval career, but the removal of the family to St. Petersburg brought to the young man, now reaching maturity, a further opportunity to follow his bent of composition. He studied under Balakiref, while attending Naval College, and although sent on a three years' cruise at the completion of his college course, he could not turn his back upon music. In 1866 he settled in the capital and devoted himself to the piano and composition. He contracted a lasting friendship with Moussorgsky, which was mutually helpful. His first opera to be produced was "The Maid of Pskof" (1873); followed by "A Night in May" and "Christmas Eve Revels." In 1871 he became Professor of Composition in the St. Petersburg Conservatory; and until the year 1890 was a conductor of the Russian Symphony. Several contemporaries including Moussorgsky and Borodin are indebted to him for aid in revising or completing their works. He wrote 13 operas, the more important being; "Snegurotchka" (The Snow Maiden), (1880); "Mlada," (1892); "Sadko," (1897); and "Kastchei," (1902); and "Le Coq d'Or," (1908). He also wrote many orchestral numbers, and was highly regarded both as musical mentor and composer. Rimsky-Korsakoff died near St. Petersburg, now Petrograd, June 8, 1908.

A NIGHT IN MAY

Folk Opera in Three Acts. Music by Rimsky-Korsakoff. Book adapted from Gogol's Malo-Russian tales. Mariensky Theatre, St. Petersburg, January, 1880. Moscow, 1898. Drury Lane Theatre, London, June 26, 1914.

ARGUMENT This is a graceful, humorous and fantastic skit laid in a village of Little Russia. It opens with a dance by merrymakers. The peasants believe that the spirits of unhappy maidens who have met their death by drowning in the near-by lake reappear as water nymphs. The village belle, Hanna, is courted by Levko, the Mayor's son. The father opposes the match, but pays court to the girl, himself. A crowd of roisterers led by Kalennik, the village "cut-up" and drunkard, waylay the Mayor. In retaliation he locks his son, Levko, up. He escapes and wanders disconsolately by the lake singing to the accompaniment of his bandorra. Here occurs the high spot of the opera. He sees a vision of water nymphs, who dance a lovely ballet, as they tell him to "Sing on!" Pannochka, their leader, who, according to legend, had once lived in a castle by the lake, then gives him a sealed letter, which, when delivered to his father, brings about a happy ending. The opera is a happy contrast to the more serious Russian music, and reveals the composer as a genuine humorist.

THE SNOW MAIDEN

(Snegurotchka—Snay-goo'-rotch-kah.)   Fairy Opera in Prologue and
Four Acts.   Music by Rimsky-Korsakoff.   Book by Ostrovsky.   Im-
perial Theatre, St. Petersburg, January 29, 1882.   At the Metropolitan,
New York, in French, January 23, 1922.

SCENE: Berendeys, a Russian province.
TIME: Legendary.

CAST   SNEGUROTCHKA, *the Snow Maiden* (Soprano).
KING WINTER, *her father* (Basso).
FAIRY SPRING, *her mother* (Contralto).
BOBYL, *a villager* (Baritone).
BOBYLICKA, *his wife* (Contralto).
LEL, *a shepherd* (Tenor).
KOUPAVA, *a village maid* (Mezzo-Soprano).
MIZGUIR, *a Tartar merchant* (Tenor).
THE CZAR.
THE CZAR'S ADVISER.
LORD CARNAVAL.
A Woodland Sprite, Other Spirits, Villagers,
Courtiers, Musicians, etc.

ARGUMENT   A charming fairy tale is here interwoven skillfully
into a melodious score—the whole reflecting one
of the lighter moods of Russian folklore.

Prologue   *A moonlit night in the "Red Mountain."*   In the distance
is seen the village of Berendeys, ancient capital of the Czar.
Although springtime is near, Fairy Spring confesses to the shivering
birds that the cold season is due to her wrongdoing.   Some years before,
she had fallen in love with King Winter and borne him a daughter,
Snow Maiden.   Since that time King Winter had lingered ever longer
in the north.   He warns her to guard their child from the rays of
Yarila, the Sun God.   The Snow Maiden now enters and bids her father
a tender farewell.   He leaves her in the care of a shepherd, Bobyl, and
his wife.

In this Prologue are heard: the charming song by the Snow Maiden,
"To go berrying"; and the rich chorus voicing their farewell to Carnival.

Act I   *Outskirts of a Village.*   None of the villagers can quite understand the lovely Snow Maiden.   She inspires love, but is un-

able to feel any warmth of heart, herself. The advances of Lel, the shepherd, who sings pleading songs, only move her to tears, but frozen ones. At the betrothal ceremony of Koupava and Mizguir, a rich Tartar merchant, the Tartar is so entranced by the Snow Maiden's beauty that he is ready to leave his bride for her; but the Snow Maiden remains cold, despite the urgings of her foster parents to such a rich match.

In this Act is heard the lovely "Song of the Lark," by the Snow Maiden:

Act II *The Czar's Palace.* The kindly old Czar has been very despondent over the condition of his country. Year by year the winter grows longer and the summer shorter. He is convinced that the Sun God is offended, but does not know how to placate him. At this juncture, the spurned bride, Koupva, comes pleading justice. Mizguir will not take her back, and is banished. The Snow Maiden now enters, and Czar and court alike are spellbound by her beauty and charm. On learning that her heart is frozen within her, the Czar suspects that here may lie the secret of the Sun God's displeasure. He announces a great reward to the successful suitor who shall win her and cause her heart to melt.

The Czar's song, "Full of wonders," has an orchestral accompaniment of unusual charm.

Act III *The Sacred Forest. Night.* On the eve of summer the villagers and court are gathered for a festival to greet the dawning days of warmth. Lel, the singer, is present and, at the Czar's request, he sings a legend of a far-off day when the clouds and the thunder conspired together to bring summer. The Czar is so pleased that he bids Lel choose for himself any one of the maidens for a bride. Much to the inner dismay of the Snow Maiden, he passes her by and selects Koupava. At the gay party's dances, the Maiden sits by dejectedly. Mizguir attempts again to win her, but in vain.

One of the gems of this Act is Lel's song, with pipe accompaniment, "Clouds plotted with thunder."

Act IV *Valley of the Sun God Yarıla. Early Morning.* The Snow
Maiden comes at dawn to a lonely lake to summon her mother,
Fairy Spring. When the latter rises from the water, the girl begs her
to bestow upon her the power to love. Her mother finally yields to
her entreaties, though sadly, and the girl goes away with a joyous step.
Before the Czar and his court she confesses that at last her heart is warm
and free, and that she loves Mizguir. Just at that moment a bright ray
of sunlight falls upon her. As she sings a plaintive farewell, she
slowly melts away before their eyes. Mizguir in despair plunges into
the water seeking her, and drowns. But the good Czar tells the people
not to mourn; this sacrifice has been necessary to appease the Sun God;
and hereafter he will smile upon their land. The plaintive lament,
"Death of the Snow Maiden," is a high point.

A moving chorus by the villagers in praise of the Sun God ends the
piece. The choruses are often accompanied by guzlis. The music is
truly national, although it deals with legend. It is rich in lyrical
melody.

SADKO

(Sahd-ko')

Legendary Opera in Seven Scenes. Music by Rimsky-Korsakoff.
Book by composer and W. T. Byelsky. Private Opera House, Moscow,
December 26, 1897. New York, at the Metropolitan, season of 1929–30.

> SCENE: Novgorod, Russia.
> TIME: Legendary.

> CAST   THE KING OF THE OCEAN (Basso).
> VOLKHOVA, *his favorite daughter* (Soprano).
> SADKO, *a minstrel* (Tenor).
> LUBAVA, *his wife* (Mezzo-Soprano).
> NEJATA, *a guzli player* (Contralto).
> A VIKING MERCHANT (Basso).
> A HINDU MERCHANT (Tenor).
> A VENETIAN MERCHANT (Baritone).
> AN APPARITION (Baritone).
> THE TWO ELDERS (Tenor and Basso).
>   Buffoons, Merchants, Townspeople, Singers,
>   Daughters of the King of the Ocean, etc.

ARGUMENT   Again, as in "Snow Maiden," the composer makes
use of a native legend to weave a fantasy of tableau
and music, of unforgettable charm.

Scene 1 *Guild Hall in Novgorod.* While the merchant princes of
Novgorod are feasting and making merry, they ask a guzli
player from Kiev to entertain them with a song.   He sings of old, heroic
days and they vigorously applaud.   Sadko, another street singer, now
enters and they bid him sing also.   But his song is fantastic; he belittles
the city's commerce, and says he would transport their ships to the wide
ocean and make them all wealthy.   As he is down at the heels they
laugh him to scorn.

Scene 2 *The Shores of Lake Ilmen.* On a clear summer night Sadko
wanders along the lake shore, playing on his guzli.   He sings
of his unhappy lot and implores aid.   A wind ruffles the waves and a
group of swans swim toward him.   When they reach land they are
changed into lovely maidens; one being Volkhova, daughter of the
King of the Ocean.   She promises him her love, and tells him that he
will catch three golden fish and voyage to distant lands.

Scene 3 *Room in Sadko's Humble Cottage.* While Sadko has remained out all night dallying with the Sea Maidens, his wife,
Lubava, awaits his return.   She sings sadly of her fears.   At last with
the dawn he returns and her song is changed to one of joy; but he thrusts
her roughly aside.   The sound of the bell for early mass reminds him
that now is the time to greet the people and tell them the great secret
he has learned—and away he dashes from the disconsolate Lubava.

Scene 4 *The Port of Novgorod.* An early morning throng of merchants, townspeople, singers, and four buffoons, jostle one
another by the side of the quay where large sailing craft are moored.
Into the throng comes the excited Sadko, shouting that he has a wonderful secret to tell.   He can catch fish of solid gold from the lake.   As a
roar of laughter greets this statement, he wagers his head against their
ships that he can prove his claim.   They send him out in a boat, a net is
cast, and, sure enough, he catches the golden fish.   With the fleet that is
suddenly his, he plans to go on a voyage, and summons other men of
courage to join him.   Then he asks three foreign merchants to tell of
their country.   In turn, a Viking, a Hindu, and a Venetian praise their
land; and Sadko and his band decide upon Venice.

Their songs, among the most typical and popular of this composer's
music, are titled: "Song of the Viking Guest," "Song of India," and
"Song of the Venetian Guest":

Song of the Viking Guest

Song of India

Song of the Venetian Guest

Scene 5 *On Board Sadko's Ship, the Falcon.* Twelve years have
passed by. Sadko has amassed great wealth, but now lies be-
calmed, and the superstitious sailors declare it is because they have not
shared their wealth with the King of the Ocean. So treasures are cast
overboard, but with no result. Then lots are cast, and the lot falls
upon Sadko. Undaunted he is sent overboard and floats away on a
plank, playing his guzli. His aria is a notable one. He hears Volkhova's voice calling him, and sinks into the deep; while the released
Falcon sails on her course.

Scene 6 *Undersea Palace of the King of the Ocean.* This entire tableau is a fantasy, filled with sprites, fish, maidens, and elves,
dancing before the King and Queen. Sadko, seemingly quite at home,

sings at the King's request and so delights him that he gives Sadko the hand of the Sea Princess in marriage. Faster and more furious grow the music and dancing, until great waves are stirred up on the surface above. An Apparition is seen, who strikes the guzli from a player's hands. He then informs the King that Sadko must be allowed to return to his native land.

Scene 7 *The Shores of Lake Ilmen. Early Morning.* Volkhova has returned with Sadko to the lake near his home, but realizes that she must give him up to his home and wife. She sings a Lullaby (Berceuse) beginning, "Sleep came to the shores of the lake"—

She ends by telling him that she will always be near him. Then the rosy light of dawn breaks, the sun rises, and she is changed first into a mist, then into the great River Volkhova. Thus she will always be by his side. Sadko awakening is greeted joyfully by his faithful wife, Lubava, and shares her rapture. The past seems like a dream, but proves a reality when his ships come sailing in, one by one, laden with wealth. His neighbors surround him with songs of acclaim.

LE COQ D'OR
(*Luh Coak Dore*)

("The Golden Cockerel.") Opera Pantomime in Prologue, Three Acts, and Epilogue. Music by Rimsky-Korsakoff. Book by V. Bielsky, based on a poem by Pushkin. Zimin's Theatre, Moscow, May, 1910. New York, the Metropolitan, in French, March 6, 1918.

SCENE and TIME: Legendary.

CAST KING DODON (Baritone).
PRINCE GUIDON (Tenor).
PRINCE AFRON (Baritone).
VOEVODA POLKAN, *the general* (Baritone).
AMELFA, *the royal housekeeper* (Contralto).
THE ASTROLOGER (Tenor).
THE QUEEN OF SHEMAKHAN (Soprano).
THE GOLDEN COCKEREL (Soprano).
Soldiers, Citizens, Fairies, Dancers, etc.

ARGUMENT The author states in the preface to this opera, which is presented by dancers in pantomime, as the singers remain seated: "The purely human nature of Pushkin's 'Golden Cockerel'—that instructive tragi-comedy of the unhappy consequences following upon mortal passions and weaknesses—permits us to place the plot in any region and in any period."

Prologue Before the curtain, the lusty crowing of a cock is heard, mingled with bizarre melodies. An Astrologer steps out to inform his hearers that through his magical powers they will be wafted away to a place in the olden time. Then as the instruments continue with their wild strains, the curtain rises.

Act I *The King's Palace.* King Dodon much prefers his ease on a couch, or a hearty dinner, to the cares of state. His more active enemies take advantage of his lethargy to attack him on all sides. He asks advice of his sons, but they disagree, and Polkan, the General, disdains all their counsel. As they wrangle, an Astrologer brings to the king a Golden Cockerel that has power to foretell events and to give warning of danger. The King is delighted, and has the bird installed in a lofty tower. It is so efficient that the monarch says, "Why worry," and has his bed brought out into the throne room and goes comfortably to sleep. But he is hardly asleep before the cock sounds the tocsin. The enemy is at hand. The King, grumbling, sends his two sons off to war, and finally goes himself.

Act II *A Narrow Defile.* The King arrives too late to aid his sons, and finds their dead bodies. As he reproaches himself he notices a tent on the hillside; and to his astonishment a beautiful woman appears. It is the Queen of Shemakhan. Raising her arms in invocation to the Sun, she sings an exquisite, exotic aria, marked by unusual chromatics: "Hymn to the Sun"—

King Dodon is so overpowered by her beauty and singing, that he is persuaded to dance with her. Almost exhausted, he yet finds breath to propose to her. She seems to hesitate, but finally says she will accept him, if he commands the execution of General Polkan.

Act III *A Public Square.* The King returns to the city with his new Queen, and the populace turns out to welcome them—a gorgeous pageant marked by rich music (Bridal Cortege):—

But the Queen soon tires of this new life and her aged spouse. The Astrologer now returns and claims as a reward for the Golden Cockerel, the person of the Queen herself. Dodon, enraged, kills him with a blow. The magic bird revenges his master's death by attacking the monarch, who falls to the ground as though struck by a thunderbolt. Darkness falls, and when the light returns, both the bird and the Queen have disappeared.

Epilogue   Here the Astrologer returns to life and states that the whole thing is a fable.

IGOR STRAVINSKY

Igor F. Stravinsky is one of the most fertile of latter-day Russian composers. His songs, symphonies, and incidental music have made him popular with many discerning musicians. Others, however, find some of his more modernistic works difficult to follow. He was born in Petrograd, June 17, 1882. His ballet-burlesque, "Petrouchka," was produced in 1912. "Le Rossignol" was originally a ballet, as he excels in this type of composition.

LE ROSSIGNOL
(*Luh Ro'-seen-yole*)

("The Nightingale.") Fairy Opera in Three Acts by Igor Stravinsky and S. Mitousoff, after the fairy tale by Hans Christian Andersen. Originally composed as a ballet, 1909; rewritten as an opera and produced at Paris and Drury Lane, London, 1914. At the Metropolitan, New York, March 7, 1926.

SCENE: China.
TIME: Legendary.

CAST THE NIGHTINGALE (Tenor).
THE KITCHEN-MAID (Soprano).
THE FISHERMAN (Tenor).
THE EMPEROR OF CHINA (Basso).
THE CHAMBERLAIN (Basso).
THE BONZE (Basso).
Japanese Ambassadors, Courtiers, Etc.

ARGUMENT The authors of the libretto have followed closely
the delightful fairy tale of Hans Christian Ander-
sen, and have lost none of the whimsicality and tender charm of the
original.   Even the fact that there is an obvious moral to the little tale
fails to detract from its beauty.

Act I *The Edge of a Forest by the Seashore at Night.* A fisherman is
singing, and soon the Nightingale's voice is heard.   A little
group of people appear—a deputation from the Chinese Court headed
by the Kitchen-maid, the Chamberlain, the Bonze, and a few courtiers,
has come to seek the Nightingale in the hope that his singing may cheer
the Emperor in his sadness.   The Nightingale agrees to return with
them to the Court, though he says his song sounds better in the quiet
forest.

Act II *Entr'acte.   The stage is veiled by tulle curtains.*   The populace beg of the Kitchen-maid, now promoted to Chief Court
Cook, a description of the wonderful bird, and are disappointed to
learn that he is quite insignificant in appearance.

[*The tulle curtains slowly rise and disclose the fantastic porcelain
palace of the Chinese Emperor.*]

At a sign from the Emperor the Nightingale sings.   The beautiful
song so touches the Emperor that he offers the bird any favor that he
may desire, but the Nightingale declares that the tears in the Emperor's
eyes are sufficient reward.   At this moment Japanese ambassadors enter,
bringing to the Emperor of China an artificial nightingale from the Emperor of Japan.   The mechanical bird is made to sing, and during its
song the real Nightingale flies away.   His absence is perceived by the
Emperor with annoyance, and a decree of banishment is pronounced,
while the artificial nightingale is given a place by the Imperial bedside.

Act III *The Imperial Sleeping Chamber in the Chinese Palace—
Moonlight.*   The sick Emperor lies upon his bed, and at one
end of it sits Death, crowned with the imperial crown and holding the
imperial sword and standard in his hands.   The spirits of his past deeds

speak to the Emperor, who calls for music to drown their cries. His summons is answered by the voice of the Nightingale, who has stolen back from exile and sings to him from the garden. When he ceases Death asks for another song. The Nightingale demands the crown of the Emperor as the price for singing, then the sword and standard. During the last words of the Nightingale's song, Death silently disappears. The Emperor begs the Nightingale to remain at Court, but the bird refuses this, promising instead to return and sing every night. The courtiers enter in solemn procession, thinking to find their Emperor dead, and see him standing in full imperial regalia in the middle of the room. . . . In the distance the fisherman's song is heard.

"Le chant du Rossignol"—chorus with orchestra—is in record form.

PETROUCHKA
(Pa-trooch'-kah)

A Ballet Burlesque by Stravinsky. First produced at Petrograd, in 1912. At the Metropolitan, New York, 1919.

ARGUMENT   This is an ironical pantomime given in the form of a puppet show. The puppet master is exhibiting his little figures before a gaping crowd in a public square of Petrograd. When his curtain rises, a dainty dancing girl is seen—and opposite her two men—one of them, Petrouchka, the noble lover, and the other a swarthy and gigantic Moor, whose regard for her bodes no good. A violent quarrel ensues between the two suitors, and naturally the sympathies of the audience are with Petrouchka. But alas! The gigantic Moor overpowers him, thrusts him in prison and—while he bemoans his hard fate and lack of favor with the ballerina—finally kills him. This tragic end to poor Petrouchka's suit causes consternation among the spectators, who are only reassured when the puppet master parts the curtains and shows them that the slain suitor is nothing but a dressed-up doll.

SERGE PROKOFIEFF

Prokofieff (b. 1891) has been styled one of the advance guard in musical futurism. He is a native of Sontsavka, in southern Russia; studied piano at an early age, and made several European tours as a concert pianist—one in the United States, in 1918. He has written works for both the piano and the orchestra, also operas including: "Maddalena," "The Gambler" (Petrograd, 1916), and "The Love for Three Oranges" (Chicago, 1921); a ballet, "Le Bouffon"; and a descriptive piece, "Peter and the Wolf," frequently played.

THE LOVE FOR THREE ORANGES

(L'Amour des Trois Oranges.) Burlesque Opera in Prologue and Four Acts. Music by Prokofieff. Book by composer, after the tale by Carlo Gozzi. Chicago Auditorium, December 30, 1921, the composer conducting. This also witnessed the American début of Nina Koshetz, as "Fata Morgana." The same company, with the composer wielding the baton, presented it at the Metropolitan, New York, February 14, 1922.

ARGUMENT In the Prologue we are introduced to four opposing groups: first, the Glooms in somber robes, who urge that the forthcoming play shall be a tragedy; second, the Joys in bright robes, who clamor for a comedy; third, the Empty Heads, who ask for a farce; and, fourth, the Jesters, or Cynics, who quell the hubbub, so that some sort of a piece may go on.

The Three Oranges are really three princesses, who are under the spell of the wicked enchantress, Fata Morgana. A Prince desires to free them, but he himself is seemingly ill beyond cure. The court physicians tell the King that the only thing which will make the Prince well is a hearty laugh; but that is impossible, as the young man was born without any sense of humor at all. The ensuing action is the attempt on the part of clowns, masqueraders, magicians, and others to stir the Prince's risibles. The Prince at last bursts out laughing at a silly antic of Fata Morgana, which so provokes her that she invokes a curse upon him. Then she tells him that he will not be happy until he finds and falls in love with one of the Three Oranges, and his love is returned. This at last is accomplished.

Among the best-known musical numbers of this opera are: the extremely modernistic "Waltz Scherzo," as danced by the imps; and a strikingly fantastic "March and Scherzo," played by the orchestra as an entre-acte.

OTHER NATIONS

HISTORICAL PREFACE

It is difficult to make hard and fast distinctions as to country in the case of many composers. While one may be born and receive his musical education in one land, his life work may largely be in another. Such is the case of several whom the reader will find listed in this volume under the United States.

From Spain, however, we have one outstanding name which has remained identified with that country. Enrique Granados in both life and work is typically Spanish. A sketch of him follows.

From Holland comes Richard Hageman, but it will be noted that since 1916 his work and residence have been in the United States.

A Czech composer, Jaromir Weinberger, is another case in point. He has been composing and teaching in America since the year 1922.

The two great world wars have, in fact, profoundly dislocated lodgings and races, and America has continued to be the land of freedom and opportunity. Our listings, therefore, have not been dictated by chauvinism, but as a matter of convenience.

In the case of England, the reader is referred to the Light Opera section, as practically all examples from that country fall more logically there than in the more serious or classic mood we style "Grand."

ENRIQUE GRANADOS

Granados was widely known in his native country before attracting attention abroad. He was born in Lerida, Catalonia, Spain, July 27, 1867. He began the study of the piano at an early age at the Barcelona Conservatory; and later composition at Madrid. In 1900 he founded and conducted the Society of Classical Concerts, Barcelona. He also toured various cities as a concert pianist with success. He first attracted attention in opera with his "Maria del Carmen" (Madrid, 1898) which went the rounds of Spanish theatres.   Inspired by the etchings of Goya, he wrote a series of musical studies later incorporated into his "Goyescas."   This and his delightful "Danzas Espanolas" are his chief claims to fame.   In 1915 he accepted an invitation from the Metropolitan Opera House, New York, to visit that city and superintend the première of "Goyescas."   He did so, but with tragic consequences to himself.   On his way home, his ship, the *Sussex*, was sunk by a German torpedo in the English Channel, and he perished, March 24, 1916.

GOYESCAS

Folk Opera in One Act of Three Scenes.   Music by Granados.   Book by Fernando Periquet.   Première in New York, the Metropolitan, under direction of composer, January 28, 1916.

ARGUMENT   The character studies of the eminent Spanish painter Goya (d. 1828) are the inspiration of this work, hence its name.   It is a lively presentation of native life in both scenes and music.   For its New York presentation Granados wrote an overture, which is now considered one of his finest works.   The story involves flirtations and quarrels, a theme by no means limited to Spain. The text is in Spanish.

Scene 1   *A Street in the outskirts of Madrid.*   The citizens are enjoying a fiesta in characteristic fashion.   Paquiro, the toreador, is flirting with every woman in sight, and they are smirking and pirouetting in return.   The majas and majos are dancing and singing, meanwhile playing a popular game of tossing a pelele, or straw-man, up and down in a blanket.   The toreador's flirtations are interrupted by the arrival of Pepa, his reigning sweetheart, in a dogcart, and she is warmly greeted.   But, "Make way!" is heard and with much pomp a sedan-chair is borne in carrying a lady of society, Rosario, who has agreed to meet an admirer, Fernando, a captain of the royal guards.   But the fickle Paquiro, runs to greet her and to remind her that she has once promised him her company at a candle-light ball.   Fernando overhears him and, in a rage, informs him that he, Fernando, will be the lady's escort.   Pepa also is in a pet and a good, four-cornered quarrel ends the scene.

Scene 2   *The Ball.*   The Captain makes good his boast and brings Rosario to the dance.   At once his quarrel with the jealous Paquiro flares up again.   As they square away at each other, the sensu-

ous Spanish dance music provides a dramatic foil. The duel is arranged, while Pepa is torn with rage and fear, and Rosario swoons away.

Scene 3. *Rosario's Garden.* Just before he meets the toreador, Fernando pays a visit to Rosario. Their tender avowals are
interrupted by the solemn tones of a bell—it marks the hour of the field
of honor. Fernando tears himself away, while his sweetheart despairingly follows. The duel is off-stage, but again the music interprets the
action. A cry is heard from Fernando, and a shriek·from Rosario. She
carries him in wounded, and as they sink together on a stone bench, he
breathes his last.

Recorded music from this opera: a delightful intermezzo with 'cello
solo by Pablo Casals; and a brilliant piano number played by José
Iturbi, "La maja y el ruisenor."

JAROMIR WEINBERGER

A Czech composer, born in Prague, in 1896. Weinberger was a pupil
of Kricka and Hofmeister. He wrote numerous pieces for the orchestra, such as "Don Quixote"; pantomimes, sonatas, and folk songs. His
fame, however, rests on "Schwanda," a close product of the soil. In
1922 Weinberger came to America to accept the professorship in composition in the conservatory at Ithaca, New York. In 1937 his opera,
"Wallenstein," was performed in Vienna.

SCHWANDA

(The Bagpiper.) Folk Opera in Two Acts and Five Scenes. Music
by Jaromir Weinberger. Book by Milos Karës. National Theatre,
Prague, April 27, 1927. At the Metropolitan, New York, November 7,
1931.

SCENE: A Czech Village.
TIME: Legendary.

CAST SCHWANDA, *the bagpiper of Strakowitz*·(Tenor).
DOROTA, *his wife* (Soprano).
BABINSKY, *a robber* (Baritone).

A QUEEN (Mezzo-Soprano).
A SORCERER.
A JUDGE.
A HEADSMAN.
THE DEVIL (Basso).
THE DEVIL'S SECRETARY.
  Guards, Courtiers, Attendants, Demons,
  Villagers, etc.

ARGUMENT   "Schwanda" is a delightful folk opera based upon
           the familiar theme of the power of music over
humans and demons alike.   It is the "Pied Piper" theme handled upon
a somewhat broader pattern.   The music is thoroughly in keeping with
the rustic spirit, one Bohemian dance with its rollicking bagpipe background being a perennial favorite with orchestras.   Indeed it seems
probable that this dance will remain in repertory long after the entire
work may be absent from the stage.

Act I   *Scene 1.   Schwanda's Farm.*   The peaceful morning scene in a
           Czech farmyard is rudely broken as soldiers enter in search of a
notorious robber, Babinsky.   Dorota, the good-looking wife of the
farmer, avers that she hasn't seen any robber.   They go away, and immediately after the coast is clear, Babinsky slides down out of a tree.
He makes love to the young woman and urges her to run off with him,
but she will not.   After a while the farmer himself enters, and the robber tries another tack.   He tells him his talents are wasted here; if he
will go with him to the court of Queen Ice-Heart, his pipes will win him
fame and fortune.   While Dorota is in the house, the two men depart.
As soon as she finds them gone, she resolves to follow.
   Scene 2.   The Queen's Court.   Queen Ice-Heart is sad.   She has sold
her living heart to a Sorcerer, who now rules her.   Schwanda enters
and his merry piping soon dispels her gloom.   The Sorcerer goes away
defeated.   The Queen is so delighted with her cure that she kisses
Schwanda and offers him half the throne.   Unfortunately, Dorota appears just at this time, and objects.   The furious Queen orders the
piper's trial and death.
   Scene 3.   Square outside the City Gate.   The luckless Schwanda is
about to lose his head, at the hands of a swarthy Headsman who awaits
the signal.   He is granted a last request.   He wishes to play his pipes;
but they cannot be found; the Sorcerer has hidden them.   In despair he
resigns himself and down goes the executioner's arm—but instead of his
wielding an axe, it is a broom cleverly substituted by Babinsky.   The
latter then turns over the pipes to Schwanda, and as he begins to play,
willy-nilly, the Queen and all her train dance back into the city, leaving

Schwanda, Dorota, and Babinsky outside the walls. Dorota chides her husband for getting into this fix, but he says that if he ever kissed the Queen, "may the Devil take him to Hell on the spot!" Instantly the pavement opens and amid a sulphurous flame down he goes. Babinsky tries again to take advantage of the situation and win Dorota, but she is so inconsolable, he agrees to go to Hell and bring the piper back to her.

Act II *Scene 1. Hell.* Schwanda arouses the Devil's ire by refusing to play for him. He is about to be tortured. Babinsky arrives and says that he will play cards with the Devil, staking his own and Schwanda's souls against one-half of the Satanic kingdom. They play and the Devil wins, but the robber proves that he has been cheating and the Devil is declared the loser. Babinsky magnanimously gives back the half kingdom; he doesn't know what to do with it, anyway. Schwanda thereupon plays so merry a tune on his pipes that all the imps and demons dance, and the two humans are released and sent back to earth.

Scene 2. The Farmyard. Babinsky is persistent; he again plots to win Dorota for himself. He tells Schwanda that since twenty minutes in Hell are the same as twenty years, he will not be interested further in his wife; she is now bald and deaf and lame. But Schwanda still wants her. Now Dorota herself hastens up, as blooming and fair as ever. She throws herself into her husband's arms, and the robber, shaking his head, goes gloomily away. Neighbors rush in to greet the reunited pair, and their cries of joy mingle with those of the chickens, ducks and other farm denizens.

Recorded music; orchestral selections; songs for baritone—"Ich bin der Schwanda," and "Wie kann ich denn vervessen?"; and Polka and Fugue.

THE UNITED STATES

HISTORICAL PREFACE

"Opera *in* the United States" is a more exact term, than "of"—since it must be admitted that this country has excelled in the production of foreign works, while being woefully lacking in native ones.   In this we resemble England.   One wonders why the genius of the Anglo-Saxon does not lend itself readily to classic opera.   Since the turn of the century and particularly because of the impact of two great wars, New York has become the musical center of the world, in opera, symphony, and concert, yet despite this fact America has still to produce one outstanding grand opera.

In the formative years of our country it was natural that we should turn to Europe for inspiration.   One of the earliest such examples was an oratorio opera written by Francis Hopkinson, a signer of the Declaration of Independence.   It was titled "The Temple of Minerva," composed in honor of our alliance with France, and performed in 1781, with General and Mrs. Washington and the French minister in the audience.   A few years later during the Presidency of Washington, a ballad opera with native theme, "Tammany," was written by James Hewitt, and performed in the old John Street Theatre, New York, 1794. Two other works of this time were: "The Archers of the Mountaineers," based on Schiller's "Wilhelm Tell"; and "Edwin and Angelina," on Goldsmith's "Vicar of Wakefield"—both by foreign composers.

Meanwhile companies from abroad were already touring our coast cities.   In New Orleans by the year 1810 grand opera had already become established.

William Henry Fry's "Leonora" is now recognized as the first native opera.   Written in 1845, from the play by Bulwer-Lytton, "The Lady of Lyons," it was performed at the Chestnut Street Theatre, Philadelphia, June 4, 1845.   Nevertheless Fry was so susceptible to foreign traditions that he allowed his work to be translated into Italian, and thus it was sung in the Academy of Music, New York, in 1858.   A second work by him, "Notre Dame de Paris," was based upon Victor Hugo's story.

In the year 1855 it is refreshing to note a truly native work, "Rip Van Winkle," by George Frederick Bristow.   Shown at Niblo's Garden,

New York, it won popular acclaim and ran for a month, showing even then how eagerly Americans awaited American opera. Notwithstanding this promising fact, no other outstanding work is chronicled for the next forty years. Then we find Walter Damrosch producing his "Scarlet Letter" with his own company. Damrosch seems to be the John the Baptist of the new era. His lifework as composer, conductor, producer, and interpreter is not finished even as this is written.

The Academy of Music continued to open its hospitable doors to foreign works, and to frown upon native ones. We have already noted that "Leonora" was admitted there only in a foreign translation. The Metropolitan Opera House was thrown open in 1883, but for many years maintained this tradition. Our singers were trained abroad and more than one of them chose foreign-sounding names—plain "Richard" becoming "Riccardo." The dearth of native talents in composition, as well as an opera-going fetich, was to blame for this.

It was not until the year 1910 that the New York temple of music was persuaded to admit an American work, and that only a one-acter, "The Pipe of Desire," by Frederick Shepherd Converse. This opera was awarded a medal by David Bispham, a stalwart exponent of native music, but despite the fanfare, the "Pipe" went out after only two performances. His "The Sacrifice," with a California theme, was presented in Boston, the following year.

In 1911, Victor Herbert's "Natoma" was shown, first in Philadelphia, then in New York, with an excellent cast and an Indian theme; but neither this nor his "Madeleine" was continued in repertory—despite the fact that Herbert was, and is, the most illustrious of our composers of operetta. Reginald DeKoven, who also excelled in Light Opera, contributed two in the Grand field, "Rip Van Winkle" and "The Canterbury Pilgrims."

A possible dozen other works comprise the product, and again world conflicts may be to blame for the poor showing of the past quarter-century, for the story is similar in other countries. Horatio Parker has given us "Mona"; Henry K. Hadley, "Cleopatra's Night"; Charles Wakefield Cadman, "Shanewis"; Louis Gruenberg, "The Emperor Jones"; Deems Taylor, "The King's Henchman"; John Laurence Seymour, "In the Pasha's Garden"; Howard Hanson, "Merry Mount."

Nor should we overlook some of the lighter works which yet deserve serious consideration, for example, George Gershwin's "Porgy and Bess," a truly native work which will be sung at least in part, long after many more ambitious efforts are covered with dust. Other composers, also, have filled our ears with tuneful music—Rudolf Friml, Jerome Kern, Sigmund Romberg, Richard Rodgers, come at once to mind. In the section of this volume devoted to the lighter vein we shall have

something more in detail to say about them.   For in Light Opera and
Musical Comedy, at any rate, the stages of the United States are filled
to overflowing.

VICTOR HERBERT

Victor Herbert (1859–1924) came of Irish stock, but from the year
1886 his work was identified with America.   His fame rests upon his
many successful operettas and the reader is referred to the Light Opera
section for a more complete biographical sketch.   He made two incursions into the more serious field: "Natoma" and "Madeleine."

NATOMA
(Nah-toh'-mah)

Romantic Opera in Three Acts.   Music by Herbert.   Book by
Joseph D. Redding.   Philadelphia Opera House, February 25, 1911.
Metropolitan, New York, February 28, 1911.   The cast at both places
was from the roster of the Chicago Opera Company, with Mary Garden
as "Natoma"; Lillian Grenville, "Barbara"; John McCormack, "Merrill"; Sammarco, "Alvarado"; Huberdeau, "Don Francisco."

SCENE: Southern California.
TIME: 1820, during Spanish Occupation.

CAST   NATOMA, an Indian maiden (Soprano).
BARBARA, her mistress (Soprano).
PAUL MERRILL, lieutenant U.S.N. (Tenor).
DON FRANCISCO, Barbara's father (Basso).
FATHER PERALTA, a Monk (Baritone).
JUAN BAUTISTA ALVARADO, a Spaniard (Tenor).
JOSÉ CASTRO, his companion, a half-breed
(Baritone).
PICO, a Spaniard (Baritone).
KAGAMA, a Spaniard (Baritone).
Spanish Citizens, Indians, American Soldiers,
Nuns, Servants, etc.

ARGUMENT   "Natoma" is so entitled from the chief character, an Indian maiden, who typifies the higher and poetic side of her people. The opera's plot represents a fusing of three diverse strains, the Indian, Spanish, and American (English), and is also interesting as having an English libretto.

Act I   *The Island of Santa Cruz.*   Don Francisco, a wealthy Spaniard, has sent his daughter off to a convent on the mainland to perfect her education. She is now expected back and all are eagerly anticipating her arrival: her father, who has sadly missed her; Alvarado, a young Spaniard who has long paid her court, but in vain; and Natoma, her Indian maid and companion, who worships her devotedly. There is still another who awaits Barbara's arrival with some interest—Lieutenant Merrill, of the United States Navy, whose duties bring him to these still-Spanish shores. Natoma has lost her heart to the officer, but he treats her as a mere child of the forest. She launches into a glowing description of her mistress' charms, until she suddenly realizes that this handsome young American will fall a victim to them and forget her, Natoma. Thenceforth, her heart is torn between two emotions, love and loyalty.

Barbara arrives amid great acclamation. She and the lieutenant speedily become interested in each other, just as Natoma had feared. In the evening a dance is given, and Alvarado realizes that he has a formidable rival. He is repulsed by Barbara and plots with Castro, his half-breed servant, to abduct her. Natoma overhears the plot and plans to frustrate it.

Chief musical numbers: the Spring Song, by Natoma: "I list the trill of golden throat"; and Paul's Address, "No country can my own outvie"; and Spanish dances.

Act II   *Public Square in Santa Barbara.*   It is Fair day at the old Spanish town of Santa Barbara, and interest in the occasion is heightened by a visit from the American marines. A dance is held in the open square, each young Spaniard inviting his lass to join him in the whirling figures. Alvarado attempts to show in public that he has a claim upon Barbara by inviting her somewhat peremptorily to dance. She hesitates, but when her father consents, she reluctantly becomes his partner. His manner angers her and she breaks away from him. He tries to compel her, and when she refuses, watches her like a hawk to seize and carry her away. Castro and several of his accomplices are at hand. To divert the general attention, Castro now challenges any one to join him in the dangerous dagger dance. A circle is formed and he thrusts his dagger in the ground defiantly. After a pause, Natoma rushes forward and thrusts her own weapon by its side. Then they dance warily around, each seeking to become possessed of the other's weapon. Finally, Natoma springs forward like a cat, knocks the half-breed's weapon aside, and dashing across to Alvarado, who is about to abduct Barbara, stabs him to the heart. The villagers crowd forward to seize her, but Merrill and his marines protect her from violence. The priest appears at the church door saying: "Vengeance is mine, I will repay, saith the Lord," and Natoma seeks sanctuary within the walls of the Church.

The "Dagger Dance," sung and acted with two flashing blades, is the high point musically of Act II. The song of the Váquero is also notable.

Act III *Interior of the Church.* Natoma crouches alone in the Church, still torn by an inner conflict. The fierce blood of her ancestors yet courses through her veins and she dreams again of the old life of the forest. She has no remorse for her bloody deed, but she does not wish to give up the lieutenant, even to her beloved mistress. The priest enters and she rails at him, but his stern words of admonition finally reach her heart and she decides to renounce all and enter the Church. The worshipers arrive, among them Barbara and Merrill, but the Indian girl gives them no heed. Mass is celebrated and the sisterhood is seen proceeding through their sunlit garden. Then Natoma bids her mistress farewell and goes through the open doors to take the veil. The "Natoma Theme" with orchestra brings the final curtain.

There are recordings of "The Spring Song" (Alma Gluck), "Paul's Address" (John McCormack) and orchestral numbers.

MADELEINE
(Mad-lane)

Lyric Opera in One Act. Music by Herbert. Book by Grant Stewart, after the play by A. Decourcelles and L. Thiboust. Metropolitan, New York, January 24, 1914, with cast of that company, headed by Frances Alda.

SCENE: Paris.
TIME: New Year's Day, circa 1760.

CAST MADELEINE FLEURY, *a prima donna* (Soprano).
NICHETTE, *her maid* (Contralto).
CHEVALIER DE MAUPRAT, *an admirer* (Tenor).
DUC D'ESTERRE, *an admirer* (Basso).
DIDIER, *a painter* (Basso).

ARGUMENT   This little lyric piece depicts one day's experience in a public singer's life, and shows that the applause of thousands does not compensate for the loss of a single friend. *Salon of an Opera Singer.* It is New Year's Day, and Madeleine Fleury, a favorite diva of the hour, has received many costly presents. Nevertheless she finds difficulty in finding a friend to dine with her. She asks her admirer, the Chevalier de Mauprat, who declines because he has promised to dine at home with his mother.   Next she asks the Duc d'Esterre, who makes the same excuse.   She cajoles, pleads, and even threatens to ask his rival Fontanges, but without avail.   She does, in fact, write to Fontanges, but he pleads the same engagement.   In desperation she asks her maid, Nichette, and the latter says the same thing, that she had previously promised to dine at home with her mother that day.   Madeleine throws herself upon the sofa in a burst of tears, and is found disconsolate by the poverty-stricken painter, Didier, who has known her since childhood.   He states that he also is to dine with his mother, but asks her if she will not join them.   Touched, she declines, but he has given her an idea.   Nichette presently returns to say that her mother has given her permission to dine with her mistress, but Madeleine excuses her.   The singer takes down her mother's portrait from the wall, and places it on the table opposite her plate.   She, too, will have her mother's company, and she will not be alone.

"A perfect day," sung by Frances Alda, is recorded.

REGINALD DE KOVEN

De Koven (1861–1920) is more widely known for his light opera, "Robin Hood," which was first produced by the Bostonians with great success, and still remains a standard of this type.   De Koven also wrote many successful songs.   "The Canterbury Pilgrims," which represents his first successful excursion into the realms of grand opera, was produced in New York in 1917.   "Rip Van Winkle" followed, three years later, and the month of his death.   (For a more complete account, see Light Opera.)

THE CANTERBURY PILGRIMS

Dramatic Opera in Four Acts.   Music by De Koven.   Book by Percy
Mackaye, after Chaucer.   Metropolitan, New York, March 8, 1917.

SCENE: England.

TIME: April, 1387.

ARGUMENT "The Canterbury Tales" of Geoffrey Chaucer is
          the foundation of this opera.   To quote Mr.
Mackaye, the librettist:

"In writing 'The Canterbury Pilgrims' one of my chief incentives was
to portray, for a modern audience, one of the greatest poets of all times
in relation to a group of his own characters.   As a romancer of prolific
imagination and dramatic insight, Chaucer stands shoulder to shoulder
with Shakespeare.   For English speech he achieved what Dante did for
Italian, raising a local dialect to a world language.

"In the spring of 1914, at the suggestion of Mr. De Koven, I re-
modeled my play, 'The Canterbury Pilgrims,' in the form of opera,
condensing its plot and characters to the more simple essentials appropriate to operatic production.   Thus focused, the story depicts Chaucer—the humorous, democratic, lovable poet of Richard Second's
court—placed between two contrasted feminine characters, the Prioress,
a shy, religious-minded gentlewoman, who has retired from the world,
but has as yet taken no vows; and the Wife of Bath, a merry, sensual,
quick-witted hoyden of the lower middle class, hunting for a sixth husband.   These three, with many other types of old England, are pilgrims, en route from London to the shrine of Thomas à Becket, at Canterbury.

"Becoming jealous of the Prioress, the Wife of Bath makes a bet with
Chaucer concerning the gentlewoman's behavior—a bet which she wins
by a trick in the third act, only to lose it in the fourth."

The plot hinges upon the machinations of the Wife of Bath, who decides that Chaucer will serve admirably for husband number six.   He,
however, entertains a respectful devotion for the Prioress, who is a gentlewoman of the time without Church vows.

Failing to win Chaucer's regard by fair means, the Wife of Bath has
recourse to strategy.   She wagers with the poet that she will get from
the Prioress a bracelet which the latter wears upon her wrist.   Should
the Wife win, Chaucer must marry her.   By underhanded methods,
Alisoun wins her wager, and Chaucer is in much distress of mind at the
prospect of marrying her.   Finally he appeals to his king to settle the

contention.   Richard decrees that if the Wife of Bath marries again she must choose a Miller—a decision that is greeted joyfully by a certain white-hatted swain who has long cast eyes upon the buxom Wife.   The poet and the Prioress are then reconciled.

RIP VAN WINKLE

A "folk" opera in Three Acts.   Music by De Koven.   Book by Percy Mackaye.   Chicago Opera Company, January 2, 1920.   In New York by same company at Lexington Theatre, January 30, 1920.

SCENE: The Catskills.
TIME: Eighteenth Century.

ARGUMENT   This American opera has an American setting, and is thus native in every particular.   It is based upon the well-known story by Washington Irving, but with many changes.

Act I   *A Village Green.*   Rip Van Winkle, a happy-go-lucky idler, who is yet beloved by all the children of the village, is to marry Katrina, daughter of Nicholas Vedder.   Katrina is a good manager, but somewhat shrewish in disposition.   Her younger sister, Peterkee, is as irresponsible as Rip, and is a partner with the latter on a truant fishing expedition.   Rip has, in fact, totally forgotten about his wedding for the nonce.   Katrina hauls him over the coals, while her father settles with Peterkee.

A goose-girl greets the crestfallen Rip, and he soons forgets his woes in a dance with the children.   He tells them the story of Hudson and his crew of the *Half Moon,* who visit the Catskills every twenty years for a game of bowling.   It is this game which sounds like thunder in the mountains.   At the height of his yarn the children are terrified by a thunder clap, and Hudson himself appears.   The children flee, but Rip and Peterkee remain and are invited by Hudson to visit his party in the mountains.   He promises Rip a magic flask.   Katrina enters as the ghostly captain vanishes.   She gibes at Rip's story and tells him that if he is not back by the next night she will wed Jan, the schoolmaster's son.   Rip and Peterkee set forth for the hills.

Act II   *Scene 1.*   After the storm Rip and Peterkee leave his hut and continue their way.

Scene 2.   They encounter Dirck Spuytenduyvil, mate of the *Half Moon,* carrying two kegs of liquor, which Rip helps him to carry to the top of the mountain.

Scene 3. The Mountain Top by Moonlight. Hendrick Hudson and his ghostly crew welcome Rip and Peterkee to their party of ninepins. Hendrick and Dirck plot to bring about the future wedding of Rip to Peterkee instead of to Katrina, by detaining Rip on the top of the mountain until their return twenty years later. To carry out this design, Peterkee is allowed to win the magic flask in a bowling match with Dirck, who then conducts her down the mountain in safety. Rip, enthused in his game as always, is given a sleeping potion, the ninth draught of which overwhelms him with slumber just as the *Half Moon* comes sailing across space.

Act III *Scene 1. Twenty years later.* At sunrise on the mountain peak, Rip is awakened by sprites, who take flight as he rouses into consciousness. Rising painfully, he is bewildered to find himself old, white-bearded and in tatters. Calling for Peterkee, he hobbles down through the mists which half conceal the ruined chimney and walls of his hut.

Scene 2. Meanwhile, Peterkee, who is now a young woman, comes searching for the magic flask. Finding it in the chimney niche, where she left it, she prays that Rip, so long lost, may yet return. Rip appears before her but she does not recognize the tattered stranger. They are on the point of recognition when her father enters, chiding Peterkee for running away from her approaching wedding.

Scene 3. On the village green a wedding party awaits Peterkee, who, despite her protests, is about to be married to Hans, a younger son of the schoolmaster, Van Bummel. At this moment Rip enters, tattered and torn. He has come to claim Katrina, still not realizing that twenty years have elapsed. She meanwhile has married Jan, and is the mother of a numerous family. Amid the general jeers, Peterkee is the only one who befriends him. She bestows on him the magic flask. Rip drinks and is restored in a twinkling to his lost youth. Hudson and his crew appear, and the hand of Peterkee is bestowed upon Rip.

WALTER DAMROSCH

Although of German extraction, Damrosch has been identified with American music since his youth, and during his later life he came to be recognized as its dean. He was born in Breslau, January 30, 1862, the son of the eminent conductor, Leopold Damrosch. He came to America at the age of nine, with his father, who was conducting at the Metropolitan Opera House. It was not long before he began to assist his father, and, upon the latter's death, took over many of his tasks, although only twenty-three. Damrosch had a long and successful career as conductor of orchestras and oratorio societies. His first opera, "The Scarlet Letter," was produced in 1896. A light opera, "The Dove of Peace," was produced in Philadelphia and New York, in 1912, "Cyrano" in 1913. In addition to these he composed incidental music to various other works. Damrosch died in New York, December 22, 1950.

THE SCARLET LETTER

Opera in Three Acts. Music by Walter Damrosch. Book by George Parsons Lathrop, after Hawthorne. First produced by Damrosch's company in New York, March 6, 1896.

SCENE: Boston.
TIME: Seventeenth century.

CAST   ARTHUR DIMMESDALE (Tenor).
HESTER PRYNNE (Soprano).
ROGER CHILLINGWORTH (Baritone).
REVEREND JOHN WILSON (Basso).
GOVERNOR BELLINGHAM (Basso).

Act I *Market Place, Boston.* An angry crowd waits without the prison clamoring against Hester Prynne, adulteress. She is conducted to a scaffold in the public square, with the Scarlet Letter on her breast. Arthur Dimmesdale and the Governor watch the scene from a balcony. Hester is bidden to reveal the name of her paramour, but refuses. The Governor commutes her sentence but bids her leave the community.

Act II *Hester's Hut in the Forest.* As Arthur is on his way to see Hester, who has been shunned by all, he is confronted by Chillingworth, who tries to wrest his guilty secret from him, unsuccessfully. In a pathetic scene between Arthur and Hester the two lovers plan to escape by ship across the ocean. Arthur learns that Chillingworth is her husband.

Act III *Same as Act I.* As Hester is about to take ship she learns with dismay that Chillingworth is advised of their plans and is going on the same vessel. Arthur, who has been in failing health, then summons Hester again to the public scaffold and, despite her protests, proclaims his share in her shame; then sinks down and expires. Hester produces a bottle of poison, drinks it, and proclaims: "Thou shalt not go alone!"

CYRANO

(Sear-ah-no)

Romantic Opera in Four Acts. Music by Walter Damrosch. Book by W. J. Henderson, after the play by Edmond Rostand. Metropolitan, New York, February 27, 1913, with Alda, Martin, and Amato.

SCENE: France.
TIME: 1640.

CAST CYRANO DE BERGERAC (Baritone).
CHRISTIAN, *a suitor of Roxane* (Tenor).
DE GUICHE, *a suitor of Roxane* (Basso).
ROXANE (Soprano).
Her Duenna (Contralto).
RAGUENEAU, *a pastry cook* (Tenor).
LISE, *his wife* (Soprano).
LE BRET, *friend of Cyrano* (Basso).
MONTFLEURY, *an actor* (Tenor).
Cavaliers, Musketeers, Actors, Cadets, Citizens.

ARGUMENT This story follows fairly closely the play by Rostand, which has achieved such striking success.

Act I *Interior of Hotel de Bourgoyne.* Cyrano, a swashbuckling Gascon with an enormous nose, is displeased by an actor's performance in a small play, and also because the man, Montfleury, has cast eyes on Roxane, Cyrano's cousin. De Guiche interposes and in a duel is slightly wounded by Cyrano. De Guiche musters a company of one hundred, but Cyrano says he will fight them all.

Act II *Ragueneau's Pastry Shop.* Cyrano has never dared to confess his great love for Roxane, on account of his huge nose. However, he gives vent to his feelings in a letter, but just then she enters and dashes his hopes by confessing that she is attracted by Christian, a rather empty-headed gallant. This young man is going to the wars in Cyrano's own company, and the Gascon promises Roxane he will keep an eye on him. He even overlooks some studied insults on Christian's part; and goes so far as to indite his love letters.

Act III   *A Square in Old Marais.*   Roxane comes from her home near by and is accosted by De Guiche. She dissembles and asks him to keep Cyrano's company from the front. After his departure Christian enters, while Cyrano lingers in the background. The young wooer is so dull that Cyrano is forced to prompt him in his speech. The lovers plan to wed at once, and their ceremony takes place within, while Cyrano halts De Guiche, by pretending to be moonstruck.

Act IV   *Scene 1. Camp of the Gascony Cadets.*   Cyrano fulfills his promise to both the lovers by writing at least one letter a day from Christian to Roxane. Just before a battle which is imminent a coach dashes up and Roxane appears. Her lover's impassioned letters have so stirred her that she must see him again at any cost. Christian realizes that it is not him, but Cyrano, whom the girl really loves. He goes into battle and is slain. Roxane is prostrated with grief.

Scene 2. A Convent Garden.   Cyrano, wounded in battle, seeks shelter in a convent. Two other wayfarers enter—Roxane and Ragueneau. Roxane sorrows over her cousin, but he tries to talk only of Christian. At her request, he reads the last letter she received and, as he reads on, darkness falls, and she realizes that the letter must be his own and not the cadet's. He tries to deny it, but she sees his sacrifice clearly at last. She kisses him tenderly as his soul takes flight.

The Man Without a Country.   See page 603.

HORATIO PARKER

    Horatio William Parker was born in Auburndale, Mass., September 15, 1863. He graduated at the Royal Conservatory, Munich, in 1885, and became Professor of the Theory of Music at Yale University, in 1894. He was awarded a prize of $10,000 by the Metropolitan Opera Company, in 1911, for the best opera written by an American composer. This was "Mona." Three years later he was again successful in competition, winning a prize for a like sum from the National Federation of Women's Clubs, for his opera, "Fairyland." He was the author of a considerable volume of church music, oratorios, cantatas, and shorter pieces. Parker died December 18, 1919.

MONA
(*Mo'-na*)

Dramatic Opera in Three Acts.   Music by Parker.   Book by Brian Hooker.   The "Ten Thousand Dollar Prize Opera" of the Metropolitan Opera House, New York.   Première, March 14, 1912.

SCENE: Southwestern Britain.
TIME: Circa 100 A.D.

CAST   ROMAN GOVERNOR (Baritone).
QUINTUS, *his son, known to the Britons as Gwynn* (Tenor).
ARTH, *a British Tribesman* (Basso).
ENYA, *his wife* (Soprano).
GLOOM, *their son, a Druid* (Baritone).
CARADOC, *chief bard of Britain* (Baritone).
NIAL, *a changeling* (Tenor).
MONA, *Princess of Britain* (Mezzo-Soprano).
Soldiers, Druids, Bards, Britons.

ARGUMENT   "Mona" tells the dramatic story of an early princess of Britain, who endeavors to win by war the freedom of her people, and who finds too late that the gentler arts of love which she forswore would have won the prize she sought.

Act I   *Interior of Arth's Forest Hut.*   While the fiery Britons chafe under the military sway of Rome, the Druids seek a chieftain who shall again lead them against the invaders.   They find one in Mona, last of the line of the warlike Boadicea, who has been reared as the foster child of Arth and Enya.   Mona is beloved by Gwynn, a man of peace who endeavors to reconcile the Romans and the Britons.   Unknown to her he is the son of the Roman Governor by a captive British woman and has more than once stood between the warring factions. He endeavors to persuade Mona to forsake her warlike traits and wed with him, but she feels that her destiny is linked with her country, even as was that of Boadicea.

Act II   *A Druidic Temple in the Forest.*   The Roman Governor finds that the Druids are again holding their ancient rites, a sign that an uprising is planned.   But Gwynn, his son (known to the Romans as Brennius) believes that he can obtain peace for the country by winning the heroic Mona as his wife.   The Governor, cynical, lets him try the plan. Mona is found by Gwynn after one of the Druidic conclaves and is compelled to confess her love, after a stormy scene of wooing. But she instantly repents her womanly weakness when Gwynn tells her he is Roman born. She summons her people who take Gwynn prisoner.

Act III *The Forest before a Roman Town.* Nial, the half-witted changeling, and Enya, watch the battle with the Romans at the walls of the town. The Romans have been warned and drive the Britons back. Mona is carried in by the retreating forces but is unwounded. To her aid comes Gwynn, who has been released in the mêlée, and once again offers her his love and protection. He confesses his identity to her but she will not believe. She thinks he has been a spy, and in an excess of mistaken devotion to her country she slays him unresistingly. The Romans pursue the enemy, and Mona is brought face to face with the Governor and learns the truth—that Gwynn was the best friend of Britain and with him perished the hope of peace. Mona realizes that by denying her womanhood she has missed happiness for herself and the true welfare of her country.

FAIRYLAND

Allegorical Opera in Three Acts. Music by Parker. Book by Brian Hooker. Los Angeles, 1915.

SCENE: A Mountainous Country in Europe.
TIME. Circa 1300.

CAST ROSAMUND, *a novice* (Soprano).
AUBURN, *the king* (Tenor).
CORVAIN, *his brother* (Basso).
ROBIN, *a woodsman* (Baritone).
MYRIEL, *the abbess* (Contralto).
Nuns, Soldiers, Foresters, Villagers, Fairies, etc.

ARGUMENT This opera is a combination of allegory and fancy. It does not succeed in either realm, despite some pleasing music.

Act I *A Valley.* Corvain has designs upon the throne of his country and plots to usurp the place of his brother Auburn the king, who is a dreamer. The nuns from a neighboring abbey enter in solemn procession, but Rosamund, a novice, is still longing for the world that she has forsaken. Corvain stands in their path, and the abbess challenges his presence there. Corvain openly boasts his designs upon his brother's throne. While they talk, Auburn enters, and is spurred by the abbess to take action against Corvain. The latter flees, but when night falls he returns, strikes the king down, and seizes the crown. A light gleams in a nearby shrine. Corvain hastens away. A fairy scene ensues, in which Auburn becomes king and Rosamund queen of Fairyland.

Act II *Hall in a Castle.* Corvain is seen attired in the robes of royalty and granting audience. Rosamund enters in sore distress, seeking the way to Fairyland. Auburn also comes in attired as a pilgrim. He does not recall her as his spouse in Fairyland, and when she tries to open his eyes, the abbess seizes her in the name of the Church. When Auburn tries to dispute the throne with Corvain, the latter overmasters him.

Act III *Public Square before the Abbey.* Rosamund has been condemned to death for being untrue to her vows. She stands tied to a stake as the abbey bell rings. The abbess offers pardon if she will recant, but the girl refuses. As the abbess departs, Auburn comes stealthily to her. His eyes are open at last, and he recognizes her as his queen of Fairyland. Corvain arrives with a strong guard. They seize the king and he is tied to the stake also; but when they would kindle the fagots, roses bloom, fairies appear, and the two victims step forth in regal robes as monarchs of Fairyland.

FREDERICK S. CONVERSE

Frederick Shepherd Converse was born in Newton, Massachusetts, January 5, 1871. He graduated at Harvard, and then went abroad to study music, at Munich. He composed various works with considerable success for the piano; and in the vocal field, songs, cantatas, and oratorios. In the realm of opera his achievement was only temporary. His "The Pipe of Desire" (1910) won the distinction of being the first opera by an American to receive its production in America. The following year his opera, "The Sacrifice," was produced, but neither work continued in repertory. Converse died in Westwood, Massachusetts, June 8, 1940.

THE PIPE OF DESIRE

Dramatic Opera in One Act. Music by Converse. Book by George Edwards Barton. Metropolitan, New York, March 18, 1910, with Martin, Homer, Whitehill, and Witherspoon.

SCENE: A Woodland.
TIME: Spring.

CAST IOLAN, *a peasant* (Tenor).
NAOIA, *his sweetheart* (Soprano).
THE OLD ONE (Basso).
Elves, Nymphs, etc.

ARGUMENT The scene of this fairy opera is laid in a sylvan glade; the time is the spring of the year. Elves flit hither and yon, at their various tasks. They are awakening Nature from her winter's sleep. Iolan. a peasant, comes in singing. He is to wed his sweetheart, Naoia, on the morrow, and his heart is glad. He beholds the elves at work, and the latter are reproached by the Old One, who carries the magic Pipe of Desire. He plays upon the Pipe, and it is snatched from his hands by Iolan, who would test its power. The Old One warns him that it has fatal powers. The peasant nevertheless persists, and at last hears entrancing music and beholds a vision of himself in later years rich, with Naoia by his side. He calls her to him, but when she comes she is in rags and wounded. The playing of the Pipe has brought misfortune to her. She soon dies in her lover's arms, and his spirit follows her.

THE SACRIFICE

Dramatic Opera in Three Acts. Music by Converse. Book by Composer. Boston Opera House, March 3, 1911.

SCENE: Southern California.
TIME: 1846.

ARGUMENT "The Sacrifice" is a colorful opera dealing with the transitional period in Southern California when the old Spanish civilization, fostered by the Mexicans, gave way before the aggressive American arms.

Act I *Garden of Senora Anaya's House.* Chonita, a beautiful Mexican senorita, has left her own home to visit her aunt in Southern California—chiefly in order to be near her lover, Bernal, a Mexican officer. Meanwhile the old order of things is passing in this section and American soldiers are in control. Bernal is forced to visit his sweetheart clandestinely. Chonita is also beloved by Captain Burton, an American officer, who calls upon her and makes love to her, while the Mexican hides in a grove nearby. Chonita dallies with him in order to be assured of his protection during the troublous times; but this explanation made later to Bernal only renders him the more jealous and furious.

Act II *Interior of a Church.* The American soldiers have converted a Mission church into a barracks, demolishing shrines and altars. The curtain rises upon a typical camping scene in which the soldiers tell of their last fight. Dancing and singing girls enter and the soldiers follow them to the garden. Chonita and her servant Tomasa now enter to learn particulars of the recent fight. Burton tells Chonita that Bernal has been killed, and learns that the Mexican was her lover. But Bernal was only wounded and presently creeps into the church. Chonita hides him in a confessional. The soldiers suspect the presence of a spy, but Bernal betrays himself by springing upon the Captain when the latter returns to renew his court with Chonita. The girl interposes between the rivals and is accidentally wounded by Burton. The Mexican is captured by the soldiers.

Act III *The Bedchamber of Chonita.* The Mexican girl is conveyed to her room where she lies in a delirious condition. She believes that Bernal is being shot as a spy. A priest has been sent for and presently appears, followed secretly by a band of Mexicans. The priest sends a request to the American officer to allow Bernal to visit the sick girl. Burton brings the prisoner in person, and the two Mexican lovers forget all the others in their joy of meeting again. Burton realizes that he stands between the two and happiness, and is unselfish enough to wish for the girl's welfare at any cost. The way is suddenly cleared when the band of Mexicans, hidden without, charge upon the house. Burton makes no resistance but offers himself to the nearest Mexican weapon and is slain. Chonita understands the greatness of the sacrifice and, supported by her lover, totters over to kneel beside the body and offer a prayer for the noble American's soul.

HENRY K. HADLEY

Henry Kimball Hadley was born in Somerville, Mass., in 1871. He studied music in Boston and Vienna. He is chiefly known as a song writer and composer for the piano, having written over 150 such pieces. He also composed ballets and orchestral numbers, and two operas, "Azora" and "Bianca," prior to "Cleopatra's Night." Hadley died in New York, September 6, 1937.

AZORA

The Daughter of Montezuma. Legendary Opera in Three Acts. Music by Hadley. Book by David Stevens. At the Metropolitan, New York, 1917, by the Chicago Opera Company.

Azora, the lovely daughter of the Aztec ruler, Montezuma, is loved by Xalca, Prince of Tlascala, and she reciprocates. Their evil genius, Ramatzin, an Aztec general, is also desirous of winning the girl. He instigates Canek, high priest of the Sun, to thwart Xalca. An invasion is threatened by the Tarascans, and Xalca leads the army against them; being promised a suitable reward. He returns victorious and demands the hand of Azora, but Ramatzin and Canek again interpose, and Montezuma says the Sun God has demanded their hearts in a human sacrifice. They are bound to the altar and await the fatal stroke, when the sun's rays fall upon it. Just before the fatal moment, Cortez and his Spanish troops rush in, and the lovers are saved.

CLEOPATRA'S NIGHT
(Clee-o-pah'-trah's Night)

Romantic Opera in Two Acts. Music by Hadley. Book by Alice Leal Pollock, after the story by Theophile Gautier. Metropolitan, New York, January 31, 1920, with Frances Alda, Orville Harrold, and Jeanne Gordon.

SCENE: Egypt.
TIME: Antiquity.

Act I *Cleopatra's Summer Palace.* The Egyptian Queen has retired to her baths to rest and refresh herself against the coming of Marc Antony on the morrow. Suddenly an arrow falls close beside her, but it bears only the message, "I love you," on a bit of papyrus. Before the Queen can recover from her surprise at this audacity, a young hunter appears, who confesses that he has shot the love message, and pleads his fierce passion for the Queen by way of excuse. "Do you love me enough to die for me?" asks the Queen. "I do," answers Meiamoun boldly. "Then I will give myself to you tonight," responds Cleopatra, "if you are content to die tomorrow." The young man accepts her terms, although Mardion, a lady-in-waiting who loves him, tries to dissuade him. Unsuccessful, she stabs herself as Meiamoun and Cleopatra float away on the royal barge.

Act II *Terrace of the Palace. Morning.* The young hunter, attired like a prince, is seated by the side of the Queen watching the dancing girls, when a slave enters bearing the poisoned draught. Cleopatra relents and would postpone his doom, but news of the arrival of Antony prevents. Meiamoun drains the cup and falls lifeless.

CHARLES W. CADMAN

Charles Wakefield Cadman has specialized in Indian music and his songs and other compositions in this field have been deservedly popular, since they reflect the spirit of the native American. Cadman has visited Indian reservations and secured phonograph records of the tribal lays. He was born in Johnstown, Pa., December 24, 1881, and studied harmony and orchestration at Pittsburgh. His "Shanewis," an opera in two scenes, was produced in New York in 1918 and 1919. He has written two other operas, "The Garden of Mystery" and "The Red Rivals" (Daoma). Cadman died in Los Angeles, December 30, 1946.

SHANEWIS
(Shah'-nee-wis)

(The Robin Woman.) An American Opera in Two Scenes. Music by Cadman. Book by Nelle Richmond Eberhardt. Metropolitan, New York, March 23, 1918.

SCENE: Western America.

TIME: The Present.

ARGUMENT　Shanewis is an Indian girl who has had exceptional advantages in education. She has been befriended by an American lady and thus had the opportunity to cultivate her rich voice. She is called "The Robin Woman." Shanewis falls in love with the son of her patron, not knowing that he is already betrothed to Amy Everton, an American girl. Meanwhile Philip, an Indian suitor, pleads his cause in vain, and urges her to make use of a bow and poisoned arrows, but she disdains him. In anger at his rival's perfidy in keeping Shanewis in ignorance of his other love affair, the Indian grasps the weapons and slays the deceiver.

"The Spring Song of the Robin Woman," sung by Elsie Baker, is recorded.

A Witch of Salem.　See page 603.

RICHARD HAGEMAN

Hageman is better known as both pianist and conductor, than as a writer of opera. He was born in Leeuwarden, Holland, July 9, 1882. Until the age of ten he was the pupil of his father, who was director of the Amsterdam Conservatory. He made his debut as pianist at the ripe age of six. Later he studied at the Brussels Conservatory, and became conductor of the Royal Opera House, Amsterdam, in 1904–5. He came on a tour to the United States, two years later, and, in 1916, accepted the post of assistant conductor at the Metropolitan, which he held for five years. He has conducted orchestras in various cities and, since 1939, has lived in Hollywood, writing incidental music for films. He has also become an American citizen. His one opera of note is "Caponsacchi."

CAPONSACCHI
(Cap-on-sah'-kee)

Tragic Opera in Prologue, Three Acts, and Epilogue. Music by Hageman. Originally titled, "Tragedie in Arezzo." English text by A. F. Goodrich, from Browning's "The Ring and the Book." A German text by W. Wolff and J. Kapp was produced at Freiburg, 1932;

Vienna, March 19, 1935, when it bore its present title, "Caponsacchi." At New York, the Metropolitan, in English, February 4, 1937.

ARGUMENT The book follows the story by Browning. Both the Prologue and the Epilogue reveal the trial of Guido, a dissolute Italian, and Caponsacchi, a saintly but quite naïve monk. In the plot, the pawn is the lovely, childlike wife of Guido, Pompilia. He continually abuses her, as her purity of character shames him, and also he cannot get hold of her family's wealth. She is pregnant and now desires above all things to shield her coming child. She appeals to the priest, Caponsacchi, to protect her from her husband; and together they undertake a foolish journey to Rome. Guido lays a trap for them, but when he seeks to surprise the pair, the innocent Caponsacchi disarms him in a duel. In the Third Act matters reach a climax. Pompilia's son is born; she is at the home of her parents; but she is still in deadly fear of her husband. She again sends for the priest, and when a knock is heard at the door, thinks it is he. But Guido rushes in, seeking the whereabouts of the child. When she will not tell him, he murders her father and mother before her eyes. She still defies him, to protect her son. He orders his followers to kill her also; but at this moment Caponsacchi rushes in, ready to slay Guido. He is prevented only by the arrival of the police.

In the Epilogue while the two men are still on trial, Guido's followers outside howl for his freedom, and death for the recreant priest. Caponsacchi's evidence is unsupported by any proof, but when all seems lost, a curtain at the rear parts, revealing the Pope. He has heard all the evidence, and now vindicates Pompilia, condemns Guido, and bestows his papal blessing on the priest.

Helen Jepson has made two recordings of songs: "This very vivid morn," and "Lullaby."

LOUIS GRUENBERG

Although born in Russia, August 3, 1883, Louis Gruenberg came to America as a child and was educated here. He studied piano and composition abroad under Busoni, and made a European tour as a pianist. Later he returned to America and made his home in Brooklyn. He wrote numerous orchestral pieces, concertos, chamber music, and songs. His fairy opera, "Die Hexe," was followed by "Jack and the Beanstalk," the words by John Erskine. It was produced by the Juilliard School, in 1931. His opera, "Emperor Jones," created a sensation during the spring season of 1933.

THE EMPEROR JONES

A musical tragedy in two acts, with prologue and interlude, after the play by Eugene O'Neill.   Music by Gruenberg.   Libretto by Kathleen de Jaffa.   Metropolitan, New York, January 7, 1933, with Tibbett as the "Emperor."

SCENE: An island in the West Indies.
TIME: Recent.

CAST   BRUTUS JONES, *Emperor* (Baritone).
HENRY SMITHERS, *a Cockney trader* (Tenor).
AN OLD NATIVE WOMAN (Soprano).
CONGO WITCH DOCTOR (Dancer).
Soldiers, Natives, Ghosts of the Formless Fears, Jeff, Convicts, Planters, Slaves, etc.

ARGUMENT   This work may be described as a tragedy with music.   The tone effects merely furnish the background for an elemental struggle of a human soul.

Prologue   A concealed chorus chants vindictively: "De Emperor, he must die!"

Act I   *Room in Palace.*   The audience chamber of the Emperor Jones is shown as a large, high-ceilinged room, rather bare and set off in the center by a massive throne.   It is deserted.   An old woman glides in and is seized, a few moments later, by Smithers, the disreputable, white hanger-on of the Emperor.   At first she is sullenly silent, then as he threatens her with the whip she shows him that the palace is without its retinue of servants and that the distant tom-toms presage a revolt. Smithers summons his master, who enters in all the barbaric elegance and swagger of such a potentate.   Although sensing that trouble is brewing, Jones maintains his bluster.   He says that he has made all plans for his get-away and that no ordinary bullet can harm him; only a silver bullet, and he has provided that for himself.   Then he tells of his former lawless life in the States, including jail-breaking and murder, but threatens Smithers with death if he blabs. The cringing Smithers promises silence. As the monotonous tom-toms grow more insistent and Jones realizes that he is deserted and in imminent danger, he says: "I resigns de job of Emperor dis minute!" But even then he saunters off with a great air of bravado, hat cocked on one side, and whistling.

Interlude Again comes the angry muttering of the unseen chorus: "Dis man must die!" This recurs from time to time in the ensuing action.

Act II *The Forest at Night.* Jones enters still whistling but walking rapidly and looking all about as if in search of something. Far-off tom-toms keep their incessant beating. He turns over one white stone after another hunting for a cache of food, but without success. As hunger and fatigue creep upon him he loses his self-assurance. The somber tree trunks with their draperies of moss lend themselves to fantastic shapes, which finally become the Formless Fears. They creep writhingly up toward him until in a frenzy he fires a shot; they vanish. Ere he has recovered from this fright he sees the ghost of Jeff, the pal he has murdered over a crap game. He shoots a second time, and Jeff disappears. Meanwhile, he has stripped himself piece by piece of his royal trappings, and is now naked to the waist. Again his frenzied eyes behold a scene from his past—that of the convict gang and the guard whom he has brained with a shovel. He tries to re-enact this deed, but as the guard stands defiant he fires for the third time, and these wraiths vanish. But he now realizes that his shots have drawn attention to his location, and he begins to run madly here and there, and to sing the Negro spiritual, "It's me, O Lawd, standin' in the need of prayer!" As he crouches in fear and weariness, another scene unfolds—a Southern plantation of ante-bellum days. Fashionably dressed ladies and gentlemen are clustered around a slave block. The auctioneer makes Jones take his place on the block, and in a rage he wastes two more of his precious bullets; the crowd vanishes; but the exultant chorus of spectres chant, "Five bullets gone!" He realizes that only one remains —the silver. As he falls groveling upon the ground, the Congo Witch Doctor appears and dances around his body. Jones stares as though hypnotized. The tom-toms are nearer, more overpowering, as soldiers and natives close in upon the fugitive. Screaming a final prayer to God, he cries, "De silver bullet. You won't git me! I'se Emperor yit!" Then he fires this last missive into his forehead and falls lifeless.

The baritone song (by Lawrence Tibbett) "Standin' in the need of prayer," is recorded.

DEEMS TAYLOR

Deems Taylor has the somewhat unusual distinction of being a native of New York City. He was born there, December 22, 1885. His elementary studies were at the Ethical Culture School, and he graduated from New York University. During his college course he wrote the music for four comic operas, and one of them, "The Echo," was given Broadway representation by Charles Dillingham. His work after college, however, was in journalistic channels; he wrote for the New York *Press,* the *Tribune* (later as war correspondent, 1916–17), *Collier's Weekly,* musical critic for the *World,* and, in 1927, he became editor of *Musical America.* He wrote several successful cantatas and songs, a symphony, "Through the Looking Glass," and incidental music. In 1925, the Metropolitan Board of Directors gave him the great honor of commissioning an opera which, in advance, they agreed to produce. The result was the very successful, "The King's Henchman" (1927). "Peter Ibbetson" (1931) followed; then "Ramuntcho" (1942) by the Philadelphia Opera Co. Taylor has served as broadcaster and interpreter on many music programs and is recognized as one of the foremost American composers.

THE KING'S HENCHMAN

Lyric Drama in Three Acts. Music by Deems Taylor. Book by Edna St. Vincent Millay. Produced by direction of the Metropolitan Opera Company "for its exclusive use," and presented, February 17, 1927. In the cast were Tibbett, as "Eadgar"; Johnson, as Æthelwold"; and Florence Easton, as "Ælfrida."

        SCENE: England.
        TIME: Tenth Century.

    CAST   EADGAR, *King of England* (Baritone).
             DUNSTAN, *Archbishop of Canterbury* (Baritone).
             ÆTHELWOLD, *Earl of East Anglia* (Tenor).
             ORDGAR, *Thane of Devon* (Baritone).
             MACCUS, *servant to Æthelwold* (Baritone).
             THORED, *Master-of-the-Household to Ordgar.*

HWITA, *cup-bearer to the King.*
ÆLFRIDA, *daughter of Ordgar* (Soprano).
ASE, *servant to* ÆLFRIDA (Contralto).
Lords and Ladies of Eadgar's Court, Retainers,
Villagers, Servants.

ARGUMENT   Although of American composition, "The King's
Henchman" takes for its theme a love story of old
England of the Tenth Century.   It reveals the struggle between love
and duty, as in "Tristan and Isolde."

Act I   *Hall of King Eadgar at Winchester.*   Eadgar, King of England,
is a widower who wishes to marry again.   He has heard reports
concerning the beauty of Ælfrida, daughter of Ordgar, and wishing to
satisfy himself as to the truth of these rumors before asking her hand,
he commissions Æthelwold, his henchman, to go in his stead.   Æthelwold, who is the foster-brother of the King and his close friend, is reluctant to take this mission, as he is a soldier and unversed in the ways
of women.   He may not know whether the maiden is fair, and he may
not say the right thing.   However, his regard for the King overcomes
his timidity, and he consents to set forth.   He and the King pledge a
parting cup, according to old Saxon custom, and he rides forth at dawn
followed by his trusty squire, Maccus.

Act II   *A Forest in Devonshire.*   After an arduous journey of a month
the two horsemen near their destination on Hallowe'en.   The
fog, however, is so thick that they do not know where they are.   Tired
out, Æthelwold lies down on the ground to sleep, while Maccus goes
farther to seek a path.   After an interval Ælfrida enters with her maid,
Ase.   She is obeying an old custom of Hallowe'en, in which a maiden
by weaving certain spells may obtain a vision of the man she is to marry.
During her song of invocation the fog lifts and she sees the young nobleman lying asleep.   She believes him to be a spirit, but is so enraptured
that she kisses him.   He awakens and thinks in turn she is a sprite, who
has cast a spell over him.   They soon realize their mutual love, and
embrace; but just then Ase is heard calling, "Ælfrida!" and he knows
that his dream lady is none other than the one he was sent to claim for
the King.   As she departs, he is in despair.   When Maccus returns, he
is told that they must go at once.   On their way, the voice of Ælfrida
is heard calling him.   He bids his squire return to the King and say that
Ælfrida is not comely enough for the King; he himself will wed her.

Act III   *Ordgar's House in Devonshire.*   It is spring.   Æthelwold
and Ælfrida are wed and happy, but he is tormented with

thoughts of his treachery to his lord. She, too, is discontented, as she had thought that her husband would take her to the Court. At last he consents to take her to Flanders. As they make preparations, Maccus announces the King's arrival on a visit. In a panic, Æthelwold asks his wife to stain her face with walnut juice. Her father, however, wishes her to look her best. The two men go out to pay their respects to Eadgar, and as the three return, the door of Ælfrida's apartment opens and she appears radiantly beautiful. Her vanity has gotten the better of her caution. After the first amazed glance, the King sadly reproaches his henchman for his faithlessness. The latter stabs himself. Eadgar does not try to stop him; he rebukes Ælfrida for her part in the tragedy, and bids his men bury the body of his henchman with all honors.

Two baritone arias (by Lawrence Tibbett)—"Oh! Caesar, great art thou!" (Act I); and "Nay, Maccus, lay him down" (Act III) are in record form.

PETER IBBETSON

Romantic Drama in Three Acts. Music by Deems Taylor. Book by Constance Collier and Taylor, from the novel by Du Maurier. Metropolitan, New York, February 7, 1931. In the cast were Johnson, Tibbett, and Lucrezia Bori. The work won an award of Five Thousand Dollars from the Juilliard Foundation.

SCENE: England and France.
TIME: 1840–1887.

CAST PETER IBBETSON, *a gentleman of French and English blood* (Tenor).
COLONEL IBBETSON, *his uncle* (Baritone).
MARY, *Duchess of Towers* (Soprano).
MRS. DEANE, *a wealthy widow* (Mezzo-Soprano).
MRS. GLYN, *her mother* (Contralto).
ACHILLE GREGOUX, *an inn-keeper* (Tenor).
MAJOR DUQUESNOIR, *a veteran* (Basso).
THE PRISON CHAPLAIN (Basso).
PASQUIER DE LA MARIERE, *Peter's father* (Baritone)
MARY PASQUIER, *Peter's mother* (Soprano).
MME. SERASKIER, *Mimsey's mother* (Soprano).
Mimsey and Gogo, Dream Children; Guests, Servants, Prison Officials, etc.

ARGUMENT Based upon a popular novel of its day, "Peter Ibbetson" is a romance of frustrated love which found its true fulfilment on the wings of tragedy and behind prison walls.

Act I   *An English Drawing Room.*   At a ball given by Mrs. Deane in her country home, Colonel Ibbetson, a middle-aged fop, tries to monopolize attention.   He reads a poem which he claims as his own, but his nephew, Peter, arriving late, says the poem is by another.   Furiously the Colonel turns upon him, and later tells Mrs. Deane that Peter is his own son, the result of one of his many conquests.   Meanwhile, Peter has told her of his own early life in France, and of a childish sweetheart whom he will never forget.   Among the last arrivals is Mary, Duchess of Towers.   She and Peter exchange glances, wondering if they have ever met before.

Act II   *Scene 1.   An Inn near Paris.*   On a visit to Paris Peter goes to his old home, but finds nothing of his former life.   He does meet Major Duquesnoir, but the veteran does not recognize him.   Peter chances to see the Duchess of Towers and, puzzled by her effect upon him, falls asleep.   The next scene is his dream.

Scene 2.   A Garden at Passy.   Peter, a boy of twelve called Gogo, plays in a garden with Mimsey, whom he adores.   He sees his father and mother.   His dream idyll is shattered by the arrival of Ibbetson, who speaks insultingly to Peter's mother.   With a cry the boy rushes to her aid.   The Duchess stands idly by looking on.

Scene 3.   Same as Scene 1.   Peter awakens as the Duchess enters the inn seeking shelter from a storm.   She recalls having seen him at Mrs. Deane's ball.   As they chat they realize that they are the boy and girl sweethearts of long ago.   He relates his dream, and she completes it.   Their astral bodies have been meeting.   However, she now tells Peter she is married to another and must not see him again, even in his dreams.

Act III   *Scene 1.   Colonel Ibbetson's Rooms in London.*   Mrs. Deane and her mother come to the Colonel's home to try to regain some letters.   They show Peter one, in which the Colonel claims that Peter's mother was his mistress.   The ladies take their leave soon after Ibbetson returns.   Peter confronts him with the slander, and in a quarrel strikes him fatally with his cane.

Scene 2.   Chaplain's Room, Newgate Prison.   Peter has been sentenced to death for the murder of his uncle.   He refuses to tell his motive.   At dawn, when he is led to the scaffold, Mrs. Deane tells him his sentence has been commuted to life imprisonment.   He at first pleads that he be allowed to die; but the lady tells him, Mary bids him continue to sleep and "dream true."

Scene 3. A Lake near Paris. In his second dream, Peter returns to the little lake where he and Mimsey played as children. No one recognizes him. Mary hurries to him, greets him tenderly, and tells him she will never leave him again. Their dream life is the only important one.

Scene 4. A Cell in Newgate. Thirty years have passed by. Peter, still a prisoner and now an old man, lies dying. Mrs. Deane brings him a last message from his beloved, who has just passed on. He does not need to be told this; she has been with him constantly in his dreams, until the previous night; and now in a last vision she smiles upon him. While Mrs. Deane rushes for the doctor, the walls dissolve, and Mary and Peter, young again, step out into the sunshine.

An orchestral suite from this opera is recorded.

RAMUNTCHO

Lyric Drama in Three Acts. Music and book by Taylor, from a novel by Pierre Loti. Philadelphia, by the Philadelphia Opera Co., February 10, 1942.

SCENE: The Basque village of Etchézar.
TIME: Early part of present century.

ARGUMENT The story is that of the love of the young Ramuntcho for a village maiden, Gracieuse. He is a smuggler and, in the opening scene, we find him and his companions engaged in this lucrative but dangerous traffic. They narrowly escape capture by the Spanish customs officers. In the next scene, a village square, our hero is found in a game of pelote. He willingly turns from this pastime to greet his sweetheart, Gracieuse, but her mother, Dolores, is bitterly opposed to the match. Not only is Ramuntcho a smuggler, he is likewise the illegitimate son of an old friend of hers. He tells Gracieuse that if she will marry him, he will give up smuggling and take his three years' service in the army.

The first two scenes of the Second Act witness the parting of the lovers. The third scene follows a lapse of two years. Gracieuse has heard nothing from her lover and wonders what has happened to him. Her mother, Dolores, has been confiscating his letters and burning them. In despair Gracieuse finally enters a convent to "find peace and comfort close to the arms of God."

In the Third Act, a year later, Ramuntcho comes home to find the deception practised upon them. He wants to take his sweetheart away from the nunnery by force, but she respects her vows. She still loves him and is partly reconciled, but she says: "I have taken my vows, Ramuntcho. I belong to God forever."

The music is enlivened by arias, duets, songs by the soldiers, and other "set pieces" in the lyric style. It has no leit-motifs, except for an identifying phrase for Ramuntcho, which appears first in the overture. There is also a limited use of Basque folk songs and dances, skillfully arranged.

JOHN LAURENCE SEYMOUR

Seymour is a California composer, who was born in 1893. He studied composition and the violin in Los Angeles. He was graduated from the University of California in 1917, and two years later received an M.A. degree from the same institution. In 1926 he was appointed Director of the Department of Dramatic Art of the Sacramento Junior College; and in addition to this he has been lecturer on music and dramatics at the University of California. He has written songs and chamber music, and six operas. "In the Pasha's Garden" was his first work to receive Metropolitan recognition.

IN THE PASHA'S GARDEN

Tragic Opera in One Act. Music by Seymour. Book by Henry Chester Tracy after tale by H. G. Dwight. Metropolitan, New York, January 24, 1935. In the cast were Helen Jepson and Lawrence Tibbett.

SCENE: Constantinople.
TIME: Uncertain.

CAST A PASHA (Baritone).
HIS WIFE (Soprano).
HER LOVER, *a Frenchman* (Tenor).
A EUNUCH (Basso).
Servants.

ARGUMENT   *A Pasha's Garden.*   The unfaithful wife of a
Pasha makes an appointment with her lover, to
meet her in the kiosk of the garden.   They are overheard in their
rendezvous by a eunuch, who informs his master.   On the Pasha's approach, the woman, in alarm, persuades her lover to conceal himself in
a large chest; then to allay her husband's suspicions she suggests that
they dine in the kiosk.   Acting on covert hints from the eunuch, but
giving no outward sign, he obtains the key of the chest from his wife,
on a pretext, and then orders his servants to bury it in the garden.
Horrified but helpless, the woman stands by and watches her lover being
entombed alive.

HOWARD HANSON

Hanson is one of the later American composers, born in Wahoo,
Nebraska, in 1896.   His musical education begun in the West was continued at the Institute of Musical Art, New York.   For three years he
studied in Europe, as a Fellow of the American Academy, Rome.   At
twenty-eight he was made Director of the Eastman School of Music,
Rochester.   He has written several orchestral suites and chorals.   His
first opera, "Merry Mount," was heard in 1934.

MERRY MOUNT

Dramatic Opera in Four Acts.   Music by Hanson.   Book by Richard
L. Stokes, after a story by Hawthorne.   Metropolitan, New York, Feb-
ruary 10, 1934.   In the cast were Tibbett, "Wrestling Bradford,"
D'Angelo, "Praise-God Tewke," and Gladys Swarthout, "Plentiful
Tewke."

SCENE: A Massachusetts Village.
TIME: May, 1623.

CAST   FAINT-NOT-TINKER, *a sentinel* (Baritone).
SAMOSET, *an Indian chief* (Basso).
DESIRE ANNABLE, *a sinner* (Soprano).
JONATHAN BANKS, *a dissenter* (Tenor).
WRESTLING BRADFORD, *a preacher* (Baritone).

PRAISE-GOD-TEWKE, *an elder* (Baritone).
PLENTIFUL TEWKE, *his daughter* (Mezzo-Soprano).
MYLES BRODRIB, *a captain* (Baritone).
PEREGRINE BRODRIB, *his son* (Soprano).
LOVE BREWSTER, *a young woman* (Soprano).
BRIDGET CRACKSTON, *her grandmother* (Contralto).
Other Puritans, Indians, Fiends of Hell, etc.

ARGUMENT This opera is of interest because it draws its inspiration from one of the earliest American
themes. It depicts the religious intolerance of the first Puritan colony.

Act I *The Village. Noon.* It is a Sabbath day and the Puritan folk
are seen emerging from their log church. The central structure is surmounted by a cannon. One or two Indians are present; and
two white offenders are awaiting punishment—a woman at the whip-
ping post, and a man in the stocks. Wrestling Bradford, still thinking
that more preaching is needful, begins to harangue the crowd. He
stops to deal with the man and the woman. He then confesses to Elder
Tewke that while outwardly a man of God, inwardly he is very much a
man of flesh. Of late he has been tempted by the pagan goddess, Astoreth herself. Tewke advises him to get a wife and offers the hand of his
own daughter, Plentiful. The girl is willing, but Bradford, after embracing her, says that she "has no medicine for his wound." The stern
orderliness of the day is disturbed by the entrance of a jester, Jack
Prence, who has come over from London with some Cavaliers. He
plays with the village children, and is soundly reproved by Bradford.
Lady Marigold enters and is so incensed that she strikes the preacher
with her riding crop. A general mêlée between Cavaliers and Puritans
is narrowly averted. But Bradford, far from being offended by the lady
who struck him, falls an immediate victim to her charms. She tells
him, disdainfully, "Come at sundown and wed me to Lackland." This
makes Bradford still more determined to have it out with the Cavaliers.

Act II *The Maypole. Afternoon.* A Maypole has been set up on a
small hill called "Merry Mount." Indians are present, led by
Samoset. The pole is a setting for the wedding of Lady Marigold, but
the Puritans see in it still another mark of ungodliness. Bradford, entering, denounces it as a "staff of Hell," and his men hack it down. In
the fight the Cavaliers are defeated. Brodrib strikes the Indian chief,
Samoset, and the latter leaves, nursing revenge.

Act III *Scene 1. The Forest. Twilight.* Bradford makes advances
to Lady Marigold and is repulsed. Lackland rushes in to aid
her and is killed by the pike-thrust of a guard. Tewke reproaches

Bradford for his treatment of Plentiful and his present conduct.   The preacher tries to pray, but falls into a troubled sleep.

Scene 2.   Bradford's Vision.   Night.   The Valley of Tophet.   The forces of Hell surround Bradford, led by Lucifer.   Finally appears Astoreth—and her face and figure are those of Lady Marigold.   Wild with desire to possess her, the preacher signs Lucifer's book, forswearing God and cursing the New England colony.   The demon then places her hand in his as they sing of the wine of life.

Act IV   *The Village.   Night.*   Samoset and his braves have attacked and set fire to the settlement.   The first part of Bradford's curse has come true.   As the colonists bemoan their ruined homes, he staggers in.   When they ask him to pray for them, he confesses his sin and shows the mark of Satan on his brow.   Marigold enters bemoaning Gower; she swoons at Bradford's confession.   The enraged Puritans are for stoning them both, but Bradford forestalls human punishment by seizing her bodily and, exclaiming, "Come, drain with me the wine of death!" he leaps with her into the flames.

Recorded music: baritone solo (by Lawrence Tibbett).   " 'Tis an earth defiled"; and a suite including the overture, children's dances, Love Duet, prelude to Act II, and Maypole Dances.

GIAN-CARLO MENOTTI

Menotti offers another example of a foreign-born composer whose work is identified with America.   Born in Milan, Italy, July 7, 1911, he came here when seventeen and became a naturalized citizen.   He wrote his own libretti and practically all in English.   He studied composition at the Curtis Institute, Philadelphia, and his first opera, "Amelia Goes to the Ball," was produced there in 1937.   "The Old Maid and the Thief," a radio novelty, came in 1939.   Other operas: "The Island God" (1942), "The Medium" (1946), "The Telephone" (1947), "The Consul" (1950).

AMELIA GOES TO THE BALL

(Amelia al Ballo.) Opera buffa in One Act. Music and book by
Menotti. First produced at the Curtis Institute, Philadelphia, April 1,
1937. At the Metropolitan, New York, March 3, 1938.

SCENE: Milan.
TIME: The Nineties.

CAST   AMELIA, *a society lady* (Muriel Dickson).
HER HUSBAND (John Brownlee).
HER LOVER (Mario Chamlee).
A FRIEND (Helen Olheim).
THE CHIEF OF POLICE (Norman Cordon).
THE COOK (Lucielle Browning).
THE MAID (Charlotte Symons).

ARGUMENT   An amusing little farce set to sparkling music.
The story concerns the burning desire of Amelia
to go to a certain dance. All other considerations are secondary.
When the curtain rises, the lady is seen making her toilet. Her husband impatiently awaits her. He is in party dress, but visibly unhappy;
he has discovered a compromising note written by another admirer to
his wife. She brushes his complaints aside. When he insistently demands the name of her lover, she agrees to tell him, provided their plans
for the evening are unchanged. But when she confesses that it is a man
living in an apartment upstairs, her irate husband dashes out armed
with a pistol to shoot him. Amelia is distraught, not at the coming
encounter, but because it may interfere with the ball. The young man
lets himself down on a rope and pleads with her to elope with him, but
she replies, "some time next week." The husband rushes in, tries to
shoot, his gun jams, and the two men decide to talk things over. In a
huff, Amelia hits her husband over the head with a vase and knocks him
out. Her shrieks bring the Police Chief and his men. To explain
away the situation, Amelia tells him that the young man is a burglar
who has assaulted her husband. He is taken into custody—but the lady
still weeps and wails. When the Chief finds that her grief is occasioned
by the fact that she will now not be able to go to the ball, he gallantly
says that he will escort her there, himself.

A joyous, bubbling overture sets the mood for the piece, which is in
the best traditions of the old opera buffa. Since both plot and score
were by the composer, he has welded genuinely comic situations with
melodious interludes. The climactic scene, for example, where Amelia

smashes the vase over her husband's head is so cleverly managed in the
score that even those familiar with it would get an added thrill.   The
piece may be described as a satire on womankind, midway between
"Cosi fan Tutte" and "The Secret of Suzanne."   It should also be noted
that Menotti wrote his story originally in Italian.   It was translated
into English by George Mead, and so sung.

THE ISLAND GOD

Tragic Opera in One Act and Three Scenes.   Music and libretto by
Menotti.   English text by Fleming McLeish.   Metropolitan, New
York, February 20, 1942.

> SCENE: an island in the Mediterranean.
> TIME: the present.

> CAST   ILO, *a fugitive* (Leonard Warren).
> TELEA, *his wife* (Astrid Varnay).
> LUCA, *a fisherman* (Raoul Jobin).
> A GREEK GOD (Norman Cordon).
> VOICE OF A FISHERMAN (John Carter).

ARGUMENT   This work has been described as more truly a
cantata, than an opera.   There is very little action and Virgil Thomson, in the New York *Herald Tribune,* remarks
that the composer "proved in 'Amelia' his sense of theatrical values,
but he has not proved in 'The Island God' that he can do without a
plot."
   Through the sea fog an exhausted pair stumble on to a desolate seashore.   They are Ilo, a fugitive, and his wife, Telea, fleeing from oppression in their native land.   Ilo finds the ruins of a temple, and calls
upon an unknown god to come and help him restore it.   The god
answers his summons and together they begin work.   The stage setting
remains in succeeding scenes.   In the second scene, Luca, a fisherman,
enters and finding Telea alone tells her that he is ready to bring aid to
them, but Ilo on his return declines it.   In the third scene, Luca and
Telea, now lovers, are fearful of Ilo, who is still busied with his work on
the temple.   Telea prompted by Luca throws a net over Ilo's head and
the two bind him up in it, then flee.   The wrathful Ilo reproaches
his god, only to learn that the deity is afraid of him; he only exists
through the faith of Ilo.   The latter throws down the altar—and man
and god perish together.
   The music interprets the stormy mood of the story, with much blaring
of brass and heavy orchestration.

THE OLD MAID AND THE THIEF

Musical farce in One Act. Music and book by Menotti. First pro-
duced as a radio operetta, an innovation, by the National Broadcasting
Company, April 22, 1939. First stage performance by Philadelphia
Opera Company, February 11, 1941.

SCENE: An American cottage.
TIME: The present.

CAST   MISS TODD, *an old maid* (Contralto).
      LAETITIA, *a servant* (Soprano).
      BOB, *a tramp* (Baritone).
      MISS PINKERTON, *a village gossip* (Soprano).

ARGUMENT   The subtitle of this humorous skit well describes
the theme: "How a virtuous woman made a thief
of an honest man." Miss Todd, a spinster, and her pert maid, Laetitia,
are tired of living alone. When Bob, a harmless tramp, seeks shelter,
they ask no questions, telling the neighbors that he is a cousin from
Australia. Miss Pinkerton, a village gossip, thinks differently and
spreads the word that he is an escaped convict. Despite the ugly rumor, Miss Todd and Laetitia are much taken with the man and wait
on him hand and foot. When he asks for a drink, Miss Todd, though
a temperance leader, raids a liquor store. The theft is laid to the
tramp, though he is innocent. He learns that the police are on his
trail, so resolves that if he is to be labelled a thief, he might as well be
one. He ransacks Miss Todd's house and runs away with Laetitia.

THE MEDIUM

Tragic Opera in Two Acts. Music and book by Menotti. First
produced at the Brander Matthews Theatre, Columbia University,
May 8, 1946; next by the Ballet Society at the Heckscher Theatre, New
York, in conjunction with "The Telephone," by the same composer,
May 1, 1947. The two operas then went to the Ethel Barrymore
Theatre for a successful run.

SCENE: Parlor of a spiritist medium.
TIME: The present.

CAST   MADAME FLORA, *a medium* (Contralto).
      MONICA, *her daughter* (Soprano).
      TOBY, *a deaf-mute*.
      MR. and MRS. GOBINEAU; MRS. NOLAN; *clients*.

ARGUMENT   Although in two acts, the plot runs consecutively
in the parlor of Madame Flora, a spiritist me-
dium. With the aid of her two confederates, Monica, her daughter,
and a deaf-and-dumb boy, Toby, she holds fraudulent seances and
fleeces her clients. Toby despite his handicap has fallen deeply in love
with Monica. During one of the spirit manifestations, the medium
herself is terrified by feeling a clammy hand reaching out and stran-
gling her. She screams, the hand ceases its grip, and in her terror she
tells her clients it is all a fraud. They refuse to believe her confession,
but she now thinks the trick was done by Toby and her life is in danger. She beats the boy unmercifully, in spite of Monica's pleas in his
behalf, which only enrage her further. He is turned out of the house.
Flora tries to find solace in drink, falls into a stupor, and Toby returns
to seek Monica. Her mother, partially sobered but still in a frenzy of
fright, draws a revolver and fires into the screen which has been a backdrop for her seances. There is a crash and the body of Toby tumbles
out and sinks at her feet.

THE TELEPHONE

Musical farce in One Act. Music and book by Menotti. First produced by the Ballet Society at the Heckscher Theatre, New York, May
1, 1947, as a curtain-raiser for "The Medium."

CAST   LUCY (Soprano).
BEN (Baritone).

ARGUMENT: Ben is in despair because his lady love is so ad-
dicted to the telephone; the line is always busy.
If he calls on her, he has no time to pop the question, for the phone
interrupts. At last he calls her number from the neighborhood booth,
luckily gets her, and she accepts him. He is going on a business trip,
but makes a note of her number and tells her that he will ring her up
every day. Presumably the course of true love then runs smoothly.

THE CONSUL

Musical Drama in Three Acts. Music and book by Menotti. Produced at the Ethel Barrymore Theatre, March 15, 1950.

SCENE: A city in Europe.
TIME: The present.

CAST   JOHN SOREL (Conell MacNeil).
MAGDA, *his wife* (Patricia Norway).

THE MOTHER (Marie Powers).
CHIEF POLICE AGENT (Leon Lishner).
FIRST POLICE AGENT (Chester Watson).
SECOND POLICE AGENT (Donald Blackey).
NIKA NAGADOFF (Andrew McKinley).
THE SECRETARY (Gloria Lane).

ARGUMENT Although titled a Musical Drama, this is Opera and an excellent example of American work. The action is laid "somewhere in Europe," but it is sung in English. The plot is simplicity itself, the harrowing struggle of a wife to join her husband by obtaining a visa in a consulate—an ironical commentary on official brutality and redtape. The Consul himself never appears, but the spirit of the office is represented by a careless and unsympathetic Secretary.

Act I The scenes in this and later acts shift from a shabby apartment to the consulate and back again. The acts are connected by musical interludes and the entire action takes place within a few weeks. John Sorel is a fugitive trying to escape the toils of the police and begin life anew in a land of freedom, presumably America. The police watch his home. In the first scene a crash of tools reveals him hiding from them. He tells his wife, Magda, that he will try to communicate with her, but she is fearful. She goes to the consulate repeatedly in an effort to get her much-prized visa, but is put off indifferently by the Secretary and given endless forms to fill out.

Act II *A month later, evening.* The Grandmother sings a lullaby to Magda's baby who is dying. Later both infant and Grandmother die. Magda has a strange dream where John comes in with his "loving sister"—but she resembles the Secretary and has evil features. After she awakes, the Chief of Police enters with brutal questioning. After her child's death, Magda goes again to the consulate. A fantastic interlude is seen, where a magician and hypnotist, Nika, casts a spell over all present and they imagine themselves in a ballroom and dance wildly until the Secretary coldly stops them and tells them to get their papers ready. The magician rapidly pulls a rabbit and other gim- cracks from his clothing, but no official papers.

Act III Magda is warned that she must at all cost prevent her husband from communicating with her, or all is lost. But it is too late. The police have been tipped off and are keeping close watch. Magda makes a last desperate attempt to get aid from the consulate, only again to be thwarted by the Secretary who tells her airily that her case will be attended to "in the morning." As she returns home, her telephone rings repeatedly; she knows the answer; it must be her husband who is in custody. "I never meant to do this!" she moans and turns on the gas in her stove. The final suicide scene occupies fifteen minutes of slow music by the orchestra, some singing, and choreography. The dream of a happier land and the constant frustration and final tragedy are admirably portrayed by the score.

PART TWO

LIGHT OPERA

AND

MUSICAL COMEDY

INTRODUCTORY NOTE

In the last edition of my *Opera Synopses* I made a new departure in the inclusion of a separate section devoted to Light Opera. It was so well received that it was followed, in 1936, with an entire volume devoted to *Light Opera and Musical Comedy*—a pioneer in its field. Both were offered without apology. I felt and still feel that no study of contemporary music, or even that of the ancients, can ignore this, shall I say, more frivolous field. As John Tasker Howard said at the time: "Highbrowism which debars such refreshing works from consideration as opera is mere snobbishness." And an observation made by Deems Taylor, several years ago, is still pertinent—all the more so since he has been both interpreter and composer of operas in more serious vein:

"The one class of composer whom the American does take seriously is the writer of musical comedy and popular songs, not only because he can make money but because he provides honest, understandable entertainment for man and beast. That, perhaps, is why our light music is the best of its kind in the world. The self-styled music-lover in this country too often brings little genuine comprehension to music. He is likely to be a highbrow with all the mental obtuseness and snobbishness of his class. He divides music into 'popular'—meaning light—and 'classical'—meaning pretentious. Now there is good music and bad, and the composer's pretensions have little to do with the case. Compare, for example, the first-act finale of Victor Herbert's 'Mlle. Modiste' with such vulgar rubbish as *Donna e mobile*. Yet because the last is sung by tenors of the Metropolitan the highbrow solemnly catalogues it as 'classical'—abolishing the work of Herbert, Berlin, and Kern, three greatly gifted men, with the adjective, 'popular.' " [*]

A difficulty encountered at the outset lay in the definition of terms. What is Grand Opera? What, Light? And Light Opera in latter years has merged into another, more popular medium, Musical Comedy. This last is so ephemeral, so fruitful, that the problem of selection is extremely difficult. I clip this remark from a theatrical review of some years ago: " 'Mexicana' may be classed with the thousand-and-one pieces

---

[*] From *Civilization in the United States,* ed. by H. E. Stearns. 1922. Harcourt, Brace & Co.

of its kind that crop up season after season, no one knows from where, run for a few weeks, and then disappear forever." As I scanned the pages of *The Theatre, The Billboard,* and many another chronicle, the old saying kept recurring, "Here today and gone tomorrow." Files of thirty, forty, and fifty years ago teem with references which are now forgotten or unintelligible. And as I write today, there are at least ten musical shows currently playing in New York.

The technical definition of Grand Opera is a composition in which no word is spoken—all is sung. So strict were the French in obeying this rule that they did not admit "Carmen" into Grand Opera, because of a few spoken lines, but relegated it to the Opéra Comique, despite its tragic ending.

Light Opera, as we Americans interpret it, has a happy ending—at least, not a tragic one; it is sentimental, humorous, even frivolous. A good example of the more serious type is De Koven's "Rob Roy." Thence it ranges downward through Musical Comedy—a peculiarly American type—Musical Plays, Extravaganzas, and Revues. The fields overlap bewilderingly. For example, it is hard to make a strict classification of Gershwin's "Of Thee I Sing"—yet it won a Pulitzer prize.

Following the fascinating subject country by country, we find many examples of classical opera which are really Light. All of Mozart's operas—even "Don Giovanni"—might be so listed. In the same land, Lortzing, Flotow, Von Suppé, Johann Strauss, Richard Strauss, and even the mighty Wagner, were among those who essayed the lighter form. The Viennese type with its lilting waltzes is well known.

Light Opera really originated in Italy where crude attempts at comic dialogue punctuated by music, called *Intermezzi,* were offered as early as the sixteenth century. They were curtain-raisers, or interludes to lighten the more serious fare. Later they were styled *Opera Buffa,* and were made use of by the masters as a sort of diversion. Scarlatti, a prolific composer of Grand Opera, wrote a comic skit, in his old age, for his theatre, in which he burlesqued his own lofty manner. This was early in the Eighteenth Century, about the time when Pergolesi was writing his "La Serva Padrona," which won favor also in Paris and London. It was produced in England only a few years after John Gay brought out his "Beggar's Opera." And, to complete the record, "La Serva Padrona" was resurrected a few years ago by the Metropolitan with renewed success after all these years. It was like a salute from one of the early masters of Light Opera to the composers of today!

Each land has its own characteristic reactions to the lighter form. In Germany, the sentimental opera, or that of Viennese type. In Russia, folk lore. In England, the Ballad Opera. In America, a little bit of everything, with emphasis on Musical Comedy. I have traced these nationalistic trends in separate Prefaces in later pages.

And when considered separately as "Light Opera and Musical Comedy," how rich the prospect! Take a single period in the eighties and nineties when the Savoyards were presenting Gilbert and Sullivan in England, and each successful opera was just as promptly pirated on this side of the water; when Offenbach's and other tuneful French works were put on here with equal success, ably aided and abetted by Lillian Russell, Fanny Rice, Henry Hallam, and the rest; the time also which saw Francis Wilson in "Erminie" setting up a continuous record for all time.

And year by year since the turn of the present century, the brilliant list—both of operettas and actors—has grown. Yet we have accepted this form of entertainment given so lavishly with little attempt to evaluate it. And meanwhile it has invaded still other fields. It is stepping pridefully into motion pictures, and the narrow stage of "Naughty Marietta" has expanded to stride the broad Atlantic. Its message throbs in our radio tubes, and the familiar airs become part and parcel of our dinner table and our evening hour. It is knocking at the door with television. Light Opera is in the air and on the air!

GERMANY AND AUSTRIA

HISTORICAL PREFACE

Since composers in Germany and Austria use a common tongue, and their works are produced without regard to politics or boundaries, they are considered jointly, for convenience. Although there was no definite school of light opera, as in Italy and France, Teutonic composers turned easily and naturally to the gayer moods, and we find such moods infiltrated through the whole fabric of their music. Mozart, an Austrian, despite the poverty and tragedy of his life, turned so naturally to the light and graceful that he might easily have become a true composer of Comic Opera. Two of his works which we list in succeeding pages illustrate this trend. His "Marriage of Figaro" might well be included also; while his "Don Giovanni," despite the latent tragedy of its theme, is likewise treated in comic vein. Beethoven's "Fidelio" and Weber's "Der Freischütz" lean to the romantic rather than the tragic.

With the beginning of the Nineteenth Century, advance is rapid in both schools. Taking them in chronological order, and referring the reader to later pages for further details, we have: Lortzing, who wrote seven or more lighter operas which have lived for the succeeding hundred years; Nicolai, who was Director of Opera in Berlin about 1850 and among others wrote "The Merry Wives of Windsor"; Flotow, of the immortal "Martha"; Von Suppé, who has often been compared with Offenbach of France both for the large volume of his operatic works and the profound influence that he exerted; Genée, who is better known as librettist than composer, but who yet produced the score of "Nanon" and other meritorious works; and Cornelius, "The Barber of Bagdad." All these men were born within the first quarter of this magnificent century!

And we have merely begun. In the year 1825 came Johann Strauss, the "Waltz King," who was born "into the purple" as his father had been a famous composer. Johann began his remarkable career at nineteen and, in middle life at the height of his fame as writer of dance melodies, he turned to Comic Opera with equal success. His works, such as "The Bat" and "The Queen's Lace Handkerchief," became as popular in America as at home.

Goldmark, who was a Hungarian, is known abroad for one Light Opera, "The Cricket on the Hearth." Smetana, a Czech, is included here, since his "Bartered Bride" first achieved wider recognition in the German tongue. Victor Nessler was widely heard in his native Germany fifty years ago, but only one or two of his works remain on the boards—"The Piper of Hamelin" and "The Trumpeter of Säkkingen." Millöcker was one of the operatic princes of his time, earning a fortune with his "Beggar Student" and a dozen others which were as eagerly heard in London and New York, as in Vienna. Brüll wrote "The Golden Cross." And this brings us only to the half-way mark, in point of births, in this prolific Nineteenth Century.

Meanwhile, that greatest of figures in German Opera, Richard Wagner, was in his heyday. And let it be noted that one of his epoch-marking operas is generally listed as "Comic"—"Die Meistersinger." It is one that the present writer has heard many times and loves; yet it is not included in these pages, for despite its overwhelming melody it has seemed more—shall we say—like an elephant walking across the stage. For all his towering genius, Wagner was not of Light Opera stamp.

Richard Strauss of later years, whose works have left an important impress, enters the Light Opera zone with his graceful "Rosenkavalier." Humperdinck's fairy opera, "Hänsel and Gretel," also qualifies.

In recent years we come to a group of younger men whose scores run from operetta to musical comedy. Several such are listed: Reinhardt, with his tuneful "Spring Maid"; Lehar, who set the capitals of the world to whistling and singing with his "Merry Widow"; Oscar Straus, who wrote Viennese waltzes in classic style, then gave us the delicious "Chocolate Soldier"; Leo Fall, who wrote "The Dollar Princess"; and Emmerich Kalman, a Hungarian, who has written delightful Gypsy and folk music in "Sari."

The foregoing is not offered as a full list. Enough has been shown, however, to illustrate that the lighter trend of musical thought, in Germany, has easily kept pace with the more serious mood. It has been a full and constantly flowing stream which has gladdened the heart of the world.

WOLFGANG A. MOZART

Mozart was "a genius by the grace of God" and, though cut off at an untimely age, left a profound influence upon both Grand and Light Opera. His touch was never heavy; and in order to emphasize this side of his genius, we have included two lighter works in this section.

THE SERAGLIO

(Or, "The Elopement from the Seraglio.") Comic Opera in Three Acts. Music by Mozart. Book by Lentzner, adapted by other hands. A "command" opera produced before Emperor Joseph II, at the National Theatre, Vienna, in 1782.

SCENE: The Palace of Pasha Selim, on the Bosphorus.
TIME: The Eighteenth Century.

CAST PASHA SELIM (*speaking part*). OSMIN, *his gardener* (Basso). BELMONTE, *betrothed to Constance.* PEDRILLO, *his manservant, temporarily in the suite of Constance* (Baritone). CONSTANCE, *a Christian lady held captive by the Pasha* (Soprano). BLONDE, *her maid* (Soprano). Janissaries, Ladies of the Harem, etc.

ARGUMENT The plot of this little opera is extremely simple, the action brisk and gay. Mozart is said to have had a share in the libretto. Light as it is, "The Seraglio" may be regarded as a beginning of the German school, a definite break from conventions.

Act I Belmonte is seeking everywhere for his sweetheart, Constance, who is being held by Selim. Belmonte lurks about the latter's garden, but is thwarted by Osmin, the steward of Selim's estate. Then Pedrillo, Belmonte's man, brings him news. While Selim strives vainly to win Constance's affection, Belmonte seeks entrance in the guise of a workman; but the suspicious Osmin will not let him in.

The music includes: an aria, "Here shall I see you"; aria, "Who a love has found"; duet, "Confounded be you and your song"; chorus, "Sing to the great Bassa"; aria by Constance, "O forgive!"; and a trio, "March!"

Act II Blonde, Constance's maid, repulses Osmin. Constance implores her to help her out of her own predicament. Later, Pedrillo, who is the maid's suitor, comes to aid the plot. He gets Osmin drunk and out of the way.

Music: aria, "By tenderness"; aria, "Sorrow is my lot"; aria, "What happiness!"; drinking song, "Live, Bacchus!"; and quartet, "Oh, Belmonte, oh, my life!"

Act III Belmonte succeeds in effecting the escape of Constance; but Pedrillo and Blonde are caught by Osmin, as he regains sobriety. The other two lovers are brought in by the guard. Selim recognizes Belmonte as the son of an ancient enemy, and at first orders his execution; then moved by the sorrow of the lovers he forgives them, and all four are set at liberty.

The musical numbers include: a song by Belmonte, "When tears of joy"; song by Pedrillo, "Captive in the land of the Moors"; song by Osmin, "Ho, how I triumph!"; duet, "Oh, what a fate!"; and finale, "Never will I thy kindness forget."

COSI FAN TUTTE

(Co'-see fan too'-tee)

(They all do it; also known as "The School for Lovers.") Comic Opera in Three Acts. Music by Mozart. Book by Da Ponte. Given as a "command" performance for Emperor Joseph II of Austria, at the Court Theatre, Vienna, January 26, 1790. At the Metropolitan, New York, March 24, 1922.

SCENE: Naples.

TIME: The Eighteenth Century.

CAST ISIDORA (Soprano) *and* DORABELLA (Mezzo-Soprano), *two sisters from Ferrara.* DESPINA, *their maid* (Soprano). FERNANDO, *officer, in love with Dorabella* (Tenor). GRATIANO, *officer, in love with Isidora* (Basso). DON ALFONSO, *a cynical philosopher* (Baritone).

ARGUMENT This sparkling opera was a "command" performance, produced for the Emperor Joseph II of Austria, to whom Mozart had been appointed "Kammer-Musicus" in 1787. Unfortunately the Emperor died less than a month after its first performance, his successor had no taste for music, and Mozart reaped no benefit.

Act I The Scene of this Act is frequently shifted. The action opens in a café of Naples; then goes to a garden by the sea; then to the home of Isidora and Dorabella. The cynical Don Alfonso wagers with Fernando and Gratiano that the constancy of the two ladies with whom they are in love would be susceptible of attack. They vigorously deny this slur. Very well then, says the Don, let them place themselves at his orders and keep their eyes open. The Don then informs the ladies that their suitors have received marching orders, and must depart for the front without delay. A touching scene of farewell follows: the ladies, with many tears, vow eternal fidelity; the gentlemen are equally fervent: Don Alfonso looks on with a grim smile. Hardly have the two officers disappeared than Despina, who is in the plot, introduces two "foreign" gentlemen, who immediately begin to pay exaggerated court to Isidora and Dorabella. They are, of course, Fernando and Gratiano in disguise. Being repelled, they pretend, in their despair, to take poison, and to be on the point of death. Despina, disguised as a doctor, restores them to life by mesmerism. The music, following a lively overture, bubbles and sparkles throughout.

Act II The Scene is laid in the house and garden of the two sisters. The "foreigners" are still importunate. The ladies begin to waver. As a token of her regard Dorabella gives the disguised Gratiano, actually her sister's lover, a locket in the shape of a heart. It contains a portrait of Fernando; but what of that? Isidora, too, relents. The impetuous "foreigners" demand that a Notary shall be sent for, to draw up the marriage contract without delay. The Notary arrives; it is the versatile Despina in another disguise. The contract is drawn up and a banquet is made ready. Then in comes Don Alfonso with the startling news that Fernando and Gratiano are on their way home, and may arrive at any moment. The "foreigners" beat a hasty retreat, the "Notary" conceals "himself" as best he can. And lo! here are Fernando and Gratiano, returned from the wars, and much intrigued at the state of affairs which they discover. They seize the marriage contract; they drag forth the "Notary"; then they rush off to look for the impudent rivals whose names they have found in the contract.

To the no small astonishment of the ladies, Despina now throws off her disguise. But their astonishment is greater still when Fernando and Gratiano come in, speaking and acting for all the world like the "foreigners" of whom they had gone—or pretended to go—in pursuit. Soon the tangle is unravelled. Don Alfonso has assuredly won his wager! However, he succeeds in reconciling the lovers, for, as he remarks with tongue in cheek, it really is no use to be angry with women for flirting. *Cosi fan tutte*—"they all do it!" In a later version, the ladies are shown as cognizant to the plot, and carry it on to its climax in order to shame their doubting lovers. The music again is light, without any outstanding numbers, save a difficult aria sung by Despina, "Would a maid be worth the winning?"

Recorded music: overture; "In nomini, in soldati" (Bori); "Come scoglio in moto resta" (Ina Souez); "Un aura amorosa" (Patzak); "Ei parte, senti," recitative, and the aria, "Per pieta, ben mio."

ALBERT LORTZING

Lortzing, although little known in this country, is a household name in Germany. He is recognized there as their light opera composer par excellence. He is master of airy, graceful themes and sparkling situations. Lortzing was born in Berlin, October 23, 1803, and died in the same city, January 20, 1851. His seven principal operas have had frequent revivals in Germany. The most popular are "Czar and Carpenter," "Undine," "The Poacher," and "The Armorer."

CZAR AND CARPENTER

(Czar und Zimmerman, or The Two Peters.) A Comic Opera in Three Acts, both music and libretto being written by Albert Lortzing. It was composed for Christmas, 1837. Produced at Berlin, in 1839.

CAST   PETER I, *the Czar of Russia, traveling under the incognito of* PETER MICHAELOFF, *a carpenter.* PETER IVANOFF, *a journeyman carpenter.* VAN BETT, *the Burgomaster of Sardam.* MARIE, *his niece.* GENERAL LEFORT, *Russian Ambassador.* LORD SYNDHAM, *English Ambassador.* MARQUIS DE CHATEAUNEUF, *French Ambassador. The Widow* BROWN. Others.

ARGUMENT   The scene of this amusing piece is Sardam; the time, 1698. The story relates to an adventure of Peter the Great, who liked to visit foreign ports incognito, and incidentally learn shipbuilding. At Sardam he meets up with another carpenter, Peter Ivanoff, who is somewhat of a rascal. The latter is in love with Marie, the Burgomaster's daughter. She is a flirt and likes to arouse his jealousy. In order to further his cause, he pretends to be the Czar in hiding. Meanwhile, ambassadors of other powers get wind of the real Czar's presence. With this as the initial situation, a lively contretemps results; but all ends satisfactorily in true comic opera fashion.

Musical numbers: Act I. chorus of carpenters, "Comrades, grasp the axe"; aria, "Jealousy is a plague"; Burgomaster's song ending, "I am wise, no one deceives me"; duet, "Shall I make a full confession?"; finale,

"The people gather to the festival." Act II. wedding chorus, "Long live joy!"; song by tenor, "Farewell, my girl of Flanders"; sextet, "The work that we begin"; Marie's bridal song, "Charming blushes tinge my cheek"; finale, "For some time have I seen strange faces." Act III. Burgomaster's song, "Hail the day"; Peter's song, "Once I played with the sceptre"; duet, "May a lonely maid dare?"; chorus, "To greet our Hero."

UNDINE

Fairy Opera in Four Acts. Words and Music by Lortzing, after the well-known tale by Fouqué. Hamburg, 1845.

Hugo von Ringstetten, a knight errant, meets Undine, a village maiden. They become mutually attracted, and the knight weds her. Undine then confesses that she has no soul; she belongs to a race of water sprites, or "Undines." She can obtain her soul only on considera-tion that her husband remains true to her. He promises this fidelity, but has previously been favored by the Duke's daughter, who tries once more to win his affections. She succeeds temporarily and Undine is forced to descend to the watery regions. Although haunted by remorse, the Knight feels in duty bound to wed the Duke's daughter; but on the night of the wedding, Undine reappears; he is drawn irresistibly into her arms; and they go together to the fairy kingdom below the sea.

The music has a pleasing, haunting quality, with some excellent numbers. In the First Act we hear a quintet and chorus, "What joy, what rapture!"; song by Hugo, "I rode to the lists"; duet and chorus, "The capital is well known"; chorus, "It is wine!" In the Second Act: a duet, "What do I see?"; recitative by Undine, "Know there are beings like you"; quartet, "Overcome with fright"; a ballet and romanza, "There lives on the shore"; and finale, "Miscreant, how dare you!" In the Third Act: chorus, "Drink merrily"; song, "Father, mother, have I none"; duet, "I will not leave thee"; song by Undine, "What do I see?"; and song by the water spirit, Kühleborn, "It is performed!" The Fourth Act: a lovers' duet, "In my young days"; drinking song, "Fill the beakers"; and final denunciatory song by Kühleborn, "You have sinned!"

THE ARMORER

(Der Waffenschmied.) Comic Opera in Three Acts. Words and music by Lortzing. Leipzig, 1846.

An amusing sketch of mistaken identities, the time being the Sixteenth Century, the scene Worms. The Count von Liebenau is in love with Mary, the pretty daughter of an armorer, Stadinger, and in order to win her, takes service in the shop under the name of Conrad. He woos her first as a Count, and then as a smithy. Mary thinks the Count's estate too high for her, but confesses her love for Conrad. The Count pretends to be jealous; and the armorer favors neither man; he has picked out another, George, who is actually the Count's servant. The confusion of persons and interests waxes furious until the Count, to end the matter, pretends to attack the house. The armorer is forced to yield up his daughter, and great is his surprise as well as that of Mary, to learn that the Count and the smithy are one and the same person.

A chorus of journeymen opens the opera, "Sparkle, flame! Glow, iron!," followed by song by armorer, "Bring quickly hat and coat"; aria, "We are born only once"; aria, "I am dissatisfied with the world"; trio, "In nightly darkness"; and Mary's song at close, "He is so good." In the Second Act: a duet, "You know he loves you"; sextet, "The man seems to be witless"; duet, "You are an industrious fellow"; song with chorus, "A Young Popinjay"; and finale, "His cheeks are reddened with anger." In the Third Act: song by Mary, "We poor girls"; chorus, "Good that I meet you"; song, "I also was a youth"; and closing song with chorus, "Gladly gave I riches and power."

OTTO NICOLAI

Although dying at the age of thirty-nine, Otto Nicolai was greatly esteemed in his own land, Germany, for his light operas and other compositions. He was born in Königsberg, June 9, 1810, and died in Berlin, May 11, 1849. He studied in Italy and for a time was Court Capellmeister in Vienna, where he founded the Philharmonic Society, in 1842. Five years later he was called to Berlin to be Director of Opera. His most important operas are: "Der Templer" (1840), "Die Heimkehr des Verbannen" (1842), and his masterpiece, "The Merry Wives of Windsor," the first performance of which was given only two months before his death.

THE MERRY WIVES OF WINDSOR

Comic Opera in Three Acts. Music by Nicolai. Book by Mosenthal, after the play by Shakespeare. Berlin, March 9, 1849. New York, April 27, 1863.

CAST Sir John Falstaff. Fenton. Shallow. Slender. Doctor Caius. Ford. Mistress Ford. Page. Mistress Page. Anne Page. Others.

ARGUMENT This story follows fairly closely the play of Shakespeare, so does not need retelling here. The scene is Windsor, England; the time, the Seventeenth Century. It is chiefly concerned with the misadventures of the amorous Sir John at the hands of the merry wives; the romantic interludes being supplied by the love affair of Anne and Fenton.

The music well describes and enlivens the comic situations. In the First Act we find Mistress Ford and Mistress Page splitting their sides over letters received by both from Falstaff. (Duet: "This is really too bad!") There is a tender duet between Fenton and Anne: "If your soul has ever felt." An aria by Mrs. Ford: "Mirth and jollity are the spice of life," sung in the florid, Italian style, follows. The Act ends dramatically with sextet and chorus, after Mrs. Ford flies into a rage at her husband for suspecting her honor.

The Second Act opens with a lively drinking song by Falstaff and his followers. When one of them falls under the table dead drunk, the music changes into a mock dirge as they carry him off. A spirited buffo duet follows between the knight and Ford, wherein Falstaff relates his mishap in the clothes hamper. The only other number of consequence is the tender aria by Fenton, "Hark, the lark in yonder grove!"

In the last Act, which is short, there is a delightful trio sung by the two women plotters and Falstaff, "The bell has pealed the midnight chime"; a ballad, "Of Herne, the hunter, a legend old"; and the lovely fairy ballet and chorus which concludes the opera, "About, ye elves!"

FRANZ VON SUPPÉ

Von Suppé has been often compared with Offenbach because of his fecundity and wide popularity in his own country. Each is a force to be reckoned with in the development of Light Opera, although most of their work is now tradition. Von Suppé was born in Dalmatia, April 18, 1820. Again like Offenbach, he was the director of several theaters, which served as the vehicle of his works. He wrote no less than one hundred and sixty operas, operettas, vaudeville skits, and the like. His first success, "Das Mädchen vom Lande," brought out in Vienna in 1847, is now forgotten. A musical comedy, "Paragraph 3" (1858), brought him his first wide fame. Thereafter works poured from his fertile brain and pen. Some of the best were: "Die Afrikareise," "Bellman," "Fatinitza," "Franz Schubert," "Leichte Kavallerie," "Vineta," "Donna Juanita," "Das Pensionat," "Boccaccio," "Pique Dame"; and the shorter operettas, "Flotte Bursche," and "Die Schöne Galathea." He composed several overtures, one being that of the "Poet and Peasant," which despite its florid style still remains popular. Von Suppé died in Vienna, May 22, 1893.

THE BEAUTIFUL GALATEA

(Die Schöne Galathea.)   Comic Opera in Two Acts.   Music by Von Suppé.   Book by Zell and Genée.   Vienna, 1865.

A well-known tale of mythology has here been turned into a clever operetta; both story and music combining to form one of the brightest pieces of its time.

The sculptor, Pygmalion, has been at work for months on his masterpiece, the statue of a lovely woman. He ends by falling in love with it. One day while he is absent from his studio, Ganymede, his servant, brings the art patron, Midas, in to see the work. He offers to buy it, but Pygmalion spurns the offer and is indignant that any eyes save his should have seen "Galatea." Now that she has been violated by other eyes, he is ready to destroy the statue, but a song of choristers stays his hand. Instead, he prays Venus to imbue the lovely figure with life. The goddess does so, and the awakening Galatea sees the sculptor first, and loves him.

In the Second Act, while Galatea is gathering flowers in the garden, Ganymede enters. The fickle girl transfers her affections to him. Then the wealthy Midas enters, and recognizing her, offers her jewels. While she accepts his gifts, she refuses his attentions, but dallies coquettishly. Pygmalion watches her actions; his own love turns to disgust; and he prays Venus to turn her back into stone. Venus does so, and the lovely Galatea, now impervious marble, is sold to Midas.

FATINITZA

Comic Opera in Three Acts. Music by Von Suppé. Book by Zell and Genée. Vienna, January 5, 1876. Adapted to American stage by Harry B. Smith—who also adapted "Boccaccio"—and the two were then considered "among the best comic operas ever written." Fritzi Scheff starred.

Vladimir Samoiloff, a Russian officer, masquerades in woman's attire under the name of Fatinitza, and meets the General Kantschakoff, who falls desperately in love with the fair one. Vladimir gets away from the General, and meets with the latter's niece, Lydia. The two fall in love, but only after a variety of amusing complications and the General has been assured that Fatinitza has died of a broken heart through separation from him, the old man consents to the union of his niece with Fatinitza's "brother," Vladimir.

Among the musical numbers are: First Act, Vladimir's song, "Lost is the dream that bound me"; the General's entrance in pompous vein, "Thunder! Lightning! Who goes there?"; Lydia's sleighing song, "When the snow a veil is flinging"; and a humorous quartet, "Not a look shall tell"; Second Act, chorus, "Washing, dressing"; duet, "New doubts, new fears"; sextet, " 'Tis well"; and the famous Bell Sextet, "Silver tinkling"; Last Act, Lydia's bell song, "Chime, ye bells"; trio, "Again, Love, we meet"; and a brilliant finale, "Joy, joy, joy to the bride!" The famous March Trio, which was "played the world over," was an afterthought and was placed in the score in one of the final rehearsals.

BOCCACCIO

Light Opera in Three Acts. Music by Von Suppé. Book by Zell and Genée. Carl Theatre, Vienna, February 1, 1879. Comedy Theatre, London, April 22, 1882 (106 performances). In an American adaptation by Harry B. Smith, Fritzi Scheff starred. This opera had the distinction of being presented in the original at the Metropolitan, New York, January 2, 1931, with Maria Jeritza as "Fiametta."

CAST GIOVANNI BOCCACCIO, *an author*. PIETRO, *Prince of Palermo*. SCALZA, *a barber*. BEATRICE, *his wife*. LOTTERINGHI, *a cooper*. ISABELLA, *his wife*. LAMBERTUCCIO, *a grocer*. PERONELLA, *his wife*. FIAMETTA, *a Florentine girl*. Students, Citizens, Courtiers, Actors in a Pantomime, etc.

ARGUMENT Of the large number of operas and skits produced by this prolific composer, "Boccaccio" has best endured the test of time. Based on the life of a famous writer, as shown in Boccaccio's own book, "L'amoroso Fiametta," the roguery of the scenes is enhanced by characteristic music. The action takes place in Florence, of the Fourteenth Century.

Act I To celebrate the feast of their patron saint, the citizens of Florence rise early and throng the streets. The plots of three beggars are interrupted by the opening chorus, "Joyful day." A street crier enters hawking the latest scandalmongering novel by Boccaccio, much to the indignation of various gentry, who do not like to find their "secret" sins thus unmercifully lampooned. Meanwhile other scandals in real life go on. Scalza, the barber, going home unexpectedly, finds his door closed against him. He summons his wife by a serenade, "Sweet and fair one." Beatrice, the wife, has been entertaining Boccaccio and Leonetto, but the three quickly stage a scene to outwit the husband. Beatrice screams for help, while the two gallants fight a pretended duel. They with a group of students sing, "Let the swords flash and clash." After the fake duel is ended amid much laughter, Boccaccio confesses he is in love with a fair unknown. Now comes his chief song telling how he writes his stories, "Yonder stands a comely youth." He ends it with, "I simply write what you dictate."

Fiametta, the girl whom Boccaccio loves, passes by on her way to church, with Peronella. She tells Peronella that she does not wish to wed Pietro, who has been picked out for her by the all-powerful duke, his father. She sings plaintively, "Had I but thy love." When Boccaccio enters, he and she in an interchange of song confess their love for each other. Pietro, who reaches the city about this time, is mistaken for Boccaccio, and the infuriated men whom he has lampooned set upon the innocent Pietro. A male chorus, " 'Tis time to take revenge!" is quite effective here. Pietro is rescued, and the act ends with the citizens consigning the offended books by Boccaccio to the flames.

Act II Boccaccio and Leonetto have taken Pietro under their wing. They sing a serenade under the windows of their respective loves, but much of their banter is satirical. It develops that Pietro has an affair with the cooper's wife. The cooper's song with chorus by his workers is a "striking" piece. After a waltz song by three of the women principals, the cooper, who is befuddled with drink, goes away. Pietro loses no time in calling on Isabella, the wife. The cooper returns unexpectedly, and Pietro takes refuge inside a barrel. On being discovered, Isabella states that the gentleman has just bought the barrel and is examining it from the inside.

Amid other nonsense Boccaccio contrives to meet Fiametta; they with Pietro and Isabella sing an ensemble beginning, " 'Tis useless that I try." Fiametta, who proves to be the illegitimate daughter of the duke, is summoned to the palace. The act closes in a riot of song and action; the men who are still pursuing the luckless Boccaccio again being out-witted by him and his friends, who disguise themselves as devils.

Act III Prince Pietro summons Boccaccio to court, and informs him that he, Pietro, is to wed Fiametta; and furthermore that he will take Isabella along as a lady's maid. Although the Prince knows that Boccaccio and Fiametta are in love with each other, he requests the poet to write a play in honor of the royal nuptials. Boccaccio hides his own feelings and consents. Meanwhile, he and Fiametta find a mo-ment alone together. She learns for the first time that he is the famous or notorious Boccaccio, and turns away. But he promises her that from that time forth he will only write his novels, and not live them! A duet ensues, "Florence has beautiful women." After a final scornful inter-view with the men who have been pursuing him, Boccaccio sings a waltz song, "My fair Florentine maiden." Then in a pantomime, he shows up the prince's amorous adventures with the cooper's wife. Luckily Pietro can take a joke. He relinquishes Fiametta to the writer, and re-sumes his intrigue with Isabella. A chorus, "Wit, Humor, Truth are his weapons," ends the opera.

DONNA JUANITA

Comic Opera in Three Acts. Music by Von Suppé. Book by Zell and Genée. Vienna, circa 1883. An English version was presented in both England and America, and a new version by Arthur Bodanzky and sung in German at the Metropolitan Opera House, New York, in 1931. Madame Jeritza sang.

The action takes place in 1796, in San Sebastian. Its English gov-ernor, Sir Douglas, an elderly fop, holds as a prisoner of war Gaston du Faure, a young French officer. Gaston has wooed and won Petrita, sister of the innkeeper, Gil Polo. But Sir Douglas himself is making eyes at the young girl; while Lady Olympia, his wife, who in her hey-day was a dancer, strives to win the affections of Gaston. As if this were not enough, Gaston's younger brother, René, comes on the scene. In order to avoid capture, he has disguised himself as a Spanish lass, "Donna Juanita." So successful has been his make-up that more than one officer has tried to make love to him. While he is laughing and talking with his brother, Petrita sees them and becomes wildly jealous.

The Second Act shows a drawing-room in the Mayor's (Pomponio's) palace. Marco, a student, with his friends sings a serenade in honor of the fair Spanish girl. Both the Mayor and the Colonel have hired them to do so. Presently Donna Juanita appears fetchingly attired and while "she" eats a hearty breakfast and tells wonderful stories about her past, the two old Romeos pay her ardent court. Later Juanita attends a meeting of a sisterhood of conspirators made up of aristocratic dames and daughters, and is elected President. "She" tells them that the latest thing in Madrid court circles is for the President to kiss the youngest and fairest of the members. Riego, a public scribe, and Gil Polo, the innkeeper, bring in a company of soldiers disguised as pilgrims, and the Act ends in a wild Spanish dance.

Merrymaking is the keynote of the final act. A festival is being celebrated, an old Spanish custom in which the grown-ups dress and behave as children; and the children as grown-ups. By this time, Gaston and Petrita have become reconciled. In the midst of a ballet, shots are heard offstage. René reveals his identity and tells Sir Douglas that he is a prisoner of the French Army. The French General enters and makes René a lieutenant. Happy songs and dances close this diverting opera.

FRANZ F. R. GENÉE

Franz Friedrich Richard Genée is better known as librettist than composer. With Zell, he wrote numerous books for Millöcker, Von Suppé, and Johann Strauss. He first studied medicine, then turned to music. He was born at Danzig, February 7, 1823, and died at Baden, June 15, 1895. From 1848 to 1867, he was connected with theatres in various parts of Europe. His operas include: "Der Geiger aus Tirol" (1857), "Die Generalprobe" (1868), "Am Runenstein"—with Flotow—(1868), "Der Seekadett" (1876), "Nanon" (1877), and "Die Piraten" (1887).

NANON

Comic Opera in Three Acts. Music by Genée. Book by Zell. Vienna, 1877. New York, the Casino, 1886 (150 times). In the cast were Pauline Hall, Sadie Martinot, and Francis Wilson.

The scene is Paris of the Seventeenth Century. The Golden Lamb is an inn near the city run by Nanon, whose wit and beauty are famed. The Marquis de Marsillac, director of the Royal Theatre, takes his nephew, Hector, out to see her. Thither also goes the famous court beauty, Ninon de l'Enclos, who suspects her own lover, the Marquis d'Aubigné, of being attracted there. Ninon is informed that Nanon is to marry a salesman, Grignan, so returns to the city with her doubts allayed. Grignan, however, is in reality the Marquis, who is planning to abduct her. But after singing a serenade to her, he is surprised into a proposal of marriage. Preparations are made for the ceremony, but the Marquis gets out of it by a trumped-up arrest over a duel.

In the Second Act we see Ninon's sumptuous drawing-room. Several persons known to history are presented in the brilliant group. Among them is the Marquis, who is reproached by the beauty for having been away so long. To cover his confusion, he sings to her the same serenade with which he won the heart of the country lass. The Marquis is jealous of Hector, because he pays court to both Nanon and Ninon, and challenges him to fight. During their absence, Marsillac tries to sing the serenade, but is only laughed at for his pains. Meanwhile, Nanon has entered to secure help from Ninon for her fiancé, Grignan, and is much bewildered by the turn of events. When the young Marquis returns from the duel, he is asked to clear up the mystery of the song. Hector, who has been wounded, is brought in under arrest, but refuses to reveal the name of his opponent.

In the Third Act, Madame de Maintenon receives an Abbé, who sings to her the same serenade in the form of a hymn. The King and his courtiers arrive. Marsillac comes in to obtain pardon for Hector, and the King grants it. Ninon and Nanon both present themselves seeking pardon for the same man, the scapegrace, D'Aubigné. When Louis also grants this, Ninon surrenders it to her rival. But the young Marquis finds that he prefers Nanon, and she becomes the Marchioness d'Aubigné.

The music is light and brilliant. The idea of a repeated serenade was used later by Herbert in his opera of that name. Other numbers are: the minstrel's song, "Ah, what a joyful day!"; some merry drinking songs; Nanon's ballad, "Once before this tavern straying"; the jolly chorus of country cousins; Gaston's ballad, "All that Frenchman"; Hector's song, "Young appearing"; and the brilliant finale.

PETER CORNELIUS

Peter Carl August Cornelius came of notable stock; his father was a noted actor, his grandfather an engraver. Peter was born in Mainz, in 1824, and at first intended to follow in his father's footsteps, but turned aside from acting to poetry and music. In 1852 he came in touch with Liszt, who exerted a profound influence upon his career. With Liszt as conductor, his first opera, "The Barber of Bagdad," was produced at Weimar, in 1858. It was misunderstood and hissed; which made Liszt so indignant that he resigned his position. Later the opera came into its own. In Vienna and Munich Cornelius came in contact with Wagner. His opera, "Le Cid," was produced at Weimar. To "Gunlod" he devoted the last nine years of his life. He died, October 26, 1874. Cornelius was versatile in talent. His poetry ranked high.

THE BARBER OF BAGDAD

Comic Opera in Two Acts. Music by Cornelius. Book by composer. Weimar, December 15, 1858, where at first it was received coldly, but later won success. At the Metropolitan, New York, January 4, 1890.

CAST THE CALIPH. BABA MUSTAPHA, *a cadi.* MARGIANA, *his daughter.* BOSTANA, *a relative.* NUREDDIN, *a noble.* ABUL HASSAN, *a barber.* Others.

Nureddin is very ill and says that only the lovely Margiana can cure him. Bostana brings him the welcome news that the girl will receive him, and the sick man summons the talkative barber to shave him. After a series of musical interludes in which the barber learns all about the love of Nureddin, the barber, who is "swift with his razor but a thousand times quicker with his tongue," sets up such a flow of talk that the lover is distracted.

In the Second Act, an apartment in the cadi's house, Margiana awaits her suitor while her father goes to the mosque to prayer. Now Nureddin comes, but almost at the moment the barber's voice is heard without. "Oh, Allah save us from the flood of his talk!" bewails Nureddin. Worse luck still, the cadi himself returns. The lover takes refuge in a chest. The barber rushes in, thinking that the screams of a servant outside are the death cries of Nureddin. Abul accuses the cadi. The confusion causes a crowd to collect, and the Caliph is summoned. The chest is opened and Nureddin is disclosed, not dead but nearly suffocated. The Caliph then says that this must be the girl's dowry, and asks the cadi to accept the young man as his son-in-law. The barber is seized, but the Caliph pardons him and orders him to come to the palace, to entertain him with stories.

The music throughout is lively and entertaining.

JOHANN STRAUSS

Johann Strauss has come down to fame as the "Waltz King," rather than as operatic composer. He it was who wrote the melodious "Blue Danube," "Wine, Woman, and Song," and a long list of brilliant waltzes which still live. As for his operas, they are now a matter of record, although at the time they vied with his shorter works in popularity. Johann Strauss came of musical stock. His father of same name was famed all over the continent as conductor and composer; and his two brothers were likewise celebrated for their waltz music. The younger Johann was born in Vienna, October 25, 1825, and died there, June 3, 1899. He made his début as conductor at nineteen and spent nearly his whole life in his native city, with the exception of ten years in St. Petersburg. In 1870 at the height of his fame as composer of dance music, he turned aside to writing light operas and operettas. The best known are: "Indigo" (1871), "Die Fledermaus" (1874), "Prince Methusalem" (1877), "Das Spitzentuch der Königen" (1880), "Der Lustige Krieg" (1881), "Eine Nacht in Venedig" (1883), "Der Zigeunerbaron" (1885), "Furstin Ninetta" (1893), "Waldmeister" (1895), and "Die Göttin der Vernunft" (1896). A modernized version of the lives of the Strausses, father and son, "The Great Waltz," with book by Moss Hart (1935) ran for a year in New York and also won wide favor on the road. Performed at St. Louis Municipal Theatre, in 1940.

DIE FLEDERMAUS
(Dee Flay'-der-mouse)

(The Bat.) Comic Opera in Three Acts. Music by Johann Strauss. Book by Haffner and Genée. Adapted from a French "ribald farce" by

Meilhac and Halévy, "Le Reveillon." Vienna, July, 1874. This classic among operettas has had such an extended and varied career, that full explanation is desirable. It has made history in more than one direction. As to title it has been shown under more guises than any other work. It is probably better known in America as "The Bat," a literal translation from the German, than any other. In the original "Fledermaus" version its first showing was coolly received; but its later success was so great that, by 1880, it had been shown on 171 German stages. It was first sung in America at the Thalia Theatre, Brooklyn, October, 1879. It was received in Paris with wild acclaim. Hardly less enthusiastic were the London audiences. In April, 1885, it was sung in New York, in English, the cast including Rosalba Beecher, Ida Valerga, Irene Perry, Agnes Folsom, Mathilde Cottrelly, Charles Plunkett, and DeWolf Hopper. A British version, "Night Birds," was shown at the Lyric, London, 1911. The following year at the Casino, New York, it became "The Merry Countess"; sung 135 times, the cast including Fritzi von Busing and the Dolly Sisters. In 1929, as "A Wonderful Night," it was put on the Majestic stage, New York. As "Champagne Sec," in 1933, at the Morosco, New York. And latest (at this writing!) as "Rosalinda." (See separate entry below.) The 1885 production was under the direction of Heinrich Conreid, at the Casino. The Metropolitan, New York, produced it in February, 1905, and forty-five years later, December 20, 1950, with some interpolations.

ARGUMENT   Baron von Eisenstein is sent to jail for eight days for insulting an official; his lawyer, Doctor Blint, who stutters, being partly responsible for his predicament. Another friend, the Notary Falke, however, induces him to delay his sentence one day in order to go to a ball. Falke had gone to a masquerade disguised as a bat, a few months before, and the Baron had compelled him to go home in broad daylight in this costume; so Falke is still waiting to "get even." The Baron sadly notifies his wife that he is on his way to prison, but, instead, heads for the dance. Rosalinde, his wife, is visited by a young admirer, Alfred, and when Frank, the warden of the prison, comes to the house seeking Eisenstein, Alfred says that he is the man wanted, in order to avoid compromising the lady. Rosalinde then goes masked to the same ball her husband is attending, to get an eye on him. Still more complications ensue, in true comic opera fashion, until all is cleared up. But Falke has had his revenge, and the luckless Baron is compelled to go to jail to serve his sentence.

The music is a gay mixture of waltzes, polkas, and other dance music, interspersed with light but pleasing songs. In the First Act, Alfred sings a serenade, "Dove that has escaped." The Baron, Baroness, and lawyer sing, "Well, with such an attorney." Falke and the Baron sing, "Come with me to the ball." There are also a lively drinking song, and Rosalinde's, "In tête-à-tête with me so late."

In the Second Act: chorus, "The repast is before us"; the host's song, "I love to invite my friends"; the maid, Adele, and chorus, "My dear Marquis"; Hungarian czarda, "Sounds from home"; drinking song, "In the fire stream of the grape"; a ballet, and a waltz finale, "Ha, what joy!"

In the Third Act: Adele's song, "I am an innocent from the country"; trio, "A strange adventure"; and finale, "Oh, Bat, oh, Bat, let thy victim escape!" The overture to this sparkling opera is a favorite number with orchestras.

ROSALINDA

(The Bat.) This latest American version of the Strauss operetta was sponsored by the New Opera Company and shown at the Forty-Fourth Street Theatre, New York, October 28, 1942, for 265 performances. It was adapted from a version of Max Reinhardt, by G. Reinhardt and J. Meehan, Jr. Added lyrics by Paul Kerby.

SCENE: A Vienna Summer Resort.

TIME: 1890.

CAST ALFREDO ALLEVANTO (Everett West). GABRIEL VON EISENSTEIN (Ralph Herbert). ROSALINDA VON EISENSTEIN, *his wife* (Dorothy Sarnoff). ADELE, *her maid* (Virginia MacWatters). FIFI, *her sister* (Shelley Winter). BLINT, *a lawyer* (Leonard Stocker). FALKE, *friend of Eisenstein* (Gene Barry). FRANK, *jail warden* (Paul Best). PRINCE ORLOFSKY, *who likes gay life and the ladies* (Oscar Karlweis). Chorus, Dancers, and others.

ARGUMENT The story follows in general the original, with some modernizations and Americanisms. A Prologue shows the outside of Eisenstein's home, at sunset. The lovelorn suitor of his wife, Rosalinda, sings outside her window.

Act I *The Living-room of the House.* While the Baron is facing jail sentence, his wife is in a pet. She wants to go to a ball. She and her pert maid talk things over. Their lively duet becomes a trio when he joins them in, "Oh, jiminy! How sad it is to part like this!" He would have been sadder, if he had realized that the moment he was gone, Alfredo steps in and makes himself much at home. The latter and Rosalinda sing a "Drinking Song," but their further revelries are interrupted by Frank, who ushers the supposed Baron off to jail.

Act II   *Ballroom of Prince Orlofsky's Palace.* The music ensemble here is much like the original. The Prince cuts a droll figure with his "hit" song, "Each to his own taste, sir. Chacun à son gout!" This is followed by a "Laughing Song." Rosalinda comes to the ball, masked; her maid, Adele, dressed like a fine lady. While the latter plays her part to the distraction of various men, Rosalinda herself is pursued by none other than her husband, the Baron. He becomes so smitten by her charms that, when she pretends to swoon, she gets from him his prized watch. Her aria, "Songs of My Homeland," is delightful. A ballet is followed by the finale to this Act: "The lords in ancient fables," sung by the Prince and Adele; then a chorus, "Champagne is king!"

Act III   *Warden's Office at the Jail.* While the others are merrymaking, Alfredo is paying for his gallantry in jail. An interlude is offered by Adele, in a character skit where she acts and sings, the country girl, the queen, the great lady. The Baron comes disguised as a notary to take Alfredo's confession. There is a comical interplay of emotions as he learns the truth from the unsuspecting prisoner—that Rosalinda is the lady of the interrupted tryst. She also is present, but stays her husband's wrath by producing his watch as evidence of his own philandering. A trio, "Revenge!" and the usual comic-opera reconciliation brings the piece to a pleasant close with, "Your aviary we all agree is certainly a joy to see."

PRINCE METHUSALEM

Comic Opera in Three Acts. Music by Johann Strauss. Vienna, 1877. At the Casino, New York, 1883 (102 performances). In the cast were Mathilde Cottrelly, Lily Post, Julie de Ruyther, Rose Beaudet, Francis Wilson, A. W. Maflin, Jay Taylor, Harry Standish, and Ellis Ryse.

The story is located nowhere in particular and involves two petty rulers, Sigismond and Cyprian. The former's army is small and finances ditto, so he desires to marry his daughter, Pulcinella, to Methusalem, the neighboring prince's son.

There is much more to it, punctuated with lovely choruses, quintets, duets, and arias. Both Pulcinella and Methusalem have excellent opportunities, as for example, the girl's romanza in the Second Act; and the man's martial air, "I'm General here!" with soldiers' chorus, in the last. Francis Wilson scored a "hit" in the topical song, "The Dotlet and I."

THE QUEEN'S LACE HANDKERCHIEF

(Das Spitzentuch der Königin.)   Comic Opera in Three Acts.   Music by Johann Strauss.   Book by Genée and Bohrmann-Riegen.   Vienna, October 2, 1880.   Casino, New York, October 22, 1882.   It was one of the popular light operas of its day.*

ARGUMENT   A clever intermingling of historical romance with delightful melody has made this one of the most enduring of the Strauss operas.   The scene is Portugal at a time when the domineering Philip II of Spain seeks to get that country into his clutches.   The premier, in fact, is in league with Philip, and makes a tool of the weak Portuguese monarch, who is too fond of good eating, especially truffles, to care for affairs of state.   Another important figure in the plot is Cervantes, the famous Spanish author, who has been banished from Spain and is now attached to the Queen's household.   He is reader to the Queen, and is also in love with Irene, a lady-in-waiting. The two try to aid the royal couple and circumvent the wily minister. The Queen, in a sentimental moment, writes upon her handkerchief, "A Queen doth love thee, yet thou art no King," and places it in a copy of "Don Quixote," which its author has been reading to her.   The fateful message falls into the hands of the minister.   The Queen is sent to a convent, while Cervantes and his faithful Sancho Panza escape and join a band of robbers.   The bandits capture her majesty and the maid, while on their way to the convent.   The ladies are disguised as hostess and maid of an inn, at which the King stops while on a hunting trip. They serve him some of his favorite dishes.   The King is then advised of the plot of his premier, and the Queen's message is explained to his satisfaction: she has loved him all the time, but he has not acted the King.

As in other works, much of the music is in waltz tempo.   Outstanding numbers are: the Queen's humorous ballad, "It was a wondrous fair and starry night"; the King's comic truffle song; an epicurean duet between him and his minister; an aria by Cervantes, "Once sat a youth"; and finale to the First Act; a pleasing little romanza by Cervantes, "Where the wild rose sweetly doth blow"; trio and chorus, "Great professors,

---

* This opera had the distinction of opening the then barely completed Casino. The auditorium was so cold that after a few performances the company went to neighboring cities, returning for another opening, December 28.   Rudolph Aronson was manager of this famous playhouse, and his book, *Theatrical and Musical Memoirs,* gives many interesting facts, also a long list of the best English, French, and German light operas.

learned doctors"; a duet between the King and the poet, "Brighter glance"; Sancho's humorous, "In the night his zither holding"; a coloratura song by the Queen, "Seventeen years"; two closing choruses in march time, "Now the King all hail!"; and a rousing bull-fight melody.

THE MERRY WAR

(Der Lustige Krieg.) Comic Opera in Three Acts.   Music by Johann Strauss. Book by Zell and Genée. Vienna, November 25, 1881. New York, the Casino, 1885 (69 performances).   In the cast were Gertrude Orme, Lily Post, Mathilde Cottrelly, Rose Beaudet, Fred Leslie, William T. Carleton, and Signor Perugini.

The scene is laid in Genoa in the Eighteenth Century. The story relates to a quarrel between two petty states.   It is hardly necessary to analyze this in detail.   Both the action and the music are "merry" and tinkle with waltz and other dance rhythms.   Widely popular in the closing years of the last century, the opera is known today only for occasional pieces played from it.   It contains some of the most delightful of the Strauss melodies.   Especially popular was a waltz song, sung by Signor Perugini, which aroused the same enthusiasm as Lehar's waltz in "The Merry Widow" of later years.

THE GYPSY BARON

(Der Zigeunerbaron.) Comic Opera in Three Acts. Music by Johann Strauss. Book by Schnitzer. Vienna, October 24, 1885. New York, the Casino, circa 1886 (86 times).   Its performances in the next few months totaled over 500.   In the cast were Pauline Hall, Mae St. John, Billie Barlow, Agnes Folsom, Rose Beaudet, William Castle, Francis Wilson, and W. H. Fitzgerald.   Revived at City Center, New York, November and December, 1944.

This sprightly work deserves a better fate than oblivion.   Its plot is unusually good, rising to a consistent climax.   It relates the familiar story of a boy, Sandov, taken from his ancestral home.   When he returns as a man, he finds the castle rundown and in the possession of Gypsies.   The score is rich in songs, Gypsy melodies, and waltz and other dance music.   Two popular songs are "Love can be dreamed," and "Your eyes light in my own."

KARL MILLÖCKER

Millöcker easily ranks as one of the foremost composers of German light opera. He was born in Vienna, May 29, 1842; studied at the Vienna Conservatory, and later held positions as choirmaster in several Austrian cities. He composed fourteen or more operettas which were successful both at home and abroad, among them, "Apajune, the Waterman" (1880), "The Beggar Student" (1882), "The Black Hussar" (1884), "Poor Jonathan" (1890), "The Du Barry," "Cousin Bobby" "Gasparone," and "The Vice Admiral." Millöcker was one of the most popular of composers during his lifetime. He is said literally to have worked himself to death. His royalties amounted to over $50,000 a year, and he lived in princely style. He died in Baden near Vienna, December 31, 1899.

THE BEGGAR STUDENT

(Der Bettelstudent.) Comic Opera in Three Acts. Music by Millöcker. Book by Zell and Genée. Vienna, 1882. London, the Alhambra, April 12, 1884 (112 performances). New York, at the Casino, under the direction of Heinrich Conreid, in the season of 1885–6 (110 performances). In the cast were Bertha Ricci, Rose Leighton, Rose Beaudet, Mathilde Cottrelly, Fred Leslie, William T. Carleton, W. S. Rising, and Harry Standish. This opera had an elaborate revival at the Casino, New York, March 22, 1913, when De Wolf Hopper was the "General," Kate Condon, the "Countess," and George MacFarlane, "Symon."

SCENE: Krakow.
TIME: 1704.

CAST GENERAL OLLENDORF, *a military governor.* COUNTESS PAL-
MATICA. LAURA, *her daughter.* BRONISLAVA, *her sister.* SY-
MON SYMONOVICZ, *a poor student.* JANITSKY, *his friend.* Others.

ARGUMENT General Ollendorf is in a rage. He has been flaunted
by Laura, to whom he has paid unwelcome attentions,

and despite the genteel poverty of the girl and her mother, the Countess Palmatica. So the General contrives a dirty little plot. He prevails upon Symon, an impecunious student, to play the rich gentleman and court and win the girl. Symon agrees, only stipulating that he take with him his friend, Janitsky, to pose as his secretary.

The two young adventurers are welcomed by the Countess and her daughters, and both men promptly fall in love, and are loved in return. The General, meanwhile, has financed Symon and when the funds give out, the student is in despair. He writes a note to Laura telling her of his share in the deception and begging forgiveness. The General intercepts the note, allows the young couple to get married, and then exposes Symon. He is driven out in disgrace and contemplates suicide. His friend, Janitsky, is more resourceful. He aids the King to regain his throne; Symon's aid is likewise enlisted; and the grateful monarch bestows a title upon Symon. When he presents himself again at the home of the Countess, all is forgiven.

The chief musical numbers are: a sprightly overture which is still popular; the General's entrance song, "And they say that towards the ladies"; duet by Symon and Janitsky, "Confounded cell, at last I leave thee"; trio of ladies, "Some little shopping"; aria by Laura, "But when the song is sweetly sounding"; finale to the First Act; Laura's humorous song in the Second, "If joy in married life you'd find"; duet, "This kiss, sweet love"; two topical songs by Ollendorf, "One day I was perambulating" and "There in the Chamber Polish"; the involved but clever finale to this Act; and in the Third, Bronislava's song, "The Prince a beggar's said to be," and Symon's lament, "I'm penniless and outlawed, too."

THE BLACK HUSSAR

Comic Opera in Three Acts. Music by Millöcker. Vienna, 1884. It met with favor in both England and America.*

The action takes place during 1812–13. Von Helbert, an officer in the Black Hussars, tries to incite an uprising in Trautenfeld, a German village. Hackenback, the magistrate, wishes to avoid an open rupture with the French and Russian troops which occupy the town. The French are hunting Helbert, but the latter ingeniously has the description of the magistrate inserted in the public notice. Hackenback is

---

* Harry B. Smith tells of the shouts of joy which greeted De Wolf Hopper at his entrance as the "Black Hussar," in the New York performance. He was clad in a suit of armor representing a stove with the front door open showing a blazing fire within.

so politic that he has a reversible panel in his house; one side bearing the likeness of the Czar, the other that of Napoleon. Unluckily he has the Czar's portrait out when the French arrive. The climax is brought about by the throwing off of all disguises by Helbert and his fellow conspirators, as the Black Hussar regiment arrives to take the town. The comedy element results from the love-making between Minna and Rosetta, the magistrate's two daughters, and the German officer and his comrade, Waldermann.

The opera is notable for the close-knit texture of its plot; the sparkle and glamor of its presentation; and the loveliness of its music.

THE DU BARRY

Romantic Opera in Nine Scenes. Music by Millöcker. Book by Paul Knepler and J. M. Welleminsky. Vienna, circa 1885. Berlin, 1931. An English version was presented at the George M. Cohan Theater, New York, in 1932, with the "Du Barry" rôle taken by Grace Moore.

CAST THE KING. CHOISEUL, *the Premier.* COUNT CHAMARD. BORDENEAU. MARSHAL OF LUXEMBOURG. MARQUIS DE BRISSAC. MARIE JEANNE VAUBERNIER. COUNT DU BARRY. RENÉ LAVALLERY MADAME LABILLE.

The story follows the historical one of the favorite of King Louis XV. The First Scene opens with a charming overture and chorus of girls, "Reminiscence"; song by Jeanne, "Today I'm happy"; the King's entrance march; and a quartet of girls and chorus. In the Second are a dance; a song by René; duet and chorus by the girls; and a duet between Jeanne and René. The third contains pleasing songs by René, "How lovely is everything"; and by Jeanne, "Love little Jeanne." The Fourth is marked by a male chorus, "Wink both your eyes." The Fifth has a girls' chorus, and a song by Jeanne, "Hy Heart." The Seventh, a waltz song by Jeanne, with chorus; and a duet between her and René, "I recall every moment." The last Scene has a song by Jeanne leading up to the brilliant finale, "Yes, she is the Du Barry."

The music sparkles throughout, and has an elaborate setting. A feast to the eye as well as to the ear.

POOR JONATHAN

(Der Arme Jonathan.) Comic Opera in Three Acts. Music by Millöcker. Vienna, 1890. New York, the Casino, 1891.

In the '90's this was a reigning sensation, having a New York run of
208 times; and being popular on the road.   It had a star cast including
Lillian Russell, Fanny Rice, George Gaston, and Jefferson De Angelis.
While the opera has some pleasing music, it is now almost forgotten.

IGNAZ BRÜLL

Brüll won fame as both pianist and composer.   He was born in
Moravia, November 7, 1846, and as a young man made concert tours as
a pianist.   Later he engaged in teaching, in Vienna.   He wrote many
pieces for the piano, and six or more operas, which were performed with
varying success between 1864 and the end of the century.   Of these,
"Das Goldene Kreuz" is the most important.   Brüll died in 1907.

THE GOLDEN CROSS

(Das Goldene Kreuz.)   Light Opera in Two Acts.   Music by Brüll.
Book by Mosenthal.   Berlin, December 22, 1875.

The story is an adaptation of a French comedy of the same name.   It
is quite simple.   The scene is a French village, in the year 1812.
Nicholas, a mill-owner, is summoned to the colors on the very day of
his marriage to Theresa.   Her sister, Christine, tries to get one of her
own suitors to go in his stead, promising to wed the man who brings
back to her the golden cross which she has worn.   A young noble, Gontran, thereupon says he will take the cross, and joins the company in
which Bombardon is sergeant.   At the end of three years, Gontran returns severely wounded, but without the cross.   The sergeant, Bombardon, bears it; but he himself is a cripple.   Christine will not go back
on her word, and says she will accept him.   Just then Gontran appears,
as if from the dead, and the two young people are joyfully united.

The music is as simple and charming as the story.   The dialogues are
generally spoken, and arias, duets and choruses intermingle in agreeable variety.

HEINRICH REINHARDT

A popular German composer, who was born in 1865, and died in 1922. He wrote many songs and other music of lighter vein, but is known abroad for only one opera, "Das Süsse Mädel" (1910).

THE SPRING MAID

(Das Süsse Mädel.) Light Opera in Two Acts. Music by Reinhardt. Book by Harry B. Smith, from the German by Wilhelm and Willner. Tremont Theater, Boston, December 5, 1910, starring Christie Mac-Donald. In New York at the Liberty Theater, December 26, 1910. William Burress had the comedy rôle.

CAST PRINCESS BOZENA. PRINCE NEPOMUK, *her father.* PRINCE ALA-DIR. ANNAMIRL, *a fountain girl.* BARON RUDI. ROLAND, *an English actor.* URSULA. SPAETLING, *a local detective.* EVAKATI, *a hotel keeper.* Others.

ARGUMENT According to an old legend, the site of the famous spa, Carlsbad, was once a wild forest, in which hunters pursued the plentiful game. A huntsman pursuing a fawn was implored by nymphs to spare it. Later a water sprite led him to a rock which, when struck, emitted a stream of water—the famous Carlsbad Spring.

The action of our opera, however, is modern and centers around a gay Princess and her impecunious father, who come to the waters at the time when the annual pageant is being put on, celebrating the Spring's discovery.

Musical numbers: First Act: opening chorus, "The Cure"; "The Loving Cup"; "Day Dreams"; trio, "We're on the track"; duet, "The next may be right"; Bozena and chorus, "The Fountain Fay"; Bozena and Aladir, "Two little love bees." Second Act: chorus, "Folk Songs"; "Dance with me"; quartet, "Take me, Dear"; duet, "Day Dreams"—with its refrain "Visions of bliss," the "hit" of the opera; "The Interrupted Allegory"; duet, "Hungaria."

FRANZ LEHAR

Franz Lehar was born in Komorn, Austria, April 30, 1870. He showed early aptitude for music, composing songs at six. At twelve he entered the Prague Conservatory. Later he studied under Dvorak. His father was conductor of a regimental band, and for a time he played in it. He also appeared as a solo violinist, at eighteen. Then he became a musical director in various theaters. His first serious opera, "Der Kurassier," was a failure. "Kukuska," later called "Titania," produced in 1899 in Budapest, was not very successful. He then turned to Light Opera, and his "The Merry Widow" made him world famous. Others are: "Gypsy Love" (1911), "The Count of Luxembourg" (1912), "The Maid of Athens" (1914), co-composer, "Eva," and others. Lehar died in Bad Ischl, October 24, 1948.

THE MERRY WIDOW

(Die Lustige Witwe.) Viennese Operetta in Three Acts. Music by Lehar. Book by Victor Leon and Leo Stein. Daly's, London, June 8, 1907 (778 times). First showing in America, New Amsterdam Theatre, New York, October 21, 1907, with Donald Brian as the Prince, and Ethel Jackson as "Sonia" (242 times). Revived in 1929 and 1931; also at Carnegie Hall, July 15, 1942; August 4, 1943; and by the New Opera Company at City Center, New York, October 7, 1944.

CAST BARON POPOFF, *Marsovian ambassador.* NATALIE, *his wife.* PRINCE DANILO, *attaché.* SONIA, *a young widow.* CAMILLE DE JOLIDON. MARQUIS CASCADA. RAOUL DE ST. BRIOCHE. KHADJA. MALITZA, *his wife.* NOVA KOVICH. OLGA, *his wife.* Various others, including Maxim show girls.

ARGUMENT Charming in music, intriguing in lines and situation, this work was a reigning favorite when produced both abroad and in New York, and still remains in repertory. The scene is laid in Paris—first at the Marsovian Embassy; then in the gardens of Sonia's residence; and finally in the Café Maxim.

Sonia, a pretty young widow now living in Paris, is quite a catch, not merely on account of her good looks but also her inheritance of some twenty million francs. Baron Popoff, the ambassador from her native country, Marsovia, has received instructions from his government, to see to it that Sonia weds with another Marsovian and thus keeps her money in that country. Prince Danilo is the man they have picked out for her. But, womanlike, she doesn't want her destiny made to measure; and further she wants to have her fling in Gay Paree—which she does. At the last, however, she and the Prince decide to take each other for better or for worse.

As already stated the music is of high order. The best numbers are— Act. I. opening chorus, "Now, ladies and gentlemen"; duet, Natalie and Camille, "A dutiful wife"; Sonia and chorus, "In Marsovia"; Danilo, "Maxim's"; Camille, "Home"; finale, "Ladies' Choice." Act II. Sonia and chorus, "I bid you wait"; duet, "Vilia"; Song, "The Cavalier"; March and septet, "Women"; duet, Natalie and Camille, "Love in my heart." Act III. sextet of girls and chorus, "The Girls at Maxim's"; dance by Fifi leading to chorus, "Butterflies"; Chorus, "Quite Parisian"; the famous "Merry Widow Waltz" and duet, Sonia and Danilo, "I love you so"; finale, "You may study her ways."

GYPSY LOVE

Operetta in Three Acts. Music by Lehar. Book by Robert and Harry B. Smith, from the German of Willner and Bodansky. Globe Theatre, New York, October 17, 1911. Daly's, London, June 1, 1912, where it ran 299 times. In New York, Marguerite Sylva took the part of "Zorika"; Harry McDonough, "Niklas"; Arthur Albro, "Jozsi"; and Frances Demarest, that of the dashing young widow. Revived at St. Louis Open-Air Theatre, in 1946.

This opera is more serious in theme than "The Merry Widow." Its music is Hungarian in texture, and at times rises almost to Grand Opera, with its wild czardas and the languorous lassan of Hungary. The original book is superior to the American version, which has been cheapened with local quips.

Musical numbers include: song by Zorika, "River, tell me"; duet, "There is a land of fancy"; duet and chorus, "Love is like a rose"; Zorika, "Melody of love." In Second Act, "Drinking Song"; Jozsi and chorus, "Gypsy Love"; trio, "There was a maiden"; duet, "Give me your roses." In Third Act, Fedor's song, "Reminiscence"; quintet, "Matrimony"; and final chorus.

THE COUNT OF LUXEMBOURG

Musical Romance in Two Acts. Music by Lehar. Book by Glen Macdonough, after the German of Willner and Bodansky. Vienna, 1909; London, Daly's, May 20, 1911 (340 times); New York, 1912. In the latter, Ann Swinburne was "Angèle"; Frank Moulan and George L. Moore were also in the cast. Revived at Jolson Theater, New York, February 17, 1930.

CAST   RENÉ, *Count of Luxembourg*. ARMAND BRISSARD, *an artist.* THE GRAND DUKE, *an old roué.* ANGÈLE DIDIER, *an opera singer.* JULIETTE VERMONT. Others.

ARGUMENT   This gay operetta, while not of the enduring quality of "The Merry Widow," attained considerable success. The action is in Paris and involves the gay and Bohemian life there. The First Act is placed in Brissard's studio; the Second, in Angèle's apartments; and a final scene, also given as a Third Act, is in the corridor of the Grand Hotel.

Brissard, an artist, is down on his luck. Yet he gives his last penny to his friend, René. The artist himself is in love with Juliette, but she is too practical to tie herself down to an impecunious artist. Meanwhile, the old rounder, the Grand Duke, wants to marry Angèle Didier, the singer, but as he does not like to take a commoner, he hits upon the scheme of having her wed somebody else with a title, then get a divorce. Count René is offered twenty thousand pounds to be "it"; and so on through a merry tangle.

There are several excellent musical numbers, such as the song in the First Act, "Day Dreams"; and a duet, "Say not love is a dream." Frank Moulan had two droll topical songs: "I am in love," and "Rootsie Pootsie." Other numbers are: "Shall we dance?"; "Bohemians"; the chorus, "Carnival!"; Juliette and chorus, "Pierre"; quintet, "A check on the Bank of England"; Angèle, "Today I become a bride"; duet, "Are you Herr Baron?"; duet, polka time, "I was a lion in the Salon"; chorus, "Flattery"; duet, "Were you already mine"; duet, "Fragrance"; finale, "Little Maid." An effective waltz by the two principals down a flight of stairs is reminiscent of "The Merry Widow," and has continued to rival it in popularity.

OSCAR STRAUS

Oscar Straus, who was born in 1870, is a German composer, who has carried out the Straus traditions in writing largely in waltz vein.   His "A Waltz Dream" (1908) is of this Viennese type; also, "The Last Waltz," which was produced at the Century Theater, New York, May 10, 1921. Another work produced also in America is "Teresina."   But his larger fame in America rests upon his brilliant "The Chocolate Soldier" (1909).

A WALTZ DREAM

Light Opera in Three Acts.   Music by Oscar Straus.   Book by Felix Doermann and Leopold Jacobson.   English adaptation by Joseph Herbert.   Hick's Theatre, London, March 7, 1908 (148 times).   New York, Broadway Theatre, April, 1908.

CAST   JOACHIM XIII, *a European prince.*   HELENE, *his daughter.*   COUNT LOTHAR.   LIEUT. NIKI.   LIEUT. MONTSCHI.   FRANZI, *woman orchestra leader.*   Courtiers and others.

ARGUMENT   Lieut. Niki, of the Austrian army, has been commanded by his emperor to wed Princess Helene, of a small neighboring state; and at the curtain's rise we are shown the wedding.   But it is a one-sided match.   While the princess is willing, the officer is irked.   He wants to get back to his beloved Vienna, and this longing is intensified by hearing the soft strains of a waltz played by a ladies' orchestra.   He prevails upon his brother officer, Montschi, to stay by, while he steals off to see Franzi, the girl violinist who leads the musicians.   A love affair rages between them, but at the last Franzi learns that he is the Prince Consort, and is persuaded to return to Vienna.

The music is lively, with waltz tempo predominating.   In the First Act we hear the trio and chorus, "The gay Hussar"; a duet, "A love of my own"; a comical trio, "Our unlucky dynasty"; and the high point, the waltz duet between Niki and Montschi, "The Waltz Dream." In the Second, a spirited march; then a lover's duet, "My dear little maiden"; and another march with trio and chorus, "The big bass drum." In the Third, chorus, "Hush it up"; trio, "Will she come or not?"; duet, "Burness and vagabond"; and finale introducing again the haunting strains of "The Waltz Dream."

THE CHOCOLATE SOLDIER

Comic Opera in Three Acts. Music by Oscar Straus. Book by R. Bernauer and L. Jacobson; English version by Stanislaus Stange. Based on Shaw's "Arms and the Man." Casino, New York, September 13, 1909 (291 times). Revived in 1921 and 1930. In the later cast were Donald Brian and Tessa Kosta. London, the Lyric, September 9, 1910 (500 performances). Has remained a favorite operetta frequently produced; latest New York revival, June 23, 1942.

CAST COL. CASIMIR POPOFF. AURELIA, *his wife.* NADINA, *his daughter.* MASCHA, *a cousin.* LIEUT. BUMERLI. CAPT. MASSAKROFF. MAJOR SPIRIDOFF. LOUKA. STEPHAN. Others.

ARGUMENT While Bulgaria and Serbia are at war, in 1885, Bumerli, a Serbian, nicknamed "The Chocolate Soldier" from his love of sweets, in trying to escape the enemy takes refuge in Nadina's room. The girl aids him to escape, lending him her father's coat, which contains some family pictures. Resulting misunderstandings are lively and amusing. Both story and music combine to provide an unusually successful work.

The music in the First Act begins with trio and chorus, "What can we do without a man?" Then comes the famous, stirring aria by Nadina, "My Hero!"—and a duet between her and Bumerli equally well known, "Sympathy." The Second Act has a march and chorus, "Our heroes come"; sextet, "Alexius the heroic"; duet, "Never was there such a lover"; sextet, "The tale of a coat"; and duet, "The Chocolate Soldier." The Third Act brings in a duet between Alexius and Mascha, "Falling in love"; Nadina's aria with duet with Bumerli, "The Letter Song"; and closes with "Thank the Lord, the war is over!"

LEO BLECH

Leo Blech, who was born in Aachen, April 22, 1871, belongs to the modern school of German composers. He has written shorter pieces and orchestral selections, but is known in America almost exclusively for one opera, "Versiegelt." At one time he was a conductor of German opera in the Metropolitan, New York.

VERSIEGELT
(Fair-zee'-gelt)

(Under Seal.) Comic Opera in One Act. Music by Leo Blech. Book by Richard Batka and Pordes-Milo, after the story by Rauppach. Hamburg, November 4, 1908.

SCENE: A German village.

TIME: 1830.

ARGUMENT A little village comedy of customs and manners is here given an appropriate musical setting.

An attractive young widow, Frau Schramm is the object of the attentions of Herr Braun, the Burgomaster of the town. While flattered, she has thus far refused him a definite answer. Meanwhile, his daughter, Else, is loved by Bertel, the town clerk, but this match does not please the exalted mayor. He visits his wrath upon the head of Bertel's mother, Frau Willmer, who comes to tell her troubles to Frau Schramm. The Burgomaster is about to seize Frau Willmer's belongings for unpaid taxes, and she begs her neighbor to conceal a huge wooden wardrobe, her most cherished possession. Frau Schramm consents, and the bulky piece of furniture is dragged in. But Lampe, the bailiff, discovers its whereabouts, and posts off to report to the mayor. When Braun calls, he is not nearly so much concerned with the wardrobe as with the pretty widow. A knock is heard. The mayor does not want to be discovered, so hides in the wardrobe. Lampe enters and places an official seal upon its doors. Later Else and Bertel arrive, and the widow prompts them to play the part of dutiful children for the imprisoned man's benefit. They would not think of eloping without his consent,

Oh no!—but they will not release him until he grants this consent and settles a dowry upon his daughter. He makes the best of a bad bargain, and when Lampe and the neighbors enter, Bertel pretends that it was he who was in the wardrobe. All is explained amid general rejoicing.

LEO FALL

Leo Fall, born in Germany in 1873, was early successful in the English field. Several of his works have been adapted to the American stage with success, among them, "The Dollar Princess," "The Merry Peasant," "The Girl in the Train," "Madame Pompadour," and "The Doll Girl." Fall died, September 16, 1925.

THE DOLLAR PRINCESS

Musical Comedy in Three Acts. Music by Leo Fall. Book by George Grossmith, Jr., after the German by A. M. Willner and F. Grünbaum. First produced in Germany, in 1907. In New York at the Knickerbocker Theatre, August 6, 1909 (250 times). At Daly's, in London, September 25, 1909 (428 times).

CAST   JOHN W. COWDER, *president of the Coal Trust.* TOM, *his indigent brother.* DICK, *his nephew.* FREDDY SMYTHE. MARQUIS DE JOLIFONTAINE. LORD HERBERT FITZ JONES, *office boy for Cowder.* IVAN TARTAROFF. PAILLARD. ALICE COWDER, *J. W.'s daughter.* DAISY, *his niece.* OLGA LABINSKA, *a Russian adventuress.* Others.

ARGUMENT   The first two Acts take place in and about Cowder's home in New York. The Third Act is in the Franco-British Exhibition, London. The action, which is involved and unimportant, chiefly concerns the heart affairs of the "Dollar Princess"— Alice, the spoiled daughter of the coal magnate. She usually gets what she wants; but when she sets her cap for the impecunious but proud Freddy Smythe, he leads her a merry chase before he capitulates. The machinations of the Russian "countess," Olga, further enliven things.

Musical numbers: First Act: Alice and chorus, "Typists have to work away"; Alice, "A self-made girl"; Freddy, "My dream of love"; Freddy and Alice, "Inspection"; a medley finale, in which Cowder introduces the countess to his guests, ends with, "Won't we splash the cash about. America, look out!"

Second Act: opening chorus, "Tennis"; Alice and Freddy, "Typewriting"; Daisy and Marquis, "Paragraphs"; quartet, "The Dollar Princess"; finale, "We are Tip, we are Top"—ending, as Cowder says that Olga is to be his bride, with "Hail to Olga from the Volga!"

Third Act: opening chorus, "At this gorgeous exhibition"; Ivan and men, "Not here, not here!"; Freddy, "Love's Race"; sextet, "The Red, White and Blue"; quintet, hornpipe, "A boat sails on Wednesday"; Daisy and Marquis, "Reminiscence"; Olga, "The Lion's Queen"; Alice and Freddy, "Then you go?"; finale, "Hip, hip, hurrah!" (One or two of the closing numbers were written by Jerome Kern.)

ITALY

HISTORICAL PREFACE

Although Italy is recognized as the birthplace of European Opera and has remained a dominant home, it is not, singularly enough, one of the chief breeding places of modern lighter works. The Italian genius has run to *bel canto* (good song), to impassioned phrases, to dramatic climaxes of singer and orchestra. So busied has it been with these, that the lighter and more frivolous moods have almost passed them by. And this despite the fact that *Opera Buffa* had its habitat in Italy, even as did *Opéra Bouffe* in France.

Medieval and modern opera is believed to have reached Europe by way of Greece and Italy. Great Greek tragedies such as "Agamemnon" and "Antigone" had choruses which were sung to the best music of their day. Spoken dialogues were interwoven with orchestration. The song, the dance, the festival, all foreshadowed the opera. Centuries were to pass, nevertheless, until the divine seed took root in this newer form.

One of the first significant dates was about the year 1285, when a French *trouvère* (not an Italian) brought to the French court there two or three pastorals with music, which suggest the comic opera. One of these was entitled "Le Jeu de Robin et de Marion." The composer, or producer, Adam de la Halle, merely strung some of the old Robin Hood ballads together into a loose plot. If this were indeed the birth of Light Opera, the thing is significant: In an Italian setting a Frenchman brings out a work with English background!

However, we must go on to the end of the Sixteenth Century before we come to the true beginnings of Italian opera. In Florence a group of music enthusiasts strove to bring back the classic style of musical declamation. They were known as the *Camerata,* and in their ranks were a poet, Rinuccini, and a musician, Peri, who brought out a work, "Dafne," which was privately performed in 1597. The music of this is lost, but their second work, "Euridice," is still extant. Except for a few bars of chorus, the work is largely recitative with accompaniment.

Monteverde produced his "Arianna" in 1607, which marked a definite advance in both score and orchestra. Opera was on its way. Cavalli, his pupil, carried on the good work to Venice; and in that city the first opera house, the Teatro di San Cassiano, opened its doors, in 1637. In

Rome no opera was performed until 1632. But during this century the new form of entertainment flourished. Strolling players, singers, dancers and musicians went through the country giving operettas from improvised stages, much as we see it in the story of "I Pagliacci."

Most of these works were serious, and in order to relieve the tension on the audience amusing interludes were introduced. Cavalli was one of the first to recognize this need and bring in the comic element. In 1639, two others, Mazocchi and Marazolli, presented in Florence one of the very first of light operas, "Chi Sofre Speri." It was the forerunner of *Opera Buffa,* but fifty years were to elapse before the Italians took this type of opera to their hearts. In the meanwhile, interludes, or *intermezzi,* diverted their ears and minds from the serious moments.

Logroscino, a Neapolitan, is credited with the founding of true *Opera Buffa.* His texts, broadly comic, were woven into musical farces of one act each, with music leading up to a climactic finale, as in our modern works. Pergolesi (1710–1736) who followed, dying in his twenties, yet achieved the first classic note in this new form. His "Sallustia," a more serious work composed when he was only twenty-two, was followed by "La Serva Padrona," which has had a successful revival in our own time.

Among the other pioneers in *Opera Buffa* were Jomelli, Scarlatti, Greco, Porpora, Piccini, Sacchini, and Guglielmi, most of whom did work in both the serious and the lighter schools. The next commanding name is that of Cimarosa (1749–1801), his greatest work being the delightful "Il Matrimonio Segreto." He is said to have written no less than seventy-six operettas. Paisiello, a contemporary, was even more prolific, but his works are now forgotten. Some were revived in Rome, fifty years ago, and were well received. He made good use of the concerted finale in his works.

With Rossini we usher in the modern school, but with it witness the death of *Opera Buffa.* We look almost in vain for enduring works in this gayer manner. As a young man Rossini received commissions to write five light operas, one of them being "Tancredi." His later masterpiece, "Il Barbiere di Siviglia," both "comic" and "grand" went a long way beyond *Opera Buffa.* Rossini, like succeeding Italian composers, was too much absorbed in the serious, to turn aside. Verdi, the dean of them all, has given us only one example, in "Falstaff." Donizetti had a light and graceful touch. Works by the Riccis, Mascagni, and Wolf-Ferrari, are also noted, but they are merely stray flowers in the vast meadows of Italian music.

There is no such flowering as followed *Opéra Bouffe* and the *Opéra Comique* in France; the long list of similar works in Germany; and the joyous moments of the music hall in England and America, coming down to our own musical comedies and *revues.*

GIOVANNI BATTISTA PERGOLESI

One of the earliest exponents of Italian *opera buffa*, Pergolesi was born in Jesi, January 3, 1710; dying, March 16, 1736. His first bent was church music, an oratorio, "San Guglielmo," being composed in 1731. However, in this same year he turned aside to an original field. His operetta, "La Serva Padrona," is one of the first successful works in this new school.

THE MAID-MISTRESS

(La Serva Padrona.)   Comic Opera in One Act.   Music by Pergolesi. Book by G. A. Federico.   Naples, 1733.   Revived in London, in 1873; and within our own day at the Metropolitan, New York, in the spring of 1935.

There are only three persons in the cast, and one of these is silent; no chorus.   Uberto, the master of the house, is waiting for Serpina, the maid, to bring him his chocolate.   She is tardy, so he sends his valet, Vespone (the mute character), to fetch her.   Serpina is pert.   She is tired of waiting on Uberto, and wants to be the lady of the house.   She contrives a plot with the silent valet.   He is dressed as a soldier and presented to Uberto as her intended husband.   Then she describes all the supposed "Captain Tempest's" bad qualities, and so works on the master's sympathies—emphasized by the fact that the fiery Captain draws his sword threateningly—that Uberto decides to make the maid his own wife.

The running dialogue is marked by music of crystal clarity and charm. There are few arias and no duets or other concerted work.   The two voices are bass and soprano, with interwoven orchestral effects.

Excerpts from this opera are in record form; also the aria, "Stizzoso, mio stizzoso."

DOMENICO CIMAROSA

A Neapolitan composer who won wide fame in *Opera Buffa*, Cimarosa came of poor working folk; he was born in 1749, and worked his way through the then celebrated Conservatorio Santa Maria di Loretto. His first light opera, composed at twenty-three, at once brought recognition. During the next twenty-five years he averaged an opera a year. He was called to the Court of Catherine II, at St. Petersburg, and later to that of Leopold II, at Vienna. It was here that he brought out his greatest work, "Il Matrimonio Segreto" (1792), which ranks in importance among early works with Pergolesi's "La Serva Padrona." Cimarosa died in 1801. He is said to have written no less than seventy-six light operas.

THE SECRET MARRIAGE

(Il Matrimonio Segreto.) Opera Buffa in Two Acts. Music by Cimarosa. Book by Giovanni Bertati, after an English comedy. Vienna, 1792; Naples, 1793; Italian Opera House, New York, 1834; and revived just 101 years later in the Metropolitan Opera House, New York.

After a light, merry overture reminding the hearer of Mozart, the curtain rises upon a simple, amusing story. It deals with the troubles of Paolino, a young lawyer, who has secretly married the lovely Carolina, one of the two daughters of the grasping Neapolitan merchant, Geronimo. The merchant's other daughter, Elisetta, is not so attractive, to put it plainly, and the lawyer tries to ingratiate himself with his unsuspecting father-in-law by arranging a match between her and Count Robinson, an English nobleman. A good, fat dowry is in prospect; but when the Englishman appears on the scene he at once prefers Carolina, and tells Geronimo that he will marry her for only one-half the stipulated amount. As if this were not trouble enough for Paolino, an elderly aunt of Carolina's, Fidalma, takes a violent fancy for him. While Robinson tries to persuade Elisetta to refuse him, by reciting a long list of his shortcomings, Paolina and Carolina try to run away from it all. They are caught, and the paternal wrath descends. But finally all is forgiven; their wedding is proclaimed to the world; and the Englishman must perforce content himself with the plainer sister.

The music, as said before, reminds one of Mozart, without the latter's staying qualities. But it is simple, direct, lively, and in the best manner of the early school of *Opera Buffa.* The composer made use of effective arias, masterly ensembles, while throughout his orchestration was skillful.

The overture may be heard in record form.

GAETANO DONIZETTI

Born in Bergamo, Italy, in 1797, and dying in his native town, in 1848, Donizetti is identified with both the Grand and the Lighter schools of opera. A more complete sketch of his life will be found under Grand Opera. He was equally facile in serious and lighter veins. In the latter he is best known for his "L'Elisir d'Amore" (1832); "La Figlia del Reggimento" (1840); and "Don Pasquale" (1843).

THE ELIXIR OF LOVE

(L'Elisir d'Amore.) Opera Buffa in Two Acts. Music by Donizetti. Book by Romani. Milan, May 12, 1832. London, December 10, 1836. New Orleans, March 30, 1842. A revival of this opera was presented at the Metropolitan Opera House, New York, in 1904, with a notable cast including Sembrich, Caruso, Scotti, and Rossi.

SCENE: A Village in Italy.

TIME: Early part of Nineteenth Century.

CAST ADINA, *an heiress.* NEMORINO, *a peasant.* BELCORE, *a sergeant.* DULCAMARA, *a traveling doctor.* GIANETTINA, *a peasant girl.* A NOTARY. A Moor, Villagers, etc.

ARGUMENT Donizetti was at his best, not in his tragic operas, but in his lighter ones. One of the brightest, most captivating of these is "The Elixir of Love," dealing with the familiar theme that the course of true love never did run smooth. Its amusing situations are delightfully blended with the music.

Act I *A Village Street.* Adina, an heiress, cannot make up her own mind about romance, though fond of reading love-stories. She is being wooed by a young peasant, Nemorino, but fears that he is seeking her hand only because of her money. From a distance is heard the voice of the lovelorn swain: "How I love her!" (Quanto e bella.) She is only amused by his attentions, as she has just been reading "Tristan and Isolde," wherein the knight wins the lady by a magic potion. With a burst of martial music, Sergeant Belcore enters bearing a bouquet— also bent on winning Adina. In despair of this new obstacle, Nemorino seeks the aid of a quack doctor, Dulcamara. They have a lively duet: "Thank you kindly." The grateful swain has obtained, as he thinks, an elixir of love that will make him irresistible. It is, however, only a bottle of wine, which so stimulates him that he treats Adina very cavalierly the next time they meet. In a huff she accepts the sergeant, who prevails upon her to set the wedding-day at once, as he must depart with his troops. A florid duet between Adina and Nemorino is heard near the end of this Act; following a tearful plea from him: "Adina, only trust me" (Adina credimi).

Act II *Scene 1. Interior of Adina's Home.* As the curtain goes up, the guests at Adina's wedding sing a chorus of rejoicing. The quack, Dulcamara, comes in with a bit of music which, he says, is the latest hit in Vienna, a duet in barcarole style. He and Adina try it— an old favorite song: "I have riches, thou hast beauty" (Io son ricco, e tu sei bella). While Adina, Belcore, and the notary retire to sign the contract, Nemorino enters in despair. He finds the quack doctor calmly enjoying the viands, and beseeches him to give him another bottle of the elixir, still more powerful. He has no more money, and the doctor refuses. In order to obtain the money, Nemorino enlists in Belcore's company. The duet between Belcore and Nemorino while the latter enlists for an advance of twenty crowns—the sum the rascally quack has demanded—is another operatic gem. It is titled, "Twenty Crowns" (Venti Scudi).

Scene 2. A Village Street. The girls of the village learn that an uncle of Nemorino's has just died, leaving him a considerable fortune. He himself has not learned it, being under the influence of that powerful second bottle. As he comes up the street they crowd around him with many attentions. He attributes his sudden access of popularity to the elixir, and even the doctor now decides it has some virtue. The quack tells Adina of the young man's devotion and offers her some of the elixir, but she refuses, as she thinks that she has lost him forever. However, the lovers come to an understanding, and Adina repays the sergeant the advance made for Nemorino's enlistment. The sergeant is forced to step aside, and the entire village attributes the happy result to the marvelous Elixir of Love. Thereupon the doctor does a land-office business.

One of the gems of the last scene is the tenor aria, "A furtive tear" (Una furtiva lagrima).

THE DAUGHTER OF THE REGIMENT

(La Figlia del Reggimento.) Opera Buffa in Two Acts. Music by Donizetti; words by Bayard and Jules H. Vernoy. Opéra Comique, Paris, February 11, 1840; Niblo's Gardens, New York, September, 1843; London, in English, at the Surrey Theatre, December 21, 1847. First American performance, New Orleans, March 7, 1843. Both Jenny Lind and Adelina Patti sang the rôle of the "Daughter" with great success. It has been in frequent repertory in the present century.

SCENE: The Swiss Tyrol.
TIME: 1815.

CAST   MARIE, the "Daughter of the Regiment." SULPICE, Sergeant of Grenadiers. TONIO, a Tyrolese peasant. MARQUISE DE BIRKENFELD. HORTENSIO, steward to the Marquise. CORPORAL. Soldiers, Peasants, Friends of the Marquise, etc.

ARGUMENT   A light opera which bids fair to be perennially successful. It is the only one of Donizetti's operas which challenges "Lucia" in popularity.

Act I   During the Napoleonic wars the Swiss Tyrol was occupied by the French. In one of their regiments was a girl, Marie, who had been found in infancy on a battlefield by Sulpice, a sergeant, and his regiment had thereafter adopted her. In a song, "The Camp was my birthplace," and duo between her and the sergeant, the facts of her early life are related. It ends with the stirring duet, "Vivandiere of the regiment, rataplan, rataplan!" Marie is the pet of the whole regiment, but is unhappy in a secret love affair with Tonio, a Tyrolese peasant. In a duet the two young people confess their passion: "No longer can I doubt it." Tonio, for venturing into the French camp, is seized as a spy, and is saved from short shrift only by Marie's intervention. He now asks to enlist with them, but is told that he cannot wed Marie without the consent of the entire company.

The lovers confront still other difficulties. The Marchioness of Birkenfeld appears with a letter, said to have been found on the child years before, proving that she is the Marchioness' niece. The lady carries the girl off, to the despair of Tonio and the disgust of the regiment.   The lusty "Rataplan" chorus and Marie's aria, "A long farewell," are among the closing numbers of this act.

Act II   In a handsome drawing room of the Marchioness' castle, Marie is like a caged bird.   Sulpice, her foster father, who is also here recovering from a wound, observes her life here with deep distaste.   She is being taught to dance and sing like a lady born, when all the while her heart is with the regiment.   What is her joy, therefore, to hear once again the familiar "rataplan!" of the drums and the shrilling of the fifes. In march her old comrades, headed by Tonio, who had been promoted to captain.   Tonio hopes that his rank will entitle him to Marie's hand, but the haughty Marchioness says that she is betrothed to a Duke; and further that Marie is really her own daughter.   But the grande dame is not to have her own way.   The soldiers' entering song proves this: "We have come our child to free."   Then the girl sings the touching aria, "When I was left, by all abandoned."   The Marchioness sees her past in its true light and consents to her daughter's happiness.   Despite the protest of her ladies-in-waiting, "This wedding shocks us!" Tonio and Marie are united.

DON PASQUALE

Opera Buffa in Three Acts.   Music by Donizetti.   Book by Camerano, after "Ser Marc' Antonio."   Théâtre des Italiens, Paris, January 4, 1843.   London, June 30, 1843.   New York, in English, March 9, 1846.   Revived at the New Theatre, New York, 1909.   Later at the Metropolitan Opera House.

SCENE: Rome.
TIME: The present.

CAST   DON PASQUALE, *an old bachelor.*   DR. MALATESTA, *a physician.*
ERNESTO, *nephew of Pasquale.*   NORINA, *a young widow.*   A NOTARY.   Citizens, tradespeople, servants.

ARGUMENT   "Don Pasquale" is a gay little farce of manners which has been given a characteristic and worthy musical setting, the action being well represented by the score.

Act I   *Don Pasquale's Apartments.*   The finicky old bachelor, Don Pasquale, has worked himself up into a fine rage because his nephew, Ernesto, is not marrying to suit him.   Ernesto wishes to wed Norina, a bewitching young widow.   Dr. Malatesta, a family friend of all parties, contrives a plot in the young man's behalf.   The physician urges the Don himself to marry a lady of his choosing, a supposed sister of Malatesta's. This pseudo-sister and bride is none other than Norina, who is instructed to make life a burden for the old gentleman.

Musical numbers: song by Malatesta, "Oh, like an angel of beauty!"; Pasquale, "Oh, how I feel the glow!"; duet, "How? You will? Marry me"; an aria by Norina, "Ah, beneath all eyes"; duet, Norina and the Doctor, "See, I am ready with love to surround him."

Act II *Don Pasquale's Apartments.* True to her role, Norina begins to carry things with a high hand. She refuses to accept any of the Don's affectionate advances, and behaves like a shrew. Ernesto, who is a bewildered onlooker, is invited by her to be her escort on a shopping expedition. Meanwhile she lays out such an extravagant scheme for keeping house that the Don flies into a passion, declaring that she will bankrupt him.

Musical numbers: Ernesto alone, then Pasquale, Norina, and the Doctor, "Take courage"; finale, "On one side."

Act III *Scene 1. Don Pasquale's Apartments.* Norina is found surrounded by tradespeople to whom she has given large orders. The Don enters and during a quarrel she boxes his ears, and leaves him disconsolate. The doctor enters and tries to pacify him, but the Don insists that Norina shall quit his house.

Scene 2. A Balcony. While Ernesto is serenading Norina, the Don taxes her with being faithless; but in the course of explanations, he discovers that his marriage contract has been only a sham, and he is only too glad to get out of the bargain and unite the two lovers with his blessing.

Musical numbers: chorus, "Bring the jewels at once"; duet, "Dear wife, may I ask?"; duet, "Softly in the dark"; serenade by Ernesto, "As Luna laughs"; duet, Ernesto and Norina, "Do I read in your looks?"; finale, "Heaven, what do you say?"

LUIGI AND FREDERICO RICCI

Two brothers of this name, of Naples, are credited jointly with the tuneful opera buffa, "The Cobbler and the Fairy." Luigi Ricci (1805–

1859) wrote some thirty lighter operas, which are now forgotten. Frederico Ricci (1809–1877) composed many orchestral and shorter pieces. The brothers conjointly produced four operas.

THE COBBLER AND THE FAIRY

(Crispino e la Comare.) Opera Buffa in Three Acts. Music by L. and F. Ricci. Book by Piave. Venice, 1850; Paris, 1865; New York, the Metropolitan, 1918.

CAST CRISPINO, *a cobbler*. ANNETTA, *his wife*. COUNT DEL FIORE. FEBRIZIO, *a physician*. MIRABOLANO, *an apothecary*. DON ASDRUBALE, *a miser*. LA COMARE, *a fairy*. BARTOLO, *a mason*. LISETTA, *ward of Don Asdrubale*. Doctors, Scholars, Villagers, etc.

ARGUMENT A pleasing little fairy opera which carries its own moral—beware of ingratitude and vainglory. Text and score are welded into a harmonious whole.

Act I In Venice during the Seventeenth Century, Crispino, a worthy cobbler, has a hard time making ends meet. His wife helps by singing ballads in the streets. Their landlord, an old skinflint, is about to put them out of their home, and Crispino, in despair, threatens to throw himself into a well, when a Fairy appears and promises to aid him. She plans to make him a famous physician, and at the good news Crispino and Annetta take heart again.

The opera opens with a chorus of apothecary's apprentices; followed by a romance by the Count, "Fair as an angel"; a melody in which Crispino bewails his ill luck; a canzonetta by his wife, followed by a duet between them; a comic song by Dr. Febrizio; and a joyous duet between Crispino and Annetta, after the Fairy's visit.

Act II True to her word, the Fairy has made a doctor out of the cobbler, and here he is installed in his own office. The delighted Annetta sings a lively ditty, which is interrupted by the entrance of a patient, a workman who has met with an accident. A baritone solo is followed by duet with soprano, and a chorus accompaniment. While the cobbler-doctor makes marvelous cures, a trio of doctors jeer at him. But the new doctor prospers.

Act III Crispino becomes puffed up over his success. He builds a fine house, and puts on airs. Annetta remains unspoiled. She sings a pretty song, "Try my fritolas," in which she tells the merits of a cake she has baked. But when she invites some of her friends to their fine new house, her husband drives them out. The good Fairy then appears. She decides that only harsh measures will bring him to his senses.

The second scene reveals a cavern. The Fairy shows the frightened cobbler two lamps: one burning brightly is Annetta's; a dim one is his own. When he would take oil from his wife's lamp, the Fairy upbraids him, and suddenly her face turns into that of a skull. In a doleful ballad he asks for only half an hour more of life, so that he can see Annetta and his children once more. The Fairy forgives him; a sudden shift of scene reveals his home with him in a chair just awaking from a dream. While he manifests his joy at the transformation, Annetta sings a brilliant song of thanksgiving, in waltz time: "Oh, the joy of this moment!"

ERMANNO WOLF-FERRARI

A German-Italian composer born in Venice, January 12, 1876. He took his name from both parents, his father being a celebrated German painter, August Wolf. He won fame with a tragic opera, "The Jewels of the Madonna," but also has several pleasing lighter works to his credit. (See Grand Opera.)

THE INQUISITIVE WOMEN

(Le Donne Curiose.) Comic Opera in Three Acts. Music by Wolf-Ferrari. Book by Luigi Sugana, after the story by Carlo Goldoni. Munich, November 27, 1903, in German. In Italian at the Metropolitan, New York, January 3, 1912.

SCENE: Venice.
TIME: The Eighteenth Century.

CAST OTTAVIO, FLORINDO, PANTALONE, LELIO, LEANDRO, *members of an exclusive club.* BEATRICE, *wife of Ottavio.* ROSAURA, *her daughter.* ELEONORA, *wife of Lelio.* COLUMBINA, *a maid.* ARLECCHINO, *a man-servant.* Other members of club, Servants, Gondoliers, Townspeople, etc.

ARGUMENT   A rollicking farce comedy, which depicts the over-
weening curiosity of a group of women concerning
a club to which their husbands belong, and the means they employ to
satisfy their curiosity.   The music is sprightly, the overture being frequently performed by leading orchestras.

Act I   This Act has two scenes.   In the first, a group of Venetian gentlemen are making merry in their club house.   In the second a
group of inquisitive wives and daughters are bothering their heads about
it.   What is going on, good or bad?   They cross-examine Arlecchino
—who is Columbina's suitor—with little success.   Ottavio, the next to
enter, also undergoes examination.   Finally, Florindo, a young gallant,
who is in love with Rosaura, calls, and between mistress and maid they
pump out of him that the password of the club is "Here's to friendship!"

Act II   In the first two scenes, we find Eleonora searching her husband's pockets for the keys to the club.   Lelio interrupts this
wifely privilege, and there is a spirited musical dialogue, after which
the testy gentleman departs.

In Ottavio's home, Rosaura and Columbina tell Beatrice that they
have learned the password.   Their next task is to get the keys.   This
Columbina accomplishes by changing the keys in her master's coat for
others.   She then plans to don male attire and go to the club.   The
other women also set forth, with the exception of Rosaura, whom they
deem too young; but she prevails upon Florindo to lend her his keys.

Act III   An uproarious farce in two scenes.   Outside the mysterious
club house keys pass from one pocket to another in bewildering fashion.   Inside the club, the women conceal themselves in an anteroom.   In their eagerness to see all that is going on, they tumble
through the door.   The startled diners term it a veritable "shower of
women."   Howbeit, they forgive them, and the women themselves are
delighted to find their fears unfounded.   All join in a dance.   Arlecchino obtains the hand of Columbina, and Florindo that of Rosaura.
The party closes with the toast, "Here's to friendship!"

The music is gay and lively, without any outstanding arias or choruses.   The club's motto, "No women admitted," becomes a sort of
musical motif.

THE SECRET OF SUSANNE

(Il Segreto di Susanna.)   Interlude in One Act.   Music by Wolf-
Ferrari.   Book by Enrico Golisciani.   Berlin, 1910.   At New York,
the Metropolitan, December 13, 1912.   Farrar and Scotti sang.

SCENE: Piedmont.

TIME: The Present.

CAST COUNT GIL, *a Piedmontese.* SUSANNE, *his bride.* SANTE, *butler.*

ARGUMENT The secret of Susanne, though quite little, makes a cloud large enough to threaten the serenity of the honeymoon, owing to an otherwise rational man's detestation of smoking. The plot light as smoke wreaths becomes all the more absurd in a later day when women are "emancipated" so far as the filthy weed is concerned. The music is of correspondingly light character.

Scene, Drawing Room in the Count's Château. Count Gil and his bride Susanne are spending their honeymoon at the Count's château in Piedmont. With the connivance of Sante, the butler, Susanne secretly indulges in her passion for smoking, but Gil detects the smell and questions Sante, who gives him to understand that no one in the house is responsible. The Count at once concludes that the culprit must be a visitor—a rival—and when on embracing Susanne he detects the odor in her hair, he finds his suspicions confirmed. Susanne, thinking her husband's accusations refer to her little weakness, makes light of the affair, but Gil, with the graver matter in mind, is amazed at her levity, and a stormy scene ensues, culminating in the overturning of flowers, furniture, and bric-a-brac. When the air is comparatively clear again, Susanne once more arouses her husband's suspicion by reminding him of an engagement with friends. He leaves her, however, and goes out. Susanne is now free to light and enjoy a cigarette. Suddenly Gil returns and pounces upon her, seizing her roughly by the hand and burning himself with the cigarette. Straightway he realizes the absurdity of his suspicions, and in penitence even goes so far as to offer to acquire the habit himself. So they light cigarettes in peace and amity.

Some of the most charming numbers have been recorded: the overture; "Gioia, la nube leggera" (sung by both Bori and Farrar); and "Il dolce idillio" (by Farrar and Amato).

L'AMORE MEDICO

(*Lah-mo-re Med'-i-co*)

(Dr. Cupid.) Opera Buffa in Two Acts. Music by Wolf-Ferrari. Book by Enrico Golisciani. After the Comedy by Molière, "L'Amour Medecin." Royal Opera House, Dresden, December 4, 1913.

SCENE: France.

TIME: The Seventeenth Century.

CAST ARNOLFO, *a wealthy landowner.* LUCINDA, *his daughter.* CLI-
TANDRO, *her admirer.* LISETTA, *her maid.* TOMES, DESFON-
ANDRES, MACROTON, BAHIS, *physicians.* A NOTARY. Friends, Servants.

ARGUMENT An amusing play of manners, based upon Molière's
famous comedy in which a selfish father, who tries to
keep his daughter from marrying, is outwitted by Dr. Cupid. Incidentally, the author satirizes the medical profession of his day.

Act I *Villa of a Wealthy Landowner.* Arnolfo, a self-centered old
fellow, is much concerned over his daughter's indisposition.
He cannot find what is wrong with her, but she seems to be languishing
away. He still treats her like a child, although she is a young woman,
as he does not want her to grow up and leave him. When she enters,
garbed childishly, he presents her with dolls and toys, and even sings a
lullaby to her. She remains indifferent, and in an unguarded moment
he asks if some young coxcomb has gained her affections. "Yes, papa!"
she answers at once. The old man is vexed and is not improved in
humor when Lisetta, the pert maid, interposes, saying boldly that what
Lucinda needs is a husband. Away he goes in a rage. Presently a
serenade is heard. It is the voice of Clitandro, a young gallant, who
throws a rose through the window. Lucinda is so perturbed that she
cannot answer him. Arnolfo returns and soliloquizes about the time
when his daughter will be too old to marry and so will take care of him,
as all daughters should. While thus musing he falls asleep, and is only
awakened by Lisetta's outcries. Her mistress is very ill. "A doctor! a
doctor, quick!" There is general confusion, and the act ends with the
entrance of four doctors, while Lisetta departs slyly to fetch a fifth of her
own choosing.

Act II *Salon in Arnolfo's Home.* The four doctors are discovered in
learned and solemn consultation. At first each listens to the
others with deference, but as they fail to agree the argument becomes
heated and blows are imminent. When Arnolfo enters to learn their
verdict they confuse him with high-sounding Latin words, and end by
demanding big fees—which he pays before he realizes that they haven't
told him what to do for his daughter. Lisetta now ushers in Clitandro,
dressed as a physician. He says that he is a doctor of sick hearts. Arnolfo retires to an anteroom and watches uneasily while the new doctor
holds the fair patient's hand unnecessarily long. Clitandro finally
states that Lucinda's malady is mental. She only imagines that she
wants a husband—so the best way to cure her is to pretend to give her
one. He himself will be the victim, if she will ask for his hand. This
the patient agrees to do, and Arnolfo, entering into the spirit of the joke,

agrees to bestow half of his property on the couple. A notary is called in to draw up the various contracts, all of which are supposed by the father to be bogus. A ceremony is performed, and then Lisetta ushers in a group of merrymakers who are in the plot, and who tell the astounded father that the marriage is genuine. He tries to pursue the couple, but is hemmed in on all sides; while Lisetta gives him one of his dolls to console him.

FRANCE

HISTORICAL PREFACE

Under Italian Opera we have noted that the earliest operetta now recorded was produced by a Frenchman at the French court in Naples. It was "Le Jeu de Robin et de Marion," at the end of the Thirteenth Century. The French school of Light Opera, indeed, was directly influenced by that of Italy, but had more abundant examples.

Following the popularity of these early forms in Italy, visiting musicians came to Paris and for a time Italian operas were popular with the French court. This was at the end of the Sixteenth and beginning of the Seventeenth Centuries. In 1600, Rinuccini, who wrote the book for Peri's opera, "Euridice," came to Paris in the suite of Marie de Medici, and was one of the first to introduce the new form of entertainment. Italian dramas as well as operas became a staple court diet.

Meanwhile, a typical French form of entertainment was appearing—the ballet. But one of the first of these, "Le Ballet Comique de la Reine," was in charge of an Italian, Baltazarini (1581). During the reign of Louis IV, when fashions became more Gallic, Italian works declined and native talent was encouraged. The poet, Perrin, and the musician, Cambert, wrote a pastoral which so pleased Louis that, in 1669, Perrin was granted a royal charter to found a national academy of music. Cambert's "Pomone" and "Les Peines et Plaisirs d'Amour" won wide favor.

Not yet, however, was French talent firmly in the saddle. German composers such as Gluck and Mozart had sprung into mastery; while great Italians such as Rossini and Spontini had likewise arisen. Their operas transplanted to Paris made it hard for the native fledglings to be heard. And it was an Italian, Jean Baptiste Lully, who is credited with having founded Grand Opera in France, in 1672. He was a master of the ballet, the *divertissement*, the minuet; and he did much to make the overture an important feature of opera.

It remained for Monsigny (1729–1817) to establish a native school of *Opéra Comique*, or *Opéra Bouffe*. He did this by a skillful blending of the best of both Italy and France. He produced a long list of French musical farces between the years 1759 and 1779; amassed a fortune for himself; and on his retirement had the satisfaction of seeing this new school firmly established. Grétry (1741–1813), who followed him, carried it to a higher level. His music was fuller than that of Monsigny; his texts better constructed. Of the fifty or more operas that he wrote, "Le Tableau Parlant" (1769), and "L'Amant Jaloux" (1778), take rank as the best of their day. Grétry tackled more serious works such as "Richard Cœur de Lion" and "Peter the Great" with some success.

With Cherubini, a Florentinian who did the bulk of his work in Paris, we begin a long list of composers who have made modern French *Opéra Comique* what it is. Cherubini was a voluminous composer. His "Les Deux Journées" (1800) won high praise. Boieldieu's "La Dame Blanche" and Auber's sparkling pieces headed by "Fra Diavolo" carried the fame of French light opera into other lands. In England these and other such works became steadily popular. Hérold's "Zampa" was also widely performed; only its brilliant overture is played nowadays.

With Offenbach we come to the giant of them all. He was equally popular in England and in America. To this country he brought his own company. He wrote over one hundred operettas and shorter pieces and nearly half of these are still listed.

In the case of others, the mere mention of the opera will reintroduce the composer. "The Daughter of Madame Angot" and "Giroflé-Girofla"—Lecocq. "Olivette" and "The Mascot"—Audran. "The Chimes of Normandy"—Planquette. Massenet first won fame with his comic opera, "The Great Aunt," before he turned his attention to Grand Opera. Then there was François Chassaigne; his comic operas, "Nadjy" and "Falka," were brought over to New York in the early Casino days and lavishly produced with casts headed by Lillian Russell, Marie Jansen, Fanny Rice, and James T. Powers. "Nadjy" ran 256 times, and "Falka" 110; yet in the succeeding years they have passed off the stage. They like many another, once-popular work, must be denied detailed description here.

André Messager is an example of another, once popular composer, now only a memory. His "Madame Chrysanthème" (see Grand Opera), produced in Paris in 1893, was performed by the Chicago Opera Company in 1920. His delicate "Véronique" was a favorite on the English stage, as also were "Mirette" and "La Bearnaise." The latter may be remembered for its duet, "Draw to me near"; the lovely soprano solo, "The Two Birds"; the trio, "Asleep"; and the dreamy berceuse, "Hush and Sleep." It is a pity that this dainty opera cannot be revived. He also wrote one with a story from an American source, "Monsieur Beaucaire," based on Booth Tarkington's novel.

For reasons of space we have not attempted a complete list; we have tried instead to give a representative one. They will serve to illustrate, if nothing else, that French opera has preserved an admirable balance between the grave and the gay.

LUIGI CHERUBINI

Although born in Florence, September 14, 1760, Cherubini is classed with French composers, as the bulk of his work was done in Paris. He became director of the Conservatoire there in 1822. He was a voluminous composer of long and short works, his most important operas being, "Demophon" (1788), "Lodoiska" (1791), "Ali Baba" (1794), "Medea" (1797), "Les Deux Journées" (1800), "Anacreon" (1803), and "Faniska" (1806). Cherubini died, March 15, 1842.

THE WATER CARRIER

(Les Deux Journées.) Comic Opera in Three Acts. Music by Cherubini. Book by Bouilly. Paris, January 16, 1800. It was tremendously popular in its own day, beginning with a run of 200 performances. It was known in Germany as "Der Wasserträger; and in London, where it was performed in 1801, as "The Water Carrier." It was this opera which caused Beethoven to say that Cherubini headed the list of living operatic composers.

ARGUMENT   The story concerns the adventures of Michele, a water carrier of Paris, whose son, Antonio, is engaged to Angeline. Michele's daughter, Marcelline, is interested in Count Armand, who is an object of persecution on the part of Cardinal Mazarin. In a climactic scene, the Count is conveyed out of the city in Michele's water barrel.

This opera is now chiefly remembered for its lovely overture, which still finds place on orchestral programs. It contains other music which deserves revival, such as the trio in the First Act, "O my liberator!" a dramatic ensemble at the beginning of the Second Act, with soldiers' chorus; a trio and march at the end of this act; the Wedding Chorus in the Third Act; a picturesque chorus by the soldiers; and a quartet and brilliant choral number at the close.

FRANÇOIS ADRIEN
BOIELDIEU

Boieldieu was widely popular in his lifetime.   He was born at Rouen,
December 16, 1775, and died near Paris, October 8, 1834.   He spent
practically his whole life in France, with the exception of eight years
when he was conductor of the Imperial Opera at St. Petersburg, Russia.
Of his numerous operas, three are still remembered for their graceful
overtures: "The Caliph of Bagdad," "John of Paris," and "The White
Lady."

THE WHITE LADY

(La Dame Blanche.)   Comic Opera in Three Acts.   Music by Boieldieu.   Book by Scribe, after Scott's novels, "The Monastery" and "Guy
Mannering."   Opéra Comique, Paris, December 10, 1825.   In English,
under the title, "The White Maid," at Covent Garden, London, January 2, 1827.   The opera was quite as popular in England as in France,
as the scene was laid in Scotland, and Scotch airs were introduced.
"George Brown" was a favorite rôle of Wachtel, who sang it also in
America.   The opera continued popular in France for over fifty years,
being performed over 1300 times.

ARGUMENT   The Laird of Avenel, who has been a zealous follower
of the Stuarts and is proscribed after the Battle of
Culloden, confides the family treasure to Gaveston, his steward.   This
is hidden in a statue known as "The White Lady"—a legendary figure
believed by the villagers to be the protectress of the family.   Gaveston
tries to force the sale of the castle, but is prevented by the arrival of a
mysterious stranger, George Brown, who at the auction outbids him.
Anna, the ward of Gaveston, aids George, appearing to him in the guise
of the White Lady.   At the last, George is disclosed as the rightful heir,
and Anna weds him.

The overture is charming and songs are delightful, many being Scotch
by descent.   In the First Act a chorus of mountaineers is heard, "Let

the music play"; George's opening song is "Ah, what joy to be a soldier!"; a ballad by the White Lady, with choral response, "Where yon trees"; and a trio leading to finale, "Heavens! what do I hear?" In the Second Act are heard a plaintive aria, "Poor Margaret, spin"; a trio, "Hark, they ring the bell"; a cavatina for tenor, "Come, O gentle Lady!"; a duet, "From these halls"; and a striking ensemble for seven voices and chorus. The Third Act begins with a sentimental aria, "With what delight I behold"; and leads up to one of the finest concerted numbers founded upon the familiar ballad, "Robin Adair."

DANIEL F. E. AUBER

Daniel François Esprit Auber, a remarkably prolific composer, was born January 29, 1782, at Caen, Normandy. His parents planned for him a business career, but his aptitude for music led to his studying under Cherubini. He was thirty-eight before he had achieved his first success in opera, "La Bergère Chatelaine." In 1822 he became associated with Eugene Scribe, the librettist, and the two produced many light and romantic operas in rapid succession, chief among them being: "Masaniello" (1828), "Fra Diavolo" (1830), "The Masked Ball" (1833), "Lestocq" (1834), "The Bronze Horse" (1835), "The Ambassadress" (1836), "The Black Domino" (1837), "The Crown Diamonds" (1841), "The Devil's Portion" (1853), and "Marco Spada" (1853). "Fra Diavolo," however, is the only one that seems to have won a permanent place. Auber died in Paris, May 13, 1871.

FRA DIAVOLO

("Brother Devil," or "The Inn of Terracina.") Light opera in Three Acts. Music by Auber. Book by Eugene Scribe. Opéra Comique, Paris, January 28, 1830. New York, in English, old Park Theatre, June 20, 1833. Widely popular in this country during the mid-century.

CAST FRA DIAVOLO, *a bandit chief.* GIACOMO, *a bandit.* BEPPO, *a bandit.* LORD ALLCASH, *an English tourist.* PAMELA, LADY

ALLCASH, *his wife.* LORENZO, *captain of the Carbiniers.* MATTEO, *an innkeeper.* ZERLINA, *his daughter.* FRANCESCO, *a miller.* Servants in the inn, Peasants, Bandits, Carbiniers, etc.

ARGUMENT "Fra Diavolo," one of the most tuneful of the light operas, is written around the adventures of a famous Italian bandit, the terror of the countryside. Despite the heavy reward offered for his capture, he remains at liberty by adopting numerous disguises. In the present adventure he travels under the name of the Marquis of San Marco. The Overture remains one of the best-loved of all the lighter ones written in the past century.

Act I At Matteo's inn in Italy a chorus of Carbiniers and others sing a drinking song: "Drink for joy bestowing." Lorenzo, their captain, says that they are soon to start on their quest of the notorious bandit, Fra Diavolo, to win a reward of twenty thousand crowns. He is risking his life, he avers, but life has lost its attraction for him, as Matteo has declined to give him the hand of his daughter, Zerlina. A duet between the two sweethearts follows. At this moment two English travelers, Lord and Lady Allcash (called "Cockburn" in some scores) arrive in much confusion, proclaiming that they have been robbed. (Song by Lady Pamela: "Oh, what a frightful land for strangers!") Lord Allcash has another grievance in the over-zealous attentions to his wife, of a traveling companion, the Marquis of San Marco. He and his lady bicker over the matter in a duet, "I don't object, I don't object." The debonair Marquis arrives, not at all disturbed by the contretemps, and orders a hearty dinner, while the vivacious Zerlina tells him stories about the notorious bandit chief, Fra Diavolo, who is a continual danger. Her recitative, "On yonder rock reclining," ends with "Diavolo! Diavolo!" The Marquis ends her song with a stanza of his own. Pamela enters and is startled to see her quondam suitor; but the Marquis, picking up Zerlina's mandolin, sings of "The gondolier, fond passion's slave." His regard for her, however, does not prevent his taking from her her last remaining jewel, a medallion, despite her protests. The soldiers now return with the tidings that they have dispersed the robbers. Final chorus: "Victory!"

Act II Zerlina shows the English couple to their room before going to her own. The girl herself is overjoyed at the success of her lover, and looks forward to her wedding day. Meanwhile, the Marquis, who is actually Diavolo, hides himself in her room, with two of his bandits. They are intent on finishing their robbery. Zerlina, unconscious of their presence, sings happily, " 'Tis tomorrow." As she slowly disrobes she remarks complacently that, "For a servant, there's no denying, here's a shape that's not much amiss!" The three bandits stifle a laugh and Zerlina turns in alarm, then becoming reassured by the silence kneels in prayer to the Virgin. After she has fallen asleep, one of them offers to strike her with his dagger, but a soft repeated prayer from her turns aside his evil design. An alarm follows and soldiers and others rush into the chamber. Diavolo stands at bay with his two men; but the jealousy of both the lord and Lorenzo is aroused by the presence of these men in the sleeping apartments. To cover his plot, the supposed Marquis says that he has an assignation with Zerlina. The enraged Lorenzo challenges him to a duel, which is arranged for the following day.

Act III "Proudly and wide my standard flies!" exults Diavolo in song. He has thrown aside his disguise and now in his native hills lies in wait for any luckless wayfarer. A wedding procession approaches. It is that of Zerlina and—not Lorenzo—but a well-to-do miller, Francesco, whom her father is compelling her to marry against her will. (Chorus: "Oh, holy Virgin!") After their departure, the disconsolate Lorenzo appears and sings, " 'I'm thine' she oft would say." He still thinks her unfaithful, and in an impassioned scene with her he reproaches her until she is in despair. Lorenzo, meanwhile, has not been idle. Recognizing the two rascals who were with Diavolo, he employs them to lure their chief into an ambush. The stratagem is successful. The chieftain is captured and all doubts are cleared. The English couple are amazed to find in him their traveling companion. Zerlina's innocence is established. She and Lorenzo find each other's arms. A quintet by the principals, "With gratitude now blended," is followed by the concluding chorus, "Victory! With heart and voice loud rejoice!"

THE BLACK DOMINO

Light Opera in Three Acts. Music by Auber. Book by Scribe. Paris, 1837.

ARGUMENT   The story relates the escapade of Angela, an abbess of Madrid, who goes to a masked ball and falls in love with Horatio, a young noble. She goes to another such affair in the hope of meeting him again, and only escapes detection by her black mask. After further complications, the Queen releases the Abbess from her vows and she weds her lover.

In the First Act there is a tuneful trio, "Is everything ready?"; also an aria by Angela, "A Fairy"; and a duet by Angela and Horatio,

"Break this silence at last."   In the Second, a chorus, "Awake who loves and lives"; a quartet, a chorus, "Quiet and low," and song by Angela, "Ha, dastard!"   In the Third, aria by Angela, "Oh this night!"; chorus of nuns, aria by Horatio, "Sweet strains," and finale by Angela and girls, "Dear sisters, hear what the Queen has ordered."

THE CROWN DIAMONDS

Comic Opera in Three Acts.   Music by Auber.   Book by Scribe and St. George.   Although first produced in Paris, in 1841, the English public took it to its heart, and it was one of the most successful operas of its day.   Princess Theatre, London, May 2, 1844.   Ten years later it had a notable revival, with a still more brilliant cast, and ran one hundred times.

ARGUMENT   **Act I**   The scene is Portugal; the time, 1777.   Don Henrique, a nephew of the Minister of Police, has lost his way in a mountain pass.   He stumbles upon a gang of counterfeiters, who are ready to kill him, when his life is saved by Catarina.   While posing as leader of the band, she is in reality the Queen of Portugal, who takes this scheme to substitute false gems for the crown diamonds, and thus obtain money to save her throne.   The gang is surrounded by troops, but makes its escape disguised as monks.   The music is charming throughout.   It has a good opening in the Don's song, "Roll on, roll on!"   Rebolledo, the chief of the coiners, sings effectively, "O'er mountain steep."   Catarina's first song tells her life story.   A chorus and rondo, "The young Pedrillo," leads on to a finale by the supposed pilgrims, "Unto the hermit of the chapel."

Act II   In the Coimbra Castle love affairs are at sixes and sevens.   Don Henrique, though pledged to Diana, for reasons of state, finds that he cannot get the mysterious Catarina out of his mind.   Likewise, Diana is loved by another gallant, Don Sebastian.   The report of the theft of crown diamonds is causing great excitement.   Catarina seeks refuge here, in spite of Don Henrique's warning that she is in the house of the Minister of Police.   Later she escapes.   The music includes a gay song by Don Henrique, "The Brigand," a quintet, "O surprise unexpected!" a florid song by Catarina, "Love, at once I break thy fetters," a duet, "If I could but courage feel," and a fine ballad by Don Henrique, "Oh, whisper what thou feelest!"

Act III   In the royal palace at Lisbon Diana awaits an audience with the Queen.   After a medley of confused identities has been satisfactorily cleared up, the mystery of the jewels is solved; Don Sebastian gets the hand of Diana; and the Queen refuses the hand of the Infante of Spain, in favor of Don Henrique, who has loved her for herself alone. The music includes Diana's opening song, "When doubt the tortured frame is rending"; a romantic aria by the Queen, "Love, dwell with me"; a martial "royal entrance" leading up to a brilliant finale.

LOUIS J. F. HÉROLD

Hérold was born in Paris, January 28, 1791, and died in the same city, January 19, 1833. He was a composer of great promise who died on the threshold of his career. He won the Grand Prix de Rome, in Italy, in 1812, and collaborated with Boieldieu in one opera, "Charles de France," but alone wrote many ballets, operas, and shorter works. His major compositions were "Zampa" (1831), and "Les Pré aux Clercs" (1832).

ZAMPA

Comic Opera in Three Acts. Music by Hérold. Book by Melesville, based on the tale, "The Statue Bride." Paris, May 3, 1831, and was a reigning favorite there and later in London and New York.

ARGUMENT   The story, which reminds one remotely of "Don Giovanni," tells the exploits of a notorious Sicilian bandit, Zampa, who adds kidnaping and betrayal to his other crimes. Albina, one of his victims, has died; a statue is erected to her memory. The bandit, in mockery, places a ring on the statue's finger; whereupon the image raises its arm menacingly. Meanwhile Signor Lugano is held for ransom, and Camilla, his daughter, promises to marry Zampa, to obtain his release. But Alfonso, her lover, interposes; her father is rescued; and the vengeful statue seizes the robber chief and carries him down to destruction.

This opera scored an enormous success when first produced, but is now only a tradition. Its tuneful overture, however, persists. Other charming bits are: the opening chorus; an aria by Camilla, "To Happiness"; quartet, "Here it is"; a canticle with harp accompaniment, "At the feet of the Madonna"; a melodious nocturne, "Where go you, poor Gondolier?"; a serenade, "Deepest night"; and a cavatina, "Why tremble?"

JACQUES HALÉVY

Halévy was of Jewish stock, born in Paris, 1799, and dying there, 1862. His chief operatic work was "La Juive," a tragic opera which has remained in repertory. (See Grand Opera.) In the same year he produced a lighter work, "L'Éclair," which is so dissimilar that many critics could not believe they were by the same hand. Halévy wrote a score of operas in all, which are now forgotten.

L'ÉCLAIR

Comic Opera in Three Acts. Music by Halévy. Book by Planard and St. George. Opéra Comique, Paris, December 16, 1835.

ARGUMENT   The story has a local interest in having its scene near Boston, Massachusetts, in the year 1797. The cast consists of a quartet, without chorus: Madame Darbel, a young widow; Henrietta, her sister; George, their English cousin; and Lionel, an American naval officer.

Henrietta likes the country, while her sister prefers the city. In the opening scene the respective merits of each section are melodiously debated. Their cousin George arrives from England to inform them that they and he have inherited their uncle's property, on condition that one or the other shall marry George. His aria is followed by a trio, "I hail from England's shores." During a thunderstorm, Lionel is rescued by Henrietta, but has lost his sight. Before this mishap, Lionel sings a stirring barcarole, "They say the sea is beautiful." In the Second Act, his sight is restored, but he mistakenly believes that Madame Darbel is his rescuer. Henrietta wanders off disconsolately. Although she is wooed by George, she has learned to love Lionel. In this Act are heard a quartet, "Be quiet, be still"; a duet, "Oh, how my heart is filled with joy!" and amusing counter arias by George and Madame Darbel on the joys of fidelity. In the final Act all these misunderstandings are cleared up; Henrietta and Lionel are united; ditto, George and Madame Darbel. An aria by Lionel, "When still the night with covered veil," and his, "Call me thine own," are the most effective bits in this Act.

ADOLPHE CHARLES ADAM

Adam was born in Paris, July 24, 1803, and passed away in the same city, May 3, 1856. As a youth he studied the organ in the Paris Conservatoire, and also came under the influence of Boieldieu, who urged him to go into his own field of opera. He devoted himself to lighter operas, some of which were highly successful, although now forgotten. A one-act work, "Pierre and Catherine" (1829) was followed by a score of others, such as "Le Chalet" (r834); "Le Postillon de Longjumeau" (1836), his most enduring work; "Le Brasseur de Preston" (1838); "Le Roi d'Yvetot" (1842); "Cagliostro" (1844), and "The Nuremburg Doll" (1852).

THE POSTILION OF LONGJUMEAU

Comic Opera in Three Acts. Music by Adam. Book by Le Leuven and Brunswick. Opéra Comique, Paris, October 13, 1836; Academy of Music, New York, 1875. Theodore Wachtel made the rôle of the Postilion famous, he himself having been a postilion before taking up singing. He sang the part over twelve hundred times.

CAST   CHAPELOU, *a postilion.* BIJOU, *a wheelwright.* MARQUIS DE CORCY. MADELEINE, *a hostess.* BOURDON, *an opera singer.* ROSA, *a maid.* Others.

ARGUMENT   The plot of this early light opera is much better than the average. It contrasts the dramatic with the humorous; and its music is sprightly and no less unexpected in its effects.

Act I   The scene is Longjumeau, a French village, at the time of Louis XV, 1776. The postilion, Chapelou, who is gifted with a fine natural voice, is taking to the marriage altar Madeleine, who has been hostess of the inn.   The Marquis de Corcy, who is a grand opera impresario, has to stop to have a carriage wheel repaired, and is so pleased with Chapelou's singing, that he persuades the postilion to forsake his bride and come with him to Paris.

The two most famous musical numbers in this Act are: Madeleine's song, "Husband ever dear"; and the lively Postilion's song with whip-snapping accompaniment.

Act II   The whole company are found in Paris.   Chapelou has become a great singer, under the name of St. Phar.   Bijou, the wheelwright, rejoices in the name of Alcindor.   Madeleine is Madame de Latour.   The chief trouble is that Chapelou does not recognize his own wife in her transformed status; and the Marquis is making violent love to her.   The misguided St. Phar is his rival.

Musical numbers: Madeleine, "I will see him again"; Chorus, "Oh, what misery!"; St. Phar, "From early dawn"; Duet, "Oh, most beautiful of women!"; Chorus, "My wishes are fulfilled."

Act III   In a country house the tangled web becomes clear.   St. Phar finds that he has been making love to his own wife, and has actually married her twice, under different names.

Musical numbers: Chorus, "O what joy!"; St. Phar, "I am now one of the aristocracy"; Quartet, "Hanged, hanged!"; Duet, "You see me in anguish"; Finale, "Quick, in the name of the King."

JACQUES OFFENBACH

No record of Light Opera would be complete without mention of Jacques Offenbach and his works.   He may be said to have founded the modern French school of *Opéra Bouffe*.   He was to France what Sullivan was to England, and Herbert to the United States.   Offenbach was born in Cologne of Jewish parents, June 21, 1819, but went to Paris at the age of fourteen and spent his life there.   He studied in the Conservatoire, played the 'cello in the Opéra Comique and, in 1849, became orchestral leader in the Théâtre Français.   Six years later he opened his own theater, the Bouffes-Parisiens, to form an outlet for the works which now were pouring from his pen. From 1872 to 1876 he managed the Théâtre de la Gaité, then came to America for a tour, being warmly welcomed. He died in Paris, October 5, 1880. He produced over one hundred musical works, nearly all of which were successful. The following are typical: "Le Mariage aux Lanternes" (1857); "Orphée aux Enfers" (1858); "Geneviève de Brabant" (1859); "Les Bavards" (1863); "Lischen et Fritzchen" (1864); "La Belle Hélène" (1864); "Barbe-Bleue" (1866); "La Vie Parisienne" (1866) which was revived in New York in 1945; "La Grande Duchesse de Gérolstein" (1867); "La Perichole" (1868); "La Princesse de Trebizonde" (1869); "Les Brigands" (1869); "Mme. Favart" (1879); and "Les Contes d'Hoffmann" (1881), his closing work and his masterpiece. (The last-named will be found under Grand Opera.) Offenbach's operettas were widely popular in America, during the eighties and nineties, being identified in New York with the Casino and Lillian Russell.

ORPHEUS IN HADES

(Orphée aux Enfers.)   Opéra Bouffe in Three Acts.   Music by Offenbach.   Book by Cremieux.   Bouffes-Parisiens, Paris, October 21, 1858.

ARGUMENT   This opera is considered to have some of the most typical music and delightful drolleries of this composer. It is a travesty upon the gods and goddesses of Olympus. They are invested with human attributes and made to take part in the joys and squabbles of every-day life. It is a mixture of burlesque, satire, and shrewd humor, enlivened by sprightly music. Typical numbers are: the opening aria by Eurydice, "She whose heart dreams"; the pastoral ditty by Aristeus; the hunting song of Diana, "When Diane comes into the plain"; the rollicking melody sung by John Styx, "When I was King of Boetia"; Eurydice's charming, "Pretty fly, with gilded wing"; the drinking song in the infernal regions, "Hurrah for the wine!"; Eurydice's wicked, "Bacchus has appeared to me"; and the medley finale, as Orpheus heads back for daylight and home.

LA BELLE HELÉNÈ

Opéra Bouffe in Three Acts.   Music by Offenbach.   Book by De Meilhac and Halévy.   Paris, December 17, 1864.   London, the Alhambra, August 16, 1873 (109 performances).   Following its London success, it was produced in New York, where it was well received but not phenomenally so. As recently as April 24, 1944, it was given an elaborate revival in New York, with considerable liberties taken with the original text, under the title, "Helen Goes to Troy," and ran for several weeks.

ARGUMENT   A burlesque of the heroes and heroines of antiquity. In the first act, the fair Helen is seen at the shrine of Jupiter in Sparta.   An augur has told her that she is to run away from her husband, Menelaus, and go with Paris to Troy.   She tries to avoid her fate, and even when Paris comes disguised as a shepherd, she will not yield to him, although she scolds her husband for getting in the way of her manifest destiny.   Other mythical events are lampooned in similar fashion, until Venus again interposes and orders her away to Troy with Paris.   So she goes, leaving Menelaus in a rage.   Agamemnon exclaims, "Well, there is nothing for it but to prepare for the Trojan War!"

Musical numbers: Helen's song of mourning, "Divine Love"; Paris' fable, "Three Goddesses on Mount Ida"; the march and chorus, "Behold the Kings of Greece!"; Helen's mock sentimental song, "We are born"; a droll goose-step march by the Kings; a chorus, "Your crown a garland of roses"; Helen's song, "A Wise Husband"; Orestes' aria, "Despite this ardent flame"; a trio, "While Greece is a camp of carnage"; and the spirited finale, "Our hatred flames."

BLUEBEARD

(Barbe-Bleue.)   Opéra Bouffe in Four Acts.   Music by Offenbach. Paris, 1866.

ARGUMENT   The Knight, Bluebeard, having poisoned five wives and still in quest of the right one, summons the peasants of his estate to choose a Rose-Queen.   The lot falls upon a rustic maiden, Bouloutte.   The Knight crowns her and makes her Wife Number Six.   Fleurette, another village girl, is discovered to be the daughter of King Bobeche, and is removed to his court.   Prince Saphir, who, disguised as a shepherd, has long loved her, follows her to court.   Thither also comes Bluebeard with his new wife, who astounds everybody with her free and easy manners.   He decides to get rid of her, like the rest. Bouloutte is duly poisoned by an Alchemist, but awakes in a cavern with the five earlier wives, none of whom has been actually put to death. Bluebeard is nonplussed by this abundance of wives and is forced to forego his contemplated marriage with the princess.   The latter's hand is then bestowed upon Prince Saphir.

A duet between Saphir and Fleurette opens the piece, "With roses newly blooming"; followed by a chorus of peasant girls; Bluebeard's song, "The Legend of Bluebeard"; the Princess' song, "My shepherd here"; a jolly quartet, "Ran, plan, plan!"; Bluebeard and chorus, "Coming in the olden fashion"; a Wedding Chorus, "To the altar"; and the droll "Bluebeard's Lament."

THE GRAND DUCHESS OF GEROLSTEIN

Opéra Bouffe in Three Acts.   Music by Offenbach.   Book by Meilhac and Halévy.   Varietés, Paris, April 12, 1867.   New York, the Casino, circa 1887, it was given a sumptuous America début, with large cast including Lillian Russell, Fanny Rice, Isabelle Urquhart, Henry Hallam, George Olmi, and Charles Renwick.   It ran 145 times.

ARGUMENT   Here again the powers of burlesque, of this composer, are seen at their best.   The action is laid in the imaginary duchy of Gerolstein, and begins with a pompous review of the army.   A recruit by the name of Fritz arouses the tender regard of the Duchess, who advances him to rank in the army with bewildering rapidity.   Finally she makes him General, then Baron, to the dismay of the other officers.   Fritz, however, is in love with Wanda, a peasant girl. His fortunes fall as rapidly as they have risen, but at the last he is allowed to wed his sweetheart; while the Duchess for reasons of state marries within her own rank.

The music is in keeping with the lighthearted mockery of the plot. It begins with the pompous "Pif, paf, pouf" song of General Boum. Then follow: the Duchess's air, "Ah, how I love my soldiers!"; the duet, "Ah, what a famous regiment!"; the famous sabre song, "Behold, the sabre of my father!"; Fritz's lively aria, "In orderly array"; a romanza, "Tell him"; trio, "Max was a soldier of fortune"; the Duchess's ballad, "It was one of mine"; and Fritz's song to her, "Well, your Highness, here I am!"

LA PERICHOLE

Opéra Bouffe in Three Acts.   Music by Offenbach.   Paris, in 1868.

ARGUMENT   Piquillo and La Perichole, two street singers with pleasing voices, come to the city of Lima, Peru, to take part in the festivities celebrating the birthday of the Viceroy.   They sing in the public square, but get no money and are almost starved. He goes to sing elsewhere in the streets, while she sinks down exhausted on a bench.   The Viceroy sees her and, struck by her beauty, requests her to come with him to his palace.   She goes, buoyed up by the hope of a square meal, and thinks she can outwit the Viceroy if he proves troublesome.   In order to further his scheme and keep within the law, the official sends out his men to find some poor man who, for a consideration, will "marry and leave" La Perichole.   They find Piquillo, who, despondent, is about to hang himself.   He is rescued, plied with wine, and taken to the palace where he unknowingly weds La Perichole. When Piquillo comes out of his stupor and is informed that he has married the Viceroy's favorite, he is amazed; but this turns to hot indignation when he discovers that she is none other than his sweetheart.   He is about to spoil all her plans to escape, but she prevails upon him to wait.   She then appeals to the better nature of the official, who sends them out with his full pardon and a princely present.   The story, while simple, is both pathetic and comical, and ranks with the really first-class libretti.

The music is typically brilliant, beginning with the lively "Song of the Three Cousins."   Then come a drinking song; a duet between Piquillo and La Perichole, "Cavalier and Captive"; "The Letter," by La Perichole; the "Tipsy Song" by her; and the final chorus in the First Act, "Ah, how charming a wedding!"   In the Second Act: women's chorus, "Ah, Signor, pray open your eyes"; and "Ah, Monsieur, good morning!"; Piquillo's amusing "couplets"; and merry chorus.   In the Third Act: La Perichole's song, "Piquillo, cease this foolish anger"; chorus, "When the hour of the feast approaches"; and the lovely duet by the two lovers, "A King was wont to stray."

THE PRINCESS OF TREBIZONDE

Opéra Bouffe in Three Acts.   Music by Offenbach.   Paris, 1869. New York, the Casino, May 5, 1883 (50 times).   In the cast were Lillian Russell, Laura Joyce, Madeline Lucette, Emma Carson, John Howson, Digby Bell, George Olmi, and A. W. Maflin.

ARGUMENT   In a village square a troupe of jugglers hold forth; they are Cabriolo, the proprietor, his two daughters, Regina and Zanetta, and his assistants, Tremolini and Paola.   But the show business is languishing as, in a lottery office across the way, they are raffling off a castle.   Prince Raphael and his tutor, Sparadrap, enter; and the Prince goes into the juggler's booth and is delighted with the beauty of a "wax" figure representing the Duchess of Trebizonde.   But the figure is the living girl, Zanetta.   The jugglers take into their till a lottery ticket with the number 1313, and it proves to be the lucky one entitling them to the castle.   The next two Acts are lively comedy, showing the strollers enjoying their good fortune; and the love affair between Zanetta and the Prince which, of course, turns out happily.

The music has a profusion of choruses, quintets, and duets: the chorus of huntsmen in the Second Act; the duet, "Angel adorable"; the rondo on "The Princess of Trebizonde"; Raphael's comic "Toothache Song"; and the song of the merrymakers in the final Act.

THE BRIGANDS

(Les Brigands.)   Opéra Bouffe in Three Acts.   Music by Offenbach. Book by Meilhac and Halévy.   English version by W. S. Gilbert. Paris, 1869.   New York at the Casino, circa 1888 (167 times).   In the cast were Lillian Russell, Fanny Rice, Isabelle Urquhart, Sylvia Gerrish, Henry Hallam, George Olmi, A. W. Maflin, and Charles Renwick.

ARGUMENT   The scene is laid in and near Mantua, Italy, and con-
                     cerns the adventures of a band of brigands headed by
Falsacappa and Fiorella, his daughter.   It is enlivened by typical music.
In the First Act we hear Fiorella's song, "A hat and a bright little feather"; the song of Fragoletto, the young farmer who falls in love with her, "When you in my cottage employed"; rondeau by Fiorella; chorus, "Come sing."   In the Second, duet between the two lovers, "Ho, la! Ho, la!"; chorus of brigands, "If you go"; Fiorella's song, "Indeed, I cannot tell you clearly."   In the Third, opening chorus, "Aurora appears"; the dialogue and chorus, "Please explain"; and the rollicking finale.

FELIX MARIE MASSÉ

Known also as Victor, Massé was born in Lorient, France, March 7, 1822, and died in Paris, July 5, 1884.   He served as chorus-master at the Opera, and taught at the Conservatoire.   His first opera, "La Chambre Gothique" (1849), was a success.   Others were: "Galatée" (1852), "Les Noces de Jeannette" (1853), "Miss Fauvette" (1855), "La Reine Topaze" (1856), "Paul and Virginia" (1876), and "Une Nuit de Cléopatre" (1877).

THE MARRIAGE OF JEANNETTE

(Les Noces de Jeannette.) Music by Massé. In One Act. Opéra
Comique, Paris, February 4, 1853. New York, 1861, with Clara Louise
Kellogg as "Jeannette," and Dubreul as "Jean," a boorish rustic, who at
first is willing to wed Jeannette, but changes his mind. The operetta
was revived some twenty-five years later, in America, by the American
Opera Company, then directed by Theodore Thomas; and was a prime
favorite as a "curtain-raiser."

LA REINE TOPAZE

(Queen Topaze.) Music by Massé. This operetta is still recalled
for its haunting melody. Produced at the Théâtre Lyrique, Paris, December 27, 1856, it is said to have led to the election of Massé to the
French Academy. It was sung also in England and America with pronounced success. The rôle of Queen Topaze was a favorite with such
prima donnas as Miolan-Carvalho and Parepa-Rosa.

ARGUMENT   In the story, the Queen is stolen by a band of Gypsies,
and the music is particularly effective. "The Song of
the Bee" is a brilliant aria for soprano. Another important number is
"The Carnival of Venice," which was later embroidered with variations
by the violinist, Paganini, and is well known as "a piece de resistance."
This opera deserves a better fate than oblivion. It was frequently
performed in the eighties and its music is still recalled by many per-
formers.

CHARLES LECOCQ

Lecocq was born in Paris, June 3, 1832. As a youth he showed high
promise, winning Conservatory prizes and excelling as an organist. At
the age of thirty-five he won place as one of the most successful composers of comic opera of his day. His chief operas were: "La Fleur de
Thé" (1868); "Le Barbier de Trouville" (1871); "Les Cent Vierges"

(1872); "La Fille de Mme. Angot" (1873); "Giroflé-Girofla" (1874); "La Petite Marie" (1876); "La Marjolaine" (1877); and "Le Petit Duc" (1878). He also wrote many lesser numbers. He was made Chevalier of the Legion of Honor in 1894. He died in Paris in 1911.

THE PEARL OF PEKIN

(La Fleur de Thé.) Comic Opera in Three Acts. Music by Lecocq. Book by Chivot and Duru. English version by Charles A. Byrne. Paris, 1868. The English version, freely adapted, was very popular in both England and America, during the last half of the Nineteenth Century, but is now only a tradition.

ARGUMENT La Fleur de Thé—or, the Pearl of Pekin, as she is known to us of America—is the daughter of Tyfoo, Governor of Pekin, who frequently remarks that he is "as knowing as the Sphinx." She has been carefully secluded until maturity and, according to an old Chinese custom, is to wed the first man she sees. Her father has planned a political match with Sorsoriki, a Japanese dignitary, but the Pearl mixes up plans by running away from the palace. She takes refuge in a cabaret run by the quartermaster of a French ship, Petit Pierre. He is a veritable Don Juan, but has a jealous wife, Finette. She accuses him, in the presence of the Governor, of harboring Chinese women; and Tyfoo is horrified to find that the refugee is his own daughter.

A Chinese law says that Pierre must wed her, or be impaled; but meantime there's his wife! All are taken to the palace, and the ceremony is performed—only, Finette is smuggled in as the bride. Pierre is rescued and taken back on shipboard; and the Pearl must perforce wed her Japanese suitor.

The music includes some of the sprightliest numbers that Lecocq has written. For the American version some additional songs were written by Gustave Kerker.

THE DAUGHTER OF MADAME ANGOT

(La Fille de Mme. Angot.) Comic Opera in Three Acts. Music by Lecocq. Book by Girardin, Clairville, and Konig. Théâtre Parisiennes, Brussels, November, 1872; Folies Dramatiques, Paris, February 23, 1873; Philharmonic, London, October 4, 1873 (235 times); Casino, New York, circa 1890 (61 times). In the latter cast were Camille

D'Arville, Marie Halton, Eva Davenport, Grace Golden, Henry Hallam, George Olmi, and A. W. Maflin.

CAST CLAIRETTE ANGOT, *betrothed to Pomponnet.* ANGE PITOU, *a poet.* MLLE. LANGE, *a favorite actress of Paris.* POMPONNET, *a hairdresser.* LARIVAUDIÈRE, *a citizen.* LOUCHARD, *police officer.* HERSILIE. BABET. TRENITZ, *officer of the Hussars.* Market Men and Women, Citizens.

ARGUMENT This pleasing work is a typical French opera boufle. The scene is Paris after the troubled days of the Revolution. The Directory has been established, with Barras at its head.

Act I On a market corner in Paris a group of tradespeople celebrate in song the approaching nuptials of Clairette and Pomponnet. Clairette is the daughter of the late Madame Angot, and rebels at wedding this barber, as she loves Ange Pitou, a poet. Clairette thanks her friends for their good wishes, but bemoans her fate in her opening song, "I owe you all my sincere thanks." An obstacle to the wedding presents itself. On looking into the records of Clairette's birth, her true father cannot be established. Although she has been reared as "a child of the market," this is not enough for the officials. A song by one of the market women and chorus tells of the famous Madame Angot: "Fish of all kinds she carried." The refrain which recurs is, "Very pretty, but not refined!"

Ange Pitou, who hawks his verses about town, is continually in trouble with the authorities. He gets out of jail again just in time to find that his sweetheart is about to be married. He voices his grief in "Yes, 'tis true I love Clairette." She enters and a tender duet reveals their affections. The audacious poet has written a song telling that Mlle. Lange, the favorite of Barras, has had an affair with Larivaudière. To avoid marriage with Pomponnet, Clairette sings this song ("In days gone by") knowing that she will be arrested. A medley of soldiers, citizens, led by Clairette, "I go cheerfully to prison," greets the curtain.

Act II Mlle. Lange, in her luxurious drawing-room, is more interested than incensed at the bold girl who has dared to sing about her. (Chorus: "Nobody would believe it.") A humorous interlude is furnished by the vainglorious Trenitz, an officer in the Hussars. While he preens himself, the chorus echoes his charms. ("Glory to the executive power.") Pomponnet now comes in to intercede for his prospective bride; he wants to throw the blame for the offending song upon its composer. He sings, "She is innocent." When Clairette is finally brought in, and the two women are alone, they recognize each other as old school friends. (Duet: "Oh, happy days of childhood vanished.") Later the poet himself appears to intercede for his sweetheart, and finds to his surprise that the maligned actress is really a very charming woman. She also is pleased with his demeanor, and they sing a fervent duet. Larivaudière arrives suddenly, and in the mix-up of interests a quintet is sung: "Yes, 'tis on her account alone." All the various conspirators then turn upon the luckless Pomponnet, who enters, and cause his arrest for having on his person a copy of the offending song.

At a meeting of political conspirators, who include some of the same group, affairs grow still more complicated. (Chorus: "When one's conspiring.") Before they can proceed with their plot against the government the house is surrounded by Hussars. The quick-witted Mlle. Lange tells her friends to hide their collars and other badges and turn the meeting into a wedding ball in honor of Clairette and Ange Pitou. A colorful medley waltz and chorus with soldiers and conspirators intermingled close the act.

Act III Clairette is released from prison, but is disconsolate. She has reason to believe that her poet is fickle; that he has turned his attentions to the actress. In a garden before a cabaret she greets some of her old friends of the market. She sings, "You brought me up above my station." Pomponnet, who has likewise been imprisoned for her sake, is now at liberty, and when she sees him her heart is touched by his faithfulness. Larivaudière, who is beginning to realize that he, too, is being hoodwinked, lends his aid to them. Clairette writes a series of decoy notes, one of which brings Ange Pitou and Mlle. Lange together. They greet each other with impassioned song, only to be surprised by the others. Clairette voices the scorn with, "Ah! then 'tis you, Madame Barras, wanting three strings unto your bow!" In the dispute which arises, Clairette renounces her recreant lover, and discovers that she is quite willing to go ahead with her postponed wedding to the honest barber. A chorus of delighted tradespeople and others terminates the opera.

GIROFLÉ-GIROFLA

Opéra Bouffe in Three Acts. Music by Lecocq. Book by Vanloo and Aterrier. Théâtre des Fantasies, Brussels, March 21, 1874. Paris, November 11, 1874. New York, Park Theatre, 1875. While this opera was popular for some years thereafter, it is now a tradition. Lillian Russell sang in it. In a later adaptation by Harry B. Smith, Fritzi Scheff starred.

ARGUMENT   The scene of this pleasing musical skit is Spain, of
about the year 1850.   Briefly, it is a farce based on mistaken identities and set off with melodious music.   Giroflé and Girofla
are twin sisters so much alike that they have to wear scarfs of different
shades.   One is betrothed to Marasquin, a wealthy banker; and this
alliance is much needed by the girls' indigent father.   The other twin is
pledged to Mourzouk, a fire-eating Moor, who is making it hot for the
father, otherwise.   Giroflé is hastily married off to the banker, but her
sister is carried off by pirates.   When the Moor arrives demanding his
bride, her sister is palmed off on him—almost!   There is a great stew
among the three—the one girl and the two insistent men—until her
twin is conveniently rescued from the pirates, and all ends happily.

The music is much better than the average, often rising to brilliant
heights: Act I. Ballad, "When the day is finished"; Chorus, "To the
Chapel"; Pirate's chorus, "Among the delicate things we do"; Duet,
"Our marriage is concluded."   Act. II. Bacchanalian chorus, "Listen to
this music" ending in a gay dance; Quintet, "Matamoras, our great Captain"; Drinking song—still a favorite—"See how it sparkles!"; Duet,
andante, "O Giroflé, O Girofla!"; Chorus of wedding guests, "It is the
cannon."   Act III. Rondo, "O my Father, now you ask"; Duet, "My
lovely Giroflé"; and a smashing finale.

THE LITTLE DUKE

(Le Petit Duc.)   Comic Opera in Three Acts.   Music by Lecocq.
English text by Fred Williams and T. R. Sullivan.   Renaissance Theatre, Paris, January, 1878.   New York, the Casino, circa 1890.   In the
cast were Georgine Von Janaschowsky, Agnes Folsom, Genevieve Rey-
nolds, and Billie Barlow.   This opera has many pleasing airs, and was
long popular in both England and America.

ARGUMENT   The action takes place in the Court of Louis XIV.
The first scene discloses a sumptuous apartment in
Versailles.   The pages are singing and making eyes at the maids of
honor, and declaring that, although young, they have as much right to
wed as the youthful Duke of Parthenay, who is to be married that night
to the Lady Blanche, for reasons of state.   (Chorus: "Here comes the
youthful bride and groom.").   The boyish groom (the part being taken
by a girl with contralto voice) after the two are left alone tries to make
love, but with poor success.   (Duet: "I love thee.   Is that so difficult to
say?")   The Duchess runs out of the room, and the pages sing a mock-

ing chorus.   Other comedy elements are the antics of the Duke's tutors
who now find themselves out of a job.   The little Duke is consoled over
his wife's actions by being made colonel of a regiment.   Closing chorus
of this Act: "Our colonel see!"

In the Second Act the Duchess is found ensconced in a Luneville
school, taking part in a singing lesson.   She is to be separated from the
little Duke for two years, and is beginning to regret it.   Dragoons surround the school, but those who are admitted have their eyes bandaged,
and all indulge in a dance which is a sort of blindman's buff.   The
schoolmistress, Chanoinesse de Lausac, says that she will defend her
charges to the last.   (Chorus: "To arms!")   The school then prepares
for a siege.   At this juncture, the Duke is admitted, disguised as a peasant girl.   (Aria: "Dear ladies, list to my simple song.")   The young
couple find opportunity to meet, but the Duke is discovered.   He and
his Duchess sing a parting song, "Alas! she speaks the truth."

The Third Act reveals a military encampment.   The Duke's mentor,
Montaland, with male chorus, sings "The Song of the Little Hunch-
back."   The little Duke has gone through his first battle, and sings,
"I've through the fiery ordeal passed."   But he generously gives credit
to Montaland for the victory.   Later the Duchess, who has run away
from school, joins him in his tent.   (Duet: "But yesterday, my love.")
A brilliant ensemble closes this delightful opera.

GEORGES   BIZET

Georges Bizet (1838–1875) is listed under Grand Opera, in this volume, with biographical sketch and synopsis of his most famous work,
"Carmen."   It is interesting to note in passing that this was originally
labelled, Light, and had spoken dialogue which banned it from the
strict ranks of Grand repertory.   As a matter of operatic record we are
including here a modern treatment of this opera, "Carmen Jones,"
which had a long run of over five hundred performances in New York;
this in sharp contrast to the initial performances of the original, which
were not successful and caused the composer to die, brokenhearted.
He was not to witness the work's later and continued fame.

CARMEN JONES

Musical Play in Four Acts. Music follows the original score of Bizet, with new orchestral arrangements by Robert Russell Bennett. Text adapted by Oscar Hammerstein 2d. Produced by Billy Rose at City Center, New York, December 2, 1943; later at Broadway Theatre.

ARGUMENT   The locale of this version of "Carmen" is Harlem in New York. The characters are taken by Negroes, and local manners and customs are substituted for Spain. Typical titles of songs: "Dat's love," "Dere's a café at de corner," and—instead of the toreador—"Get your program for de big fight," (a boxing match) and "Dat's our man!"

Mr. Hammerstein says that melodies with few exceptions were sung in the accustomed order, small deviations only being made when deemed necessary in transporting Carmen to a modern American background. In the elimination of recitatives from the original, he maintains that it was not taking so great a liberty, since Bizet himself had spoken dialogue in his first version. The work was not converted into Grand Opera until after the death of the composer.

If Bizet in the spirit could return and witness this modernization, one wonders what would be his sensations!

EDMOND AUDRAN

Audran was a reigning prince of Light Opera in the closing years of the last century. Born in Lyons, April 11, 1842, dying in Tierceville, August 17, 1901, he was the son of Marius Audran, a composer and tenor singer. Edmond was educated at the École Niedermeyer, Paris, where he won a prize for composition at seventeen. He started his career as organist in a church in Marseilles, writing masses and other church music. Turning to lighter songs, he soon became widely known as a composer of opéra bouffe. Twenty or more light operas are credited to him, most of which found favor in both England and America. They include: "The Grand Mogul" (1876), produced with great success in London, in 1881; "La Cigale," which also had an immense vogue abroad; "La Poupée," widely produced by both professionals and amateurs; "Uncle Celestin"; "Olivette," and "La Mascottë—the two latter having phenomenal runs in England and America.

OLIVETTE

(Les Noces d'Olivette.) Light Opera in Three Acts. Music by Audran. English adaptation by H. B. Farnie. Opéra Bouffe, Paris, November 13, 1879; the Strand, London, September 18, 1880 (466 times). In America it was equally popular and frequently revived.

CAST CAPTAIN DE MERIMAC, *of the man o' war, Cormorant.* VAL-
ENTINE, *his nephew.* DUC DES IFS. COQUIELICOT. MARJEVOL,
Mayor of Perpignan. OLIVETTE, *his daughter.* BATHIELDE. COUNTESS
OF ROUSILLON. VELOUTINE, *housekeeper.* MOUSTIQUE. Others.

ARGUMENT The action of this light, graceful opera takes place in
Perpignan, a village of Rousillon. The time is that
of Louis XIII.

Act I The villagers are excited over the announced nuptials of
Olivette, the Mayor's daughter, and the bluff but no longer
young sea captain, De Merimac. Olivette herself does not approve; she
is in love with Valentine, the Captain's nephew. As a further complication, the Countess is also setting her cap for the young man. Valentine
takes a hand by impersonating his uncle and in this guise wedding
Olivette, with the full approval of the Countess.

Musical numbers: "Gossip Chorus"—a jolly opening piece; Olivette,
"The convent slept"; Marine madrigal, "The Yacht and the Brig";
Countess (waltz song) "O heart, wherefore so light?"; the Duke's comical
ditty, "Bob up serenely"; Valentine's serenade, "Darling, good night";
"Wedding Bells," chorus.

Act II At a ball given by the Countess in honor of the wedding, Valentine finds that he has to be two persons at once. This he
manages to accomplish by constant change of attire. But at this juncture the real Captain turns up, and is naturally bewildered to find that
he is already married and everybody is celebrating the event except
himself. Olivette tries to get rid of him. The Countess, too, gets in
the way and a plot is hatched to get rid of her likewise.

Musical numbers: chorus, "Soon the bride"; quintet, "It is he";
Countess, "Wayward women"; finale, "What joy in honeymooning!"

Act III The Countess is imprisoned on board the *Cormorant*. Olivette and Valentine disguise themselves as sailors, but he is

detected and the plot gets still more mixed. Olivette does not help matters by removing her sailor's disguise, only to assume that of the Countess. When the last make-up is removed, the two young people are allowed to stay wed, while the Captain is advised to "marry the sea."

Musical numbers: chorus, "Jamaica Rum"—sung as a "Grogorian Chant!"; Countess, "Nearest and dearest"; Olivette and chorus, the old-time favorite, "The Torpedo and the Whale"; quartet, "No, no, 'tis you"; march militaire and finale, "All is ended."

THE MASCOT

(La Mascotte.) Light Opera in Three Acts. Music by Audran. Paris, December 29, 1880, where it was received with wide favor. During the next twenty years in France it was performed 1700 times. An English version at the Comedy Theatre, London, October 15, 1881, ran 199 times. New York, Abbey's Park Theatre, in 1881. "The Mascot" was taken by Fay Templeton. It had a run of over two years and both Nat Goodwin and Henry E. Dixey starred as "Lorenzo." Some twenty years later an "elaborate revival" was given in New York with an excellent cast headed by Raymond Hitchcock and Flora Zabelle.

CAST LORENZO, *Prince of Pembino.* FREDERICK, *Prince of Pisa.* PIPPO, *a shepherd.* ROCCO, *a farmer.* PARAFANTE, *a sergeant.* MATHEO, *an innkeeper.* FIAMETTA, *daughter of Lorenzo.* BETTINA, *the Mascot.* Peasants, lords and ladies, soldiers, etc.

ARGUMENT This tuneful opera describing the checkered fortunes of an irrepressible girl long enjoyed popularity in both its French and English versions, and has been transplanted successfully to other lands. It is still regarded as a Light Opera classic.

Act I The scene is Pembino, Italy. The time, the Fifteenth Century. As the curtain rises on an Italian farmyard scene, a chorus gaily sings, "Now the vintage time is over," but despite their gaiety, Rocco, owner of the farm is depressed. His barn is burned; his sheep are lost; and he is facing a lawsuit. His shepherd, Pippo, returns without the money for which he has been sent to town; but he tells his master he has brought something far more valuable. It is a Mascot in the shape of a pretty girl, and she will surely bring him good luck. Bettina now enters pursued by some of the village swains who sing teasingly, "Come now, my beauty!" She sauces back at them in song until at last she seizes a bucket of water from Rocco's hand and dashes it in their faces. Rocco admires her spunk and wonders if she will bring him better fortune, after all.

Prince Lorenzo and his party enter from a hunting trip and wish to rest at the farm. The chorus sings, "When the gay sport of hunting is over." Lorenzo's theme song is "Wise men of all ages." His daughter, Fiametta, also enters with her suitor, Prince Frederick. Lorenzo complains of the same thing that Rocco does—ill luck—while the latter is beginning to think that with the advent of Bettina his own luck is commencing to change for the better. Fiametta, meanwhile, is much taken with the young shepherd, Pippo; but the latter reassures the jealous Bettina in a duet, with a barnyard motif, "Gobble, gobble!" Rocco's new hopes are further dashed when Lorenzo decides to take the Mascot back to court with him.

Act II "Oh, what a beauty!" sings the opening chorus in the prince's palace. It is in praise of the Countess of Panada, the new title of our Bettina. She still wins all hearts; even the pages are writing love letters to her. Rocco, who has been taken along too and made Court Chamberlain, is disgusted and wants to take the girl back to his farm. She, too, is unhappy, because Fiametta still pursues Pippo. "Ah! let me be!" sings Bettina. A court masque is presented, and Pippo takes one of the leads, as "Saltarelle," singing, "All hail to you, my lords!" He is recognized by Bettina, and they sing a duet, "Knowest thou those robes?" They are surprised by Lorenzo and Rocco, and Pippo is arrested. A further complication ensues when the jealous Fiametta tries to force Pippo to make love to her, telling him that Bettina is to wed Lorenzo. Frederick, meanwhile, presents himself for his marriage with Fiametta. The general mix-up is ended by Pippo, who seizes Bettina in his arms and jumps out of a window into a river below. The music in the latter part of this lively act reflects the interplay of emotions.

Act III At an inn near Pisa a chorus of soldiers sings, "Fill the cups full, overflowing," a rollicking drinking song. Frederick, incensed at his repulse by Fiametta, is making war on her father. He enters with the song, "Good day, my braves!" Pippo and Bettina, none the worse for their ducking in the river, now appear and are recognized by the Prince. Others also are discovered near camp. They are Lorenzo, his daughter, and Rocco, disguised to represent poor minstrels. Lorenzo, convinced that without the Mascot he is lost, has taken this means to escape his enemy. A medley of songs ensues. Pippo and Bettina announce their intention of getting married, but Pippo is told that the virtues of his Mascot will vanish, if he so much as kisses her; but he takes the chance regardless. His song as a bridegroom is, "I near the goal." A quartet follows with the bride and groom, and Lorenzo, and Rocco singing, "How is this, Pippo?" followed by "Ah! with wrath

I'm fairly choking." Fiametta sees that her own pursuit of the shepherd is hopeless, so bestows her hand on Frederick. The two noblemen patch up their differences, and all echo Lorenzo's parting words, "Mascots we must believe in!"

LA CIGALE
(*La See-gahl*)

(The Grasshopper.) Romantic Opera in Three Acts. Music by Audran. Book by Chivot and Duru. English version by Burnand and Gilbert à Beckett. Paris, circa 1882, then in London and New York, where it met with wide favor.

ARGUMENT   This tuneful opera is now unfortunately only a tradition. It is built around the fable of the Ant and the Grasshopper. The scene opens with the marriage of Charlotte, the "Ant," to William. Her cousin, Marton, the "Grasshopper,"—*La Cigale*—is more frivolous-minded and announces that she is going upon the stage. Then ensues a complication of loves and jealousies, demanding unusual acting as well as singing ability—perhaps one reason why the opera is not produced more often.

Music is lively and plentiful. A children's chorus near the beginning, "Hey, boys, gay boys," is followed by Charlotte's song, "The Golden Harvester"; Marton, "The merry cricket"; Vincent, "Bird voices"; chorus, "Dance and sing"; Marton, "Three to one"; and finale, "La Gloria." Second Act, opening chorus, "Bells for our fête are ringing"; Franz, "Trifle not with love"; Marton's charming gavotte song, one of the best remembered, "Mother dear"; quartet, "Too little foresight"; and trio, "Excuse me." Third Act, Franz, "List to me"; concerted piece, "The grasshopper and the butterfly"; a dream song by Marton, "My dear old home"; and finale, "Oh, day of joy!"

ROBERT JEAN PLANQUETTE

The name of Planquette inevitably calls to mind only his great classic, "The Chimes of Normandy," yet in his lifetime he was known for at least a dozen operettas. Planquette was born in Paris, July 31,

1850, and passed away in the same city, January 28, 1903. He wrote many songs and light orchestral numbers. His operettas include: "The Chimes of Normandy" (1877), "Rip Van Winkle" (1881), "Nell Gwynne" (1884), "Paul Jones" (1887), "Merrie England," and "The Old Guard."

THE CHIMES OF NORMANDY

(Les Cloches de Corneville.)   Light Opera in Three Acts.   Music by Planquette.   Book by Clairville and Babet.   Folies Dramatiques, Paris, April 19, 1877.   The Folly, London, February 28, 1878, in English (705 times).   Transplanted to America, it was an instant "hit," with long runs in cities, and frequent renewals by both professional and amateur singers.

CAST   HENRI, *Marquis of Villeroi*.   GASPARD, *a miser*.   GERMAINE, *his niece*.   SERPOLETTE, *the village "good-for-nothing."*   JEAN GRECHINEUX, *a fisherman*.   THE BAILIFF.   Villagers, Fishers, Servants, Officers, etc.

ARGUMENT   A perennially pleasing light opera is this, depicting the fisher and peasant folk in a little town of old Normandy, time of Louis XV.   Its initial situation in which is shown the "Corneville Market, Grand Hiring of Maidservants, etc." is reminiscent of "Martha."   An excellent plot is welded to tuneful music.

Act I   As the Corneville Fair opens, the men and girls who wish to obtain service are zealously parading their wares in a tuneful chorus: "All who for servants are inquiring."   Serpolette, the village gossip and cut-up, enters, and although the other girls criticize her behind her back, they are ready enough to listen to her tittle-tattle.   She claims that there is a mystery surrounding her own birth, and sings, "I may be a princess."   She proves, at any rate, that she is abundantly able to take care of herself with her sharp tongue.

Her venom is next directed toward the old miser, Gaspard, who has half starved his niece, Germaine, and now intends to bestow her hand upon the ancient Bailiff.   Germaine herself vows that she will wed no one unless it be the young fisherman, Jean Grechineux, in gratitude for once saving her life.   He enters singing a barcarole, "On billows rocking."   A duet follows between the two, "I vow to keep the faith then spoken."

In the guise of a wandering seaman, Henri, the Marquis of Villeroi, now comes back to his ancestral home.   None recognizes him, but when he says that he is on his way to the old castle, they tell him it is haunted.

Strange lights are often seen flickering in the windows; and Germaine, with the chorus, sings to him one of the finest bits of the opera: "Yes, that castle old by wizard is enchanted," ending with the melodious, "Ding, dong!"—the greeting of the bells when the rightful master shall return. "Quite a romantic legend!" avers the stranger; and he responds with a waltz rondo: "With joy my heart has often bounded."

A commotion without is followed by a struggling group. Serpolette is pursued by Gaspard in a rage; and Jean is seized by the scruff of the neck. Serpolette has seen the love-making between Germaine and Jean, and feels it her duty to "tell the world." The miser aims a blow at her, and it hits the Bailiff. (Chorus: "Such conduct is quite sad in one about to marry.")

The second scene of this act takes place at the Fair. The young fisherman is discovered fleeing from jail, and in a song he announces that in order to escape from his enemies he will have to take service with some one as a coachman. He hides as other men and maidens enter, all again chanting their virtues as servants. A notary states that all contracts must endure for six months. Henri comes in and engages Jean as his coachman, and Serpolette as maid. The latter is overjoyed, as she thinks she has put one over on the "superfine Germaine." But the latter, who has escaped from the cruelty of her uncle, also takes service at the castle. The act ends with the miser trying to get his hands upon his niece, and a spirited chorus ("Yes, old Gaspard, you are wrong") preventing him.

Act II A great hall covered with dust is the sight which greets the Marquis, as he undertakes to explore his castle. With him comes a group bearing torches and singing, "Let our torches light up the gloom." Germaine hangs back but is reassured by Henri. As all leave to explore the other rooms, she remains, to sing, "From pallid cheek you may be telling." She leaves and in the gloom a trio—Serpolette, Jean, and the Bailiff,—collide. Recovering from their shock, Serpolette sings, "Not a ghost at all!" The Bailiff is now confronted by Henri, who reveals his identity and reproaches the officer for letting the castle fall into such neglect. The Bailiff answers with a buffo song, "Oh dear! oh dear! that riot and that rabble." In a recitative and chorus, Henri and the others say that the armed statues are "not phantoms," but "silent heroes from the mighty past." Henri finds an old document showing that an heiress was entrusted to Gaspard to rear as a simple peasant girl. Serpolette thereupon boldly claims that she is the person described and a Marchioness. Henri hears her claims with distaste; he is strongly drawn toward Germaine, and she to him, although she thinks that, from gratitude, she should give her hand to

Jean. A duet between the Marquis and his "serving maid" is one of the charming bits of this act.

Jean, meanwhile, through his fear of ghosts, is cutting a poor figure. Henri sees his trepidation but, far from shielding him, places him in a suit of armor to keep watch for the real "phantom." The unwilling spy presently sees the old miser enter by a secret way. It is he who has made use of the castle for many years, to hide his gold. Now he spreads it out on the table, before Jean's terrified eyes, and croons over it: "Love, honor, happiness—what are they all compared with gold?" The hidden fisherman joins him in a duo. As it ends, the castle bells ring out, and Gaspard starts back in dismay. Shrieking, "The ghosts! The ghosts!" he struggles between his fear and his desire to save his hoard. The others surprise him, and as the chorus exclaims: "Yes, we are ghosts! Vengeance is sped!" the old man falls senseless amid his bags of gold.

Act III The setting of a brilliantly lighted banquet hall of the castle is in sharp contrast to the former scene. The Marquis has come into his own and is giving a great entertainment to all his retainers. But before it begins, poor old Gaspard wanders in singing a ballad of "the good old times." He has lost his reason. The belle of the ball is Serpolette, who flaunts her new-found rank as Marchioness. Jean is now her faithful satellite. She sings, with chorus, her saucy "Cider Song." Later, alone, Jean sings of the time he rescued Germaine from the sea ("That night I'll ne'er forget"). The Marquis, who was the actual rescuer, strikes him, and Jean sneaks off. A duet follows between Henri and Germaine, in which the girl still protests that she cannot wed him, because of her uncle's conduct. Gaspard, however, in a moment of sanity, recognizes the nobleman and confesses that Germaine and not Serpolette is the missing heiress. All ends as it should. Both Serpolette and Jean are forgiven, as well as the old miser; Germaine accepts the Marquis; and the finale brings in the bell refrain, "Ding, dong!"

RIP VAN WINKLE

Comic Opera in Three Acts. Music by Planquette. Paris, in 1881; and London, in 1882. Later version in America, 1933.

ARGUMENT This opera deserves mention on account of an elaborate revival given it in St. Louis and other American cities, by J. J. Shubert; and also the fact that its theme is American. However, in the modernized version, presented in the summer of 1933,

Rip begins his adventures in the present time; he is, in fact, a radio announcer.   In order to evade his wife's party-giving proclivities, he wanders off into the Catskills.   Then follows the story much after Irving.   But when Rip comes home, the colonists are free of King George; they are preparing to hold an election; and returns are coming in over the radio! An Epilogue brings it back to the present.

The music is typical of this gifted composer.   It includes, in the First Act, chorus and solos, "Far and near"; Rip's song, "Oh, where's my girl"; Gretchen and chorus, "Legend of the Catskills"; and rondo led by Katrina.   In the Second Act, Gretchen's ballad, "Now the twilight"; trio, "Now won't you come?"; sea song, Rip and Hudson, "Blow high, blow low"; and sextet leading to finale.   In the Third Act, Rip's song, "Truth in the well"; and trio, "I know you not."

NELL GWYNNE

Comic Opera in Three Acts.   Music by Planquette.   Book by H. B. Farnie.   London, 1884.   New York at the Casino circa 1891, where it ran for 43 performances.   In the cast were Mathilde Cottrelly, Laura Joyce Bell, Billie Barlow, and Digby Bell.

ARGUMENT   This sprightly opera has been more of a favorite in England than in America, as it deals with an English theme.   It portrays the adventures of that actress who was a favorite of Charles the Second; and brings in other historical personages of the day, such as Buckingham and Rochester.

The music is introduced by a drinking song, "Fill up each flagon," followed by an aria, "To you, ladies"; Nell's rondo, "Only an orange girl"; quartet, "Oh, heart, my lover's near!"; serenade, "Sweetheart, if thou be nigh"; the "Song of the Clock"; Nell's romance, "First love"; a hunting chorus beginning the Third Act; Nell's "The broken cavalier"; a charming minuet leading up to quartet and finale.

HENRI RABAUD

Rabaud was born at Paris, October 10, 1873.   After completing his musical training he became conductor of the orchestra at the Opéra

Comique, Paris. In 1918 he came to America to conduct the Boston Symphony Orchestra. His operas include: "La Fille de Roland" (1904); "Le Premier Glaive" (1908); and "Marouf" (1914). He is also the composer of orchestral numbers, quartets, and other incidental music. Rabaud died in September, 1949.

MAROUF, THE COBBLER OF CAIRO

Comic Opera in Five Acts. Music by Rabaud. Book by Lucien Nepoty, after a tale in "The Arabian Nights." Opéra Comique, Paris, 1914. At the Metropolitan Opera house, New York, December 19, 1917, with a cast including Frances Alda, Kathleen Howard, Leon Rothier, and Giuseppe de Luca (as the Cobbler).

CAST   MAROUF, *a cobbler.* FATIMAH, *the kill-joy, his wife.* THE SULTAN. PRINCESS SAAMCHEDDINE. THE VIZIER. ALI, *a merchant.* AHMAD, *a pastry cook.* Merchants, Courtiers, Drivers, Slaves, Ladies of the Harem, etc.

ARGUMENT   A light opera partaking of the flavor of "Arabian Nights" in the droll series of misadventures which befall the luckless cobbler. The music is incidental to the action, and is so nearly "classic" that it has been well received at the Metropolitan, although it is not now in active repertory.

Act I   In a poverty-stricken cobbler's booth in Cairo, Marouf strikes a few half-hearted blows with his hammer, the while he bemoans his fate. Cairo is full of seductive damsels, and here he is blessed with a wife who has an ugly face and a disposition of the same stripe. On one unlucky occasion when he brings home the wrong kind of rice cake, she flies into a rage and posts off to tell the Cadi that her husband has been beating her. The over-credulous official thereupon orders a public bastinado for the poor cobbler, and Marouf decides that this is the last straw. He runs away. Musically this act is one of recitative and colloquy, with no outstanding aria or chorus.

Act II   Taking refuge on a sailing ship Marouf departs for other and, he hopes, friendlier strands. Their ship is wrecked and he is cast ashore clinging to a spar. When he comes to his senses he finds himself in the city of Khaitan, a mythical place "somewhere between China and Morocco." He has been rescued by a well-to-do merchant, who proves to be a boyhood friend, Ali. The latter palms him off as the richest merchant in the world. He arrays him in gorgeous attire and has him flinging gold pieces right and left as he rides down the street. Other traders are all eager to deal with him; and the Sultan and his Vizier are so impressed that they invite him to dine at the palace. The musical numbers are similar in treatment to those of the first act, and include much musical banter, but little concerted work.

Act III In the Sultan's palace the erstwhile cobbler is living a life of luxurious ease. The Sultan is so taken with him that he gives him the hand of his daughter. When the canny Vizier begins to doubt the visitor, whose rich caravan is still "on the way," the Sultan grows angry and proclaims the nuptials for that very day. A ballet ensues. After the dance the princess and the cobbler have an amusing conversation. She is still veiled and Marouf is afraid that he has again drawn a hook-nosed harridan. But when she is at last persuaded to unveil, her unexpected beauty overpowers him and he falls in a swoon. Some confused words reveal to the princess his identity, but her heart goes out to him regardless. This scene with its background of ladies of the harem is one of brilliance.

Act IV The cautious Vizier and his master discuss ways and means in a garden before the harem. The wedding gifts and largess have been so bountiful that the royal treasury is empty—and still Marouf's caravans do not arrive! The Sultan is still credulous, however. The princess is summoned and she concocts a great tale about a robbery which occurred to the caravan, but other treasure is on its way. Later, Marouf confesses all to her, and she decides to run away with him, to escape her father's vengeance.

Act V While the two elopers are making their way across the desert on horseback they are sheltered one night by a poor Bedouin. Marouf offers to plow his field for him in return for his hospitality. While plowing, the share strikes an iron ring which opens a door disclosing a stairway leading to an underground vault. The ring also has magic power. When rubbed, the Bedouin is transformed into a powerful genie, who says that he serves the master of the ring. A hidden treasure of vast size is disclosed, and a caravan of goods, such as Marouf and his friend, Ali, have been bragging about, is conjured up out of the desert. As a final climax, however, Marouf's triumph is postponed, and wellnigh fatally. The Vizier captures him and takes him back to the court. His friend, Ali, is also seized, and the heads of both are in imminent danger of leaving their bodies, on the headsman's block, when the caravan really appears. Marouf is vindicated, and even Ali apologizes for doubting him. The over-zealous Vizier is himself sentenced to receive a hundred lashes. A chorus of praise to Allah the Mighty closes the story.

MAURICE RAVEL

Hailed as "the foremost French composer since Debussy," Maurice Ravel has challenged attention in every field of composition that he has undertaken. He was born in Ciboure, Basse-Pyrenees, March 7, 1875. He studied both the piano and the orchestra, writing among other pieces a "String Quartet in F," a "Mother Goose" Suite for orchestra, songs for "Scheherezade," a one-act ballet, "Daphnis and Chloe," "Pavane for a Dead Infanta," and an opera, "L'Heure Espagnol." To the man in the street he became best known for his tumultuous short, descriptive "Bolero." Ravel lived for some years just outside of Paris, and was of retiring disposition. He toured America as pianist and conductor, in 1927. He died in Paris, December 28, 1937.

L'HEURE ESPAGNOL
(Lur-es-pan-yole)

(The Spanish Hour.) Folk Opera in One Act. Music by Ravel. Book by Franc-Nohain. Given at the Opéra Comique, Paris, 1911, for 10 performances. Chicago, January 5, 1920, by the Chicago Opera Company, who brought it to New York, the Lexington Theatre, January 28, 1920. Has since been performed in various lands and translations.

ARGUMENT The scene is the cluttered-up shop of Torquemada, an absent-minded clockmaker of Toledo; the time, the 18th Century. This is his day for going out to mend the town clocks— likewise the day that his wife, Concepcion, has set aside to enjoy her clandestine love affairs without his interference. The first visitor, however, is Ramiro, a muleteer, come to get his watch fixed, much to the annoyance of Concepcion. While the man awaits the clockmaker's return, her lover, Gonsalve appears and, noting that the coast is not clear he quickly hides in one of the big grandfather's clocks. Ramiro obligingly and unsuspecting, carries him, clock and all up to the lady's room. Another gallant, Inigo, a portly banker comes in, and is also hidden in a clock, and carried off. By this time, Concepcion has become so smitten with the muleteer's strength, that she transfers her affection to him. In the general confusion, Torquemada returns but doubtless thinking there is safety in numbers he accepts the situation and the curtain falls on a charming quintet.

Ravel himself said of the piece: "Of course I meant the whole thing as a farce, a musical parody, and as such it must be played and judged." The vision of singers popping in and out of timepieces and declaiming their lines is alone mirth-provoking, and their tender sentiments are accompanied by cleverly woven dance rhythms.

ENGLAND

HISTORICAL PREFACE

Any consideration of operas as a whole relating to England has been relegated to this Light Opera section, for candor compels the statement that, despite the traditional English love for music and the hospitable doors of Covent Garden to the works of every nation, England has yet to produce an enduring opera of major caliber. Handel, that outstanding figure of the Eighteenth Century whose work is identified with England, though an importation, wrote—in addition to his famous oratorios, church music, and suites—several operas beginning with "Almira" and "Nero," now forgotten. The trend of nearly all of the composers who followed him was definitely Light.

The origins of English Opera must be sought in the tales, songs and dances of the strolling minstrels and players. Long before the time of the famous Elizabethan playwrights, ballads were recited in some castle yard or village green, often with simple musical accompaniment. In court circles the Masque came to hold the same position as the Ballet on the other side of the Channel.

One of the first of these which has definite record was a Masque written by Ben Jonson, with musical score by Lanière. It was closely akin to opera. However, the honor of being the first true English opera is generally accorded to "Dido and Æneas," by one of the greatest of her earlier musicians, Henry Purcell. Produced in 1679, it was a by-product of the Restoration. The second Charles, impatient at the rather stodgy style of musical counterpoint of the court musicians, sent Pelham Humphrey over to Paris to learn the secret of Lully's great success in opera there. Purcell was a pupil of Humphrey's and this opera was a result. It was not followed, however, by other long works; but rather by incidental music of light, graceful, but not permanent character.

Any history of English Opera must perforce give early mention to "The Beggar's Opera," which is the first of them in many essentials. It is a ballad opera, loosely constructed, with its tunes arranged by Dr. Pepusch, a German. Its text is a satire. First produced in 1728, it set all London agog, then Paris. We refer you to a later page for a further account of this remarkable work. Handel, who was essaying

465

opera at this time, found his efforts hampered by "The Beggar's" success.

The first half of the Nineteenth Century saw England definitely launched in the field of opera, with such composers as these: John Gay, who wrote "The Beggar's Opera" and "Achilles"; Rutland Boughton, who wrote a music drama, "The Immortal Hour"; and Gustav Holst, who won recognition for "The Revoke," "The Youth's Choice," and "A Perfect Fool." One of the first to make both himself and his country famous in Light Opera was Julius Benedict, with his "The Lily of Killarney," "The Gypsy's Warning," and others. He was of German descent, but was knighted for his musical work in England. Another was Balfe, of Ireland (but we presume that England will still claim him!) whose "Bohemian Girl" sang itself around the world. Wallace, another contemporary, wrote the tuneful "Maritana," among others which made him popular during his lifetime.

Others whose work should be noted in any history of lighter opera claim consideration. Dame Ethel M. Smyth wrote some delightful music for her works such as "The Boatswain's Mate" and "Fête Galante." Ralph Vaughan Williams has a highly creditable ballad opera in "Hugh the Drover." Alfred Cellier wrote several operas in the eighties, such as "In the Sulks," "The Carp" and "Dorothy." Arthur Goring Thomas wrote "Esmeralda" and "Nadesha." Frederic H. Cowen wrote "Garibaldi" and "Harold." Edward Solomon wrote "The Nautch Girl" and other operas which were produced with success in America—perhaps partly because his wife, the famous Lillian Russell, starred in them. They belong to the eighties and include "Claude Duval," "Virginia," "Polly," "Pepita," "The Red Hussar," "Billee Taylor," and "The Vicar of Bray." Howard Talbot was a talented composer of a later day, who collaborated with Monckton in "The Arcadians," and "Mousmé," and also wrote "A Chinese Honeymoon," "The White Chrysanthemum," "Her Ladyship," and other successes. An opera which still marks a milestone in musical history is "Erminie," by Jakobowski. The story of its enormous run in New York, after a triumph at home, is a lively tradition in the annals of the theatre.

Other more recent composers will be found in later pages, so will not need mention here. They serve further to illustrate the fecundity of the English school in the lighter field.

We have purposely reserved for the last the name of that giant among English composers and of the world in this special field—Sullivan. So fortunate was he in his choice of librettists that the name of Gilbert will be linked with his for all time. Their operas, which are listed in full in the succeeding pages, have some rare quality which make them deathless. It would be superfluous to comment further, except to refer the reader to the record of their works. The mere reading of a page will suffice to set ringing in one's ears a host of familiar melodies.

JOHN GAY

Many works of musical reference do not include the name of John Gay, as he ranks as librettist, rather than as composer. However, his name is connected inseparably with one of the earliest of English works, "The Beggar's Opera." His work here was more nearly that of borrower and arranger. Its popularity was due both to the biting satire of its lines and the familiar Scotch and English tunes. Gay was born in Barnstable, Devon, in September, 1685. He died in London, December 4, 1732. "The Beggar's Opera" was brought out in 1728. A sequel, "Polly," was stopped by the government, but its score was printed in 1729. When again performed, in 1777, it was a failure, as its satires were then out of date.

THE BEGGAR'S OPERA

A Ballad Opera written by John Gay, with sixty-nine tunes arranged by Dr. Christopher Pepusch, who also wrote the overture. Produced by John Rich at the Theatre in Lincoln's Inn Fields, January 29, 1728.* In Paris in 1750. Revived repeatedly, notably in 1886 with Sims Reeves as Macheath. Again with success by Nigel Playfair at the Lyric Theatre, London, in 1920, where it ran for over three years. Greenwich Village Theatre, New York, December 27, 1920. A parody, "The Three-Penny Opera," at the Empire Theatre, New York, in April, 1933.

CAST MACHEATH, *a highwayman.* PEACHUM. MRS. PEACHUM. POLLY PEACHUM. LOCKIT. LUCY LOCKIT. FILCH. THE BEGGAR. DRAWER. JENNY DIVER. DIANA TRAPES. Others.

---

* The original run was 62 performances—a record for those times. The local saying was that it "made Gay rich, and Rich gay." Lavinia Fenton, who was the original Polly Peachum, won the heart of a lord and became the Duchess of Bolton. Her portrait painted by Hogarth is still extant.

ARGUMENT   This early classic in the Light Opera field was written
              by Gay as a lampoon against foreign affectation, par-
ticularly the Italian school of opera; and also as a satire on social and
political conditions.   The plot concerns one, Macheath, notorious but
fascinating highwayman, who is loved by all the ladies.   Even when
apprehended and placed behind the bars, two rival sweethearts present
themselves.   A cynical jailer and an outrageous hangman supply the
grim comedy.

As to music, Gay borrowed where he chose and freely.   The lyric,
"Let us take the road," is reminiscent of Handel.   That beginning,
"Virgins are like the flowers of May," of Purcell.   Other popular numbers are: "Lillibullero," a political air; "Green Sleeves," "Hither, dear
husband," and "When a wife's in a pout."

JULIUS BENEDICT

A composer, performer, and teacher of music who was held in high
esteem in England for over forty years, Benedict, nevertheless, was not
of English blood.   He was born in Stuttgart, November 27, 1804, and
spent his youth in Germany.   Such was his promise musically that, at
seventeen, he was taken by Weber "more as a son than pupil."   He
went to Italy, where his first opera, "Giocinta ed Ernesto," was performed unsuccessfully (1829).   He lived for a time in Paris, then (1835)
went to London, where he made his home.   He was knighted in 1871.
His English operas include "The Gypsy's Warning," "The Brides of
Venice," "The Crusaders," "The Lily of Killarney," and "The Bride
of Song."   Benedict died in London, June 5, 1885.

THE LILY OF KILLARNEY

Romantic Opera in Three Acts.   Music by Benedict.   Words by D.
Boucicault and John Oxenford.   Covent Garden, London, February 8,
1862.

CAST   HARDRESS CREGAN.   CORRIGAN, a "middle man."   MYLES, in
           love with Eily.   O'MOORE.   DANNY, a boatman.   FATHER
TOM.   EILY O'CONNOR, the "Colleen Bawn," the Lily of Killarney.

MRS. CREGAN, *Hardress' mother.* SHEELAH. ANN CHUTE, *an heiress.*
Others.

ARGUMENT   Long a favorite abroad, this Irish opera has now chiefly
a reminiscent interest.   The somewhat sticky senti-
mentality of its plot is relieved by a freshness and vivacity of song.

Act I   The scene is rural Ireland; the time, the early part of last century.   At Tore Cregan, the ancestral home of Hardress, guests
are greeting the return of the "bachelor" heir, little dreaming that he
has been secretly married to the beautiful "Colleen Bawn."   This
secret causes endless trouble as others try to arrange a match between
him and the wealthy Ann Chute.

The music is brightened by many Irish folk melodies, cleverly interpolated.   Principal numbers in this Act: serenade and duet: "The
moon has raised her lamp above"; Myles, "It is a charming girl I love";
Eily, "In my wild mountain valley he sought me"; Eily—the well-
known melody, "The Cruiskeen Lawn"; and stirring chorus.

Act II   At Tore Cregan, Hardress is reluctantly paying court to Ann,
but haunted by memories of Eily.   Danny, the boatman, plots
to remove Eily, and in the second scene puts his plot into action.   She
is carried to a lonely cavern.

A ringing hunting song and chorus introduces this Act.   Other numbers are: Danny's recitative and songs, "The Colleen Bawn"; and "Yes,
I'll do my duty"; and a dramatic medley and finale.

Act III   Again at Tore Cregan, Hardress, believing Eily to be dead,
is about to be married to Ann.   But Danny, dying, confesses
the plot; and later Eily is restored to Hardress' unworthy arms.

Musical numbers: serenade by Myles, "Your slumbers, och!"; Hardress' beautiful aria, "Eily Mavourneen, I see thee before me"; and a
melodious trio leading up to finale.

MICHAEL WILLIAM BALFE

An Irish composer, born in Dublin, May 15, 1808, Balfe came to
notice as a boy musical prodigy, playing the violin in public at the age
of nine.   He had also begun to compose music.   He went to London
to continue his studies, when fifteen, and two years later proceeded to

Italy, where he had the advantage of the finest teachers, among them Galli and Rossini. He was the possessor of a rich baritone voice, and at nineteen we find him singing in the Italian Opera, at Paris, with applause. From the year 1830 he produced many musical compositions —ballet music, songs, operas, and operettas. The most lasting operas have been: "The Bohemian Girl" (1843), "The Rose of Castile" (1857), and "The Talisman" (1874). Only the first of these is produced today. In 1846 Balfe was appointed conductor of the London Italian Opera. He died in England, October 20, 1870.

THE BOHEMIAN GIRL

Romantic Opera in Three Acts.   Music by Balfe.   Book by Alfred Bunn.   Drury Lane Theatre, London, November 27, 1843, where it ran for nearly a year.   The original company then brought it to New York, at the Park Theatre, November 25, 1844, where it duplicated its "huge success."   It has been revived repeatedly in Europe and America, its total productions placing it near the top.   In France it won for Balfe the Cross of the Legion of Honor.

CAST   COUNT ARNHEIM, *Governor of Presburg*.   THADDEUS, *a Polish exile*.   FLORESTEIN, *the Count's nephew*.   DEVILSHOOF, *chief of the Gypsies*.   CAPTAIN OF THE GUARD.   ARLINE, *the Count's daughter*.   BUDA, *her nurse*.   THE GYPSY QUEEN.   Gypsies, Huntsmen, Officers, Guests.

ARGUMENT   "The Bohemian Girl" is the romantic story of a highborn child kidnaped by the Gypsies, whose after life is an intermingling of court and rustic environment.   It has remained one of the most popular of the lighter operas.

Act I   The scene is Presburg and vicinity; the time the Eighteenth Century.   On the grounds of Count Arnheim's estate on the Danube, a group of the Count's retainers sing a spirited chorus, "Up with the banner!"   Presently he enters with his little girl, Arline, whom he bids farewell and entrusts to her nurse, Buda.   After they have left the scene, Thaddeus, a Polish fugitive, rushes in seeking to escape from the Austrian soldiery.   He is set upon by a Gypsy band, headed by Devilshoof, who sing the familiar chorus, "In the Gypsy's life you read the life that all would like to lead."   At first they intend to rob Thaddeus, but end by disguising him as one of themselves, and thus he eludes his pursuers.

Florestein, the Count's nephew, now rushes in exclaiming that Arline has been attacked by a vicious stag.   Thaddeus seizes a rifle, rushes after the hunters, and kills the animal. He restores Arline, who is slightly wounded in the arm, to her father. In gratitude the Count asks him to dine with the huntsmen, but when a toast is proposed to the Emperor, Thaddeus keeps his seat. The others surround him with drawn swords (Chorus: "Down with the daring slave!").

The Count interposes, as also does Devilshoof, who rushes in. The latter is imprisoned for his temerity, but soon escapes and is seen carrying off Arline across a gorge in the mountains. The Count's prayer, "Thou who in might supreme," is followed by the closing chorus, "Follow, follow, with heart and with arm."

Act II Twelve years pass by before we meet again with the Gypsies, in a camp in Presburg. The child has grown into a beautiful woman, and her devoted guard is Thaddeus. The Gypsies have reared her as one of their own. While Arline is sleeping, Florestein comes upon the scene, drunk. He is relieved of all his valuables, but the Gypsy queen orders them returned. All are given back except a medallion. When Arline awakes she tells Thaddeus of a strange dream. Her aria is one of the famed bits of all light opera, "I dreamt that I dwelt in marble halls." She and Thaddeus confess their mutual love, but he will not tell her all her past, fearing to lose her. (Duet: "Where is the spell.") Their hands are joined in the Gypsy rite of betrothal by the queen, who, however, is jealous and vows revenge.

The scene shifts to another street. Arline in fanciful dress leads a band of Gypsies, who sing again, "In the Gypsies' life you read," followed by an aria from Arline, "Come with the Gypsy bride."

Again the scene changes to the Fair, which is thronged with sightseers. The Gypsies entertain with songs and dances. Florestein, who is one of the visitors, attempts some familiarities with Arline, who slaps him. The Gypsy queen then gives the medallion to the girl, so that Arline may be accused of robbing the gallant. The plot succeeds; Florestein recognizes the jewel, accuses her, and she is arrested.

In the final scene of this act, we find Count Arnheim in his apartments at the Hall of Justice. He stands gazing at a portrait of his long-lost daughter. As he muses he sings another favorite aria, "The heart bow'd down by weight of woe." At this juncture a band of soldiers bring the supposed Gypsy girl into his presence, charged with the theft of the medallion. She pleads her innocence, and her story and the scar upon her arm enable the Count to recognize his daughter. While he clasps her in his arms, Thaddeus, Devilshoof and others join in the closing medley, "Praised be the will of Heaven!"

Act III Arline is seen surrounded by every luxury in the splendid castle, but her heart is sad. She remembers her old, free life, and her love for Thaddeus. He, also, is longing for her and is emboldened to come with Devilshoof and implore her to rejoin them. To answer his reproach, "I thought you had forgotten me," she answers "Forgotten?" Then comes another unforgettable song—the haunting refrain, "When other lips and other hearts,"—ending, "You'll remember me." Immediately, the Count, Florestein, and guests enter. Devilshoof leaves by the window, but Thaddeus conceals himself in a cabinet. The Gypsy queen now endeavors to cast fresh shame on Arline by disclosing her lover. A quintet and chorus follow, "Though every hope be fled." Thaddeus now reveals his true rank, that of a Polish noble (Solo: "When the fair land of Poland was plowed"). The Count finally relents and agrees to give him the hand of Arline. A trio celebrates this event, "Let not the soul over sorrows grieve." The Gypsy queen, in a rage, attempts to shoot Thaddeus, but as Devilshoof wrests the weapon from her hands it goes off, killing her instead. A joyful chorus concludes the tuneful opera.

WILLIAM VINCENT WALLACE

Wallace was the son of an Irish bandmaster, born in Waterford, Ireland, March 11, 1812. He early showed great talent for the violin and played a concerto in public in Dublin, whither his father had removed. Becoming soured on the artistic life young Wallace, in 1835, went to "the Bush" in Australia near Sydney, but his talents could not remain in obscurity; he was rediscovered and in a few years went back to London where, in 1845, he wrote "Maritana," which met with immediate success and set a high mark in English operas. Others of tuneful but not so lasting quality were "Matilda of Hungary," "The Desert Flower," "Lurline," and "The Amber Witch." Wallace was a great traveler. He died in the Pyrenees, October 12, 1865.

MARITANA

Romantic Opera in Three Acts. Music by Wallace. Words by Fitzball, from the French play, "Don César de Bazan," with interpolated lyrics by Alfred Bunn. Drury Lane Theatre, London, November 15, 1845; and in New York, May 4, 1848, with the original cast headed by Mr. and Mrs. Seguin.

CAST THE KING OF SPAIN. DON CÉSAR DE BAZAN, *a good-natured rake.* DON JOSÉ DE SANTAREM, *his friend.* MARQUIS DE MONTE-FIORI. CAPTAIN OF THE GUARD. ALCADE. LAZARILLO, *a poor boy.* MARITANA, *a Gypsy singer.* MARQUIS DE MONTEFIORI. Others.

ARGUMENT This was Wallace's first opera, and it won an instantaneous success. Many of the separate numbers, such as "Scenes that are brightest" and "Let me like a soldier fall," were heard in every Victorian drawing-room, and have not yet exhausted their appeal. The scene of the opera is Madrid of the Seventeenth Century.

The text follows the drama closely and may be summarized as follows: Don César, a swashbuckling soldier of fortune, in trying to befriend a lad of the streets, gets into a quarrel and duel with the Captain of the Guard. He is sentenced to death, while Maritana, a street singer, tries vainly to ransom him. Don José, the villain of the piece, plots to have Don César go through a mock marriage with the girl, and then be shot by the firing squad—to feather his own nest. His plot involves the honor of the Queen. Don César escapes death, informs the King of the conspiracy, is pardoned and made Governor of Granada. Maritana, saved from the King's clutches, is restored to the knight.

The opera abounds in pleasing music and is perhaps the most successful of all the English operas before Sullivan. It begins with Maritana's song, "It was a knight of princely mien." She also sings a delightful romanza, "I hear it again, 'tis the harp in the air." Others are: duet between Maritana and Don José, "Of fairy wand had I the power"; Don César's drinking song, "All the world over"; chorus, "Pretty Gitana, tell us"; the strong medley which closes the First Act, when Don César is arrested.

In the Second Act, a lovely song by Lazarillo, "Alas! those chimes so sweetly pealing"; trio, "Turn on, old Time, thine hour-glass"; the Don's ever popular plea to avoid a shameful death, "Let me like a soldier fall!"; the ballad (written by another hand), "In happy moments, day by day"; quartet and chorus, "Health to the lady!" chorus, "Ah, what pleasure!"; an aria by the King, "The mariner in his bark"; and a rousing quintet and chorus, "What mystery must now control."

The high mark of the Third Act is Maritana's well-loved aria, "Scenes that are brightest"; followed by a duet, Don César and Maritana, "This heart with bliss o'erflowing"; and Don's sentimental ballad, "There is a flower that bloometh"; and the closing chorus. In brief, this work of a century ago has enough music to outfit two average works of the present day.

ARTHUR S. SULLIVAN

With Arthur Seymour Sullivan we reach the peak of English Light Opera, and one of the peaks of the world itself. His works written in collaboration with William S. Gilbert, equally famed as a librettist, have become classic examples of their type and are perennially popular. Arthur Sullivan was born in London, May 13, 1842; was a member of a boy choir and at the age of thirteen published his first composition. The following year he won a scholarship at the Royal Academy of Music. He was a prolific composer of songs, oratorios, and incidental music, and after producing a one-act operetta, "Cox and Box," in 1867, he began the famous partnership with William S. Gilbert, which resulted in the works still known and loved under their joint names: "Trial by Jury" (1875); "The Sorcerer" (1877); "H. M. S. Pinafore" (1878); "The Pirates of Penzance" (1879); "Patience" (1881); "Iolanthe" (1882); "Princess Ida" (1884); "The Mikado" (1885); "Ruddigore" (1887); "The Yeomen of the Guard" (1888); and "The Gondoliers" (1889).* Another seldom produced was "Utopia Limited, or The Flowers of Progress." Sullivan wrote only one grand opera, "Ivanhoe" based upon Scott's novel and for which Gilbert was not librettist, but it was not successful. He also wrote the music for a romantic music drama, "The Beauty Stone," book by A. W. Pinero, which was produced at the Savoy Theatre, London, May 28, 1898; and "The Rose of Persia," book by Basil Hood. Sullivan was knighted by Queen Victoria in 1883. Gilbert also received knighthood, but after her death; it was said that

---

* Most of the Gilbert and Sullivan operas were originally produced at the Savoy Theatre, London, and the company was locally known as the "Savoyards." The names in this famous group of singers and actors deserve recording in any book devoted to Light Opera. They include George Grossmith, Richard Temple, Louie and Courtice Pounds, Jessie Bond, Rosina Brandram, Agnes Fraser, Isabel Jay, Ruth Vincent, Rutland Barrington, George Passmore, and Robert Evett. This company was succeeded by the D'Oyly Carte Company, which played regularly in London and New York until the outbreak of the Second World War.

some of his political satires displeased her Majesty. Sullivan died in London, November 21, 1900.

COX AND BOX

(or,"The Long Lost Brothers.") Farcical Operetta in One Act. Music by Sullivan. Book by F. C. Burnand. London, in 1867.

ARGUMENT This story is based on a farce by J. Maddison Morton, "Box and Cox." The characters are: James John Cox, a journeyman hatter; John James Box, a journeyman printer; and Sergeant Bouncer. The two journeymen are boarders with the Sergeant. Since one works by day, and the other by night, the thrifty landlord puts them up in the same room, unbeknown to each other. Things disappear and complaints naturally arise, until on a holiday the two meet and find that they are long-lost brothers. There is a lady in the case, but she remains off-stage.

The music is amusing and shows Sullivan in facetious vein. The songs alternate solos, duets and trios, beginning with Bouncer's song, "Rataplan," and including the comical trio, "Who are you, sir?"

TRIAL BY JURY

Dramatic Cantata in One Act. Music by Sullivan. Book by Gilbert. Royalty Theatre, London, March 25, 1875. Revived at the Savoy, October 11, 1884 (150 times).

CAST The Learned Judge. Counsel for the Plaintiff. Foreman of the jury. Edwin, *the Defendant*. Angelina, *the Plaintiff*. Jurymen, Court Attendants, etc.

ARGUMENT This is the only Gilbert and Sullivan opera without any dialogue. It thus follows "Grand" lines—but only thus. Run off in less than an hour, it is generally used as a "curtain-raiser."

The scene is a court of justice, in London, during a trial. Edwin and Angelina are betrothed, but he is showing signs of coolness and looking appreciatively upon another. So the fair Angelina hales him into court on a breach of promise suit. The subsequent action is clever satire. The Judge shows that he himself is not averse to feminine charms, and is visibly moved when Angelina pleads her case. Edwin tries to defend himself on the specious plea that he is but obeying the laws of nature, "for nature is constantly changing!" He is quite ready to rectify things by wedding Angelina today, and the other fair one tomorrow. This further confuses matters, and as the Judge is in haste to adjourn court, he settles the case by declaring that he will marry Angelina himself. Thus everybody is happy.

Musically the skit sparkles throughout. It is good-natured fooling, from the time that the Foreman chants, "Just like a father I wished to be," through the Judge's explanatory ditty, "When I, good friends, was called to the Bar," the Usher's solo with chorus, "Now, Jurymen, hear my advice"—the Jury agreeing, "From bias free of every kind this trial must be tried," to the joyous and absurd finale.

THE SORCERER

Comic Opera in Two Acts. Music by Sullivan. Book by Gilbert. Opera Comique, London, November 17, 1877 (175 times). George Grossmith was the "Sorcerer." New York at the Casino, February 21, 1879, first run disappointing (21 times), but later it attained popularity with a New York cast including Lillian Russell ("Aline"), John Howson (the "Sorcerer"),* Laura Joyce, Madeline Lucette, Lily Post, Digby Bell, George Olmi, Charles Campbell, and A. W. Maflin.

CAST   SIR MARMADUKE POINTDEXTRE. ALEXIS, *his son.* LADY SANGA-
         ZURE. ALINE, *her. daughter.* WELLS, *the Sorcerer.* MRS.
PARTLET, *the pew-opener.* CONSTANCE, *her daughter.* DR. DALY, *the
Vicar.* Friends, Servants, etc.

ARGUMENT   A tuneful opera with droll situation, which still ap-
                peals to many amateur as well as professional com-
panies. It has an excellent comedy character.

Act I   On the grounds of Sir Marmaduke's estate, in England, all is
           joy. The villagers are assembled to celebrate the betrothal of
his son with Aline. They sign the marriage contract amid general felicitations. Alexis begins to wonder if, after all, marriage is not governed too much by social barriers. He suggests that the firm of J. Wellington Wells be called in: they are well established sorcerers who make
a potion which will cause persons to fall in love without prejudice to
rank or wealth. He obtains from Wells some of the elixir and pours it
into the tea which is served at the betrothal banquet.

---

* Harry B. Smith says: "The sensational feature of 'The Sorcerer' was John Howson's 'J. Wellington Wells.' The actor's make-up as the old, reliable family sorcerer
was an exact reproduction of the physiognomy of the Rev. T. DeWitt Talmage, who
had been cartooned into notoriety."

The First Act's musical numbers include: opening chorus: "Ring forth, ye bells"; Constance: "When he is here"; Dr. Daly: "Time was when Love and I"; Aline: "Happy young hearts"; mixed chorus: "With heart and with voice"; Alexis: "For love alone"; a rapid-fire patter song by Wells: "My name is John Wellington Wells"; finale: "Now to the banquet we press."

Act II The curtain rises on a market place in the village. (Often the setting of Act I is retained.) Peasants enter dancing, but oddly assorted: an old man with a young girl; and *vice versa*. Sir Marmaduke's guests enter, also badly mixed up. The sorcerer's potion has taken good effect.

Sir Marmaduke is ready to wed Mrs. Partlet, the aged pew-opener; Aline bestows her smiles on the vicar; and when Wells comes upon the scene, he is pounced upon by Lady Sangazure. Alexis sees, too late, all the mischief, and implores the sorcerer to remove the spell. He says that it cannot be done unless or until somebody sacrifices himself to the Evil One. As nobody wants to be the victim, they take a vote of the guests, and Wells is elected. A trap opens in the floor and down he sinks into a ruddy glow; while the others untangle their recent mésalliances.

Musical numbers include: ensemble led by Constance: "Dear friends, take pity"; quintet: "I rejoice that it's decided"; Lady Sangazure and Wells: "Oh, I have wrought evil with my spells"; Aline: "Alexis, doubt me not"; chorus: "Oh, joyous boon!"; and recitative by Alexis, "Prepare for sad surprises," leading up to a brilliant finale.

H.M.S. PINAFORE

(or, "The Lass That Loved a Sailor.") Comic Opera in Two Acts. Music by Sullivan. Book by Gilbert. One of the most popular of all light operas. Opera Comique, London, May 25, 1878 (700 times) and in New York, January 15, 1879, where it had a long first run.

CAST THE RIGHT HONORABLE SIR JOSEPH PORTER, *Admiral of the Fleet.* CAPTAIN CORCORAN, *of the "Pinafore."* JOSEPHINE, *the Captain's daughter.* RALPH RACKSTRAW, *Able seaman.* DICK DEADEYE, *Able seaman.* BOB BECKET, *Carpenter's mate.* BILL BOBSTAY, *Boatswain's mate.* TOM TUCKER, *Midshipman.* SERGEANT OF MARINES. HEBE, *Sir Joseph's first cousin.* LITTLE BUTTERCUP, *a Portsmouth bumboat woman.* Sir Joseph's Sisters, his Cousins, his Aunts; Sailors, Marines.

ARGUMENT   "Her Majesty's Ship Pinafore" is a good-natured satire on English political and marine affairs, and also of pomposity.   It vies with "The Mikado" in being the most popular and oft-repeated of the Gilbert-Sullivan operas.   The stage setting for both Acts is the deck of her Majesty's warship *Pinafore,* off Portsmouth, England.

Act I   When the curtain rises, the sailors led by the Boatswain are discovered cleaning brasswork, splicing rope, etc.   As they work they sing: "We sail the ocean blue."   Enter Little Buttercup, a bumboat woman, "the rosiest, the roundest, and the reddest beauty in all Spithead."   She now sings one of the best-known of the Sullivan songs: "I'm called Little Buttercup."   The sailors are all in high spirits, with the exception of Dick Deadeye, whose looks are against him, and Ralph Rackstraw, who has dared to fall in love with no less a person than Josephine, the daughter of his Captain.   In a recitative, echoed by the crew, he has "loved a lass (alas!) above his station."   The Captain himself, who presently appears singing his introductory song: "I am the captain of the *Pinafore*"—and who hardly ever uses "a big, big D——," is having his own troubles.   He wants his daughter, Josephine, to give her hand to the Admiral of the Fleet; whereas Josephine with the perversity of youth replies that she has already given her heart to a common sailor. But she tells her father that she will carry her love in secret to the tomb.

Now in comes Sir Joseph Porter with much pomp, singing, "I am the monarch of the sea"—and attended by a flock of female relatives, "his sisters and his cousins and his aunts."   He tells how he rose to his present lofty estate from "When I was a lad, I served a term," to "Now I am the ruler of the Queen's Navee!"   The pompous official once more tries to win Josephine's hand, but is repulsed.   In a duet between the girl and Ralph a mutual passion is disclosed.   She repulses him, however, until he puts a pistol to his head, when she dashes back on stage crying, "Ah! stay your hand! I love you!" (Echoed by chorus).   A chorus of joy ensues, the single jarring note being that of the heavy villain, Dick Deadeye.   He resolves to frustrate the lovers' plan to elope.

Act II   It is night time on deck.   The Captain is discovered with Little Buttercup, who is regarding him with affection while he sings, "Fair moon, to thee I sing," and wondering why, when all is so serene above, things his way should be at sixes or at sevens.   Then ensues a duet between the two: "Things are seldom what they seem."   Sir Joseph now comes forward to tell the Captain that he is disappointed with Josephine and her actions.   The Captain replies that his exalted rank must be in her way, and that he should tell her that "love levels all ranks."   Both go back stage while Josephine sings: "The hours creep on apace." Then the two men unite with her in a trio, telling her about the love-levelling business, which she is delighted to hear about, but for a different reason. After Josephine and the Admiral have departed, Dick Deadeye comes to tell the Captain of the plot that is brewing. The Captain thereupon pulls a cloak around him, gets a cat-o'-nine-tails, and prepares to surprise the crew and elopers. A comical by-play ensues: "Silent be, it was the cat!" When the Captain finally throws off his coat and confronts the eloping couple, Ralph defies him with a spirited song, "I am an Englishman!" Which the crew avows is greatly to his credit. The Admiral, who now enters, is not of the same mind. He falls into a rage and orders Ralph handcuffed and imprisoned. But his rescue is effected from an unexpected quarter. Little Buttercup reveals a secret of "A many years ago," when she "mixed two children up." They were the Captain and Ralph, who, as a consequence, were each occupying the other's place. The Admiral thereupon releases Ralph and places him in command of the ship, while the luckless Corcoran is demoted to the rank of common sailor. The latter then seeks solace in the love of Little Buttercup. Josephine and Ralph fly into each other's arms, singing, "Oh joy, oh rapture unforeseen!"— while the crew after a medley of former airs reaffirm the fact that, "It's greatly to his credit that he is an Englishman!"

THE PIRATES OF PENZANCE

(or, "The Slave of Duty.") Comic Opera in Two Acts. Music by Sullivan. Book by Gilbert. Of special interest in being the only one produced in New York first, in the vain attempt to protect copyright, as all their operas were being pirated. Fifth Avenue Theatre, New York, December 31, 1879, under personal direction of both Gilbert and Sullivan. Then in London at the Opera Comique, April 3, 1880 (363 performances).

CAST   RICHARD, *a Pirate Chief.* SAMUEL, *his Lieutenant.* FREDERIC, *a Pirate apprentice.* MAJOR GENERAL STANLEY, *of the British Army.* EDWARD, *a Sergeant of Police.* MABEL, *youngest daughter of Stanley.* KATE, EDITH, ISABEL, *daughters of Stanley.* RUTH, *a piratical "maid-of-all-work."* Pirates, Policemen, Citizens, and others.

ARGUMENT   "The Pirates of Penzance" has no motif. It is merely light and tuneful nonsense, but its rollicking airs and delightful drollery have made it a permanent favorite on the light opera stage. Its setting is the coast and interior of England.

Act I On a rocky shore on the coast of Cornwall a band of pirates make merry over the coming of age of Frederic, an apprentice. Led by Samuel they sing, "For today our Pirate 'prentice." Frederic, however, tells them that there has been a mistake; he was intended as a pilot, and not as a pirate. Ruth corroborates this in her song, "When Frederic was a little lad." Frederic then tells them that he is a slave of duty and may have to exterminate them. But the pirate king and chorus aver: "Oh, better far to live and die under the brave black flag." A duet follows by Frederic and Ruth, in which she pleads for his love. But his eyes are opened to younger feminine charms when the daughters of General Stanley come on. (Chorus: "Climbing over rocky mountain.") Mabel with chorus sings one of Sullivan's most appealing arias, "Poor wand'ring one." Frederic speedily falls in love with her, and a duet with chorus follows. The pirates return and decide to marry the other girls, "against their will." (Chorus: "Now here's a first-rate opportunity.") But the General induces the pirates to relent in a droll patter song, "I am the very pattern." He tells them that he, as well as they, is an orphan. A medley of all singers brings the act to a peaceful close.

Act II In a chapel on the General's estate, he bemoans his deception; he has told the pirates a lie; he is no orphan. Frederic now enters and bids Mabel farewell, as he is away to lead an expedition against his former mates. (Chorus of police: "Tarantara! Tarantara!" with Mabel and other girls singing, "Go, ye heroes!") But Ruth and the pirate king come back to confront Frederic with a paradox (Trio: "Ha, ha, ha, a paradox!"). They have discovered that Frederic's birthday falls upon February 29, and since he has had only five birthdays, he can be only five years old—so too young to be anything but a pirate's apprentice! Frederic, again a slave of duty, thereupon resumes service as a pirate, and tells the king that the General has deceived him. The pirate chief resolves to exact swift and terrible vengeance for such duplicity. After a duet between Mabel and Frederic, in which she tries to dissuade him from his new course, the police enter again singing, "Tarantara!" (Sergeant's song: "When a fellow's not engaged.") They creep up on the pirates, each company singing its own song. A combined male chorus is led by the General, who sings, "Softly sighing to the river comes the lonely breeze." The girls in night dresses also enter with, "Now, what is this?" After a struggle between pirates and police, the freebooters are bidden to yield in the Queen's name—which they promptly do. On their promise to reform, the General bestows his daughters' hands upon them. Frederic, the slave of duty, gets Mabel, and a final medley ends, "Take heart!"

PATIENCE

(or, "Bunthorne's Bride.") "Comic Æsthetic" Opera in Two Acts.
Music by Sullivan. Book by Gilbert. Opera Comique, London, April
23, 1881, (578 times). Its literary and other allusions were so British,
however, that it has not been a success in New York. It was shown at
the Casino for 22 performances. In the cast were Mary Beebe, Laura
Joyce Bell, Rose Leighton, Irene Perry, Ethel Clare, and Digby Bell.

CAST REGINALD BUNTHORNE, *a fleshly poet.* ARCHIBALD GROSVENOR,
an idyllic poet. PATIENCE, *a dairymaid.* COLONEL CALVER-
LEY, *an officer of Dragoons.* MAJOR MURGATROYD, *an officer of Dragoons.* DUKE OF DUNSTABLE, *an officer of Dragoons.* ANGELA, SAPHIR,
ELLA, JANE, *"rapturous maidens."* More "Rapturous Maidens," Dragoons, and others.

ARGUMENT This story is hardly intelligible today, and the opera
persists on account of its music. It was written as a
satire upon the fleshly school of poetry as represented by Oscar Wilde
and his admirers, in contrast with the æsthetic culture of Swinburne and
others, which likewise raged at the time of the opera's writing. The
scene is England of that day.

Act I A chorus of maidens opens the piece; the scene being the
grounds of Castle Bunthorne: "Twenty lovesick maidens we."
All are wild over Reginald, the fleshly poet. Patience views them with
pity; her heart is untouched. (Recitative: "Still brooding.") So engrossed are the girls with their ideal that they scorn the Colonel and his
dragoons when they come upon the scene. (Chorus: "The soldiers of
our Queen.") Bunthorne enters reading a book and followed by some
of the girls. The Colonel sings of the joys of war: "When I first put the
uniform on." The poet replies: "Am I alone?" He makes love to
Patience, who is indifferent. A duet between Patience and Angela follows: "Long years ago." Grosvenor, the rival poet, now appears and
likewise pays attention to Patience; their duet being one of the droll
bits: "Willow, willow, waly." Bunthorne, wearing a rose garland and
with his faithful retinue, again appears, the action leading up to finale:
"Let the merry cymbals sound"; followed by sextet and chorus.

Act II Jane, the oldest of the maidens and a trifle too old for her own
peace of mind, rails at the other girls for deserting Reginald
for his rival. ("Sad is that woman's lot.") Sure enough—the girls are
now following Grosvenor, beseeching him to "Turn, oh turn in this

direction!" His amusing ballad follows: "The magnet and the churn." Patience is perplexed by the claims of the rivals, and sings: "Love is a plaintive song." A trio, the two officers and the duke, is followed by a quintet—with Angela and Saphir—"Our heartfelt sympathy." The rival poets finally meet and come to a state of truce. (Duet: "When I go out of door.") Grosvenor agrees to have his long hair shorn; he next appears in quite ordinary rig, and his train of girls are also sensibly dressed. Since he has become quite commonplace, Patience says that there is nothing now to prevent her loving him. (Finale, "In that case unprecedented.")

IOLANTHE

(or, "The Peer and the Peri.") Comic Opera in Two Acts. Music by Sullivan. Book by Gilbert. Savoy Theatre, London, November 25, 1882 (398 times).

CAST   STREPHON, *a shepherd, half mortal, half fairy.* THE EARL OF MOUNT ARARAT, *a Peer.* THE EARL OF TOLLOLLER, *a Peer.* THE LORD CHANCELLOR. PHYLLIS, *the Ward of the Lord Chancellor.* PRIVATE WILLIS, *of the Guard.* THE TRAIN-BEARER. THE FAIRY QUEEN. IOLANTHE. CELIA. LEILA. FLETA. Chorus of Peers and of Fairies.

ARGUMENT   A sly dig at peerdom and pretense, welded to thoroughly delightful music.

Act I   A dainty, tripping chorus of fairies, on an Arcadian field, heralds the opening of this musical tale. Iolanthe, one of the fairies, has disobeyed their laws; she has married a mortal. For this sin she was banished from Fairyland, and at the time our story opens she is doing penance at the bottom of a river, where she has been confined for the past twenty-five years. She rises from the deep clad in rags and sues her Queen for pardon, in a recitative, "With humbled breast." The Queen is moved to pity, and Iolanthe's rags fall from her, to reveal a shimmering fairy as of yore. She confesses that she has had a son by this early union, who is now twenty-four—a young shepherd, Strephon by name. He is presented to the fairies (Solo and chorus: "Good morrow") and tells them that he is in love with Phyllis, "a ward in Chancery," and the fairies promise aid. (Chorus: "Farewell, attractive stranger.")

As they withdraw, Phyllis appears and in a duet with Strephon they promise each other that they "are to be married today." This is followed by, "None shall part us from each other." Their tryst is interrupted by the stately entering march of the Peers, supported by the grandiloquent chorus, "Loudly let the trumpets bray," and with the admonition, "Bow, ye lower middle classes!" The Lord Chancellor, who now struts and in a volley of rapid words avers that he is "the Law's true embodiment." However, he and all the other Peers are themselves in love with Phyllis, so are not disposed to view with equanimity her wedding with a shepherd. After the lords retire with much dignity, Strephon pleads his cause, but without avail. The Lord Chancellor says that he has always done his duty strictly. (Solo: "When I went to the Bar as a very young man.") He then stalks off leaving Strephon in tears. His mother, Iolanthe, returns to comfort him and assure him of her support. Phyllis, who sees him thus in earnest converse with a young and beautiful fairy, believes him faithless. Other fairies enter to give their aid in the tangle, followed by the group of Peers. The Act ends with an ensemble of fairies and mortals.

Act II In the Palace Yard, Westminster, a chorus of elated fairies celebrate Strephon's success in the world. He has been elected to Parliament by their aid, and is meeting with great renown—much to the disgust of the Peers. In a chorus the Peers and the peris square off against each other, "Here's a pretty kettle of fish!" Meanwhile, Phyllis has thrown Strephon over and is engaged to two of the noblemen —Ararat and Tolloller—but cannot decide which of them to marry. They wrangle with each other and with the Lord Chancellor, for her hand. Strephon again meets Phyllis, by accident, and reveals to her the secret of his birth—that he is half-fairy, half-mortal, and that it was his mother, Iolanthe, whom she had seen. Phyllis finally believes him and says that they had better marry before they change their minds. (Duet: "If we're weak enough to tarry, ere we marry.") Their next problem is to get the consent of the Lord Chancellor, but that is difficult. After carrying on a heated debate with himself, that official has decided that it would not be beneath his dignity to wed his ward. Iolanthe intercedes with him in a recitative, "My Lord, a suppliant at your feet I kneel," and braves the fairy death penalty by revealing herself to him as his bride of twenty-five years ago. The Chancellor is overjoyed to see her again, and now consents to Strephon's suit, but at this moment the Fairy Queen enters and sternly bids Iolanthe prepare for death. ("Once again thy vows are broken.") The sentence, however, is stayed in an unexpected manner by other fairies, who confess that they, too, have yielded to the blandishments of mortals and have accepted the Peers. The Queen in resignation to the inevitable bestows her own hand upon Private Willis, a sentry whom she has already admired. The concluding chorus by all emphasizes the refrain, "If you've two beaux to every string."

PRINCESS IDA

(or, "Castle Adamant.") Comic Opera in Three Acts. Music by Sullivan. Book by Gilbert. Savoy Theatre, London, January 5, 1884 (246 performances); in New York, February 11, 1884.

CAST KING HILDEBRAND. KING GAMA. PRINCESS IDA, *his daughter.* HILARION, *Hildebrand's son.* AVAC, GURON, SCYNTHIUS, *sons of Gama.* CYRIL, FLORIAN, *friends of Hilarion.* Ladies, Gentlemen, Servants, etc.

ARGUMENT The authors styled this "a respectful operatic perversion of Tennyson's 'Princess.'" It is now regarded as perhaps the least meritorious of the Gilbert and Sullivan operas. The setting is ancient England.

Act I In a pavilion of King Hildebrand's palace all are agog over the expected arrival of King Gama with his daughter, Ida, whose hand has been promised to Hilarion, Hildebrand's son. When Gama finally arrives, the princess is not with him, and he says that she has decided to remain at Castle Adamant to take charge of a woman's college. Gama and his three sons are thereupon held as hostages, while Hilarion with two friends set out for Castle Adamant to see what all the shouting is about.

Musical numbers in this Act include; Hilarion's ballad, "Ida was a twelvemonth old"; trio by Gama's sons, "We are warriors three"; and Gama's topical song, "If you give me your attention."

Act II In the gardens of Castle Adamant two of the lady professors are disclosed in earnest converse with their pupils. Hilarion and his two friends scale the walls, disguise themselves as girls, and mingle with the pupils. They meet Princess Ida and are easily persuaded by her to enroll in the institution. Later she finds that the three new pupils are men. In her dismay she falls off a bridge into a stream, and is rescued by Hilarion. Nevertheless, she orders his arrest. The arrival of Hildebrand and others stays her hand.

Musical numbers include: the Princess' aria, "At this my call"; songs by Lady Blanche and Lady Psyche; Hilarion's "Whom thou hast chained must wear his chain"; quartet, "The world is but a broken toy"; quintet, "The woman of the wisest art"; and Cyril's song, "Would you know the kind of maid."

Act III Still at Castle Adamant, the Princess and her pupils try to withstand the inevitable; but there are too many members of the opposite sex present. Gama proposes a test of arms between his three sons and Hilarion and his two friends. Gama's sons are defeated, whereupon Ida agrees to resign as head of her college and accept Hilarion.

The musical numbers include: the Princess' song, "I built upon a rock"; Gama's "Whene'er I spoke sarcastic joke"; the ladies' and soldiers' chorus, "When anger spreads his wings"; and the finale, "With joy abiding."

THE MIKADO

(or, "The Town of Titipu.") Comic Opera in Two Acts. Music by Sullivan. Book by Gilbert. Savoy Theatre, London, March 14, 1885 (672 times). New York, August 19, 1885.*

CAST THE MIKADO OF JAPAN. NANKI-POO, *his son, "a wandering minstrel."* KO-KO, *the Lord High Executioner.* POOH-BAH, *Lord High everything else.* YUM-YUM, *Ko-Ko's ward, "from school."* PEEP-BO, PITTI-SING, *her friends, the other little maids from school.* KATISHA, *a lady at court.* PISH-TUSH, *a courtier.* Courtiers, Citizens, Servants.

ARGUMENT The action of this ever-popular work, which easily ranks with the best liked of all operettas, takes place in the courtyard and garden of the Lord High Executioner, Ko-Ko, in Titipu, Japan. It is a burlesque on things Japanese, as at that time conceived, and a jest at officials who try to take on too much authority.

Act I The first curtain rises upon a courtyard scene, where Japanese nobles of the old school are discovered in fantastic attitudes suggested by native drawings. While they introduce themselves, Nanki-Poo enters. Although apparently a wandering minstrel, he is really the son of the Mikado. He sings, "A wandering minstrel I." He seeks Yum-Yum, a ward of Ko-Ko, with whom he has fallen in love. While

---

* De Wolf Hopper later made "Ko-Ko" one of his star rôles. Elaborate precautions were taken to protect American rights for this as well as other G. and S. operas, but without success. Harry B. Smith tells of some of these attempts, which themselves have the humor of a comic opera. Hearing that a company had obtained the score and was preparing to present "The Mikado" in America, Mr. D'Oyly Carte smuggled a company on shipboard in disguise and brought it to New York for its first production, while the rival company was still rehearsing. Another incident Smith relates is of a company in the Middle West being deprived of Japanese dress, performing it with the cast and chorus attired in "Pinafore" costumes.

he is conversing with the nobles, Pooh-Bah enters. He informs the young man that Ko-Ko is now the Lord High Executioner, and that he himself is Lord High everything else. He will tell him about Yum-Yum for a consideration. On receipt of a tip he sings, "Young man, despair!" Yum-Yum is destined to wed the Lord High Executioner. That official now arrives heralded by the chorus, "Behold the Lord High Executioner!" and himself singing of his strange reversal of fortune. From a cheap tailor, "Taken from a country jail," he has now reached this high estate. The only trouble, as later develops, is that Ko-Ko is so chicken-hearted he cannot bear the sight of blood. Consequently there have been no executions under his rule—a fact which displeases the Mikado. Ko-Ko avers, however, that "I've got a little list" of victims who "never would be missed." Now enter Yum-Yum and her two chums, Peep-Bo and Pitti-Sing, with the well-known refrain, "Three little maids from school are we." Nanki-Poo presently appears and is recognized by all the girls as the musician who had won Yum-Yum's attention. As soon as the two lovers are alone, he confesses his true rank to her, telling her that he has been forced to flee his father's court to avoid marrying an elderly spinster, Katisha. In a duet beginning, "Were you not to Ko-Ko plighted," he tells Yum-Yum, "I would kiss you fondly thus," and she demurely responds, "I would kiss you fondly thus." The fond dream of the twain is disturbed by the entrance of Ko-Ko, who has troubles of his own. He has received word from the Mikado that unless he executes someone within the next month he will be deposed. Nanki-Poo now offers himself, to relieve this dilemma. He says that if he is allowed to wed Yum-Yum and live with her a month, he will allow Ko-Ko to execute him. Ko-Ko wryly accepts the bargain, and the chorus make merry at this turn of events: they are going to have both a wedding and an execution to witness. The only disturbing element is the dramatic entrance of Katisha, with, "Your revels cease!" She is determined to reclaim her suitor.

Act II   A charming picture is revealed by the second curtain. Yum-Yum is in her garden surrounded by her maidens, making her toilet for the wedding. They sing, "Braid the raven hair." The bride, looking in her mirror, is quite satisfied with her own looks, singing, "We really know our worth, the sun and I!" (quartet, Yum-Yum, Pitti-Sing, Nanki-Poo and Pish-Tush: "Brightly dawns our wedding day.") The ardor of the lovers is cooled, however, by Ko-Ko, who announces that he has just discovered an ancient law to the effect that when a married man is beheaded, his wife must be buried alive. Yum-Yum and others sing: "Here's a how-de-do! Here's a pretty mess!" Nanki-Poo magnanimously offers to stab himself instead, but Ko-Ko points out, that would not help *him;* there must be an execution. When Nanki-Poo then says calmly, "Do it now," Ko-Ko weeps and confesses that he never even killed a blue bottle. Then he brightens up with a happy thought. There needn't be any execution; they will fake one, and Pooh-Bah, who is every other official in the city, will witness it. Pooh-Bah, as usual, is willing to do so, for a consideration. They have no sooner completed the plot than in comes the Mikado with his court. (Song, "Obedience I expect; I'm the Emperor of Japan.") In a longer ditty he avers that "A more humane Mikado never did in Japan exist." Ko-Ko now presents himself in triumph with papers proving that he has carried through his first beheading stunt. He describes in horrid detail how "I gnashed my teeth, when from its sheath I drew my snickersnee." The other leads and chorus back him up with other gory details. "This is all quite interesting," remarks the Emperor, but he says he has come on an entirely different matter; he wants to find his son who has run away from court. Katisha now discovers that it is none other than this son, they are all talking about. The Mikado then decrees that the Lord High Executioner shall be put to death in boiling oil, or something equally lingering and pleasant for his blunder. (Glee: "See how the Fates their gifts allot.") After the Emperor has gone to lunch, which he says can be placed ahead of Ko-Ko's torture, Nanki-Poo and Yum-Yum are seen starting off on their honeymoon. An argument ensues between the prince and the executioner, and Nanki-Poo says that the only way Ko-Ko can save his skin is to marry Katisha. They sing the rollicking duet, "The flowers that bloom in the spring," with chorus. Ko-Ko then makes comic love to Katisha, singing the "Titwillow" song. Katisha capitulates. After his luncheon the Mikado is informed that Nanki-Poo is very much alive and happily married. Pitti-Sing leads the finale, "For he's gone and he's married Yum-Yum!"

RUDDIGORE

(or "The Witch's Curse.") Comic Opera in Two Acts. Music by Sullivan. Book by Gilbert. Savoy Theatre, London, January 22, 1887 (283 performances). In New York, February 21, 1887.

CAST   SIR RUTHVEN MURGATROYD. ADAM, *his servant.* HANNAH, *an aged soothsayer.* DESPARD, *brother of Sir Ruthven.* RICHARD, *his foster brother.* ROSE, *a foundling maiden.* MAD MARGARET, *a village girl.* Villagers, Servants, etc.

ARGUMENT   In this rather labored work, relieved by sparkling music, the librettist and composer satirized the old Eng- .

lish melodramas, with their witches' curses, legendary crimes of the
nobility, and the like. It is really burlesque melodrama, and while
not often produced today, was regarded by Gilbert as one of his three
best operas.

Act I   The action opens in Cornwall. The founder of the house of
Murgatroyd was such a crimester that a heavy curse hangs
over the line. The present incumbent, Sir Ruthven, is a very mild-
tempered young man who seeks to evade the family curse by living
quietly under the name of Robin Oakapple. His brother, Despard,
thinking him dead, succeeds to the title. Robin is in love with a village
maiden, Rose, but does not prosper in his suit. Richard, a foster
brother, lately returned from a life on the sea, offers to plead his suit;
but, instead, pleads his own so successfully that Rose favors him.
Despard now learns that his elder brother, "Robin," is not dead, so
relinquishes the estate.

The principal musical numbers in this Act are: Hannah's eerie
legend, "Sir Rupert Murgatroyd"; Richard's salty song of the sea, "I
shipped, d'ye see, in a revenue sloop"; the bridesmaids' chorus, "Hail
the bridegroom! Hail the bride!"; Mad Margaret's "Cheerily carols
the lark"; male chorus, "When thoroughly tired of being admired";
Sir Despard's song with refrain, "Oh, why am I moody and sad?"; the
madrigal, "Where the buds are blossoming"; and the duos and trios
leading up to a brilliant finale.

Act II   In the second act, which takes place in the picture gallery of
Ruddigore Castle, Robin and his faithful servant, Adam, are
seen trying to adjust themselves to the situation and the family curse.
His ancestors, whose portraits hang upon the walls, admonish him that,
in order to live up to the curse, he ought to commit some daily crime;
and that he will probably die in agony unless he commits a good one,
such as abducting a lady. As one by one they come to life, it is proven
that they really ought not to have died at all. Robin is greatly cheered
to find that the curse doesn't amount to so much; and Rose decides that
he is not so bad a fellow, and she can be quite happy with him.

The musical numbers include: the opening duet between Robin and
Adam, "I once was as meek as a new-born lamb"; a pleasing love duet
between Richard and Rose, "Happily, coupled are we"; Sir Roderick's
haunting refrain, "When the night wind howls"; the patter song sung
by Robin, Despard, and Margaret, "My eyes are fully open to my awful
situation"; the ballad by Hannah, "There grew a little flower"; and a
finale no less brilliant than the first, beginning with the aria by Robin,
"Having been a wicked baronet a week."

THE YEOMEN OF THE GUARD

Or, "The Merryman and His Maid." Comic Opera in Two Acts. Music by Sullivan. Book by Gilbert. Savoy Theatre, London, October 3, 1888, (423 times); New York, at the Casino, October 3, 1889, (100 performances). In the New York cast were Bertha Ricci, Sylvia Gerrish, Isabelle Urquhart, J. H. Riley, George Broderick, Henry Hallam, George Olmi, and Charles Renwick.

CAST   SIR RICHARD CHOLMONDELEY, *Lieutenant of the Tower.* COLONEL FAIRFAX, *a prisoner.* SERGEANT MERYLL, *of the Yeomen of the Guard.* PHOEBE MERYLL, *his daughter.* LEONARD MERYLL, *his son.* JACK POINT, *a strolling jester.* WILFRED SHADBOLT, *Head Jailer and Assistant Tormentor.* ELSIE MAYNARD, *a strolling player.* DAME CARRUTHERS, *Housekeeper to the Tower.* KATE, *her niece.* FIRST AND SECOND YEOMAN. FIRST AND SECOND CITIZEN. THE HEADSMAN. Yeomen of the Guard, Citizens, etc.

ARGUMENT   Here the grim Tower of London is forced to contribute its quota of amusement, some of which takes place around the headsman's block. The time is the Sixteenth Century. Sullivan was very proud of "The Yeomen," and its plot is one of the best. It introduces a note of sadness and sentiment.

Act I   Colonel Fairfax, a gallant soldier, is a prisoner of the Tower under sentence of death on the charge of sorcery, due to his delving in alchemy. Sergeant Meryll and others of the Guard are in sympathy with him and look hourly for his reprieve, which does not come. The sergeant's son, Leonard, arrives and connives with him to aid in the escape of Fairfax. Leonard hides and the prisoner is given a uniform like his and his beard is shaved off, after which Fairfax is palmed off as the returned yeoman. However, before this is accomplished, Fairfax is hastily married to Elsie, a strolling player. It is strictly a marriage of convenience, as Elsie is paid a hundred crowns and is assured that within an hour she will be a widow. The Colonel, on his part, contracts the hasty alliance in order to circumvent a rascally kinsman who has committed him to the Tower that his estate may be confiscated. While the ceremony is being performed, Phoebe, the Sergeant's daughter, purloins the dungeon keys from Wilfred, her ardent admirer, and soon after the prisoner escapes in his disguise of a yeoman, Phoebe, who is something of a flirt, ardently kisses her supposed brother, while Elsie swoons at the realization that she is married to a man she doesn't know, and who is still very much alive.

This opera contains some characteristic and delightful bits, the choruses in the First Act being especially vigorous: "Tower warders under orders"; "When our gallant Norman foes"; "Here's a man of jollity"; the duet, Elsie and Point, "I have a song to sing"; Point's "I've jest and joke"; Elsie's tuneful ballad, " 'Tis done, I am a bride"; Phoebe's graceful solo, "Were I thy bride"; and the final trio, "To thy fraternal care."

Act II Again the scene is the Tower, by moonlight. Two days have gone by without trace of the missing prisoner. Fairfax in his disguise seeks just as busily as the others. Elsie mopes about, and Fairfax falls in love with her, deciding finally to woo his own bride incognito. He is succeeding when another absurd plot is hatched. Jack Point contrives with Wilfred to make her a "widow." An arquebus is fired in the distance, and Wilfred runs in to announce that he shot the prisoner while attempting to escape, and the body is sunk. Jack corroborates this, but their plot is hoist by its own petard. Elsie, now thinking herself actually a widow, accepts Fairfax. The latter obtains a reprieve and discloses his identity. Phoebe has to content herself with Wilfred; and Jack is left out in the cold.

The best musical numbers are: Jack's rollicking ditty, "Oh, a private buffoon!"; Fairfax's ballad, "Free from his fetters grim"; a quartet, "Strange adventure!"; a trio, "If he's made the best use of his time"; a quartet, "When a wooer goes a wooing"; and the smashing medley and finale, "Heighdy! Heighdy! Misery me!"

THE GONDOLIERS

Or, "The King of Barataria." Comic Opera in Two Acts. Music by Sullivan. Book by Gilbert. Savoy Theatre, London, December 7, 1889 (554 times). It was the last joint production of composer and librettist.

CAST The Duke of Plaza-Toro, *a Grandee of Spain.* The Duchess of Plaza-Toro, *his wife.* Casilda, *their daughter.* Luiz, *their attendant.* Don Alhambra del Bolero, *the Grand Inquisitor.* Inez, *the King's foster mother. Venetian Gondoliers:* Marco Palmieri. Giuseppe Palmieri. Antonio. Francesco. Giorgio. Annibale. Ottavio. *Contadine:* Gianetta, Tessa, Fiametta, Vittoria, Giulia, and others. Gondoliers, Men-at-Arms, Heralds, etc.

ARGUMENT "The Gondoliers" makes use of the familiar comic opera situation of a mix-up of identities in childhood, to weave a droll series of resulting contretemps. The action shifts from

Venice to an imaginary island. The time is 1750. This final offering
of the two great co-workers is regarded as one of their best.

Act I On the Piazetta at Venice a group of laughing contadine, or
flower girls, make merry. (Opening chorus: "List and learn,
ye dainty roses.") While they sing a band of gondoliers joins them.
Two of the men, Marco and Giuseppe, after their duet, "We're called
gondolieri," break the news to the girls that they seek brides, but it is
impossible to choose, when all are so fair. A game of blindman's buff
is thereupon staged, and the girls agree that the two who are caught
shall be "it." Gianetta and Tessa are finally captured, and agree to wed
the two brothers in true comic opera style.

Now enter the Spanish Duke of Plaza-Toro, his wife, daughter, and
"suite" consisting of Luiz, the young drummer. The Duke is too impoverished to afford a larger ménage. (Quartet: "From the sunny
Spanish shore.") The optimistic Duke hopes to replenish his coffers
by a speedy union between his daughter, Casilda, and the wealthy but
mysterious King of Barataria, to whom she was wedded in infancy.
Their quest is now to find the missing king. But Luiz is unhappy because he has aspired to her hand. After a quartet celebrating the
prowess of "The Duke of Plaza-Toro," Luiz is overjoyed to find that
Casilda reciprocates his love. As they rush into each other's arms they
sing, "O rapture, when alone together."

Don Alhambra, the Grand Inquisitor, who comes from the Ducal
Palace with the Duke and Duchess, says that there is a hitch in the
plans, as the king cannot be found. He had been entrusted in childhood to the care of a gondolier, and the boy had gotten mixed up with
another lad. Sings Don Alhambra: "I stole the Prince and brought
him down, and left him gaily prattling." Casilda is informed that she
is wedded to one of two gondoliers—Marco or Giuseppe—but nobody
knows which. A recitative by Casilda, "But, bless my heart, consider
my position!" is followed by a quintet, "Life's a pudding full of plums."
The gondoliers themselves now return and are informed of the predicament. Marco and Giuseppe are bidden to proceed to the island realm
of Barataria, to determine which of them is the king. They reluctantly
agree, as they are quite pleased with the two flower girls whom they
have just married. The latter are no less disturbed. Gianetta sings,
"Kind sir, you cannot have the heart our lives to part." This is followed by a quartet, Marco, Giuseppe, Gianetta, and Tessa, "Oh, 'tis a
glorious thing, I ween." A closing chorus sings, "Then away we go to
an island fair."

Act II The curtain rises on the court of Barataria, with Marco and
Giuseppe reigning jointly (as no one sees any other solution

for it) and giving general satisfaction. They have brought a lot of their gondolier comrades along, given them court jobs, and a good time is being had by all. Their opening chorus shows that this ideal monarchy "is tempered with Republican Equality." Giuseppe sings of his kingly duties, "Rising early in the morning," at some length. The court is, however, a bit dull, they confess, without feminine society. Marco sings, "Take a pair of sparkling eyes."

They are delighted, therefore, by the entrance of their two brides of three months, who have braved the perils of the deep with other contadini to follow them. The brides rush into the two kings' arms and then sing, "After sailing to this island." All dance a cachuca, but their felicity is interrupted by the entrance of Don Alhambra, who, supported by the two monarchs, sings the topical song, "There lived a king, as I've been told." The Inquisitor announces that Casilda has also come to the island and is prepared to marry formally the one who is the rightful king. Since both prospective grooms are happily married, this presents difficulties. (Quartet, "In a contemplative fashion.") The entrance of the Duke, Duchess, and Casilda in much state is punctuated by the chorus, "With ducal pomp and ducal pride." The Duke and Duchess sing a topical song, "Small titles and orders." A quintet by the two pairs of wedded lovers, and Casilda, seeking to find a way out of the mess ("Here is a case unprecedented") is succeeded by a solution of their problem. The old family nurse, Inez, enters, and in a recitative points out that neither of the gondoliers is the missing prince, but he is none other than Luiz. He ascends the throne, which the two former monarchs cheerfully yield. They prefer the simple life and their brides; while Luiz and Casilda are united. The closing chorus hails the new king and sings the old songs of the gondolieri.

EDWARD SOLOMON

Edward Solomon (1853–1895) wrote the music of six or more operettas which won considerable popularity in the eighties and nineties, in both England and America. In New York and elsewhere in the States this popularity was partly due to the fact that Lillian Russell, then his wife, starred in them. One of the earliest was "Billee Taylor," described as a nautical comedy; the book being by Henry P. Stephens; and the producers the D'Oyly Carte Company (1880). This was followed by "Lord Bateman" (1882) with the same librettist; "The Maid and the Moonshiner," adapted for the American stage (1886) by Charles H. Hoyt; and "Pickwick," some three years later. But his most enduring piece is probably "The Nautch Girl" (1891). His elaborate Drury Lane show, "Mr. Bluebeard," was adapted for the American stage and produced here with success in 1903.

THE NAUTCH GIRL

Comic Opera in Two Acts. Music by Solomon. Book by George Dance. Produced in both London and New York circa 1891.

The plot is laid in India. Punka, the Rajah, a comedy part, has a son, Indru, who has fallen hard for a Nautch dancing girl, Beebee. This is one of the Rajah's worries, the other being the theft of a diamond. He suspects the Grand Vizier, Pyjama, a poor cousin who has been given this job of Vizier. The gem belongs to the god, Bumbo, who has an active part in what follows.

There are twenty or more musical numbers of tuneful quality, the dances and male songs being particularly effective. Bumbo's songs are for a bass-baritone. In the First Act we hear: Indru's song, "This is the place," followed by "Bow not, good people"; Beebee's dainty, "One, two, three," followed by a lovers' duet, "When our shackles are undone"; Punka's pompous entrance song with chorus, "Room for Punka!"; a quartet, "Now when a young man says"; and delightful finale, "Merrily, merrily peals the bell."

In the Second Act: chorus, "We are Punka's poor relations"; the Vizier's song, "The secret of my past success"; fine songs by Bumbo— "It was all my eye," "Put upon the shelf," and "Crocodile"; dancing number with chorus, "If we travel"; an Indian lullaby, "Gently bear my lady"; and finale, "This is the idol grave and staid."

JULIAN EDWARDS

An English composer, born in 1855, Edwards was educated abroad and did his first musical work there. He came to America in 1888, living in Yonkers, New York, until his death, in 1910. He tried his hand first at cantatas and operas in serious vein. These operas include: "Corinne" (1880), "Victorian" (1883), "Elfinella" (1893), "King Rene's

Daughter" (1893), "The Patriot" (1907). His lighter works by which he is best known are: "Jupiter" (1892), "Friend Fritz" (1893), "Brian Boru" (1893), "The Goddess of Truth" (1896), "Princess Chic" (1900), "Madeleine" (1902), "Dolly Varden" (1902), and others.

DOLLY VARDEN

Comic Opera in Two Acts.   Music by Edwards.   Book by Stanislaus Stange.   London, 1901.   New York, Herald Square Theatre, January 27, 1902.   The latter cast was headed by Lulu Glaser.

CAST   CAPTAIN RICHARD BELVILLE, *an English officer.*   CAPTAIN HOR-
        ACE HARCOURT, *of the Navy.*   LORD GAYSPARK.   JOHN FAIR-
FAX, *Dolly's guardian.*   LETITIA FAIRFAX, *his sister.*   DOLLY VARDEN.
Others.

ARGUMENT   A light and charming musical romance telling of the
            tangled love affairs of a beauty, Dolly Varden, who
comes to London, time of George the First, and replaces her many rural
swains with city ones equally fervent.   Fairfax, her guardian, is in
love with her himself, but is finally circumvented by young Belville, a
dashing officer.   The story also deals with the heart affairs of Letitia
Fairfax.
   There is an abundance of pleasing music, though of no great depth.
First Act: Gayspark and girls, "Swing, my pretty one"; Harcourt and
chorus, "My ship's the girl for me"; Belville, "Dolly Varden"; Dolly
and girls, "The Country Girl"; Dolly and Dick, "What love means";
Fairfax, "When we met in lover's lane"; Dolly and chorus, "The Can-
nibal Maid."
   Second Act: quartet, "Lovable Love"; Letitia and chorus, "The
Navy"; quartet, "For the benefit of man"; Dolly, "The lay of the Jay";
Dick, "The girl you love"; Fairfax and men, "The Song of the Sword";
octet, "Brides and Grooms."

ETHEL M. SMYTH

Ethel Mary Smyth won renown both in England and abroad for her composing and other writings.   She was born in London, in 1858, but received much of her musical education abroad; attending the Leipzig Conservatory. Her first two operas, "Fantasio" and "Der Wald," were produced in Germany, in 1898 and 1901. A lyrical tragedy, "The Wreckers," was first produced at Leipzig, in German, in 1906; and three years later at London, in English. "The Boatswain's Mate," a comic opera, was staged in London during the dark days of the first World War. She wrote "Fete Galente" and other short operas and an Autobiography in two volumes. In 1922, George V created her a Dame of the British Empire in recognition of her work for both literature and the stage. Dame Ethel Smyth died, May 8, 1944, at the age of 86.

THE BOATSWAIN'S MATE

Humorous Opera in Two Acts. Music by Ethel M. Smyth. Dramatized by the composer from W. W. Jacob's story of the same name. Shaftesbury Theatre, London, January 28, 1916.

CAST   HARRY BENN, *ex-boatswain.* NED TRAVERS, *a discharged soldier.* MRS. WATERS, *landlady of "The Beehive."* MARY ANNE, *maid at "The Beehive."* A Policeman, Farm-laborers, and others.

ARGUMENT   The composer has followed Mr. Jacobs' popular story as closely as the exigencies of opera will allow, and the music is cleverly adapted to the theme.

The First Act takes place outside a little inn, "The Beehive." Harry Benn, a boatswain, has been wooing the landlady, but is so unsuccessful that he persuades Ned Travers, a discharged soldier, to aid him. The latter is to "rescue" Mrs. Waters from Ned, and thus curry favor.

The Second Act relates a series of misadventures. The landlady armed with a gun proves quite capable of defending herself. It is all "foolery" and some delightfully characteristic music is interwoven.

FETE GALANTE

A "Dance Dream" in One Act. Music by Ethel M. Smyth. Book by Edward Shanks, from a story by Maurice Baring. Birmingham, England, June 4, 1923.

The action takes place in a moonlit garden of the last century. It introduces a King, Lover, Pierrot, Harlequin, Queen, Columbine, four Puppets, and the mute Pantaloon. Although set in an atmosphere of light frivolity, the action becomes ever more sinister, and ends in tragedy. However, it is relieved by the unreality of its figures and the lilting strains of melody interspersed.

EDWARD JAKOBOWSKI

Jakobowski, who is also known as Ed. Belville, said to be his true name, was an industrious composer of light opera in the latter part of the last century. Although born in London, 1858, and classed as English, his parents were Viennese of Polish extraction. He studied for some years at the Vienna Conservatory, winning prizes in harmony and orchestration. He early tried his hand at light opera, first at Paris unsuccessfully, then in London where he made his home. Among his works are "The Three Beggars," "Dick," "Mynheer Jan," and "Formosa." But his fame rests upon a single work—his sensational hit, "Erminie."

ERMINIE

Comic Opera in Two Acts. Music by Jakobowski. Book by Claxson Bellamy and Harry Paulton. Comedy Theatre, London, November 9, 1885, where its great success resulted in its opening with an American cast, at the Casino, New York, May 10, 1886.*

CAST MARQUIS DE PONTVERT. ERMINIE DE PONTVERT, *his daughter.* EUGENE MARCEL, *his secretary.* VICOMTE DE BRISSAC. DELAUNAY, *a young officer.* DUFOIS, *Landlord of the Lion d'Or.* CHEVALIER DE BRABAZON. RAVANNES, *a vagabond.* CADEAUX, *his comrade.*

---

* The continuous runs here and in Boston and Philadelphia totaled 1256 performances—a record. Rudolph Aronson, the American producer, paid the composer $120,000 in royalties. The New York cast included: Francis Wilson, as "Cadeaux"; Pauline Hall, as "Erminie"; Marie Jansen, as "Javotte"; and William S. Daboll, as "Ravannes." "Erminie" was revived at the Park Theater, New York, January 3, 1921, with Francis Wilson again as "Cadeaux," and De Wolf Hopper as "Ravannes." Aronson, who was one of the foremost producers of light opera in America, in the eighties, calls "Erminie" "the most successful operetta of modern times." It ran here and on the road for several years, and was extensively "pirated." Aronson tells an interesting story of the great blizzard that hit New York in March, 1888, and stopped the show temporarily. On the night of the storm's height, only two performers showed up— Francis Wilson and Louise Sylvester, the latter in a state of collapse. And the audience consisted of three stalwart Canadians, who evidently took such storms as a matter of course. They were given tickets to the next performance.

CERISE MARCEL, *Erminie's companion.* PRINCESS DE GRAMPONEUR.
JAVOTTE, *Erminie's maid.* Waiters, maids, soldiers, peasants, guests, etc.

ARGUMENT This droll story, based on an old melodrama, "Robert
Macaire," relates the escapades of two vagabonds in
polite society.

Act I In the opening scene before the Lion d'Or inn, the villagers
make merry with the song, "Around in a whirl." Javotte,
Erminie's maid, comes in with the tidings that the Marquis is to bring
some distinguished guests to the fair. The nobleman and his daughter, Erminie, now enter, the latter's opening song being the charming
ballad, "Ah! when Love is young." It later develops that the Marquis
plans to bestow his daughter's hand upon the scion of another house,
whom she has never seen. She, perversely, loves Eugene, her father's
secretary. In a duet, "There is a sweet remembrance of the past," they
pledge their affections anew. Following a chorus of the soldiers, the
Marquis sings a ringing refrain, "Dull is the life of a soldier in peace,"
followed by chorus, "All for glory!" Two rogues enter, Ravannes and
Cadeaux, who are destined to upset the apple-cart considerably. Their
"Thieves' Duet" is echoed by a chorus, "Downy jailbirds of a feather."
After Erminie has sung her "Dream Song," one of the chief numbers,
and she and others have gone to her father's chateau to prepare for the
wedding, the two vagabonds waylay Ernest de Brissac, her intended
suitor, take his clothes away from him and tie him to a tree. When he
escapes, the villains boldly denounce him as the thief who has robbed
them, and the act ends with the luckless Ernest in custody.

Act II Ravannes, clad in the stolen attire of the young Vicomte, presents himself at the chateau as the expected guest. Cadeaux
is his noble friend. Erminie is not at all pleased with her suitor's
appearance or the turn of events. Eugene disconsolately sings, "The
Darkest Hour." And while the servants hail the bride with "Joy attend
on Erminie," she voices the plaintive and familiar melody, "Dear
mother, in dreams I see her." During the festivities Ernest arrives, only
to be confronted and denounced by the audacious Ravannes. The latter, however, is such a good fellow that he nearly gets away with his plot
and he and his pal all but succeed in robbing the house, before their
true identity becomes known. A song and whistling chorus, "What
the Dickey Birds Say," enliven things here. With the tangle straight-
ened, love affairs run smoothly. Erminie is allowed to wed Eugene;
and Ernest wins Cerise, her friend, and the girl he has wanted all along.
A vocal gavotte, "Join in pleasures," is one of the closing numbers.

IVAN CARYLL

Ivan Caryll was born in England, in 1861, and while identified with English music of the lighter vein, spent many of his later years in France, having two homes there—one being a castle in Normandy, and the other a villa on the Mediterranean. He was interested in operettas and French farces. His first production in England, which met with fair success, was "The Lily of Leoville" (1886). It was followed by "Monte Cristo Jr.," "Little Christopher Columbus" (1893), one of his most successful; two in which he collaborated with Lionel Monckton, "The Circus Girl" and "A Runaway Girl"; "The Girl from Paris," "Chin Chin," "The Pink Lady," "The Duchess of Dantzic," "Jack o'Lantern (starring Fred Stone), "The Earl and the Girl," "The Gay Parisienne," and "Oh! Oh! Delphine." While several of these made pronounced "hits" at the time, they were ephemeral. Caryll died in New York, November 29, 1921. Harry B. Smith speaks of his wide circle of friends in all walks of life.

A RUNAWAY GIRL

Musical Comedy in Three Acts. Music by Caryll in collaboration with Lionel Monckton. It made a sensational hit, at the Shaftesbury Theatre, London, in 1898, where it made a "runaway" of 593 performances. It also won wide favor in America; it was produced in New York during the season of 1898-9; then came a long road tour. Its catchy music, such as "The soldiers in the park," was heard everywhere.

ARGUMENT Winifred Gray, an orphan, and ward of Lord and Lady Coodle, runs away from a convent to join a wandering band of minstrels. She is accompanied by a lay brother, Tamarind. The minstrels meet up with a Cook's Tour, which included the Coodles, and Guy Stanley, their nephew, who promptly falls in love with the minstrel queen—our Winifred. As a matter of fact, a match had been arranged between him and Winifred, much to his disgust. Of course, he does not recognize her in her present station, and equally of course, musical comedy situations follow.

This operetta owed its popularity to its plenitude of musical hits. In the First Act: Winifred and chorus, "The sly cigarette"; chorus, "The convent bell"; Guy and chorus, "Not the sort of girl"; Winifred and chorus, "I'm only a poor little singing girl"; Winifred and Guy, "No one in the world"; and the rollicking song and dance, "Follow the man from Cook's." In the Second: trio, "We have left pursuit behind us"; Dorothy and chorus, the great hit, "Soldiers in the Park"; Winifred and chorus, "Beautiful Venice"; her droll topical song, "The boy guessed right"; topical song between Flipper, the comedian, and Alice, "The pickaninnies"; and chorus, "Oh, I love society!"

THE PINK LADY

Musical Comedy in Three Acts. Music by Caryll. Book adapted from the French of Berr and Guillemand by C. M. S. McLellan. New Amsterdam Theater, New York, March 13, 1911. In the cast were: Hazel Dawn, who took the part of "Claudine," the "Pink Lady"; Alice Dovey, as Lucien's fiancée; Alma Francis, as "Serpolette"; Ida M. Adams, as "Desirée"; William Elliott, as "Lucien." It was presented in London, at the Globe Theatre, April 11, 1912, and ran 124 times. It was performed at the St. Louis Open-Air Theatre in 1945.

ARGUMENT This plot is unusually clever, being based on a sophisticated French farce. It relates the adventures of Lucien, who takes his former innamorata, the "Pink Lady," to a restaurant, where they run into his present fiancée. Both the ladies thereafter have a good deal to say in the matter. The curtain rises on a brilliant scene in the Forest of Compiègne. The Second Act is laid in a Parisian furniture shop; the Third in a sumptuous Ball of Nymphs and Satyrs.

The music also is better than the average. In the First Act are heard: "Bring along the camera"; "I'm going to be married in June"; "When Love goes a-straying"; "Gently"; and one of the gems of the work, "The Girl from Saskatchewan." In the Second Act: quartet, "The Intriguers"; chorus, "Donny did, Donny didn't"; the famous "Kiss Waltz," in which the Pink Lady undertakes to coach one of the males in osculation; and "The Duel." The Third Act introduces a lively Parisian two step; "I like it"; and the perennial favorite, "Beautiful Lady."

THE EARL AND THE GIRL

Musical Comedy in Two Acts. Music by Caryll. Book by Seymour Hicks. Adelphi Theatre, London, in 1903 (371 performances). It was also popular in New York.

This show emphasizes the comedy parts, headed by Jim Cheese, a dog trainer, with Bunker Bliss, a character comedian, and Liza Shoddam, Jim's soubrette sweetheart. The action starts with the arrival from Paris of Richard Wargrave and Elphin Haye, elopers. Gay "patter" and lively music follow swiftly.

THE DUCHESS OF DANTZIC

Romantic Light Opera in Three Acts. Music by Caryll. Book by Henry Hamilton. London circa 1912.

An opera dealing with Napoleon and extending over the years 1792 to 1807. It is another version of the popular tale of Catherine, the laundress, who came to be known as Madame Sans Gène. The music is pleasing throughout and contains some excellent choruses.

OH! OH! DELPHINE

Musical Comedy in Three Acts. Music by Caryll. Book by C. M. S. McLellan, after the French farce, "Villa Primrose." Shaftesbury Theatre, London, in 1913 (174 times). New York, the Knickerbocker Theatre (248 times).

A spicy, sophisticated farce with music which keeps its French smartness under a thin British veneer. It relates chiefly to the amorous adventures of Colonel Pomponnet and the demure Delphine.

In the First Act are heard the song by Pomponnet, with chorus, "Please turn your backs"; the models' song, "Posing for Venus"; duet, "Oh! Oh! Delphine"; and trio, "Why shouldn't you tell me that?" In the Second, chorus, "Poor Bouchotte!"; duet, "Can we forget?"; and the saucy song by Bouchotte and maids, "Everything's at home except your wife." In the Third, duet, "The Venus Waltz"; Bouchotte and chorus, "Then all come along"; duet, "Captain Dinklepop"; and finale.

EDWARD GERMAN

A composer who has taken high rank in his own country, being knighted in 1928, German was born in Whitchurch, Shropshire, February 17, 1862. He entered the Royal Academy of Music, at eighteen, where he studied for seven years. His musical career began as a violinist in an orchestra. He conducted musical festivals and wrote incidental music for Shakespeare's plays produced by Sir Henry Irving. He collaborated with Sullivan on "The Emerald Isle" (1901); and wrote "Merrie England" (1902), "A Princess of Kensington" (1903), and the one opera for which he is chiefly known abroad, "Tom Jones" (1907). German died in London, November 11, 1936.

TOM JONES

Comic Opera in Three Acts. Music by German. Book by Robert Courtneidge and A. M. Thompson, based on the novel by Fielding. Apollo Theatre, London, April 17, 1907 (110 times). Astor Theatre, New York, November 11, 1907.

ARGUMENT This story does not need rehearsing, as it follows fairly closely the main lines of Fielding's classic novel. The book is clever and the music "exquisite," according to one critic. It was very popular in England. It proved an admirable vehicle for the composer to indulge his taste in old English dances and madrigals.

The music also includes pleasing solos and rollicking choruses. In the First Act, Squire Western and chorus, "On a January morning"; Tom and chorus, "West country lad"; Sophia, "Today my spinet"; and madrigal, "Here's a paradox." In the Second Act, opening chorus, "Hurry, bustle"; Sophia, "Dream o'day Jill"; laughing trio, "You have a pretty wit"; Tom, "A soldier's scarlet coat"; and Sophia, "Love maketh the heart a garden fair." In the Third, Tom's song, "If love's content"; a barcarole, trio, "Says a well-known saw"; and smashing finale.

LIONEL MONCKTON

Monckton was born in 1862, and died, February 15, 1924. He was well known in his own country as both composer of songs and operettas, and musical critic. He collaborated with Ivan Caryll in "The Circus Girl" and "A Runaway Girl"; and wrote "A Country Girl," "The Quaker Girl," "The Cingalee," and others which scored successes. His

most popular work was "The Arcadians," in which he was assisted by
Howard Talbot.

THE ARCADIANS

Musical Play in Three Acts. Music by Monckton and Talbot.
Book by Mark Ambient and A. M. Thompson. Shaftesbury Theatre,
London, April 28, 1909 (809 performances). It also had a good run
at the Liberty Theater, New York, beginning January 17, 1910. In
the cast were: Julia Sanderson, as "Eileen Cavanagh"; Frank Moulan, in
the comedy part, "Simplicitas," an Arcadian; Alan Mudie, as "Jack
Meadows"; Ethel Cadman, and Audrey Maple.

ARGUMENT   The First Act is laid in Arcadia; the Second, in the
                 Askwood Race Course; and the Third, in the Arcadian
Restaurant. The inhabitants of Arcadia live remote from the world
and its temptations; they dance and sing in primeval simplicity. They
cannot believe their ears when Sombra, one of their girls, tells them that
she has heard of a strange country, England, where people do not tell
the truth; they have an ingenious substitute called a lie. The simple
Arcadians express a desire to see a being from this queer land, and Fate
answers them by dropping James Smith from an airplane into their
midst.

The piece is of "show girl" type and was very popular in its day.
Music is light and catchy, including: Act I, opening chorus, "Arcadians
are we"; Time and chorus, "Since the days before the Flood"; Sombra's
song, "The Pipes of Pan"; Simplicitas' funny, "I'm a case of complete
reformation." Act II, Eileen's "The dear little girl with a bit of a
brogue"; Sombra's "Far away in Arcady"; duet, "You're taking such
good care of me"; "What charming weather"; "Arcady is ever young."
Act III, Chrysea's song, "When first I came to London Town"; "Eileen's
"When I wander in my garden"; quintet, "Tho' truth is not in great
demand"; and spirited finale, "Truth is so beautiful!"

THE QUAKER GIRL

Musical Play in Three Acts. Music by Monckton. Book by J. T.
Tanner. Adelphi Theatre, London, November 5, 1910 (536 times).

ARGUMENT   A light and pleasing comedy dealing with the tribu-
                 lations of Prudence, a Quaker girl, who is cast out of
the sect because of an innocent love affair with Tony Chute. She is

given a job with Madame Blum, a Parisian dressmaker. The Princess Mathilde, Captain Charteris, her fiancé, and others higher up, are involved.

The music as well as costuming is charming. In the First Act we hear a song by Mathilde, "O Time, Time!"; a duet between her and Charteris, "Wonderful"; Prudence's demure entrance song, "A Quaker Girl"; and topical song, Jeremiah and chorus, "Just as father used to do." In the Second Act, Phoebe's song, "Or thereabouts"; Prudence's "Ah, oui"; waltz song, "Come to the ball"; and quintet, "Barbizon." In the Third Act, duet, "Mr. Jeremiah"; Prudence's, "Tony from America"; and a dance duet, "The first dance."

THE CINGALEE

Musical Play in Two Acts. Music by Monckton. Book by James T. Tanner. London, circa 1911.

ARGUMENT   A work of lighter musical comedy style with unusually tuneful melodies, but not of lasting merit. The scene is laid in Ceylon. Nanoya, a Cingalee girl, has been betrothed at the age of four, and grows up to find that her proposed husband is the pompous Boobhamba. To escape him she assumes the disguise of a tea girl on her own plantation, which has been fraudulently leased to the handsome young Englishman, Harry Vereker.

A good deal is said about Ceylon in the music, from the opening chorus, "Sleepy Ceylon" and Harry's song, "Pearl of Sweet Ceylon," on. The march and chorus introducing the high-and-mighty Boobhamba, "Hail the Noble!" is one of the best bits. Nanoya's song, "Cinnamon tree," is pleasing. In the Second Act we hear: chorus, "Sing to Boobhamba"; song by Nanoya and the other tea girls, "The dance I'll lead him"; Harry's "My dear little Cingalee"; a comical duet, "Gollywogs," and others.

LESLIE STUART

Stuart's baptismal name was T. A. Barrett. He was born in Southport, in 1864; studied the organ, and at fifteen became organist in St. John's Cathedral, Salford. Later he served in similar capacity in

Manchester. He is chiefly known for his sensational success, "Florodora" (1899). Other works include: "The Silver Slipper" (1901), "The Belle of Mayfair" (1906), "Havana" (1909), and "The Slim Princess" (1911). Stuart died, March 27, 1928.

FLORODORA

Musical Comedy in Two Acts. Music by Stuart. Book by Owen Hall. Lyric Theatre, London, November 11, 1899 (455 times); Casino, New York, November 10, 1900. It was a road success for the next eight years, and was revived at the Century Theater, New York, April 5, 1920. In the original New York cast were R. E. Graham, Cyril Scott, William and May Edouin, Guelma L. Baker, and Edna Wallace Hopper. The famous sextet of girls is said to have supplied more than one member for the "upper ten" matrimonial market.

CAST   CYRUS W. GILFAIN, *proprietor of the perfume and of the Island of Florodora.* FRANK ABERCOED, *his manager.* LEANDRO, *overseer.* CAPTAIN ARTHUR DONEGAL, *of the Life Guards.* ANTHONY TWEEDLEPUNCH, *a phrenologist.* ANGELA GILFAIN. DOLORES, *a native girl.* LADY HOLYROOD. Six men clerks. Six native girls. Six girl friends of Angela. Others.

ARGUMENT   One of the most delightful light operas produced at the turn of the century, and its music has proved enduring—some of it traditional in its appeal. The First Act takes place in the little island, "Florodora," in the Philippines. The Second switches to Abercoed Castle, Wales.

Act I   Gilfain, an overshrewd Englishman, has obtained the famous perfume, "Florodora," from its rightful owner, whose daughter, Dolores, is in his employ. He has sent as his manager, Frank Abercoed, who is really Lord Abercoed. Frank and Dolores fall in love with each other. Meanwhile, Tweedlepunch, a detective disguised as a sort of traveling showman, is on a still hunt for the girl who is the rightful owner of the perfume. Gilfain bribes Tweedlepunch to get the girl married off and out of the way. Lady Holyrood also joins the plot; she wants Frank, herself. When Frank refuses, Gilfain discharges him. He starts back for England. So does Dolores.
    Musical numbers: male sextet, "The credit's due to me"; Dolores, "The silver star of love"; duet, Dolores and Frank, "Somebody"; chorus, "Come and see our island"; duet, "Galloping"; trio, "I want to marry a man, I do"; Angela and chorus, "The fellow who might"; Abercoed—the haunting melody—"The shade of the palm."

Act II Abercoed Castle, Frank's ancestral domain, has likewise come into possession of Gilfain. Now he won't allow the young man to enter. Undaunted, Frank breaks in, with Dolores and Tweedlepunch. The latter tells a ghost story which so frightens Gilfain that he confesses his misdeeds and restores his ill-gotten property. All is forgiven. He weds Lady Holyrood; Frank and Dolores achieve happiness; and Captain Donegal gets Angela.

Musical numbers: Lady Holyrood and chorus, "Tact"; Gilfain, "The Millionaire"; double sextet—the famous and familiar—"Tell me, pretty maiden"; Lady Holyrood, "I've an inkling"; duet, "We get up at 8 A.M."; song, "The fellow who might"; duet, "We're both on the stage"; Dolores, "The Queen of the Philippine Islands"; Donegal and chorus, "I want to be a military man"; Dolores, "He loves, he loves me not"; Dolores, "The Island of Love."

THE BELLE OF MAYFAIR

Musical Comedy in Two Acts. Music by Stuart. Book by Brookfield and Hamilton. Its American premiere, at Daly's Theater, New York, December 3, 1906, was marked by a notable cast including Irene Bentley, Christie MacDonald, Bessie Clayton, Valeska Suratt, May Hobson, and Frank Shea.

The scenes are laid in England and deal with society folk there. In the First Act are found: "Eight little debutantes are we"; "I'm a Duchess"; "In Gay Mayfair"; "The Weeping Willow"; and quartet, "Come to St. Georges." Second Act: duet, "My little girl is a shy little girl"; quintet, "We've come for Court"; Duchess, "Why do they call me a Gibson girl?"; finale, "Come to St. Georges."

THE SLIM PRINCESS

Musical Comedy in Three Acts. Music by Stuart. Book after George Ade, by Henry Blossom. Globe Theatre, New York, January 2, 1911, with Elsie Janis starring as "Princess Kalora," who refuses to fatten; William Pruette, as the fierce Oriental parent; Joseph Cawthorne, as the German tutor; and Queenie Vassar.

In the First Act occur the male chorus, "When the Guards are passing by"; quartet, "Love's Lesson"; and "My Yankee Doodle Girl." In the Second, duet, "We will not live in a bungalow"; quartet, "Nursery Rhymes"; and octet, "Say, little girl." In the Third, "A certain sort of father"; "Romance is not over"; and the chorus, "Queen of my Dreams."

HOWARD TALBOT

Howard Talbot (1865–1928) was well known in England about the turn of the century for his own compositions and his joint work with Lionel Monckton and others. One of his earliest successes was "A Chinese Honeymoon," which also met with favor on the other side of the Atlantic. This came out in 1899, and was followed by "Kitty Grey" (1900), aided by Monckton and others; "The Blue Moon" (1905); "The Girl Behind the Counter" (1906); "The Belle of Brittany" (1908); "A Daughter of the Gods"; and several others ending with "Her Ladyship," in 1928, the year of his death.

A CHINESE HONEYMOON

A Musical Comedy in Two Acts, which requires only brief comment today. The plot concerns members of a typical Chinese Court, with the addition of Hi Lung, the Lord High Admiral, who is really an Englishman. The story is rather "wooden" but is relieved by catchy melodies and dances. The sextet in the First Act, "A Chinese Honeymoon"; and songs by the soubrette, Fi-Fi, "I want to be a lidy" and "Martha spanks the grand pianner," and an octet and chorus in the Second, are best remembered.

SIDNEY JONES

Sidney Jones was born in Leeds, England, in 1869; the son of a musician; and began to study at an early age to be a conductor. He was first connected with theater orchestras, but in later life he devoted himself to composition. In addition to songs, ballets, and shorter works he has composed a dozen or more operas with marked success.

The list includes: "A Gaiety Girl" (1893), "An Artist's Model" (1895), "The Geisha" (1896), "A Greek Slave" (1898), "San Toy" (1899), "My Lady Molly" (1902), "See See" (1906), "The King of Cadonia" (1908), "A Persian Princess" (1909), "The Girl from Utah" (1913), and "The Happy Day" (1916)—the last two in collaboration with Paul Rubens. Jones died in London, England, January 29, 1946.

THE GEISHA

Japanese Musical Play in Two Acts. Music by Sidney Jones. Book by Owen Hall. Daly's Theatre, London, April 25, 1896 (760 performances). Marie Tempest was "O Mimosa San." It was given an elaborate revival in New York, at the Forty-fourth Street Theater, March 27, 1913. James T. Powers was "Wun Hi"; Lina Abarbanell, "Molly"; Carl Gantvoort, one of the officers; and George Williams, "Takemini."

CAST O MIMOSA SAN, *proprietress of a tea house. Four Geisha girls.* LADY CONSTANCE WYNNE, *an English tourist. Four lady guests.* JULIETTE DIAMANT. MOLLY SEAMORE. FAIRFAX, *and three other officers of H. M. S. "The Turtle."* WUN HI, *owner of tea house.* MARQUIS IMARI, *Governor of province.* TOMMY STANLEY. CAPTAIN KATANA. TAKEMINI. NAMI. Others.

ARGUMENT This "Japanese musical play" offers an interesting parallel to Sullivan's "The Mikado" and also to Spenser's "The Little Tycoon," both of which preceded it by about ten years. The action is slight, gay, and amusing; the music tuneful. The First Act takes place in the Tea House of Ten housand Joys, in Japan. The Second represents a Chrysanthemum Fête in the Palace Gardens. The trouble is all caused by the efforts of a rascally old Marquis to close up a Geisha tea shop, in order to get possession of O Mimosa San, who is a general heartbreaker. Officers from a British warship threaten "to blow the old beggar to pieces." The escapade of Molly Seamore, masquerading as a Geisha girl, further complicates the business.

Musical numbers are varied and pleasing. A few of the chief ones in the First Act are: opening chorus, "Happy Japan!"; Fairfax and officers, "Jack's the boy"; Mimosa, "The Amorous Goldfish"; Mimosa and Fairfax, "Kissing"; Geisha chorus, "If you will come to tea"; chorus, "Oh, will they sell our master?"; Molly and Fairfax, "Toy Duet"; Mimosa, "A Geisha's life"; Molly and chorus, "I'm the smartest little Geisha in Japan"; medley and finale, "Sorry and sad," ending, "Fast the sun is setting."

Act II　Opening chorus, "Day born of love"; Molly, "I'm a monkey on a stick"; Geishas, "Geishas are we"; English girls and officers, "Now you must go"; Fairfax, "Star of my soul"; Wun Hi and chorus, "Chin, Chin, Chinaman"; Fairfax and chorus, "Love, love!"; Molly and chorus, "The Interfering Parrot"; chorus, "Before our eyes"; quartet, "What will the Marquis do?" chorus, "It's coming off today."

SAN TOY

Chinese Musical Play in Two Acts.　Music by Sidney Jones.　Book by Edward Morton.　Daly's Theatre, London, October 21, 1899, where it duplicated its forerunner's success, being produced 768 times.　Marie Tempest took the part of "San Toy."　Also quite successful in New York and "on the road."

CAST　EMPEROR OF CHINA.　YEN HOW, *a Mandarin*.　SAN TOY, *his daughter*.　SIR BINGO PRESTON, *British consul*.　CAPTAIN BOBBY PRESTON, *his son*.　FO HOP, *a Chinese student*.　SING HI.　LI. WUN LUNG.　Yen How's six little wives.　Other Chinese.　POPPY. DUDLEY, *her maid*.　English ladies.　Others.

ARGUMENT　Sidney Jones followed his success in the Japanese field, "The Geisha," with a no-less-brilliant Chinese musical play.　The First Act represents a street in Pynka Pong, wherever that may be.　The Second, a Hall in the Emperor's Palace, Pekin.　Yen How, a Mandarin of the first class, has a daughter, San Toy, whose beauty and accomplishments attract the attention of the Emperor, who sends for her.　Yen How, however, has other plans for her; so sends word that his child is a boy, and not a girl, and so disguises her.　He leaves her with a British consul, whose son, Bobby, promptly falls in love with her.　Fo Hop, a student, also determines to wed her, and his plots cause further trouble.　San Toy is taken to Court, where the jealous ladies there plot in their turn to be rid of her.　At last the Emperor relieves the strain by giving her hand to Bobby.

Musical numbers in First Act: opening chorus, "We'll keep the feast in Pynka Pong"; quintet, "The Mandarin"; Dudley, "The Lady's Maid"; Poppy, "A posy from over the sea"; Yen How and wives, "Six little wives"; San Toy, "The petals of the plum tree"; Bobby, "Love has come from Lotus Land."

In Second Act:　chorus of Mandarins, "We're the cream of courtly creatures"; Dudley, "Rhoda and her pagoda"; March and chorus, "The Emperor's Own"; Poppy and chorus, "The whole story"; San Toy and Bobby, "The little China maid"; quartet and chorus, "Back to London"; Yen How, "I mean to introduce it into China"; San Toy, "The one in the world"; Bobby, "The Butterfly"; San Toy, "It's nice to be a boy sometimes."

RALPH VAUGHAN WILLIAMS

Williams was born near Cirencester, England, October 12, 1872. He was educated at Cambridge, "majoring" in music. He continued his studies at the Royal Conservatory, London. He wrote many symphonies, ballets, quartets, and two works for the stage, classed as "music dramas"—"Hugh the Drover," and "The Shepherds of the Delectable Mountains," the latter having a Bunyanesque flavor.

HUGH THE DROVER

Romantic Ballad Opera in Two Acts. Music by Williams. Book by Harold Child. His Majesty's Theatre, London, July 14, 1924.
SCENE: Cotswold, England.
TIME: April, "bout 1812."

ARGUMENT The story is essentially English, threaded with folk-songs, ballads, and traditional airs. The color and atmosphere have the clarity and brightness of an old engraving. The story is laid at the time of the Napoleonic wars and reflects their impact upon a typical countryside. In a small town a fair is in progress, and one feature of it is a prize fight between the local champion—hailed by the chorus as "the Cotswold pride"—and Hugh the Drover. After a lively fight not bound by prize-ring rules, John the Butcher, the "pride," is knocked out by Hugh, but accuses the latter of being a French spy. In the second Act, Hugh is found in the stocks; but is set free by Mary, the Constable's daughter. After more complications, marked by pleasing arias and choruses, the worthy Drover wins the hand of Mary. But his life has been a roving one, and henceforth she is ready to share it. Singing hand in hand they take the road together.
Musical excerpts from this opera are available in record form.

NOEL COWARD

Noel Coward is better known as playwright and actor, than as operatic composer. He was born in Teddington, England, in 1899, and
at the ripe age of ten left the Croydon School to begin his career as
actor, appearing in a village fairy play. At eighteen he had written a
play, "The Last Track," and was fully embarked on the dramatic sea.
He became famous in both England and America for his dramas and
acting, and turned his hand to songs and incidental music. He produced one operetta, "Bitter Sweet," in 1929.

BITTER SWEET

Operetta in Three Acts. Music and book by Coward. "Entire production by Noel Coward." His Majesty's Theatre, London, August,
1929; Tremont Theatre, Boston, October 21, 1929; Ziegfeld Theatre,
New York, November 5, 1929 (159 times). In the American production Evelyn Laye starred as "the Marchioness." It was revived at the
Municipal Open-Air Theatre, St. Louis, in August, 1945.

ARGUMENT   Dolly Chamberlain, promised in marriage to one man
                         and in love with another who is the leader of a night-
club band, tells her troubles to her Aunt, the Marchioness of Shayne,
who is credited with an exotic past.   In order to help her niece, the
older lady tells her of her own love affairs. As a young girl she has
eloped with a music teacher, Carl Linden. Their married life is
brief, as Carl gets into a quarrel with another man, in a Vienna café, for
an insult to the girl, and Carl is killed. After other adventures she
becomes a prima donna on the opera stage and finally attracts and weds
the Marquis of Shayne. But as she recalls her present gilded life with
her early love and ambitions, there is a "bitter-sweet" taste in her mouth.

Act I has three scenes: 1, Lady Shayne's House in Grosvenor Square—
1945 (in last version); 2, Music Room of the Millick's House in Belgrave
Square—1878; 3, Ballroom of Millick's House—1878. Musical numbers: "The Call of Life," "If You Could Come With Me," "I'll See You
Again," "What Is Love?"

Act II has two scenes, in Herr Schlick's Café in Vienna—1883. Music: "Ladies of the Town," "If Love Were All," "Evermore and a Day," "Tokay," "Kiss Me."

Act III has two scenes, the first being in Lord Shayne's House—1898; the second reverting to the opening scene of the play. The music begins with the rousing old tune, "Ta Ra Ra Boom De Ay," and includes "Zigeuner" and reprises of earlier melodies.

OTHER NATIONS

FRIEDRICH SMETANA

Friedrich Smetana is considered the most famous exponent of the Czech school, which is allied with the German. He was born in Leitomischl, March 2, 1824; and died in Prague, May 12, 1884. Of his numerous works, only one opera is now known to the American public, "Die Verkaufte Braut" (The Bartered Bride), first sung in the Czech language at Prague, in 1866, and revived in the German tongue, at Vienna, in 1893. Other works are: "Dalibor" (1868) and "The Kiss" (1876). Says one critic: "Poor Smetana. Nature had put on his brow the stamp of genius, but he never lived to see his glory. After grief and sorrow and direst need he died in a mad-house, and now posterity heaps laurels on his grave. 'The Bartered Bride' has been presented in Prague over three hundred times, and it begins to take possession of every noted stage in Europe."

THE BARTERED BRIDE

(Die Verkaufte Braut.) Light Opera in Three Acts. Music by Smetana. Book by K. Sabina. Prague, May 30, 1866. Metropolitan, New York, February 19, 1909. Emmy Destinn was "Maria."

CAST KRUSCHINA, *a peasant.* KATINKA, *his wife.* MARIA, *their daughter.* MICHA, *a landowner.* AGNES, *his wife.* WENZEL, *their son.* HANS, *son of Micha by a former marriage.* KEZUL, *a marriage broker.* SPRINGER, *a theatrical manager.* ESMERALDA, *a dancer.* MUFF, *a comedian.* Villagers, Players.

ARGUMENT "The Bartered Bride" has achieved a world-wide popularity both as opera and concert music, and deservedly so. It is chockful of vivacious melody and local color, and likewise reflects Bohemian national life. Beginning with the lively overture, the dances, folk-tunes and interplay of dialogue speedily put the auditor in the frame of mind to enjoy the village story that follows.

Act I A spring festival is being celebrated in the village square, and all is joyous. Every heart is merry save only that of Maria, the daughter of Kruschina, a well-to-do peasant, for on this day a suitor chosen by her parents and unknown to her is to claim her hand. She loves Hans, who is poor and obscure. Her parents now enter with Kezul, the village marriage-broker, who has arranged the match with Wenzel, son of the rich farmer Micha. When they tell Maria of the match she objects, and Kezul learns that it is on account of Hans.

An opening Festival chorus, "See the buds are opening," is followed by a pleasing aria sung by Maria, "Indeed I will trust thee"; a trio, "All is as good as settled"; and a dashing finale by the chorus.

Act II To further the marriage, Wenzel, the awkward, stammering bride-groom-to-be, is brought face to face with Maria, but does not know who she is. She worms his secret from him and persuades him to look elsewhere for a sweetheart. Meanwhile, Kezul has been working upon Hans and finally prevails upon him to forego all claim upon Maria, "in favor of Micha's son," by bribing him with three hundred guilders. All present turn from him in disgust as he coolly signs away his prospective bride and pockets the money.

Musical numbers: song by Wenzel, "Dear son"; a duet between Maria and him, "I also knew a dear sweetheart"; song by Hans, "It must succeed"; and a gay choral number.

Act III A traveling showman's troupe is performing in the village square. Wenzel especially is delighted with the performance, on account of a Spanish dancer, Esmeralda. The manager engages the lad to take the part of a dancing bear, and promises him the hand of Esmeralda. At this moment his parents approach with the marriage papers, but he refuses to sign them and runs away. Meanwhile, Maria is in tears over the action of her lover, Hans, but will not make another choice. Hans now reappears upon the scene, still without showing any remorse. He repeats that she shall wed with "Micha's son," as the document reads, and finally discloses himself as the long-lost son of Micha by a former marriage. His stepmother is angry over the trick but is later appeased; the bride is reconciled to her "sale," and only Kezul retires crestfallen.

Musical numbers: song by Wenzel, "Ah, what ails me?"; quartet, "This comes like a thunder clap"; sextet, "Consider a little while"; song by Wenzel, "Be without fear"; trio, "Blessed be they who love and trust"; duet, Maria and Hans, "My dearest sweetheart"; and finale, "Willingly come we!"

CARL GOLDMARK

Carl Goldmark was born in Keszthely, Hungary, May 18, 1832.   He is known chiefly as the composer of three operas: "The Queen of Sheba," "Merlin," and "The Cricket on the Hearth."   The first-mentioned was produced in Vienna, in 1875, where also "Merlin" had its première. "The Cricket on the Hearth" has been transplanted to this country, where it was sung in New York in 1910. Goldmark died in Vienna, January 2, 1915.

THE CRICKET ON THE HEARTH

(Das Heimchen am Herd.)   Light Opera in Three Acts.   Music by Goldmark.   Book by A. M. Willner, after the story by Charles Dickens. Berlin, June 27, 1896.

CAST   JOHN, *a mail-carrier*.   DOT, *his wife*.   TACKLETON, *a manufacturer of dolls*.   MAY, *a girl in his employ*.   EDWARD PLUMMER, *her suitor*.   THE CRICKET, *a guardian spirit*.   Chorus of Cricket Elves, Villagers, etc.

ARGUMENT   The well-known story by Dickens has been followed in this opera, which is an intermingling of romance and domestic felicity.   The action takes place in England of a hundred years ago.

Act I   John, the mail-carrier, and his wife, Dot, live contentedly in their modest home, but for the wish to have a child.   After a Prologue by a chorus of elves without, the Cricket (a soprano voice) tells them that she is their guardian spirit, in the song, "I am the Cricket." Dot tells her that she is secretly in hopes that her home will be blessed with a child.   Dot's friend, May, enters, bemoaning the fate that she is compelled to marry her employer, Tackleton, a doll manufacturer; she has waited vainly seven years for the return of her sweetheart, Edward Plummer.   Later, Edward turns up but in the disguise of a sailor. (Song, "Home, sweet home.")

Act II   In a garden scene a supper in honor of the approaching wedding is being served, with John, Dot, May and Tackleton at the board. A fifth is the mysterious stranger, who proves to be a disturbing element. The quintet sings, "My heart beats." Even John becomes jealous; but the Cricket sings a lovely lullaby and shows him in a dream his son-to-be, driving the mail cart.

Act III   In a room in John's house, May still laments her fate. Just then she hears a song outside, by the sailor. It is one he had used to sing to her: "List to the song of the sea." She recognizes him and they sing a joyful duet, "Oh, speak, my adored one!" When Tackleton drives up for his bride, he is greatly chagrined as Edward calmly appropriates both the girl and the carriage, while villagers prevent his following them. The pleasant opera ends with a domestic tableau and a ringing chorus by their friends and well-wishers.

EDVARD GRIEG

Edvard Grieg (1843–1907) was famed as a composer of songs and instrumental pieces celebrating his native land, Norway. After he had been gathered to his fathers for nearly two-score years, his melodies were garnered and arranged into an operetta, "The Song of Norway," which has been successful on Broadway and will doubtless be so "on the road." The music is faithful to his spirit and his land, and will make many other thousands more familiar with his genius.

THE SONG OF NORWAY

Operetta in Two Acts. Music adapted from Grieg by Robert Wright and George Forrest; orchestration and choral work by Arthur Kay. Book by Milton Lazarus, from play by Homer Curran. Premiere at Curran Theatre, San Francisco, July 3, 1944, by San Francisco Light Opera Association. Imperial Theatre, New York, August 21, 1944.

     SCENE: Norway and later Rome.
     TIME: 1860–1.

CAST EDVARD GRIEG (Lawrence Brooks). RIKARD NORDRAAK (Robert Shafer). NINA HAGERUP (Helena Bliss). FATHER GRIEG (Walter Kingsford). MOTHER GRIEG (Ivy Scott). COUNT PEPPI (Sig Arno). LOUISA GIOVANNI (Irra Petina). FREDDY (Frederic Franklin). 15 others, villagers, dancers.

ARGUMENT Considerable liberties have been taken with the life-story of Edvard Grieg, famous Norwegian composer, but the result is a pleasing blending of native life with his music. The adapters of these melodies have done a painstaking service. A detailed list of sources is given below.

The story itself is slight. Grieg is represented as a rather tumultuous and erratic young man, who is torn between love of home and country, and desire to spread his musical wings—much to the distaste of his prosaic father, who wants him to follow his own trade. Edvard is in love with Nina, his rival and devoted friend being Rikard, the more admirable and unselfish of the two. Nina and Edvard are betrothed and all apparently goes well until the entrance of another tumultuous person, the prima donna, Louisa. She kidnaps Edvard under guise of needing an accompanist for her concert tours, and they go to Italy. But thanks to Rikard, Edvard is finally reunited with Nina and returns home to devote his talents to the music of his native land.

Act I has two scenes. (1) Troldhaugen. After a Prelude, Rikard sings to children "The Legend" (from "A minor concerto") and he, Edvard and Nina sing "The Hill of Dreams" (from same concerto). (2) Square on outskirts of Bergen. "Freddy and his fiddle" (Norwegian dance); "Now" by Louisa and villagers ("Waltz Opus 12"); "Strange Music"—the "hit" song of the operetta—a duet between Edvard and Nina ("Nocturne" and "Wedding in Troldhaugen"); "Midsummer's Eve" (" 'Twas a lovely eve in June" and "Scherzo"); "March of the Trollgers"—an amusing scene of a "Cake Lottery" with "Song of the Mountaineers" leading to a delightful folk finale with reprise of "Strange Music" and "Midsummer's Eve."

Act II has 5 scenes, alternating from Rome to Grieg's home in Norway. (1) The Introduction is based on "Papillon"; "Bon Vivant," part one, from "The Water Lily"; part two, from "The Brook"; song, "Three Loves," from "Albumblatt" and "Poem Erotique." (2) A humorous, "Chocolate pas des trois" ("Monte Pincio"). (3) In this scene the Italian ballerina "puts on an act" and avers she cannot dance to that barbarous Grieg music. Nevertheless, an artistic ballet is finally achieved and we hear three familiar selections from the "Peer Gynt Suite." An aria which Edvard had long denied his sweetheart, "I love you," is another of the many high spots in the music. Then, in scene 4, we find Father and Mother Grieg rejoicing in an oldtime Christmas at home, with the pleasing, "At Christmas time, at Christmas time!" (from "World Wanderings"). In the last scene, the great composer is seen at his piano pouring out his "Song of Norway."

EMMERICH KALMAN

Kalman, a Hungarian, born in 1882, was a prolific writer of operettas, successful in Vienna, Berlin, and abroad. He is chiefly known in America for his "Sari." Others of his works are "The Gay Hussars" (1909), "Miss Springtime" (1916), "Her Soldier Boy" (1917), "The Riviera Girl" (1917), "A Little Dutch Girl" (1920), "The Gypsy Princess" (1921), "Countess Maritza" (1926), "The Circus Princess" (1927), "Paris in Spring" (1931), and "The Devil Rider" (1932).

SARI

Operetta in Two Acts. Music by Kalman. Book by Julius Wilhelm and Fritz Grünbaum. English version by C. C. S. Cushing and E. P. Heath. Liberty Theatre, New York, January 13, 1914. Revived, same place, January 28, 1930. Mitzi Hajos was "Sari." Also at St. Louis Open-Air Theatre, in 1945.

CAST　PALI RACZ, *Gypsy violinist.* LACZI, *his son.* SARI, *his daughter.* JOSKA, *a friend.* JULISKA, *his daughter.* GASTON. COUNT IRINI. CADEAUX. Others.

ARGUMENT　This pleasing operetta has been described as "Hungary brought to America." Its theme and groundwork are musical. Pali Racz, a famous Gypsy violinist now up in years, does not realize his infirmities. He wishes to marry a girl; and also hold his place as a virtuoso. But in a concert when he is tardy, his son, Laczi, outshines him as a violinist. Pali thereupon throws his beloved Stradivarius into the flames, and allows his son to wed the girl, Juliska. But the piece, in America, was really the vehicle for the outstanding talents of Mitzi Hajos as singer and dancer. Her Hungarian folk dance, "Ha-za-za!" became famous. The music throughout is haunting, pathetic, and delightful. "Love's Own Sweet Song" will certainly live in many hearts.

THE UNITED STATES

HISTORICAL PREFACE

Students and critics of Grand Opera have approached—and still approach—the American field with caution. What we have done is clearly not commensurate with the best that Europe has produced. For one thing, our culture is still too young; and we have been too busy with other affairs. With the turn of the century, increasing attention has been paid to native work, and we have had promising material from Damrosch, Herbert, De Koven, Parker, Converse, Hadley, Cadman, Deems Taylor, and others. But Grand Opera in this country, it may as well be confessed, is still in formative process.

This is not the case, however, in the fields of Light Opera and Musical Comedy; for here our stage has sprung into a commanding position. Not that it has been a closed market. Our enterprising producers comb the stages of the world in their effort to find new operettas. The best ones of the past century or more are being revived and refurbished. But side by side with this we have evolved a group of skillful and prolific composers whose works hold their own with the best of other lands.

Perchance this but reflects the timbre of the American folk. We are not serious minded. We work like fury during the day, but at night want frivolity. Even Musical Comedy, which is a grade below the true Light Opera, is not colloquial enough. So we have "plays with music," "revues," "follies," and "vanities." The resultant product speaks for itself; let us consider the men and their work as catalogued in these pages. As in other parts, the composers are given chronologically and thus form a sort of running history of American Light Opera.

Our chronicle seems to begin at the half-way mark of last century. Within ten years—from 1852 to 1861—were born eight men, at least two of whom still rank as leaders. They are Willard Spenser, William Furst, John Philip Sousa, Gustave Kerker, Woolson Morse, Victor Herbert, Ludwig Englander, and Reginald De Koven.

Spenser, the earliest, was an important figure in his day; and let it be said in his favor that he was a staunch exponent of "clean" shows—a good example that others of our pioneers followed. His "Little Tycoon" has been produced by professionals and amateurs literally thousands of times. Furst delighted his day with the more sophisticated "Isle of Champagne." And who that beheld it will ever forget

"Wang," Morse's contribution, with the tall De Wolf Hopper cutting up "didoes" with the diminutive Della Fox! In the list of the unforgettable must also come Kerker's "The Belle of New York," which Londoners took even more warmly to their hearts. Englander's joyous "Strollers" and "Rounders" were hardly less popular.

"The March King," Sousa, challenges attention. His operettas have that same virile quality of his band music. Yet "El Capitan" and "The Bride-Elect" are passing into that purgatory of forgotten operas, musty library shelves.

Victor Herbert, who was born two years before De Koven, is our dominant figure in this field. He is the nearest prototype, in America, to Sullivan, Offenbach, and Von Suppé, in their respective lands. He wrote no less than thirty-five operettas, at least a third of which are still in active repertory. Amateur companies all over the country turn to him for inspiration and material. The radio continually retails his melodies. And now the "movies" have rediscovered him. Strange to say, however, England has remained cold to him. He has not transplanted to foreign soil readily. He is an indigenous growth.

De Koven has not nearly the quantity of material to his credit, as has Herbert. De Koven left four works which bid fair to endure. "Robin Hood," his masterpiece, still holds its own as one of the most popular of American comic operas. If he had written nothing else he would still rank as one of our leaders.

Among other operettas which we heard "only yesterday" and would not willingly forget are those of that merry chap, Gustav Luders—"The Prince of Pilsen," "The Burgomaster," "King Dodo," "The Sho-Gun," and "Woodland." Who, also, will forget the capers of "The Sultan of Sulu," Wathall's creation; or the haunting strains of "Madame Sherry," by Karl Hoschna?

The turn of the century ushered in a coterie of talented composers who have done much to give the American stage prestige and popularity—Friml, Kern, Romberg, Berlin, Gershwin, and Rodgers. Each has an individual style, but also that precious gift of melody and song. Friml intrigues with the plaintive strains of "Rose Marie," or the more martial notes of "The Vagabond King." Kern teases and charms by turns, in his "Sally," "Show Boat," "Cat and Fiddle," and "Music in the Air." Romberg displays a wide gamut of ability from "My Maryland" and "The New Moon" down the long list to "Desert Song." Berlin gets into the list almost by accident. He has been too busy writing songs to turn definitely to Musical Comedy. However, his characteristic music in "Face the Music" and "As Thousands Cheer" must be mentioned. Gershwin in his crashing, smashing "Of Thee I Sing" made Musical Comedy history and won a Pulitzer prize. Richard Rodgers, famed for his earlier "Connecticut Yankee," has reached the topmost rank in this field with "Oklahoma!", "Carousel," "South Pacific," and, in 1951, "The King and I." And judging from the universal approval the end is not yet.

No record would be complete without mention of the work of George M. Cohan; yet it is hard to classify, as it merges from the field of Drama to that of Musical Comedy, and back again. Cohan himself was probably better known as actor than composer, though his song, "Over There" of the First World War was sung also in the Second. Born in 1878 of an actor family, he first attracted notice in vaudeville as one of the "Four Cohans." Then came his popular plays with music: "Little Johnny Jones" (1904); "Forty-five Minutes From Broadway" (1905); "George Washington, Jr." (1906); and a long list of other works during a third of a century until his death, November 5, 1942. In 1927 he brought out a musical play, "The Merry Malones," and, the next year, "Billie." He was a typical American producer of the "play with music."

The eminent Austrian violinist, Fritz Kreisler, has also contributed to American operetta. He collaborated with Victor Jacobi in "Apple Blossoms," the book by William Le Baron, which was played in 1919 and 1920 in both New York and Boston. Harry Tierney and Joseph McCarthy wrote a highly successful musical show, "Rio Rita," which Ziegfeld produced at his theatre, beginning in November, 1927. "Irene" is also to their credit. The list is almost endless.

Still another popular type is the musical extravaganza. "The Wizard of Oz," based upon a favorite juvenile story, packed the houses around the turn of the century, and first brought those sterling comedians, Montgomery and Stone, into nationwide fame. Its music was by A. Baldwin Sloane and Paul Tietjens. Later when presented at St. Louis (1942) and also as an elaborate screen play, other music was supplied by Harold Arlen. One of the great stage successes of all time was "Chu Chin Chow," music by Frederic Norton, book by Oscar Asche. It made its bow in New York, in 1917, and for the next five years was eagerly sought by managers in this country, Canada, and England. It was revived in London, in 1940; and three years later in the St. Louis Municipal Theatre. Then it became a cinema.

Recent years have shown every type of entertainment employing the musical score, making it impossible to fix a definite line of demarcation. Musical technique itself has not escaped. The artists of "jazz" and "swing" lay their predatory fingers upon even the classics. Chopin's melodies are "adapted" to current songs. Mendelssohn's "Spring Song" has been "modernized." Gilbert and Sullivan have been "burglarized" by adapters who presumably are not smart enough to write their own tunes, and we see "The Mikado" and "Pinafore" masquerading in almost unrecognizable dress. The latest example at this writing is the "lifting" of Bizet's "Carmen," transplanting it to Harlem, and giving it Negro actors and mutilated dialect. One wonders where this sort of "adaptation" will stop!

Light Opera in America has a rich heritage from the past, and such an array of composers today, that a tampering which borders on sacrilege seems needless. Our native music has come of age. Let it rest sturdily upon its own feet.

Meanwhile for the opera-goer and opera-lover the horizon is constantly expanding. To the stage has been added the screen, the audience automatically being lifted from the thousands into the millions. Stage successes like "Naughty Marietta" are presented in technicolor and with elaborate scenic effects impossible on the stage. Another praiseworthy example makes us familiar with great musicians—Paderewski, Chopin, Schubert, Grieg, and our own George Gershwin; while the most eminent pianists of the day interpret their music. Plays and novels are being translated to the film, often with a wealth of incidental music, as for instance, "State Fair."

And just around the corner is television! Who would undertake to predict its possibilities? The easy-chair at home may rival a seat at the opera. Truly the musical horizon of America—and of the world—is constantly widening!

WILLARD SPENSER

One of the first American composers to write successful light opera, Willard Spenser was born in Philadelphia, in 1852, and died in that city, December 16, 1933. A prophet honored by his own, his "The Little Tycoon" when produced in 1886 was an immediate success. "The Princess Bonnie" which was produced at the Chestnut Street Theater, Philadelphia (1894), was hardly less successful, with a run of 1039 performances. "Miss Bob White" and "Clarabel" followed. Spenser's operas were noted for their clean and ingratiating quality. In them played Bob Graham, Digby Bell, J. H. Riley, Raymond Hitchcock, Frank Daniels, William Hodge, Marguerite Sylva, Eleanor Mayo, and others, most of whom were just then winning their spurs in this field.

THE LITTLE TYCOON

Comic Opera in Two Acts. Words and music by Spenser. Temple Theatre, Philadelphia, January 4, 1886. Its first run was 500 performances, a record at that time. Since then it is estimated that professional and amateur performances have totaled over 7000. In point of time as well as high achievement, the "Tycoon" deservedly begins our record.

CAST GENERAL KNICKERBOCKER. VIOLET, *his daughter*. ALVIN BERRY, *a Wall Street broker*. RUFUS READY, *his college friend*. LORD DOLPHIN. TEDDY MULDOON, *his valet*. DOLLY DIMPLE, *her school friend*. MISS HURRICANE, *a chaperone*. Others.

ARGUMENT An American-Japanese opera composed at the same time as "The Mikado" by Sullivan. It is a satire on pretension and title worship with a good plot and a melodious score.

Act I The action opens on board an ocean steamer bound for America. General Knickerbocker, of the old-line Knickerbockers of New York, has a fair daughter, Violet, for whom he is determined to make a brilliant match. Violet, however, is in love with Alvin Berry, a young New Yorker whom she has met abroad. Returning from Europe on the same ship is Lord Dolphin, an Englishman. The General throws Violet at the nobleman's head, but Alvin tries to frighten the latter away. Alvin only gets himself arrested on a charge of smuggling.
Musical numbers: opening chorus, "On the sea"; Violet, "Doomed am I to marry a lord"; Violet with chorus sing the ever-popular, "Love comes like a summer night"; Lord Dolphin and Teddy, another popular hit of the day, "Heel and toe we always go"; Violet and Alvin, "Love reigns"; finale, "Oh, why this apprehension!"

Act II The action switches to General Knickerbocker's home in Newport; the first scene in the drawing room, the second in the garden. Alvin, disguised as Dolphin, gains entrance into the villa, but is chased off by the guards. As a final ruse, he plays on the General's weakness for titles, and makes his next entrance (the Garden Scene) as The Great Tycoon of Japan. He now wins Violet and makes her The Little Tycoon.
Musical numbers: Violet, "Sad heart of mine"; Rufus, Alvin, and chorus, "Checkmated we"; Violet, "Tell me, Daisy"; Miss Hurricane,.

Dolly, and girls, "Speak low, walls have ears"; the Tycoon entrance march followed by chorus, "Sham, Great Tycoon!"; General and chorus, "The cats on our back fence"; finale, Violet with chorus, "Yes, I'll be The Little Tycoon."

WILLIAM WALLACE FURST

Furst was born in Baltimore, in 1852; educated at Calvert Hill in that city, and at Rock Hill College. He went to San Francisco as conductor of a theatre orchestra, where David Belasco discovered him and brought him back East to write incidental music for Belasco's plays. He became orchestra leader at the Empire Theatre, New York. His operettas include "A Normandy Wedding," "The Princess Nicotine," "Fleur de Lys," "The Little Trapper," "Fleurette," and "The Isle of Champagne." Furst died at his home in Freeport, Long Island, June 11, 1917.

THE ISLE OF CHAMPAGNE

Comic Opera in Three Acts. Music by Furst. Book by Charles A. Byrne and Louis Harrison. Manhattan Opera House, December 5, 1892. Thomas Q. Seabrooke was the "King."

On the fanciful Isle of Champagne wines and other sparkling drinks are the only known beverages. Plain water is unknown; consequently when a strange vessel is wrecked on its shores and the store of drinking water is salvaged, it creates a profound sensation. The names of the islanders are in keeping with the place: King Pommery Sec'nd; Prince Kissingen, his son; Appolinaris Frappé, his prime minister; Moet and Shandon, his standing army of two; and other bibulous ones. Survivors of the shipwreck are: Sam Binnacle, a sailor; and Abigail and Priscilla, New England girls. Between the machinations of the latter, and the effects of the strange new beverage, things happen.

In the First Act, the Royal Army of two sing, "We're the light brigade." King Pommery is greeted with the salute, "Pop! Ah!" and there are one or two lively choruses. In the Second Act is an aria, "Fly, sweet bird," and a topical song, "Old King Mumm could make things hum." In the Third, the song, "There's a land in the shimmery, silver moon."

JOHN PHILIP SOUSA

Sousa is much better known as bandmaster and "the march king," than as writer of operas. However, he produced a creditable list of the latter and left a definite impress. He was born in Washington, D.C., November 6, 1854. He early showed an aptitude for music and was a bandmaster before he was out of his 'teens. From 1880 to 1892 he led the band of the United States Marine Corps, bringing it up to a high pitch of excellence. Later as leader of his own band he toured the world For it he composed his famous marches, some of which will be found in his operas. The latter include: "El Capitan," "The Bride-Elect," "The Charlatan," "The Free Lance," "Chris," "The Glass Blowers," and "The American Maid." Sousa died in Reading, Pa., March 6, 1932.

EL CAPITAN

Comic Opera in Three Acts. Music by Sousa. Book by Charles Klein. Produced in 1896, in New York, with success. In London, the Lyric Theatre, July 10, 1899 (140 times).

CAST DON ERRICO MEDIGUA, *Viceroy of Peru.* SENOR AMABILE POZZO, *Chamberlain.* DON LUIZ CAZZARO, *Ex-Viceroy.* COUNT VERRADA. SCARAMBA, *an insurgent.* ESTRELDA, *daughter of Cazzaro.* ISABEL, *daughter of Medigua.* PRINCESS MARGHANZA, *wife of Medigua.* Others.

ARGUMENT The action takes place in Peru; time, the Sixteenth Century. The First Act is shown in the Viceroy's palace; the Second, the Gates of Tampoza; the Third, Plaza Limatamba. Don Medigua, recently appointed Viceroy, has studiously kept himself in the background, forcing his chamberlain to take the lead in political affairs. The most feared of the insurgents was El Capitan, who is now dead and buried—a fact unknown to any except Don Medigua. He himself now assumes the part of the famous bandit—and the usual complications occur. This opera contains some of the best of the stirring Sousa music:

Act I   Opening chorus, "Nobles of Castilian birth"; Isabel, "Ah, beautiful land of Spain"; Verrada, "From Peru's majestic mountains"; Don Medigua and chorus, "If you examine humankind"; finale, "Bah! bah!"

Act II   Scaramba and chorus, "Ditty of the drill"; Don Medigua and male chorus, "Behold El Capitan!"—one of the familiar Sousa marches; Isabel and chorus, "Oh, warrior grim!"; sextet, "Don Medigua, here's your wife"; finale, "He can not, must not, shall not."

Act III   Isabel, Verrada, and chorus, "Sweetheart, I'm waiting"; Don Medigua, "When some serious affliction"; Don, Estrelda, and Scaramba,—one of the topical hits—"A typical tune of Zanzibar"; finale, "We beg your kind consideration."

THE BRIDE-ELECT

Comic Opera in Three Acts.   Music and book by Sousa.   Knickerbocker Theatre, New York, December 28, 1897.

CAST.   PAPAGALLO XIII, *King of Timberio*.   GUIDO, *Duke of Ventrose*.   FRESCOBALDI, *Prime Minister*.   GAMBO.   BUSCATO.   PIETRO.   SARDINIA.   BIANCA, *Queen of Capri*.   MINUTEZZA, *Princess of Capri, her daughter*.   LA PASTORELLA, *a bandit*.

ARGUMENT   The action takes place on the Island of Capri; no particular period.   The First Act is in a street of Capri; the Second, the Fold of the Shepherdess; the Third, the Fortress of Anacapri.   The death of a pet goat belonging to King Papagallo leads to a seven years' war between neighboring kingdoms.   In order to prevent the marriage of Papagallo with Minutezza, La Pastorella, the woman leader of a band of brigands, carries him off.   There are at least three sets of lovers whose fortunes must become disentangled before the final curtain falls.   Music is lively.

Act I   Opening chorus, "If ninety-nine percent. the papers print"; chorus, "Come, Cavalier"; Papagallo, "Kind friends, this deference"; Papagallo and Minutezza, "Should you marry me"; La Pastorella, Gambo, and Buscato, "To marry or not to marry"; finale, "Oh, stars!" and "Let poets sing."

Act II   La Pastorella, "Here's a pack"; trio, "He's here"; Duet, Minutezza and Guido, "Love light my heart"; chorus, "We can not see the reason why"; Minutezza, "The Snow Baby"; finale, "Unchain the dogs of war."

Act III Male quartet, "These are our sentiments"; solo with chorus, "The iceman works"; La Pastorella and girls, "Cuckoo!"; chorus, "Love light my heart"; finale, "The God of Love presides."

THE CHARLATAN

Comic Opera in Three Acts. Music by Sousa. Book by Charles Klein. New York, circa 1900.

CAST DEMIDOFF, *Professor of Mystic Black Art.* PRINCE BORIS, *a Russian noble.* GOGOL, *his uncle.* JELLIKOFF, *an actor.* CAPTAIN PESHOFSKI, *a Cossack.* GRAND DUKE. GRAND DUCHESS. ANNA, *Demidoff's daughter.* KATRINKA, *his assistant.* SOPHIA. KOREFF and SKOBELOFF, *rival theater managers.* Others.

ARGUMENT In the village of Bokhara, Russia, during the latter days of the Czars, a marionette show and a theater run rival performances. Prince Boris is spending a few days with his Uncle Gogol and his cousin, Sophia, who has fallen in love with him. Boris has become interested in Demidoff, an exponent of Black Magic. The charlatan thereupon mixes up love affairs and other interests in true comic-opera fashion. It requires a Grand Duke and a small army to untangle the political details.

The work ranks with the best of the Sousa operas and contains ringing music—arias, duets, ensembles, and a well-known march.

GUSTAVE KERKER

Kerker came of a musical family and German stock. He was born in Westphalia, February 28, 1857, and came to America with his parents when a boy of ten. They settled in Louisville. He became leader of local orchestras, then came as a young man to New York to join forces with E. E. Rice. He was musical director at the Casino during its heyday in the '80's. A dozen or more operettas and comedies are to his credit, among them, "Castles in the Air," "The Whirl of the Town," "An American Beauty," "Fascinating Flora," "The Telephone Girl," "Kismet," and the one upon which his chief fame rests, "The Belle of New York." Kerker died in 1923.

THE BELLE OF NEW YORK

Musical Comedy in Two Acts.   Music by Kerker.   Book by C. M. S. McLellan.   Casino, New York, in 1898, with only moderate success. But in London, at the Shaftesbury Theatre, it had a phenomenal run of 697 performances.   It was successful on the road in both countries. It was revived as late as 1945, at the Open-Air Theatre, St. Louis.

The story, of frivolous type, is laid in New York.   Harry Bronson, the son of the President of the Young Men's Rescue League, which is fighting vice, gives his father plenty of mild material to combat right at home.   But after avoiding several entanglements, Harry falls in love with Violet Gray, a demure little Salvation Army girl.

The piece has some gay, intriguing music which was widely sung and whistled at the time.   It is chiefly remarkable, however, in having brought to stardom, overnight, the then unknown Edna May.   In an emergency she was given the star rôle, the Salvation Army lassie, and played the part so charmingly that she became the rage of London— literally, "the Belle of New York."

Although the cast is large, the plot is thin and serves only as a vehicle for songs and dances by some seven girl and thirteen men leads.   In the First Act we hear: "When I was born the stars stood still"; "Teach me how to kiss"; "The Anti-Cigarette Society"; Violet's demure entrance, "They all follow me"; and chorus, "We'll stand and die together."

The Second Act has a rousing chorus, "Oh, Sonny!" followed by a song by Violet and chorus, "The Purity Brigade"; another by Violet, "At ze naughty Folies Bergere"; and finale, "For in the field."

WOOLSON MORSE

Woolson Morse was born in Boston, in 1858, and at first studied paint- ing, one of his teachers being Gerome, in Paris.   But on his return to America, in 1878, he turned to music, particularly comic opera.   He painted the scenery and directed the production, as well as wrote the score.   His one great success, "Wang" (1891), was at first a failure under another title. Others were: "The Merry Monarch" (1890); "Panjan-drum" (1893); and "Doctor Syntax." Morse died in New York, May 3, 1897.

WANG

Comic Opera in Two Acts. Music by Morse. Book by J. Cheever Goodwin. Produced in New York, in 1891, with De Wolf Hopper in the title role. The diminutive Della Fox was his "foil." It had a long run, and was revived in 1904.

The story tells of the troubles, financial and otherwise, of Wang, Regent of Siam. During the youth of Mataya, his nephew and heir to the throne, Wang tries to obtain the royal treasure. He is being pressed by creditors, a sacred elephant recently purchased being his latest encumbrance. He sadly laments that he is "the man with the elephant on his hands." He marries a wealthy widow, only to find that he is out of the frying pan into the fire. With its uproarious comedy and lively music, "Wang" proved one of the outstanding hits of its time.

Musical numbers include: First Act, a song by Mataya, which was widely popular for some years, "A pretty girl, a summer's night"; duet, "Where are you going?"; and Wang's topical hit, "The man with the elephant on his hands." In the Second Act, a ballad by Marie; a trio by Wang, Mataya and Fracasse, "The man in the moon"; Jean's song, "As in waves without number"; Wang and children, "Baby, baby"; and a "Coronation March."

VICTOR HERBERT

With the name of Victor Herbert we come to the leading exponent of Light Opera in America. He is as definitely representative of the best that this country has produced, as is Sullivan in England, Offen-bach in France, and Von Suppé in Germany. Although of Irish birth, he came early to America and produced his work here. He was a de-scendant of Samuel Lover, the novelist, and was born in Dublin, Febru-ary 1, 1859. Herbert studied music in Germany and became noted as a 'cellist; came to America in 1886 and was at first known only for orchestra activities. Then came two incursions into Grand Opera, but without success. His fame, which continues to expand with the years, rests upon his light operas, operettas, and songs. His music is constantly being played and sung over the radio; and amateur operetta groups turn continually to his work. Between the years 1894 and 1917 Herbert wrote no less than thirty-five operas and operettas, not to mention the incidental music for other current Broadway (New York) productions. The best known are: "Prince Ananias" (1894); "The Wizard of the Nile" (1895); "The Gold Bug" (1896); "The Serenade" (1897); "The Idol's Eye" (1897); "The Fortune Teller" (1898); "Babes in Toyland" (1903); "Mlle. Modiste" (1905); "It Happened in Nordland" (1906); "The Red Mill" (1906); "The Rose of Algeria" (1909); "Naughty Marietta" (1910); "The Enchantress" (1912); "Sweethearts" (1913); "The Princess Pat" (1916); and "Eileen" (1917). Others followed almost each year until the last, "The Dream Girl" (1924). Herbert died in New York, May 26, 1924.

THE WIZARD OF THE NILE

Comic Opera in Three Acts. Music by Herbert. Book by Harry B. Smith. Casino, New York, November 4, 1895. Frank Daniels took the leading comedy part, "Kibosh," and won his spurs in this piece. His catch line, "Am I a wiz?" has gone into common speech. This was Herbert's first success in the operetta field. It was also produced in England, Germany, and Mexico.

CAST KIBOSH, *a Persian magician.* ABYDOS, *his apprentice.* PTOL-
      EMY, *King of Egypt.* SIMOONA, *his second wife.* CLEOPATRA,
their daughter. PTARMIGAN, *her music teacher.* CHEOPS, *royal
weather bureau.* OBELISKA, *captain of Amazons, and others.*

ARGUMENT The action takes place in Egypt, during the Ptolemies;
           but the audience speedily finds that real estate speculation and political chicanery were just as rife then as today.

Act I Kibosh, a fake magician, learns that the King has been investing
       heavily in desert lands, influenced by Cheops, the "weather bureau," who informs the monarch that the next great overflow of the Nile will make him rich. The reverse ensues; there is a drought. Ptolemy orders the forecaster to be beheaded, but Kibosh now enters in a barge stolen from Cleopatra. He saves his own head by predicting

a speedy rise of the river. This actually occurs, and the grateful king promises the hand of the princess to the fakir as a reward.

Musical numbers include: song by Cheops, Obeliska, and chorus, "Song of the Optimist"; a lively "Oriental March"; Ptolemy, Simoona, and chorus, "I am the ruler"; a droll topical song by Kibosh, "That's one thing a wizard can do"; and duet, "I have been a Maying."

Act II The roof of the King's Palace is this setting. The Nile has become so full that the people flee for their lives and the court takes refuge on the roof. Kibosh is again condemned to death, this time for overdoing it. He is spared upon divulging a plot of elopement between Cleopatra and her music teacher. Other incidents follow rapidly, and the act ends with Kibosh incarcerated in the king's pyramid, where he is doomed to be sealed up, to meet a lingering death.

An opening serenade, Abydos, Cheops, and pages, is followed by: duet, Cleopatra and Ptarmigan, "If I were a King"; quintet, "On Cleopatra's wedding day"; and chorus led by Kibosh, "My Angeline."

Act III In the interior of a pyramid, the luckless magician is preparing to meet his fate. While the workmen are filling in the wall, the King comes to see how the work progresses, and is sealed up in the tomb by mistake. He is freed and pardons Kibosh, who, glad to get out of Egypt, decides to practice in parts unknown.

The Act opens with a ringing male chorus, "Stone-cutter's song." Other good numbers are: Cleopatra's solo, "In Dreamland"; quintet, a waltz melody, "Starlight, star bright"; Kibosh, Ptolemy, and pages, "The Echo Song"; and finale, "Ah, love we know!"

THE SERENADE

Light Opera in Three Acts. Music by Herbert. Book by Harry B. Smith. Produced by the Bostonians in Chicago, then at the Knickerbocker Theatre, New York, March 16, 1897. It followed their first great success, "Robin Hood" (De Koven) and proved a worthy successor. Alice Neilsen was starred in it.

CAST   THE DUKE OF SANTA CRUZ, *a Spanish grandee.* ALVARADO, *an opera singer.* DOLORES, *the Duke's ward.* ROMERO, *President of the Royal Madrid Brigandage Association.* LOPEZ, *Secretary of same.* COLOMBO, *a former operatic tenor.* YVONNE, *his daughter.* GOMEZ, *a tailor.* EL GATO, *a bandit.* Mother Superior, ladies, servants, and others.

ARGUMENT   The "Serenade" is sung by an ardent lover to the ward of an eccentric old nobleman, who wants to marry her himself. The grandee tries to discover the identity of the singer; and meanwhile the elusive melody is heard in many unexpected places. This device provides an ideal plot as the action grows out of the music itself.

Act I   In the main office of the Royal Madrid Brigandage Association all is activity. Romero, its esteemed president, has discovered that the ancient castle where they have their headquarters is about to be used by its rightful owner, the Duke of Santa Cruz. He is bringing his ward, Dolores, hither, to separate her from an ardent suitor, Alvarado, whose baritone voice in serenade has captured her heart. Others come to the castle for refuge also, and the usual comic opera mix-up follows.

The opening chorus, "Hist, hush!" is followed by: Romero and chorus, "Song of the carbine"; mixed chorus, "Peering left, peering right"; Alvarado and chorus, "With cracking of whip"; Duke and chorus, "The funny side of that"; duet, Dolores and Alvarado, "I love thee, I adore thee"; Yvonne and others, "The singing lesson," and "Gaze on this face so noble."

Act II   The Second Act represents the gardens of a monastery and convent. Dolores is placed in the convent by her guardian. Alvarado thereupon takes refuge in the near-by monastery. The now famous serenade is taught to the monks, who sing it as a chant. The school girls in the adjoining garden take up the refrain; and the parrot shrieks it. Yvonne exchanges clothing with Dolores, and the Duke takes away Yvonne, thinking her his ward.

This Act is rich in music, beginning with a chorus of monks, "In our quiet cloister." Others: Yvonne and monks, "In fair Andalusia"; Romero and monks, "The monk and the maid"; Duke and chorus, "Woman, lovely woman"; Dolores and chorus, "The Angelus"; Yvonne's famous waltz song, "Cupid and I"; Monks' chant, "The Serenade"; quartet, "I love thee."

Act III   Yvonne is brought back to the castle, before her identity is revealed. After other complications, the brigands cut the Gordian knot by capturing the whole party. The Duke must perforce pardon the lovers and learn to like the hateful (to him) serenade.

Musical numbers: chorus, "Here merrily the bandit tribe"; Dolores, Alvarado, and chorus, "Don José of Sevilla"; Lopez, "I envy the bird"; Duke, Yvonne, and Gomez, "Dreaming, dreaming"; finale, "That for love! Pif! Paf!"

THE IDOL'S EYE

Comic Opera in Three Acts. Music by Herbert. Book by Harry B. Smith. Broadway Theatre, New York, October 25, 1897. It was written for Frank Daniels, who took the part of "Abel."

CAST ABEL CONN, *an American magician traveling in India.* NED WINNER, *an American novelist.* JAMIE McSNUFFY, *a Highland kleptomaniac.* DON PABLO PABASCO, *a Cuban planter.* CORPORAL O'FLANNIGAN. DAMAYANTI, *Nautch girl.* MARAQUITA, *daughter of Don Pablo.* Priests and Priestesses; Brahmins, Officers, Soldiers, and others.

ARGUMENT An East Indian story with emphasis placed on the comedy rôles, costumes, and specialties.

Act I A Brahmin idol has had a pair of jewel eyes of immense value. One, called the Eye of Love, has been stolen, leaving the Eye of Hate. The thief is one, Jamie McSnuffy, a Scotch, light-fingered chap. He is saved from drowning by an aeronaut, Abel Conn, who just happens to "drop in" at the right time. The possession of the ruby makes all women fall madly in love with its possessor.
 The following musical numbers are found in this Act: Maraquita, Ned, and girls, "Pretty Isabella"; Don Pablo and chorus, "Cuban Song"; Chorus of Brahmins; Abel, "Balloon Song"—"I just dropped in" (one of the "hits"); Abel and chorus, "I'm Captain Cholly Chumley"; Damayanti and chorus, "The lady and the kick"; finale, "Thou art guilty."

Act II The Second Act is laid in the Temple of the Ruby, and provides a medley of amusing and nonsensical complications.
 Musical numbers: chorus of Nautch Girls, "With dances wild"; song of Chief Priestess, "Here in the Temple I've waited thee"; Abel and chorus, in another hit, "The Tattooed Man."

Act III The last Act clears up all the mystery and furnishes the usual happy ending. There is a subplot introducing the romance of Ned, a writer, with Maraquita, the Cuban girl.
 Musical numbers: Abel and chorus, "Talk about yo' luck"; waltz sextet, "Fairy Tales"; finale, "Come, be off!"

THE FORTUNE TELLER

Comic Opera in Three Acts. Music by Herbert. Book by Harry B. Smith. Wallack's Theater, New York, September 26, 1898, and made such a success that the original company took it to England, where it was presented at the Shaftesbury Theatre. The work was written for Alice Neilsen and had a notable cast including, also, Marguerite Sylva, Eugene Cowles, Joseph Cawthorn, and Joseph Herbert. It has been frequently revived and considered one of Herbert's best.

CAST SANDOR, *a Gypsy musician.* FRESCO, *a ballet-master.* COUNT BEREZOWSKI, *a Polish musician.* CAPTAIN LADISLAS, *a Hungarian Hussar.* BORIS, *a Gypsy.* MUSETTE, *his daughter, the "Fortune Teller."* IRMA, *a pupil in the ballet school.* MLLE. POMPON, *a prima donna.* Ballet Pupils, Gypsies, Hussars.

ARGUMENT A good "story" is enriched by some of the composer's most tuneful and lasting melodies.

Act I Courtyard of Opera House, Budapesth. Irma, a pupil in a large ballet school in Budapesth, goes on with her studies for the stage, unaware that she is the heiress to a large estate. Count Berezowski, a hard-up noble turned musician, has learned of this fortune, however, and schemes with Fresco, the ballet master, to win the girl and her dot. But Irma has plans of her own. She is in love with the handsome Captain Ladislas, and he with her. In order to thwart the plotters, the two lovers run away.

First Act: Irma and chorus, "Always do as people say you should"; Ladislas and Hussars, "Hungary's Hussars!"; Sandor, "Ho, ye townsmen!"; Musette and chorus, "Here we are a Gypsy troupe," and "Romany life."

Act II Garden of the Count's Chateau. At this point a band of strolling Gypsies arrives, and Musette, the pretty fortune teller, looks so much like the run-away Irma that everybody is certain it is she. The Count triumphantly claims her, and plans for the wedding proceed apace, until Sandor, the Gypsy suitor of the fortune teller, protests. He substitutes Irma for Musette, which is satisfactory to himself but slightly confusing to others.

Musical numbers: Fresco and chorus, "Signor Mons, Muldoni"; Musette and chorus, "Serenades of all nations"; Sandor's ever pleasing serenade, "Slumber on, my little Gypsy sweetheart"; Pompon and Ladislas, "Only in the play"; Ladislas and chorus, "Speak, Irma, I implore you."

Act III An Army Camp near Budapesth. Captain Ladislas is as much at sea as are the scheming Count and Fresco. But after a series of contretemps the two girls are untangled, and each is bestowed upon her rightful suitor.

Musical numbers: Sandor and chorus, "Gypsy Jan"; Boris and Count, "The power of the human eye"; waltz song, "The lily and the nightingale."

BABES IN TOYLAND

Musical extravaganza in Three Acts. Music by Herbert. Book by Glen MacDonough. Grand Opera House, Chicago, 1903. In New York at the Majestic Theatre, October 13, 1903.

CAST UNCLE BARNABY, *a rich miser.* ALAN, *his nephew.* JANE, *Barnaby's niece.* RODERIGO and GONZORGO, *ruffians.* MASTER TOYMAKER. WIDOW PIPER, CONTRARY MARY, TOM TOM, JILL, and other Nursery Rhyme characters. Animals, Fairies, Dolls, Toy Soldiers, etc.

ARGUMENT No brief synopsis can give a clear idea of this extravaganza based upon Mother Goose Land and the adjoining grounds of Fairyland. The stage is often crowded with figures. The music is brilliant and tuneful.

Act I Four scenes are shown beginning with Contrary Mary's garden. Uncle Barnaby, the miser, is the trouble-maker. He has seized Mother Hubbard's cottage for debt. Tom, the Widow Piper's son, saves him from a ducking. Other events swiftly follow.

A country dance, instrumental, is followed by: song, "With downcast eye"; aria and chorus, "Never mind, Bopeep"; lullaby with chorus, "Go to sleep; slumber deep"; chorus, "Mary, Mary, quite contrary"; and the well-liked and catchy song by Jane and chorus of the children, "I don't care what the teacher says—I can't do this sum!"

Act II Four scenes are shown, also, in this Act—all in Toyland; the most effective being the dramatic scene of the Master Toymaker with his toys. He has been persuaded to invoke the spirit of evil into the toys which have human shapes. His incantation succeeds, and the toys thereupon turn upon him and slay him.

Musical numbers include: chorus, "Hail to Christmas!"; solo and chorus, "A legend"; Alan with chorus: "Song of the Poet"; the stirring and ever-popular, "March of the Toys" and the no-less-pleasing refrain, "Toyland!"

Act III The setting is the courtyard and Toyland Palace of Justice. Alan is accused of the murder of the Toymaker. He is taken to the scaffold, and saved at the last moment by the fact that the miser drinks poison intended for him.

Musical numbers: duet, Alan and Jane, "O we'll live in a castle in Spain"; serenade, "Mignonette"; chorus, "He won't be happy till he gets it"; chorus, "O, we are the soldiers."

MLLE. MODISTE

Light Opera in Two Acts. Music by Herbert. Book by Henry Blossom. Knickerbocker Theatre, New York, December 25, 1905. It was written for Fritzi Scheff, who was "Fifi." William Pruette was the Count. First run, 252 performances.

CAST   FIFI, *a salesgirl in a millinery shop.*   MME. CECILE, *owner of shop.*   GASTON, *her son.*   CAPTAIN ETIENNE DE BOUVRAY. COUNT DE BOUVRAY, *his uncle.*   HIRAM BENT, *an American millionaire.* MRS. BENT.   Salesgirls, Servants, Guests, etc.

ARGUMENT   This opera is one of the peaks in Victor Herbert's career. It contains a constant succession of catchy tunes. No less than six lasting "hits" are found here.

Act I   The action takes place in Paris and St. Mar. It opens in a millinery shop. One of the girls, Fifi, a pert little Parisian modiste, has two ambitions. She wants to become a great singer, one day, and she wants also very much to marry a young captain, Etienne, who has been paying her ardent court. Etienne's rich old uncle, on his part, has something to say to this; his plans do not include the modiste. Another obstacle is found in the person of Mme. Cecile, proprietress of the millinery shop, who seeks to make a match between Fifi and her artist son, Gaston. Luckily for the girl, an angel appears just then in the person of Hiram Bent, a wealthy American, who makes it possible for her to take vocal lessons.

Musical numbers: opening chorus by girls, "Furs and feathers, buckles, bows"; trio, "When the cat's away"; Etienne and chorus, "The time and the place, and the girl"; Fifi's song—one of the memorable hits—"Kiss me again"; Gaston, "Love me, love my dog"; Fifi and chorus, "Hats make the woman."

Act II   The action is transferred to the Count's castle. Fifi is found transformed, after a year of study, into the celebrated Mme. Bellini, a prima donna. As such she is invited to sing at a big charity fête, given by the Count in his castle at St. Mar. She comes to the castle and enters a room in which the Count is lying indisposed from the gout. The choleric old gentleman recognizes her and orders her out of the house. Hiram Bent again comes to the rescue; she is smuggled back in again; and as the singer, Mme. Bellini, so charms the Count that he relents and agrees to her marriage with his nephew.

After an opening chorus of footmen, the Count sings his stentorian song, which still goes the rounds, "I want what I want when I want it!" Gaston's song, "In English language," is followed by Fifi and male chorus, "The mascot and the troop"; "Ah! but in dreams so fair"; Rene and girls, "The dear little girl who is good"; Mrs. Bent and girls, "The Keokuk Culture Club"; Fifi, "The Nightingale and the star"; and finale, "Hark, the drum!"

IT HAPPENED IN NORDLAND

Comic Opera in Two Acts. Music by Herbert. Book by Glen Mac-Donough. First produced in New York, in 1904, with Pauline Frederick, Bessie Clayton, Marie Cahill, and Lew Fields.

CAST   KATHERINE PEEPFOGLE, *an American Ambassadress.* HUBERT, *her brother.* PRINCE GEORGE OF NEBULA. DUKE OF TOXEN. BARON SPARTA. CAPTAIN SLIVOWITZ. PRINCESS ALINE. DR. OTTO BLOTZ. DR. POPOFF. CAPTAIN CATLING. PARTHENIA SCHMITT. MISS HICKS. Others.

ARGUMENT   The mythical land of Nordland, somewhere in Europe, is the scene of this lively comedy. The cast is large and the action inconsequential. Suffice it to say that, in the First Act, the continued absence of the Queen is causing much uneasiness, until the arrival of the American Ambassadress, who bears such a striking resemblance to her, that she is foisted off on the court, by conspirators, as the real monarch. Amid the varied musical numbers, dances, and skits, the plot both political and theatrical ceases to bother anyone very much.

Musical numbers in the First Act: Prince and girls, "The woman in the case"; Absinthe frappé"; Dr. Blotz and chorus, "The gifted Dr. Blotz"; Baron and girls, "Slippery James"; George and Parthenia, "My catamaran"; Katherine, "As commander in chief."

Musical numbers in Second Act: girls' chorus, "The knot of blue"; Parthenia, "The Jack o' Lantern girl"; girls, "The matinee maid"; Queen and chorus, "Bandana Land"; Katherine, "The coon banshee," and "She's a very dear friend of mine."

THE RED MILL

Comic Opera in Two Acts. Music by Herbert. Book by Henry Blossom. Knickerbocker Theatre, New York, September 24, 1906.*

CAST   "CON" KIDDER, and "KID" CONNER, *two Americans doing Europe.* JAN VAN BORKEM, *a burgomaster.* BERTHA, *his sister.* GRETCHEN, *his daughter.* FRANZ, *sheriff.* WILLEM, *innkeeper.* CAPTAIN DORIS VAN DAMM. THE GOVERNOR OF ZEELAND. JOSHUA PENNEFEATHER, *an English solicitor.* TINA, *a barmaid.* COUNTESS DE LA FERE.

ARGUMENT   This opera proved to be one of the biggest successes of Herbert's career. It was the greatest money-maker. The plot is picturesque; the action at times "acrobatic," and the music delightful.

Act I   The scene is Holland and at the Sign of the Red Mill. Con and Kid are stranded in a Dutch town. Unable to pay their innkeeper, they try to get away by climbing out of the window. The burgomaster catches them and sends them to jail. The innkeeper is merciful and says that they can work out their board bill by taking service with him. Con is made an interpreter, and Kid, a waiter. They try to save Gretchen the pretty daughter of Jan, the innkeeper, from marrying the Governor, whom she dislikes. They promise to aid her to elope with Captain Van Damm, instead. Jan overhears the plot and informs the burgomaster, and Gretchen is locked up in the mill, for safe-keeping. The two Americans, who are quite acrobatic, rescue her on the huge wings of the mill.

Musical numbers: opening chorus of girls, "By the side of the mill"; Tina and girls, "Mignonette"; Burgomaster and Willem, "You never can tell about a woman"; Kid and Tina, "Whistle it"; Bertha, "A widow has ways"; Doris and Gretchen's haunting duet, "The Isle of our Dreams"; Con, Kid, Tina, and Bertha, "Go while the goin' is good"; finale, "Moonbeams."

Act II   In the great hall of the Burgomaster's house all is in readiness for the wedding of the Governor to Gretchen, but the bride

---

* David Montgomery and Fred Stone starred in this production, which ran in New York for 274 performances. Montgomery and Stone had made their first smash hit in "The Wizard of Oz" and were greatly beloved. Here they added to their reputation and following. "The Red Mill" has been a prime favorite with amateur companies. It was revived professionally in the fall of 1945, at the Ziegfeld Theatre, New York, with Dorothy Stone, Fred's daughter, starring.

has flown. The furious father offers a reward for her capture. Con and Kid are first disguised as Italian organ-grinders, and then appear as Sherlock Holmes and Dr. Watson. After more foolery, the Governor of Zeeland arrives to clear up matters in his own way. The lovers are united and everybody is happy as the curtain falls:

Musical numbers: Bertha and chorus, "The Legend of the Mill"; Con and Kid, "Good-a-bye, John"; Tina and chorus, "I want you to marry me"; Governor and men, one of the hits, "Every day is lady's day with me"; a charming duet between Bertha and the Governor, "Because you're you"; Con, Kid, and chorus, "The streets of New York"; wedding march leading to finale, "In old New York."

THE ROSE OF ALGERIA

Original title, "Algeria." Comic Opera in Two Acts. Music by Herbert. Book by Glen MacDonough. First produced at the Broadway Theater, New York, by Lew Fields, in 1909. In the cast were William Pruette, Ida Brooks Hunt, Eugene P. Arnold, and Florence Nash.

CAST ZORADIE, *a Sultana.* GENERAL PETITPONS, *Governor of Algeria.* CAPTAIN DE LOME. MILLICENT MADISON, *an American girl.* CARROLL SWEET. DE LONG GREENE. VAN COURTLANDT PARKE. MR. AND MRS. BILLINGS F. COOINGS. ALI KOHJA, *Chief of Police.* Others.

Act I The action opens in a walled oasis of the Sahara. Zoradie has become so infatuated by the songs and poems of a mysterious "El Mokani," that she vows to marry none other but him. The action is complicated and amusing. Musical hits in this Act include: Mrs. Cooings and chorus, "The same old two"; "I've been decorated"; "Rose of the World"; De Lome and chorus, "The Boule Miche'"; Millicent, "You'll feel better then."

Act II Exterior of a palace in Algeria. Despite the turmoil of the preceding Act, "El Mokani" has not been found, and Zoradie is in a temper. Affairs finally work out satisfactorily, when he is revealed to be De Lome. Musical numbers: De Lome and male chorus, "Love is like a cigarette"; Millicent and girls, "Ask her while the band is playing"; Zoradie and chorus, "Twilight in Barakeesh"; duet, "The foolish gardener"; Van and girls, "Little bird of Paradise"; quartet, "Bohemia, good-bye!"; finale, "My life, I love thee."

NAUGHTY MARIETTA

Light Opera in Two Acts. Music by Herbert. Book by Rida Johnson Young. New York Theatre, New York, November 7, 1910, by Oscar Hammerstein, who starred Emma Trentini. Orville Harold was the male lead.

CAST CAPT. RICHARD WARRINGTON, *an American officer.* LIEUTENANT GOVERNOR GRANDET. ETIENNE, *his son, known also as Bras Pique, the pirate.* SIR HARRY BLAKE, *an Irish adventurer.* SILAS SLICK, *Warrington's servant.* RUDOLFO, *keeper of a marionette theater.* MARIETTA D'ALTENA. LIZETTA. ADAH. Casket Girls, Citizens, Pirates, Soldiers.

ARGUMENT This easily ranks as one of the best of Herbert's operas, dividing honors with his "The Serenade," "The Fortune Teller," and "Mlle. Modiste."

Act I The action takes place in New Orleans, about 1750; the opening scene is the Place d'Armes. Capt. Dick Warrington has been sent to New Orleans to capture the notorious pirate, Bras Pique. He meets there, for a second time, an irresponsible, high-born girl, Marietta, who has left the convent in order to see the world. She has come to America with a group of "Casket Girls," sent by the King of France to be married to young settlers. She persuades Dick to get her a boy's disguise. Rudolfo, a marionette showman, passes her off as his son.

The work has many pleasing airs, from its opening, which is a lovely tone picture of dawn through to the last haunting refrain, "Ah, sweet mystery of life!" In the First Act: Capt. Dick and men, "Tramp, tramp, tramp!"; Casket girls and men, "Taisez vous"; Marietta's charming introductory song, "Naughty Marietta"; Marietta and Dick, "It never, never can be love"; Comedy duet, "If I were anybody else" (a parody on grand opera); Adah, " 'Neath the Southern moon"; and the stirring finale with Marietta's famous obbligato with chorus, "Italian street song."

Act II In the Marionette Theater, first scene, the naughty Marietta speedily proves the undoing of Rudolfo, as she cannot or will not pull the puppet wires properly. The man in despair turns to Dick, who is likewise helpless, but is sure of one thing—that he does not love the teasing girl.

The second is a ballroom scene. Etienne has been strutting about town secure in his incognito. None knows he is Bras Pique, certainly not Captain Dick. All the town turns out to a ball, and of course, the irrepressible Marietta. Etienne auctions off his quadroon slave, Adah, so that he can marry Marietta. Captain Dick buys Adah, to free her. Marietta, misinterpreting his action, tells Etienne she will wed him. Adah prevents this by revealing the pirate's identity to Dick. The Lieutenant Governor, however, will not arrest Etienne, as he is his own son. The pirate makes his exit, but Dick and Marietta find that they love each other, after all.

Musical numbers: Marietta and Rudolfo, "The Dance of the Marionettes"; Marietta's dance with pleasing instrumental "Dream Melody"; male chorus, "New Orleans jeunesse dorée"; Lizetta, "The sweet bye and bye"; quartet, "Live for today"; Dick's popular love song, "I'm falling in love with someone"; and the no-less popular air by him, which leads up to the finale, "Ah, sweet mystery of life!"

"Naughty Marietta" is now probably the best known of the Herbert operettas, as well as of all light opera—a determining factor being the fine presentations on the screen, to which the excellent plot lent itself admirably. The leads here were taken by Jeannette MacDonald and Nelson Eddy.

SWEETHEARTS

Romantic Opera in Two Acts. Music by Herbert. Book by Harry B. Smith and Fred de Gresac. Academy of Music, Baltimore, March 24, 1913; New Amsterdam Theater, New York, September 8, 1913. Christie MacDonald took the part of "Sylvia"; Tom McNaughton, "Mikel"; Lionel Walsh, "Percy"; and Thomas Conkey, the Prince.

CAST SYLVIA, *the lost princess.* DAME PAULA, *Proprietress of the "White Geese" laundry. Her six daughters.* MIKEL MIKELOVIZ, *a political conspirator.* PRINCE FRANZ. LIEUTENANT KARL. HON. PERCY ALGERNON SLINGSBY. CANICHE. VAN TROMP. LIANE, *a milliner.* Others.

ARGUMENT This operetta suffered a temporary eclipse for a few years, but has come back to current repertoire, particularly with amateur companies.

Act I Dame Paula, who runs a laundry in Bruges, known as the "White Geese," finds an infant girl that has been abandoned there.   Although she has six daughters of her own, she adopts the foundling, who is called Sylvia.   She grows up not knowing her parentage.   She is actually Crown Princess of Zilania, and is presently enmeshed in a political plot.   It is complicated by the fact that Prince Franz, who is heir presumptive to the throne, while traveling incognito has fallen in love with her.

Several charming musical bits enliven this opera.   In the First Act: opening chorus of laundresses, "Iron, iron, iron!"; Soldiers and laundresses, "On parade"; Liane and laundresses, "There is magic in a smile"; Sylvia and chorus, "Sweethearts"; Prince and chorus, "Every lover must meet his fate"; Sylvia and laundresses, "Mother Goose"; and a charming duet between Sylvia and Franz, "The Angelus."   The Finale rises almost to Grand Opera heights.

Act II   The chateau of Prince Franz in Zilania.   Sylvia, who has been in a convent for a year, is presented at court as the Prince's fiancée.   Dame Paula now identifies Sylvia as the lost princess and the real heir to the throne; but the girl is quite willing to merge her claims in with Franz.

The opening chorus, "Pretty as a picture," is followed by: chorus of wedding guests, "Welcoming the bride"; Sylvia and chorus, "In the convent they never taught me that"; Slingsby's topical song, "I don't know how I do it, but I do"; Sylvia and Franz, "The cricket on the hearth"; quartet, "Pilgrims of love"; and Sylvia's charming ditty, "The ivy and the oak."

THE PRINCESS 'PAT'

Comic Opera in Three Acts.   Music by Herbert.   Book by Henry Blossom.   Cort Theatre, New York, January 29, 1915, starring Eleanor Painter, as "The Princess."

ARGUMENT   The setting of this comedy of action is on Long Island; the time the present.   Bob and Tony, two gay adventurers, are putting as much distance behind them as possible from Broadway, while pursued by Si Perkins, a hick sheriff.   Running out of gasoline they take refuge in a woodland near the estate of General Holbrook.   At his home they meet with the sympathetic daughter of the General, Grace, who happens to be the betrothed of Tony's father.   She has agreed to marry him in order to get money to pay off the mortgage on the Holbrook estate—a well-worn stage device.   She confides her dilemma to her friend, Patricia O'Connor, who is the wife of Prince di Montaldo. Pat decides to do a little flirting on her own account, in order to make her husband jealous. One farcical situation succeeds another, but everybody is happy as the curtain falls.

Music, Act I.—a duet, "Allies"; "I'd like to be a quitter"; song by Pat, "Love is best of all"; and duet, "For better or for worse."

II.—Chorus, "Estellita"; "Neapolitan love song"—one of the delightful bits—the humorous, "I wish I was an island in an ocean of girls"; song by Pat, "Flirting"; and a charming duet, "All for you."

III.—"In a little world for two"; the topical song, "The shoes of Husband Number One are worn by Number Two"; and the finale, "Two laughing Irish eyes."

EILEEN

Romantic Comic Opera in Three Acts. Music by Herbert. Book and lyrics by Henry Blossom. Shubert Theatre, New York, March 19, 1917 (64 times). Starring Grace Breen, as "Eileen Mulvaney," and Walter Scanlan, as "Captain Barry O'Day."

ARGUMENT The three episodes of "Eileen" are set forth in a time of upheaval and romance in Ireland, the Rebellion of 1798. Act I is at the Sign of the Black Bull Tavern; Acts II and III, the Castle, interior and gardens.

Captain Barry has been enlisted with the fighting Irish in France, and now comes home to get recruits, despite the price set upon his own head. Two spies of the English Colonel Lester inform him that Barry is at the Black Bull. Meanwhile, Lady Maude Estabrooke and her niece, Eileen Mulvaney, while driving in their jaunting car are surrounded by noisy peasantry, who have no love for the English. Barry comes to their rescue, and a love affair develops between the two young people, which further complicates matters. The action is fast and amusing; the music a faithful reflex of the plot.

Musical numbers, Act I.—Chorus, "Free Trade and Misty Morn"; "My little Irish rose"; and "Ireland, my Sireland."

Act II.—Chorus, "Too-re-loo-re"; "Eileen, Alanna, Asthore"; "If Eve had left an apple on the bough"; "I'd love to be a lady."

Act III.—Chorus, a three-part number ending in a "Serenade"; "In Erin's Isle"; duet, "Thine alone"—one of the most melodic bits—and an ensemble, "When Ireland stands among the nations of the world."

LUDWIG ENGLANDER

Ludwig Englander was born in Austria, in 1859. His first work in music was conducting small orchestras. He left Vienna in 1882, removing to New York, where he led the orchestra of the Thalia Theatre. His first operetta produced there, "The Princess Consort," had only moderate success. Most of his earlier works produced in the nineties are now forgotten: "1776," "The Monks of Malabar," and "Miss Innocence." Later ones which have been put on the Broadway stages with considerable success include: "The Strollers," "The Office Boy," "The Cadet Girl," "The Rounders," "Half a King," "The Little Corporal," "A Madcap Princess," "The Casino Girl," "The Jewel of Asia," and others. Englander died, September 13, 1914.

THE STROLLERS

Musical Comedy in Three Acts. Music by Englander. Book adapted from the German by Harry B. Smith. Knickerbocker Theatre, New York, by Francis Wilson's Company, June 24, 1901. Wilson took the part of "Lump." Irene Bentley also starred; and the cast included Marie George, and Eddie Foy.

CAST   AUGUST LUMP, *a stroller.* BERTHA, *his Gypsy comrade.* KAMFER, *a jailor.* ROLAND, *a magistrate.* PRINCE ADOLAR DE BOMSKY. MIMI, *a dancer.* ANNA. Others.

ARGUMENT   Two light-hearted "strollers," Lump and Bertha, get into a series of scrapes by trying to cash a thousand-mark note which they have found on the highway. Their adventures and droll disguises are only a part of the riotous fun, which takes place at a German resort and village. The story was later modernized and the locale placed in Florida.

Musical numbers: First Act: "Gossip Chorus" and march; Lump, Bertha, and chorus, the theme song, "Song of the Strollers"; duet, "Heaven's best gift"; Second Act: Roland and male chorus, "Hail to the bridegroom"; Lump and chorus, "English coon song"; Bertha and officers, "A lesson in flirtation"; trio and chorus, "The bold hussars"; Third Act: chorus and ballet, "In ev'ry age"; Lump and chorus, "When the orchestra plays"; finale, "Strollers we!"

REGINALD DE KOVEN

De Koven was a prolific composer of songs and of operas in both serious and lighter vein. His fame, however, rests upon his lighter works. He was born in Middletown, Connecticut, April 3, 1861; his full name being Henry Louis Reginald De Koven. At the age of eleven he was taken abroad and there educated; graduating from Oxford in 1879. His musical education was continued in Stuttgart and Frankfort, and later he studied Light Opera under Genée, Von Suppé, and Delibes. He returned to America in 1882, and resided here until his death, January 16, 1920. In 1902–4 he conducted the Washington (D.C.) Symphony Orchestra. Later he was musical critic of the New York *World*. In the heavier field he wrote "The Canterbury Pilgrims" (1917), and "Rip Van Winkle" (1920), the year of his death (See Grand Opera). But his fame rests upon his light opera, "Robin Hood" (1890), now recognized as one of the best American works in this field. "The Fencing Master" was one of his earlier successes. Other operettas reached nearly a score, including: "The Begum" (1887), "Don Quixote" (1889), "The Algerian" (1893), "Rob Roy" (1894), "The Highwayman" (1897), "The Three Dragoons" (1899), "Foxy Quiller" (1900), "Maid Marian" (1901), "The Student King" (1906), "The Golden Butterfly" (1907).

ROBIN HOOD

Comic Opera in Three Acts. Music by De Koven. Book by Harry B. Smith. Chicago Opera House, June 9, 1890.*

CAST   The original cast was: ROBIN HOOD, *leader of an outlaw band* (Edwin Hoff). THE SHERIFF OF NOTTINGHAM (H. C. Barnabee).

* Produced by The Bostonians it was their tour de force for many years and was, in effect, the yardstick of American operettas. The Bostonians included Henry Clay Barnabee, Eugene Cowles and Jessie Bartlett Davis. Such was its success that this company regarded the opera for twenty years as its "gold mine." Its continued production by professional and amateur companies has totaled thousands of performances.

LITTLE JOHN (W. H. MacDonald). WILL SCARLET (Eugene Cowles). FRIAR TUCK (Geo. B. Frothingham). GUY OF GISBORNE (Peter Lang). ALLAN-A-DALE (Jessie Bartlett Davis). DAME DURDEN (Josephine Bartlett). ANNABEL (Grace Reals). MAID MARIAN (Marie Stone).

ARGUMENT   The story of this melodious opera is that of the famous English outlaw, Robin Hood. The scene is England of the time of Richard the First.

Act I   In the market place of Nottingham all is gaiety. Villagers are singing in praise of May Day and their fair (" 'Tis the morning of the fair"). Friar Tuck sings his lusty song, "As an honest auctioneer," as Robin Hood and some of his men enter. They are joyously hailed, for is not Robin the foe of the rich and the friend of the poor? Robin has turned to outlawry because he has been despoiled of his earldom. An arch-enemy of Robin is the Sheriff of Nottingham, who is now planning a marriage between his ward, Guy of Gisborne, and the lovely Maid Marian. As soon as Robin sets eyes on Marian, he decides that here again he must interfere with the Sheriff's plans. Robin and his men have a spirited entrance song, "Come the bowmen in Lincoln green." An opening duet between Robin and Marian, "Though it was within this hour we met," is followed by a buffo song and chorus, "I am the Sheriff of Nottingham." Guy's feeble wooing ends with the gay waltz song, "Sweetheart, my own sweetheart." Robin confronts the Sheriff and demands his earldom. Flouted, he and his men sing, "An outlaw's life's the life for me."

Act II   Amid the sheltering trees of Sherwood Forest the outlaws sing a lively hunting chorus, "Oh, cheerily soundeth the hunter's horn!"—followed by a droll tale in song led by Scarlet, "The Tailor and the Crow," with humming chorus. Then comes one of the famous bits, "Brown October Ale," sung by Little John, with chorus. In rapid succession in this charming Act now come the "Tinkers' Song" and an elaborate sextet, "Oh, see the lambkins play." Maid Marian has followed Robin to the greenwood, and declares that she will never leave him. Her "Forest Song" is followed by Robin's serenade, "A troubadour sang to his love." The Sheriff and his men have pursued the outlaws, but are themselves captured. Robin's men jeer at their plight ("Let us put him in the stocks"). Guy and a band of archers in their turn rout the outlaws.

Act III   The last Act, in the courtyard of the Sheriff's castle, opens with a vigorous bass aria, by Will Scarlet, the "Armorer's

Song"—"Let hammer on anvil ring!"; followed by Allan's pleasing fantasy, "The legend of the chimes," with bell accompaniment. A duet by Robin and Marian ensues, "There will come a time." Guy, however, has the upper hand. He seizes the unwilling Marian and leads her to the door of the church, where she is to become his bride—by order of the Sheriff and the King himself. Robin, however, manages to get to the King on his return from the Crusades; he tells Richard his story, and obtains the royal pardon and title to his lands. Armed with these and the bows and arrows of his followers, he rescues Marian. Before the wedding Allan sings the ever-popular aria (not in original score), "Oh, promise me!" A jolly country dance and chorus lead up to the finale, "Now let each bonny bridegroom take his bonny bride."

MAID MARIAN

Comic Opera in Three Acts. Music by De Koven. Book by Harry B. Smith. Philadelphia, November 4, 1901. In New York, at the Garden Theatre, January 27, 1902.

CAST ROBERT OF HUNTINGTON (*Robin Hood*). THE SHERIFF OF NOTTINGHAM. SIR GUY OF GISBORNE. LADY MARIAN FITZWALTER. DAME DURDEN. *Outlaws:* LITTLE JOHN, WILL SCARLET, FRIAR TUCK, ALLAN-A-DALE, *and others.* Crusaders. Saracens.

ARGUMENT This opera is a sequel to "Robin Hood" and the action closely follows that story. Robin is not content with his good fortune in winning Marian, but thinks that his duty to his King should be shown by joining a Crusade to the Holy Land.

Musical numbers include: Act I, "The Cellarer's Toast," with Scarlet, Friar Tuck, and chorus; Maid Marian's "Song of the Falcon"; the Sheriff's intriguing, "I am the Sheriff mild and good"; Little John and men, "Forester's Song"; and a pleasing madrigal sung as a quintet, "Love may come, and love may go." Act II, Scarlet and chorus, "The Monk and the Magpie"; Robin's spirited ballad, "Song of the Outlaw"; Allan's lovely song, "Tell me again, sweetheart"; Maid Marian's and Robin's duet, in waltz time, "True love is not for a day"; and Robin and chorus, "Song of the Crusader." Act III, music is largely choral, with Yuletide songs predominating. An effective solo with chorus is "Under the mistletoe bough"; another, "The Cobbler and the Flies." The finale with interwoven medley begins, "Now chime the wedding bells."

ROB ROY

Romantic Opera in Three Acts. Music by De Koven. Book by Harry B. Smith. Herald Square Theater, New York, October, 1894. The cast included Lizzie MacMichol, Juliet Cordon, William Pruette, Richard Carroll, and Joseph Herbert.

CAST ROB ROY MACGREGOR, *a Highland chief.* PRINCE CHARLES EDWARD STUART, *called "The Young Pretender."* DUGALD MACWHEEBLE, *Mayor of Perth.* JANET, *his daughter.* FLORA MACDONALD, *an adherent of the "Pretender."* CAPTAIN RALPH SHERIDAN, *of his Majesty's Grenadiers.* LOCHIEL, *a Highlander.* SANDY MACSHERRY, *town-crier.* Soldiers, Servants of the Mayor, Clansmen, and others.

ARGUMENT The action takes place in or near the city of Perth, Scotland, at the time of the Scottish uprising on behalf of "The Pretender," to restore the Stuarts to the English throne. Both music and action are more pretentious than the usual light opera. It contains some of De Koven's best work, but is not now in active repertory. The more memorable musical numbers are: Act I, Flora and chorus, "Who's for the chase, my bonny hearts?"; Flora and Prince, duet, "Then I will live, Love, for thee"; Town Crier, "Ding, dong!"; Sheridan and soldiers, "We come to the sound of the drum"; Rob Roy and Highlanders, "The white and the red, Huzzah!"; Ballad, Janet, "My hame is where the heather blooms"; Mayor and servants, "My hairt is in the Heelands." Act II, Janet and chorus, "The Merry Miller"; Prince and chorus, "Lay of the Cavalier"; Mayor and others, "Song of the Balladmongers"; Rob Roy and chorus, "Come, lads of the Highlands"; quintet, "My true love is a shepherdess"; Flora, "Dearest heart of my heart." Act III: Prince and Flora, "Who can tell where she dwells"; "Song of the Turnkey"; Mayor and Sandy, "Serenade"; Rob Roy and Janet, "Rustic Song"; finale, "Away!"

THE HIGHWAYMAN

Comic Opera in Three Acts. Music by De Koven. Book by Harry B. Smith.* Broadway Theatre, New York, December 13, 1897.

---

* Harry B. Smith says: "Many consider this to be the composer's best opera. It was **for** this piece that the character of 'Foxy Quiller' was invented and his name was

ARGUMENT The action takes place in various parts of England: the Cat and Fiddle Tavern, Act I; Forests on York Road, Act II; and the Park of Beverley Manor, Act III. The plot concerns the fortunes of a soldier of fortune, Dick Fitzgerald, who has been ruined by a gambler, Hawkhurst. Dick becomes a highwayman and achieves notoriety as "Captain Scarlet." His pardon has fallen into the hands of his arch-enemy, Hawkhurst, but Lady Constance disguises herself as Scarlet and holds up a coach, in order to get the paper. Other complications, of course, follow. Foxy Quiller is a would-be-clever constable. There is some excellent music in this opera.

GUSTAV LUDERS

Although born in Germany (1866), Gustav Luders came to America as a young man and his musical career has been identified with this country. He was first a director of a light opera company in the Middle West, his home being Milwaukee. In 1889 he went to Chicago, where he met Frank Pixley, who was afterwards to work with him successfully as librettist. Their joint works are "The Prince of Pilsen," "King Dodo," "The Grand Mogul," "Marcelle," "Woodland," "The Burgomaster," and "The Gypsy." George Ade supplied the book for "The Fair Co-ed," "The Sho-Gun," and "The Old Town." Luders died, January 24, 1913.

THE PRINCE OF PILSEN

Musical Comedy in Two Acts. Music by Luders. Book by Frank Pixley. Produced in Boston, in 1902. At the Shaftesbury Theatre, London, May 11, 1904 (160 times). Revived at the Jolson Theatre, New York, January 14, 1930; and at the St. Louis Open-Air Theatre, in 1937.

ARGUMENT "The Prince of Pilsen" was a side-splitting piece in its day, due partly to the antics of the traveling brewer, incorporated in the slang of the day as a pseudonym for any one who considered himself phenomenally shrewd." The operetta was given a notable revival, May 2, 1917, at the Forty-Fourth Street Theatre, New York. Jerome Sykes and, later, Jefferson de Angelis was "Foxy Quiller"; and John Charles Thomas was "Dick."

Hans, who constantly wants to know, "Have you ever been to Cincinnati?" The story opens with a party of American girls taking a Cook's Tour abroad. Hans is mistaken for the Prince, and the usual comedy mix-up ensues. The music is hearty and vivacious, with some excellent male choruses. "Oh, Heidelberg!" has taken its place with the best of student songs, and the operetta would be worth while if it had given us nothing else. There is a charming duet, "Keep It Dark"; a pleasing refrain, "Message of the Violets"; and other catchy airs.

THE BURGOMASTER

Musical Comedy in Prologue and Two Acts. Music by Luders. Book by Frank Pixley. First produced in 1900, in New York.

ARGUMENT   The curtain of the Prologue rises upon the Dutch city of New Amsterdam (later New York) in 1660. Peter Stuyvesant is having so many troubles with the English, Swedes, and Indians, that he decides to chuck it all. He and his secretary, Doodle, drink so much of a drugged firewater that they go to sleep, and remain that way for about two hundred and fifty years.

The First and Second Acts show us New York of today. Workmen digging in City Hall Park exhume the two Dutchmen, who proceed to take a lively interest in present-day affairs.

Musical numbers: Prologue: chorus of Dutch girls. "Good-bye, Mr. Amsterdam"; Peter, "Keep cool"; Chief Bluefeather and Indians, "We're civilized now"; Drinking song; First Act: Willie and chorus, "The Land of the Midnight Son"; Daisy and girls, "The little soubrette"; College boys, "In dear old college days"; Peter and chorus, "The Tale of the Kangaroo"; Second Act: Talkington and chorus, "We haven't discovered him yet"; Ruth, "I love you, dear"; Ruth and Willie, "Cupid does not marry."

KING DODO

Comic Opera in Three Acts. Music by Luders. Book by Frank Pixley. Daly's Theatre, New York, May 12, 1902, with Raymond Hitchcock as "King Dodo." An immensely popular piece in its day, with droll situations and costumes, and lively music.

ARGUMENT   The trouble all starts when the aged King Dodo, determines to regain his youth at all hazards. He keeps the Court Physician in constant dread of a violent end, if a potent elixir is not discovered. In the Second Act, Dodo is brought in as prisoner of Queen Lili, of a neighboring realm. She likes them old, and is ready to marry him; but just then somebody gives him a draught from the Fountain of Youth; he turns into a youth; and the Queen will have none of him, until another ducking in the same spring makes him again an old-timer.

Musical numbers: First Act: chorus, "Look in the book and see"; topical song, "The eminent Dr. Fizz"; duet, "Two hearts made one"; finale medley including, "Old Father Time"; Second Act: song, "A true barbaric soldier"; Queen, "For love I live alone" and "Claim thou thine own"; topical song, "The Tale of a Bumblebee"; Third Act: chorus, "We are conspirators"; serenade, "True as the stars above."

THE SHO-GUN

Comic Opera in Two Acts. Music by Luders. Book by George Ade. Wallack's Theater, New York, October 10, 1904, produced by Henry W. Savage, featuring Trixie Friganza, as "Omee-Omi."

ARGUMENT The scene is laid on the imaginary island of Ka-Choo, near Korea. The action relates to an invasion, also imaginary, of an American expedition—the said forces consisting of one person, William Henry Spangle, a chewing-gum salesman. Through a series of comic situations he reaches the exalted office of Sho-Gun just in time to greet the Marines sent to rescue him. The piece is a sly satire on various things American—the worship of titles, business enterprise, advertising, politics, and other Yankee foibles superimposed on the Orient. Described by George Ade as "a playful treatise upon the gentle arts of promoting and trust building."

Musical numbers: First Act: Tee-To, "I'll live for you"; Tee-To, "I am yours truly"; Spangle, "The irrepressible Yank"; Omee-Omi, "The man she'll never meet"; Omee-Omi and Spangle, "Love must be blind"; Second Act: chorus of Sing-Song Girls; duet, "Crime is merely a disease"; Spangle and chorus, "The games we used to play"; octet, "Go where fate may lead"; chorus, "The Sho-Gun of Ka-Choo"; sea song, "The Jackie."

WOODLAND

A Forest Fantasy in Two Acts. Music by Luders. Book by Frank Pixley. New York Theatre, November 21, 1904 (83 performances). Revived in 1926, at the Municipal Theatre, St. Louis.

A novelty piece in which the characters represent birds, in costume and action.   The story relates the troublous events during the reign of King Eagle, when a Blue Jay is elevated to office and threatens the succession of the King's son.   The First Act shows the Royal Court.   Judge Owl is on the bench, and is censuring various fowls for being late.   The King announces the homecoming of the Prince, to take charge of the army.   Meanwhile, all view with some interest a huge shell which occupies the center of the stage.   It is presently cracked, and out steps Blue Jay, who from that moment on keeps things lively.   Many of the familiar birds are imitated in the ingenious costuming.

The music in the First Act includes an opening chorus by all the birds; the Nightingale's song, "Time is flying"; Blue Jay, "Florrie is a flapper"; duet, Wren and Blue Jay, "Bye, bye, Baby"; Peacock, "Will you be my little bride?"   Second Act: Sparrow and chorus, "Clear the way"; Rooster and chorus, "You never can tell till you try"; Blue Jay, "When you're all dressed up"; Blue Birds, "The Message of Spring"; Dove and chorus, "The Tale of the Turtle Dove"; and finale.

KARL HOSCHNA

Hoschna comes of Bohemian stock.   Both his grandfather and his father were musicians in that country.   He was born circa 1870.   He studied at the Vienna Conservatory and won a grand prize.   Later he became proficient on the oboe, playing with an Austrian army band. He came to America in 1896 and for two years played in the Victor Herbert orchestra.   He wrote nearly a score of operettas and musical plays, among them, "The Yama Yama Man," "Three Twins," "The Girl of My Dreams," "Bright Eyes," "Dr. De Luxe," "Jumping Jupiter," "The Belle of the West," "Back Again," "Katie Did," and his most successful work, "Madame Sherry."   Hoschna died in New York, December 23, 1911.

MADAME SHERRY

Musical Comedy in Three Acts.   Music by Karl Hoschna.   Book by Otto Harbach.   Based on a French vaudeville by Hugo Felix, and some of his music is retained in score.   Colonial Theatre, Chicago, April 10, 1910; New Amsterdam Theatre, New York, August 30, 1910. Lina Abarbanell and Ralph C. Herz headed cast.

Edward Sherry is a man about town in New York, the nephew and heir of Theophilus Sherry, an eccentric millionaire, who also has a niece, Yvonne, who has been in a convent.   Others in the cast are: Leonard Gomez, son of the President of Venezuela; Pepita, his sweetheart; and Lulu, an actress and dancer.   To hoodwink his uncle, Edward presents Catherine, his Irish landlady, as "Madame Sherry."

The music is gay and vivacious.   In the First Act is heard that beguiling ditty, "Every little movement has a meaning all its own"; also "Birth of the Butterfly," "Theophilus," and "The smile she means for you."   In the Second Act: "The Other Fellow," "The Dublin Rag," "The Birth of Passion," and "Off for a sail."   In the Third: "Tonight," "Loading up the Mandy Lee," "We are only poor, weak mortals," and "The Seduction."

ALFRED G. WATHALL

Wathall is an English composer, whose work belongs to America. He was born near Nottingham, January 30, 1880.   At the age of ten he came with his parents to America, and appeared as a solo violinist. He pursued his later musical studies in Europe, but returned to this country.   He lived in Chicago, where he was organist and choirmaster in churches.   He was also on the faculty of Northwestern University. He composed many songs, anthems, and cantatas.   His first opera was "The Belles of Stamboul" (1898); his most notable success, "The Sultan of Sulu" (1903).   Wathall died in 1938.

THE SULTAN OF SULU

Musical Satire in Two Acts.   Music by Wathall.   Book by George Ade.   Wallack's Theater, New York, February, 1903, by the Castle Square Opera Company, with Frank Moulan as the Sultan.

ARGUMENT   The action takes place in the gardens of the palace of Sultan Ki-ram, on the island of Sulu in the Philippines. Colonel Budd, a big, blustering American, is over here for business reasons, accompanied by his good-looking daughter, Henrietta. The amusing business of the piece is the contrast between the bumptious American tourists, and the Court of the Sultan.

Musical numbers: First Act: Henrietta and chorus, "Palm branches waving"; female quartet, "Schoolma'am's Song"; Ki-Ram, "Smiling Isle of Sulu"; "Schoolma'ams, "In our little school"; Second Act: opening chorus, "Slumber Song"; Ki-Ram, "R-E-M-O-R-S-E"; native war song, "Allah strike for thee"; quartet, "Foolish wedding bells."

RUDOLF FRIML

Charles Rudolf Friml was born in Prague, Bohemia, December 7, 1879. At the age of twenty-two he came to America and his work has been done here. He first studied the piano, and came as accompanist for the violinist, Jan Kubelik, for whom he played five years. He has written numerous compositions for the piano, violin and 'cello, and has been a featured pianist with various orchestras, but his outstanding success has been in the field of Light Opera, being recognized as one of the most melodious of contemporary composers. He first won recognition with "The Firefly" (1912), which was followed by "The Ballet Girl" (1914), "High Jinks" (1914), "Katinka" (1915), "The Peasant Girl" (1916), "You're in Love" (1917), "Glorianna" (1918), "Tumble Inn" (1919), "June Love" (1920), "Cinders" (1923), "Rose Marie" (1924), "The Vagabond King" (1925), "The Wild Rose" (1926), "The White Eagle" (1927), "The Three Musketeers" (1928), and others.

THE FIREFLY

Comic Opera in Three Acts. Music by Friml. Book by Otto Harbach. Empire Theatre, Syracuse, October 14, 1912; Lyric Theatre, New York, December 2, 1912. Emma Trentini took the part of "Nina." Others in cast were Roy Atwell, Audrey Maple, Vera de Rosa, and Craig Campbell. Has been repeatedly revived by both professional and amateur companies. A screen version has also been made of "The Firefly," with pronounced success—adding to it the popular "Donkey Serenade."

ARGUMENT The action shifts from New York to Bermuda; time, the present. Act I takes place on the Recreation Pier, foot of 23rd Street, New York; Act II. in the Bermuda estate of Mrs. Oglesby Van Dare, a New York society leader; and Act III., in the Van Dare home in New York. The story revolves around the adventures of Nina, a street singer, who, disguised as a boy, goes as a stowaway to Bermuda, on the same boat with a group of society folk. Nina is accused of theft and of being the notorious pickpocket, Tony. She is finally cleared, her identity is revealed, and she wins her hero, Jack Travers, who has been pledged to Geraldine, the rather plain niece of Mrs. Van Dare. This opera has won wide popularity by reason of its wealth of engaging music. The libretto is clean, bright and amusing.

Act I Thurston and chorus, "Call me uncle"; Nina, "Love is like a firefly"; Suzette and Jenkins, "Something"; sextet, "We'll barricade her"; Nina's superb song, "Giannina mia"; finale, "I've found it at last."

Act II Sybil and chorus, "In sapphire seas"; Tea girls and guests, "A cup of tea"; Nina and soldiers, "Tommy Atkins on a Dress-Parade" (march); Geraldine and Thurston, in the unforgettable "Sympathy"; Jack, "A woman's smile"; Nina and male quartet, "We're going to make a man of you"; Franz and men, "The beautiful ship of Toyland"; finale, "See my cloak."

Act III Thurston and chorus, "I love pretty lips"; Nina's waltz song, "The dawn of love"; Nina and Jack, "Like a dream it seems"; finale, "When a maid comes knocking at your heart."

KATINKA

Musical Comedy in Three Acts. Music by Friml. Book by Otto Harbach. Produced in New York, in the fall of 1915.

ARGUMENT One of the most successful of the earlier works by this composer, and still recalled for its gaiety and charm. The story shifts between Russia and France. Boris, a Russian ambassador, is to be married to Katinka. Among the guests is Ivan Dimitri, who really loves her, and who would have won her, but for some intercepted letters. Then enters the *deus ex machina* in the person of Thaddeus T. Hopper, a wealthy American chap. He agrees with Ivan to abduct Katinka, on the day of her wedding, and does so. But when he arrives with her at Anzuli, matters are badly complicated by the presence of Hopper's wife, who is something of a virago. Later Katinka becomes a singer in a Paris café; and is united to Ivan.

There is an abundance of bright music, some of the haunting quality for which this composer is famed. In the First Act are: a male quartet, "In this ruby cup of wine"; a duet between the lovers, " 'Tis the end, so farewell"; and a colorful Russian dance. ˙ In the Second: the opening chorus, "On high in minaret"; a humorous duet between the Hoppers, "The weekly wedding"; the exceptional number, "Allah's Holiday"; and song by Katinka and chorus, "Rackety Coo." In the Third: chorus of Vienna girls, "In Vienna girls are brightest"; Ivan's song, "My Paradise"; Mrs. Hopper and chorus, "I want to marry a male quartet"; concerted number, "Pay to the order of"; and finale, "On my heart."

ROSE MARIE

Musical Play in Two Acts. Music by Friml. Book by Otto Harbach. Imperial Theatre, New York, September 2, 1924. Mary Ellis took the part of "Rose Marie"; Arthur Deagon, that of the Sergeant; Edward Hawley, that of "Black Eagle."

ARGUMENT   The scene of this simple love story is laid in various parts of Canada. In the first part we are in Saskatchewan and the Canadian Rockies. Then we follow Rose Marie and her musical fortunes to Quebec, the first scene of the Second Act being in a novelty shop in Quebec, eight months later. A glittering ballroom scene in the Chateau Frontenac is followed, after an indicated lapse of a month, by a return to the mountains, the Kootenay Pass. This operetta won favor by reason of its contrasts—the simplicity of the wilds, with the sophistication of society.

Music of perennial loveliness is interwoven: "Rose Marie, I love you," the "Indian Love Call," which is one of those little gems that will live; the rhythmical "Totem Tom Tom"; the sentimental ballad, "The Door of My Dreams"; the rousing "Song of the Mounties"; and the comedy song, "Why Shouldn't We?" (written by Herbert Stothart).

"Rose Marie" has since widened its audience into the millions through the fine screen version, in which the leads were taken by Jeannette MacDonald and Nelson Eddy.

THE VAGABOND KING

Musical Play in Two Acts (given as four parts). Music by Friml. Book by Brian Hooker and W. H. Post, based on McCarthy's, "If I Were King." Casino, New York, September 21, 1925. Dennis King took the rôle of "Villon." Later given successfully at the Winter Garden Theatre, London. Frequently revived, the latest New York date being June 29, 1943. At St. Louis Open-Air Theatre, in 1944.

ARGUMENT This sprightly story follows fairly closely the thread of the well-known novel "If I Were King." It tells the adventures of that vagabond poet, François Villon, and his ragged followers, to aid the King in his struggle against Burgundy. In jest, Louis XI commands that Villon be made King for twenty-four hours; and at the end of that time he is to be hanged if he cannot win the hand of the haughty lady, Katherine.

The music is as spirited as the text, the refrain by Villon and his followers, "Song of the Vagabonds," bidding fair to become a permanent musical possession. Others are: "Love for Sale," sung by Huguette; the lovely "Huguette Waltz," which is one of the high points of the operetta; "A Flagon of Wine," sung by Tabarie; three songs by Katherine, "Some Day," "Tomorrow," and "Only a Rose"—the last being another prime favorite; "The Hunting Song," a serenade to Lady Mary, a beautiful "Nocturne," and a duet, "Love Me Tonight." In brief, one of the very best works of this brilliant composer, and of the contemporary stage.

THE THREE MUSKETEERS

Light Opera in Two Acts. Music by Friml. Book by William A. McGuire, after the novel by Dumas. First produced at the Lyric Theatre, New York, in March 13, 1928. Dennis King took the rôle of "D'Artagnan." Presented at St. Louis Open-Air Theatre, in 1941.

ARGUMENT The narrative is based on the exploits of Dumas' famous Musketeers. In the First Act is a ringing song by the Musketeers, "All for one, and one for all." Other melodies in this Act are: "Summer Time," "Gascony," "Heart of Mine," "Vesper Bell," and "Love is the sun." In the Second Act a male chorus gives a lusty drinking song, "With red wine." Then come a duet between

D'Artagnan and Constance, "Kiss before I go"; D'Artagnan and his
men, "My Sword!"; and the songs, "Queen of my heart" and "Every
little while." Two other "hit" songs of this very tuneful production
are "Ma Belle" and "Your Eyes."

JEROME KERN

Jerome David Kern was born in the city of New York, January 27,
1885. After studying the piano in the New York College of Music, he
went abroad for a year. Returning to his native city, he obtained work
as a staff musician, "dressing up" the works of foreign composers for
local production. Soon came scores under his own name. Kern was
prolific in lighter opera and allied fields. One of his first successes was
"The Red Petticoat" (1912). Then "The Girl from Utah" (1914), in
which Julia Sanderson plaintively sang, "They didn't believe me!"
Others are: "Very Good, Eddy" (1915), "Oh, Boy!" (1917), "Oh, Lady,
Lady!" (1918), "Sally" (1920), "Sunny" (1925), "Sweet Adeline" (1929),
"The Cat and the Fiddle" (1931), "Music in the Air" (1933) and "Roberta" (1933). However, "Show Boat" (1927) is his *magnum opus* and
has made Light Opera history. He also wrote the music for the screen
play, "I Dream Too Much," starring Lily Pons (1935). About this time,
Hollywood called him and he wrote much incidental music for the
films—to the loss of the "spoken" stage. He made his home there, but
returning to New York to supervise a revival of his "Show Boat," he
was seized with sudden illness and died in a hospital, November 11,
1945. Subsequent to his death a musical play for the screen in technicolor—"Centennial Summer" (1946)—was presented, with his music
and an excellent cast. A hobby of Kern's was rare-book collecting, and
a sale of some of his rarities, in 1929, brought over $1,500,000.

SALLY

Musical Comedy in Three Acts. Music by Kern. Book by Guy
Bolton. New Amsterdam Theatre, New York, December 21, 1920,
where it ran for several months, before being presented with equal

success on the road. It met with warm favor also in London, at the Winter Garden, where it opened, September 10, 1921, running 387 times. Presented at St. Louis Open-Air Theatre, in 1942.

This is a singing and dancing show. The leads were taken by Marilyn Miller ("Sally"), Leon Errol ("Constantine"), and Irving Fisher ("Blair"). Sally Green is an alley waif who gets a dish-washing job in the Elm Tree Inn, but it is not to her liking. She is pert, clever, and a good mimic and dancer, so she wants to step out. She is befriended by Connie, the worst of waiters, who claims to be a foreign Duke and who likes to step out, too, in fine clothes and mingle with the select. In one of these fine homes he introduces Sally as a Russian dancer. Blair Farquar, the scion of the house, has already met Sally, and their turbulent love affair finally reaches its proper climax at the Little Church Around the Corner.

The gay, intriguing music has several memorable numbers such as: the song and dance of Sally and the Settlement girls, "Joan of Arc"; duet between Sally and Blair, the theme song, "Look for the silver lining"; and the male chorus led by Blair, "Sally," in the First Act. Sally and the boys, "A wild, wild rose"; duet, Sally and Blair, "Whip-poor-will," in the Second. A lovely "Butterfly Ballet" (by Victor Herbert) and the finale, "The Little Church Around the Corner," in the last Act.

SUNNY

Musical Comedy in Two Acts. Music by Kern. Book by Otto Harbach and Oscar Hammerstein 2nd. New Amsterdam Theatre, New York, September 22, 1925, where it had a run of several months. Also successful in the Hippodrome, London. Revived in 1929.

A singing and dancing show. It had an excellent cast including Marilyn Miller ("Sunny Peters"), Joseph Cawthorn ("Siegfried Peters"), Clifton Webb ("Harold"), Jack Donahue ("Jim Deming"), Paul Frawley ("Tom Warren"), and Mary Hay ("Weenie Winters"). The plot concerns the fortunes of a winsome circus girl, Sunny Peters, a bareback rider. She is recognized, on the grounds at Southampton, England, by members of a New York regiment as their World War entertainer in France. Tom Warren, one of their number, is present and Sunny is again attracted to him. To avoid marriage with the circus owner she stows away on a ship sailing for America. The usual complications of a musical play follow.

In the First Act after an opening song by Tom and the boys, "Sunny," we hear the melodious theme song (Sunny and Tom), "Who stole my heart away?"; a duet, Jim and Weenie, "Let's say goodnight till it's morning"; and song by Marcia, "Be still, my heart."

The Second Act has a popular duet between Harold and Weenie, "Two little blue birds"; then one by Sunny and Jim, "When we get our divorce"; a repetition of the theme song, "Who?", one of the best songs, "D'ya love me?", and a finale, "Hunt Ball," and "The Chase."

SHOW BOAT

Musical Play in Two Acts.　Music by Kern.　Book by Oscar Hammerstein 2nd, based on Edna Ferber's novel of the same name.　Ziegfeld Theatre, New York, December 27, 1927.　It scored an outstanding success, "grossing $50,000 a week."　Was revived in 1932, with nearly the same cast; and again in New York, with elaborate settings, at the Ziegfeld Theatre, January 5, 1946.　Kern had come east to superintend rehearsal, but died, the preceding November.

The original cast included Charles Winninger ("Captain Andy Hawks"), Howard Marsh ("Gaylord Ravenel"), Norma Terris ("Magnolia"), Helen Morgan ("Julie"), Edna May Oliver ("Parthy Ann Hawks"), Jules Bledsoe ("Joe"), "Queenie," "Kim," and others.　In the later performance Paul Robeson took the part of "Joe."

This work has been spoken of as "the best that America has yet done," in the perfection of its plot and setting.　Music and action are closely welded and reflect life upon the Mississippi in its "show boat" days. The fortunes of Cap'n Andy and his troupe on the "Cotton Blossom" and through nearly fifty years are depicted.　The romance of Gaylord Ravenel, light-hearted gambler, and Magnolia, the "leading lady"; and their later life in Chicago and that of their daughter, Kim, follow Edna Ferber's story.

The First Act has eight scenes, opening on a levee, in "the late '8o's," and then aboard the "Cotton Blossom."　An opening chorus, "Cotton Blossom," is followed by a duet between Ravenel and Magnolia, "Only Make Believe," which has remained widely popular.　Then comes Joe and the Jubilee Singers in a song that has already become classic, "Old Man River"; the renditions by both Jules Bledsoe, the original "Joe," and later by Paul Robeson, are famous.　Next, a quintet, "Can't help lovin' that man"; a male chorus led by Ravenel, "Till good luck comes my way"; and a duet between the lovers, "You Are Love."

The Second Act, which introduces nine scenes, opens with the Midway at the Chicago Fair of 1893; shows scenes in the Trocadero Music Hall; and comes back to the old "Cotton Blossom" in the year 1927.

Here some of the old songs are sung by Kim, who is a coming young star. The opening chorus, "At the Fair," is followed by the familiar quartet, "Why do I love you?"; the Jubilee Singers in "In Dahomey"; Queenie and the same singers, in "Hay, Feller!"; and a repetition of "Old Man River" and other "hits" of the First Act.

"Show Boat" is, in brief, one of the milestones of the American stage. Its songs are constantly sung by ambitious singers in concert and over the air; and it has had an elaborate screen production.

THE CAT AND THE FIDDLE

A Musical Love Story in Two Acts. Music by Kern. Book by Otto Harbach. Globe Theatre, New York, October 15, 1931, where it had a season's run.

While partaking of both play and operetta, this is particularly charming, with more than one melody of persistent appeal. Shirley Sheridan, an American girl who has won some success as a writer of popular songs, comes to Brussels to study music. On the quay she chances to meet Victor Florescue, a young Roumanian composer, who takes his work very seriously indeed. He is engaged on an operetta, "The Passionate Pilgrim." In his studio, later, he is much annoyed by hearing some frivolous airs wafted across the court from a neighboring studio. Daudet, his producer, listens to the score of the opera, but thinks it too heavy. Just then he, too, hears the tinkling music from across the way. "That's what we want!" he exclaims. Victor is still further put out, when he discovers that the musical neighbor is the American girl. A later scene shows the production of "The Passionate Pilgrim," and shows also how the course of true love cannot run smooth when there are musical and professional jealousies in the way.

In the First Act are: a military march, "I watch the love parade"; a canzonetta, the popular theme song, "The night was made for love"; aria by Victor, "The breeze kissed your hair"; trio, "Try to forget"; and "Poor Pierrot." The Second Act introduces the saucy refrain, by Shirley, "She didn't say yes, she didn't say no"; Victor, "A new love is old"; duet, "One moment alone"; and the amusing song by Shirley and chorus, "Ha! Cha! Cha!"

MUSIC IN THE AIR

Musical Comedy in Three Acts. Music by Kern. Book by Oscar Hammerstein 2nd. Forty-Fourth Street Theatre, New York, September 4, 1933.

The cast was a notable one including: Reinald Werrenrath, who, however, had a minor rôle, "Cornelius," the bird man; Walter Slezak ("Karl Reder," the schoolmaster); Al. Shean ("Doctor Lessing," the music teacher); Tulio Carminati ("Bruno Mahler," the playwright); Ann Barrie ("Sieglinde," Lessing's daughter) , and Natalie Hall ("Frieda Hatzfeld," the star). There are many other speaking and singing parts.

A refreshing little musical story of rustic life. It opens in a village of the Bavarian Alps and an old-fashioned singing school. Sieglinde, the daughter of the music teacher, is a charming girl with a pleasing voice, good enough for the village choir, but she is stage struck. So Karl, her sweetheart, goes with her on the long walk to Munich. Here they encounter city life and ways, strange and alarming. The girl sees the seamy side of the stage and after she has tried her wings out, but found them not strong enough to sustain her, she goes back contentedly to the village, and Karl.

In the First Act we hear a choral, "Melodies of May"; the teasing theme song, "I've told every little star"; song, "I am so eager"; and a duet and chorus, "There's a hill beyond a hill." In the Second, a duet repeating "I've told"; Bruno's "Letter Song"; Frieda, "I'm alone"; Bruno, "One more dance"; Frieda, "Night flies by"; Third Act: chorus, "When spring is in the air"; solo and duet, "The song is you"; and a final duet bringing in again the theme song.

ROBERTA

Musical Comedy in Prologue and Two Acts. Music by Kern. Book by Otto Harbach. From the novel by Alice Duer Miller. New Amsterdam Theatre, New York, November 18, 1933. In the cast were Fay Templeton, the veteran actress who played "Aunt Minnie"; Tamara, Lyda Roberti, and Robert Hope. Performed at St. Louis Open-Air Theatre, in 1945.

ARGUMENT   This may be briefly described as a "glorified fashion show." Its action is laid chiefly in a high-grade dressmaking establishment, affording opportunities for parades of lovely dresses and lovelier girls. John Kent, an American football star, is jilted by Sophie Teale, and goes to Paris to visit his Aunt Minnie. She is an elderly lady who owns this exclusive dress shop, "Roberta's," and she now wills the business to John and to her chief designer, Stephanie, who is really a Russian princess in exile. The later affairs of business and of the heart occupy the show.

The most popular song, "Smoke gets in your eyes," is sung with guitar accompaniment by Tamara in the Second Act.*   Other pleasing songs are: "Let's begin," "You're devastating," "Yesterdays," "Something had to happen," "The touch of your hand," "I won't dance," "Lovely to look at," and "Hard to handle."

SWEET ADELINE

Musical play in Three Acts.   Music by Kern.   Produced in New York in 1929.

A highly pretentious offering, which despite the length of its run must be classed with the few failures of this composer.   It had a crowded stage, one of the principals being Helen Morgan.   The plot was a blending of old times with new, something as in "Show Boat."   But the production was noisy, in part due to the device of distributing the orchestral strains to various parts of the auditorium by means of loud speakers.

SIGMUND ROMBERG

Born in Hungary, in 1887, and educated at Bucharest University, Sigmund Romberg came to America as a young man and his musical career is closely linked with New York productions.   He had been educated as an engineer, with bridge building in view, but on coming to this country, in 1909, he turned to music as a means of livelihood, playing the piano in small orchestras, then writing incidental music for "revues."   His first opera was "The Midnight Girl" (1913).   That he has pronounced gifts in the operetta field is shown by a partial list of his works, which include: "Maytime" (1917); "Blossom Time" (1921); "The Rose of Stamboul" (1922); "The Student Prince" (1924); "Princess Flavia" (1925); "The Desert Song" (1926); "My Maryland" (1927); "The New Moon" (1928); "Melody" (1933); "Sunny River" (1941); and "Up in Central Park" (1945).   In recent years Romberg has turned to a new

* A recent story going the rounds on Broadway is to the effect that, before production, the stage manager vigorously balked at the inclusion of this song, and it was only at Kern's insistence it was retained—later to become the one song most remembered, whistled and sung.

medium with success—radio operettas—one such work being "Viennese Nights." A recent chronicler credits him with having a musical hand in no less than 77 shows, which would rank him as one of the most prolific composers of any period.

MAYTIME

A Play with Music, in Four Acts. Music by Romberg. Book and Lyrics by Rida Johnson Young and Cyrus Wood. Shubert Theatre, New York, August 16, 1917. With Peggy Wood, as "Ottilie," and Charles Purcell, as "Richard Wayne."

ARGUMENT   This is one of those nostalgic pieces whose plot, of a love frustrated, has a universal appeal, coupled with some of the best of Romberg's earlier music. One song, "Will you remember?" is deathless.

The action of the four acts, "or episodes," begins in the year 1840 and continues through the century. The locale is the fine old home of the Van Zandts in Washington Square, New York. While the Second Act takes us to Mme. Delphine's Night Club (time 1855) the Third is back in the mansion, in the '80's; and the last Act shows it converted into a modern dress-making shop, with the turn of the century.

John Wayne, a cooper, is in debt to his employer, Colonel Van Zandt, and gives the latter a deed to his home, as security. John's son, Richard Wayne, is an apprentice in the cooperage, but ambitious and likewise much in love with the Colonel's pretty daughter, Ottilie. While Ottilie is entertaining some of her girl friends, a sudden gust of wind blows papers from her father's desk into the garden. Matthew Van Zandt, a charming ne'er-do-well, retrieves them with one exception, a blue paper lying at the foot of an apple-tree. Ottilie and Richard find this paper, which later proves to be the deed to the Wayne home, and bury it in a little box with a ring, the while they pledge their eternal love for each other.

In the second episode we are carried forward fifteen years. Ottilie, despite her love for Richard, has been compelled to marry Claude, another Van Zandt. The Colonel still rules the roost. The two unhappy lovers meet only briefly.

In the third episode we find another lapse of time, twenty-five years. Claude, a gambler, has died, leaving Ottilie penniless. The old home with its apple-tree still standing is about to be sold at auction. Unknown to her, Richard comes upon the scene and buys it, deeding it back to her.

The fourth episode, or act, again sets the clock forward. The mansion has been transformed into a dress-making establishment by Ottilie's grand-daughter, who takes the trade name of Mlle. Brown. Richard Wayne's grandson is in love with her and tries to help the business by sending his friends to the shop. She, however, will not marry him while her house is encumbered by debt. Then workmen digging in the old garden find the casket with its ring and the deed, which restores the family fortunes; and the lifetime sweethearts through their descendants find that they have indeed "remembered."

Music, Act I, "In our little home, sweet home"; "It's a windy day on the battery"; "Gypsy song"; and the duet, "Will you remember?" II.: the humorous, "Jump Jim Crow!"; "The Road to Paradise"; "Spanish Dance"; "Will you remember?" III.: Chorus at the auction; "Reminiscence." IV.: Chorus of girls, "Selling gowns"; "Dancing will keep you young"; "Only one girl for me"; and the theme song, "Will you remember?"

BLOSSOM TIME

Musical Play in Three Acts. Music by Romberg. Book by Dorothy Donnelly. Music based upon airs by Franz Schubert. Ambassador Theatre, New York, September 29, 1922. Later, March 2, 1931; December 26, 1938; September 4, 1943. In the original cast, Olga Cook took the part of "Mitzi"; Bertram Peacock, "Franz Schubert"; Howard Marsh, "Baron Franz."

CAST FRANZ SCHUBERT, *the composer.* BARON FRANZ SCHOBER, *his friend.* KRANZ. VON SCHWIND. BINDER. ERKMANN. COUNT SHARNTOFF. HANZY. NOVOLNY. MITZI. BELLABRUNA. FRITZI. KITZI. GRETA. MRS. KRANZ. Others.

ARGUMENT While clever and entertaining, this work represents a somewhat garbled version of both the life and music of the famous composer, Schubert. He is shown as a brilliant but obscure fellow, who does not get along with the ladies, and particularly the one whom he secretly loves, because of a homely face set off by a stub nose. In the climactic scene he plays the theme melody based upon his "Unfinished Symphony"—"This is my song of love"—while watching and aiding his handsomer friend woo his sweetheart. It is somewhat like the situation in "Cyrano de Bergerac." "The Serenade," "Ave Maria," and other Schubert music, are drawn upon. "Tell me, Daisy," is a song in lighter vein. Other melodies are "Keep it dark," "Serenade," "My springtime thou art," and "There is an old Vienna."

THE STUDENT PRINCE

Operetta in Four Acts.   Music by Romberg.   Book by Dorothy Don-nelly.   Based on Mansfield's play, "Old Heidelberg."   Jolson's The-ater, New York, December 2, 1924.   Ilse Marvenga took the part of "Kathie"; Howard Marsh, the Prince.   Revived at Majestic Theater, January 29, 1931, June 8, 1943.

CAST   PRINCE KARL FRANZ.   DOCTOR ENGEL.   GRAND DUCHESS ANA-
           STASIA.   KATHIE, *a waitress*.   PRINCESS MARGARET.   CAPTAIN
TARNITZ.   GRETCHEN.   TONI.   DETLEF.   LUTZ.   Others.

ARGUMENT   The setting of this work is youthful and vivacious; the
                      music in full keeping.   From the students' song, "Old
Heidelberg," to the end, the melodies have charm and appeal.   The
story concerns a young prince who enrolls in this famous university and
takes his place in college life as one of the fellows.   He falls in love with
Kathie, the pretty maid in the college inn.   She reciprocates his affection, which is pure and sweet.   But their romance is brief.   His grandfather, the King, dies, and he is summoned back to court to take up the
crown and affairs of state.   Furthermore, he is betrothed to a princess.
His rustic sweetheart has to give him up.

   The music includes: the "Student Marching Song," "Golden Days,"
the lively "Drinking Song," the well-remembered "Deep in my heart,"
"Come, boys, let's be gay boys," and a melodious "Serenade."

THE DESERT SONG

Musical Play in Two Acts.   Music by Romberg.   Book by Otto
Harbach and Oscar Hammerstein, 2nd.   Casino, New York, Novem-
ber 30, 1926.   In London at the Theatre Royal, April 7, 1927.   In
New York Robert Halliday sang the leading rôle.   Revived in New
York, in January, 1946.

ARGUMENT   The scene is North Africa; the time, 1925.   Described
                      as a "musical play," this piece has much more actual
story, atmosphere and local color than the average.   The music is so
interwoven as to become an integral part; and the haunting "Desert
Song" permeates it.

Act I   The First Act, in three scenes, takes place, first, in the retreat of
          the famous bandit chief, "Red Shadow," then in General Bira-

beau's house. For some months the French have been endeavoring to capture Red Shadow, but without success. In the opening chorus, Sid, his lieutenant, with the Riffs, sings the "Feasting Song." Red Shadow enters, and his men sing "The Riff Song." Red Shadow learns from his men that Margot is to be wed to the Governor. He makes the Riffs promise not to harm her. After the bandits leave, the stage is occupied by Captain Paul and his men, who are chasing them. They sing, "Oh, pretty maid of France!" The second and third scenes are of lighter texture. Susan sings, "Has anybody seen my Bennie?" The girls sing, "Why did we marry soldiers?" Margot and the other girls don French soldier uniforms. They sing, "Handsome cavaliers, aren't we fine?" Margot sings, "Romance." Later comes a trio, "My passion is not to crash on." Red Shadow boldly invades the Governor's palace, to prevent the wedding of Margot, whom he loves. Red Shadow is, in fact, a Frenchman, a deserter from the army, and a price is upon his head. After an impassioned song, "My desert is waiting, dear," which ends in a duet, he abducts her from the palace.

Act II This Act is in five scenes opening in the harem of Ali Ben Ali. Red Shadow, who is his ally, brings Margot hither and seeks refuge, which is granted. The opening song is by Ali and others, "Eastern and Western Love." Red Shadow seeks to win Margot's love, but she repulses him. (Margot: "The Sabre Song.") She tells him that she loves Pierre. He chivalrously says that he will bring Pierre to her, and promptly does so. But Margot finds that she is cold to Pierre; her heart turns toward Red Shadow, in spite of herself. Red Shadow, who returns, triumphantly sings, "Blue Heaven and you and I!" At this juncture General Birabeau himself arrives (Song: "I have come to take Margot home"). Red Shadow drops his sword and will not fight the General, even after the latter strikes him. This episode leaves Red Shadow disgraced in the eyes of his men. He goes into exile, and here he voices the melodious "One alone, to be my own." Margot is disconsolate. She sings, "Kissing a moonlit sky." Later Red Shadow is captured and then discovered to be Pierre, the General's son. He and Margot are united. The finale brings in again the refrain, "One alone to be my own!"; also "Farewell," by Red Shadow and the Riffs.

MY MARYLAND

Operetta in Three Acts. Music by Romberg. Book by Dorothy Donnelly. Produced at the Casino, New York, September 12, 1927, where it ran until following June; later at Shubert Theatre and quite successful on the road.

ARGUMENT   The action revolves around the Frietchie family home
            ⟩ in Frederick, Maryland, then a storm center between
North and South, in Civil War times.   Barbara Frietchie is the belle
of the town and an ardent States Rights girl.   Her brother Arthur is
now fighting in the South.   Jack Negly, also a Confederate, has been
suing for her hand, and her father is agreeable to the match.   But just
at this juncture, Captain Trumbull, commanding Union troops, comes
in and takes control of Frederick.   Jack escapes through the lines.
Arthur is later smuggled home, wounded.   Trumbull falls in love with
the beautiful, spunky Barbara, who waves her flag from the balcony;
and she with him in spite of her family.   The Captain learns about
Arthur and is torn between love and duty.   In the end both are reconciled.

The First Act reveals a street in Frederick, in the evening.   The
music includes: "Mr. Cupid"; "Won't you marry me?"; the rousing
chorus, still a favorite, "Your land and my land!"; "The same silver
moon" (another enduring favorite); and "The Mocking-bird."

The Second Act, the House of a Clergyman in Hagerstown; the next
morning: "Strawberry Jam"; "Mexico"; "Something old, something
new"; and "Old John Barleycorn."

The Third Act, the Frietchie home in Frederick: "Song of Victory";
"Ker-choo!"; "Boys in Gray"; "Mother" (another charming song); "The
Bonnie Blue Flag"; and a chorus, "Hail, Stonewall Jackson!"

THE NEW MOON

Musical Romance in Two Acts.   Music by Romberg.   Book and
lyrics by Oscar Hammerstein 2d, Frank Mandel, and Lawrence Schwab.
Imperial Theatre, New York, September 19, 1928, for a long run.
Theatre Royal, Birmingham, England, 1929; and elsewhere.   Evelyn
Herbert took the part of "Marianne"; Robert Halliday, "Robert," a
bondservant; William O'Neal, "Philippe," friend of Robert.

ARGUMENT   "The New Moon" has been frequently revived and is
            justly regarded as containing some of Romberg's best
music, in abundant quantity.   The opening scene is New Orleans; the
time, 1788.

Monsieur Beaunoir, a wealthy citizen of New Orleans, has a number
of bondservants shipped across from turbulent France.   Among them is
Robert, who has fallen in love with his master's lovely daughter,
Marianne; and she is also attracted to him.   Captain Duval arrives
from France on his ship the "New Moon" in quest of an escaped Revolu-

tionist, Chevalier Robert Missen. Beaunoir lines up his servants for inspection, but Robert eludes the net. The scene changes to a tavern, where Robert denounces a certain Ribaud as a spy. Then it shifts again to the Beaunoir mansion where a dance is going on. Robert manages to gain entrance and steal a kiss from his sweetheart.

The Second Act opens with a scene on shipboard. Ribaud has arrested Robert and is taking him to France for trial. Philippe, a friend of Robert, overhauls them in his vessel, sends Captain Duval and Ribaud ashore on a Florida reef, and with the liberated men sets up camp on a small island. After more stormy action, another ship from France arrives and announces that France is now a Republic; and the islanders headed by Robert (united with Marianne) set up their own government as part of the Republic.

Music, Act I: a song by Robert, "Marianne"; by her and chorus, "The girl on the prow"; "Gorgeous Alexander"; "An interrupted love song"; "Tavern Song"; one of the great "hit" numbers, by Philippe and chorus, "Softly, as in a morning sunrise"; the rousing male chorus, "Stout-hearted men!"; the lovely, "One Kiss," by Marianne and chorus, with its also charming duet by the lovers, "Wanting you!"

In Act II: the humorous skit, "Funny little sailor man"; the perennial favorite, crooning melody, "Lover, come back to me!"; "Love is quite a simple thing"; and "Try her out at dancing."

UP IN CENTRAL PARK

Musical Play in Two Acts. Music by Romberg. Book by Herbert and Dorothy Fields. Century Theatre, New York, January 27, 1945.

SCENE: Central Park and downtown New York.

TIME: 1870-1.

CAST ROSIE MOORE (Maureen Cannon). BOSS TWEED (Noah Beery). JOHN MATTHEWS (Wilbur Evans). THOMAS NAST (Maurice Burke). ELLEN LAWRENCE (Elaine Barry). JOE STEWART (Fred Barry). BESSIE O'CAHANE (Betty Bruce). Tammany and City Officials, Bagpipers, Children, Others.

ARGUMENT A large and gaily costumed company under the direction of Michael Todd put on this show which was hailed as "one of the happiest events of the season." The story concerns the efforts of Matthews, a New York Times reporter, and Nast, a Harper's Weekly cartoonist, to expose and overthrow the vicious Tweed Ring which had all the city offices in its clutches. History relates the sequel and how our heroes saved the city hundreds of thousands of dollars, and put the Boss behind the bars. The play gives added and pleasing touches, such as the scene with the five children. The Times reporter finally marries Rosie Moore, daughter of a Tammany politician. The singing and acting of Maureen Cannon, who had won fame in Chicago, were noteworthy. The settings and costumes were patterned upon the famous Currier and Ives lithographs, and the show as a whole offered a pleasing parallel to another current attraction, "Bloomer Girl."

The First Act in 5 scenes was mostly in Central Park. Music: Bessie and chorus, "Up from the gutter"; Rosie's "Carrousel in the Park"; a trio, "It doesn't cost us anything to dream"; Boss Tweed and his group of Tammanyites, "Boss Tweed"; John's "When she walks in the room"; the duet by Bessie and Joe, followed by a costume dance, "Currier and Ives"; one of the "hit" songs, "Close as pages in a book"; a chorus with dance, "Rip Van Winkle"; a humorous skit by girls, "The Fireman's Bride"; and finale.

In the Second Act of 6 scenes we witness other Park settings; interior of the Times office, and a July picnic by the sachems of Tammany. Music: a chorus, "When the Party gives a party"; "Maypole Dance"; "The big backyard," by John and chorus; "April Snow"; "The birds and the bees"; and reprises of earlier songs.

IRVING BERLIN

Although not classed as a writer of opera, Irving Berlin's work in adjoining fields should be mentioned. Born in Russia, May 11, 1888, christened Izzy Baline, he was brought to New York as a child of five. He received the briefest of education in the city schools, and there was nothing to distinguish him at the time from other East Side street urchins. He started as a singing waiter in a saloon, then began composing such songs as "Alexander's Rag-Time Band," "Oh, How I Hate to Get Up in the Morning,"—a popular song of the First World War— and many others which were speedily sung and whistled all over the land. Some of the best known are: "All Alone," "Remember," "Always," and "White Christmas." Berlin has since written incidental music for revues. He owns his own publishing house. He followed his patriotic service in the First World War with no less work "for the boys" in the Second War; the high spot being a huge revue, "This is the Army!", the entire proceeds being devoted to the service, as also were the royalties from his nationally sung song, "God Bless America!" His stage plays have been chiefly "Face the Music" (1932), "As Thousands Cheer" (1933) and, after his war work was completed, "Annie Get Your Gun" (1946).

FACE THE MUSIC

Musical revue in Two Acts. Music by Berlin. Book by Moss Hart. New Amsterdam Theater, New York, February 17, 1932. In the cast were Mary Boland and J. Harold Murray. It was a satire on current political scandals.

In the First Act the chorus singing "Lunching at the Automat" leads up to one of the song hits, "Let's have another cup of coffee." Other songs are: "You must be born with it," "A roof in Manhattan," and "Soft lights and sweet music." The Second Act introduces: "I say it's spinach," "Dear old Crinoline Days," "I don't want to be married," and "Manhattan Madness."

AS THOUSANDS CHEER

Musical revue in a Prologue and Two Acts. Music by Berlin. Book by Moss Hart. Music Box, New York, September, 1933. In the cast were Marilyn Miller, Clifton Webb, Helen Broderick, and Ethel Waters.

A satirical review of people and things, mostly New Yorkers. Impersonations of prominent people from Gandhi and Rockefeller down are interspersed with crazy, hilarious, irreverent lines and melodies. Miss Broderick, as the Statue of Liberty, sang, "We'll all be in Heaven when the dollar goes to Hell." Marilyn Miller and Clifton Webb had duets such as, "How's chances?" "Easter Parade," and "Our Wedding Day." Ethel Waters sang, "To be or not to be," "Heat Wave," and "I've got Harlem on my mind." Among the concerted works are "The Funnies," in the First Act, and the closing song, "Not for all the rice in China."

ANNIE GET YOUR GUN

Musical Play in Three Acts. Music and lyrics by Berlin. Book by Herbert and Dorothy Fields with Ray Middleton. Imperial Theatre, New York, June, 1946.

The story is based upon the picturesque career of Annie Oakley, the dead-shot who was a feature of Buffalo Bill's Wild West Show. Ethel Merman took the part of "Annie." The score is enlivened by typical Berlin melodies. An interesting fact is that it was produced by Rodgers and Hammerstein.

Miss Liberty. See page 595.
Call Me Madam. See page 596.

COLE PORTER

A contemporary composer and lyricist who may be said to have succeeded despite his surroundings. Born, June 9, 1893, on a 700-acre farm near Peru, Indiana, his family was well-to-do and socially prominent. At first he was regarded distrustfully by producers as a playboy seeking amusement by writing for the stage, but he speedily proved that music was a vocation and not an avocation. He studied the violin at six. In 1909 he graduated from Worcester (Massachusetts) Academy; and got his A.B. at Yale, four years later. He began the study of law, but promptly dropped it for his first love. At Yale he wrote the popular songs, "Bingo" and "Bulldog Yale." He studied music at the Harvard Music School, 1915–16; and later at the Schola Cantorum, Paris. In 1916 he wrote his first musical show, "See America First"; followed by "Hitchy-Koo" (1919); "Greenwich Follies" (1923); "Paris" (1928); "Wake Up and Dream" (1929); "Fifty Million Frenchmen" (1929); "The New Yorkers" (1930); "Gay Divorcée (1932); "Nymph Errant" (1933); "Anything Goes (1934); "Jubilee" (1935); "Red Hot and Blue" (1936); "Leave It to Me" (1938); "Du Barry Was a Lady" (1939); "Broadway Melody" (1940); "Let's Face It" (1941); "Something for the Boys" (1943); "Mexican Hayride" (1944); and others, including some "screen" music. In the First World War, Porter enlisted in the Foreign Legion, and later in the French Army, serving until 1919. Since then he has been identified with Broadway. In 1946 a motion picture based upon his life story was presented.

JUBILEE

Musical Play in Two Acts. Music by Porter. Book by Moss Hart. New York, 1935. Mary Boland was the star. St. Louis, 1945.

ARGUMENT   A gay and amusing satire on the English royal house. The Jubilee of King Henry's reign is only one week away, but the preparations are rudely interrupted by two cut-up princelings, who throw a threatening note attached to a stone through a palace window.   The Prime Minister is alarmed and, fearing a plot, orders the royal household off for safety to Feathermore, a gloomy castle in the North.   But the family have other notions.   They start off on a jaunt of their own, as "the Smiths."   The King has always wanted to do rope and string tricks.   The Queen has long had a desire to meet Charles Rausmiller, a swimming and movie star.   Prince James is interested in an American dancer of the opposite sex.   Princess Diana is smitten with one Eric Dare, a youthful actor-composer.   As the Smiths they go to a Grecian ball, where the Prime Minister discovers them and again orders them to make themselves scarce.   At Feathermore the King manages to help them escape by means of one of his rope tricks. Finally everything is explained; he confers titles on their holiday companions, and all ends merrily.

Songs which have made this piece remembered include: "Begin the Beguine," "When Love Comes Your Way"; "Just One of Those Things," "Me and Marie," and "A Picture of Me without You."

RED HOT AND BLUE

Musical Play in Two Acts.   Music by Porter.   Book by Howard Lindsay and Russel Crouse.   Alvin Theatre, New York, October 29, 1936.

This show deserves mention although not one of his most successful. Lindsay and Crouse are skilled playwrights, famed among other things for their "Bringing Up Father."   The musical was elaborately staged with a large cast.   Ethel Merman took the part of a raucous young sentimentalist, "Nails" O'Reilly Duquesne.   Jimmy Durante was "Policy" Pinkle, the pride of the state prison polo team.   In one scene he doubles as a witness on his own behalf before a senatorial investigating committee; then acts as the prosecutor for the state.   He sings, "A Little Skipper from Heaven Above."   Two of Ethel Merman's best songs were: "Down in the Depths of the 90th Floor," and "Ridin' High."

LEAVE IT TO ME

Musical Play in Two Acts.   Music by Porter.   Book by Belle and Samuel Spewack.   Imperial Theatre, New York, November 9, 1938. Revived in September of next year.

Alonzo P. Goodhue (part taken by Victor Moore) is socially and politically the best horseshoe pitcher in Topeka, Kansas, and quite content with his lot, if there are stakes and shoes upon it. However, his wife is ambitious. She pulls the wires to have him appointed Ambassador to the Soviet Republic. He balks and conspires with Buckley Joyce Thomas, a smart newspaper correspondent, to have himself recalled. He kicks a Japanese diplomat in the belly—but Cordell Hull approves of that. Then Alonzo shoots at a Russian bigwig, but hits a Trotskyite instead—and all America from the President down acclaims him a hero. In desperation he tries idealism and doing his one good deed a day—and his popularity thermometer drops to zero. There was a cast of about thirty, and fair dancing and singing; but Victor Moore's drolleries "made the show."

DU BARRY WAS A LADY

Musical Play in Two Acts. Music by Porter. Book by Herbert Fields and B. G. DeSylva. 46th Street Theatre, New York, December 6, 1939.

ARGUMENT   The action shifts from the Club Petite, New York, to the Petit Trianon, near Paris. A large cast was headed by Ethel Merman, who took the part of "May Daly" and later "Comtesse Du Barry"; and Bert Lahr, first plain "Louis Blore" and then "His Majesty, the King of France." Betty Grable was "Alice Barton" and later, the "Marquise de Vernay." Benny Baker shifted from "Charley" to the role of the "Dauphin."

Act I has 6 scenes, its best music being: "Every day a holiday," "It ain't etiquette," "When love beckons," "Do I love you," and "DuBarry was a lady."

Act II, a ballet is followed by DuBarry's satirical, "Give him the oo-la-la," and her humorous "hit," "Katie went to Haiti"; "It was written in the stars," and the duet between the two stars, "Friendship."

MEXICAN HAYRIDE

Musical Play in Two Acts. Music by Porter. Book by Herbert and Dorothy Fields. Winter Garden, New York, January 27, 1944.

ARGUMENT   This typical Porter show was put on with a large cast, with chorus and dancers. In the cast were: "Montana" (June Havoc); "Joe Bascom" (Bobby Clark); "David Winthrop"

(Wilbur Evans). Joe has run away from the States to Mexico to escape the troublesome attentions of the F.B.I. But though a fugitive he yet finds time to engage in many rackets. His various disguises afford some of the humor of the piece.

The First Act has 6 scenes laid in and around Mexico City. Music: "Sing to me, guitar"—which has proved a popular Cole Porter number—"The Goodwill Movement," "I love you," and "There must be someone for me."

Second Act: scenes in Xochimilco, the floating gardens just outside the city; and Taxco, the typical village to the south. "What a crazy way to spend Sunday!" "Abracadabra," and "Count your blessings" are some of the best musical numbers.

Kiss Me, Kate. See page 597.
Out of This World. See page 598.

GEORGE GERSHWIN

Born in Brooklyn, New York, September 26, 1898, George Gershwin received his education in the city schools, but early turned aside to devote himself to piano and harmony, playing where he could. At sixteen he took a position with Remick & Sons, and soon began composing in the "jazz" manner. A friendship with Paul Whiteman induced him to write a "jazz rhapsody," which turned out to be his sensational "Rhapsody in Blue" (1923). A "Piano Concerto in F" followed. Gershwin then turned to musical comedy with success, his works including: "La, La, Lucille" (1919), "Lady, Be Good" (1924), "Song of the Flame" (1925), "Oh, Kay!" (1926), "Treasure Girl" (1928), "Strike Up the Band" (1930), "Of Thee I Sing" (1931), Pulitzer Prize winner; "Let 'Em Eat Cake" (1933), "Porgy and Bess" (1935). The last-named was his most ambitious venture in this field and in its interpretation of Negro life and melody challenges some of the best work of the Grand school. Gershwin was a talented pianist, playing his own compositions at symphonic concerts. He also had a talent for painting. He died in Hollywood, California, July 11, 1937.

OH, KAY!

Musical Comedy in Two Acts. Music by Gershwin. Lyrics by Ira Gershwin. Book by Guy Bolton and P. G. Wodehouse. Shubert

Theatre, New York, October 18, 1926. With Gertrude Lawrence, as "Kay"; Oscar Shaw, as "Jimmy Winter"; Victor Moore, as "Shorty McGee," a bootlegger; and Betty Compton, as "Molly."

ARGUMENT The curtain rises on a deserted house on the beach near Southampton, Long Island, which is being used as a hideout and cache for the liquor smuggled in by the Duke, an English rum-runner. Right in the midst of activities, the owner of the house, Jimmy Winter, arrives with his bride, Constance. To cover up the gang, Shorty McGee poses as the butler. Further to complicate matters, Kay, the sister of the Duke, rushes in, after pistol shots are heard from a pursuing revenuer. Jimmy recognizes her as the girl who had once saved his life, and to put the officer off the trail says that she is his wife. Of course there is a later accounting with the irate Constance and her father. There are an added marital mix-up and various complications, before Jimmy and the others can say, "Oh, Kay!"

Music, Act I.—Chorus, "The Woman's touch"; "Don't Ask"; "Dear little girl"; "Maybe"; "Clap yo hands!" (chorus); and "Do-do-do." Act II.—"Bride and Groom"; "Fidgety Feet"; "Someone to watch over me"; "Heaven on Earth"; and the finale, "Oh, Kay!"

OF THEE I SING

Musical Burlesque in Two Acts. Music by Gershwin. Book by George S. Kaufman and Morris Ryskind. Lyrics by Ira Gershwin. New York, the Music Box, December 27, 1931. Later at the Forty-Sixth Street Theatre. Won the Pulitzer Prize. Also at the St. Louis Open-Air Theatre, in 1938.

CAST JOHN P. WINTERGREEN, *the President* (William Gaxton). ALEX. THROTTLEBOTTOM, *the Vice President* (Victor Moore). DIANA DEVEREAUX, *the Queen of Beauty*. MARY TURNER, *who becomes the President's wife*. THE CHIEF JUSTICE. SENATOR LYONS. SENATOR JONES. LOUIS LIPPMAN. FRANCIS X. GILHOOLEY. MATTHEW ARNOLD FULTON. SAM JENKINS. MISS BENSON. Senators, Supreme Court Justices, Congressmen, Lobbyists, Beauty contestants, and many others.

ARGUMENT A pungent and delightful satire and travesty upon American politics, sparing none, not even the President and the Supreme Court. While many of its allusions were of the particular year, much of it is applicable to any period.

Act I The action, which endeavors to show a cross-section of America in the throes of a Presidential election, shifts rapidly from the Main Street of a typical town to Atlantic City; then to Madison Square

Garden, New York; and finally to Washington. It begins with an ardent campaign for "Wintergreen for President." Meanwhile, some beauty contest managers have announced that the winner will be the prospective President's bride. But Wintergreen objects; he wants only Mary Turner; she makes corn muffins. Diana, the beauty winner, threatens suit for breach of promise. Election returns show triumphant election of Wintergreen—and Mary.

Musical numbers: In addition to original music, other popular melodies are introduced, as Sullivan's "Hail, hail, the gang's all here!"; and Sousa's "Stars and Stripes Forever!" Original themes: opening medley in modern manner; Diana and girls, "Who is the lucky girl to be?"; chorus, "Love is sweeping the country"; Mary, Wintergreen, and chorus, "Of Thee I Sing"; march finale, Entrance of Justices.

Act II The action shifts from the White House, Washington, to the Senate, and finally back to the Yellow Room of the White House. President Wintergreen is at the helm, but his chief difficulty now is evading the Diana issue. The French Ambassador has taken up her cause; her rejection is an insult to his country, as he has found that Diana is "the illegitimate daughter of an illegitimate son of an illegitimate nephew of Napoleon!" In the political crisis Wintergreen is urged to leave Mary, or resign. He refuses. The Senate proceeds to impeach him—and is calling the roll when Mary enters and says, "Stop! My husband is in a delicate condition. He is about to become a father!" The Senate immediately reverses its sentiments, and the story ends with Mary presenting to the expectant country, not one baby, but two. The Supreme Court determines the sex of the infants by a strictly party vote.

Music: French Ambassador, "She's the illegitimate daughter"; Throttlebottom, "I simply can't be bothered with names that do not rhyme"; Diana, "Jilted, jilted!"; Wintergreen and chorus, "Posterity is just around the corner"; chorus, "Trumpeter, blow your horn"; chorus, "Of Thee I Sing!"

PORGY AND BESS

Folk Opera in Three Acts. Music by Gershwin. Book by DuBose Heyward, after the play, "Porgy." Additional lyrics by Ira Gershwin. Alvin Theatre, New York, October 10, 1935. Revived, January 22, 1942; September 13, 1943.

CAST PORGY (Todd Duncan). CROWN (Warren Coleman). SPORTIN' LIFE (John W. Bubbles). BESS (Anne Brown). JAKE (Edward Matthews). Many other Negroes of "Catfish Row."

ARGUMENT   Described as an American folk opera, this reveals a
            cross section in Southern Negro life. The scene is
Catfish Row, Charleston. The plot alternates humor, pathos, and
tragedy. The music closely interprets the varying moods, running the
gamut of spirituals, melodies in minor key, "blues," and syncopated
rhythm. It is now recognized as a classic example of its type, and rivals
many Grand operas, but for convenience is included here.

Act I   It is a summer's evening on Catfish Row. While Clara sings a
         lullaby to her baby, a crap game is in progress. Porgy, a crip-
pled beggar and "crap-shooter," enters in his little wagon drawn by a
goat. He joins the game where his good luck persists; and meanwhile
is accused of being "soft on Crown's Bess." The game ends in a fight
between Crown and Robbins. The latter is killed, and Bess seeks sanctuary with Porgy. On the following night, while the Negroes by means
of a "saucer burial" are getting funds together to inter Robbins, detectives enter to get evidence.
   The music includes a charming lullaby sung by Clara: "Summer
Time." Jake and his fellow fishermen sing one of the big numbers, "A
woman is a sometime thing." Porgy's entrance song is, "They pass by
singing." A chorus, "Gone, gone, gone!" is followed by Serena's song
with ensemble, "My man's gone now."

Act II   Porgy and Bess live together happily, and although her former
          alliance was irregular, a lawyer persuades them to buy a proper
divorce from Crown. But another disturbing element enters in the
form of Sportin' Life, a "dope" peddler. In the Second Scene, the
Negroes are enjoying an all-day picnic in Palmetto Jungle. On the way
back Bess is seized by Crown, who has been in hiding. She comes back
to Porgy, a few days later, in a delirium. Serena leads the prayers for
her. Bess recovers, but a hurricane strikes Catfish Row. While the
storm rages, the Negroes shout and pray. But Crown comes in and ridicules their fright. Jake's boat is wrecked, and Crown rushes out to aid
in rescue.
   The musical numbers include: the song by Jake and the other fishermen, "It takes a long pull to get there"; Porgy's droll avowal, "I got
plenty o' nuthin' "; duet between him and Bess, "You is my woman
now"; Sportin' Life and chorus, "It ain't necessarily so"; duet, Porgy and
Bess, "I loves you, Porgy"; and the singing of the frightened Negroes,
one of the high spots, "Oh, de Lawd shake de Heaven" and "Oh, dear
Jesus!"

Act III   In Three Scenes the rest of the story is told. It opens with
           the wailing of women, mourning the storm's toll. While

Bess sings to the baby, Crown returns, is encountered by Porgy, and is slain. Later the coroner tries to bring Porgy to confront the corpse, and when Porgy refuses he is arrested. While he is in jail the insidious dope merchant, Sportin' Life, leaves some of the white powder on Bess's doorstep, and later prevails upon her to run away with him to New York. Porgy is finally released and comes home only to find it deserted. Hitching up his goat to his cart, he starts north in search of the recreant Bess.

Musical numbers include: a chorus, "Clara, don't you be downhearted"; a duet between Sportin' Life and Bess, "There's a boat that's leavin' soon"; trio, "Where's my Bess?"; and Porgy's mournful aria with chorus, "I'm on my way."

VINCENT YOUMANS

Vincent Youmans was born in New York City, September 27, 1898, the son of a well-known hatter. He was educated here and, in 1917 at the outbreak of the First World War, enlisted in the Navy. However, he had already shown promise of his musical gifts and was retained as entertainer in the Great Lakes Training Station. Later he obtained valuable experience in stage work as an assistant to Victor Herbert. One of Youmans' earliest successes was "Two Little Girls in Blue," in collaboration with Ira Gershwin. "Wildflower" (1923) was followed the next year by his immensely popular "No, No, Nanette!" Then came "A Night Out" (1925), "Oh, Please!" (1926), "Hit the Deck" (1927), "Rainbow" (1928), "The Great Day" (1929), "Smiles" (1930), and "Through the Years" (1932). His strenuous work broke down his health and he was compelled to retire, his last music being heard in a film play, "Flying Down to Rio." In 1944 he put on an elaborate "Ballet Revue" in Baltimore, but it never reached Broadway. Youmans died in Denver, April 5, 1946. His life story was then being filmed under the title of "Sometimes I'm Happy," the name of one of his songs.

NO, NO, NANETTE!

Musical Comedy in Three Acts. Music by Youmans. Book by Otto Harbach and Frank Mandel. Garrick Theatre, New York, April 20,

1924 (321 times). Also produced at the Palace Theatre, London, thence to nearly every large city in Europe, and to South America and New Zealand. Several road companies toured the United States.

In the cast were Phyllis Cleveland ("Nanette"), John Barker ("Tom") and Charles Winninger as the comedian. Louise Groody starred as dancer.

The story is presented in three settings: Home of James Smith, New York City; Lawn of Chicadee Cottage, Atlantic City; and the Living Room of Chicadee Cottage. Music in the First Act includes: the opening chorus, "Pauline"; "The Call of the Sea"; "I've confessed to the breeze"; "Too many rings and Rosie"; "The boy next door"; "No, no, Nanette"; and a favorite, "I want to be happy." In the Second Act: "Lilies of the Field"; "The deep blue Sea"; and the perennial favorite, "Tea for Two." In the Third Act: "Hello, hello, Telephone Girlie!"; "Pay-day Pauline"; and "Take a little one-step."

THROUGH THE YEARS

Romantic Musical Play in Three Acts. Music by Youmans. Lyrics by Edward Heyman. Book by Brian Hooker. Based upon the successful play, "Smilin' Through." Manhattan Theatre, New York, January 28, 1932. Natalie Hall was "Kathleen"; Charles Winninger, "Dr. Harding."

The action goes back forty years, to carry the theme of an old wrong righted. The First Act includes the songs: "Kathleen Mine"; "I'll come back to you"; and "Kinda like you." The Second Act introduces the haunting melody which will persist, "Through the Years"; and "You're everywhere." The Third, "The Road to Home," and another popular number, "Drums in my heart."

RICHARD RODGERS

Richard Rodgers, an outstanding contemporary composer of lighter music, is a product of New York City. He was born here, June 28, 1902; his father was a physician. In his early teens he showed marked aptitude for composing, and at Columbia University in his freshman year, at seventeen, wrote the lyrics for the varsity show, for which he was classed "a prodigy." His "Poor Little Ritz Girl" followed, on Broadway. He also met while there Lorenz Hart, the librettist, and a friendship and musical partnership was instantly struck up which lasted until Hart's death, in 1944. They were styled the "Gilbert and Sullivan of America" and are credited with over a thousand songs and thirty shows. After Columbia, Rodgers studied in the Institute of Musical Art under Frank Damrosch. Some of his best-known earlier shows are: "The Garrick Gaieties" (1925)—214 times; "Dearest Enemy" (1925) with its perennial favorite song, "Here in my arms"; "Peggy Ann" (1926); "A Connecticut Yankee" (1927); "Present Arms" (1928); "Heads Up" (1929); "Simple Simon" (1930); "America's Sweetheart" (1931); "On Your Toes"; "Too Many Girls" (1939); "Higher and Higher" (1940); "I'd Rather Be Right"; "By Jupiter" (1942). After one-half of this prolific pair, Lorenz Hart, passed on, Richard Rodgers was fortunate in linking up with Oscar Hammerstein II, and the two have since made stage history with the phenomenal successes "Oklahoma!", "South Pacific," and (in April, 1951) "The King and I"; not to overlook "Carousel" and music for the film "State Fair." This remarkable output has placed Rodgers and Hammerstein first among contemporary composers and librettists.

A CONNECTICUT YANKEE

Musical Play in Prologue, Two Acts, and Epilogue. Music by Rodgers. Lyrics by Lorenz Hart. Book by Herbert Fields, from Mark Twain's "A Connecticut Yankee at King Arthur's Court." First performed at the Stamford (Conn.) Theatre, September 30, 1927; then at Vanderbilt Theatre, New York, November 3, 1927. Revived at Municipal Opera, St. Louis, 1936; and at Martin Beck Theatre, New York, November 17, 1943.

SCENE: Hartford, Connecticut, 1927,
    Camelot, England, 528.

CAST "THE YANKEE" (William Gaxton). DEMOISELLE ALISANDE (Constance Carpenter). KING ARTHUR (Paul Everton). SIR LAUNCELOT (William Roselle). MERLIN (William Norris). MORGAN LE FAY (Nana Bryant). QUEEN GUINIVERE (Celeste Dueth); others.

In the later cast the leads were taken by Vivienne Segal and Dick Forran. A world-war tinge was given it by making all the American actors officers in the U.S. Navy. A few songs were added.

ARGUMENT   The story in general follows the well-known one by Mark Twain, wherein a shrewd Yankee is suddenly set back a thousand years in time, and placed within the chivalric but crude court of King Arthur. After the first shock of readjustment, which lends itself to comic situations, the Yankee sets himself the task of introducing modern machinery and customs into Camelot. The librettist and composer have inserted some notions of their own, at which the humorist from Missouri would doubtless have chuckled.

The Prologue finds us in the Grand Ballroom of a Hartford hotel, the chief music being, "A Ladies' Home Companion" and the long-time favorite among Rodgers' songs, "My heart stood still."

Act I has two scenes: on the road to Camelot, in the year of our Lord, 528, and the courtyard of King Arthur's castle. "Thou swell!" a greeting song, is introduced here; followed by a male chorus, "At the Round Table," and the song, "On a desert isle with thee."

Act II. in three scenes, gives us: a look-in at the Royal Factory, with the Yankee industriously at work; the road to Camelot; and the Palace of Morgan le Fay. Music: "Nothing's wrong," "I feel at home with you," "Evelyn, what do you say?" Finally, "Ye lunchtime follies," "You always love the same girl," and "The Camelot Samba."

OKLAHOMA!

Musical Play in Two Acts. Music by Rodgers. Book by Oscar Hammerstein 2d, after the play by Lynn Riggs, "Green Grow the Lilacs." St. James Theatre, New York, March 31, 1943, by Theatre Guild. Within a few months, two other companies—one for U.S.O. camps; the other on tour in various cities.

SCENE: Indian Territory—later Oklahoma.

TIME: Turn of the century.

CAST   AUNT ELLER (Betty Garde). CURLY, *a cowpuncher* (Alfred Drake). LAUREY (Joan Roberts). WILL PARKER (Lee Dixon). JUD FRY (Howard de Silva). ADO ANNIE CARNES (Celeste Holm). ALI HAKIM, *a Persian peddler* (Joseph Buloff). IRA SKIDMORE, FRED, SLIM, GERTIE CUMMINGS, ELLEN, KATE, and others; Chorus and Ballet.

ARGUMENT   This musical play was a Pulitzer Prize winner, and up to the time this book goes to press has smashed one record after another for enduring popularity. It has achieved at least three desirable objects: its plot is excellent; it is well integrated with the music, which is also of a high order of excellence; and the story is clean and wholesome. Add to these good singing, clever acting, both comedy and drama, and an artistic ballet, and one has an unbeatable combination—as the box office shows.

Act I *Scene 1. Front of Laurey's Farm House.* Instead of a typical Broadway show with the curtain rising on a dancing and singing ensemble, we see a midwestern farmyard. Aunt Eller is seated at a churn, working away. She is interrupted by Curly, the cowpuncher, who jumps over the fence; he is looking for Laurey, his disdainful sweetheart who believes in keeping him at arm's length. But he is in high spirits. "Oh, what a beautiful morning!" he sings. Laurey appears at the door. "I thought you was somebody," she sniffs. He tries to persuade her to go to a dance with him in (the second "hit" song) "The Surrey with the Fringe on the Top." Others come on stage. A descriptive cowboy's song, "Kansas City" is followed by the droll, "I Cain't say No," by Ado Annie. Ali Hakim, a Persian peddler, the male comedy character, enters. Between selling his customers shoddy goods and dodging shotgun weddings, his life is not a bed of roses. His latest marital threat is Ado Annie. "Ain't it wonderful," she avers, "to be a peddler's bride?" But he protests vocally with "It's a scandal! It's an outrage!" The farmhands at first sympathize with him, but their attention is distracted by word of an auction of box-lunches put up by the girls. Gertie Cummings, meanwhile, has set her cap for Curly. Laurey doesn't like this; nor does she like the attentions of a disreputable farmhand, Jud Fry, who boasts that he is going to take her to that dance. However, she still treats Curly cavalierly and sings, "Many a New Day"—with dance by the girls. When Curly protests her treatment, the charming duet follows: "People will say we're in love."

Scene 2. The Smoke House. In Jud's living quarters there is a spirited dialogue between him and Curly, who warns him to stay away from Laurey and meets threat with threat. An unexpected foil to their quarrel is the lugubrious song, "Pore Jud is Daid!"

Scene 3. Grove on Laurey's Farm. A pleasing interlude is shown here. Laurey has supposedly been given a light sleeping potion by the peddler and what follows is a dream sequence. A lovely song by her and her girl companions, "Out of My Dreams," is the prelude. In her dream she sees her two suitors striving to win her, and the evil Jud triumphing over Curly. A ballet-pantomime portrays the struggle.

Act II *In Three Scenes—Skidmore Farm House; Kitchen Porch; Laurey's Farm House.* A song by Curly and the men, "The Farmer and the Cowman," is followed by a comic song between Ado Annie and Will. She tells him that the peddler match is off, but she has threatened to be such a light-of-love, that he warns her, "With me it's all or nuthin' "—and she comes right back at him in similar vein. Ali, however, has gotten entangled again, this time for keeps. He has been hooked by Gertie and comes on stage the picture of distress. The picnic boxes put up by the girls are offered to the highest bidder, and the tug of war comes between Jud and Curly. Jud empties his pockets, and so does Curly—the latter finally offering a cowpuncher's dearest possession—his gun. He gets Laurey's box and plans to take her to the dance. Later, Jud tries to overpower her at the side-porch; Curly comes to her rescue and she falls willingly into his arms. A reprise of "People will say we're in love" follows. Aunt Eller, who all along has been a quiet backstage force, tells them that they couldn't find a better place to start in life than this new state of Oklahoma. A wedding and chivaree ensue, then the final dramatic moment. Jud, drunk and dangerous, comes upon the evening scene brandishing a long knife and tries to kill Curly; but the latter overpowers and stabs him fatally. The sheriff is on the point of haling Curly off to jail, on his wedding night, but the other men interpose; a court can be held right there; and Curly is acquitted. Friends drag in the famous surrey with the fringed top, and deposit the happy couple in it. The smashing song, "Oklahoma!" with a medley of other favorites, rings down the curtain.

CAROUSEL

Musical Play in Two Acts.   Music by Rodgers.   Book by Oscar Hammerstein 2d., based on Ferenc Molnar's play, "Liliom." Produced by the Theatre Guild at Majestic Theatre, New York, April 19, 1945.

SCENE: Coast of New England.
TIME: 1873–88.

CAST   BILLY BIGELOW ("Liliom"), *a carnival barker* (John Raitt).
      JULIE JORDAN, *his wife* (Jan Clayton). CARRIE PEPPERIDGE (Jean Darling). MRS. MULLIN (Jean Casto). JUGGLER (Lew Foldes). FIRST POLICEMAN (Robert Byrn). DAVID BASCOME (Franklyn Fox). HANNAH (Annabelle Lyon). LOUISE (Bambi Linn). CARNIVAL BOY (Robert Pogent). NETTIE FOWLER (Christine Johnson). ENOCH SNOW (Eric Mattson). JIGGER CRAIGIN (Murvyn Vye). Two Heavenly Friends, others, chorus, ballet directed by Agnes De Mille.

ARGUMENT   "Liliom" of the Molnar play becomes "Billy" and the scene is shifted from Austria to a New England summer resort. After a Prelude, the First Act is divided into two scenes; the Second into six. All are in and around the coast, one scene being on an island in the bay. In the third scene of Act II we are shown "up there," with Billy residing briefly in Heaven.

The story follows that of Molnar, with American slang and "trimmings." Billy is a tough customer, who coaxes the crowd into the carnival. Julie Jordan, a flirt, falls under his spell and he finally marries her. When he learns that he is about to become a father, he is, as always, short of funds. He aids in an attempted robbery and then commits suicide to avoid arrest. After fifteen years spent in Purgatory he is admitted into the Heavenly gates, and while there is permitted to look "down here" and among other things witness an artistic ballet. He sees his daughter for the first time, and is told that he may redeem his soul by doing one good deed. On earth he meets the girl, now on the threshold of womanhood, and offers her a star. When she refuses it, he slaps her and goes back to Purgatory.

The music of Act I includes: "You're a queer one, Julie Jordan," sung by her and Carrie; "When I marry Mister Snow" (Carrie); a duet between Julie and Billy, "If I loved you"; a delightful song by chorus with dance, "June is bustin' out all over"; a duet between Carrie and Snow, "When the children are asleep"; and a hornpipe song by men, "Blow high, blow low!"

Act II: the girls and chorus, "This was a real nice clambake"; "There's nothing so bad for a woman" (Jigger and others); Julie's pathetic aria, "What's the use of wond'rin'?"; "You'll never walk alone"; and "The highest judge of all."

ALLEGRO

Musical Play in Two Acts. Music by Rodgers. Book by Oscar Hammerstein II. Directed by Agnes de Mille. Majestic Theatre, New York, October 10, 1947.

CAST JOSEPH TAYLOR, JR. (John Battles). JOE'S FATHER (William Ching). JOE'S MOTHER (Annamary Dickey). JOE'S WIFE (Roberta Jonay). JOE'S GRANDMA (Muriel O'Malley). JOE'S CHUM (John Conte). NURSE (Lisa Kirk). Others with chorus of forty; twenty-four dancers; one hundred in entire cast.

ARGUMENT An ambitious production put on expensively and with novelty. The stage remains bare save for two small platforms with large screen for backdrop, on which are depicted scenes from Joe Jr.'s life. His baby face is thrown on the screen (the year 1905) and the ensuing thirty years carry him through college, courtship, marriage, and later events. The story is unfolded by a combination of spoken word, picture, a chorus in the Greek manner, and choreography. At times, the hero's unspoken thoughts are thus interpreted.

Joe's father is a small-town doctor, and the son also studies medicine. He weds a girl with social aspirations, who persuades him to be a big-town specialist. He treats a series of wealthy neurotics until, disillusioned, he goes back home to take up practice with his father. There are side issues shown in rapid interplay on the screen, or sung by the chorus, with no pronounced undertones or overtones, in quick, lively style suggested by the title, Allegro.

SOUTH PACIFIC

Musical Play in Two Acts. Music by Rodgers. Lyrics by Hammerstein. Book by Hammerstein and Joshua Logan, adapted from "Tales of the South Pacific," by James A. Michener. Majestic Theatre, New York, April 7, 1949. A sensational, "history-making" success, also shown by touring companies.

SCENE: Islands of the South Pacific.

TIME: Recent World War, during action against the Japanese fleet.

CAST ENSIGN NELLIE FORBUSH, *an army nurse* (Mary Martin). EMILE DE BECQUE, *a French planter* (Ezio Pinza; later, Ray Middleton). BLOODY MARY, *a native camp-follower* (Juanita Hall). LUTHER BILLIS, *a Seabee* (Myron McCormick). LT. JOSEPH CABLE, *of the Navy* (William Tabbert). CAPT. GEORGE BRACKETT (Martin Wolfson). LIAT, *Mary's daughter* (Betta St. John). COM. WILLIAM HARBISON (Harvey Stephens). Large number of Seabees, Soldiers, Nurses.

ARGUMENT Based on another Pulitzer Prize winner, this play achieved such early and continued box-office demands that it seems destined to outstrip "Oklahoma!" and set up a record perhaps for all time. It combines continuous, smooth-moving action with well-integrated music: Richard Rodgers at his best. The staging, in a word, is excellent affording lively interplay for numerous scenes which in less capable hands could be confusing.

Act I *Scene 1. Front of Emile's Home.* Emile de Becque, an expatriated Frenchman of middle age, is living in quiet retirement in a lovely home on a small island of the South Pacific. In earlier life he had killed a man in self-defense and fled France. He has made a comfortable fortune in the islands, planter style, and taken a native woman as mistress, who dies a few years later, leaving two children, Ngana and Jerome, both under ten as the story opens.   They speak only French and when the curtain rises are singing a charming ditty, "Dites-Moi Pourquoi."   After their servant, Henry, takes them to bed, Emile enters followed by Ensign Nellie Forbush, the latter one of a group of nurses stationed here with American troops.   Nellie is a girl from Little Rock, who is one of the liveliest of this band and, although years younger than this Frenchman, who is grizzled at the temples, is attracted by him and his manner of living.   On his part he has "fallen for" Nellie and makes no secret of his feelings in one of the hit melodies, "Some Enchanted Evening."   She in turn is attracted and promises to think it over.   Succeeding scenes follow so rapidly that it is easier to follow the plot outlines.

The *Second Scene* is another spot on the shore with the volcanic Bali Ha'i in the distance.   The men are at leisure in the camp, sailors, marines, Seabees, poking good-natured fun at Bloody Mary ("Bloody Mary Is the Girl I Love"), a squat, middle-aged islander who sells souvenirs such as grass skirts and shrunken human heads.   Mary learns her English from the boys and they roar with laughter when she calls someone a "stinky bastard."   Follows a roaring men's chorus, "There's Nothing Like a Dame," led by Luther Billis, an impudent chap whose tongue perpetually gets him into trouble.   They are all curious about the distant isle with its twin peaks, which is out of bounds and said to be peopled with lovely dames.   Bloody Mary adds to their desire by singing a haunting melody, "Bali Ha'i."   Lt. Cable, who "just flew in," now reports to Capt. Brackett and they discuss the importance of using Marie Louise Island, twenty-four miles away ("Bali Ha'i") for reconnaisance purposes to get intelligence of Japanese fleet movements. Since the Frenchman, Emile, has been long resident in the islands, they consider him the logical man to go over.   Nellie enters and is asked to "spy" on Emile and learn if he is politically sound.   In *Scene 7,* one of the most laughable, Nellie decides that Emile is taking up too much of her thoughts and resolves "I'm Gonna Wash That Man Right Outa My Hair"—with the aid of soap and a shower.   While she is being dried off, Emile enters unnoticed.   When others have gone, she tries to follow instructions and quiz him about his past.   He talks freely, but does not mention his two children.   When alone on stage she sings, "I'm In Love With a Wonderful Guy."   Emile is called into the Captain's office, but declines the mission to the other island, because of his hatred of warfare and his love for Nellie.   An interlude to the main plot now comes on.   Bloody Mary has a daughter, half-French, half Polynesian, named Liat who, Mary decides, would be a good wife for the handsome Lieutenant Cable.   She employs native methods to bring them together to a rendezvous in her hut. The girl is charming and although she speaks no English, her pantomime and demeanor captivate him. During their tryst he sings, "Younger Than Springtime." In the final scene of the lengthy act, at Emile's home, he amuses Nellie by mimicking her "Wash My Hair" song and dance. She is ready to admit her love for him when the two native children are brought in. Nellie thinks them cute and interesting, but when Emile tells her they are his own, she is horrified and runs off stage, while the curtain falls.

Act II   The first four scenes center around a stage show given by the Seabees. It is hilarious but is interrupted by lighting failure. Backstage, the unhappy Frenchman entrusts a bouquet for Nellie to Billis, who promises to deliver it later. Mary, Liat, and Cable enter, and Mary tries to promote the union between the young couple with her song, "Happy Talk," with Liat executing a charming pantomime dance. The lieutenant has fallen in love with the girl, but cannot consent to marriage with her. He gives her his wrist watch, which Mary angrily throws to the floor with "Stingy bastard!" Cable, disconsolate and alone, sings a reprise of "Younger Than Springtime." A humorous song follows as part of the inner stage show, Luther Billis in "Honey Bun." Nellie does a droll dance in sailor's costume. Later, Emile's flowers are given to her, but in a short, tense scene she tells him she cannot marry him. Alone he sings, "This Nearly Was Mine." He is joined on stage by Cable, who is likewise heartbroken, and the two resolve to undertake the dangerous mission to the other island. In succeeding scenes which interplay rapidly, the central point is the radio communications office. The two men have landed and Emile's voice is heard giving detailed advice of enemy movements. Nellie, who has learned after some days of Emile's departure, listens in on one of Emile's messages. In the midst of his story that Cable has been killed, the radio stops abruptly. The Seabees and other troops are given marching orders, but Nellie resolves to stay and care for Emile's two children, as she fears that he is dead. The final scene shows her placing their supper "sur le tobler" and trying to speak French and join in with the opening ditty, "Dites-Moi Pourquoi." Emile enters backstage, comes around and quietly seats himself at the table. His uniform is in tatters. Nellie silently looks across at him, then pushes the bowl of porridge over to him. He begins to eat using the ladle. Old familiar strains of "Some Enchanted Evening" are heard as they clasp hands.

HAROLD ARLEN

Harold Arlen, a stage name which he took in early life, was born in Buffalo, New York, February 15, 1905. At seven he sang in his father's choir; at fifteen he was playing the piano in night clubs and organizing his own band. In 1927 he came to New York, where his knack in organizing novelties for the stage soon brought him into notice. One of his first "hits" was "Stormy Weather," with its song, "I Love a Parade." He wrote the score for the Winter Garden revue, "Life Begins at 8.40" (Bert Lahr in the cast); and "Hooray for What!" (with Ed Wynn starring). In 1935 he went to Hollywood, writing for the films. His song, "Over the Rainbow," in "The Wizard of Oz" was sung and whistled all over the country. He has been called "one of the best of Broadway's tunesmith's." His melodies are warm and sensitive. The musical play, "Bloomer Girl" (1944) is his most recent and outstanding success.

BLOOMER GIRL

Musical Comedy in Two Acts. Music by Arlen. Lyrics by E. V. Harburg. Orchestration by Russell Bennett. Book by Sig Herzig and Fred Saidy, from the play by Lilith and Dan James. Shubert Theatre, New York, October 5, 1944.

SCENE: Cicero Falls, New York.
TIME: 1861.

CAST HORATIO APPLEGATE (Matt Briggs). SERENA APPLEGATE (Mabel Taliaferro). *Their six daughters,* OCTAVIA, LYDIA, JULIA, PHOEBE, DELIA (Nancy Douglass), and EVELINA (Celeste Holm). DOLLY BLOOMER (Margaret Douglass). DAISY (Joan McCracken). GUS (John Call). JOSHUA DINGLE (Robert Lyon). JEFFERSON CALHOUN (David Brooks). POMPEY (Dooley Wilson). Five sons-in-law of Applegate. Others, Chorus, Dancers.

ARGUMENT "Bloomer Girl" owes its long success to a good plot and music, plus quaint costuming dating from the period of the Civil War when women were about to get out of voluminous hoopskirts into the far more daring costume indicated by the title.

The First Act has six scenes, in and around the Applegate mansion in Cicero Falls, a small manufacturing town in upper New York state. Horatio has six daughters, five of whom he has married off to salesmen in his hoopskirt factory; thus keeping the family in the business. But Evelina, the sixth of the flock, rebels; she has come under the influence of her Aunt Dolly, a radical and progressive champion of women's rights not only in clothing but in politics. Among other activities Dolly is aiding in the underground runaway slave movement. Caught red-handed she is hustled off to the local jail, where she proves as great a problem as when at liberty. And Evelina, too, has her troubles. She outrages her father by appearing in pantalettes, not only scandalizing both parents, but showing to Horatio a possible ruin of his hoopskirt business. Further, she finds herself falling for a handsome young slaveholder from the South, Jeff Calhoun, who has come North in search of his runaway slave, Pompey.

Music: song by Serena and her daughters, "When the Boys Come Home"; an opening duet between Evelina and Jeff; "The Farmer's Daughter," by the five sons-in-law; a delightful bit, "It was good enough for Grandma," Evelina and girls; the rousing bass song by Pompey, "The Eagle and Me"; "Right as Rain," duet between Evelina and Jeff; "T'morra', t'morra'" sung by Daisy; "The rakish young man with the whiskers," by Evelina and Jeff; the male chorus, "Pretty as a Picture," with waltz and final ballet.

The Second Act has four scenes. We find the principals parading in the Cicero Falls park dressed in their Sunday best. The jail episode is a thing of the past, but there are still repercussions. In the third scene, a play within a play, there are bits from "Uncle Tom's Cabin" with a dramatic auction of slaves. Jeff frees Pompey and love at last finds its way through difficulties.

Music: a humorous song by the citizens, "Sunday in Cicero Falls"; "I got a Song," by the Negroes; "Lullaby," by Evelina; in the small stage show—"Simon Legree," "Liza Crossing the Ice," "I Never Was Born," "Man for Sale!" The last scene introduces a Civil War ballet and reprises from earlier songs.

RECENT MUSICAL COMEDIES

IRVING BERLIN

MISS LIBERTY

Musical Comedy in Two Acts and Twelve Scenes. Music by Berlin. Book by Robert E. Sherwood. Staged by Moss Hart. Imperial Theatre, New York, July 15, 1949.

CAST   MAISIE DELL, *of the "Police Gazette"* (Mary McCarty). JAMES GORDON BENNETT (Charles Dingle). JOSEPH PULITZER (Philip Bourneuf). HORACE MILLER, *a "Herald" reporter* (Eddie Albert). BARTHOLDI (Herbert Berghof). MADAME DUPONT (Allyn McLarie). THE COUNTESS, *her grandmother* (Ethel Griffis). Others, Singers, Dancers.

ARGUMENT   An ambitious performance which had only moderate success. The time is 1885, in New York, during the intense rivalry of Pulitzer of the "World" and Bennett of the "Herald." The Statue of Liberty has been completed in Paris by Bartholdi, but now lies in packing cases awaiting its pedestal in New York Harbor. Public funds have been solicited to build the pedestal, and the two publishers almost come to blows. Horace Miller, a news photographer of the "Herald," gets an idea and with the help of Maisie Dell of the "Police Gazette" goes over to Paris to bring back the girl who posed as model for Miss Liberty. However, Madame DuPont, the girl produced, proves to be the wrong one. The romance between Horace and the French girl is all but wrecked, but at the final curtain he gets her, leaving the lively Maisie cold. As an aside, the grandmother of the French girl almost steals the show with her leering comments on men and affairs generally. The play ends with a patriotic note of appeal to the American spirit of freedom and our land the haven of the world's oppressed, reminiscent of the poetic lines on the pedestal; but this note, however good, is not in tune with the farcical musical itself.

There are eighteen musical numbers, the best songs being: "A Little Fish in a Big Pond," "Let's Take an Old-fashioned Walk," "Paris Wakes Up and Smiles," "Just One Way to Say I Love You," "Homework," and "You Can Have Him."

CALL ME MADAM

Musical Comedy in Two Acts and Thirteen Scenes. Music and lyrics by Berlin. Book by Howard Lindsay and Russel Crouse. Imperial Theatre, New York, October 12, 1950.

CAST   Mrs. Sally Adams (Ethel Merman). The Secretary of State (Geoffrey Lamb). Supreme Court Justice (Owen Coll). Congressman Wilkins (Pat Harrington). Henry Gibson (William David). Kenneth Gibson (Russell Nype). Senator Gallagher (Ralph Chambers). Senator Brockbank (Jay Velie). Cosmo Constantine, *Prime Minister* (Paul Lukas). Princess Maria (Galina Talva). Hugo Tantinnin (E. A. Krumschmidt). Sebastian Sebastian (Henry Lascoe). Pemberton Maxwell (Alan Hewitt). Other Actors, Singers, and Dancers.

ARGUMENT   The most widely-publicized musical of the year 1950, "Call Me Madam," had an unprecedented advance sale of a million dollars, topping even the already legendary "South Pacific." It is a good-natured lampoon directed at the society lady appointed our minister to Luxembourg. The plot is simple. A Washington City wealthy widow and party-giver is rewarded by the administration by being sent as ambassador to Lichtenburg. She sets her cap for the prime minister of that country, personally, while officially she tries to lend a hundred million dollars to them. This would-be kindness has the reverse effect upon the prime minister, and she is recalled to Washington—but eventually wins out.

The leading part is taken by Ethel Merman, well-known as Annie in "Annie Get Your Gun." She is well cast as the lady diplomat who alternates slang with culture; gets tangled up in a very long train to her official dress; has long telephone conversations with "Harry"; tries to democratize the duchy to her own brand of thinking; and in general "raises a riot." Mixed up with it is a Congressional investigating committee; also the love affair of her Harvard assistant, "Kenneth," with Princess Maria, that inspires the loveliest melodies of the show.

The performance is well staged. It is a pleasant satire on present-day officialdom—a mélange of money, money, love, love, politics, politics, but it must be admitted that, without the lively, dominating presence of the lady diplomat, it would not live up to its promises. However, it sends its audiences away happy. They recall a parting fling of the lady when she says to the officious chargé d'affaires, "Call me Madam—and smile!"

Songs: "You're Just in Love," "It's a Lovely Day To-day," "The

Hostess With the Mostes' " (Miss Merman's hit song), "The Best Thing For You Would Be Me," "Can You Use Any Money Today?", "They Like Ike" (which might be a good campaign song for a certain general), "Marrying for Love," and the rhythmic dance number, "The Ocarina."

COLE PORTER

KISS ME, KATE

Musical Comedy in Two Acts. Music and lyrics by Porter. Book by Sam and Bella Spewack. Century Theatre, New York, December 30, 1948.

CAST   FRED GRAHAM (Alfred Drake). HARRY TREVOR (Thomas Hoier). LOIS LANE (Lisa Kirk). RALPH (Don Mayo). LILLI VANESSI (Patricia Morison). HATTIE (Annabelle Hill). In "Shrew": BIANCA (Lisa Kirk). BAPTISTA (Thomas Hoier). KATHARINE (Patricia Morison). PETRUCHIO (Alfred Drake). Players, Singers, Dancers.

ARGUMENT   This is a play within a play. Scenes in broad comedy from Shakespeare's "The Taming of the Shrew" are sandwiched between the bickerings of two temperamental lovers in real life. Katharine, the Shrew, is no more in need of a sound spanking than Lilli, her present-day counterpart—but they both get it.

A vainglorious actor and his recently divorced wife are cast for parts opposite each other in a revival of Shakespeare's play, in a Baltimore theatre. The scenes shift from the Bard's stage to the backstage dressing rooms and alleys. Since the two principals are legally separated, it would seem that their personal feelings would have no part in the inner play. However, when the ex-wife finds her ex-husband paying too much attention to Lois, a night-club entertainer, the pot boils over and the two former mates begin slugging each other, both off-stage and on. On the side, Fred's name has been forged to an IOU for a gambling debt, and when the gangsters try to collect the note, Fred is torn between righteous wrath and the fear of losing Lilli's talents in the show. It is uproarious comedy with the original play burlesqued, but Shakespeare himself would doubtless have chuckled over it.

A generous sprinkling of choruses, dances, and songs enliven the performance. The opener, "Another O'p'nin, Another Show," is followed by "Why Can't You Behave," "Wunderbar" (particularly good), "I've Come to Wive It," "I Hate Men," and "Kiss Me, Kate," in the first act. In the second: "Too Darn Hot," a rather broad song and dance; "Always True to You (in My Fashion)," "So in Love," a reprise of Lilli's earlier song; "Brush Up Your Shakespeare," and "Where Is the Life I Led," sung earlier in the act by Drake, well-known for his part in "Oklahoma!"

OUT OF THIS WORLD

Musical Comedy in Two Acts and Eighteen Scenes. Music by Porter. Book by Dwight Taylor and Reginald Lawrence. Century Theatre, New York, December 21, 1950.

A Christmas-time production which had some good singing and dancing as "props" to a humorous tale of an amorous adventure of Jupiter of Greek mythology. The god (George Jongeyans) sings impressively while disguised as a mortal who poses as the husband of a pretty Greek maiden (Patricia Gillette). Meanwhile, the angular, jealous Juno (Charlotte Greenwood) in a characteristic comedy role makes things lively for the loving couple. Some excellent songs include: "No Lover for Me," "I Am Loved," "Where, Oh, Where," and "They Couldn't Compare to You." The dancers present pleasing ballets in Greek costume with more modern antics.

BURTON LANE

An American composer born in New York, February 2, 1912. Lane received his education at the Dwight School, studying music with Simon Bucharoff. At the age of fifteen he was on the staff of a musical publication. He contributed songs to various stage plays, "Three's a Crowd," "Earl Carroll's Vanities," and others. He went to Hollywood to write music for the films, in 1933, and has since lived in Beverly Hills, California. "Finian's Rainbow" came out early in 1947.

FINIAN'S RAINBOW

Musical Play in Two Acts and Ten Scenes. Music by Burton Lane. Book by E. Y. Harburg and Fred Saidy. Lyrics by Harburg. Forty-Sixth Street Theatre, New York, January 10, 1947.

CAST SUNNY (Sonny Terry). BUZZ COLLINS (Eddie Bruce). SHERIFF (Tom McElhany). SUSAN MAHONEY (Anita Alvarez). HENRY (Augustus Smith, Jr.). FINIAN MCLONERGAN (Albert Sharpe). SHARON MCLONERGAN (Ella Logan). WOODY MAHONEY (Donald Richards). SENATOR BILLBOARD RAWKINS (Robert Pitkin). OG, *the Leprechaun* (David Wayne). Sharecroppers and others; Singers, Dancers.

ARGUMENT A whimsical play introducing an Irish flavor into a town of our deep South, "Missitucky." The opening scene, the Meetin' Place in Rainbow Valley where both whites and Negroes live, finds some strange visitors—Finian McLonergan and his daughter Sharon, from the mythical town in Ireland, Glocca Morra. Finian has stolen a pot of gold from Og, the Leprechaun, and Og is hot on his trail. Finian has heard about the huge golden treasure at Fort Knox, and thinks that if he can plant his crock it too will germinate. He buys land from the sharecroppers, hides the magical vessel, and soon we witness a sleepy southern town taking on the airs of wealth. Missitucky goes on the gold standard; tractors and other luxuries are speedily bought; the mail-order house of Shears and Robust gets out its big catalogues; flashy clothes are worn—but trouble brews. Senator Rawkins, who hates the blacks, is on the point of tricking Finian and the others by getting title to the property. The pot's magical powers are invoked. Its owner can have three wishes granted before it loses its magic. Finian makes his first wish, that the greedy Senator be turned into a Negro evangelist and learn for himself what it means to be black—done! Og, who has gotten possession of the crock, makes the second wish—that a deaf-mute girl with whom he has fallen in love be made to hear and speak. The third and final wish is invoked to save Sharon from the wrath of the Senator's minions. This brief outline does not attempt to cover the play and interplay of a confused but intriguing story. It is, in fact, a satire on present-day politics, left-wing Socialism, sharecropping, polltax, anti-Negro legislation, the T V A, and sudden wealth. Nevertheless the curtain falls on a pleasurable evening.

"How Are Things in Glocca Morra?", the opening song, speedily found its way into the country's "top" tunes. "Look to the Rainbow" is a charming duet. The Negro choruses are good, beginning with a trio, "The Begat." Others: "When the Idle Poor Become the Idle Rich," "Something Sort of Grandish," "If This Isn't Love," "Old Devil Moon," and "Necessity."

FRANK LOESSER

Loesser, an American composer, was born in New York, June 29, 1910. He was educated at the College of the City of New York, and while there wrote music for college shows. He was a private in World War II, and composed several memorable songs for the infantry, including "Rodger Young" and "Praise the Lord and Pass the Ammunition." His Broadway full-scale production "Guys and Dolls" appeared in 1950.

GUYS AND DOLLS

Musical Comedy in Two Acts and Seventeen Scenes. Music by Loesser. Book by Jo Swerling and Abe Burrows, based on Damon Runyan's story, "The Idyll of Miss Sarah Brown." Forty-Sixth Street Theatre, New York, November 24, 1950.

CAST   NATHAN DETROIT, crap-game manager (Sam Levene). MISS ADELAIDE, *his sweetheart* (Vivian Blaine). SKY MASTERSON, *big-time gambler* (Robert Alda). SARAH BROWN, *a Salvation Army lassie* (Isabel Bigley). Many others, Broadway characters, the Mission Band, Singers, Dancers.

ARGUMENT   A lavish production of typical Broadway type and concerned with life in and about the bright lights, being a musical setting for characters made familiar in Damon Runyan's sketches. There are two romances interlinked with a lot of other stage material. In the first, we witness the troubles of Miss Adelaide, a night-club singer who has been engaged to Nathan Detroit, who runs "floating" crap-games and is content to keep the lady dangling in a betrothed state for the past fourteen years. She voices her trouble in the song, "Take Back Your Mink" and complains that she is catching cold from a naked finger—one that hasn't been properly clothed with a wedding ring. She emphasizes her plight with a take-off on strip tease.   Her other songs are: "A Bushel and a Peck," "Marry That Man To-day" (duet with Sarah Brown), "Sue Me" (duet with Nathan), and "Adelaide's Lament."

The other romance involves Sky Masterson, big shot in gambling circles who will bet on anything, even that he can persuade a sweet Mission lass to take a trip with him to Havana.   Her own bewilderment when she finds herself falling in love with such an impossible character is pleasingly shown in song and story.   There is a rousing hymn of true revivalist type, "Follow the Fold"; others, "If I Were a Bell," "The Oldest Established," "I'll Know," and "Sit Down, You're Rockin' the Boat."

The book is both "tender and tough," a spicy mixture of the seamy side of New York, yet with heart-warming interludes.

FREDERICK LOEWE .

Of Austrian parentage, Frederick Loewe has since the age of twenty been identified with American music. He was born in Vienna, June 10, 1904, and studied the piano with Ferrucio Busoni and Eugene d'Albert, winning the Hollander Medal in Berlin, in 1923. The next year he came to New York, where he has supplied music for such productions as "Salute to Spring," "Great Lady," and "The Life of the Party"; also writing suites for the piano and playing. A piano recital was given by him in Carnegie Hall, in 1942. "Brigadoon" was given stage production in 1947.

BRIGADOON

Musical Play in Two Acts. Music by Frederick Loewe. Book and lyrics by Alan Jay Lerner. Ziegfeld Theatre, New York, March 13, 1947.

CAST TOMMY ALBRIGHT, *an American tourist* (David Brooks). JEFF DOUGLAS, *his friend* (George Keene). ARCHIE BEATON (Elliott Sullivan). HARRY BEATON (James Mitchell). ANDREW MACLAREN (Edward Cullen). FIONA MACLAREN (Marion Bell). JEAN

MacLaren (Virginia Bosler). Meg Brockie (Pamela Britton). Charlie Dalrymple (Lee Sullivan). Maggie Anderson (Lidije Franklin). Mister Lundie (William Hansen). Singers, Dancers.

ARGUMENT   A play of fantasy which appeals to the imagination as well as to the senses; the scene, a Scottish village over which a spell has been cast; the time, the present. Tommy and Jeff, two American travelers on a vacation jaunt, come to Brigadoon on the day of a festival and wedding. There is an eerie feeling about it that puzzles them. Lundie, the schoolmaster, finally tells them that Brigadoon comes back to life only once in a century and for a single day. Two centuries earlier, in 1747, the dominie had prayed that the village be preserved from witchcraft by remaining unchanged. The miracle had happened and it was still as it had been at that time, preserved from the turmoil of the rest of the world. However, if a native should leave the place, it would cease to exist. If an outsider entered, he must remain and also come to life only once in a century. This last item is bad news for Tommy, as he has fallen for a pretty villager, Fiona, and despite the fact that he is already engaged to a girl back in New York. How true love of the Scottish brand triumphs over miracles and other obstacles is the theme of an engaging and poetic play.

Some excellent music is interspersed with spirited dancing. Songs: "Waitin' for My Dearie," "The Heather on the Hill," "Come to Me, Bend to Me," "I'll Go Home to Bonnie Jean," "Almost Like Being in Love," "From This Day On," "The Love of My Life," "There But for You Go I," and "Brigadoon."

RECENT AND REVISED GRAND OPERA

CHARLES W. CADMAN

A WITCH OF SALEM

Dramatic Opera in Two Acts. Music by Cadman. Book by Nelle Richmond Eberhart. Produced at Chicago by the Chicago Civic Opera Company, December 8, 1926.

CAST   ARNOLD TALBOT (Tenor).
        SHEILA MELOY (Soprano).
        CLARIS WILLOUGHBY (Soprano).
        Townsfolk of Salem, Massachusetts.

ARGUMENT   The scene is Salem, the time 1692, when the witch-hunt of history rocked the sleepy little town to its foundations. Involved in it are the three principals of this opera. Claris Willoughby is the daughter of a well-to-do Puritan. His ward is Sheila Meloy, lately come over from Ireland, who finds the severe life of the colony foreign to her former life. Sheila had fallen in love, as a girl, with Arnold Talbot, and is embittered to find him engaged to marry her cousin, Claris. When the witch-hunt is at its height, Sheila accuses her cousin of being a witch, and says that there is a red cross upon her breast, a birthmark, in fact, being there. Poor Claris is promptly tried and just as promptly sentenced to hang. While the noose is being adjusted, the remorseful Sheila confesses her wrongdoing to Arnold and tells him that if he will kiss her once, she will go with this upon her lips and take her cousin's place on the scaffold. The rather implausible story is sung and enacted with dramatic force.

WALTER DAMROSCH

THE MAN WITHOUT A COUNTRY

Opera in Two Acts. Music by Damrosch. Book by Arthur Guiterman from the classic story by Edward Everett Hale, of the same title. Metropolitan, New York, May 12, 1937.

CAST   PHILIP NOLAN, *a Lieutenant of Marines* (Tenor).
MARY RUTLEDGE, *his betrothed* (Soprano).
HARMAN BLENNERHASSET (Tenor).
AARON BURR (Baritone).
COLONEL MORGAN (Bass).
COMMODORE STEPHEN DECATUR (Spoken).

ARGUMENT   The plot can be briefly summarized as following the well-known short story by Hale, of the man who in an unguarded moment forswears allegiance to the United States and shouts, "I never wish to hear that cursed name again!" The army officers take him at his word. He is placed on board a Navy vessel and never allowed ashore, while all references to his country are kept carefully from his ears.

The time is 1807; the opening scene in the home of Harman Blennerhassett, on the Ohio River. Practically all of the characters are historic, that of Philip Nolan being fictional. The intrigue against the United States known as the Aaron Burr plot is fomenting, with its center here. Young Nolan, a lieutenant in the Marines is involved. He is in love with Mary Rutledge, who begs him to have nothing to do with the conspiracy, but he persists. When he is arrested he voices his defiance and thereafter is "the man without a country."

The second act takes place several years later. Of all the wars and rumors of wars, and the growth of his native land, Nolan knows nothing, and his longing for word becomes intense. A new poem by Walter Scott falls into his hands, with the famous lines:

"Breathes there a man with soul so dead
Who never to himself hath said,
'This is my own, my native land.' "

He falters and turns away sobbing. His punishment is complete. At the siege of Tripoli against the pirates, Commodore Decatur relents and lets him take part in the battle. He fights heroically until cut down by a bullet. Dying he hears Mary's voice as in a dream telling him he is pardoned.

OTTORINO RESPIGHI

Ottorino Respighi has come to be regarded as one of the most talented of contemporary composers. Born in Bologna, Italy, July 9,

1879, he studied the violin, played in quintets in European concerts, and in 1932 toured America as a soloist. He earned fame for his numerous orchestral suites, the best known being "The Fountains of Rome" and "The Pines of Rome." He was made a member of the Royal Academy of Italy in 1932. Three operas, "Re Enzo" (1905), "Semirama" (1910), and "La Fiamma" (1934), were little known outside of Italy. His best-known opera, "La Campana Sommersa" ("The Sunken Bell") was produced in Germany and America. Respighi died in Rome, April 18, 1936.

THE SUNKEN BELL

(La Campana Sommersa.) Legendary Opera in Four Acts. Music by Respighi. Book by Claudio Guastalla, based upon the drama by Gerhart Hauptmann of the same title. First performed in Hamburg, in 1927. At the Metropolitan, New York, in November, 1928.

CAST   HEINRICH, *the bell-caster* (Tenor).
MAGDA, *his wife* (Soprano).
RAUTENDELEIN, *an elf-child* (Soprano).
THE WITCH, *her grandmother* (Mezzo-soprano).
NICKELMANN, *the old man of the well.*
THE FAUN (Tenor).
THE PASTOR (Bass).
THE BARBER (Tenor).
THE SCHOOLMASTER (Baritone).
Mortals, elves, witches.

ARGUMENT   The scene and time of this charming fantasy are in the realm of dreams. By an ancient well is seated a pretty elf-child, Rautendelein, who is troubled over the misfortune that has come to the bell-caster, Heinrich. While taking his latest and best bell up a hillside to the church, a mischievous Faun has overturned his cart and the bell has dropped into a lake. Rautendelein has fallen in love with the foundryman and determines to aid him. While he lies asleep upon the ground she draws a magic circle around him, although warned by the Witch, her Grandmother, that he is a mortal and must die. The Witch then spirits the bell-caster away.

The second act takes place in Heinrich's home. His wife, Magda, listens intently for the sound of the bell, but he rushes in all but dead to tell her that the bell is sunk and he has lost his power to cast another. The Pastor brings a girl into the house, who proves to be Rautendelein, whose love for him gives him new life and courage.

In the third act, Heinrich has abandoned Magda and their children to live in the mountains with Rautendelein. The elves help him to make finer works, but the Pastor urges him to give up this life of sin and return to his family. The bell-caster refuses saying: "If I desist from this work, may the sunken bell ring again." When the wrathful neighbors come to kill him and destroy his new temple on the mountain, he is aided by spirits in defeating them. However, when later the images of his children stand before him bearing an urn containing tears of his dead wife, who has thrown herself into the lake, he repents, regains his mortal self—and the tolling of the sunken bell is heard.

In the final act, same setting as the first, Rautendelein has gone back to her first lover, the old man of the well. Heinrich, deserted by all, comes to see her once more before he dies. The Witch permits him to do so. The elf-child at first reproaches him for having driven her back into the well, then relents and presses a kiss upon his dying lips.

BENJAMIN BRITTEN

British composer born November 22, 1913, Lowestoft, England. He was educated in Gresham's School, Norfolk; later in Royal College of Music, 1930–33. He studied composition under John Ireland; piano under Arthur Benjamin. First public performance in 1934 at the Florence Festival, and then in Barcelona and London. Britten has written widely for the films, stage, radio, piano, symphonic concerts. His "Ballad of Heroes" was given in 1939. Since then he has composed three operas, "Peter Grimes," "The Rape of Lucretia," and "Albert Herring," the first-named being the most important and given in England in 1945 with "considerable acclaim." In December, 1950, New York audiences were given a novelty, "Let's Make an Opera," with music by Britten.

PETER GRIMES

Tragic Opera in a Prologue and Three Acts. Music by Britten. Book by Montagu Slater, from George Crabbe's poem, "The Borough." Composed for the Koussevitsky Music Foundation and performed at Sadler's Wells Theatre, London, June 7, 1945; at the Berkshire Music Center in America, August 6, 1946; at the Metropolitan, New York, February 12, 1948.

SCENE: A Suffolk fishing village.

TIME: Circa 1830.

CAST PETER GRIMES, *a fisherman* (Tenor).

JOHN, *a boy apprentice* (Silent).

ELLEN ORFORD, *a schoolmistress* (Soprano).

NED KEENE, *an apothecary.*

MRS. SEDLEY, *a village gossip* (Contralto).

SWALLOW, *a lawyer.*

CAPTAIN BALSTRODE, *a retired skipper* (Baritone).

REV. HORACE ADAMS, *a rector.*

HOBSON, *a carrier* (Bass).

BEN BOLES, *a fisherman and Methodist* (Tenor).

"AUNTIE," *landlady of "The Boar"* (Contralto).

Her two nieces, townspeople, and fisherfolk.

ARGUMENT The story reveals a cross-section of English village life, a little over a century ago. The central figure, Peter Grimes, is a social misfit, a recluse with a bad reputation. Rumor has it that he mistreats the boys whom he obtains from an orphanage, although he maintains that he cannot afford to hire a man to help him with his nets.

The prologue set in the borough hall shows Peter being cross-examined by Swallow, the lawyer, regarding the mysterious fate of an apprentice. Peter sullenly protests his innocence and through lack of evidence is dismissed with a sharp warning. His neighbors shake their heads. A long, slow-moving melody pervades the prologue, and later harps suggest the glitter of the sea.

Act I *Scene 1. The Beach with exterior of buildings.* Peter has few friends to help him secure another boy. Ned Keene, the apothecary, is willing to give him another chance. His two staunchest allies are Ellen Orford, a widow and teacher, with whom he is in love; and Captain Balstrode, an old salt, who bluntly advises him to leave town and either enter the Navy or become a privateer. But Peter is obstinate. He is going to fish for all the fish in the sea and then marry Ellen. Ellen tells him that she is going with Hobson, the public carrier, to the orphanage to get a new boy.

Scene 2. Interior of Tavern. A storm is raging and the townspeople are huddled inside. Peter dripping enters to await the boy. Word comes that the storm has swept away a portion of the cliff near Peter's hut. However, the carrier arrives safely with the apprentice,

John, much to general disapproval. There is a rousing chanty in this scene, "Old John has gone fishing."

Act II   *Village Street outside of Church.*   It is Sunday morning and a clear day.   People are going to church, while bells chime in with the melody.   Ellen notices that the new boy, John, is dressed in clean clothes and allowed to rest on Sunday, as Peter had promised, but she also sees that the boy is unhappy and his neck is bruised.   She confronts Peter, who now enters, but the man has one of his irrational streaks and angrily maintains that the boy is now his property and he can do as he pleases; then he seizes the lad and returns home.   The people coming from church are furious and threaten to go to the hut and thrash Peter.   Balstrode tries to calm them.   They march down the street to the beat of Hobson's drum.

Scene 2.   Peter's Hut (made from an inverted boat).   An orchestral interlude ceases and Peter is shown roughly shaking the frightened boy and telling him to take off those fine clothes and "on with this jersey." A shoal of fish is in the offing and, Sunday or no Sunday, they must after them; he must get rich.   Then the beat of Hobson's drum is heard and the angry mutterings of the mob.   Alarmed, Peter shoves the boy out a side door and follows him to the cliff's edge.   A wild scream is heard. The men burst in to find the hut empty.   The Captain peers out the side door; he surmises the truth but keeps his counsel.

Act III   *Scene 1.   Outside Moot Hall.*   The music affords relief from previous tenseness.   A dance is going on within, which the crowd watches through the windows; music gay and lively.   Ellen and the Captain, however, are much perturbed.   They have searched for three days and Ellen reports that she has found the boy's jersey washed up on the strand.   Mrs. Sedley, the busybody who has been active in other situations, overhears her and now loudly demands that a further search be made.   An interlude notes the passage of several hours.

Scene 2.   On the Beach.   A heavy fog hampers the seekers.   A horn wails dismally.   Peter wanders in haggard but sullen.   The crowd shouts, "Peter! Peter Grimes!"   Ellen and the Captain still try to shield him, but the situation has grown so ominous that Balstrode takes him aside and advises him to get into his boat, go out to sea, and never return.   He consents.   Dawn breaks; the fog lifts; the villagers take up their daily tasks; Ellen and the Captain sadly leave the scene with, "The sea is so deep, so deep!"

THE RAPE OF LUCRETIA

Tragic Opera in Two Acts. Music by Britten. Book by R. Duncan, from Obey's "Le Viol de Lucrece." Performed at the Glyndebourne Opera House, in July, 1946.

The plot follows the familiar theme, the scene Rome, about 500 B.C. Tarquin the Tyrant while a guest in the house of Collatinus, the General, violates Lucretia, the latter's wife. On the General's return she appears dressed in deep black, tells of her misfortune, and stabs herself. A Chorus after the manner of the Greek tragedies foretells the action.

ALBERT HERRING

Comic Opera in Three Acts. Music by Britten. Book by E. Crozier from a tale by Guy de Maupassant. First performance in 1947.

Turning aside from serious work to this light comedy, Britten is regarded as not successful. Nevertheless there are moments of excellent music. In a sparkling farce of village life, the action hinges upon the vain attempt on the part of a committee to find an acceptable Queen of May. Whenever any local girl is mentioned, a sour old maid smirches her reputation. Who then is pure? In despair they turn from the fair sex and choose a King of May—one Albert Herring who apparently is blameless as he has been tied closely to his mother's apronstrings. Albert is at first dismayed, but being duly crowned and allotted many unaccustomed privileges, he decides to sow a wild oat or two for himself.

LET'S MAKE AN OPERA

Musical Play in Two Acts. Music by Britten. Book by Eric Crozier. John Golden Theatre, New York, December 13, 1950.

On the assumption that audiences like to participate in a show, they are here given full opportunity to do so. The whole first act might be called rehearsal, the folks out front being told what roles they are to assume, whether singing or imitating forest calls. Act II then puts on this dual performance, an operatic skit about an English chimney sweep who is befriended by lads and lasses in England, the time being 1810. As a novelty it attracted attention, but more as a diverting "parlor game."

BERNARD ROGERS

Bernard Rogers is an American composer who was born in New York City, February 4, 1893. He studied at the Institute of Musical Art, New York, and in Cleveland with Ernest Bloch. He has won several awards, the Pulitzer Scholarship, the Guggenheim Fellowship, and the Eastman Award. He is teacher of composition at the Eastman School of Music. His first opera, "The Marriage of Aude" (1931) won the Bispham Medal. He has been on the Editorial Board of *Musical America*. "The Warrior" was written in 1946 and produced in 1947.

THE WARRIOR

Tragic Opera in One Act. Music by Rogers. Book by Norman Corwin. Metropolitan, New York, January 11, 1947.

CAST   SAMSON, *a Jewish warrior* (Baritone).
DELILAH, *a Philistine woman* (Soprano).
Other Philistines.

ARGUMENT   The story follows that of the Old Testament telling of Samson's betrayal by Delilah. In the opening scene, the siren is shearing off the warrior's locks while he sleeps. A second scene reveals him as a prisoner, mocked and bound and finally blinded by redhot irons. A third episode is his trial in prison where Delilah pours out her scorn upon him. The final scene is the famous last act of the warrior. His hair has grown long again, he seeks forgiveness of Jehovah, and at a great festival of his enemies he thrusts aside the pillars and brings the temple crashing down.

KURT WEILL

Kurt Weill was born in Dessau, Germany, March 2, 1900, the son of a cantor. His musical gifts were shown at such an early age that, at

ten, he wrote his first opera, which earned him a scholarship at the
Berlin Conservatory where he studied under Humperdinck.   At 26,
his opera "Protagonist" was produced, and he wrote an opera each
year until Hitler's crusade against the Jews forced him to leave Germany, in 1933.   In Paris he wrote some ballet music.   In 1937 he collaborated with Max Reinhardt with the score for the spectacular pageant of Jewish history, "The Eternal Road."   This and other work
brought him to America, and he became a naturalized citizen in 1943.
He wrote the music for "Johnny Johnson," "The Lady in the Dark,"
"Street Scene," "One Touch of Venus," and "Lost in the Stars."   He
was actively associated with the Playwrights Company.   Weill died
April 3, 1950.

LOST IN THE STARS

Musical Tragedy in Two Acts.   Music by Kurt Weill.   Book by
Maxwell Anderson, based on Alan Paton's novel, "Cry, the Beloved
Country."   The Music Box, Ocotber 30, 1949.

CAST   STEPHEN KUMALO (Todd Duncan).
       JOHN KUMALO (Warren Coleman).
       JAMES JARVIS (Leslie Banks).
       EDWARD JARVIS (Judson Rees).
       NITA (Elayne Richards).
       GRACE KUMALO (Gertrude Jeannette).
       LINDA (Sheila Guyse).
       ABSALOM KUMALO (Julian Mayfield).
       IRINA (Inez Matthews).
       Numerous others, including singers.

ARGUMENT   The story follows faithfully the original book by
           Paton, regarded by critics as one of the most sig-
nificant and important novels of the past decade or two.   It tells of a
simple Zulu preacher, a Negro, who goes on a visit to Johannesburg,
the metropolis of the gold-mining in the Transvaal.   He is seeking his
son, Absalom, who meanwhile has gotten into bad company, is impli-
cated in a slaying during a hold-up, convicted, and sentenced to hang.
The desolate father and the white man, Jarvis, whose son has been
slain, finally come to a mutual understanding and respect.   The scenes
where Stephen tries to give up his pastorate and the final meeting between him and Jarvis are particularly moving.   It is a strong, sincere
play of elemental emotions, excellently staged, acted, and sung.   The
cast is distinctive, headed by Todd Duncan, originally of "Porgy and

Bess," who cancelled a concert tour in Australia to create his role; and Leslie Banks, who came over from England. Most of the company are Negroes, good singers and actors, the chorus especially good. It is hard to particularize, but in the opening scene are the songs, "The Hills of Isopo," "Thousands of Miles," and the resounding, "Train to Johannesburg"; in the second, "The Little Grey House," "Who'll Buy?" and "Trouble Man"; the finale, "Lost in the Stars." In Act Two, "The Wild Justice," Stephen's pathetic prayer, "O Tixo, Tixo, Help Me," the chorus in the prison, "Cry, the Beloved Country"; "Big Mole," a song by a teenage boy, "Alex" (Herbert Coleman) that almost stopped the show; "A Bird of Passage," and the final reprise, "Thousands of Miles."

INDEX OF CHARACTERS

(GRAND OPERA)

613

INDEX